TRAVELING LITERARY AMERICA

A Complete Guide to Literary Landmarks

TRAVELING LITERARY AMERICA

A Complete Guide to Literary Landmarks

B. J. Welborn

jefferson press

ISBN 0–97189–742–5
Library of Congress Catalog Card Number: 2005929156

Illustrations by William Parker
Author's Photo by Barry Ahrendt
Front Cover Design by Kelly Kornegay
Book Design by Fiona Raven

First Printing September 2005
Printed in Canada

Published by Jefferson Press

jefferson press
P.O. Box 115
Lookout Mountain, TN 37350

To Katie and Georgie

ACKNOWLEDGMENTS

A nostalgic nod goes to two women who passionately taught me high school English many years ago in my little hometown, Dunn, N.C.: Irene G. Dixon and Opal Weeks. Although Miz Dixon and Miz Weeks have passed from this world and Dunn High School has fallen prey to school consolidation, social progress and bulldozers, these teachers' efforts to light a love of literature in one student live on. I am sure the flames they kindled decades ago helped illuminate this book.

For the unfailing support of my husband, Barry Ahrendt, I am, as always, grateful. I also express an indebtedness to my late father, Ed Welborn, who imparted to me his enthusiastic curiosity about nearly everything, making my life richer and more productive. And I give a salute of gratitude to the many museum curators, site volunteers, professors and other knowledgeable sources without whose help this guide to literary America would not be possible.

Lastly, I thank Henry David Thoreau, John Steinbeck, Mark Twain, Herman Melville, Theodore Dreiser, James Baldwin, Edith Wharton and the other literary giants who helped mold me and inspire this book.

CONTENTS

Contents

Contents

Contents

Contents

Contents

Contents

PREFACE

Writers are an interesting, determined and imaginative lot. So are the places where they lived, loved and worked. A visit to the homes they left behind reveals volumes about who they were, the passions that drove them, and the ideals that inspired them. Luckily for us, we can visit these homes and other literary places all across America. They have been preserved and restored by admirers who often saved these historic jewels from destruction.

Book lovers and curious travelers can experience these literary landmarks: homes — some just as the authors left them (Longfellow, for instance), memorials, poetry walks (Edna St. Vincent Millay), exhibits (L. Frank Baum), and museums (Carl Sandburg) dedicated to many of our nation's influential writers. *Traveling Literary America* describes more than 200 literary sites in nearly all 50 states. These places give us insights into the famous and not-so-famous people who contributed to American and world literature.

Traveling Literary America will guide you from Plimoth Plantation in Massachusetts, where William Bradford penned one of our country's earliest histories, to John Steinbeck's boyhood home in California's Salinas Valley. You will find out why William Faulkner wrote on the walls of his study in his Oxford, Miss., mansion and learn about the many places in Willa Cather's corner of Nebraska — officially called "Catherland" — as described in her novels. From Harriet Beecher Stowe's dwellings in Maine and Ohio, to Edgar Allen Poe's hideaways in Philadelphia, Richmond, Va., and New York, to sites along the Laura Ingalls Wilder Highway in the Midwest, to the stone house poet Robinson Jeffers built with his own hands along the Pacific coast, you'll read about intriguing and sometimes amazing places.

In this unique guide you'll also find:
- The most comprehensive listing available of literary sites in America. These include not just the well-known places, but literary secrets, like the Mississippi barber shop of diarist William Johnson, a free black man in the Civil War era; the only home that WWII journalist Ernie Pyle ever owned, now a branch library in Texas; the humble, Georgia manse where young Erskine Caldwell lived; and colonial novelist William Gilmore Simms' former plantation in South Carolina.

- Places relating to writers whom young people currently study in school, going beyond Nathaniel Hawthorne and F. Scott Fitzgerald to such writers as Zora Neale Hurston and Richard Wright.
- Detailed directions to sites, contact information, hours of operation and where to find more facts on the Internet.
- Guides to towns written about by such intensely autobiographical writers as Thomas Wolfe (Asheville, N.C.), Jack Kerouac (Lowell, Mass.), Sherwood Anderson (Clyde, Ohio) and Carson McCullers (Columbus, Ga.).
- Unusual literary treasures such as the Yiddish Center in Amherst, Mass., which has saved 1.5 million Yiddish books from destruction; America's first public library in Newport, R.I., still in operation; and the world's largest collection of items connected to Elizabeth and Robert Browning in Waco, Texas.
- A look at diverse literary sites in such major literary cities as Boston, New York, New Orleans and San Francisco.
- Links to various sites related to Mark Twain from New York, to Missouri to California; *Peripatetic Poe*, following the gloomy genius along the East Coast; and *Hemingway Homes* from Illinois to Florida, Arkansas and Idaho.
- A section for each entry titled **The Writer And His Work** that includes key biographical facts, a list of works, and explanations of the writer's contribution to literature.
- A **Frame of Reference** to clearly identify the period in which the writer lived or wrote.
- Descriptions include **The Best Stuff**, a section offering insights into events that occurred at the site or details of special interest.
- Emphasis on the interconnections between writers. For instance, Tennessee Williams documented D.H. Lawrence's death in one of his plays; Booker T. Washington (*Up From Slavery*) asked Paul Lawrence Dunbar to write a poem for the dedication of Tuskegee Institute; and Thomas Bailey Aldrich's book, *Bad Boy,* inspired Twain's *Tom Sawyer.*
- **Hot Tips** on where to find literary collections via the Internet, as well as in libraries.
- Sidebars explaining literary phenomena in America, including Transcendentalism, Romanticism, Naturalism, and The Beat Generation.
- Suggestions for side trips. For instance, visitors to the Margaret Mitchell House in Atlanta can find area museums that feature *Gone With The*

Wind memorabilia. Tips on where to stay and eat are included when a site is off the beaten path.
- Lists of books about authors and their homes in a **Further Reading** section.

Please note that some of the sites described in this book are privately owned and are not open to the public. When this is the case, it is clearly noted. Please do not knock on the doors of private homes. Since the hours and days of operation of public sites might change without notice, you should contact the site or consult its official Web site before visiting.

Here's hoping that you enjoy your literary travels across America as much as I did. Happy trails!

Emerson House

NEW ENGLAND

MONTE CRISTO COTTAGE

Eugene O'Neill Boyhood Home

Eminent American playwright Eugene O'Neill spent his boyhood summers, from 1888 to 1917, at a cottage in coastal **New London, Conn.**, at 325 Pequot St. The Monte Cristo Cottage ($) today is open seasonally for guided tours. O'Neill set two of his most famous plays in the cottage, his comedy *Ah! Wilderness* (1933) and his semi-autobiographical *Long Day's Journey Into Night* (1956). O'Neill also used incidents, locations, and people he knew from New London in many of his 40 plays. O'Neill is the only American playwright to win the Nobel Prize for literature. He also won four Pulitzer Prizes.

O'Neill was the third son of a traveling actor and drug-addicted mother. He once wrote that the cottage, built in the 1840s, was the only home he ever knew. Some say the ghosts of the tormented O'Neill family still haunt the cottage.

The cozy house was named Monte Cristo Cottage after O'Neill's matinee-idol father James O'Neill's most popular role, the dashing Edmund Dantes in *The Count of Monte Cristo*. The house features a Eugene O'Neill portrait and poster gallery, multimedia presentation, and a permanent exhibition on the playwright's life and works. The Eugene O'Neill Theater Center in nearby Waterford, Conn., has owned and operated the National Historic Landmark since 1974.

The cottage is open for guided tours from the day after Memorial Day through Labor Day, Tuesday through Saturday, 10 a.m. to 5 p.m. and on Sunday from 1 p.m. to 5 p.m. Closed major holidays. Tour schedule varies after Labor Day. For more information, contact the Monte Cristo Cottage, 325 Pequot Ave., New London, CT 06320. Tel. (860) 443-0051 or Eugene O'Neill Memorial Theater Center, 305 Great Neck Road, Waterford, CT 06385. Tel.: (860) 443-5378. E-mail: info@oneilltheatercenter.org. On the Net: www.oneilltheatercenter.org/prog/monte/montprog.htm. For details about O'Neill and other O'Neill sites, see California in the Pacific section of this book. ◙

WALLACE STEVENS WALK

Hartford Traces Poet's Inspirational Commute

A dedicated group in **Hartford, Conn.**, is developing the two-mile loop Wallace Stevens walked from his home at 118 Westerly Terrace to his office at 690 Asylum Ave. downtown as the Wallace Stevens Walk in the distinguished poet's honor. On Stevens' weekday commute to and from the Hartford Accident and Indemnity Company, he composed verse in his head. Stevens joined the firm in 1916, became vice-president in 1934, and worked for the company until his death in 1955. In his spare time, he composed poetry.

From mid-1916 through 1917, Stevens managed to publish a poem a month. But his first collection, *Harmonium,* was not published until 1923, when he was 44. Although Stevens was first and foremost a conservative businessman and lawyer, he won the Pulitzer Prize in 1954 for his *Collected Poems.* He turned down a year's professorship at Harvard, saying he couldn't take time off from his job, and he never traveled outside the United States. He produced most of his poetry between the ages of 60 and 75 as his business duties declined. He did not permit other writers or those involved with his poetry to visit him at home.

Today Stevens is widely regarded as a major, 20th-century poet and perhaps as the mild-mannered man who once had a scuffle with brusque Ernest Hemingway and came away with a black eye and broken hand. His naturalist poems treat philosophical matters in a witty and profound way. Stevens gradually transformed his playful use of language to a more reflective, though abstract style. Influenced by imagism and French symbolism, Stevens wrote *Sunday Morning*, his breakthrough work. Stevens' collections include: *Ideas and Order* (1935); *Owl's Clover* (1937); and *The Man With The Blue Guitar and Other Poems* (1937). Among his best-known poems are: *Notes toward a Supreme Fiction; The Auroras of Autumn; An Ordinary Evening in New Haven; The Planet on the Table*; and *A Primitive Like an Orb.*

Stevens was born in Pennsylvania in 1879 and died in 1955 in Hartford. He is buried in the 1865 Cedar Hill Cemetery, 453 Fairfield Ave., in the southwest part of the city.

The Stevens Walk will feature 13 stone markers along his daily route from his large, two-story white wood house to the Hartford insurance company. Each marker will have a stanza from his poem, *Thirteen Ways of*

Looking at a Blackbird. A Hartford firm has completed preliminary design work and fundraising continues.

For more information, contact Friends and Enemies of Wallace Stevens, 500 Main St., Hartford, CT 06103. On the Net: www.wesleyan.edu/wstevens/stevens.html. ◮

HARRIET BEECHER STOWE CENTER

Last Home for Author of 'Uncle Tom's Cabin'

LOCATION Central Connecticut, in Hartford, at 77 Forest St., in Nook Farm, a 19th-century neighborhood of writers and reformers. The homes of **Mark Twain** and **Noah Webster** are also in the neighborhood, named after the "nook" in the Park River. Take I-91 to intersection with I-84. Take I-84 West to Sisson Avenue (exit 46). Right onto Sisson Avenue. Right onto Farmington Avenue. Right onto Forest Street.

The Harriet Beecher Stowe Center ($) is open Tuesday through Saturday from 9:30 a.m. to 4:30 p.m., and from Memorial Day through Columbus Day as well as December on Monday, from 9:30 a.m. to 4:30 p.m.; Sunday from noon to 4:30 p.m. Closed Jan. 1, Easter Sunday, July 4, Thanksgiving Day, and Dec. 24-25.

For more information, contact the Harriet Beecher Stowe Center, 77 Forest St., Hartford, CT 06105. Tel. (860) 522-9258. On the Net: www .harrietbeecherstowecenter.org.

FRAME OF REFERENCE Harriet Beecher Stowe lived in this house from 1873, when she moved here from her custom-built dream home, Oakholm, also in Hartford, until her death in 1896. The writer and her retired husband, Calvin, lived here with their two adult twin daughters, Eliza and Harriet. The house was built in 1871.

SIGNIFICANCE Although Stowe wrote more than 30 books during her half-century of writing, she became an international celebrity for *Uncle Tom's Cabin* (1852). The sensational best seller was based on Stowe's experience with the Underground Railroad and interviews with escaping slaves when she was a young woman living in Ohio. Her father, Lyman Beecher, a celebrated minister and staunch abolitionist, was then president of Lane Seminary in Cincinnati. The book, which portrayed the physical, sexual, and emotional abuse endured by enslaved people, sold more than 10,000 copies in the first week after publication. During the last half of the 19th century, Stowe was the most widely read American author in Europe and Asia.

Uncle Tom's Cabin took America by firestorm, igniting pubic passion as no literary work had done. The book galvanized the abolitionist cause and contributed to the outbreak of the Civil War. President Abraham Lincoln reportedly greeted Stowe as "the woman whose little book started the Civil War."

Stowe also penned other novels, biographies, poetry, hymns, essays, and children's stories. She was known for her excellent depictions of rural New England life. Her other topics were homemaking, education, child rearing and religion.

ABOUT THE SITE The Stowe Center includes the Harriet Beecher Stowe House, the 1884 Katharine Seymour Day House and eight Victorian flower gardens, all on 2 1/2 acres. Day was Stowe's grandniece and founder of The Stowe Center. The house is one of six remaining Victorian homes at Nook Farm.

The three-story Stowe House has a simple facade of white painted brick with sage green shutters and gingerbread trim. The Victorian cottage-style house has 17 rooms and halls and was modest by the standards of the Nook Farm neighborhood. (For proof, look across the lawn at the opulent Mark Twain House.) The gardens surrounding the house reveal Stowe's fondness for and knowledge of Victorian-era plantings.

On the first floor, you'll find front and rear parlors, each with distinct functions. The front parlor was reserved for receiving distinguished guests, of which there were many, and hosting formal events. Today it serves as an exhibition gallery. The rear parlor functioned as a family living room for reading, playing games and taking tea. In these rooms, original Stowe family furnishings and artworks, many collected during the Stowes' extensive travels, reflect several centuries. Paintings include a copy of Madonna of the Goldfinch by Raphael and a Venus de Milo reproduction. You'll also see oils and watercolors that Stowe herself painted.

The formal dining room features a Victorian sideboard with carvings of birds and fruit, Stowe's dining table and a set of period chairs with a three-arm gasolier light in the ceiling. Woodwork designs of oak and cherry enrich interiors throughout the house.

The pinewood kitchen exemplifies the model of efficiency put forth by Harriet and her sister, Catharine Beecher, in their book, *The American Woman's Home* (1869). Kitchen tools and utensils lay in specified order on open shelves, and bins are within easy reach. A grand staircase leads to the second and third floors.

Next to Stowe's bedroom on the second floor, her sitting room features cottage-style furniture, which she decorated. Here you'll find reproductions of classical ruins, a common purchase of Victorian-era travelers, and Stowe's hand-painted scenes of Maine, Florida and Scotland. In her bedroom, a Ward's case (terrarium) brims with native ferns and mosses.

The bedrooms open to a central hall/sitting room, now the research reading room. The grand staircase continues to the third floor, where the former billiard room is used for collection storage.

Guided tours also include the first floor of the granite and brick Day House, which houses a research library, archives, and site offices. The carriage house serves as the visitor center. Here you can see the exhibition *Uncle Tom's Cabin: A Moral Battle Cry for Freedom*. Artifacts portray the public reaction to Stowe's blockbuster novel. A display features Stowe's silver ink stand and the first chapter of *Uncle Tom's Cabin*, printed in the National Era magazine.

HOT TIPS Guided tours begin in the carriage house. You must make an appointment to access the research library by calling (860) 522-9258, ext. 309. Hours are Monday through Wednesday from 9 a.m. to 4 p.m. The library holds 19th-century materials on African-American and women's history, the Stowe and Beecher families, more than 180,000 manuscripts, 12,000 books and 100 scrapbooks. The site offers many student and special programs. For other Stowe sites, see Maine and Ohio in this book.

THE BEST STUFF Stowe's small spindle writing desk and chair.

THE WRITER AND HER WORK
BORN: June 14, 1811, in Litchfield, Conn.; one of 11 children
DIED: July 1, 1896, in Hartford, Conn.
EDUCATED: Hartford Female Seminary
MARRIED: Calvin Stowe; seven children
IMPORTANT WORKS: *The Mayflower* (1843); *Uncle Tom's Cabin* (1852); *The Key To Uncle Tom's Cabin* (1853); *Dred: A Tale of the Great Dismal Swamp* (1856); *The Minister's Wooing* (1859); *Oldtown Folks* (1869); *The Pearl of Orr's Island; Palmetto Leaves; The First Christmas In New England; Pink and White Tyranny*
INTERESTING BIO FACT: Although Stowe was busy rearing seven children and managing a household, she made time to write. Her husband, a biblical scholar, unwaveringly encouraged her writing career, which was most unusual at the time. In a letter to her in 1850, Calvin Stowe wrote, "My dear, you must be a literary woman. It is so written in the book of fate ... Make all your calculations accordingly."

FURTHER READING *Harriet Beecher Stowe and the Beecher Preachers* by Jean Fritz (1998); *The Stowe Debate* by Mason I. Lowance (1994)

ELSEWHERE IN THE AREA Old State House (1796, oldest in America), 800 Main St.; Museum of American Political Life; Sarah Whitman Hooker Homestead. Other houses at Nook Farm include those of Isabella Beecher Hooker, Harriet's sister; William Gillette, a playwright/actor; and Charles Dudley Warner, journalist/writer. ⬦

MARK TWAIN HOUSE

Where Literary Lion Wrote 'Huckleberry Finn'

LOCATION Central Connecticut, in the capital city of Hartford. From I-84 near the downtown area, take Forest Street to Farmington Avenue and turn left to the site, or take Sisson Avenue north to Farmington and turn right.

The Mark Twain House ($) is open for guided tours in April and November on Monday, and Wednesday through Saturday, 9:30 a.m. to 4 p.m., and on Sunday, noon to 4 p.m. From May through October and in December the house is open Monday through Saturday, 9:30 a.m. to 4 p.m. and Sunday noon to 4 p.m. The site is closed Jan. 1, Easter Sunday, Thanksgiving Day, Dec. 24 and 25.

For more information, contact The Mark Twain House, 351 Farmington Ave., Hartford CT. 06105. Tel. (860) 247-0998, ext. 26. E-mail: info@marktwainhouse.org. On the Net: www.marktwainhouse.org.

FRAME OF REFERENCE Samuel Langhorne Clemens commissioned this lavish mansion in 1873 and lived in it with his family from 1874 until 1891. Twain sold the house in 1903 when he moved to Europe. The Friends of Hartford bought the site in 1929, and the house served as the Mark Twain Branch of the Hartford Public Library. After full restoration, the nonprofit Mark Twain Memorial opened the house, a National Historic Landmark, to the public in the 1960s.

SIGNIFICANCE Clemens, who wrote under the pen name Mark Twain, is generally considered the greatest American writer of the 19th century. During the 20 amazingly productive years he lived in Hartford, he wrote seven major works in this house, including *The Adventures of Tom Sawyer* (1876), *The Adventures of Huckleberry Finn* (1884), and *A Connecticut Yankee in King Arthur's Court* (1889). *A Connecticut Yankee* was a powerful indictment of political and social injustice.

Twain was the first great American writer born and reared west of the Appalachian Mountains and the first to write in the American vernacular. Twain led an incredibly exciting and adventuresome life, and his writings reflect this. Twain's utterly American wit raised the level of humor in his work to high art. The literary lion's works have been translated into more than 60 languages. His book and lectures made him an international celebrity in his lifetime, and he continues to be read and studied worldwide.

ABOUT THE SITE Following the celebrated success of *Tom Sawyer* and his lecture tours throughout America, Twain set about building a dream home. He bought land in Hartford's West End at Nook Farm, an upper-class neighborhood of distinguished intellectuals, writers and reformers. He commissioned leading New York architects to design his Victorian mansion, blending whimsical details from around the globe: turrets, balconies, a wrap-around verandah and patterned brickwork.

Twain asked Associated Artists, an influential design firm directed by Louis Comfort Tiffany, a notable contributor to the Art Nouveau style, to decorate the major rooms of his asymmetrical, 19-room mansion. The house today has been retored to look as it did in 1881, the year Tiffany founded his firm. Louis Tiffany, famous for his glassmaking, was the son of Charles L. Tiffany, who founded Tiffany and Co. in New York. Twain paid a then-whopping $122,000 for the house, land and furnishings. More than 10,000 Victorian-era objects fill the mansion. Many belonged to the Clemens family.

The spectacular entrance hall incorporates red walls, a high ceiling with stenciled patterns of blue, and ornamental details carved by Leon Marcotte of New York and Paris. The rich wood paneling was stenciled in silver. Associate artists also stenciled the drawing room with East Indian motifs of silver over salmon pink. Here you'll see crystal chandeliers, a piano, cream upholstered furniture and a floor-to-ceiling mirror on the far wall. The mirror was a wedding gift brought from the Clemens' house in Buffalo, N.Y.

The library, where Twain recited poetry and read his new works to family and friends, boasts a towering mantel carved in Scotland for the dining room at Ayton Castle. Twain bought the mantel in Europe. Twain and wife Livy's second-floor bedroom accommodates the original, elaborately carved bed Twain purchased in Venice. Twain died in this bed at another home, **Stormfield**, in Redding, Conn. Twain built that house upon his return from Europe. Twain called the huge bed "the most comfortable bedstead that ever was."

The Twains left Nook Farm for Europe in 1891. The publishing company he founded in 1884 collapsed, and he lost a fortune he had invested in the Paige compositor, an automatic typesetting machine. His financial losses resulted in bankruptcy. Visitors can see one of the 3-ton typesetters at the site. The advent of the linotype machine ensured the doom of Twain's Paige typesetter.

HOT TIPS For tickets, enter through the back door on the ground floor. Allow one hour for your visit. Visitors must negotiate three flights of stairs for the full tour.

Kids will enjoy the booklet, *Mark Twain's Activities for Good Little Boys and Girls*, available at the site.

The museum's Education Department has created a comprehensive set of teaching materials for use in the classroom or home school, for grades 3 through 5. Contact the site for details. The Museum Shop at the site offers mail order service. You can request a free book list by e-mail at shop@marktwainhouse.org.

THE BEST STUFF Twain placed his private office/billiard room on the third floor, away from the bustle of a busy household. In this masculine room with balcony, he wrote at his desk, relaxed, and often enterained friends until the wee morning hours. The billiard table was a gift from an admirer.

THE WRITER AND HIS WORK

BORN: Nov. 30, 1835, in Florida, Mo.

DIED: April 21, 1910, in Redding, Conn.; buried Elmira, N.Y.

EDUCATED: Largely self-educated

MARRIED: Olivia Langdon, 1870; one son, three daughters

IMPORTANT WORKS: *The Adventures of Huckleberry Finn, The Adventures of Tom Sawyer, A Connecticut Yankee in King Arthur's Court, Innocents Abroad, Roughing It, The Celebrated Jumping Frog of Calaveras County, Tom Sawyer Abroad, A Dog's Tale, King Leopold's Soliloquy, The Prince and the Pauper, The Private History of a Campaign That Failed, Life on the Mississippi, Merry Tales, An American Claimant, The 1,000,000 Bank Note, Pudd'nhead Wilson, Personal Recollections of Joan of Arc, Following The Equator, What Is Man?, Chapters from My Autobiography, Christian Science, A Horse's Tale, Is Shakespeare Dead?, Extract From Captain Stormfield's Visit to Heaven, Letters From The Earth; The Death of Jean.* Twain wrote five travelogues, detailing his experiences in America's West, along the Mississippi, in Europe, the Middle East and Asia.

ACCOLADES: Honorary degrees from Yale, University of Missouri, and Oxford

INTERESTING BIO FACT: Bankruptcy, the death of his daughter Susan in 1906 and of his wife in 1904, turned Twain's once optimistic outlook and writing into deep pessimism. Twain wrote his last work, *The Death of Jean*, mourning the passing of his youngest daughter, Jean, in 1909. He vowed never to write again.

FURTHER READING *The Singular Mark Twain* by Fred Kaplan (2003); *Mark Twain and the American West* by Joseph L. Coulombe (2003); *The Complete Essays of Mark Twain* edited by Charles Neider (2000); *Mr. Clemens and Mark Twain* by Justin Kaplan (1991); *Biography of Mark Twain* by Albert Bigelow (1910)

ELSEWHERE IN THE AREA Harriet Beecher Stowe Center and Noah Webster House at Nook Farm; Old State House museum downtown

• A TWAIN RIDE •

Mark Twain traveled and lived throughout America, absorbing the places, people and experiences that became fodder for his writing. Other Twain sites in this book include Hannibal, Mo.; San Francisco and Sonoma, Calif.; as well as the campus of Elmira College in Upstate New York. ◩

All modern American literature comes from one book by Mark Twain called 'Huckleberry Finn'.

— ERNEST HEMINGWAY

SIGNS OF STORMFIELD
Trail Tells Story of Last Twain Home

Mark Twain was still in Europe when he set about building a new home in New England. He planned a magnificent Italian villa on a 350-acre country estate on a ridge overlooking what is now the Saugatuck Reservoir in **Redding, Conn.**, in southwestern Connecticut near Danbury. Twain named his estate, designed by the son of his friend, John Howells, Stormfield. He moved to Redding in June 1908 at the urging of his friend and official biographer, Albert Bigalow Paine, a Redding resident.

Twain lived at Stormfield only two years before he died in his bed there on April 21, 1910. His daughter, Clara, who lived in Europe, summered at the estate for years, then sold it. In 1923, the new owners undertook a renovation, during which a fire burned the house to the ground. Twain had installed an acetylene lighting system, the latest modern convenience, and when the blaze broke out, the highly flammable gas fed the fire. The mansion quickly was engulfed in flames.

Today, the curious can savor Twain's days in Redding on a 4-mile hiking trail that traverses a big part of Twain's original property. An owner of Stormfield sold 161 acres to the Town of Redding in 1974 in an open-space acquisition. The hiking trail, part of the town's extensive trail system, is accessible on Fox Run Road via Route 53 to Diamond Hill Road.

In 1924, new owners built a 5,600-square-foot Italian villa on some remaining acreage from Twain's estate. The mansion's exterior design of stucco and its tile roof closely resemble the original Stormfield. The villa, which stands today, remains private and is not open to the public. You can glimpse the renovated house from the hiking trail in fall and winter, after trees lose their leaves.

The owners later sold the house and the 65 remaining acres to the current owners in the 1980s. These owners split the Stormfield property and sold part of it for private construction. Their 40-acre lot included two of Stormfield's original outbuildings, on private property; the others had been demolished over the years.

A visit to the **Mark Twain Library,** at the corner of Route 53 and Diamond Hill Road in Redding, also allows a glimpse of Twain's last years in New England. Twain and some of his friends started the library in 1909 and Twain donated many of his own books to start the collection. Twain named the little library the Jean Clemens Twain Memorial Library, dedicated to his late daughter. The original structure was renovated and twice expanded. It remains open to the public. To reach the Twain library, call (203) 938-2545. E-mail: askSam@marktwainlibrary.org. On the Net: www.marktwainlibrary.org. For more information on Stormfield, go to www.historyofredding.com. ◪

NOAH WEBSTER HOUSE

Birthplace of Creator of America's First Dictionary

The restored, 18th-century house where the creator of America's first dictionary, Noah Webster, was born and spent his childhood functions as a busy museum and history center today in **West Hartford, Conn.** The Noah Webster House ($), part of the historic Nook Farm neighborhood, is located at 227 South Main St. The museum is 1 mile north of I-84. Take exit 41 and follow signs.

Webster's father, a farmer and weaver, built the two-story wood house in 1748 and Noah was born in the house on Oct. 16, 1758. The family of seven lived there until 1790. Noah left Hartford in 1774 to attend Yale, Connecticut's only college at the time, and he was a Yale student during the Revolutionary War. After graduating in 1778, Webster taught school in Connecticut and later studied law.

As an adult, Webster, father of eight children, disapproved of America's one-room schools, with their inferior books from England and untrained teachers. So in 1783, he wrote a landmark textbook, *A Grammatical Institute of the English Language.* Most people called it the "Blue-backed Speller" because of its blue cover. For the next 100 years, the Blue-backed Speller taught America's children how to read, spell and pronounce words. Until the speller came to the classroom, children in different parts of the country learned to spell and say words in different ways. Webster's efforts standardized the American language.

Webster began to write his dictionary at age 43. He labored over his masterpiece for the next 25 years, writing in three different homes, and finally completing it in 1825 while researching in England. His two-volume *An American Dictionary of the English Language* contained 70,000 definitions and required Webster to learn 26 languages. Webster's magnum opus, published in 1828, followed Webster's *A Compendious Dictionary of the English Language*, the first truly American dictionary, published in 1806.

Webster's dictionary first distinguished American usage from British. Webster used American spellings like "color" instead of the English "colour" and "music" instead " of "musick." He also added American words reflecting American experience that weren't in English dictionaries like "skunk" and "squash." The current descendant of Webster's seminal work, the Webster's Third New International Dictionary, defines about 470,000 words.

Other works by Webster include: *A History of the United States*; a version of the Bible, which he saw as his most significant work; and a book of essays completed only weeks before he died on May 28, 1843, in his home in New Haven, Conn.

The Noah Webster House is open Monday, Tuesday, Thursday, and Friday, from 10 a.m. to 4 p.m., and Saturday and Sunday from 1 p.m. to 4 p.m. in July and August. Open Thursday through Tuesday from 1 p.m. to 4 p.m. the rest of the year. Closed federal holidays and the first five weekdays in January. The site has been operated by the West Hartford Historical Society since 1970. It was privately owned until 1960 when it was given to the town of West Hartford and is now a National Historic Landmark.

For more information, contact the Noah Webster House, 227 S. Main St., West Hartford, CT 06107. Tel. (860) 521-5362. E-mail: perkinsa@snet .net. On the Net: http//noahwebsterhouse.org. For more on Webster, see Michigan in the East North Central section of this book. ◭

THORNTON WILDER'S CONNECTICUT
Playwright Lived in Hamden

The Pulitzer Prize-winning novelist and playwright Thornton Niven Wilder, who wrote the plays *Our Town, The Matchmaker, and The Skin of Our Teeth,* graduated from Yale University in **New Haven, Conn.**, in 1920. The Wisconsin native (born 1897) also lived on and off with his devoted sister, Isabel Wilder, in **Hamden, Conn.**, from 1929 until his death from a heart attack in 1975. He is buried in Mount Carmel Cemetery in Hamden. Wilder's gravesite features a simple family headstone with the name Wilder carved on the front and surrounded by shrubbery. Wilder's footstone bears his name.

In 1986, Isabel Wilder endowed the **Thornton Wilder Writing Competition** in Hamden to inspire high school students to write creatively. Four cash prizes are awarded annually for original creative work in prose and poetry. For more information, contact Thornton Wilder Writing Competition, c/o Friends of the Hamden Library, 2901 Dixwell Ave., Hamden CT 06518. Tel. (203) 288-0556 . On the Net: www.hamdenlibrary.org. Isabel Wilder lived in Hamden until her death in 1995.

Yale houses the **Thornton N. Wilder Papers** in its Beinecke Rare Book and Manuscript Library. The papers document Wilder's personal and literary life and include letters, manuscripts, personal papers, printed material, photographs, memorabilia and recordings. On the Net: webtext. library.yale.edu/xml2html/beinecke.WILDER.nav.html. While a student at Yale in 1920, Wilder published his first full-length play, *The Trumpet Shall Sound*, in the Yale Literary Magazine. The play was produced in 1926. Wilder's best-known work, the play *Our Town*, won the Pulitzer Prize in 1938. His play *The Matchmaker* (1954), was turned into the blockbuster musical *Hello, Dolly!*. His novel *The Bridge of San Luis Rey* won the 1928 Pulitzer Prize and his play *The Skin of Our Teeth* (1942) won Wilder his third Pulitzer Prize.

In 1962 Wilder received the first National Medal for Literature at a special White House ceremony. Wilder's friends included fellow writers **Gertrude Stein**, **Ernest Hemingway** and **Willa Cather**. For more on Wilder, contact The Thornton Wilder Society, 4855 Reservoir Road, NW, Washington, D.C. 20007. ◮

SARAH ORNE JEWETT HOUSE

19th-Century Writer's Sanctuary and Setting

LOCATION Southern Maine near the New Hampshire border, in South Berwick, 15 miles northwest of Portsmouth, N.H. The site is located about 8 miles west of I-95 in the center of town, at the intersection of Routes 4 and 236.

The Sarah Orne Jewett House ($) is open June 1 through Oct. 15, Friday through Sunday, for guided tours at 11 a.m., noon, 1, 2 , 3 and 4 p.m. For more information, contact the Sarah Orne Jewett House, 5 Portland St., South Berwick, ME 03908. Tel. (207) 384-2454. On the Net: www. spnea.org/visit/jewett.htm.

FRAME OF REFERENCE Sarah Orne Jewett's grandfather bought this 1774 house in 1839. He bequeathed it to Jewett's uncle in 1854, who gave it to Jewett and her sister, Mary, when he died. The sisters moved there in 1887. Jewett spent most of her life in the house. The Society for the Preservation of New England Antiquities opened the site to the public after restoration in 1984.

SIGNIFICANCE Jewett — novelist, short-story writer and poet — wrote 30 books and 170 stories, set in impoverished, isolated rural Maine. Although she lived for long periods in Boston and Europe, she wrote many of her important works in this house in her beloved Berwick. These include her collection of short stories, *A White Heron* (1886), and the masterpiece for which she is best remembered, the 1896 novel, *The Country of the Pointed Firs*. During her career, Jewett also wrote numerous magazine pieces, especially for The Atlantic Monthly. She established herself as a popular regional writer with her incisive, colorful and sympathetic studies of small-town New England life. Today Jewett is regarded as an important representative of the Realism movement in American literature.

ABOUT THE SITE The grand two-story, white, 13-room Georgian house was built by a veteran of the French and Indian wars, John Haggens, also a sea captain. In 1790, an el addition was added and a second floor in the 1890s. Sarah and Mary Jewett decorated the house, uniquely combining 18th-century architecture, antique furniture, and interesting wallpapers with furnishings of the whimsical Arts and Crafts movement. You'll see a tulip-patterned wallpaper in the hallway along with classic arches, wood carvings and moldings. Everything in the house remains almost exactly as when Sarah died in her bedroom in 1909. This includes the rare flocked maroon and pink 18th-century wallpaper with glittering mica in Mary's upstairs bedroom.

In Sarah Jewett's rear bedroom, you'll see her writing desk and an interesting cup hanging next to her bed. The cup contains metal-nibbed pens with Jewett's teeth marks, a result of late-night writing in bed. A small formal garden in the side yard includes herbs that Jewett wrote about, as well as the lilacs, a favorite, in the front yard. The site has a small museum shop.

HOT TIPS The two-story Green Revival house next door to the Jewett House functions as the South Berwick Public Library. The 1887 house, known locally as the Jewett-Eastman house, was the home of Jewett's sister, Caroline Jewett Eastman. The future author lived in the house during much of her childhood.

As an adult, Jewett was instrumental in preserving the nearby Hamilton House, which she used as the setting for her historical romance, *The Tory Lover*. The preservation society also owns The Hamilton House and sponsors many literary events there. For online texts of some of Jewett's writings, go to www.public.coe.edu/-theller/soj/sj-index.htm.

THE BEST STUFF Jewett wrote at a desk in the second-floor hall of her Berwick home. She could look through a window overlooking the major crossroads in the heart of her village. Seated at her desk, she observed the comings and goings of ordinary people, fodder for her novels and short stories. Her original desk chair remains in the hallway.

THE WRITER AND HER WORK
BORN: Sept. 3, 1849, in South Berwick
DIED: June 24, 1909, in South Berwick
EDUCATED: Berwick Academy, 1865
IMPORTANT WORKS: *Deephaven* (1877); *A Country Doctor* (1884); *A Marsh Island* (1885); *White Heron and Other Stories* (1886); *The King of Folly Island* (1888); *Betty Lester* (1890); *A Native of Winby* (1893); *The Life of Nancy* (1895); *Country of the Pointed Firs* (1896); *The Queen's Twin* (1899); *The Tory Lover* (1901); *Tales of New England* (1890). Short stories include: *Jenny Garrow's Lover* (1868); *Tom's Husband* (1882); *The*

Landscape Chamber (1887); *A Dunnett Shepherdess* (1899); *The Foreigner* (1900); *In Dark New England Days* (1900); *William's Wedding* (1910)

ACCOLADES: First woman to receive honorary Doctor of Letters from Bowdoin College, 1901

INTERESTING BIO FACT: In 1902, Jewett was in a serious carriage accident when the horse slipped on a loose rock and stumbled. This accident resulted in dizzy spells and inability to concentrate and effectively ended Jewett's writing career. In her lifetime, Jewett formed friendships with many artists and intellectuals of her time. These included fellow writers **Willa Cather**, William Dean Howells, Henry James, Alice G. Howe, Rudyard Kipling, **Harriet Beecher Stowe** and **John Greenleaf Whittier**. She had an especially strong relationship with the widow of famous publisher James T. Fields, Annie, with whom she lived and traveled extensively.

FURTHER READING *Sarah Orne Jewett: Her World and Her Work* by Paula Blanchard (1994) Biographies; *Sarah Orne Jewett: A Writer's Life* by Elizabeth Silverthorne (1993); *Appreciation of Sarah Orne Jewett* by Richard Cary (1973); *Sarah Orne Jewett: An American Persephone* by Sarah W. Sherman (1989)

ELSEWHERE IN THE AREA Counting House Museum downtown ◿

EDWIN ROBINSON HOUSE

Childhood Home of Major American Poet

The childhood home of 20th-century poet Edwin Arlington Robinson (1869-1935) stands in **Gardiner, Maine**, at 67 Lincoln Ave. at Danforth Street. Robinson, a major naturalist poet who won three Pulitzer Prizes for his work, resisted the romantic sentimentality of earlier poets and helped energize American *fin de siècle* poetry. The Italianate-style house, a National Historic Landmark, is privately owned and not open to the public.

Robinson was noted for his mastery of verse forms and admired for his moving poetic vision. His most influential poems include: *The Children of the Night* (1897); *Captain Craig* (1902); *The Man Against the Sky* (1916); *Merlin* (1917), the first of three Arthurian tales dealing with the modern world, followed by *Lancelot* (1920) and *Tristram* (1927). His important narratives include *Amaranth* (1934) and *King Jasper* (1935). His early short poems remain among his most widely read. These include *Richard Cory* and *Miniver Cheevy*, figures of failure and tragedy.

Robinson's family moved into the Victorian house in Gardiner shortly after his birth in nearby Head Tide, Maine. Robinson's father remodeled the 1856 Victorian house into the Italianate style soon after buying it in 1870. The lovely two-story, white wood house today has black shutters and a screened side porch. Robinson grew up in Gardiner, which later provided the model for a series of poems that he wrote throughout his career. Robinson began seriously writing poetry in his childhood home at age 11 and as a teen, attended meetings of the town's poetry society as its youngest member.

Although he graduated from Harvard, Robinson lived much of his life in poverty, dedicated to his work. An unexpected support came from President Theodore Roosevelt, an admirer of Robinson's poetry. He arranged a job for Robinson at the New York Customs House (which Robinson later quit) and helped arrange the publishing of his work. Robinson also wrote several unsuccessful plays.

Robinson was awarded the Pulitzer Prize for poetry in 1921 for *Collected Poems* and in 1924 for *The Man Who Died Twice*. He earned his third Pulitzer for *Tristram*, which became a best seller.

For a photo of The Robinson House, go online to www.gpl.lib.me.us/garear.htm. ⬧

HARRIET BEECHER STOWE HOUSE

Where 'Uncle Tom's Cabin' Was Penned

The woman whom President Abraham Lincoln reportedly called "the little lady whose book started the Civil War" lived in a two-story house in Maine when she wrote her electrifying *Uncle Tom's Cabin* (1852). Today the house where Harriet Beecher Stowe lived from 1850 to circa 1852 is part of Bowdoin College in **Brunswick, Maine**, 30 miles north of Portland. The white house with 14 rooms is located at 63 Federal St. While the college considers options for renovation and use, the main house currently is closed. An annex, added in 1968 as an inn, is used for student housing.

The famous author, humanitarian, and abolitionist lived in the Federal Street house while her husband, Calvin Ellis Stowe, taught at Bowdoin College two blocks away. The Stowes moved to the house, built in 1807 in the Federal style, from Cincinnati, Ohio, where Harriet Stowe and her future husband both taught at the Western Female Institute. The house stands empty today and apparently was not all that welcoming when Stowe lived in it. In a letter dated Oct. 29, 1850, Stowe wrote that the house was cold, crowded and chaotic. She said there was a schoolroom upstairs and a dining room next door, and she could not take a nap without being disturbed.

Although Stowe wrote 30 books, she is remembered for *Uncle Tom's Cabin*, which introduced many Americans to the horrors of slavery she had heard about while living in the Midwest. In Ohio, Stowe had interviewed former slaves escaping to freedom on the Underground Railroad. Historians say the Stowes' Brunswick house might have been a stop on the Underground Railroad. The house was designated a National Historic Landmark in 1963.

Some characters in *Uncle Tom's Cabin* mirrored real-life individuals and the book told their stories as slaves. The novel was first published as a serial in the abolitionist newspaper, National Era, and became an overnight best seller in the United States and Europe. It has been translated into 23 languages.

For more information, contact the director of Facilities Administration at Bowdoin College at (207) 725-3706. On the Net: www.cr.nps.gov/nr/travel/underground/me1.htm. For more Stowe sites and details on the author, see Ohio and Connecticut in this book. ⌂

WADSWORTH-LONGFELLOW HOUSE

Childhood Home of Famous 19th-Century Poet

The **Portland, Maine**, house where the poet Henry Wadsworth Longfellow grew up welcomes visitors in the heart of the city's busting downtown area, at 487 Congress St. The grand, three-story brick house is the oldest house on the Portland peninsula and was its grandest when built in 1785 by Longfellow's grandparents, Gen. Peleg and Elizabeth Wadsworth. Longfellow's parents brought him to the house when he was 8 months old.

Longfellow, who grew up to become the most widely published and most famous American poet of the 1800's, lived in the house until he left to study at Bowdoin College in 1821. As an adult, Longfellow returned to his Portland home often and last visited only a year before his death in 1882. His love for his hometown greatly influenced his later works, and he wrote about Portland in several poems, including *My Lost Youth* and *The Lighthouse*. At age 13, Longfellow wrote his first verse in the Portland house, *The Battle of Lovell's Pond*, based on a story his grandfather had told him. Henry possibly wrote his earliest verses, including *The Rainy Day*, on the round, tilt-top table which is now in the best parlor chamber. The Portland Gazette published young Longfellow's *The Battle* in 1820.

The Georgian-style house, the first in Portland built entirely of brick (shipped from Philadelphia) has been restored to look as it did in the 1890s. Most of the furnishings are original and reflect the Victorian style favored by Longfellow's sister, Anne, who cared for the home after her parents died. Several treasures possibly from Longfellow's childhood also remain, including an early 19th century rod-back, Windsor high chair and an early 19th century, slant-top school desk. A particularly dear treasure in the house is the Henshall and Co. dinner service in the rear dining room. The set might have been a gift to Henry's parents at their marriage in 1804. Longfellow obviously treasured the table service, too. He is said to have written several lines of his poem *Keramos* about it: "Nor less the coarser household wares/ The willow pattern, that we knew/ In childhood, with its bridge of blue/ Leading to unknown thoroughfares."

When the Longfellow family lived in the house, it commanded a view of the harbor and Back Bay, which the young poet could see from the third floor where the eight children played. The third floor, with seven rooms, was added in 1815 after a fire on the roof damaged the grand house. The family gave the restored house a new Federal appearance, altering the window and door moldings. They also installed new technological advancements, such as a hot air furnace and an intricate bell system that remains today. Modern visitors also will find the Longfellows' original garden, including a calicanthus bush and a mock orange amid brick paths and benches.

Three generations of Wadsworths and Longfellows called the site home until 1901. The family then gave it to the Maine Historical Society which opened it to visitors as Maine's first "historic house museum." Longfellow is buried in the family tomb at Western Cemetery in Portland.

Many of Longfellow's poems remain among the most familiar in American literature, although his influence on modern poetry is less than that of other contemporary poets. His best-known works include *Evangeline*, *The Song of Hiawatha*, and *The Courtship of Miles Standish*. Among his popular shorter poems are *The Village Blacksmith*, *The Children's Hour*, and *Paul Revere's Ride*.

Visitors should park in two public parking garages within two blocks of the site along Cumberland Street. The first floor of the house, as well as the Maine Historical Society Museum and museum shop, are handicapped accessible. The house is open May through October, Monday through Saturday 10 a.m. to 4 p.m. and Sunday noon to 4 p.m. Special weekend hours November and December. Closed other months and major holidays.

For more information, contact the Maine Historical Society, 485 Congress St., Portland, ME 04101. Tel. (207) 774-1822. E-mail: info@mainehistory.org. On the Net: www.mainehistory.org. For more on Longfellow, see Massachusetts in this book. ◮

QUILLCOTE
Home of Kate Douglas Wiggin

Kate Douglas Wiggin, who wrote the children's book, *Rebecca of Sunnybrook Farm* (1903), spent much of her childhood in the family's Greek Revival house called Quillcote in **Hollis, Maine**. The house today is privately owned and not open to the public. The site, located east of Hollis center on Salmon Falls Road, was listed on the National Register of Historic Places in 1977.

Wiggin was born in Philadelphia in 1856 and was reared in that city, as well as in Portland, Maine, and Hollis. She returned to Hollis from New York City, where she ran a kindergarten, in 1889 following her husband's death. In Hollis, Wiggin wrote the children's book *Timothy's Quest* (1890), which was made into a silent movie, and the adult novel *The Village Watch-Tower* (1895), which was set in Hollis. *Rebecca* was also made into movies in 1922 and 1932. The setting for the book resembled Hollis.

A devoted advocate for early childhood education, she, along with her sister, Nora, founded a school for kindergarten teachers, as well as the Salmon Falls Village Library, which still serves as the town library for Hollis.

Wiggin's other works include: *The Birds' Christmas Carol* (1887/1889); *The New Chronicles of Rebecca* (1907); *The Story of Patsy* (1883/1889; for children); *The Story Hour* (1890); *Polly Oliver's Problem* (1893); *A Cathedral Courtship* (1893); *The Republic of Childhood* (1895-96, with her sister, Nora); *Hymns for Kindergartners* (18??); *Penelope's Progress* (1898) plus other *Penelope* books; *The Diary of a Goose Girl* (1902); *The Posy Ring* (1903, verses); *The Old Peabody Pew* (1907); *Pinafore Palace* (1907); *Susanna and Sue* (1909); *Arabian Nights* (1909); Mother Carey's Chickens (1911, movie 1938, 1963); *The Story of Waitstill Baxter* (1913); *Ladies in Waiting* (1918); *Homespun Tales* (1920).

Wiggin died in Harrow, England, in 1923. She is buried in Tory Hill Cemetery in **Buxton, Maine**. The plot is on Kate Douglas Wiggin Avenue, 60 feet on the left.

HOT TIP Bowdoin College provides Wiggin's personal papers online at http://library.bowdoin.edu/arch/mss/kdwg.shtml. ⌂

JOHN ADAMS BIRTHPLACE
Preserving Political and Literary Legacy

John Adams — delegate to the First Continental Congress, signer of the Declaration of Independence, early American diplomat, first U.S. vice president and second U.S. president — left behind more than a dazzling political legacy. He also left an important literary heritage. Adams created a significant body of literature with his diaries; his letters to his wife of 52 years, Abigail, and to Thomas Jefferson; his autobiography; and his essays on government. Adams' monumental diary covers more than 60 years of his extraordinary life, which ended in 1826.

You can discover John Adams, politician, diplomat and writer at the **Adams National Historical Park** ($) in **Quincy, Mass.**, 10 miles south of Boston. The park's visitor center is located in the Galleria at President's Place at 1250 Hancock St. Validated parking is in the garage at the rear of the building.

The 14-acre park, rich in natural, historic and cultural themes, comprises 11 historic structures, including the **John Adams Birthplace** where Adams was born in 1735. The site also preserves the John Quincy Adams Birthplace, where Adams' son, who became 6th U.S. president, was born in 1767; the "Old House," home to four generations of the Adams family; and the Adams Stone Library. The library contains more than 14,000 historic volumes and includes John Quincy Adams' book collection.

The Harvard-educated, honest and unbending Adams' important works include: *Dissertation on the Canon and Feudal Law* (1765); *Novanglus or a History of the Dispute with America* (1775, appearing periodically in the Boston Gazette); *A Defense of the Constitutions of Government in the United States of America* (1787-88); and *Discourses on Davila* (1790).

A collection of the writings of John Quincy Adams is included in **The Adams Papers**, a projected 100-volume edition of Adams family documents in the custody of the Massachusetts Historical Society in Boston. Harvard University began publication of the series, edited by Lyman H. Butterfield and others, in 1961.

The Adams National Historical Park visitor center and historic homes are open daily, mid-April through mid-November, from 9 a.m. to 5 p.m. The visitor center only is open mid-November to mid-April, Monday through Friday, limited hours. For more information, contact Adams NHP,

135 Adams St., Quincy, MA 02169-1749. Tel. (617) 770-1175. E-mail: ADAM_Visitor_Center@nps.gov. On the Net: www.nps.gov/adam.

FURTHER READING *The Book of Abigail and John: Selected Letters 1762-1784* edited by L. H. Butterfield, et al (2003); *John Adams* by David Mc-Cullough (2001); *The Political Writings of John Adams* edited by George W. Carey (2001); *The Adams-Jefferson Letters* edited by Lester J. Cappon (1988) ◮

GREATER BOSTON, BY THE BOOK

During the 19th-century rise of American literature, Boston reigned supreme. Such literary luminaries as Emerson, Thoreau, Hawthorne, the Alcotts, Walt Whitman and Margaret Fuller lived and wrote in the old city by the sea. The Massachusetts capital has been home to many intellectuals and writers from its illustrious Colonial times to present day. In fact, some historians trace the beginning of American literature to the *Mayflower Compact* that the male Pilgrims signed aboard the Mayflower in 1620.

Later William Bradford, governor of the Pilgrims' fledgling colony, penned one of the earliest historical works, *The History of Plymouth Plantation*. Then John Winthrop, governor of the Massachusetts Bay Colony, also wrote a journal, *History of New England*. These histories were the start of the tremendous influence Boston was to exert on American literature for hundreds of years.

No wonder the area's 19th-century doers and thinkers somewhat arrogantly dubbed Boston the "Hub of the Universe."

From Phyllis Wheatly, whose deeply moving account of her life as a slave in Boston (1761) was the first of the published slave diaries, to the leading writers of the Harlem Renaissance who studied at Harvard (Langston Hughes, for one), greater Boston has hosted a long list of important writers. Today "America's Walking City" offers plenty of literary treasures from the past. When in the Boston area, check out these sites:

BOSTON

ERNEST HEMINGWAY COLLECTION at the John F. Kennedy Library and Museum on Columbia Point. Due greatly to President Kennedy's widow, Jacqueline Kennedy, the JFK Library houses 100,000 pages of Hemingway's writings; 10,000 photographs; letters; French copybooks with handwritten drafts of *The Sun Also Rises*; and many personal items, including the novelist's flask, wallet, and a ring containing shrapnel from the leg injury he sustained in WWI. Most were gifts from Hemingway's fourth wife, Mary. The Hemingway Room welcomes researchers. Tel.: (617) 514-1600 or 1-866-JFK-1960. E-mail: kennedy.library@nara.gov. On the Net: www.jfklibrary.org.

COTTON MATHER'S GRAVE in the 1659 Copp's Hill Burying Ground in Boston's North End, near Old North Church. Mather (1663-1728), the Puritan minister who fueled the Salem witch hysteria, produced 444 volumes of written work, including *Memorable Providences, Relating to*

Witchcraft's, and Possessions (1689); *The Wonders of the Invisible World* (1693); and *Magnalia Christi Americana* (1702). Copp's Hill is part of the Boston Freedom Trail. Mather is buried alongside his influential father, Increase Mather, who was minister at Old North Church.

THE OLD BOOKSTORE, 1 School St., at Washington St., also along Boston's historic Freedom Trail. The red-brick building with gambrel roof was built in 1711 as a home and apothecary. During the mid-1800s, the landmark reigned supreme in Boston's literary scene, functioning as offices for the prestigious Ticknor and Fields publishing house. The Civil War-era publishing giant listed such clients as Ralph Waldo Emerson, Nathaniel Hawthorne, Henry Wadsworth Longfellow, Harriet Beecher Stowe, Oliver Wendell Holmes, Louisa May Alcott, and Henry David Thoreau. Today the former bookstore is home to The Boston Globe Store, founded by The Boston Globe newspaper. The store features Boston Globe page reproductions, Boston history and travel books, and Boston and New England maps. Tel. (617) 367- 4000. On the Net: www.nps.gov/bost/bost_lographics/oldcornr.htm.

BOSTON PUBLIC LIBRARY, in Copley Square. The National Historic Landmark was established in 1848 and claims many firsts: America's first publicly supported municipal library, the first public library to lend a book, the first to have a branch library, and the first to have a children's room. The huge, granite library, known for the massive lion sculptures flanking the three arches at its front entrance, serves Boston not only as an awesome resource for literature, but as a museum and architectural masterpiece in the Renaissance Revival style. The library's nearly 5,000 yearly programs and exhibits are free and open to the public.

BOSTON ATHENAEUM, 10 1/2 Beacon St. Founded in 1807 and modeled on the Athenæum and Lyceum of Liverpool in Great Britain, this National Historic Landmark is one of the oldest independent libraries in America. Its collections today comprise more than 500,000 volumes, emphasizing Boston and New England history, biography and English and American literature. Its gallery brims with fine and decorative arts. The Athenaeum is open for guided art and architecture tours, with reservations, on Tuesday and Thursday at 3 p.m. Tel. (617) 227-0270. The first floor and newspaper rooms are open weekdays, except for holidays. On the Net: www.bostonathenaeum.org.

ALCOTT RESIDENCE, in North Boston at 20 Pinckney St. The Alcotts rented rooms here when Louisa Alcott was 10, and her father, Bronson Alcott, had opened his progressive school in Boston. The Alcotts moved from this site to a faraway farm, Fruitlands, the Transcendentalists' ill-fated agricultural experiment. Later they moved to Concord, Mass. The site today is privately owned and not open to the public.

FRANCES PARKMAN HOUSE, 50 Chesnut St. Parkman (1823-93), a historian, wrote *The Oregon Trail* and *A Half-Century of Conflict*. The site is a multiple private dwelling and not open to the public.

CAMBRIDGE

HENRY WADSWORTH LONGFELLOW HOUSE, 105 Brattle St. See separate entry in this book.

E. E. CUMMINGS BIRTHPLACE, 104 Irving St., at junction of Irving and Scott streets. The house where the poet was born in 1894 and lived with his family is marked with a historic plaque on the high fence that now surrounds the grounds. The house is privately owned and not open to the public.

OLIVER WENDELL HOLMES BIRTHPLACE. The poet, physician and essayist, was born in 1841 in the old "gambrel-roofed" house in Cambridge at 8 Montgomery Place (now Bosworth Street) near Harvard. Holmes is best known for *Autocrat at the Breakfast Table* and *The Last Leaf*.

FANNIE FARMER BURIAL SITE, Mount Auburn Cemetery, 580 Mount Auburn St. Farmer (1857-1915) created the first cookbook that listed very specific and accurate measurements. Before her *Fannie Farmer Cookbook* in 1896, recipe ingredients were estimates. Tel. (617) 547-7105.

HOUGHTON LIBRARY AT HARVARD UNIVERSITY. The library on the Cambridge campus focuses on the study of Western civilization. Collections center on American, Continental, and English history and literature. Exhibits culled from its collections might include the personal effects, notes, books, and other objects of interest from such writers as Copernicus, Emily Dickinson, John Keats, Edward Lear, Dante, Tennessee Williams, Goethe, Cervantes, and Lewis Carroll. The Houghton Library's rare book collection of about 500,000 printed books includes early 2,600 books from the fifteenth century and extensive holdings of European and American imprints thereafter.

The library's Manuscript Department administers a diverse collection of more than 10 million manuscripts, with material dating from 3,000 BCE to the present. The Houghton Library is open without fee to adult researchers. Tel. (617) 495-8415. On the Net: hcl.harvard .edu/houghton.

CONCORD

The village of Concord played a central role in America's literary life in the mid-1800s. People traveled from afar to Concord just to talk with Ralph Waldo Emerson, the embodiment of the vigorous intellectual life. Literary sites in Concord, 16 miles northwest of Boston, include:

RALPH WALDO EMERSON HOUSE, 28 Cambridge Turnpike;

ORCHARD HOUSE, 399 Lexington Rd., home of Bronson and Louisa May Alcott;

WALDEN POND, along 126 just south of Route 2, and related Thoreau sites;

THE OLD MANSE, 269 Monument St., home to Emerson and Nathaniel Hawthorne.

THE WAYSIDE, Lexington Road next to Orchard House, was Hawthorne's home;

THE CONCORD FREE PUBLIC LIBRARY, 129 Main St., features books and items on the town's literary heritage. Tel. (978) 318-3342. On the Net: www.concordnet.org/library/scollect/scoll.

AUTHOR'S RIDGE AT SLEEPY HOLLOW CEMETERY, on Bedford Street (Route 62), is the burial site for Concord's literary elite.

THE CONCORD BOOKSHOP, 65 Main St., is a local landmark for book lovers. Also, in the nearby town of Harvard, Mass., you can visit Fruitlands, 102 Prospect Hill Rd., where Bronson Alcott and other Transcendentalist leaders established a short-lived Utopia in 1843. You can find more about Fruitlands and Concord literary sites under separate entries in this book.

HOT TIP The Literary Trail of Greater Boston ($) features guided, 20-mile walking/ trolley tours of area literary sites. For information, contact The History Collaborative, 175 Berkeley St., 3E, Boston, MA 02117. Tel. (617) 574-5950. On the Net: www.bostonhistorycollaborative.org. ◪

NEW ENGLAND *Massachusetts*

ORCHARD HOUSE

Home of Louisa May Alcott, Little Women

LOCATION Concord, Mass., 16 miles northwest of Boston, at 399 Lexington Road. The site is located 1 mile east of Concord Center, reached via Route 2 or the Cambridge Turnpike.

Orchard House ($) is open for guided tours April through October, Monday through Saturday, from 10 a.m. to 4:30 p.m., and on Sunday from 1 p.m. to 4:30 p.m.; from November through March, Monday through Friday, from 11 a.m. to 3 p.m., Saturday from 10 a.m. to 4:40 p.m. and on Sunday from 1 p.m. to 4:30 p.m. Closed Easter, Thanksgiving and Dec. 25. and Jan. 1 through 15.

For more information, contact Orchard House, P.O. Box 343, Concord, MA 01742-0343. Tel. (978) 369-4118. E-mail: info@louisamayalcott.org. On the Net: www.louisamayalcott.org.

FRAME OF REFERENCE Louisa May Alcott lived in Orchard House, dating from the early 1700s, with her family from 1858 to 1877. The Louisa May Alcott Memorial Association was founded in 1911 to preserve the house as a public museum.

SIGNIFICANCE Louisa May Alcott was a novelist, short-story writer and poet who wrote 270 works, although she is known mostly as the author of the books *Little Women* (1868) and *Little Men* (1871). Alcott wrote much of these two best sellers at Orchard House. She also set her autobiographical *Little Women* in the house, although the experiences she wrote about would have happened during the Alcott years at **Hillside** (see **Wayside** entry) and other places. *Little Women* has never been out of print and made Alcott a respected and financially successful writer. The book mirrors the experiences of the four March sisters — Jo (Louisa herself, the second-oldest daughter), Meg, Beth and Amy. Alcott's *Little Men* (1871) featured Jo as an adult and was even more successful than *Little Women*. Film adaptations have been made of several of Alcott's books, including four versions of *Little Women*.

Alcott turned to writing to support her poor but intellectual and idealistic family. Alcotts' father, Bronson, also a writer, was continually involved in financially disastrous utopian schemes, including pioneering schools and an experimental community named **Fruitlands** (see sidebar). Women's rights and educational reform—important social issues of 19th-century America — were two of Alcott's pet causes that often appear as themes in her work.

ABOUT THE SITE A visit to Orchard House takes you back to the time when Concord and Boston were literary America's epicenter. Not only did such luminaries as the Alcotts, Emerson, Thoreau, Hawthorne, Margaret Fuller, Julia Ward, and James Russell Lowell live in Concord, they socialized with each other, lectured the town's citizens, and most importantly, recorded their world in pivotal works of literature. They also enhanced Louisa's rich home life and education. Her father home-schooled her; Emerson's library provided philosophy books for her use; and Thoreau taught her botany.

Alcott's home, located next to Hawthorne's Wayside and across from Emerson's house, today embodies that heady mid-19th century era when Transcendental philosophy led an American Renaissance. Guided tours by costumed interpreters introduce visitors to the reform movements that the Alcotts backed, objects that were important to the family, and to the family members themselves. You'll learn about Louisa, who sequestered herself in her upstairs, corner bedroom to pen *Moods*, *Hospital Sketches* (about her Civil War experiences) and much of *Little Women* and its sequels. As you go about the nine rooms, left almost exactly as they were when the Alcotts lived in the house, you'll learn of Louisa's idealistic father; her mother, Abigail, an independent woman who was one of the first paid social workers in Massachusetts; Anna Alcott Pratt, Meg in *Little Women*, who had a talent for acting; Elizabeth Sewall Alcott, Beth in the book, who died shortly before the family moved to Orchard House; May Alcott Nieriker, the character Amy, an artist; and of course, Louisa herself, Jo the writer in *Little Women*.

The plain two-story, brown house itself comprises two joined houses, both dating to the early 1700s. Bronson Alcott bought the larger house and a small, el-shaped tenant house on the property and placed it at the rear of the main house. He named his new house after the apple orchards that stood on his 12 acres of land. (Alcott considered apples the perfect food.) During renovation, he also added arches and alcoves to create interesting little nooks and corners.

About 75 percent of the home's furnishings today were owned by the Alcotts. You'll see May's artwork on the walls, as well as her sketches preserved on window casings and doors. In the kitchen you can still see where May decorated a wooden board with a burning poker, a scene Louisa recreated in *Little Women*.

The site's museum shop stocks collectibles, books and educational materials related to the Alcotts and their world.

HOT TIPS Orchard House guided tours last 30 minutes and are usually offered every half hour from April through October. In other months, call on the day of your visit for tour times. Tour tickets are available on a first-come, first-served basis. Group size limited. Most of the site is handicapped accessible. The site offers many special programs year-round with emphasis on educational events for school groups and Girl Scouts. Alcott family papers are collected at Houghton Library, Harvard University.

THE BEST STUFF You can almost imagine Louisa writing away in her cozy, white-walled bedroom, where the tiny desk her father built remains in front of the windows. The semi-circular desk, attached to the wall, still has Louisa's ink well on it. Christmas at a decorated Orchard House is a holiday treat and the educational programs, living history tours and special events will interest people of all ages.

THE WRITER AND HER WORK

BORN: Nov. 29, 1832, in Germantown, Penn.

DIED: March 6, 1888, in Boston; buried in Sleepy Hollow Cemetery, Concord

EDUCATED: Temple School in Boston, founded by father, who also tutored her

IMPORTANT WORKS: *Flower Fables* (1854); *Hospital Sketches* (1863); *Moods* (1865); *Little Women* (1868); *Proverb Stories* (1868); *The Inheritance* (1868); *An Old-Fashioned Girl* (1870); *Little Men* (1871); *Jo's Boys* (1886); *Aunt Jo's Scrap Bag* (6 volumes, 1872-82); *Eight Cousins* (1875); *Rose in Bloom* (1876); *Silver Pitchers* (1876); *Under the Lilacs* (1878); *Meadow Blossoms* (1879); *Behind A Mask* (thrillers, 1879); *Water Cresses* (1879); *Sparkles for Bright Eyes* (1879); *Jack and Jill* (1880); *Spinning-Wheel Stories* (1884); *Lulu's Library* (3 volumes, 1886-1889); *A Garland for Girls* (1888); *Work* (1873); *A Modern Mephistopheles* (1877); *Diana and Persis* (1978); *A Long Fatal Love Chase* (1995)

INTERESTING BIO FACT: Louisa Alcott realized early that her father was too impractical to provide for his family. After the failure of Fruitlands, her lifelong concern for the welfare of her family began. To escape poverty, Alcott worked as a teacher, domestic servant, seamstress, nurse and finally turned to writing. Her career began with sensational thrillers published under the male pseudonym, A. M. Barnard. The stories proved both popular and lucrative. Alcott sold her first short story in 1852 and other salable fiction rapidly followed. She was a regular contributor to Atlantic Monthly magazine. She continued writing until two years before her death.

FURTHER READING *Louisa May and Mr. Thoreau's Flute* by Julie Dunlap (2002); *Louisa May Alcott: A Biography* by Madeleine B. Stern (1996); *The World of Louisa May Alcott* by William Anderson (1995)

ELSEWHERE IN THE AREA Minute Man National Historical Park, 174 Liberty St.; Concord Museum, 200 Lexington Rd.; Museum of Our National Heritage, 33 Marrett Road; Great Meadows Wildlife Refuge; the original Concord grapevine

• FRUITLANDS •

TRANSCENDENTALISTS' UTOPIAN COMMUNITY

In 1843, Bronson Alcott moved from Boston with his family, including 10-year-old Louisa, to a remote area near the town of **Harvard, Mass.**, to start a utopian community called Fruitlands. Alcott and a small, colorful group of people — ranging from ex-convicts to nudists, based their communal farm on the ideals of Transcendentalism. This philosophy, rooted in the Romanticism that had engulfed Europe in the late 18th and early 19th centuries, held that the individual is in direct communication with God and nature and he has no need for complacent or rigid churches or creeds. Emerson, who helped formalize Transcendentalism, urged self-reliance and nonconformity. The movement played a key role in the so-called American Renaissance of literature.

Fruitlands citizens were forbidden to eat meat or use animal products, including wool, leather, honey, wax and manure. Alcott made himself a tunic and shoes from linen cloth, which he wore everywhere. Sugar, milk, cheese, tea and coffee were forbidden. The commune planned to live *by the fruits of the land* on their farm. Each person would help grow food and build housing, but still have time to develop such talents as writing poetry or fiction, woodworking or fine art.

The high-minded social experiment collapsed after six months. But travelers in the 21st century can visit the place where the Transcendentalists worked and dreamed.

The 200-acre **Fruitlands** ($) today comprises the **Four Museums of American Art and History**. The site is located 30 miles west of Boston and 6 miles from the junction of I-495 and MA 2. Take exit 38A to Old Shirley Road. Fruitlands is 2 miles on the right.

Fruitlands includes the Fruitlands Farmhouse where the Alcotts and leaders of the transcendentalist movement attempted their new social order; the Shaker Museum, an 18th-century building filled with Shaker furniture and artifacts; the Picture Gallery of American Art, featuring works of the Hudson River School; and the Indian Museum. The site on Prospect Hill also includes a reception center, tea room (featuring Sunday brunch), a museum store and four nature trails.

From the tearoom you can catch a 50-mile panoramic view of the Nashua River Valley. The trails feature two interpreted sites: an American Indian hunting-gathering ground and a colonial farm. The farmhouse features letters and memorabilia from Fruitlands leaders, offering insight into the story behind the utopian community.

Bronson Alcott became interested in communal living after meeting Charles Lane during a teaching trip to England in 1842. Alcott considered the other utopian communities in America at the time (Brook Farm and Hopedale) lacking in ideals and "not pure enough."

But the community could not be sustained by human labor alone. Its strict diet of fruits and grains left some malnourished. Alcott and Lane also took off on lecturing tours to promote the community, leaving the women and children to do the manual labor. When Emerson visited Fruitlands in June 1843, he reportedly commented, "They look well in July. We shall see them in December."

The community called it quits in January 1844. The Alcotts moved to Concord, where Louisa wrote her famous *Little Women*. She also wrote a short account of the experimental lifestyle at Fruitlands in *Transcendental Wild Oats*.

The Fruitlands ($) is open daily from mid-May through October 31 from 11 a.m. to 4:30 p.m. on weekdays, and from 10 a.m. to 5 p.m. on weekends. For more information, contact Fruitlands Museums, 102 Prospect Hill Road, Harvard, MA 01451-1301. Tel. (978) 456-3924. On the Net: www.fruitlands.org.

HOT TIP Since Fruitlands is largely an outdoor site, you should wear comfortable shoes, dress for the weather, and bring a hat ⬧

THE WAYSIDE

Home to Alcotts, Hawthorne, Margaret Sidney

The Wayside, a rambling, two-story white wood house next to Orchard House in **Concord, Mass.**, has been home to several of Concord's leading literati. Bronson Alcott and his family owned the house, which they called **Hillside**, from 1845 to 1852. Nathaniel Hawthorne bought the house from the Alcotts. He renamed it Wayside. Hawthorne spent the last four years of his life at Wayside, from 1860 to 1864.

In 1883, Harriet Lothrop, who under the pen name Margaret Sidney created *The Five Little Peppers*, acquired it. When Sidney's husband, Daniel, died in 1892, she devoted herself to preserving The Wayside, as well as Orchard House and the "**Grapevine Cottage**." This house, located just east of Wayside on Lexington Road, was the birthplace of Ephraim Bull, father of the famous Concord grape. The Wayside, now part of the sprawling Minute Man National Park, was also once the home of the muster master, or roll caller, of the Concord Minute Men. Other illustrious residents also rented or owned the famous house.

Hawthorne bought Wayside — the only one he ever owned — from the Alcotts after returning from Salem, Mass., where he had written *The Scarlet Letter*. (See entry in this book.) The family lived at Wayside only a year before President Franklin Pierce appointed Hawthorne consul to Liverpool, England. In their absence, Hawthorne rented out the house. The family returned to Concord in 1860 and rejoined the neighborhood of famous Concord intellectuals.

In the neighborhood, the Hawthorne children — Una, Julian and Rose — played with Edward and Ellen Emerson and Louisa May Alcott and her sister May. Hawthrone fashioned a path between Wayside and Orchard House to cement the children's friendship. He, however, spent most of his time alone, much as he had in Salem, to write in the tower study he had built atop Wayside.

Several years after Hawthorne's death in 1864, his heirs sold Wayside to Mrs. Abby Gray. Her son, George Arthur, painted the murals on the ceiling of the Tower Study in memory of Hawthorne. Margaret Sydney preserved the house as it was in Hawthorne's time, and bought some of Hawthorne's furniture from his daughter Rose. The Wayside was designated a National Historic Landmark in 1963 and became a part of Minute Man National

Historical Park in 1965. It was the first literary site the National Park Service acquired.

The Wayside is open daily, May through October from 9:30 a.m. to 5:30 p.m. Closed Wednesdays and major holidays. Guided tours ($) of the house and barn last 35 minutes. You must be able to climb steep stairs in the main house, but the barn is handicapped accessible. The site offers a bookstore, restrooms and picnic area. For more information, contact Minute Man National Historical Park, 174 Liberty St., Concord, MA 01742. Tel. (978) 369-6993. E-mail: mima_info@nps.gov. On the Net: www.nps.gov/mima/wayside/Home1.htm. ⌂

EMERSON'S CONCORD
Sites Tell of Transcendentalist Icon

LOCATION The town of Concord is located in eastern Massachusetts along Route 2, 16 miles west of Boston. From I-95, take Route 2 west and follow signs.

Emerson-related sites in Concord include: the **Ralph Waldo Emerson Memorial House** ($), 28 Cambridge Turnpike at Lexington Rd.; **The Old Manse**, 269 Monument St., where he briefly lived; **The Concord Museum,** ($) Lexington Road near the Emerson House, where his study has been preserved intact; and **Author's Ridge at Sleepy Hollow Cemetery,** where he is buried, along with Thoreau, Hawthorne, Louisa May and Bronson Alcott; and the **Concord Free Public Library** downtown. The library's special collections contain manuscripts, printed volumes, photographs, ephemera, and works of art, all documenting Emerson's life and work. Emerson served on the library's committee from 1873 until his death.

The Emerson House is open mid-April through the last weekend in October, Thursday through Saturday. Call ahead to verify hours. For more information, contact Emerson Memorial House, 28 Cambridge Turnpike, Concord, MA. 01742. Tel. (978) 369-2236.

FRAME OF REFERENCE Emerson, born in Boston, and his brothers visited Concord often during their childhood. Emerson's fondness for Concord led him to settle permanently in the village in 1834. In 1835, Emerson and his family moved from The Old Manse near North Bridge to this house, built in 1828 on 2 acres of land. Emerson lived here from age 32 until his death in 1882. The Emerson Memorial Association formed in 1930 to oversee the house, still a property of the Emerson family. The house, a National Historic Landmark, opened to the public for tours in the 1940s.

SIGNIFICANCE Emerson, a poet and the most important American essayist and lecturer of the 19th century, was the leading proponent of an intellectual movement known as American Transcendentalism. (For explanation of Transcendentalism, see Fruitlands entry.) In Concord, Emerson penned his first book, the seminal *Nature* (1836), detailing his ideas and values of self-reliance and of living in harmony with nature. The book represented a decade of intense study of philosophy, religion, and literature and influenced such Idealist writers as **Thoreau** and **Walt Whitman**.

Emerson wrote his first series of essays at his home in Concord, launching a very public career that cast him not only as "The Sage of Concord" and the anchor of an intellectual community that profoundly influenced American literature and history, but also as an international celebrity. Through his presence, Emerson's village west of Boston became "the Delphi of New England," the epicenter of what many view as the American Renaissance.

Emerson co-founded the Transcendentalist periodical, The Dial, which he edited it from 1842 to its failure in 1844. At the height of his 40-year career, Emerson was giving as many as 80 lectures a year. In all, he gave about 1500 public lectures, traveling as far as California and Canada but generally staying in Massachusetts. He did all of his writing at home. The Ralph Waldo Emerson Memorial House seeks to preserve his important legacy.

ABOUT THE SITE Nearly everything in the squarish, two-story, white clapboard Georgian mansion remains as it was in 1882 when Emerson died. Although the furnishings of the actual study where he wrote have been removed to nearby Concord Museum, and Harvard University houses his personal library, the room contains a replica of his round writing table, whale-oil lamps, family books and aeolian harp.

Photographs of family and the famous fill the eight rooms open to the public and in an upstairs stairway, pictures of Abraham Lincoln, Ulysses Grant and poet Alfred, Lord Tennyson adorn the walls. Shelves of books are everywhere. Treasures include a cup that the German philosopher Goethe gave the Emerson family; a doll house with original hand-made furniture and drapes made by Emerson's daughters; a 1750 rocking horse belonging to the poet's son and an 1879 bust of Emerson by his friend and Concord neighbor, Daniel Chester French. French sculpted the Lincoln statue in the Lincoln Memorial in Washington, D.C., and the Minute Man statue at Concord's North Bridge.

A white fence surrounds Emerson's barn and the preserved garden grounds on Lexington Road, where passing tourists gawk at the famous home once owned by one of America's most famous personalities.

HOT TIPS On-street parking spaces in Concord are difficult to find. Combine a visit to the Emerson house with a stop at the Concord Museum, which has a small parking lot. For an interesting dining experience, make reservations at the historic Colonial Inn (1716) at 48 Monument Square, near the town rotary.

THE BEST STUFF The home's many bookcases have handles on the ends, a design that would allow them to be removed quickly in case there was a fire. On July 24, 1872, a blaze did break out in the house, partially destroying it. The Emersons escaped, and daring young neighbors helped rescue the books and other possessions in baskets and blankets. **Louisa May Alcott** helped save Emerson's manuscripts. Surviving Emerson letters have charred edges.

The fire damaged Emerson' health and concentration, and friends urged him to travel abroad, which he did with daughter Ellen. Meanwhile, admirers raised about $11,000 to rebuild the house. When Emerson returned to Concord in May 1873, the restored house looked as it was before the fire. Concord citizens turned out en masse to welcome their most famous resident. After Emerson's death, his descendants elected to move his entire study intact to fireproof quarters at the Concord Museum, built on land that was once Emerson's horse pasture.

THE WRITER AND HIS WORK

BORN: May 25, 1803, in Boston

DIED: April 27, 1882, in Concord; buried in Sleepy Hollow Cemetery in Concord

EDUCATED: Boston Latin School; Harvard College, 1821; Harvard Divinity School

MARRIED: Ellen Tucker, 1829, who died of TB; Lidian Jackson, 1835; four children

IMPORTANT WORKS: *Nature* (1836); *Essays* (1841); *Essays: Second Series* (1844); *Poems* (1847); *Nature: Addresses and Lectures* (1849); *Representative Men* (1850); *The Conduct of Life* (1860); *Fate* (1860); *May-Day and Other Pieces* (1867); *Society and Solitude* (1870). Famous essays include : *The American Scholar* (1837); *Self Reliance*; *Compensation*; *The Over-Soul*; *The Poet*; *Experience*. His *Divinity School Address* in 1838 first brought him fame.

INTERESTING BIO FACT: After Harvard, Emerson worked as a colleague-pastor at the Second Church of Boston and in 1829 was ordained as pastor of the Second Unitarian Church in Boston. Upon his first wife's death, Emerson, whose family had nine generations of ministers, underwent a religious and personal crisis. He also inherited property, freeing him of financial worries. He left the church and sailed to Europe. He met Thomas Carlyle and William Wordsworth, forming life-long friendships. Upon returning to Concord in 1833, he began the pivotal career based on ideals, including a radical anti-slavery stance during the Civil War, for which he is remembered.

FURTHER READING *Emerson* by Lawrence Bull (2003); *Understanding Emerson* by Kenneth S. Sacks (2003); *The Spiritual Teachings of Ralph Waldo Emerson* by Richard G. Geldard and Robert Richardson (2001)

ELSEWHERE IN THE AREA See listing under Orchard House in this book.

• WHAT IS TRANSCENDENTALISM? •

Transcendental philosophy took root in Emerson's parlor. A small group of people who regularly gathered there, including Thoreau, Bronson Alcott and Hawthorne, to discuss philosophical and religious problems. Concord neighbors nicknamed the group "the Transcendental Club." The adjective came to describe their idealistic thinking, based on the fiery energy of Puritanism, that dramatically shaped the direction of American literature.

Transcendentalism, rooted in the Romanticism that had engulfed Europe in the late 18th and early 19th centuries, held that the individual has direct communication with God and nature and has no need for complacent and rigid churches or creeds. Emerson, who helped formalize Transcendentalism, urged self-reliance and nonconformity.

For more information, go to the American Transcendentalism Web site at www.transcendentalism.org. ◪

THE OLD MANSE

Crossroads of America's Two Revolutions

LOCATION Concord, Mass., at 269 Monument St. From Concord center (Monument Square) take Monument Street north 1/2 mile. Site entrance is at left, bordering North Bridge and Minute Man National Historic Park.

The Old Manse ($) is open for guided tours mid-April through Oct. 31, Monday through Saturday, from 10 a.m. to 5 p.m. Sundays and holidays noon to 5 p.m. For more information, contact The Old Manse, P.O. Box 572, Concord, MA 01742. Tel. (978) 369-3909. Email: oldmanse@ttor .org. On the Net: www.concord.org/town/manse/old_manse.html. or www.thetrustees.org.

FRAME OF REFERENCE The Old Manse was built in 1770 for the Rev. William Emerson, spiritual leader of the Concord Minute Men and grandfather of Ralph Waldo Emerson. On April 19, 1775, the Rev. Emerson and his wife witnessed the outbreak of the American Revolution as they watched the battle of Concord from behind their home. Emerson's father, William, as well as the writer's beloved aunt, Mary Moody Emerson, were born in the Old Manse. Ralph Waldo Emerson moved to the house with his mother in Oct. 1834. He spent a year in the Manse before he remarried and moved to a house on the other side of Concord center, now known as The Emerson House.

Nathaniel Hawthorne rented the Manse with his new bride from 1842 to the fall of 1845, when he returned to Salem, Mass. His first child, Una, was born in the Manse in 1844. Emerson employed Henry David Thoreau as a handyman and gardener while the Hawthornes lived in the old house. The Emerson-Ripley-Ames family descendants summered in the house until 1939. The Trustees of Reservations bought and restored the house in 1939 and opened it to the public.

SIGNIFICANCE People around Concord like to describe their historic town as the center of America's two great revolutions: one that began in April 1775 at North Bridge and led to the nation's independence from England; and the other the Literary Renaissance that had a huge and lasting intellectual and social impact on the country. The Old Manse tells both stories.

In this house, with a clear view of the North Bridge where the first battle of the American Revolution took place, Ralph Waldo Emerson finished his first great work, *Nature* (1836). The seminal essay became the Bible of New England Transcendentalism, an essentially religious movement that profoundly influenced American literature. Hawthorne later immortalized the house by writing his book, *Mosses From An Old Manse* (1846).

ABOUT THE SITE The Old Manse today reflects the influential people who lived there and the events associated with it in its more than 230 years of existence. The stately wood frame, three-story, late Georgian-style house is painted gray and has a gambrel roof, center entrance with overhead pediments, and two chimneys, an unusual look for its era.

Many of the furnishings and furniture in the 13-room house are original, but not all are restored to the time of Hawthorne's idyllic stay. The cookstove Hawthorne put in the kitchen was later replaced, then removed to restore the older fireplace and oven. Most of the thousands of books in the house are from the Ripley family. You'll find a quarter chair owned by William Emerson, a case clock of Ralph Waldo's, and an 1862 Steinway box grand piano. The site's big barn burned down in the 1920s. The former carriage house functions as a museum shop.

Visitors are not allowed into the attic but we can learn of it in *The Old Manse*. Hawthorne described the huge garret as "an arched hall, dimly illuminated through small and dusty windows. . .there were nooks or rather caverns, of deep obscurity. . . beams and rafters, roughly hewn and with strips of bark still on them, and the rude masonry of the chimneys, made the garret look wild and uncivilized, an aspect unlike what was seen elsewhere in the quiet and decorous old house." Hawthorne also said the attic had a little, whitewashed apartment with fireplace called "the Saint's Chamber." The name reflected the times when young ministers slept, studied and prayed there.

Treasures found in the attic include a 1660 book by John Calvin and writings and art on the walls. The dusky portraits Hawthorne put in the attic are now displayed downstairs. Wife Sophia scratched some messages with diamonds on two of the western window panes of the upstairs study, and another pane was discovered in the attic and has been placed in a downstairs window. The etching is signed "Sophia A. Hawthrone 1843. Nath' Hawthorne. This is his study." You can view these today. Sophia also practiced her art in the back parlor, which was at times used as the dining room.

A historically restored vegetable garden out front reflects the one Thoreau planted in 1842 for his friends, the Hawthornes.

HOT TIPS Park in the parking lot across Monument Street. Allow 1/2 hour to see the house; a half day to tour with a visit to Minute Man park. Restrooms located near parking lot and in North Bridge Visitor Center. Picnicking is allowed in the park.

THE BEST STUFF The west windows of the second-story study where the first Rev. Emerson watched the Battle of Concord remain the same as then, though others have been enlarged. This is the same study where Ralph Waldo Emerson finished writing *Nature*, and where Hawthorne penned his works. Emerson also wrote the Concord hymn sung at the dedication of the Monument obelisk, erected on the battlefield next door, on July 4, 1837. You can read first verse of Emerson's hymn on the base of the Minute Man statue sculpted by Daniel Chester French.

You also can view the folding desk Hawthorne constructed against the study wall. (He found writing at a desk facing a window was too distracting.) Emerson's desk, however, overlooks the Concord River. Ripley's desk is downstairs.

In 1836, the Rev. Ripley gave the Battle Ground property to the town and citizens planted trees along the street in 1836. Ralph Waldo Emerson's grandmother married Ripley, the Puritan minister of Concord, after her husband's death in 1776. During his time, the house was called the Old Ripley Mansion. Hawthorne dubbed the house The Old Manse in recognition of all the ministers who had owned it. Manse is the Scottish word for a minister's home.

THE WRITERS AND THEIR WORK For information on Emerson, see Ralph Waldo Emerson House; on Hawthorne, see the House of Seven Gables entry.

FURTHER READING *The Old Manse and the People Who Lived There* by Paul Brooks

ELSEWHERE IN THE AREA See entries under Orchard House. ♤

The study had three windows. . . the third, facing northward, commanded a broader view of the river at a spot where its hitherto obscure waters gleam forth into the light of history. It was at this window that the clergyman who then dwelt in the Manse stood watching the outbreak of a long and deadly struggle between two nations. . . . Many strangers come in the summer time to view the battle-ground.

— HAWTHORNE in *The Old Manse*

WALDEN POND

Site of Thoreau's Experiment in Simple Living

LOCATION Concord, Massachusetts, 16 miles northwest of Boston, along Route 126 just south of Route 2, toward the town of Lincoln. Watch for signs. The **Walden Pond State Reservation** is open daily from 5 a.m. to half an hour after sunset. For more information, contact Walden Pond, 915 Walden St., Concord MA 01742. Tel. (978) 369-3254. On the Net: www.state.ma.us/dem/parks/wldn.htm or www.walden.org.

FRAME OF REFERENCE Henry David Thoreau lived at Walden Pond from July 4, 1845 to Sept. 6, 1847. His experiences and meditations at the pond are recounted in his literary classic, *Walden* (1854). The slow creation of Walden Pond began 10,000 to 12,000 years ago with the retreat of a glacier that covered New England. The Commonwealth of Massachusetts acquired the nearly barren property in 1922.

SIGNIFICANCE Thoreau, philosopher-poet, essayist-lecturer-critic-general handyman and leading Transcendentalist writer, is best known for *Walden*, his account of his two years of simple living at Walden Pond, and his essay, *Civil Disobedience* (1849). This essay about passive resistance, stemming from Thoreau's choosing jail instead of paying his poll tax as a protest against slavery, brought him international fame. It later inspired such political leaders and reformers as India's Mahatma Gandhi, President John F. Kennedy, Civil Rights leader Martin Luther King, Jr., Russian philosopher Leo Tolstoy and U.S. Supreme Court Justice William O. Douglas.

At Walden, Thoreau lived on 40 acres of land owned by his friend Emerson to conduct an experiment in essential living. On the shores of the pond, he read, wrote, walked, meditated, made friends with the beasts, birds and fish, and lived in a one-room cabin he built. He recorded his experiences, thoughts, and fascination with woodland life in *Walden*. At the pond, Thoreau also wrote *A Week on the Concord and Merrimack Rivers* (1849), describing a rowboat trip he had taken with his brother in 1839.

Walden, as well as Thoreau's 2 million-word journal (published 1906), helped inspire awareness and respect for the natural environment.

ABOUT THE SITE Walden Pond State Reservation encompasses the 103 foot-deep, glacial kettle-hole pond, a National Historic Landmark since 1965, and 333 acres of land. The 2,280 acres of woods around the reservation, called Walden Woods, remains undeveloped and are zealously guarded by a preservation organization.

After Thoreau's famous book, crowds flocked to the pond, and in the late 19th century, a large excursion park with a dance hall and baseball diamond attracted throngs. The park burned down in 1902, but people still flocked to the pond, threatening its fragile ecosystem and literary history. When the commonwealth took over the site in 1922, it restricted the pond's use and instituted strict crowd controls.

Visitors to Walden today can walk a trail around the pond to view wildlife and absorb the wooded place Thoreau made famous. On a gentle slope at the far side of the pond, near the commuter railroad tracks, you'll find the location of Thoreau's cabin, now marked by an inscribed fieldstone where Thoreau's hearth stood. A nearby kern, a pile of rocks to which you can add, commemorates Thoreau's legacy. Look for a dramatic outcropping of bedrock still known as Emerson's Cliff.

Above the cabin site, you can detect some of the stumps of the 400 white pines Thoreau planted in the cleared "sprout land" nearly 160 years ago. The great hurricane of 1938 leveled the trees. You can view a statue of the writer and a replica of Thoreau's little house across the highway near the parking lot, as well as at nearby Concord Museum.

Visitors still flock yearly to Walden Pond to recreate, absorb and enjoy rabbits, foxes, red tail hawks, migratory geese and rainbow trout, and revel in the area's beauty, a tradition ignited by Thoreau's sojourn.

HOT TIPS The number of visitors at Walden Pond is tightly restricted to 1,000 at a time. Call ahead when about to visit to check on parking availability or arrive early in the morning. Parking ($) is restricted to the lot off Route 126. Dogs, bicycles, floatation devices, grills, fires, off-road vehicles, motorcycles, motor boats and alcohol are prohibited. Row boats and canoes permitted. You also can swim, picnic, hike, fish, cross-country ski and snowshoe. Stay on the trails and established sitting areas and avoid all slopes where vegetation is growing. Lifeguards are on duty seasonally. The site has changing rooms.

THE BEST STUFF The Thoreau Institute at Walden Woods, less than half a mile from Walden Pond, houses the Walden Woods Project, a conservation effort, and the Thoreau Society. The Institute comprises two structures situated on 18 acres of conservation land in Walden Woods between Pine Hill and Beech Spring roads in Lincoln. The institute features the world's foremost collection of Thoreau and Thoreau-related materials, an archives and technology center, a reading room, educational programs and resources, and a gift shop. The building and the grounds, originally used as a hunting retreat, resemble an English Tudor estate. Hiking trails through Walden Woods link the institute to Walden Pond.

For more information, contact The Thoreau Society, 44 Baker Farm, Lincoln, MA 01773-3004. Tel. (781) 259-4750. E-mail: ThoreauSociety@walden.org. For information on preservation efforts, contact Walden Woods Project at the same mailing address. E-mail: Webmaster@walden.org.

Check with the site and local news media for the early morning walks around the pond with "Henry David Thoreau," an authentically clad interpreter. For more on Thoreau's famous act of civil disobedience, read or go see the 1970 play, *The Night Thoreau Spent in Jail*, written by Jerome Lawrence and Robert E. Lee.

THE WRITER AND HIS WORK

BORN: July 12, 1817, in Concord

DIED: May 6, 1862, in Concord

EDUCATED: Concord Academy; Harvard, 1837

IMPORTANT WORKS: *A Week on the Concord and Merrimac Rivers* (1849); *Walden* (1854); *On the Duty of Civil Disobedience* (1849); essays on the Maine wilderness (1864), Cape Cod (1865), and Quebec (1866); *A Plea for Captain John Brown* (1860); *Succession of Forest Trees* (1860). Published posthumously - *Excursions* (1863); *The Maine Woods* (1864); *Cape Cod* (1864); *Letters to Various Persons* (1865); *A Yankee in Canada* (1866); *Early Spring in Massachusetts* (1881); *Summer* (1884); *Winter* (1887); *Autumn* (1892)

INTERESTING BIO FACT: Thoreau couldn't support himself with his writing. Well-educated and reared in genteel poverty, he took jobs in his father's pencil factory, as a handyman and as a surveyor. He also contributed to the Transcendentalist magazine The Dial, which Emerson edited. Known as a serious, stoic, even humorless man (**Robert Lewis Stevenson** called him "skulker") in his lifetime, his lasting reputation exceeds that of an imitator of Emerson, as some critics had labeled him. He is revered as a contributor to natural history, a pioneer ecologist and conservationist and especially as an advocate of a simple life. In Walden he enjoined us to "simplify, simplify, simplify."

FURTHER READING *Henry David Thoreau and the Moral Agency of Knowing* by Alfred I. Tauber (2003); *My Contract With Henry* by Robin Vaupel (2003); *Walking With Henry* by Thomas Locker (2002); *Henry Thoreau: A Life of the Mind* by William E. Cain (2000); *The Senses of Walden* by Stanley Cavell (1992)

ELSEWHERE IN THE AREA See Emerson House entry. ⌂

> *I went to the woods because I wished to live deliberately, to front only the essential facts of life. . .*
>
> — THOREAU in *Walden*

TRACKING THOREAU

Emerson, Thoreau's first and most powerful champion, called him "*the man of Concord.*" Today, you'll find these remembrances of the Concord celebrity (locals insist you pronounce it "Thorough," as in thoroughfare) at these sites, in addition to **Walden Pond State Historic Site**:

SITE OF THE OLD CONCORD JAIL, where Thoreau spent a night in 1846 for refusing to pay the poll tax. A plaque marks the spot on Main Street downtown near the Monument Square rotary.

THE CONCORD MUSEUM houses a collection of Thoreau-related artifacts, including the narrow bed from his cabin at Walden Pond and the small desk on which he penned *Walden* and *Civil Disobedience*. You'll also see a replica of the one-room cabin on the grounds.

AUTHOR'S RIDGE IN SLEEP HOLLOW CEMETERY, on Bedford Road (Route 62), is Thoreau's burial site.

THOREAU STREET, just south of Concord Center, named in honor of the naturalist-philosopher.

THOREAU INSTITUTE AT WALDEN WOODS, in adjacent Lincoln between Pine Hill and Beech Spring streets, houses The Thoreau Society and the Walden Woods Project. The project, begun in 1994, works to preserve Walden Woods. The institute offers conference and seminar space for educational programs, as well as residence facilities for visiting scholars, teachers, and students.

THE THOREAU SOCIETY, the oldest and largest organization devoted to an American author. Established in 1941, the society, housed in The Thoreau Institute buildings, honors Thoreau by fostering education about his life, works, and philosophy and by coordinating research on his life and writings. The society/institute is a repository for Thoreauviana and relevant materials and advocates for the preservation of Thoreau country. On the Net: www.walden.org/society.

The society maintains **The Shop at Walden Pond** at 915 Walden St. in Concord, near Monument Square. Tel. (978) 287-5477. E-mail: Shop@walden.org ◮

> *I have traveled a good deal in Concord.*
>
> — THOREAU in *Walden*

LONGFELLOW HOUSE
Popular 19th-Century Poet's Historic Home

LOCATION Eastern Massachusetts in Cambridge, at 105 Brattle St. From I-90/Massachusetts Turnpike, take Allston/Cambridge exit toward Cambridge. Cross bridge, turn left onto Memorial Drive and go past intersection with John F. Kennedy Street. Bear right onto Hawthorne Street. Take next left onto Mt. Auburn Street and next right onto Willard Street. Turn right onto Brattle Street at next intersection. **The Longfellow National Historic Site** is on immediate left.

The site is open from mid-May to Oct. 31, Wednesday though Sunday, from 10 a.m. to 4:30 p.m. Closed major holidays. Entrance to the **Longfellow House** ($) is by guided tour only. For more information, contact Longfellow National Historic Site, 105 Brattle St., Cambridge, MA 02138. Tel. (617) 876-4491.

FRAME OF REFERENCE Henry Wadsworth Longfellow lived in the former "Craigie Castle," built in 1759, for nearly 50 years, from 1837 to his death in 1882. George Washington, commander-in-chief of the newly formed Continental Army, headquartered and planned the Siege of Boston here between July 1775 and April 1776. In 1913, the Longfellow children formed a trust to preserve the house. In 1972, the family's trust donated the property to the National Park Service and it became a National Historic Site.

SIGNIFICANCE In this lifetime and for years after his death, Longfellow was the most popular and widely read American poet in the world. He also was the first American to earn a substantial income writing poetry. His poems outsold those by Browning and Tennyson. Some argue that the brilliant professor, literary critic, essayist, translator and all-around intellectual holds the current title of most popular poet in American literature.

Best remembered as the author of *The Song of Hiawatha* (1855), a bestseller of the time, the Harvard professor of modern languages achieved immense popularity with long narrative poems such as *Evangeline* (1847), *The Courtship of Miles Standish* (1858), and *Tales of a Wayside Inn* (1863), which included the perennially favorite poem, *Paul Revere's Ride*. His work endures as a valuable repository of the moral and spiritual ideals of Victorian America.

ABOUT THE SITE Longfellow's two-story, yellow clapboard, 22-room mansion already claimed a rich history by the time his industrialist father-in-law gave it and 5 acres of land to him as a wedding present. Longfellow had rented lodging in the house, owned by Andrew Craigie, as a new Harvard professor and had admired it.

Visitors today cross an expanse of lawn to the house set back from Brattle Street, once known as "Tory Row," for the mansions of wealthy loyalists to King George that lined the lovely and celebrated avenue. Brattle Street remains home to many of the rich, powerful and famous in the Boston area. To enter the stately mansion of mid-Georgian Colonial architecture, you'll go past the low, white fence, negotiate three sets of low steps, and walk through a broad front door. Then take a deep breath.

The renovated parlor, study, dining room, "Lady Washington's Drawing Room" and halls on the main floor contain historic furnishings, books, portraits and the fabulous paintings and sculpture that belonged to the Longfellows. Off to the right, Longfellow's study features his writing table in the center of the room. It is heaped with books and Longfellow's papers. An inkstand that belonged to Coleridge remains on the table, surrounded by book cabinet, floor clock, portraits and a fireplace with ornate gold mirror above it.

One if the house's great treasures is an armchair hand-carved from the wood of the "spreading chestnut tree" that Longfellow wrote about in *The Village Blacksmith*.

The tree was cut down in the late 1870s when Brattle Street was widened. The children of Cambridge gave it to Longfellow on his 72nd birthday.

The dark, rich and spacious library behind the study contains 10,000 of the Longfellows' leather-bound books. A collection of outstanding Asian furniture and artwork decorates the house, including a red-lacquered side table in the red and gold dining room with rare china. The home's collection preserves about 35,000 historic items and archives about 600,000 manuscripts. The formal garden out back displays the statuary Longfellow placed in the pond. You also can tour the carriage house.

Longfellow's diary documents the many prominent guests who visited his hospitable home, including writers Emerson, Hawthorne, Julia Ward Howe, as well as Charles Sumner, the Massachusetts senator and leading anti-slavery advocate. (*The Works of Charles Sumner*, 15 vols., 1870-83).

HOT TIPS Parking is on-street and severely limited. The best way to reach the site is by public transportation. Take the MBTA Red Line subway train to Harvard Square and walk down Brattle Street to the house. The visitor center and carriage house are accessible via wheelchair ramp. The first floor rooms of the house are wheelchair accessible via a lift from the visitor center. Researchers may access the museum archives by appointment year-round on Tuesday and Wednesday, 9 a.m. to 5 p.m.

Harvard's Houghton Library preserves The Longfellow Papers. Go online to: oasis.harvard.edu/html/hou00425.html. For more on Longfellow, see Portland, Maine in this book.

THE BEST STUFF Longfellow's upstairs chamber once served as Washington's bedroom. The poet mused in *Hyperion*, which he wrote in his chambers before a picturesque window, that "the shades of Washington and William Tell seem to walk together on these Elysian Fields." The window commanded a view of the house's expansive lawn and gardens.

THE WRITER AND HIS WORK

BORN: Feb. 27, 1807, in Portland, Maine

DIED: March 24, 1882, in Cambridge

MARRIED: Mary Storer Potter, 1831, died 1835; Frances Appleton, 1843; six children

EDUCATED: Bowdoin College, 1825; studied in Europe

IMPORTANT WORKS: *Voices of the Night* (1839); *Ballads and Other Poems* (1841); *The Belfry of Bruges and Other Poems* (1846); *Evangeline* (1846); *The Seaside and the Fireside* (1850); *The Song of Hiawatha* (1855); *The Courtship of Miles Standish and Other Poems* (1858); *Tales of a Wayside Inn* (1863); *Christus: A Mystery* (1872). Shorter poems include *Day is Done*; *The Village Blacksmith*; *Hymn to the Night*; *Excelsior*; *The Wreck of the Hesperus*; *A Psalm of Life*; *My Lost Youth*; *The Arrow and the Song*; *The Jewish Cemetery at Newport*; *The Rainy Day*; *The Bridge*; *The Slave's Dream; A Cross of Snow*. Longfellow also penned a poetic translation of *Dante's Divine Comedy* (1867), for which he wrote a sequence of six sonnets.

ACCOLADES: Honorary degrees from Oxford and Cambridge; bust in Poet's Corner of Westminster Abbey

INTERESTING BIO FACT: Although Longfellow was highly praised, beloved and successful in his lifetime, his literary reputation declined after the 19th century. His verse was criticized — especially by **Edgar Allen Poe** — as simple, sentimental, often moralizing and of greatest appeal to schoolchildren. In the 1870s, adoring students nationwide celebrated his birthday as a holiday. After World War I, his poetry was rarely included in school curricula.

FURTHER READING *A Henry Wadsworth Longfellow Companion* by Robert L. Gale (2003); *Henry Wadsworth Longfellow: America's Beloved Poet* by Bonnie L. Lukes (2002); *Evangeline for Children* by Alice Couvillan et. al. (2002)

ELSEWHERE IN THE AREA See entry *Greater Boston, By The Book.* ⏃

LONGFELLOW'S WAYSIDE INN

Speaking of Longfellow, would you like to dine at the inn near Boston where the poet set his version of the Canterbury Tales? Then make your way to **Sudbury, Mass**., and visit Longfellow's Wayside Inn. The wooden, gambrel-roofed inn, which offers authentic lunches and dinners as well as unique lodging, has been in operation since 1716. It is America's oldest operating inn.

The Wayside, a nonprofit educational and charitable trust and National Historic Site, is located on Wayside Inn Road, west of The Boston Post Road (Route 20) in South Sudbury, an historic town 15 miles west of Boston. From I-90 (Mass Pike), take Route 128 north to exit 26 onto Route 20. Go right onto Wayside Inn Road to site on right.

The inn is part of the **Wayside Inn Historic District**, built in 1940 under the direction of auto manufacturer and philanthropist Henry Ford. The 106-acre district includes The Wayside Inn Grist Mill, a two-story stone structure with huge water wheel.; Martha-Mary Chapel; the 1798 one-room Red Stone School, relocated from Sterling, Mass. The school is the one described in the nursery rhyme, *Mary Had a Little Lamb*. Both are open for self-guided tours. Pick up a brochure at the inn.

The publication of Longfellow's *Tales of a Wayside Inn* in 1863 thrust the old tavern into the national spotlight. By popular demand, the establishment, named the Red Horse Inn at the time, changed its name to honor the famous poet.

A main-floor back room at the Wayside bears the name The Longfellow Parlor. In the *Tales*, Longfellow immortalized this cozy room and his Cambridge friends when he wrote of them sitting around the glowing fireplace exchanging stories. In this setting, readers learned of *Paul Revere's Ride*.

You'll find a luncheon or dinner in the Main Dining Room unforgettable. Costumed wait-staff serve visitors authentic food. You can begin your meal with a Coow Woow, perhaps America's first cocktail, or hot Indian Pudding.

The Old Bar Room to the right of the entrance was part of the downstairs of the original, two-room homestead that David How built in 1709. The inn grew by seven additions over the years to its present 14 rooms on the main floor, plus 10 guest rooms upstairs. You also can view other historic rooms, as well as the barn, gate house, Longfellow's Rose Garden and the ice house on the rolling grounds of fields, forest and babbling brooks.

For more information, contact Longfellow's Wayside Inn, 72 Wayside Inn

Road, Sudbury MA 01776. Tel: (978) 443-1776. On the Net: www.wayside .org. For reservations to dine or lodge in one of the 10 rooms at the Wayside Inn, call (978) 443-1776 or e-mail to reservations@wayside.org.

HOT TIP The Wayside Inn Archives contains more than 500,000 documents relating to the Howe family and the development of what would eventually be called Longfellow's Wayside Inn. The Wayside Inn Archives is open by appointment only. ⌂

> *As ancient is this Hostelry, As any in the land may be, built in the old colonial day, When men lived in a grander way, With ampler hospitality.*
>
> — LONGFELLOW

MEET 'WILLIAM BRADFORD'

Visit Plimoth Plantation Where Governor Penned History

Want an up-close-and-personal visit with the colonial governor who recorded some of the country's first history in his expansive journals? Then go to Plimoth Plantation ($) near **Plymouth, Mass.**, and talk to "William Bradford" himself. You can visit the modern-day interpreter, who dresses, walks and talks his historic role as Bradford in a recreated daub-and-waddle cottage on Cape Cod Bay, 3 miles south of Plymouth. Bradford's thatched-roof home is one of many authentic structures at Plimoth (Bradford's spelling), a living history museum of the Pilgrims' 17th-century village.

Bradford (1590-1657) came to New England aboard the Mayflower in 1620. While governor of the colony from 1622 to 1656, he vividly recorded in his journals the Puritan separatists' triumphs over hardships, as well as their arduous Mayflower voyage. The Pilgrims, a term Bradford coined for the group, also produced the ***Mayflower Compact***, a document for self-government signed aboard the ship. Some historians cite the 1620 *Mayflower Compact* as the beginning of American literature.

Although Bradford's manuscript probably was not intended for publication, it was printed in 1856 in London as *The History of Plymouth Plantation*. Historians of the 17th and 18th centuries used Bradford's book, noted for its fine prose, as documentation for their writings.

Plymouth, one of the New World's earliest settlements, lasted from 1620 to 1691, when it was absorbed by the Massachusetts Bay Colony. **John Winthrop**, governor of the Massachusetts Bay Colony, also wrote a journal, *History of New England*. Winthrop's journal chronicles events from 1630 until two months before his death in 1649. The bay colony also published the country's first book, the *Bay Psalm Book* (1640), for use in worship services.

Plimoth Plantation is open daily from late March through November. You can buy tickets to the plantation or to the Mayflower II, a replica of the original Mayflower, at both locations or online. The Mayflower II, as well as the famous Plymouth Rock where the Pilgrims landed, are both located on the waterfront in Plymouth. For more information, contact Plimoth Plantation, P.O. Box 1620, Plymouth, MA 12362. Tel. (508) 746-1622. On the Net: www.plimoth.org.

HOT TIPS Park free in a lot at Plimoth Plantation. Visitors with disabilities should park in the lower lot. Metered parking near Mayflower II. Wear sturdy shoes and dress for the weather.

Want to experience an authentic Thanksgiving Day feast at Plimoth? Call (508) 746-1622, ext. 8364 for details on dining and functions. E-mail: dcox@plimoth.org.

FURTHER READING *William Bradford and Plymouth* by Susan Whitehurst (2003); *William Bradford: Governor of Plymouth Colony* by Marianne Hering (2000); *William Bradford: Rock of Plymouth* by Kieran Doherty (1999) ◮

WILLIAM CULLEN BRYANT HOMESTEAD

Home of Famous Poet, Influential Editor

LOCATION In the Hampshire Hills of western Massachusetts, in Cummington, 60 miles northwest of Springfield, Mass., and .2 miles east of the intersection of Route 112 and Route 9 (Bryant Road) at 207 Bryant Road.

The William Cullen Bryant Homestead ($) is open for guided tours from the last Friday in June through Labor Day, Friday through Sunday and on some holidays from 1 p.m. to 5 p.m. From Labor Day through Columbus Day, the site is open on Saturday and some holidays from 1 p.m. to 5 p.m. Grounds, including Rivulet Trail, are open year-round from sunrise to sunset. For more information, contact The William Cullen Bryant Homestead, 207 Bryant Road, Cummington, MA 01026-9639. Tel. (413) 634-2244. E-mail: bryanthomestead@ttor.org. On the Net: www .thetrustees.org.

FRAME OF REFERENCE Young William Cullen Bryant moved with his family in 1799 to the homestead, built in 1783 by Bryant's grandfather. Bryant spent his childhood on the farm, moving to New York in 1825. His family sold the farm in 1835. Thirty years later Bryant repurchased it and summered there until his death at age 84. The Trustees of Reservations owns and operates the homestead, a National Historic Landmark, which opened for public visits in 1931.

SIGNIFICANCE Bryant — world traveler, famous poet and critic, and influential editor of the New York Evening Post — was America's earliest theorist of poetry and one of America's most important poets throughout the mid-1800s. At the Cummington homestead, 18-year old "Cullen" wrote *Thanatopsis* (1817), which became his most famous poem. Decades later, as a noted poet and influential editor, Bryant returned to his summer retreat in Cummington, where he found inspiration for some of his finest verse.

Bryant held a romantic view of nature in an age of America's westward expansion and discovery of the young country's wildness and beauty. His poetry embodies the past, Europe, and the stirring idea of Manifest Destiny. His "odes" to natural objects epitomize the general movement from Puritanism to Transcendentalism. (See Fruitlands entry in this book.)

Bryant's talent as a poet flourished alongside his law practice in Massachusetts. In 1825, as he began a new career as editor of literary publications and later as editor-in-chief and publisher at the New York Evening Post. He held his position at the Post for 50 years until his death.

Bryant was a leader of the anti-slavery Free-Soil movement within the Democratic Party, but later helped found the Republican Party. He was an early political backer of Abraham Lincoln. He also took up conservationist causes, leading to the creation of New York's Central Park, and played a major role in the creation of the city's Metropolitan Museum of Art. Artists of the Hudson River School regarded Bryant as a muse. At his death in 1878, Bryant was a national icon.

ABOUT THE SITE Although the grand house on Bryant's pastoral estate has been renovated and redecorated through the decades, the rambling, three-story wooden house has remained largely unchanged for more than 150 years. The trustees have repainted the house to the colors used in 1870 when Bryant lived there: white with brown shutters and trim.

The house began as a 1 1/2-story Dutch Colonial farmhouse set on a hillside. When Bryant bought the property, he added wings on either side, raised the whole house to add a lower floor, Paladian window and 26 rooms, and remodeled the house in Victorian style. What was once the first-floor kitchen is now second-floor bedrooms. Bryant's daughter, Julia, added the stone porch in 1894.

The site preserves 195 lovely acres of Bryant's 465-acre pastoral estate overlooking the Westfield River with views of the Hampshire Hills. Some of the land remains a working farm, with summer crops and grazing cows. Bryant's furnishings and mementos of his extraordinary life fill the house. You can see the poet's dumbbells and chin-up bar, his straw hat and berry-picking basket, rock collection, letters, passport, his mother's diary, and near-Eastern furniture and accessories that he picked up during his travels.

Bryant's library, fashioned from his physician-father's office, features his desk, book-lined shelves, oil lamp, inkwell and pens and a photograph of Julia.

You'll find 2.5 miles of footpaths and carriage roads that will take you through natural landscapes that sparked Bryant's imagination, as well as several interesting structures. These include: the 1801 barn, expanded several times; the 1831 caretaker's cottage; Bryant's school house; site of the sugar house, used to boil sap into maple syrup; a remnant of Bryant's apple orchard; the Bryant family cemetery; and the Old-Growth Forest with trees more than 200 years old. The forest inspired Bryant's poem *The Rivulet*, written at the homestead.

The Rivulet Trail near the Rivulet Brook, which provided water for the homestead, helps visitors navigate the Old-Growth Forest and natural areas. Guided tours ($) of the trail are offered seasonally.

HOT TIPS A parking area for 10 vehicles is located behind barn. Allow one hour for the guided tour of the house. No photography inside house. The site's visitor center and museum shop are open seasonally. Picnic tables. Dogs must be kept on a leash. Outdoor private functions by reservation. Seasonal hunting is permitted at this property subject to all state and town laws. Special events at the site include the Bryant Homestead Craft Festival every July and the bi-annual Christmas at the Homestead.

Other Bryant-related sites include: the Cummington Library, which Bryant founded in 1871, and the site of the poet's birthplace, marked by a stone obelisk on Potash Hill Road.

THE BEST STUFF Bryant's parents planted five maple trees in the early 19th century, one for each of their sons. (They also had two daughters.) These maples and the sugar maples that the young poet and his brothers planted along the entrance road to the homestead are nearly 200 years old.

THE WRITER AND HIS WORK For details on Bryant, see Cedermere under New York in the Middle Atlantic Section of this book.

ELSEWHERE IN THE AREA Shaw-Hudson House; Kingman Tavern Historical Museum, 41 Main St.; Susan B. Anthony Birthplace 24 miles northwest in Adams, Mass. ◢

THORNTON W. BURGESS REMEMBERED

Sites Honor Creator of 'Yankee Peter Rabbit'

LOCATION Eastern Massachusetts on Cape Cod, south of Boston. Sites include the **Thornton W. Burgess Museum** ($) along Shawme Pond on Water Street (Route 130) in **Sandwich Village** and the **Green Briar Nature Center/Briar Patch Conservation Area and Jam Kitchen** ($) at 6 Discovery Hill Road (off Route 6A) in **East Sandwich**, 2 miles from the museum.

For more information, contact the Thornton W. Burgess Society, 6 Discovery Hill Road, East Sandwich, MA 02537. Tel. (508) 888-6870. E-mail: tburgess@capecod.net. On the Net: www.thorntonburgess.org.

FRAME OF REFERENCE Thornton Waldo Burgess was born in Sandwich in 1874 and grew up in the village. He returned frequently as an adult to the place he called his spiritual home. The Thornton W. Burgess Society formed in 1976 to permanently maintain the sites for the public.

SIGNIFICANCE During his 50-year career, Burgess created an American version of Peter Rabbit and a host of animal pals to teach children lessons of conservation and a love of wildlife. Burgess wrote more than 170 books and 15,000 stories in a newspaper column, *Bedtime Stories,* about the adventures of Peter and his friends, including Jimmy Skunk, Grandfather Frog, Johnny Chuck, Sammy Jay, Reddy Fox, and Hooty Owl. In the early 1900s, Burgess's tales were the ones read at bedtime to America's children, introducing them to nature and teaching little lessons about life.

Burgess' books, including his classics *The Adventures of Peter Cottontail* and *Old Mother West Wind*, have been published around the world in many languages. Collaborating with him was his illustrator and friend, Harrison Cady, who created the familiar form of Peter Rabbit and other animal characters still popular today.

ABOUT THE SITES

THORNTON W. BURGESS MUSEUM The museum is located in the 1756 Eldred House on Shawme Pond in the historic center of Sandwich, Cape Cod's oldest town. The house, once owned by Burgess' Aunt Arabella, exhibits artifacts, art, writings and memorabilia related to his life and work. The "tussie mussie" herb garden overlooks the pond, where swans and ducks swim in their natural habitat. The museum has a gift shop.

GREENBRIER NATURE CENTER The center, on the shores of Smiling Pool, offers interpreted nature trails and a spectacular wildflower garden. Green Briar, a house dating to 1780, is also home to the Robert S. Swain Natural History Library, which has a collection of books, periodicals and other materials on the natural history of the Northeast, particularly eastern Massachusetts.

Next to Green Briar spreads the 57-acre Briar Patch Conservation Area, famous home of "Peter Rabbit" and many of the other Thornton Burgess animal characters. Walking trails are open to the public.

JAM KITCHEN The 100-year-old Jam Kitchen is a living museum where you can view the cooking process first-hand. The kitchen still operates using founder Ida Putnam's recipes and preparing the jams, jellies, relishes and pickles the "old fashioned way" in a turn-of-the-century kitchen. Green Briar's sun-cooked preserves are cooked in the oldest commercial solar-cooking operation in America. Sugar is stored in 300-pound barrels. Jam Kitchen products are sold in the gift shop or by mail order. Sales help support the Burgess society's education programs.

HOT TIPS The museum offers many special events, including Peter Rabbit's Animal Day, strawberry and herb festivals, and Burgess story times in summer months.

The nature center features natural history programs for children and classes, field trips, guided walks, and workshops for adults.

The **Burgess Birthplace** still stands at 6 School St. in Sandwich. It is not part of the public sites.

THE BEST STUFF The Jam Kitchen presents a mouth-watering series of workshops to teach jam-making by traditional Green Briar methods. Participants take home what they make, plus a recipe booklet. Contact the site for details.

THE WRITER AND HIS WORK

BORN: Jan. 14, 1874, in Sandwich

DIED: June 5, 1965, age 91, in Hampden, Mass.

EDUCATED: Business college in Boston, 1892-93

MARRIED: Nina Elvira Osborne, 1905, died 1906; Fannie H. Phillips, 1911; one son

IMPORTANT WORKS: *Big Book of Animal Stories*; *Long River Winding*; *Now I Remember* (autobiography, 1960); *The Burgess Bird Book for Children*

(2003); *The Burgess Seashore Book for Children* (1985); *Burgess Flower Book for Children* (1995); *Life, Love, and Death along the Connecticut* (2003); *The Adventures of... Reddy Fox, Bobby Raccoon; Buster Bear, Lightfoot the Deer, Jimmy Skunk, Old Mother West Wind, Peter Cottontail* and a host of animal characters

ACCOLADES: Honorary literary degree, Northeastern University, 1938; gold medal, Boston Museum of Science; distinguished Service Medal of the Permanent Wildlife Protection Fund

INTERESTING BIO FACT: As a youth Burgess earned money by tending cows, picking berries, shipping water lilies from local ponds, selling candy and trapping muskrats. William C. Chipman, one of his employers, lived on Discovery Hill Road, then a wildlife habitat of woodland and wetland. This habitat became the setting of many of Burgess' stories, including *Smiling Pool* and *Old Briar Patch.*

FURTHER READING *Peter Cottontail Mazes* by Pat Stewart (2000); *My Grandfather, Thornton W. Burgess* by Frances B. Meigs (1998); *The Cape Cod Story of Thornton W. Burgess* by Russell A. Lovell

ELSEWHERE IN THE AREA Heritage Museum and Gardens, 7 Grove St.; Sandwich Glass Museum, 109 Main St.

• BURGESS' HAMPDEN HOME •

After Thornton W. Burgess' death, the Massachusetts Audubon Society purchased his **Hampden, Mass.**, home and established the **Laughing Brook Nature Center** ($). Burgess bought his place in Hampden, just southeast of Springfield in western Massachusetts, in 1925 and made it his permanent home in 1957. Burgess' home still stands.

The 4 miles of trails in the 356-acre wildlife sanctuary are open daily from dawn to dusk year-round. The park entrance and visitor center are located at 793 Main St. Tel. (413) 566-8034. ◮

EMILY DICKINSON MUSEUM
19th-Century Poet's Birthplace, Home

Location West central Massachusetts in Amherst, reached via I-91 and Highway 116. The Emily Dickinson Museum comprises the **Dickinson Homestead** ($), at 280 Main St. and **The Evergreens** ($) next door at 214 Main St. The Evergreens was the home of the poet's brother and sister-in-law, Austin and Susan Dickinson. For more information, contact The Evergreens, P.O. Box 603, Amherst, MA 01004. Tel. (413) 256-3925. E-mail: evergreens1856@yahoo.com.

Both sites are open for guided tours March through November. Days and times vary. For more information on the Dickinson Homestead, contact the site at 280 Main St., Amherst, MA 01002. Tel. (413) 542-8161. E-mail: info@dickinsonhomestead.org. On the Net: www.dickinsonhomestead.org.

FRAME OF REFERENCE Emily Elizabeth Dickinson's paternal grandparents built the house in 1813 and her parents moved into the western half in 1830, the year the poet was born in the house. Dickinson grew up in the homestead, then lived for several years beginning in 1840 in another home in Amherst. She returned to her birthplace in 1855 and lived there until her death in 1886. The house was designated a National Historic Landmark in 1963. In 1965, the Trustees of Amherst College acquired the home and merged with The Evergreens in 2003 to form the museum.

SIGNIFICANCE Until her death, Dickinson was an enigmatic figure in the village of Amherst and unknown to the rest of the world. Although it has been estimated that she wrote more than 1,700 poems, only seven of them are known to have been published in her lifetime, all anonymously and possibly without her permission. Presumably, she feared being misunderstood, or maybe being understood.

Her public career as a poet began in 1890, when the critic and family friend, Thomas W. Higginson, helped publish 115 of her poems. Six additional volumes of her poetry were published between 1890 and 1955, when three more volumes were published. These were titled *The Poems of Emily Dickinson*, edited by T.H. Johnson.

Today Dickinson is considered one of the greatest American poets, and along with Walt Whitman, one of the two greatest poets of the 19th century. Her choice of metaphysical and sensual topics of love, life, nature and eternity was revolutionary. Dickinson's original style, particular perspective, and keen portrayal of human isolation and vulnerability culminated in a large literary legacy.

ABOUT THE SITE Emily Dickinson's grandfather, a lawyer and one of the founders of Amherst College, built the homestead as a Federal-style structure. The house, with a white-columned entrance, was probably the first brick house in Amherst. When Dickinson's parents moved back in, they added a kitchen and laundry on the back of the imposing, two-story house, as well as Italianate features, including a cupola on the roof. The conservatory they built for Emily's exotic plants no longer stands.

Although you'll find few original family pieces in the house, furnishings reflect the era and the contemplative lifestyle of the Dickinsons. In the renovated front parlor, reproductions of three family portraits adorn the white walls: Emily's father, mother and one of the poet with her brother Austin and sister Lavinia.

The two-story Evergreens, topped by a square cupola, remains as it was when it was an integral part of Dickinson's world. Austin and Susan Dickinson opened their home to an active intellectual circle and played a vital role in Amherst's social scene. The homestead's Tour Center features a museum shop and orientation exhibit.

HOT TIPS Special programs at the site include the "At Home and Glad" Tours and Tea ($) one Sunday a month, May through September; the Annual Celebration of Emily Dickinson's Birthday in December, and many lectures and activities.

You can visit the **Dickinson gravesite** in West Cemetery on Triangle Street in Amherst. The Dickinson family plot contains four headstones enclosed by an ornate iron fence. One of the smaller stones marks Emily Dickinson's grave.

Other **Dickinson-related sites** in Amherst include: College Hall, on South Pleasant Street, which was the third building of the First Congregational Church, the Dickinson family church; and the 1830 Fisher House at 227 South Pleasant St. In 1837, the Nelson sisters ran a school in this house that Emily Dickinson attended.

THE BEST STUFF In Emily's upstairs bedroom, you can see her actual bed, narrow with white linens, and one of the dresses of white, the color she preferred. Before a window, you'll see a small writing table, much like the poet's. Many family items now reside in the Houghton Library at Harvard. This writing table belonged to another family member.

The Jones Library at 43 Amity St. in Amherst, houses the **Emily Dickinson Collection**. The growing research collection comprises 7,000 items, including original manuscript poems and letters, Dickinson editions and translations, family correspondence, scholarly articles and books, newspaper clippings, theses, plays, photographs, audio and video recordings, and contemporary artwork and prints. Access is generally unrestricted; Dickinson manuscripts are extremely fragile. Contact the library at (413) 256-4090. On the Net: www.joneslibrary.org/specialcollections/collections/dickinson.

THE WRITER AND HER WORK

BORN: Dec. 10, 1830, in Amherst

DIED: May 15, 1886, in Amherst; buried in West Cemetery

EDUCATED: Amherst Academy, 1847; Mount Holyoke Female Seminary, one year

IMPORTANT WORKS: Poems include (by first lines) *I never lost as much but twice*; *Success is counted sweetest*; *I like a look of agony*; *I felt a funeral in my brain*; *A Clock stopped*; *A bird came down the walk*; *A wounded deer leaps high*; *This is my letter to the world*; *The heart asks pleasure*; *Wild Nights-Wild Nights!*; *Safe in their Alabaster Chambers*; *I've seen a dying eye*; *Remorse - is Memory - awake*; *My Cocoon tightens*; *I heard a fly buzz -when I died*; *A Route of Evanescence*; *Much madness is divinest sense*; *The Bible is an antique Volume*; *In Winter in my Room*; *My life closed twice before its close*; *Because I could not stop for death*

INTERESTING BIO FACT: After moving back to the homestead in 1855, Dickinson began writing poetry in earnest. During her most productive years, 1858 to 1865, she compiled her poems in small, sewn packets now termed "fascicles." Dickinson's flurry of writing might have resulted from a profound psychological upheaval, possibly brought on by a tragic, unrequited love. During her final decades, Dickinson reduced her social circle to her family, communicated largely through cryptic notes and fragments of poems, dressed completely in white, and never left her house and garden.

FURTHER READING *Letters of Emily Dickinson* (2003); *My Wars Are Laid Away in Books: The Life of Emily Dickinson* by Alfred Habegger (2002); *The Emily Dickinson Handbook* by Gudren Grabher (1999); *The Mouse of Amherst* by Elizabeth Spires (1999); *The World of Emily Dickinson* by Polly Longsworth (1997)

ELSEWHERE IN THE AREA 1867 First Church 165 Main St.; Sweetser Park in the Dickinson Historic District; **Noah Webster** home site, near 62 Main St. at Phoenix Row; Webster statue stands on the Amherst College campus on the north side of the Frost Library. Webster was a founder of Amherst. ◮

HELEN HUNT JACKSON HOME

The childhood home (1830) of writer Helen Hunt Jackson, a contemporary of Emily Dickinson, is located at 249 S. Pleasant St. in Amherst. Jackson, best known for her novel *Ramona* (1884), about the plight of American Indians in the West, corresponded with Dickinson in her later years. She encouraged Dickinson to publish her poetry. In 1883, Dickinson sent pressed flowers to Jackson with this cryptic note: "To be remembered what? Worthy to be forgot is their own renown -" The letters are part of the Emily Dickinson Collection at the Jones Library in Amherst.

For more on Jackson, see Colorado in the Mountain section of this book. ◭

W.E.B. DU BOIS BOYHOOD HOMESITE
Where NAACP Co-Founder, Writer Grew Up

A former farm along the Housatonic River in southwestern Massachusetts near **Great Barrington, Mass.**, was once the boyhood home of W.E.B. Du Bois, a major figure in the African-American civil rights movement during the first half of the 20th century. Du Bois (doo boys') co-founded the NAACP and also gained fame as an editor and author of numerous books.

Although today you'll find only the faintest traces of Du Bois' original boyhood home, you can hike a 5-acre wooded field where the house once stood. The site, a National Historic Landmark since 1976, is located on the north side of Route 23, 2 miles west of Great Barrington. The Commonwealth of Massachusetts owns the land.

You can also visit The **W. E. B. Du Bois River Garden**, part of the local Housatonic River Walk. For more information, contact River Walk, P.O. Box 1018, Great Barrington, MA 01230. Tel. (413) 528-3391. E-mail: river@gbriverwalk.org.

William Edward Burghardt Du Bois was born in Great Barrington in 1868, a few years after the Civil War ended. He lived on this farm in his maternal grandfather's house as a youngster until he was 17, when he left to attend Fisk University in Nashville. (He was the first African-American to receive a Ph.D. from Harvard, in 1895).

In his autobiography, Du Bois described his grandfather's home as "sturdy, small and old-fashioned. There was a great fireplace, whose wrought-iron tongs stand now before my fireplace as I write." Du Bois' family had lived near Great Barrington for more than 200 years and as an adult he often used the family home as a retreat. For Du Bois' 60th birthday, a committee of friends that included Clarence Darrow and Mary McLeod Bethune gave him the house and land as a gift. They had raised the money and bought the site from a Du Bois relative. Soon after Du Bois' death in 1963, only a stone-lined cellar hole remained of the farm. You can see this today.

Plans for the site include further archaeological study to help provide information on the African-American community that nurtured Du Bois. Findings might be used in planning commemorative buildings and exhibits.

As a founder of the National Association for the Advancement of Colored People in 1909, Du Bois served as that organization's director of publications and editor of Crisis magazine until 1934. Du Bois championed a direct assault on the legal, political, and economic system that thrived on the exploitation of the poor and the powerless. His call to arms put him in direct opposition to **Booker T. Washington,** who counseled acceptance of the social order. (For more on Washington, see Alabama in the East South Central section of this book.)

In 1944, Du Bois returned from Atlanta University to become head of the NAACP's special research department, a post he held until 1948. Du Bois emigrated to Africa in 1961. He became editor-in-chief of the *Encyclopedia Africana*, an ambitious publishing venture planned by Kwame Nkrumah, president of Ghana at the time.

Du Bois' books include: *The Suppression of the Slave Trade* (1896); *The Philadelphia Negro* (1899); *The Souls of Black Folk* (1903), *John Brown* (1909), *Quest of the Silver Fleece* (1911), *The Negro* (1915); *Darkwater* (1920); *The Gift of Black Folk* (1924); *Dark Princess* (1928); *Black Folk: Then and Now* (1939); *Dusk of Dawn* (1940); *Color and Democracy* (1945); *The World and Africa* (1947); *In Battle for Peace* (1952); and a trilogy, *Black Flame* (1957-1961).

Du Bois spent his last years in exile, unwelcome in some quarters of the U.S. black community. He died in Ghana on Aug. 27, 1963, at age 95.

For more information on the Du Bois boyhood homesite, contact Robert Paynter, Department of Anthropology, University of Massachusetts, Amherst, MA 01003. E-mail: rpaynter@anthro.umass.edu or William Strickland, W.E.B. Du Bois Department of Afro American Studies, New Africa House, University of Massachusetts, Amherst 01003. E-mail: tlovelan@afroam.umass.edu. On the Net: www.cr.nps.gov/NR/travel/civilrights/ma2.htm.

HOT TIP The University of Massachusetts Amherst houses the **W.E.B. Du Bois Papers**, in its Special Collections and Archives at the W.E.B. Du Bois Library. ◮

SPRINGFIELD, A.K.A. 'SEUSSVILLE'

Hometown Salutes Theodor Geisel

LOCATION Southwestern Massachusetts, in **Springfield**., reached by the Massachusetts Turnpike or I-91. The **Dr. Seuss National Memorial** sculpture garden is located at the Quadrangle downtown at State and Chestnut streets. The **Connecticut Valley Historical Museum** ($) on the Quadrangle, 220 State St., features an exhibition on Theodor Geisel and his work, **Seuss on the Loose in Springfield**, and special play area, **SeussScape**.

To reach the Quadrangle: From I-91 South, take Exit 7, turn left at the second traffic light onto State Street and go 3 blocks to site. From I-91 North, take Exit 4, Columbus Avenue to the third traffic light and turn right on State Street. From the Massachusetts Turnpike West, take Exit 6 to I-291. Exit 2B at Dwight Street, then turn left. Follow Dwight Street to ninth light; turn left onto State Street. From the Mass Pike East, take Exit 4 to I-91 South to Exit 7.

The Seuss memorial can be viewed from 7 a.m. to 8 p.m. daily. The Connecticut Valley museum is open Wednesday through Friday, from noon to 4 p.m., and on Saturday and Sunday from 11 a.m. to 4 p.m. The Dr. Seuss National Memorial Sculpture Garden is open daily from 9 a.m. to 5 p.m.

For more information, contact The Springfield Museums at the Quadrangle, 220 State St. , Springfield, MA 01103. Tel. (413) 263-6800. On the Net: www.quadrangle.org. Suess memorial: Tel. 1-800-625-7738.

FRAME OF REFERENCE Theodor "Ted" Seuss Geisel, a.k.a. Dr. Seuss, was born in Springfield in 1904 and grew up in the city. He left Springfield as a teenager to attend college. After his death in 1991, the Springfield Library & Museums Association resolved to honor Geisel and the Dr. Seuss National Memorial opened to the public in May 2002.

SIGNIFICANCE During his lifetime, the renowned children's author and cartoonist sold more than 200 million copies of his 46 fanciful books from the 1930s through 1970s. Geisel, a.k.a. Dr. Seuss, remains America's best-selling children's author. Nearly all of his titles are still in print and have been translated into 20 languages. He won a Pulitzer Prize, three Academy Awards and virtually every award for children's literature. Dr. Seuss's stories have charmed four generations of children and in the process, helped them learn to read.

Geisel's distinct writing style uses nonsense words and rhyme designed to instill syllable recognition in pre-readers and help them pronounce words. Geisel credited his mother with both his ability and desire to create the rhymes for which he became so well known. Henrietta Seuss Geisel often soothed her children to sleep by "chanting" rhymes remembered from her youth.

The first book Geisel wrote and illustrated, *And to Think That I Saw It on Mulberry Street*, was rejected 27 times until Vanguard Press finally published it in 1937. "Dr. Seuss" kept writing and at last hit pay dirt. A best-selling critique of children's literacy, *Why Johnny Can't Read* by novelist John Hersey, characterized school primers as bland and antiseptic. In response, publisher Houghton Mifflin challenged "Dr. Seuss" to write a reading primer using a vocabulary of only 225 words to captivate young readers. The result was Geisel's *The Cat in the Hat* (1957). The book became the prototype of the best-selling Random House series, *Beginner Books*, and changed the course of children's literature. Geisel became president of the *Beginner Books* division and remained with Random House for the rest of his career.

ABOUT THE SITES

DR. SEUSS NATIONAL MEMORIAL This outdoor sculpture garden features larger-than-life bronze statues of Dr. Seuss at his drawing board surrounded by some of his most-beloved characters, including Horton the Elephant, the Grinch, and the Lorax. Lark Grey Dimond-Cates, the stepdaughter of Dr. Seuss, created the sculptures. The memorial is located in the courtyard of the Springfield Museums at the Quadrangle. On the Net: www.catinthehat.org/history.

SEUSS ON THE LOOSE The exhibition features family photographs from Geisel's childhood and genealogical information about the Seuss-Geisel family history. You'll also find photographs and memorabilia from Kalmbach and Geisel Brewery, the family business founded by Geisel's grandfather, as well as comparisons of Dr. Seuss's fanciful illustrations with actual Springfield places.

SEUSSSCAPE This play area for young children has bright, colorful walls illustrated with scenes and creatures from Dr. Seuss's books. Activities include a push-button listening station where children can hear the Cat in the Hat talking, child-size furniture, toy display and books.

HOT TIPS Park free in the Springfield Library and Museums lot on State Street across from the library. Geisel's other homes in Springfield still stand; one on Howard Street where he was born, and another 74 Fairfield St. They are not open to the public.

The University of California, San Diego, Mandeville Special Collections Library houses the **Dr. Seuss Collection**. On the Net: http://orpheus .ucsd.edu/speccoll.

THE BEST STUFF In many ways, Springfield is Seussville. Giesel evoked images of Springfield in many of his books. His *Mulberry Street* features a look-alike of Mayor Fordis Parker on the reviewing stand, and police officers ride red motorcycles, the traditional color of Springfield's famed Indian Motorcycles. Drawings of Horton the Elephant meandering along streams in the *Jungle of Nool* mirror the watercourses in Springfield's Forest Park from the period.

THE WRITER AND HIS WORK

BORN: March 2, 1904, in Springfield

DIED: Sept. 24, 1991, in La Jolla, Calif.

EDUCATED: Dartmouth; Oxford

MARRIED: Helen Palmer, 1927, died 1967; Audrey Stone, 1968; no children

IMPORTANT WORKS: *And To Think That I Saw It On Mulberry Street* (1937); *The 500 Hats of Bartholomew Cubbins* (1938); *Horton Hatches the Egg* (1940); *McElligot's Pool* (1947); *Thidwick, The Big-Hearted Moose* (1948); *Horton Hears A Who* (1954); *The Cat in the Hat* (1957); *If I Ran The Circus* (1956); *Why the Grinch Stole Christmas* (1957); *Yertle the Turtle and Other Stories* (1958); *Bartholomew and the Oobleck* (1959); *Green Eggs and Ham* (1960); *One Fish, Two Fish, Red Fish, Blue Fish* (1960); *Dr. Seuss's ABC* (1963); *Hop on Pop* (1963); *The Fox in Socks* (1965); *The Eye Book* (1968); *The Foot Book* (1968); *My Book About Me, By Me Myself* (1969); *I Can Draw Myself* (1970); *The Lorax* (1971); *Oh Say Can You Say* (1979); *Oh, The Thinks You Can Think!* (1975); *The Butter Battle Book* (1984); *Oh, The Places You'll Go!* (1990)

ACCOLADES: Special Pulitzer Prize, 1984; Academy Award, 1945, for documentary *Your Job In Germany*; Peabody Award; seven honorary doctorates; and virtually every children's book award

INTERESTING BIO FACT: The transformation from Ted Geisel to Dr. Seuss began at Dartmouth, where Geisel edited the Jack-O-Lantern, the college's humor magazine. He signed his work simply "Seuss," a pseudonym that was both his middle name and his mother's maiden name. He signed his early drawings "Dr. Theophrastus Seuss" to lend a scientific cachet to his goofy zoology. This became "Dr. Seuss" and he used that moniker on all his children's books.

FURTHER READING *Dr. Seuss Goes To War* by Richard H. Minear (2002); *The Man Who Was Dr. Seuss* by Thomas Fensch (2001); *Oh, the Places He Went* by Maryann N. Weidt and Kerry Maguire (1995)

ELSEWHERE IN THE AREA Basketball Hall of Fame; Volleyball Hall of Fame, both in Springfield ⚐

HOUSE OF SEVEN GABLES HISTORIC SITE

Hawthorne's Birthplace, Inspiration for Novel

LOCATION Coastal Massachusetts, in Salem, 30 miles north of Boston. From Route 128 (after Route 128 splits from I-95), take Exit 25A to Route 114. Follow Route 114 East to Salem Center. Follow the "Waterfront" signs to Derby Street. Signs throughout the city direct you to the house.

The House of Seven Gables Historic Site ($) includes The **House of Seven Gables**, the house that provided inspiration for Hawthorne's novel of the same name, and the **Nathaniel Hawthorne Birthplace.** The houses are open for guided tours daily from mid-February through December, except for Thanksgiving and Dec. 25, from 10 a.m. to 4:30 p.m. with extended hours in season. Opens at noon on Sunday during winter. Closes early on Christmas Eve and Dec. 31.

For more information, contact House of the Seven Gables, 54 Turner St., Salem, MA 01970. Tel. (978) 744-0991. E-mail: info@7gables.org; group tours: reservations@7gables.org. For information on **Hawthorne in Salem**, go to www.hawthorneinsalem.org.

FRAME OF REFERENCE The House of the Seven Gables, also known as the Turner-Ingersoll Mansion for the families who owned it, was built in 1668 by wealthy sea captain John Turner. It is the oldest surviving 17th-century wooden mansion in New England.

Nathaniel Hawthorne was born in a house on nearby Union Street in Salem in 1804. He lived only a few years in the house, which was relocated next to the House of Seven Gables in 1958. During his adult life, Hawthorne lived in Salem on and off, occupying several different houses. He first left Salem in 1821 to attend Bowdoin College. Hawthorne and his wife, whom he met in Salem, lived in Concord after they married, but they returned to Salem late in 1845. In 1846 Hawthorne took the position of Surveyor of the Port at the Salem Custom House. After he lost his job in 1849 — creating a sensational stir — and his mother died, Hawthorne said he had no reason to remain in Salem, "that abominable city." Hawthorne and his family left the town for good in 1850.

SIGNIFICANCE The great American novelist who gave us *The Scarlet Letter* (1850), *The House of Seven Gables* (1851) and *Twice-Told Tales* (1837), also published more than 100 other works, including novels, short stories, essays, sketches and poems. Hawthorne was the first author to impose artistic standards on Puritan society in the New World in an authentic American voice. His writing brims with moral and psychological insight into human nature.

Born into a family whose ancestors had participated in the 17th-century Salem witch trials, Hawthorne called himself "the last Puritan." His "Puritan" tales, such as his masterpiece, *The Scarlet Letter*, severely criticize Puritan religious intolerance. Other works extol the need to cast aside old ways and embrace a new culture. He epitomizes the Romantic movement in American literature that stressed the inherent goodness of man and his place in nature.

As a youth, Hawthorne published a newspaper, The Spectator, which he distributed to family members for a few months in 1820. After a prolific career, Hawthorne cloistered himself in the study of his house in Concord, Mass., fearing his muse was on the wane. He did continue to write, however, producing works such as *Septimius Felton,* an unfinished romance.

ABOUT THE SITE Within the 2 1/2-acre historic grounds you'll find the House of Seven Gables that inspired Hawthorne's novel of the same name; Hawthorne's birthplace; two 17th-century homes, the 1682 Hathaway House and the 1658 Retire Beckett House; and restored period gardens.

THE HOUSE OF SEVEN GABLES The famous, brown three-story house that Hawthrone described in his novel probably had seven pitches in the roof when he often visited the cousins who lived there. Now it has eight. During the 18th and 19th centuries, several owners modified the house. Hawthorne's cousins, the Ingersolls, removed gables to reconstruct a front porch. In 1908 the founder of the House of Seven Gables Settlement Association, Caroline O. Emmerton, bought the house. She restored the eighth gable.

Furnishings in the house today reflect the styles of 1840, a time when Hawthorne visited his cousins there. Visitors can tour eight restored rooms to view period furnishings and also a few pieces related to Hawthorne. You'll find his writing desk, a bureau where he possibly stored his manuscript for *The Scarlet Letter*, and his cousin's leather chair where he sat to write. The site also has an 18th-century granite sea wall and two seaside Colonial Revival gardens. The museum houses more than 2,000 items, 40 framed works, 500 photographs and glass plate negatives, and more than 650 volumes in the research/rare book library.

HAWTHORNE'S BIRTHPLACE The modest two-story, red wooden house where Hawthorne was born in 1804 has been restored to look as it did in 1808, the year his mother sold the house after his sea-captain father's death. Much of the furnishings belonged to Hawthorne's maternal family, the Mannings, who took them in after Hawthorne's father died in Surinam. The period furnishings depict life in Salem for a family of modest means and emphasize Hawthorne's maritime roots.

HOT TIPS Set aside a half-day to visit all the houses and to tour the gardens. The visitor center is wheelchair accessible but the houses are not. The Garden Cafe on the grounds offers meals, desserts and tea inside or outside. A museum store is located in the Retire-Beckett home. For a day in Salem park in a downtown parking deck. The House of the Seven Gables offers tour texts in several foreign languages. For more on Hawthorne, see The Old Manse and The Wayside entries.

THE BEST STUFF A secret staircase in the House of Seven Gables wraps around a chimney and leads directly from the first floor to the third, bypassing the second floor. While renovating in the 1800s, the current owners discovered the mysterious, winding steps. Some say the Ingersolls built the steps to harbor runaway slaves. Another theory states that the Turners added the steps to allow the servants entry to a new kitchen without disturbing the family sleeping on the second floor.

THE WRITER AND HIS WORK

BORN: July 4, 1804, in Salem

DIED: May 11, 1864, in Concord, Mass.

EDUCATED: Bowdoin College, 1825

MARRIED: Sophia Peabody, 1842; three children

IMPORTANT WORKS: *Twice-Told Tales* (1837, 1842); *Mosses from an Old Manse* (1846, 1854); *The Snow-Image* (1851); *The House of the Seven Gables* (1851); *The Blithedale Romance* (1852); *The Life of Franklin Pierce* (1852); *The Scarlet Letter* (1850); *The Marble Faun* (1860); *English Notebooks, Our Old Home* (1863)

INTERESTING BIO FACT: Among Hawthorne's illustrious companions — Emerson, Thoreau, the Alcotts, Margaret Fuller — none exerted a greater personal and professional influence than **Herman Melville**.

(See Arrowhead entry in this book.) Hawthorne met Melville on a picnic at Mt. Graylock in 1850, soon after he moved to the Berkshires, where Melville lived. Melville reveals his admiration and affection for Hawthorne in the dedication of his masterpiece, *Moby-Dick*, to Hawthorne.

Some literary scholars say that surviving letters between the men, as well as allusions in Hawthorne's book, *The Blithedale Romance*, indicate a mysterious end to their friendship. Was Hawthorne too much the Puritan to remain close to the adventurous Melville? Playwrights Juliane and Stephen Glantz explore theories in their drama, *A Tanglewood Tale* (2001).

FURTHER READING *Hawthorne: A Life* by Brenda Wineapple (2003); *The Salem World of Nathaniel Hawthorne* by Margaret B. Moore (2001); *Mesmerism and Hawthorne* by Samuel C. Coale (2000)

ELSEWHERE IN THE AREA Salem Maritime National Historic Site; Salem Witch Museum; Witch Dungeon Museum; Salem Witch Trials Memorial; Salem Wax Museum of Witches and Seafarers; the many Federal-period houses along Chestnut Street; and Salem 1630 Pioneer Village at Forest River Park ◢

JACK KEROUAC'S LOWELL

'Beat' Writer's Hometown Keeps Fame Alive

Jean-Louis Lebris de Kerouac was born on March 12, 1922, in **Lowell, Mass.**, and grew up in eight different homes in America's first industrial city. He lived there again briefly in the 60s. The mill town 30 miles northwest of Boston profoundly influenced Kerouac (kair' oo ak), the leading — if somewhat reluctant — spokesman for the "Beat Generation" of the 1950s and 60s. Kerouac himself coined the term for the group of American writers who expressed their alienation from a "sick society" in their art.

Best known for his book *On The Road* (1957), Kerouac also wrote five "Lowell novels" that draw on his youth in Lowell. These are *Visions of Gerard* (1963), about Kerouac's saintly older brother, who died in childhood; *Doctor Sax* (1959), offering glimpses of the town and his young fantasies; *Maggie Cassidy* (1959), about youthful romance; *The Town and the City* (1950); and *Vanity of Duluoz* (1968), a memoir of his early years.

If you're a Kerouac aficionado, you might want to experience the three-day **Lowell Celebrates Kerouac!** festival held every fall. While in town, retro-beatniks can visit several other revered sites related to the author and his work. These include: **Jack Kerouac Park** downtown, where you'll find **The Jack Kerouac Commemorative**, part of an informal **Kerouac Downtown Walking Tour;** the **Kerouac Gravesite** in Edson Cemetery in South Lowell; and a **display of Kerouac artifacts** in The Working People Exhibit. You'll find the exhibit, part of Lowell National Historical Park, at the Mogan Cultural Center, 40 French St. The artifacts include Kerouac's typewriter and backpack.

The Kerouac Commemorative, created by Houston artist Ben Woitena and dedicated in 1988, features a path with eight triangular marble columns. The columns feature excerpts from Kerouac's work and symbols of Roman Catholicism and Buddhism, beliefs that influenced the writer. A 12-story brick and concrete warehouse, which Kerouac described as "the great gray warehouse of eternity," once stood on the park site. A Kerouac walking tour of Lowell should also include:

POLLARD MEMORIAL LIBRARY, 401 Merrimack St., which was named the Lowell Public Library when Kerouac lived in Lowell. The writer spent long hours at the castle-like library in the 1920s and 30s devouring books.

LOWELL HIGH SCHOOL, Kirk St., where Kerouac graduated in 1939. Young Kerouac was a shy but popular and bright student. He stood out in track and football, and played outfield on the baseball team. He left Lowell to attend Columbia.

KEARNY SQUARE, between the high school and the Lowell Sun newspaper building downtown, has several Kerouac associations. In the 1920s, Kerouac's father often brought the family to a popular Chinese restaurant there. In the 1930s, young Kerouac hung out with friends in the Square. In the early 1940s he worked as a Sun sportswriter.

BOOTT COTTON MILLS MUSEUM, along Bridge Street, is now part of the national park. Kerouac mentions the brick Boott Mills (1836) in *Doctor Sax* as "a maze of haze sorrow," where the red chimneys sway in "the dreambell afternoon" or, at night, the windows shine "like a lost star in the blue city lights of Lowell." Boott has been preserved as one of Lowell's many textile mills built near the Merrimack River since 1822. The last of the Industrial Revolution mills in Lowell closed in the 1950s, the years the Beat Generation took off. The city's textile heyday was around 1850. Mills began closing in 1912, most heading south.

KEROUAC'S GRAVE in Edson Cemetery in South Lowell. His simple gravestone reads "He Honored Life".

With the publication of his novel *On the Road*, critics quickly hailed Kerouac as a major American writer at the center of a new social and literary movement. The official "cool cat" of the beat movement kept the flames of fame hot with a succession of books exemplifying his spontaneous and unconventional prose. These included: *The Dharma Burns* (1958); *The Subterraneans* (1958); *Lonesome Traveler* (1960); and *Big Sur* (1962). His deeply autobiographical works reveal a peripatetic life, with warm but stormy relationships (he married three times) and social disillusionment dulled by drugs, alcohol, mysticism and dark humor. An overweight Kerouac died in St. Petersburg, Fla., of an abdominal hemorrhage due to alcoholism on Oct. 21, 1969.

For more information about the Kerouac Park and the artifact display, contact Lowell National Historical Park, 67 Kirk St., Lowell, MA 01852. Tel. (978) 970-5000. On the Net: www.nps.gov/lowe/kerouac.htm. For more information about the Kerouac festival, contact Lowell Celebrates Kerouac, P.O. Box 1111, Lowell, MA 01853. For information on a Kerouac Walking Tour, go to ecommunity.uml.edu/jklowell or www.americanwriters.org/places/kerouac.asp ◮

HERMAN MELVILLE'S ARROWHEAD
Where 'Moby-Dick' Was Written

LOCATION Berkshire Mountains of western Massachusetts, in Pittsfield, at 780 Holmes Road. From the Massachusetts Turnpike (I-90), take Exit 2 along Route 20 West for 8.5 miles. It will merge with Route 7 North. Turn right onto Holmes Road at traffic light. Site is 1.5 miles on the left. From north, take Route 2 to Route 7 South to Pittsfield-Lenox town line. Turn left onto Holmes Road at the traffic light.

Herman Melville's Arrowhead ($) is open daily from Memorial Day weekend to Oct. 31 from 9:30 a.m. to 5:00 p.m. for guided tours. Last tour 4 p.m. Call for winter hours. For more information, contact the site at 780 Holmes Road, Pittsfield MA 01201. Tel. (413) 442-1793. E-mail: info@mobydick.org. On the Net: www.mobydick.org.

FRAME OF REFERENCE Herman Melville lived at Arrowhead, built in 1780, from 1850 to 1863, when he and his family returned to New York City. Arrowhead remained in the Melville family until the 1920's, then was home to several owners. The Berkshire County Historical Society bought Arrowhead in 1975 and opened it to the public. Melville visited the Berkshires often and decided to move to Pittsfield permanently as his good friend, **Nathaniel Hawthorne**, had done, fleeing city life for a quiet place to write.

SIGNIFICANCE Melville gained great fame in his lifetime with the five books that drew on his experiences at sea, but he is best remembered for his masterpiece, *Moby-Dick* (1851). Many consider this complex maritime novel the finest piece of American literature ever written, and Melville is regarded as one of America's most influential novelists. As a major Romantic writer, most of Melville's work revolves around an allegory of self. In *Moby-Dick*, he wrote of a great white whale. Melville's works deal with man's relation to the natural world and the destruction of social restrictions.

Melville was the first Romantic writer to describe, based upon personal knowledge, the inhabitants of the South Sea islands. *Typee* (1846) was based on Melville's adventures after jumping ship in the Marquesas Islands. Unlike many other contemporary writers, such as pal Hawthorne, and Thoreau, whose books took off after their deaths, *Typee* quickly made Melville a literary celebrity in America.

At Arrowhead Melville wrote *Moby-Dick*, along with three other novels; a collection of short stories, *The Piazza Tales*; all of his magazine stories; and poetry. Many of his poems were about happy days spent at Arrowhead. Melville's last novel, *Billy Budd* (1924), published posthumously, gave him the worldwide recognition that eluded him during his life.

ABOUT THE SITE Arrowhead, which Melville named after the American Indian relics he discovered as he was plowing the fields, and the beauty of the Berkshires exerted great influence on the novelist. Melville said that the view of Mount Greylock, highest point in Massachusetts, from his study window was his inspiration for the white whale in *Moby-Dick*. He dedicated *Pierre*, his first "land" novel, to the mountain. The 44-acre site preserves Meville's two-story house, the restored barn where Melville and Hawthorne spent hours in conversation, and the scenic North Meadow with stunning views of Mount Greylock. A nature trail takes visitors through the woods that surrounded Melville's 160-acres.

Original owners built the 18th-century house in a Georgian style, and a later owner added federal-style architectural details to the exterior in the 1840s. In several works, Melville alludes to a previous owner having removed the original gambrel roof, replacing it with the roof you see today. The plain clapboard house, painted yellow with green trim, looks as it did in Melville's day. It retains original wide floorboards. Interior furnishes reflect a 19th-century Berkshires lifestyle and some were owned by the Melvilles. These include the novelist's trundle bed upstairs; a chair; one of wife, Elizabeth's, dresses; a tobacco tin and photographs.

Melville incorporated features and aspects of Arrowhead into several stories. He named his short story *The Piazza*, and the book *The Piazza Tales* (1856) for the porch he added to the north side of Arrowhead. *The Piazza* begins at Arrowhead and takes a magical journey to the mountain. Visitors can still stand on the piazza and look at the same view Melville had when he spent hours there in his rocking chair.

In the dining area, a fireplace with a famous massive chimney inspired his short story *I and My Chimney*. Melville also built outbuildings and an el addition at the rear, and he made many interior modifications.

Visitors can view a video, *The Berkshire Legacy,* recalling the times when Melville, Hawthorne, **Edith Wharton**, Daniel Chester French and Norman Rockwell worked in Berkshire County. The site also has a museum shop.

HOT TIPS Arrowhead presents a series of lectures, discussion groups, and special events year-round relating to Herman Melville and his life in the Berkshires. Arrowood's basement is home to a research library of 12,000 volumes and 14,000 photographs and documents related to Melville and Berkshire County history. The library is open to the general public.

Find out more about Melville at the **Herman Melville Memorial Room** at the Berkshire Athenaeum, 1 Wendell Ave. in Pittsfield. Since 1953, The Melville Memorial Room has offered one of the world's largest collections of Melville family memorabilia, including photographs, paintings, prints, artifacts and furniture, as well as scholarly research materials. Tel. (413) 499-9486. On the Net: pittslhg@cwmars.org.

The Athenaeum and the Berkshire Historical Society offer a **Berkshire-Melville Memorial Trail**, a driving tour of Berkshire sites meaningful to Melville. Ask for a guide at Arrowhead.

The Best Stuff Melville created a refuge from this chaos in his second-floor library/study. Today, the pale yellow room with green trim preserves a rectangular, wooden table displaying his steel-rimmed glasses, ink pot and plotter, quill pens and a penknife. You also can see a letter Melville wrote to his brother and first editions of his books.

When Melville bought the house, the room where he wrote *Moby-Dick* served as a small bedroom. Previous owners had enclosed the fireplace and built a wall through the room to create a hallway. The historical society restored the room to its Melville-era appearance, based on documentary and physical evidence.

THE WRITER AND HIS WORK

BORN: Aug. 1, 1819, in New York City

DIED: Sept. 28, 1891, in New York; buried Woodlawn Cemetery, Bronx, N.Y.

EDUCATED: Privately schooled in New York

MARRIED: Elizabeth Knapp Shaw; four children

IMPORTANT WORKS: Books of experiences at sea: *Typee* (1846); *Omoo* (1847); *Mardi* (1849); *Redburn* (1849); *White-Jacket* (1850). Other: *Moby-Dick* (1851); *Pierre* (1852); *Israel Potter* (1855); *Piazza Tales* (1856); *The Confidence-Man* (1857); *Battle Pieces* (1866); *Clarel* (1876); *John Marr and Other Sailors* (1888); *Timoleon* (1891); *Billy Budd* (1924); *Uncollected Prose* (1839-1856)

INTERESTING BIO FACT: Melville, grandson of two Revolutionary War heroes, took up writing after other career attempts went sour. He grew up in New York high society, with money, dancing lessons and servants.

When he was 11, his father went bankrupt, forcing the family, with eight children, to flee the creditors and move to Albany. Melville dropped out of school to help support the family.

Melville found jobs as a bank clerk, clerk in a cap and fur store, school teacher, merchant marine, and bowling pin setter. In 1841, he signed on the whaler Acushnet, sailing from Massachusetts, and the seeds of his writing were sown. He began to set down marvelous stories based on his adventures at the urging of his sisters. He turned out important literature for years, but his career ended early. When he died at age 72, his most recent novel had been published three decades earlier.

FURTHER READING *Monumental Melville* by Edgar A. Dryden (2004); *Herman Melville: A Biography* by Hershel Parker (2002); *New Essays on Billy Budd* edited by Donald Yannella (2002); *Call Me Ishmael* by Charles Olson (1997)

ELSEWHERE IN THE AREA Hancock Shaker Village, Route 20, Pittsfield; Norman Rockwell Museum, Route 183, Stockbridge; Chesterwood (Daniel Chester French estate), 4 Williamsville Road, Stockbridge; and Tanglewood (summer home of the Boston Symphony Orchestra) in Lenox ◭

THE MOUNT

Edith Wharton's House of Mirth

LOCATION Berkshire Hills of western Massachusetts, in Lenox, over-looking Laurel Lake, at 2 Plunkett St. Reach Lenox via I-90 (Massachusetts Turnpike).

The Mount ($) is open early May through early November from 9 a.m. to 5 p.m. For more information, contact The Mount, P.O. Box 974, Lenox, MA 01240-0974. Tel. (413) 637-1899. On the Net: www.edithwharton.org.

FRAME OF REFERENCE Edith Newbold Jones Wharton bought the 113-acre Lenox property in 1901, then designed and built The Mount on the rolling land. She and husband, Teddy, lived in the country mansion from 1902 to 1911, when she sold it and moved to France. After a series of private owners, the Foxhollow School for girls used The Mount as a dormitory until 1973. The Edith Wharton Restoration bought the property from a developer in 1980. The organization then opened the site to the public as a cultural center.

SIGNIFICANCE Wharton is considered one of the most distinguished American writers of the early 20th century. She was born into a tightly controlled society known as "Old New York" at a time when women were discouraged from achieving anything beyond a proper marriage. This Gilded Age uniquely positioned her to write from the inside about the fall of New York's post-Civil War, upper-class society and rise of a new gentry, the subject of her best works.

Wharton, who wrote more than 40 books in 40 years, is best known for her novel *The Age of Innocence* (1920), as well as *Ethan Frome* (1911) and *The House of Mirth* (1905), both written at The Mount. Wharton also wrote authoritative works on architecture, gardens, interior design and travel, as well as poems, short stories and essays.

The House of Mirth brought Wharton her first great literary success, dramatically transforming her life, giving her confidence to defy social norms and pursue a writing career. While living at The Mount, her private sanctum, she wrote five other novels, three nonfiction works and numerous short stories.

Wharton was the first woman awarded the Pulitzer Prize for fiction.

ABOUT THE SITE Wharton herself designed and oversaw construction of her elegant, three-story, white stucco country mansion of 42 rooms and the surrounding gardens. She based the design of her classical revival house with green shutters on the principles outlined in her influential book, *The Decoration of Houses* (1897), co-authored with architect Ogden Codman Jr. A treasure of American architecture and landscape design, The Mount, Wharton's "first real home," combines English, French and Italian elements with an American twist (Otis elevators).

The restored, 15,000-square-foot main house, inspired by Belton House, a 17th-century Palladian-style English country house, features classical Italian (terrazzo floors) and French influences (plenty of marble), including a grand cupola on the roof.

On the nearly 50 acres the estate now occupies, you'll find Wharton's Georgian Revival-style stable, greenhouse with potting shed; restored Italian walled garden; formal flower garden; alpine rock garden; lime walk and grass terraces. A bookstore is located in the main house, which you enter from the basement floor.

The home's symmetrical yet elegant design, as well as the grand furnishings, reflect the grandeur of America's Gilded Age. You won't find much of Wharton's furniture, but you will find outstanding examples of period furnishings.

HOT TIPS Lunch at the Terrace Café offers great views from The Mount's terrace, where Wharton entertained such notable friends as novelist Henry James. The Terrace Cafe is open mid-June through September 1 from 11 a.m. to 4 p.m., and on weekends in the fall. The site also hosts many lectures and special events.

THE BEST STUFF Wharton's meticulously restored bedroom, overlooking her gardens, features a French marble fireplace and eight richly painted oil panels set in ornate moldings original to the room. Her opulently appointed, private library (a bold assertion of independence for a woman of the era) has walls of books and a writing desk much like Wharton's. In this room, maybe with a glass of sherry on the side, she mirthfully wrote her way to greatness.

THE WRITER AND HER WORK

BORN: Jan. 24, 1862, in New York City
DIED: Aug. 11, 1937, in France
EDUCATED: Self-educated

MARRIED: Edward Wharton, 1885; divorced 1897

IMPORTANT WORKS: *The Decoration of Houses* (1897); *The Touchstone* (1900); *The Valley of Decision* (1902); *The House of Mirth* (1905); *Madame de Treymes* (1907); *The Fruit of the Tree* (1907); *Tales of Men and Ghosts* (1910); *Ethan Frome* (1911); *The Reef* (1912); *The Custom of the Country* (1913); *Summer* (1917); *The Age of Innocence* (1920); *The Marne* (1918); *The Glimpses of the Moon* (1922); *A Son at the Front* (1923); *Old New York* (1924); *The Old Maid* (1924); *The Mother's Recompense* (1925); *Twilight Sleep* (1927); *The Children* (1928); *Hudson River Bracketed* (1929); *The Gods Arrive* (1932) *The Buccaneers* (1938); *A Backward Glance* (autobiography, 1934); *Fast and Loose* (1977)

ACCOLADES: Pulitzer Prize for fiction, 1921, for *The Age of Innocence*; honorary doctorate of letters from Yale; American Academy of Arts and Letters

INTERESTING BIO FACT: Wharton's years in Paris were punctuated by a passionate affair with journalist Morton Fullerton, intellectual friendships with artists and writers, and dedication to the Allied cause during World War I. Wharton led the committee to aid refugees from northeastern France and Belgium, and created hostels and schools for them. She helped establish workrooms to employ women who had no means of support and raised funds for these projects. Traveling to the front lines to observe the fighting, Wharton wrote reports for publication in America and urged her homeland to join the war.

FURTHER READING *A Historical Guide to Edith Wharton* edited by Carol J. Singley (2003); *Edith Wharton* by Janet Beer (2002); *Edith Wharton: An Extraordinary Life* by Eleanor Dwight (1999); *The Letters of Edith Wharton* edited by R.W.B. Lewis et. al. (1994)

ELSEWHERE IN THE AREA The stately "Berkshire Cottages" of the Gilded Age endure in the area as schools and resorts; Tanglewood, nearby summer home of Boston Symphony Orchestra ◢

> *The Mount was to give me country cares and joys, long happy rides and drives through the wooded lanes of that loveliest region, the companionship of a few dear friends...*
>
> — EDITH WHARTON

JOHN GREENLEAF WHITTIER HOMES
Quaker Poet's Birthplace, Long-Time Residence

LOCATIONS Northeastern Massachusetts, near the New Hampshire border, in Amesbury and Haverhill. The **John Greenleaf Whittier Home** ($) is located at 86 Friend St. in **Amesbury**, **Mass.**, near the junction of I-95 and I-495. The site is open for guided tours May 1 through Oct. 31, Tuesday through Saturday, from 10 a.m. to 4 p.m. Last tour at 3:15 p.m. Winter months by appointment only. For more information, contact the Whittier House, 86 Friend St., Amesbury, MA 01913. Tel. (978) 388-1337. For a virtual tour of the Amesbury home, go to http://www.SeacoastNH.com. You'll also find **Whittier's Grave** in Amesbury's historic Union Cemetery on Haverhill Road.

The **Whittier Family Homestead and Birthplace** ($) is located in **Haverhill**, **Mass.**, 32 miles north of Boston and 20 miles southwest of Amesbury, at 305 Whittier Road. From I-495, take exit 52 east 1 mile. The site is along Route 110. Hours are: May 1 through Oct. 31, Tuesday through Saturday from 10 a.m. to 5 p.m.; Sunday: 1 p.m. to 5 p.m., and Nov. 1 through April 30, Tuesday through Friday and on Sunday, from 1 p.m. to 5 p.m.; Saturday from 10 a.m. to 5 p.m. Closed Mondays and major holidays. For more information, contact Whittier Family Homestead, 305 Whittier Road, Haverhill, MA 01830. Tel. (978) 373-3979. On the Net: www.haverhilltourism.com/PICwhittierbirthplace.html.

FRAME OF REFERENCE John Greenleaf Whittier moved to Amesbury with his Quaker mother, aunt and sister in 1836 and lived in his Amesbury house, built 1829, for 56 years until his death in 1892. The house has been owned and maintained by the Whittier Home Association since 1918, when it opened to the public. Whittier was born near Haverhill in 1807 and spent his boyhood on a farm in the Merrimack River Valley. His great-great grandfather built the Haverhill home in 1688.

SIGNIFICANCE Whittier, a Romantic poet, story writer, politician, abolitionist, journalist, newspaper editor, and author of more than 100 hymns, was a Victorian superstar in the last half of the 19th century. One of the era's famous "Fireside Poets," he is best remembered for his classic poem *Snow-Bound* (1866), which won him national acclaim and financial security late in life. His many anti-slavery poems and patriotic verses also won him popularity.

Whittier's reputation persists largely as a regional poet. Many of his New England ballads are set in New Hampshire, where he immortalized characters from the mountain, lakes and seacoast areas.

In 1887, the town of **Whittier, Calif**., was named for the tall and spare poet with dark eyes, known as America's Quaker Poet. Whittier wrote most of his prose and poetry, including *Snow-Bound*, in the Garden Room in Amesbury.

ABOUT THE SITES

WHITTIER'S AMESBURY HOME The three-story, white clapboard house with black shutters originally had four rooms and an attic. Whittier enlarged the house, raising the original building and adding another story. He also built a first-floor study and a garden room, where he wrote most of his works. Visitors today can tour six of the home's nine rooms.

You'll find the home and its furnishings about the same as when the Whittier family lived in Amesbury. Whittier-related items amid the modest Victorian decor include the desk where he penned *Snow-Bound*; a portrait of his mother, Abigail, above the parlor mantel; Whittier's coat lying across the bed in an upstairs bedroom; a family bedspread; the poet's bow tie and his lounge chair. Whittier, it's said, wrote during the morning in his chair by the window until around noon. A picture in the upstairs hall depicts mourners in the home's backyard at the poet's funeral in 1892. Many pictures in the house remain where Whittier hung them.

In the Manuscript Room (also the gift shop), you find a Whittier work desk, books, canes, photographs, souvenirs, locks of his hair and Whittier's death mask.

When the museum opened near the turn of the century, the el of the original kitchen was removed and placed at the back of the yard. Today the former kitchen, now the "Garden House," accommodates public functions. Visitors can view a 30-minute orientation video at the site.

The house, a stop on the Underground Railroad, is part of the Essex National Heritage Area's Early Settlement Trail, featuring several 17th-century houses.

WHITTIER'S HAVERHILL BIRTHPLACE Although Whittier wrote his most popular poem, *Snow-Bound*, in Amesbury, he set the work at the Haverhill farm where he was born and grew up. Little has changed at the homestead that five generations of Whittiers had called home. The simple two-story, white clapboard house occupies a rolling, green expanse under the shoulder of Job's Hill. A low stone wall surrounds the Colonial-era homesite.

The old New England spread, originally 148 acres, continues as a working farm. The babbling brook that turned the wheel of a grist mill for homesteader Thomas Whittier remains.

HOT TIPS Whittier-related sites in Amesbury include: 1850 Friends Meeting House, Friend Street, where Whittier served as the chairman of the building committee; "The Captain's Well", Main Street next to Middle School, subject of Whittier's best-known poem which tells of Captain Valentine Bagley's shipwreck and his vow to dig the well; Harriet Prescot Spofford Home on Deer Island, former tavern (now restaurant) that hosted Whittier, Emerson, Holmes and other literary luminaries.

In Haverhill, you can pick up a driving tour guide to sites associated with Whittier and his poems. Also, a walking tour, the **Freeman Memorial Trail**, guides you to 13 sites, marked by numbered signs, cited in Whittier's poetry or by a biographer. Pick up the guide at the Homestead.

THE BEST STUFF The Amesbury study where Whittier penned most of his works remains almost exactly as the poet left it, right down to the personal items on his desk. The room's carpets, wallpaper, maps, books and magazines look as they were in the 1800s. It seems that Whittier just removed his boots and hat upon arriving in his personal space, where fellow writers and abolitionists once visited.

THE WRITER AND HIS WORK

BORN: Dec. 17, 1807 (same year Longfellow born) near Haverhill
DIED: Sept. 9, 1892, in Hampton Falls, N.H.; buried in Amesbury
EDUCATED: Haverhill Academy
IMPORTANT WORKS: Books - *Legends of New England* (1831); *Lays of My Home* (poetry, 1843); *Supernaturalism of New England* (1847); *Leaves From Margaret Smith's Journal* (1849); *The Panorama, and other Poems* (1856). During the Civil War, Whittier published two volumes, *In War Time* (1864) and *National Lyrics* (1865), which included poems inspired

by the turbulent times. Popular poems - *Among The Hills* (1868); *Ichabod* (1850); *Maud Muller* (1854); *The Barefoot Boy* (1855); *Barbara Frietchie* (1863); *Snow-Bound* (1866)

INTERESTING BIO FACT: Whittier began his writing career as a journalist, working for the famous abolitionist William Lloyd Garrison and his newspaper, The Liberator (1831). He edited the Haverhill Gazette, the New England Weekly Review in Hartford, Conn., and the Pennsylvania Freeman in Philadelphia. He also wrote for The National Era in Washington, D.C.

Whittier was elected for a term in the Massachusetts legislature in 1835 and helped found the anti-slavery Liberty party in 1839. His career turned to writing in 1833 with the publication of his abolitionist manifesto, *Justice and Expediency*. Whittier was once mobbed and stoned for his stands, and his office in Philadelphia was burned. As a poet, he nurtured the career of fellow writer **Sarah Orne Jewett**.

FURTHER READING *John Greenleaf Whittier: A Biography* by Roland H. Woodwell (1985); *The Letters of John Greenleaf Whittier* edited by John B. Pickard (1975)

ELSEWHERE IN THE AREA Amesbury - Golgotha burying ground, Macy Street; Macy-Colby House, Main Street; Bartlett Museum (1870 schoolhouse); Mary Baker Eddy House, 277 Main St.; 1810 Old Powder House, Monroe and Madison streets; 1793 Lowell's Boat Shop, still operating on Main Street. Haverhill Area - Buttonwoods Museum; Washington Street Shoe District; Tattersall Farm; Rocks Village; Winnekenni Castle ⬧

In my boyhood, in our lonely farm-house, we had scanty sources of information; few books and only a small weekly newspaper. Our only annual was the Almanac. Under such circumstances storytelling was a necessary response to the long winter evenings.

— Whittier in preface of *Snow-Bound*

NATIONAL YIDDISH BOOK CENTER

Preserving Yiddish, Modern Jewish Literature

In 1980, a graduate student named Aaron Lansky panicked when he discovered that thousands of priceless Yiddish books were being deemed useless and thrown away throughout North America. He worried that an entire literature based on the historical language of Jews in central and eastern Europe was on the verge of extinction. He decided to do something.

Lansky took a leave of absence from his studies, and operating out of an unheated factory loft, issued a public appeal for unwanted and discarded Yiddish books. So began the nonprofit National Yiddish Book Center in **Amherst, Mass.**, 30 miles north of Springfield and 120 miles west of Boston.

Today, the 37,000 square-foot building on the campus of **Hampshire College** in Amherst attracts visitors from around the globe who wish to explore the meaning and relevance of Yiddish culture and modern Jewish literature. The center, an architecturally interesting, cedar-shingled structure that looks like a chain of linked buildings, is also the world's only comprehensive supplier of Yiddish books. Because many of the books are deteriorating , the center in 1998 launched the Steven Spielberg Digital Yiddish Library. The pioneering program is digitizing titles and making reprints available to the public on demand. The center also offers lectures, films, museum exhibits, theater, conference rooms, concerts and live performances.

When Lansky and his co-workers began their rescue in the 80s, scholars estimated that 70,000 Yiddish books were still extant and recoverable. The Center retrieved that number in six months and now has 1.5 million volumes.

The center is open to the public Sunday through Friday, from 10 a.m. to 3:30 p.m. It is closed on Shabbos (Saturday) and major legal and Jewish holidays. For more information, contact the National Yiddish Book Center, Tel. 413-256-4900. E-mail: yiddish@bikher.org. On the Net: www .yiddishbookcenter.org. ⚬

THOMAS BAILEY ALDRICH MEMORIAL

Victorian Novelist Who Inspired Twain

Thomas Bailey Aldrich was a Victorian poet, novelist, short-story writer, and magazine editor whose popular novel *Story of a Bad Boy* (1870) inspired Mark Twain to write *Tom Sawyer*. Between 1849 to 1852, Aldrich lived in his grandfather's house facing Court Street in **Portsmouth, N.H**. After Aldrich's death in 1907, his widow and friends acquired the house and opened it to the public. Today, the house, along with the Aldrich Garden and Aldrich Museum, comprise the Thomas Bailey Aldrich Memorial. The memorial is part of the Strawbery Banke Museum ($), a living history maritime village telling of New Hampshire seacoast life from 1600 to 1950.

Portsmouth's first settlers in 1630 named the settlement Strawbery Banke for the profusion of wild berries found on the shores of the Piscataqua River. Strawbery Banke Museum is located 1 hour north of Boston and 1 hour south of Portland, off I-95 at exit 7.

As a boy, Aldrich lived in the house with his grandparents from 1849 to 1852. These years were later described in his autobiographical *Story of a Bad Boy*. In 1908 the circa 1797, two- story house of white wood with green shutters and white brick chimneys was furnished to recreate the novel's setting. The surrounding Colonial Revival garden is planted with flowers Aldrich mentioned in his poetry. The brick museum exhibits Aldrich's manuscripts and memorabilia.

Aldrich, born in Portsmouth in 1836, wrote of his boyhood and his grandfather's house in *Story of a Bad Boy*, his best-known work. William Dean Howells, editor of the literary journal Atlantic Monthly, hailed it as the first truly American novel. *Bad Boy* first appeared in serial form in Our Young Folk, a 19th- century children's magazine. Aldrich's other famous works are *An Old Town by the Sea* (1883), an evocative literary picture of contemporary New England, and *Marjorie Daw and Other People*.

After Aldrich's first success with poetry in 1855, he was quickly accepted into the literary circles of New York City, where he lived at the time. After moving to Boston in the mid-1800s, he succeeded Howells as editor of The Atlantic Monthly. He also was a Civil War correspondent. After he became a famous writer, he also summered in Portsmouth with his family.

When Aldrich died at age 70, the Aldrich House had served as Portsmouth's first hospital since the 1880s. The Aldrich family repurchased it and under the direction of Lilian Aldrich, the author's widow, the home

95

was restored as a memorial to him. Mark Twain, who had said the *Bad Boy* inspired his Tom Sawyer character, was among those who came to Portsmouth for the dedication. In 1979 the house became part of Strawbery Banke.

Strawbery Banke Museum is open May 1 through Oct. 31, Monday through Saturday, from 10 a.m. to 5 p.m., and on Sunday from noon to 5 p.m. The site is open November through April, Thursday through Saturday, from 10 a.m. to 2 p.m. and on Sunday noon to 2 p.m. Closed January and major holidays.

For more information, contact Strawbery Banke Museum, P.O. Box 300 Portsmouth, NH 03802. Tel. (603) 433-1100. E-mail: hharris@strawberybanke.org. On the Net: www.strawberybanke.org/museum. ◢

Imagine a low-studded structure, with a wide hall running through the middle. At your right hand, as you enter, stands a tall black mahogany clock, looking like an Egyptian mummy set up on end.

— ALDRICH's description of his home in *Bad Boy*

JOY FARM

Summer Home of Poet E. E. Cummings

The countryside summer home of poet Edward Estlin Cummings from 1923 until his death in 1962 is now a private residence on part of Cummings' former 300-acre Joy Farm in **Silver Lake, N.H.** Cummings' white clapboard farmhouse, a National Historic Landmark since 1971, is located on Salter Hill Road just south of Madison, in the east central part of the state. The house is not open to the public.

Cummings (1894-1962) was one of America's most innovative and popular poets in the 1930s. He also was a lecturer, essayist, playwright and accomplished painter. Cummings' playful, typographically striking, and sometimes controversial verse places him among the most anthologized 20th-century poets. His poetry rejects the restraints and small-mindedness of society and celebrates the individual, as well as erotic and familiar love.

Cummings, a Harvard graduate, published the first of his 11 volumes of poetry in the anthology *Eight Harvard Poets* (1917). In the anthology, he began writing "i" in the lower case to symbolize the humbleness and uniqueness of the individual. It was not published that way because the editor thought that it was an error, but the poet used lower-case letters as a stylistic trademark.

Cummings' best-known works include *The Enormous Room* (1922), a novel/memoir based on his experiences in the French internment camp and considered one of the best works of World War I literature; *Tulips and Chimneys* (1923); & (1925); *by e e cummings* (1930); *Eimi* (1933); *Collected Poems* (1938); *50 Poems* (1940); *XAIPE* (1950); *Poems 1923-1954* (1954); *95 Poems* (1958); *Fairy Tales* (1965); *Complete Poems: 1913-1962* (1972).

Cummings summered at Joy Farm with his third (and common-law) wife, fashion model Marion Morehouse. The peace and beauty of the New Hampshire countryside and his happiness with Marion changed the tone of his verse, which became more life-affirming with high praise for what was simple, natural and unique.

FURTHER READING *Dreams in a Mirror* by Richard S. Kennedy (1994); *e. e. cummings: The Art of His Poetry* by Norman Friedman (1960). *E. E. Cummings: The Magic Maker* by Charles Norman (1973), describes the environment at Joy Farm. ◢

ROBERT FROST FARMS

Two Sites Where Famous Poet Lived and Wrote

LOCATIONS The **Robert Frost Farm** is located in southern New Hampshire along NH 28 in **Derry**, about 1.5 miles from the traffic circle and directly across from Berry Road. **The Frost Place** is located in north central New Hampshire in **Franconia**, just east of I-93 on Ridge Road. From I-93 take exit 38 to Route 116 South for 1 mile. Follow signs to The Frost Place.

The Robert Frost Farm ($) is open mid-May to mid-June on weekends only, 10 a.m. to 5 p.m. and mid-June to Labor Day, Monday through Saturday, 10 a.m. to 5 p.m., and on Sunday from noon to 5 p.m. Tours are conducted on the hour until 4 p.m. For more information, contact Frost Farm, Route 28, Derry, NH 03038. Tel.: (603) 432-3091. On the Net: www .nhstateparks.org.

The Frost Place ($), part of the town of Franconia, operates as a nonprofit museum and educational retreat. From I-93, take exit 38 and go left at ramp to Route 116. Follow signs to site. The site is open Memorial Day through June on weekends from 1 p.m. to 5 p.m., and July 1 through Columbus Day, except for Tuesday, from 1 p.m. to 5 p.m. For more information, contact The Frost Place, Ridge Road, Franconia, NH 03580. Tel. (603) 823-5510. E-mail: rfrost@frostplace.com. On the Net: www.frostplace.com.

FRAME OF REFERENCE Frost and his family lived on the Derry farm (Robert Frost Farm) from 1900 to 1911. The state of New Hampshire opened the site to the public in the 1940s. The Frosts lived on the Franconia farm (The Frost Place) from spring 1915 to fall 1920. They returned every summer until 1938. The city of Franconia bought the site in 1976 and opened it to the public in 1977.

SIGNIFICANCE One of America's leading poets and winner of the Pulitzer Prize for poetry four times, Frost was the most popular American poet since Henry Wadsworth Longfellow. His 11 volumes of verse comprise more than 350 powerful and memorable poems written over 75 years. His first book, *A Boy's Will,* was published in 1916, and his last volume, *In the Clearing,* was published in 1962, on his 89th birthday. He received a special Congressional Medal of Honor the same day.

Frost's best-known poems include *The Death of A Hired Man, After*

Apple-Picking, Mending Wall, The Road Not Taken, Birches, and especially *Stopping By Woods on a Snowy Evening*.

ABOUT THE SITES

ROBERT FROST FARM (DERRY) Frost lived and wrote at this isolated farm from 1900 until 1911. Frost's grandfather had bought the 30-acre chicken farm, which he gave to grandson Robert in 1900 because he feared the future poet would not amount to much. While here, Frost drew inspiration from the beautiful countryside and wrote more than 40 poems, including *Mending Wall, Pastures* and *Running Brook*, all actual sites on the farm. Frost lived in the simple, two-story, white clapboard farmhouse, built in 1884, with his family. While in Derry, Frost taught English at nearby Pinkerton Academy.

The house is furnished to reflect the period when the Frosts lived there and retains some original furnishings, including the dining room dishes. Furnishings that are not original were selected by Lesley Frost Ballantine, the poet's daughter, to be representative of those owned by the family. Elinor Frost's sister painted several of the small works downstairs.

Frost built the farm's barn to house his Wyandotte hens, a source of income. A patch of raspberry and blackberry bushes flourished against the southern side of the barn. Poetry-inspiring sites include the stone wall that lay between land owned by neighbor Napoleon Guay, who every spring replaced fallen stones from the wall that marked the boundary between his and Frost's farm. Just south of the farm, you'll find a stream that flows in spring but dries up in summer. Frost named the stream Hyla Brook after its "peepers," tiny tree frogs of the genus Hyla, which shrill in the spring. The brook drains a swampy area to the east. Along the brook grew alders, and in the marshy area grew the lady slippers, violets, cowslips, and ferns that delighted Frost the "botanizer."

After the Frosts sold the Derry farm in 1911, it passed through several owners until, in the 1940s, it ceased to be farmland and became instead an auto graveyard before restoration.

THE FROST PLACE (FRANCONIA) Only a few rooms of the farmhouse are open to visitors and no tours are given. First editions of Frost's work are on display, along with photographs, memorabilia, and a rare collection of Christmas card poems. To the left of the front door, you'll see the parlor where Frost wrote. In warm weather, he preferred to write on the front porch.

You can also walk the half-mile Poetry Nature Trail that winds through the 8 acres of the original 30. Stops along the trail behind the house feature Frost's poems on wooden plaques affixed to trees. The poem *The Line Gang* hangs on a telephone pole. Two poems, *Evening in a Sugar Orchard* and *Goodby and Keep Cold* are displayed where Frost actually wrote them. Signs also identify flowers and plants along the trail. In the old barn/theater you can view a slide presentation, "Robert Frost in Franconia," as well as a video scripted by Frost's great-grandson about the poet's life.

The seven-room, one-story white clapboard farmhouse is a typical 19th-century New England style. When Frost moved to the farm he already was considered one of the world's great living poets. Coming up the road to the house on Ore Hill with a view of Mount Lafayette, you'll see the old gray metal mailbox with "Frost" painted on it in black letters.

Frost left Franconia in 1920 to assume a post as poet-in-residence at Amherst College in Massachusetts.

HOT TIPS No pets at state historic sites. Every summer, the Frost Place hosts the Frost Day and a Festival of Poetry with many activities held in the old barn/theater. Soon after his wife's death, Robert Frost purchased the Homer Noble farm in Ripton, Vermont. Although in his later years Frost lived in Cambridge, MA and in Florida, the Vermont farm became for him a place of refuge and restoration, and his final permanent residence.

THE BEST STUFF When Frost wrote *Mending Wall* at his Derry farm, he was reminiscing about the regular excursions he and his neighbor made to repair the wall. Guay viewed the task as a tradition. Frost hints in the poem that he considered it needless work, but years later, thinking of the task made him long for the old wall in New England.

THE WRITER AND HIS WORK
BORN: March 26, 1874, in San Francisco
DIED: Jan. 29, 1963, in Boston
EDUCATED: One semester Dartmouth College, 1892
MARRIED: Elinor Miriam White, 1895; four children
IMPORTANT WORKS: Books of poetry - *A Boy's Will* (1916); *North of Boston* (1915); *Mountain Interval* (1916); *New Hampshire* (1923); *West-Running Brook* (1928); *A Further Range* (1936); *A Witness Tree* (1942); *Steeple*

Bush (1947); *In The Clearing* (1962); *A Masque of Reason* (1945); *A Masque of Mercy (1947)*

ACCOLADES: Pulitizer Prizes for *New Hampshire* (1924); *Collected Poems* (1930); *A Further Range* (1936); and *A Witness Tree* (1942). Congressional Medal of Honor, 1963; two unanimous votes of praise from U.S. Senate

INTERESTING BIO FACT: Frost, also a teacher and lecturer, lives on in the hearts of many Americans because of his reading of a poem, *The Gift Outright*, at the inauguration of President John F. Kennedy in 1961.

FURTHER READING *Belief and Uncertainty in the Poetry of Robert Frost* by Robert Pack (2003); *Toward Robert Frost: The Reader and the Poetry* by Judith Oster (1994); *The Breath of Parted Lips: Voices from the Robert Frost Place* by Mark Cox et al (2000)

ELSEWHERE IN THE AREA America's Stonehenge near Derry △

MACDOWELL COLONY

Inspiring Writers For Nearly A Century

The **Peterborough, N.H.**, farm that American composer Edward Mac-Dowell and his wife, Marian, bought in 1896 has offered inspiration and support as an artist colony for nearly a century. After Edward's death in 1908, Marian built a number of one-room studio cottages on the southern New Hampshire farm and invited authors, poets, playwrights, composers, painters, sculptors, architects and filmmakers to come and create. For 48 years, she traveled throughout America raising funds and support for the colony.

Through the decades, the MacDowell Colony has attracted more than 4,000 artists. Many have achieved great acclaim after their sojourn in the New Hampshire woods. More than 50 MacDowell colonists have won Pulitzer Prizes, including **Stephen Vincent Benet** (*John Brown's Body*) and **Willa Cather** (*Oh, Pioneers!*). **Edward Arlington Robinson** was one of the colony's first applicants. Alice Walker, Studs Terkel, Mary Karr and Terry MacMillan also wrote at MacDowell. **Thornton Wilder** wrote some of *Our Town* on the farm, and Aaron Copland composed parts of *Appalachian Spring* in the bucolic setting.

Today the elite colony's 450 acres of woodlands and fields offer artists seven live-in studios, plus 25 studios assigned with separate bedrooms in a common building. Based upon the artist's needs, studios can offer darkrooms, pianos, mixing board, 16mm film-editing suite, litho and plate printing press or welding and air tools and overhead crane. Interested artists must apply for acceptance. The main criterion to win a residency, which averages from four weeks to two months, is quality of work (talent).

For more information, contact The MacDowell Colony, 100 High St., Peterborough, NH 03458, Tel. (603) 924-3886; or 163 East 81st St., New York, NY 10028. Tel. (212) 535-9690. E-mail info@macdowellcolony.org On the Net: www.macdowellcolony.org. ⌂

REDWOOD LIBRARY AND ATHENAEUM
America's Oldest Circulating Library

Among the many Colonial and historical sites of **Newport, R.I.**, book lovers will want to visit the oldest lending library in America, the Redwood Library and Athenaeum, located at 50 Belleville Ave. Abraham Redwood and a group of friends and associates founded the library in 1747, and Peter Harrison, one of America's first architects, designed the white stone library, an impressive display of neoclassical architecture. Completed in 1750, the library claims to be the oldest library building in continuous use in the country.

The National Historic Landmark continues as an independent subscription library, supported by membership fees, endowments and gifts. The stately library, with columned front portico, high arched windows, and polished hardwood floors, provides a home for an important collection of 18th- and 19th-century portraits, sculpture, furniture, and other decorative arts. The light green bookshelves of the library, expanded from its original size, contain many rare and unique books among a total of 160,000 volumes, archives and manuscripts. Qualified scholars and researchers are welcome without charge.

Newport, located in southeastern Rhode Island on the Narragansett Bay, was one of the first settlements in the state, chartered in 1663. Religious refugees from the Massachusetts Bay Colony founded Rhode Island, which the British occupied during the American Revolution.

The Redwood Library is open Tuesday through Thursday from 9:30 a.m. to 8 p.m. On Mondays, Fridays and Saturdays, hours are 9:30 a.m. to 5:30 p.m.; Sundays from 1 p.m. to 5 p.m. Guided tours are available Monday through Friday at 10:30 am. Sign up at the front desk. Groups must make reservations. For more information, contact the Redwood Library and Athenaeum, 50 Belleville Ave., Newport, RI. 02840 Tel. (401) 847-0292. E-mail: redwood@redwoodlibrary.org. On the Net: www.redwoodlibrary.org.

ELSEWHERE IN THE AREA Friends Meeting House (1699); Trinity Church (1726); Touro Synagogue (1763), oldest U.S. synagogue; White Horse Tavern (1673), oldest operating U.S. tavern; the 3-mile Cliff Walk that includes such fabulous mansions as The Breakers (1895), Château-sur-Mer (1852), The Elms (1901), Marble House (1892) and Rosecliff (1902) ◢

KIPLING'S NAULAKHA
Where English Author Wrote 'Jungle Books'

English author Joseph Rudyard Kipling built a whimsical house in the 1880s in **Dummerston, Vt.**, and wrote his famous *Jungle Books* there. The house, which he named Naulakha, is available to the public today as a vacation guest house. Kipling and his new American bride, Caroline Balestier, lived in the southern Vermont town from 1892 to 1896, and their two children were born there. The Nobel Prize-winning author, who was born in India, named his house after a Hindu word meaning "precious jewel." Kipling built Naulakha with a view of New Hampshire's Mount Monadnock, a place he had heard about while in England.

In 1992, the house was purchased and restored by a British organization, Landmark Trust. The company rescues historic British properties and restores them as vacation destinations. Naulakha was the firm's first property in North America.

The Kipling home, located near Brattleboro, Vt., off I- 91 at exit 3, has most of the original Kipling furnishings, placed as they were when the famous writer lived there. The original carriage house, ice house, and tennis court (likely the first in Vermont) have been rebuilt. The trust has restored the grounds, where Kipling invented "snow golf" and allegedly introduced skiing to Vermont on skis given to him by English mystery writer Arthur Conan Doyle. The house also has an exhibit on Kipling's Vermont years.

You can rent Naulakha by the week, with shorter stays possible November through March. The house can accommodate up to eight guests in its four bedrooms. Bedrooms and bathrooms are located on the second floor, accessible only by stairs.

When he moved to Vermont, Kipling was 27 years old and already famous. His best-known works include *The Jungle Book* (1894) and *The Second Jungle Book* (1895); *The Light That Failed* (1890); *Barrack Room Ballads* (1892); *Captains Courageous* (1897); *Kim* (1901); *Just So Stories* (1902); *The Village That Voted The Earth Was Flat* (1913); and *Something of Myself* (1937). Kipling was the first English writer to win the Nobel prize in literature (1907).

The writer came to America in 1892 for a brief visit with his in-laws in New York. He decided to travel to New England to visit Mt. Monadnock, which he had read about in a poem by Ralph Waldo Emerson. He fell in love with nearby Brattleboro, then a declining resort town of 6,000 people, and decided to stay.

To build Naulakha, Kipling collaborated with New York architect Henry Rutgers Marshall, choosing the then-popular "shingle style" architecture, an outgrowth of the Arts and Crafts movement that retreated from Victorian stuffiness. The 90- by 24-foot house, which some say resembles a ship, had large, east-facing windows for bright mornings and stained, oak-paneled rooms. Kipling's long, narrow library occupied the "bow" of the ship and the kitchen its wider "stern."

Naulakha's relaxed furnishings featured floral motifs and decorations drawn from nature, and they reflected the family lifestyle (although Kipling reportedly dressed up for dinner.) A billiards table occupied the attic. Today, the architecture remains virtually unchanged. Guests can view Kipling's golf clubs and a set of 1891 Encyclopedia Brittanica, a replacement of a gift from **Robert Louis Stevenson** to Kipling.

Kipling left Vermont in 1896 after a quarrel with his brother-in-law and didn't visit again until 1899. During that visit, Kipling's daughter died of pneumonia and, brokenhearted, he left America forever. In 1903, Naulakha was sold to a family friend and later remained unoccupied for 50 years until Landmark Trust bought it.

For more information about Naulakha, contact The Landmark Trust USA, 707 Kipling Road, Dummerston, VT 05301. Tel. (802) 254-6868. E-mail: Itusa@sover.net.

FURTHER READING *Rudyard Kipling in Vermont: Birthplace of The Jungle Books* by Stuart Murray (1997) ◢

ROKEBY MUSEUM

Estate of Rowland Evans Robinson

LOCATION Vermont's Champlain Valley, in Ferrisburgh, 30 miles south of Burlington, Vt., at 4334 US 7. The museum entrance is about 3 miles north of the town of Vergennes and 2 miles south of the village center of North Ferrisburgh.

Rokeby ($) is open mid-May to mid-October, Wednesday through Sunday. Guided tours of the house are offered at 11 a.m., and 12:30 and 2 p.m. Hiking trails are open year-round during daylight hours for self-guided tours. For more information, contact Rokeby, R.R. 1 Box 1540, Ferrisburgh, VT 05456-9711. Tel. (802) 877-3406. E-mail: Rokeby@globalnetisp.net. On the Net: www.rokeby.org.

FRAME OF REFERENCE Roland Evans Robinson was a member of a family of Quaker pioneers, farmers, abolitionists and artists who lived at Rokeby from the 1790s to 1961. Robinson was born at Rokeby in 1833 and died there in 1900. The site, documenting 200 years of Vermont life, became a National Historic Landmark in 1997.

SIGNIFICANCE Robinson — illustrator, historian, conservationist and a popular writer in his time — lived and wrote at Rokeby, home to four generations of his family. Robinson's better-known works, celebrating his beloved Vermont, include *Danvis Tales, Uncle Lisha's Shop* and *Danvis Folks*. His writing and illustrations appeared in magazines, including The Atlantic Monthly and Forest and Stream. Robinson gave precise descriptions of nature, wrote in long sentences and gave his characters a complex Vermont dialect. His tales of life in Danvis, the hill town he created, made him a beloved figure in the Green Mountain State.

ABOUT THE SITE The Robinson homestead, one of the most prosperous sheep and dairy farms in the Champlain Valley by the mid-19th century, was called Rokeby after a poem by Sir Walter Scott and a manor in England. The name means a settlement of crows. Visitors today can walk 90 acres of farm pastures, orchards and hayfields by scenic trails. You can view eight agricultural outbuildings, including the smokehouse, creamery and slaughter house, as well as several foundations, wells, and a sheep dip.

The large, brown clapboard house with white trim where the family lived is fully furnished with original family belongings. These include a desk in every room, paintings (mostly by family members), books, china, kitchen utensils, linens, musical instruments, snow shoes, clothing and even Robinson's original longjohns.

The Robinsons, all Quakers, were staunch abolitionists. Rokeby was part of the Underground Railroad and offered ex-slaves jobs, education and equal treatment.

HOT TIPS Among the museum's historical 15,000 items are letters, books, magazines, scrapbooks, receipts, photographs, artwork and Robinson's complete manuscripts. The site features the Rokeby Wool Festival in July and a Pie and Ice Cream Social in August.

THE BEST STUFF Robinson loved to paint agricultural and hunting scenes and many of his paintings hang in the house. You'll find his lovely scenes of winter, of foxes and of hunting.

THE WRITER AND HIS WORK
BORN: May 14, 1833, at Rokeby
DIED: 1900, at Rokeby
EDUCATED: Trained as an engraver and illustrator in New York City
MARRIED: Anne Stevens, 1870, three children
IMPORTANT WORKS: *In New England Fields and Woods*; *Latchkey Kids*; *A Danvis Pioneer, Vermont: A Study of Independence*; *A Hero of Ticonderoga*; *Danvis Tales*; *Uncle Lisha's Shop*; *Danvis Folks*.
INTERESTING BIO FACT: Failing eyesight in his fifties forced Robinson to give up his art, and with his wife's help, he turned to writing. Anne, a painter, art teacher and Ferrisburg town clerk, took her husband's book dictation.

FURTHER READING *Folklore in the Writings of Roland E. Robinson* by Ronald L. Baker (1973); *Rowland Evans Robinson: Realist of the Outdoors* by Terence Martin (1955)

ELSEWHERE IN THE AREA Lake Champlain Maritime Museum ⌂

STONE HOUSE MUSEUM

Robert Frost's Home in 1920s

The stone house where Robert Frost lived from 1920 to 1929 in **South Shaftsbury, Vt.**, opened to the public as a museum in 2002. The house, near **Frost's gravesite** in **Bennington, Vt.**, is where the poet composed his famous poem *Stopping by Woods on a Snowy Evening* at the dining room table. The poem was part of Frost's Pulitzer Prize-winning volume *New Hampshire* (1923). Frost usually arranged poems for a book by spreading them out on the house's living room floor.

The Robert Frost Stone House Museum ($) preserves the wildly popular poet's modest, two-story stone house with pitched roof. Built circa 1769, it survives as a rare example of colonial architecture using native stone and timber. The white house looks almost as it did when Frost lived in it at the height of his career. The 7 acres surrounding the museum still feature the stone walls, birch trees, a timbered barn that Frost contemplated, as well as some of his original apple trees.

Frost wrote that in Shaftsbury, "I mean to plant a new Garden of Eden with a thousand apple trees of some unforbidden variety."

The museum today has two galleries: The J.J. Lankes Gallery in the central hall and the *Stopping by the Woods* Gallery. The Lankes room features the woodcut art of local artist J. J. Lankes, who worked with Frost "decorating" his books of poetry. The second room is dedicated to Frost's famous poem, written here in the early hours of a hot June morning in 1922. Frost had worked all night on the title poem for New Hampshire when he went outside for a breath of fresh air. Exhilarated, he returned to his dining room table with a new poem swirling in his head like fresh snow. The house also has a small book shop.

During Frost's nine years at the Stone House, he wrote two books of poetry and won his first Pulitzer Prize plus two later ones. Frost is buried behind the Old First Church in Old Bennington. His gravestone of Barre granite with hand-carved laurel leaves reads "I had a lover's quarrel with the world."

The Frost Stone House Museum is open May through December, Tuesday through Sunday, 10 a.m. to 5 p.m. For more information, contact The Friends of Robert Frost, 121 Historic Route 7A, Shaftsbury, VT 05262. Tel. (802) 447-6200.

E-mail: stopping@frostfriends.org. On the Net: www.frostfriends.org. For more Frost sites, see entries under New Hampshire and Florida in this book. ◪

Joyce Kilmer Birthplace

T. THOMAS FORTUNE HOUSE

Leading African-American Journalist

A southern New Jersey house listed in both the State Register of Historic Places and the National Register of Historic Places once belonged to the leading African-American journalist of the 19th century, T. Thomas Fortune. The house, at 94 West Bergen Place in **Red Bank, N.J.**, is privately owned and not open to the public.

Fortune (1856-1928), a freed slave and close friend of **Booker T. Washington**, published more than 20 books, as well as more than 300 editorials. Fortune is regarded as an important post-Civil War advocate for equal educational opportunity. He is credited with having coined the term "Afro-American."

Fortune, trained as a printer and educated at Howard University, went to New York in 1878 from his home state, Florida. He worked for the New York Sun and later joined its editorial staff. He edited a black daily, The Globe, and became chief editorial writer for The Negro World. In 1883, he founded The New York Age. Fortune's influential opinion newspaper protested discrimination, lynching, mob violence, and disenfranchisement. In 1890, he founded the Afro-American League, a forerunner of the NAACP.

Fortune bought the two-story, L-shaped shingle house with large attic in 1901. He lived there until 1915. The rambling house with front porch and front bay window was built in the mid-1800s and has been enlarged from its original six rooms. Its architecture represents "Picturesque Eclecticism," a high-Victorian look that combines decorative elements from a variety of styles. The main floor features two marble-faced fireplaces.

On the Net: www.redbank.com/eri.

FURTHER READING *T Thomas Fortune: Militant Journalist* by Emma Lou Thornbrough (1972) ◮

JOYCE KILMER BIRTHPLACE
Home of Poet Who Penned 'Trees'

The house where teacher/poet/journalist/essayist Alfred Joyce Kilmer was born in 1886 stands at 17 Joyce Kilmer Ave. in downtown **New Brunswick, N.J.**, 10 miles west of the southern end of Staten Island, N.Y. The city of New Brunswick owns the Kilmer birthplace and currently uses the first floor as offices for the city's Dial-A-Ride program. The Joyce Kilmer Birthplace Association began restoring the house in 1973 and completed the restoration in 1978.

Interested visitors can tour the second floor of the house, a 1780 Dutch farmhouse with Greek Revival additions. The 2 1/2-story frame house is considered one of the oldest remaining structures in New Brunswick. The front upstairs bedroom, where Kilmer was born on Dec. 6, is furnished with period pieces, including about 40 pieces of the Kilmer family's personal belongings. These include items of china, a chaise lounge, children's chairs, and clothing. You also will find poems that Kilmer penned in his own hand, including "The Peacemaker," and — drum roll — pieces of the towering white oak tree on the campus of Rutgers University that inspired his famous poem. Kilmer attended Rutgers Preparatory School and Rutgers College, now Rutgers University.

Kilmer, an accomplished journalist who once worked for the New York Times, is best remembered for his poem *Trees* (1913), part of a collection, *Trees and Other Poems*. Critics consider his war poems his best writings, among them *Rouge Banquet* (1918). Kilmer also wrote *Main Street and Other Poems* (1917); *Anthology of Catholic Poets*; and *Memories of My Father*. He was the first widely recognized American Roman Catholic poet.

Kilmer, father of five, died in 1918 on a World War I battlefield in France at age 31. He was killed during an attack on a German machine-gun nest. Kilmer had lived his first 20 years in New Brunswick. The city has honored him by changing the name of the street where his birth home is located from Codwise Avenue to Joyce Kilmer Avenue. The city also named a park and several public buildings, including the post office, after him.

To arrange a visit of the Kilmer house, contact the Dial-A-Ride program, 17 Joyce Kilmer Ave., New Brunswick, NJ 08901. Tel. (732) 745-5117. You can visit the birthplace Monday through Friday from 9 a.m. to 3 p.m.

Other tributes to Kilmer include: the Joyce Kilmer Service Area between Exits 8A and 9 on the New Jersey Turnpike; Joyce Kilmer Park, between Grand Concourse & 161st Street in Bronx, N.Y.; and Joyce Kilmer Memorial Forest, part of Nantahala National Forest in western North Carolina.

HOT TIP You can find the Joyce Kilmer Papers at Georgetown University in Washington, D.C. On the Net: gulib.lausun.georgetown.edu.

FURTHER READING *Joyce Kilmer: A Literary Biography* by John Covell (2000); *Memories of My Father* by Kenton Kilmer (1993) ◢

TERHUNE SUNNYBANK PARK

Homesite of Dog-Adventure Writer

The house where Albert Payson Terhune lived and wrote in northern New Jersey no longer stands, but dog lovers and fans of the writer who spun adventure tales about collies have honored him with a park. The nearly 10-acre Terhune Sunnybank Memorial Park, part of **Wayne Township** on the eastern shore of Pompton Lakes, was built on a central portion of Terhune's former land. Much of the Sunnybank land was lost to developers in the 1960s and Terhune's house was demolished in 1969.

Terhune (1872-1942) referred to Sunnybank as "The Place" in his stories. The popular writer is best known for his numerous adventures about dogs, including *Lad, A Dog*; *Sunnybank: Home of Lad*; and *Further Adventures of Lad*; *Gray Dawn*; *Heart of A Dog*; *My Friend the Dog*; *Dog of the High Sierras*; and *The Way of A Dog*. The Wayne Public Library houses a collection of rare Terhune works and artifacts. For more information, contact Wayne Public Library, 461 Valley Road, Wayne, NJ 07470. Tel. (973) 694-4272. On the Net: www.waynepubliclibrary.org/terhune.shtml. ◿

WALT WHITMAN HOUSE

Home of 'The Great Gray Poet'

LOCATION Western New Jersey, in Camden, just south of Philadelphia, at 330 Mickle Boulevard. From the New Jersey Turnpike, take exit 4 onto Route 73 North. From I-95, I-76 or I-295 South to I-676, take exit 5-A and follow signs to Mickle Blvd. The site is two blocks east of the Camden Waterfront along the Delaware River.

The house is open year-round, Wednesday through Sunday. Call to confirm hours. For more information, contact Walt Whitman House, 328 Mickle Blvd., Camden, NJ 08102-1126. Tel. (856) 964-5383. On the Net: www.nj.gov/dep/parksandforests/historic/whitman.

FRAME OF REFERENCE Walter Whitman bought the row house, circa 1848, in 1884 and lived in it until his death in 1892. He had moved to Camden in 1873 to visit his sick mother and decided to stay in the town near his brother, George.

SIGNIFICANCE Whitman — teacher, editor, Civil War veteran, short-story writer, essayist and poet — is famous for his first book of poetry, the seminal *Leaves of Grass* (1855), which included his popular *Song of Myself*. Although Whitman financed and typeset the book himself, it launched a career that established him as one of 19th-century America's greatest poets and literary figures. He finished his ninth revision of *Leaves of Grass* just before his death. He also is remembered for his famous poems, *When Lilacs Last in the Dooryard Bloom'd* and *O Captain! My Captain!* (1866).

Whitman was a proponent of Transcendentalism. He celebrated the high spirit of the common man in his poetry, choosing topics usually avoided by other poets of his era: everyday experiences, labor and sexuality. His celebration of democracy, freedom, the joys of life, the "American masses," as well as the individual self, define his revolutionary legacy to American literature.

ABOUT THE SITE The state of New Jersey has restored Whitman's six-room, two-story row house, a National Historic Landmark, to the time of Whitman's residency. The exterior clapboard and shutters, as well as interior walls, are painted historic colors. Wall coverings were specially printed to duplicate the wallpapers as recorded in historic photographs.

Inside the only house Whitman ever owned, you'll find original Whitman letters; many personal belongings; and his death notice, hand-written by his doctor, which was nailed to the front door. A collection of rare 19th-century photographs contains the earliest known image of Whitman, an 1848 daguerreotype.

HOT TIPS Whitman is buried in the family tomb he designed in **Harleigh Cemetery**, 1640 Haddon Ave., in Camden. For more on Whitman, see Whitmanland entry under New York in the book.

THE BEST STUFF Whitman wrote at odd hours in his bedroom, where you'll find the bed in which he died, his hat and slippers. Whitman piled books and papers all over the bedroom floor, but the poet could locate any bit of information he sought. He reportedly gave his room a nautical look.

THE WRITER AND HIS WORK
BORN: May 31, 1819, in West Hill, Long Island, N.Y.
DIED: March 26, 1892, in Camden
EDUCATED: Learned printing and building trades
IMPORTANT WORKS: Books and poetry collections - *Leaves of Grass* (1855); *Drum-Taps* (1865); *Sequel to Drum-Taps* (1866); *Democratic Vistas* (1871); *Memoranda during the War* (1875); *Specimen Days and Collect* (1882); *November Boughs* (1888); *Good-Bye, My Fancy* (1891)
INTERESTING BIO FACT: Many early readers found Whitman's sensual writing indecent, but that didn't get in the way of popularity. Today, a bridge over the Delaware River, a shopping center on Long Island, and a rest stop on the New Jersey Turnpike attest to his enduring fame.

FURTHER READING *Walt Whitman: A Life* by Justin Kaplan (2003); *The Better Angel: Walt Whitman in the Civil War* by Roy Morris (2002); *Walt Whitman* by Jerome Loving (2000); *Walt Whitman: A Gay Life* by Gary Schmidgall (1997)

ELSEWHERE IN THE AREA USS New Jersey, state aquarium on Waterfront ⌂

L. FRANK BAUM-OZ MUSEUM

Follow Yellow Brick Road to Chittenango

Lyman Frank Baum, creator of *The Wizard of Oz*, was born in Chittenango, N.Y., in 1856 and spent his early childhood on a country estate near the village. So it's only fitting that Chittenango, 15 miles east of Syracuse, N.Y., considers itself the Birthplace of Oz. That's why the sidewalks of **Genessee Street**, Chittenango's main thoroughfare, are painted yellow, and The Chittenango Foundation was formed to open the L. Frank Baum-OZ Museum ($) at 201 Genessee St. And every spring, around Baum's birthday, the foundation throws a huge **OZ Fest** to support museum efforts and honor its most famous son.

The four-day OZ Fest includes a costume contest, parade, golf tournament, and carnival. Some of the original Munchkins from the classic 1939 *The Wizard of Oz* film have attended the celebration.

The museum, nestled among downtown businesses, is a work in progress. Local supporters are scouring the countryside for Baum and Oz-related items. They already have in hand first-edition copies of all of Baum's 14 Oz books, including the first, *The Wonderful Wizard of Oz* (1900), which brought Baum worldwide popularity and fame. Baum wrote 13 Oz sequels and adapted the book for the stage. His musical extravaganza, *Oz*, toured for 9 years. In recent years, Broadway adaptations have also proved popular. After his first blockbuster, Baum wrote 13 more Oz books, two of which were published after his death.

For information on the L. Frank Baum-OZ Museum, contact the L Frank Baum-OZ Museum, 201 Genessee St., Chittenango , NY 13037. Tel. (315) 638-3423. On the Net: www.ozfest.com.

HOT TIP Every June, Aberdeen, S.D., where Baum operated a general store and managed a weekly newspaper, hosts the **L. Frank Baum Oz Festival**. **Baum's gravesite** is in Forest Lawn Memorial Park, in Glendale, Calif., near his last home, called Ozcot. ◢

CEDARMERE

William Cullen Bryant's Country Estate

LOCATION North shore of Long Island, N.Y. in Roslyn Harbor, on Bryant Avenue. Take Glen Cove Road to the third traffic light north of Northern Boulevard. Turn left, go under railroad trestle and turn left at the stop sign. Bear right onto Bryant Avenue. Site is on right beyond stop light.

Cedarmere is open May through early November on Saturday from 10 a.m. to 4:45 p.m., and on Sunday from 1 p.m. to 4:45 p.m. For more information, contact Cedarmere, Bryant Avenue, Roslyn Harbor, NY. Tel. (516) 571-8130. On the Net: www.nassaulibrary.org/bryant/cedrmer.htm.

FRAME OF REFERENCE William Cullen Bryant lived at this country estate, a second home away from the bustle of New York City, from 1843 until his death in 1878. A Quaker farmer, Richard Kirk, built the house in 1781. Nassau County acquired the property in the 1970s.

SIGNIFICANCE Bryant — poet, travel writer, famous poet, critic, and influential editor of the New York Evening Post — was America's earliest theorist of poetry and one of America's eminent poets throughout the mid-1800s. As a young man, Bryant wrote *Thanatopsis*, which became his most famous poem. Decades later, as a noted poet and famous editor of the New York Evening Post, Bryant escaped the city to Cedarmere, where he found inspiration for his writing in the area's natural beauty.

Bryant's romantic view of nature describes an age of America's westward expansion and discovery of the country's wildness and beauty. His poetry embodies the past, Europe, and the stirring idea of Manifest Destiny in this country. His "odes" to natural objects epitomize the general movement from Puritanism to Transcendentalism.

Bryant's talent as a poet flourished alongside his Massachusetts law practice. In 1825, as he began a new career as editor of literary publications and later as editor-in-chief and publisher at the New York Evening Post. In New York, he enjoyed a life of a literary celebrity and was an early member of **James Fenimore Cooper**'s Bread and Cheese Club. He held his position at the Post for 50 years until his death.

Bryant was a leader of the anti-slavery Free-Soil movement within the Democratic Party, but later helped found the Republican Party. He was an early political backer of Abraham Lincoln. He also took up conservationist causes, leading to the creation of New York's Central Park, and played a major role in the creation of the city's Metropolitan Museum of Art. Artists of the Hudson River School regarded Bryant as a muse. At his death in 1878, Bryant was a national icon; flags in New York City flew at half staff.

At his refuge from metropolitan life, Bryant carved out time to write a little poetry, penning some of his best-known poems, including *The Snow Shower.*

ABOUT THE SITE When Bryant bought the little Quaker-built house in 1843, he commissioned architect and artist Frederick Copley to build a cottage with overhanging pitched roof, bay windows and pinnacles at each gable. The house, of cream-colored clapboard with brown trim, had Georgian symmetry, with a central hallway. Bryant named his home Cedarmere for the cedar trees that ringed the estate's pond, "mere" in old English.

Through the years, he expanded and remodeled the 2 1/2-story cottage, adding a third floor, attic, wings, bay windows, carriage way, running water, flush toilets and a three-story "pear tower" to store ripening pears from his orchards. He built outbuildings and turned his lush 200 acres into a horticultural wonderland. He also built a stone bridge over the lake and planted exotic trees and flowers, later inspiration for his poetry.

In 1902, a fire almost burned the sturdy house to the ground. Only the basement, first floor front facade, hallway, parlor and Bryant's study survived the blaze. In 1903, the new owner rebuilt the house in a similar style, according to its floor plan. The house remains essentially unchanged from this time.

Visitors today can tour the rambling three-story, 24-room main house, which has two attics and five bathrooms. You can see a small bit of the original 1878 house in the parlor; the basement retains some original fieldstone. In the book-lined library/study where Bryant did most of his writing, you'll find an exhibit on the author. Some items, such as the mantel, have been reproduced, based on sketches and photographs from Bryant's day.

Other buildings at Cedarmere include a Gothic Revival mill built in 1862, an ice house, tool shed, greenhouse and boathouse.

HOT TIPS The adjacent **William Cullen Bryant Preserve**, once part of Bryant's estate, has the quaint Jerusha Dewey Cottage (1862), open to the public. You can also visit **Bryant's grave** in Roslyn Cemetery, where authors **Christopher Morley** and Frances Hodson Burnett (*The Secret*

Garden) also are buried. The **William Cullen Bryant Library**, in Roslyn, began as a Reading Room Bryant built in the 1870s. The library today houses books by and about Bryant, letters, photographs and relevant news clippings.

For more on Bryant, see **William Cullen Bryant Homestead** under Massachusetts in the New England section of this book. Bryant also used this boyhood home as a country retreat.

THE BEST STUFF The Delph tiles with Biblical inscriptions around the fireplace in the study were saved during the 1902 fire and replaced during reconstruction.

THE WRITER AND HIS WORK

BORN: Nov. 3, 1794 , in Cummington, Mass.

DIED: June 12, 1878, in New York City; buried Roslyn Cemetery on Long Island

EDUCATED: Williams College; studied law

MARRIED: Frances Fairchild, 1821; one daughter

IMPORTANT WORKS: *Lectures on Poetry* (series of lectures, 1884). Volumes of poetry include *The Fountain and Other Poems* (1842); *The White Footed Deer and Other Poems* (1844); *Thirty Poems* (1864). Bryant also translated the *Illiad* and the *Odyssey* and published three volumes of travel letters, as well as essays. Individual poems include: *Thanatopsis* (1817); *Inscription for the Entrance to a Wood* (1817); *To a Waterfowl*; *I Cannot Forget With What Fervid Devotion* (1815); *A Forest Hymn* (1825); *A Meditation on Rhode Island Coal* (1826); *To Cole, the Painter, Departing for Europe* (1829); *The Prairies* (1832); *Earth* (1834); *The Antiquity of Freedom* (1842); *Oh Mother of a Mighty Race* (1846); *Robert of Lincoln* 1855); *The Poet* (1863); *The Flood of Years* (1876)

INTERESTING BIO FACTS: Bryant published his first major poetry in a local newspaper at age 13. His father arranged the publication of his first book, *The Embargo*, an attack on President Jefferson's dealing with the Napoleonic conflict, when he was 15. As a college student, Bryant exchanged his love of poetry for a law career and its promise of money. He wrote his poetry in his leisure time. With the publication of *Thanatopsis* (1817) in the North American Review periodical, he established his reputation as a poet and as a critic. He gave up law in 1825 and moved to New York to pursue a literary life.

FURTHER READING *Intimate Friends: Thomas Cole, Asher B. Durand and William Cullen Bryant* by Ella M. Foshay (2001); *Power for Society: Selected Editorials of William Cullen Bryant 1832-1861* (1994); *William Cullen Bryant* by John Bigelow (1970)

ELSEWHERE IN THE AREA African-American Museum, Hempstead; Cradle of Aviation Museum, Garden City; Falaise-Harry F. Guggenheim Home, Sands Point; Chelsea Manor, Muttontown; Old Bethpage Village Restoration, Old Bethpage. ◮

MIDDLE ATLANTIC *New York*

FINDING JOHN BURROUGHS

Two Sites in Catskills Honor Naturalist Essayist

Nature lovers and fans of John Burroughs can visit two sites in the Catskill Mountains that were near and dear to the 19th-century naturalist essayist: a cabin Burroughs built, dubbed **Slabsides**, in the **John Burroughs Sanctuary** near **West Park, N.Y.**; and a his favorite summer retreat, **Woodchuck Lodge**. Woodchuck Lodge — on the family farm where Burroughs was born in 1837, grew up, and was buried in 1921 — is part of the **John Burroughs Homestead and Woodchuck Lodge Historic Home Site** in **Roxbury, N.Y.**

Woodchuck is awaiting renovation and is not yet open to the public on a regular basis, although you can see an exhibit on Burroughs' life and works at the site. Slabsides is open for tours on special occasions, but visitors can peer inside any time.

Burroughs' many essays comprise 23 of his 29 books. The essay collections include: *Wake Robin*; *Signs and Seasons*; *Winter Sunshine*; *Fresh Fields*; *Riverby*; *Under The Maples*; and *The Last Harvest*. His *Notes on Walt Whitman as Poet and Person* (1867) was the first published Whitman biography. He also wrote *My Boyhood: An Autobiography*. Burroughs' tantalizing message of simple values, simple means and simple ends ensured his popularity.

SLABSIDES In 1895, Burroughs built a rustic cabin on his Catskills property where he could write. Burroughs built the cabin, which he named Slabsides, near his house, called Riverby, in the hamlet of West Park. Slabsides is now part of the 220-acre John Burroughs Sanctuary, located between US 9W and the Hudson River, 10 miles northwest of Poughkeepsie.

Slabsides, a National Historic Landmark, is open to the public year-round. By peeking through the windows, you can see furnishings much as Burroughs left them. You'll see Burroughs' desk, ready for writing; his chamber pot by the bed; his cupboard stocked with his dishes; and the fireplace he built. The fireplace's stone foundation has no mortar but remains in excellent condition. A welcoming sign, quoting Burroughs reads, "If I were to name the three most precious resources of life, I should say books, friends and nature; and the greatest of them, at least the most constant and always at hand, is nature."

The preserve also offers hiking trails, waterfalls, brooks and woodlands. You can go inside the cabin on the third Saturday in May and the first Saturday in October, when it is unlocked and attended.

To reach Slabsides, begin at the post office on US 9W in West Park. Go about a mile to Floyd Ackert Road and turn west, cross the railroad tracks (where Burroughs met his guests), and turn left onto narrow Burroughs Drive. You'll find Slabsides parking up the hill on the right.

For more information on Slabsides, contact The John Burroughs Association, Inc., 15 West 77th St., New York, NY 10024-5192. Tel (212) 769-5169.

WOODCHUCK LODGE Burroughs fondly called Woodchuck Lodge, which the Burroughs family built in the early 1860s, his "little gray farmhouse." The homestead, a National Historic Landmark, has not been altered in any major way since Burroughs used it as a summer retreat as an adult. The Burroughs family has owned the lodge since it was built, except for the years 1922-1947, when Burroughs' friends Henry and Clara Ford owned it.

The home is open only for special events, so visitors are allowed only a stroll around the exterior and the lawn for picnicking. But you can hike to Boyhood Rock, where Burroughs played as a child, a mile or so from the lodge. The writer is buried at the foot of the rock. You'll find an exhibit on Burroughs' life and works, as well as hiking trails and a picnic area. It was in the Beech Woods at the site that the young naturalist witnessed dark flocks of passenger pigeons. Maybe you'll spot some of the area's famous woodchucks while hiking.

To reach Woodchuck Lodge, go to Roxbury, 35 miles south of Cobleskill, N.Y., located on I-88. You can reach Roxbury via Route 30, which intersects with I-88 north of Cobleskill.

For information on Woodchuck Lodge, contact the John Burroughs Homestead and Woodchuck Lodge Historic Home Site, John Burroughs Memorial Road, Roxbury, NY 12474. Tel. (607) 326-3722. On the Net: www.roxburyny.com or www.johnburroughs.org.

FURTHER READING *Religion of John Burroughs* by Clifford Hazeldine (2003); *Sharp Eyes: John Burroughs and American Nature Writing* by Charlotte Zoe Walker (2000)

122   **ELSEWHERE IN THE AREA** Vanderbilt Mansion, FDR National Historic Site, both near Poughkeepsie; Corvette Americana Hall of Fame near Cooperstown ⬨

COOPERSTOWN

James Fenimore Cooper Remembered

Get past the Baseball Hall of Fame Museum when you think of Cooperstown, N.Y., and think literature. Think James Fenimore Cooper. The author of the *Leatherstocking Tales* (1823-41) who became the first American writer to achieve international stature grew up in Cooperstown and spent his last years in the upstate New York village.

Cooperstown, named after the writer's father and founder, Judge William Cooper, today remembers the influential author at the **Fenimore Art Museum** ($). The museum, fashioned from a house built in 1932 on former Cooper property, serves as headquarters for the N.Y State Historical Association. The museum is located on Lake Road (Route 80), 1 mile north of Cooperstown on Lake Otsego.

At the museum, you find Cooper memorabilia, Cooper-period furniture, and paintings illustrating Cooper's novels in an exhibit titled **The Coopers of Cooperstown**. The exhibit includes a portrait by Gilbert Stuart of the author's father and the actual chair and barometer depicted in an early Cooper family portrait. The treasured **Cooper Screens** include a wood-and-paper memento screen that belonged to the Cooper family. It is one of two screens that the writer and his family decorated as a remembrance after returning in 1833 from a 7-year stay in Europe.

Other museum exhibits include: 19th-century New York art; 22 bronze portrait busts of early American statesmen, heroes and celebrities cast from life masks; and folk art. A new Indian Wing displays an expansive collection of traditional Native American art. A **Cooper exhibit** at the Historical Society's Research Library features Cooper books and manuscripts. You'll find **Cooper's grave** in the cemetery at Christ Church on River Street in Cooperstown.

Cooper (1789-1851), one of the famous Romantic "Western Frontier" writers, gets credit for inventing the modern sea novel. His wilderness novels were the first important works of that type. Although criticized for his writing blunders by the likes of **Mark Twain**, his structural elements remain standard in today's Western stories and films.

Cooper's *Leatherstocking Tales* comprise five novels that recount the adventures of Natty Bumppo and his American Indian comrades. The tales include *The Last of the Mohicans* (1826) and *The Deerslayer* (1841). Other Cooper works include *Precaution* (1820), his first novel; *The Spy* (1821), an immediate bestseller; *The Pilot* (1823); *The Pioneers* (1923); *The Prairie* (1827); *The Red Rover* (1828); *The Wept of Wish-ton-Wish* (1829); *The Water-Witch* (1831); *The Bravo* (1831); *The Chase: A Tale of the Sea* (1835); *Home as Found* (1838); *Wyandotte* (1843); *Satanstoe* (1845); and *The Redskins* (1846). He also wrote travel books, a history of the U.S. Navy and criticism. Cooper's novels have been remolded into movies, TV shows and comic books.

For more information, contact the James Fenimore Cooper Society, 8 Lake St., Cooperstown, NY 13326. E-mail: jfcooper@stny.rr.com. On the Net: www.oneonta.edu/external/cooper/cooperstown.htmlge. Reach the Fenimore Art Museum at Tel. (607) 547-1400.

FURTHER READING *The American Abraham* by Warren Motley (2003); *James Fenimore Cooper* by William B. Clymer (2000); *Cooper's Otsego County* by Hugh Cooke MacDougall (1989) ◬

FREDERICK DOUGLASS REMEMBERED

In **Rochester, N.Y.**, a room in a downtown building honors Frederick Douglass, the former slave who became one of most effective and respected black leaders of the 19th century and one of the greatest orators of his day. The little museum is located on the fourth floor of the five-story Talman Building at 25 E. Main St. in downtown Rochester, on the shores of Lake Ontario. The building is owned by a law firm and access to the museum room is by appointment. Tel. (585) 546-2500.Douglass wrote of his life in his best-known book, *Narrative of the Life of Frederick Douglass: An American Slave* (1845). In Rochester, he published The North Star newspaper and the Frederick Douglass Paper from an office he maintained in the Talman Building from 1847 to 1863. The famous abolitionist, writer, lecturer, statesman, and Underground Railroad conductor helped hundreds of runaway slaves on their way to freedom via his adopted home city of Rochester. The museum, initiated by the City of Rochester, plans to memorialize and celebrate Douglass and his vision of freedom and equality with exhibits, a library, archives and meeting space.

For more on Douglass, see Frederick Douglass National Historic Site under Washington D.C., in the South Atlantic section of this book. ⌂

FITZGERALD IN BUFFALO

Glimmers of Jazz-Age Writer

Only a glimmer of young F. Scott Fitzgerald's stay in Buffalo, N.Y., during the late 1800s remains at three separate locations where the future writer lived with his family. When Francis Scott Key Fitzgerald was not yet 2 years old, his father took a job as a soap salesman with Procter and Gamble in Buffalo. The senior Fitzgerald moved his family to what is now The Lenox Hotel at 140 North St. downtown. Back then, the elegant hotel, built in 1897, was the Lenox Apartments, rising in the midst of mansions that no longer stand. The Lenox was converted into a hotel in 1900. You can visit the 156-room Lenox today, one of the last surviving hotels in Buffalo: Tel. 716-884-1700.

In the spring of 1899 the Fitzgeralds took a flat at Summer and Elmwood in Buffalo. That house has been demolished. Procter and Gamble later transferred Scott's father and in January 1901 the family moved to Syracuse. They returned to Buffalo in 1903, when Scott was 7 years old, and lived at 29 Irving Place near the Lenox. The fashionable address was near the Procter and Gamble offices at 683 Main St. The front-gabled, Italianate structure still stands in Irving Place, a one-block street running between North and Allen Streets, one block west of Delaware Avenue. Scott attended school at the now-defunct Holy Angels Convent, at the corner of Porter and West Avenues in Buffalo, and frequented many of the houses that remain in the area.

For more information, go to the City Honors F. Scott Fitzgerald Page, on the Net at cityhonors.buffalo.k12.ny.us/city/rsrcs/eng/auth/fitz.html. For more on Fitzgerald, see F. Scott and Zelda Fitzgerald Museum under Alabama in the East South Central section of this book, and the Fitzgerald Walking Tour under Minnesota in the East North Central section. ⬦

SUNNYSIDE

Home of Washington Irving

LOCATION Tarrytown, N.Y., 25 miles north of Manhattan, along the Hudson River near the Tappan Zee Bridge. Take US 9 north to the site on West Sunnyside Lane.

Sunnyside ($) is open April through October, Wednesday through Monday, from 10 a.m. to 5 p.m. In November and December, it is open daily except Tuesdays from 10 a.m. to 4 p.m. In March, weekends only from 10 a.m. to 4 p.m. For more information, contact Historic Hudson Valley, 150 White Plains Road, Tarrytown, NY 10591. Tel. (914) 631-8200. E-mail: mail@hudsonvalley.org. On the Net: www.hudsonvalley.org. The organization is a network of six historic sites in Sleepy Hollow Country, including Sunnyside.

FRAME OF REFERENCE Washington Irving bought the then two-room, 18th-century farmhouse in 1835, and Irving descendants called the estate home well into the 20th century. In 1945 the Sealantic Fund, Inc., a private philanthropy established by John D. Rockefeller, Jr., acquired the property and in 1947 opened it to the public as a historic site.

SIGNIFICANCE Irving, the most polished and popular American prose writer of his era, brought American fiction into the mainstream of world literature. He is called the first truly American writer since he was first to earn a living with his pen. Irving wrote short stories, essays, newspaper columns, poetry, travel books, satire, history and biography, but his enduring fame stems largely from his stories *Rip Van Winkle* (1819), about a man who slept for 20 years, and *The Legend of Sleepy Hollow* (1820), about a teacher chased by a headless horseman. These tales, set in rural New York, where he lived much of his life, epitomized his romantic style and feature memorable characters who often were spoofs or stereotypes. Who can forget fussy teacher Ichabod Crane of *Sleepy Hollow*?

World citizen Irving, who lived in Europe for 17 years and held diplomatic posts in Great Britain and Spain, accentuated the cultural and social differences between the European Old World and the American New World in his writings. In America, he served for 10 years as the first president of the Astor Library, forerunner of the New York Public Library. Recognition as a humorist came with his *Deidrich Knickerbocker's A History of New York*, a satirical account of Manhattan's early Dutch settlers. Irving's fictitious historian became so popular that the word Knickerbocker came to mean New Yorker.

Irving devoted the last decade of his life to what he considered his greatest triumph, a five-volume biography of George Washington, his namesake. *The Life of George Washington* (1855–1859) long endured as the definitive work on this nation's first president. Before his death, Irving also wrote books about the American West. His lasting legacy, however, rests with his popular *Sleepy Hollow* and *Rip Van Winkle*. These literary treasures of romantic style stand as enduring hallmarks in American literature, culture, and folklore.

Irving's historically important works, among the first mature examples of American fiction, remain widely read. (Check an online bookstore and you'll find thousands of Irving entries). They still provide the subject for plays, films, made-for-TV movies, and bedtime stories.

ABOUT THE SITE As a New York City boy, Irving often visited the area he later made famous in *The Legend of Sleepy Hollow*. As an adult, he bought a two-room tenant farmhouse of pedestrian Colonial architecture. He then set about transforming the house into his "snuggery," a fairy-tale version of a Dutch bowery. The result: an eclectic, fairy-tale version of a Dutch bowery with two floors, white stucco exterior walls scored to resemble cut stone, pitched red roof, gable-stepped entrance draped with the wisteria vine that Irving himself planted, and a Spanish-style tower. Irving said the cottage of Romantic architecture was "all made up of gabled ends, and as full of angles and corners as an old crocked hat."

The manor house and grounds have been restored to Irving's day, based on sketches and writings of some of the illustrious friends who visited Sunnyside. Although a bachelor all of his life, the popular Irving kept Sunnyside abuzz with guests; admirers journeyed there just to shake his hand. **Henry Wadsworth Longfellow** was a good friend.

When you visit Sunnyside today, guides dressed in the costume of the mid-Victorian period will escort you through the famous restored house, as well as the gardens that Irving also designed. House furnishings date from the late 18th and early 19th centuries, with a mix of artifacts representing Irving's world travels and friendships.

By the time Irving died in his Sunnyside bedroom in 1859, both the man and his house had become national icons. In the 21st century, Sunnyside remains a historical, architectural and literary treasure.

HOT TIPS The site has a visitor center with gallery, a museum shop and seasonal cafe. Allow 1 hour for the guided tour, which is not appropriate for children under 10. You may take a guided tour of the house and grounds, or buy a grounds-only ticket and browse alone.

You can visit the adjacent Lyndhurst historic site by walking the Croton Aqueduct Trail. Boat trips to Sunnyside from Manhattan and New Jersey are available during spring, summer, and fall. Call 1-800-53-FERRY. Contact the site for information about social catering, weddings, commercial photography and corporate entertaining.

You can visit Irving's gravesite in **Sleepy Hollow Cemetery**, 540 N. Broadway in Sleepy Hollow, N.Y., 3 miles north of Sunnyside. On the Net: www.sleepyhollowcemetery.org.

The **Van Alen House** (1737), one of the few early Dutch farmhouses that remains unaltered, on Route 9H, might have played a role in *The Legend of Sleepy Hollow*. Locals say that Irving modeled his character Katrina Van Tassel on a Van Alen daughter, and the house was the scene of the famous party in the book.

THE BEST STUFF Sunnyside's quiet and unspoiled riverside setting makes for a fabulous getaway from modern metropolitan frenzy. You can picnic on rolling lawns among wildflowers and walkways laid out by Irving himself, or next to the pond he created and called his "Little Mediterranean."

THE WRITER AND HIS WORK

BORN: April 3, 1783, in New York City, last of 11 children

DIED: Nov. 28, 1859, in Tarrytown; buried in nearby Sleepy Hollow Cemetery

EDUCATED: Studied law

IMPORTANT WORKS: *Salmagundi* series (1807-08); *A History of New York by Diedrich Knickerbocker* (1809); *The Sketch Book of Geoffry Crayon, Gent* series (includes *Rip Van Winkle* and *Sleep Hollow*, 1819-20); *Bracebridge Hall* (1822); *Tales of a Traveller* (1824); *Columbus* (1828), *Conquest of Granada* (1829); *The Companions of Columbus* (1831); *The Albambra* (1832); *The Crayon Miscellany* (1835); *Tour of the Prairies* (1835); *Astoria* (co-author, 1836); *Adventures of Captain Bonneville* (1837); *Life of Oliver Goldsmith* (1840); *Mahomet and His Successors* (1850); *Wolfert's Roost* (1855); *Life of Washington* (5 vols. 1855-59)

ACCOLADES: Honorary degrees from Columbia, Harvard, and Oxford; Smithsonian Institution honorary member, 1849

INTERESTING BIO FACT: Irving's Scottish-immigrant parents named him in honor of Revolutionary War hero Gen. George Washington, later America's first president.

Irving reportedly told the story that when he, as a child, met Washington, the president patted him on his curly haired head and blessed him.

FURTHER READING *Washington Irving Esquire* by George S. Hellman (2001); *The Life and Letters of Washington Irving* by Pierre M. Irving (2001); *Washington Irving: Storyteller for a New Nation* by David R. Collins (2000); *Discourse on the Life, Character, and Genius of Washington Irving* by **William Cullen Bryant** (reprint 1989)

ELSEWHERE IN THE AREA Kykuit, the Rockefeller Estate, Philipsburg Manor, Union Church of Pocantico Hills, all in nearby Sleepy Hollow; Van Cortlandt Manor (18th-century tavern) in Croton-On-Hudson; Montgomery Place in Annandale-On-Hudson ◢

CHRISTOPHER MORLEY KNOTHOLE
Writing Studio of Literary Arbiter

LOCATION Long Island, in Roslyn, N.Y., at 500 Searingtown Rd. Reach the Knothole, located in Christopher Morley Park, via Route 25 A or the Long Island Expressway to Searingtown Road.

The **Knothole Museum** is open in season on Sunday from 1 p.m. to 5 p.m. For more information, contact Christopher Morley Knothole, 500 Searingtown Road, North Hills, NY 11576. Tel. (516) 571-8113.

FRAME OF REFERENCE Morley built the cabin in 1936 in the back yard of his Roslyn Estates home. Until he died in 1957, he did much of his writing in the Knothole. In 1961, friends formed the 1961 Christopher Morley Knothole Association to save the writing studio The group moved the studio to its current site in Christopher Morley Park in 1965 and opened it to the public.

SIGNIFICANCE Morley was one of the leading arbiters of literary tastes of the 1920s and 30s. The essayist-novelist-poet-playwright-actor-journalist worked as an editor for both The New York Evening Post and The Saturday Evening Post. He was a columnist for the Ladies Home Journal, and he helped found The Saturday Review of Literature, where he also was an influential columnist. He promoted the careers of many budding American writers, including **Sherwood Anderson**. He helped make **Walt Whitman** America's favorite poet. Having learned the book trade at Garden City's Doubleday, Page and Co., he went on to become a judge of the Book-of-the-Month Club for nearly 30 years. Morley also edited the 11th and 12th editions of *Bartlett's Familiar Quotations* (1937, 1948). A bona fide bibliomaniac, he also was deemed an "angloliterophile" for his love of the English language.

Morley, who lived on Long Island and commuted by train to New York City, produced 50 books, most with a humorous bent. He only hit the best-seller stratosphere once, with his blockbuster *Kitty Foyle* (1939), which sold more than 1 million copies. His essays are collected into several volumes, and he wrote plays, although he wanted to leave his mark as a poet.

When Morley died in 1957, the New York Times editorialized that "few managed to seem such a perfect representative of the literary life."

ABOUT THE SITE The Knothole looks pretty much today as when Morley wrote and met with his many friends 70 years ago. Morley considered his one-room, pine cabin his "own Walden" and equipped his little getaway with a huge writing desk, a big friendly fireplace, and built-in bunks for reading amid the shelves loaded with favorite books. Visitors today can quietly read on the bunks and view the writing table, complete with Morley's papers, pipe and inkwell. You'll also find first editions of many of Morley's works.

When he built the Knothole behind his late Victorian, brown-shingled house at 38 The Birches in Roslyn Estates, Morley didn't install a telephone. He did, however, eventually install a fantastic bathroom. American futuristic architect and inventor Buckminster Fuller in 1934 designed and gave his friend the copper "Dymaxion" bathroom you'll see near the front door. A sign near the Knothole entrance reads, in Latin "May you work hard in the library, paradise for you."

When the 98-acre park on Searingtown Road was being built in the 1960s, it turned out that one of the developers, a book lover, regarded Morley as a favorite author. So the park was named after Morley, a place befitting a functional memorial to him.

HOT TIPS Christopher Morley Park offers swimming pools, tennis courts, and an ice- skating rink. The Bryant Library in Roslyn has a Morley collection. On the Net: www.nassaulibrary.org/bryant/wcbryant.htm.

THE BEST STUFF The Dymaxion bathroom that Buckminster Fuller sent to the Knothole was a prototype for a patented, pre-fabricated model made of copper. The internationally famous Fuller, who held more than 2,000 patents and was the author of 25 books himself, designed the bathroom to be self-contained and readily movable. In 1964, when Fuller toured the world's great institutions, he made a stopover at the Knothole.

THE WRITER AND HIS WORK

BORN: May 5, 1890, in Haverford, Penn.

DIED: March 28, 1957, in Roslyn; buried in Roslyn Cemetery, Roslyn

EDUCATED: Haverford College, 1910, valedictorian; Rhodes Scholar at Oxford

MARRIED: Helen Fairchild; four children

IMPORTANT WORKS: *Parnassus on Wheels* (1917); *Shadygaff*; *Tales from a Rolltop Desk*; *Mince Pie*; *The Haunted Bookshop* (1919); *Plum Pudding*

(1921); *The Romany Stain; Songs for a Little House; Where the Blue Begins; Thunder on the Left* (1925); *Kitty Foyle* (1939, film 1940); *The Trojan Horse; Thoro-Fare; The Man Who Made Friends With Himself; The Standard Doyle Company: Christopher Morley on Sherlock Holmes* (posthumously)

INTERESTING BIO FACT: Bibliophile Morley founded several literary clubs in New York, including the Baker Street Irregulars and the Three Hour Lunch Club. A devotee of Arthur Conan Doyle, he also helped establish a group of fanatical followers of Sherlock Holmes.

Morley loved New York. He wrote of the city's restaurants, its book shops, and its people. But he also wrote of the joys of returning to the suburban life he had constructed and cherished on Long Island.

FURTHER READING *Christopher Morley's New York* by Walter Jack Duncan (1988); *Three Hours for Lunch* by Helen M. Oakley

ELSEWHERE IN THE AREA Roslyn Historic District, Smith House, Sycamore Lodge Fahnstock House, Willowmere, William Cullen Bryant home and preserve, all in Roslyn ◢

MILLAY POETRY TRAIL AT STEEPLETOP

Edna St. Vincent Millay's Country Home

American poet Edna St. Vincent Millay lived at her country home near **Austerlitz, N.Y.**, from 1925 until her death in 1950. Today, Millay's house, which she named Steepletop, and her gardens in the countryside southeast of Albany are slated for restoration. Plans are to eventually open the house to the public. Meanwhile, fans of the Pulitzer Prize-winning poet can take advantage of **The Millay Poetry Trail**, dedicated in the fall of 2003. The half-mile hiking trail behind the house wends to Millay's gravesite and features plaques with selections from her poems.

The poems mounted on cedar posts along the trail include excerpts from *Renascence* (1912), *The Little Ghost* (1917), *Afternoon on a Hill* (1917), *Elegy Before Death* (1918), *Mariposa* (1921), *Portrait by a Neighbour* (1922), *The Goose-Girl* (1923), *Counting-out Rhyme* (1928), *A Very Little Sphinx* (1929), *Through the Green Forest* (1940), and *Steepletop* (c. 1935).

Millay, one of America's most accomplished sonneteers, gained attention with the publication of her first volume of poetry, *Renascence* (1917). The Maine-born feminist (1892), agnostic and political radical lived for a while in New York's Greenwich Village, where she starred in the Bohemian cultural movement. While there, she wrote poetry, verse plays and political articles. Millay's important works include: *Second April* (1921); *Make Bright the Arrows* (1940); *Collected Sonnets* (1941); and *Collected Lyrics* (1943). The title poem of *The Harp Weaver and Other Poems* (1923) won the Pulitzer Prize.

The Millay Poetry Trail, built by the Friends of the Millay Society, which owns the property, is based on a similar trail behind the **Robert Frost** home in Franconia, N. H. The Austerlitz trail honors Millay's literary executor, Elizabeth Barnett, who safeguarded Steepletop and its contents after the death of the poet's sister, Norma Millay, in 1986.

In 1925, Millay and her husband, Eugen Jan Boissevain, bought a berry farm near Austerlitz at the height of Millay's popularity. They spent most of their married life at the farm, which they renamed Steepletop after the wildflowers growing in nearby fields. Steepletop, a two-story white clapboard house, sheltered Millay from the outside world. She wrote many of her works in her refuge, including the libretto for the opera, *The King's Henchman*. The couple also lived in Florida, the Riviera, Spain and on an 85- acre island they bought in 1933 in Casco Bay, Maine.

Steepletop, a National Historic Landmark, houses Millay's personal library, her music, clothing, household implements and souvenirs from her travels, including Zuni pots. Steepletop grounds include Millay's writing cabin; her grave, as well as the graves of her husband and mother; an outdoor pool and bar; and a dramatic sunken garden Millay had built.

For more information, contact The Friends of Edna St. Vincent Millay At Steepletop. E-mail: MillaySoc@aol.com.

HOT TIPS In 1973 Norma Millay established **The Millay Colony for the Arts** in Austerlitz. The colony helps writers, composers, and visual artists further their work in surroundings already rich with an artistic heritage. For more information, contact The Millay Colony For The Arts, Inc., 454 East Hill Rd., POB 3, Austerlitz, NY 12017. Tel. (518) 392-3103.

The Library of Congress, Manuscript Division, protects an extensive collection of **the Millay manuscripts** and materials, including poetry and play holographs, typescripts and galleys, unpublished diary-notebooks, sonnets, the original manuscript of *Renascence*, drafts of *The King's Henchmen*, photographs, newspaper clippings, financial records, and first editions of her books. On the Net: www.loc.gov/today/pr/1998.

FURTHER READING *Savage Beauty: The Life of Edna St. Vincent Millay* by Nancy Milford (2002); *What Lips My Lips Have Kissed: The Loves and Love Poems of Edna St. Vincent Millay* by David Mark Epstein (2002) ◮

THOMAS PAINE MEMORIAL

Honoring Author of 'Common Sense'

The home of the author and Revolutionary hero Thomas Paine (1737-1809), originally stood at the top of the hill on the south side of what is now Paine Avenue in **New Rochelle, N.Y.,** just northeast of Manhattan. Paine's historic cottage, which a grateful state of New York gave to him in 1784 along with 277 acres of land, was rescued and moved to its present site, 983 North Ave., in 1908. The Paine cottage today is part of the **Thomas Paine Memorial**, situated on a corner of Paine's original property. The site perpetuates the memory of the controversial man who wrote the passionate call for independence, *Common Sense* (1776).

In addition to the cottage where Paine spent his last years, the memorial also comprises the marble-and-stone **Thomas Paine Monument**, called the oldest known memorial to the seminal thinker and writer; the **Thomas Paine Memorial Building**, a museum and library; and the Paine gravesite. Visitors can view Paine's wallets, glasses, watch, gloves and his death mask in the museum.

Common Sense was the first pamphlet published in America to urge independence from Britain. Paine anonymously wrote the persuasive document, which sold a half million copies, but his secret was not long kept. Exposed as the author, Paine enlisted in the Revolutionary Army. He went on to write a series of 16 pamphlets called *The Crisis* (1776), which began with the famous line: "These are the times that try men's souls." *The Crisis* was read to Gen. George Washington's troops at Trenton to lift their spirits.

The self-taught, British-born writer also authored two of the best-known works in 18th-century America: *Rights of Man* (1791-92) and *The Age of Reason* (1794), which many regarded a blasphemy in his application of reason to religion; as well as *Agrarian Justice* and *Dissertation on First Principles of Government*.

The Paine Monument, erected in 1839 and renovated in 1905, stands near the cottage. The sculptured marble column, stone wall, and iron gate feature a bronze bust of Paine on top.

While living at the cottage in New Rochelle, Paine suffered ostracism and abuse from the community. He retreated to Manhattan, where he died childless and poor. His remains supposedly were returned to his farm for burial with barely a handful of mourners in attendance.

The Thomas Paine Memorial Building museum was dedicated in 1910 and opened to the public. It is located north of the Paine Monument at the corner of North Avenue and Valley Road and has served as headquarters for the Thomas Paine National Historical Association since 1925. The American inventor Thomas A. Edison turned the first spadeful of earth in a ceremony anticipating the museum.

The Paine museum is open May through October, on Friday, Saturday and Sunday, from 2 p.m. to 5 p.m. or by special arrangement. For more information, contact Thomas Paine Memorial Museum, 983 North Ave., New Rochelle, NY 10804. Tel. (914) 632-5376. On the Net: www .thomaspaine.org/museum.html. ◮

EDGAR ALLAN POE COTTAGE

Literary Genius' Last Home

The writer some call "America's Shakespeare," Edgar Allan Poe, lived in a small wooden farmhouse in the **Bronx, N.Y.**, from the summer of 1846 to January 1847. Poe had brought his ailing wife, Virginia, to the cottage hoping the country air would revive her, but she died of tuberculosis at age 26. Poe, deeply saddened, left the cottage. The Edgar Allan Poe Cottage ($), located at East Kingsbridge Road and Grand Concourse, is open on weekends for guided tours by reservation.

The Poes, along with Maria Clemm, Poe's mother-in-law, moved in April 1844 to New York City, where Poe was expanding his career as a writer and critic. At the Bronx cottage, the dark genius likely composed poetry and at least one short story. Two years after Virginia's death, Poe, ill and drinking steadily, died under mysterious circumstances in Baltimore, Md.

The Bronx County Historical Society, which has administered the site since 1975, has restored the white clapboard cottage with narrow front porch and green shutters to its original appearance. Inside, visitors will find authentic 1840s furnishings and possibly some original ones, including the bed in which Virginia died and the rocking chair where Poe sat vigil. In the kitchen, dishes on the table appear as if the great master of five literary genres had just stepped out for air. An orientation film is also available at the National Historic Landmark. The cottage, built in a period style typical of the Lower Hudson Valley, first opened as a museum in 1917.

The Edgar Allan Poe Cottage is open for guided tours on Saturday from 10 a.m. to 4 p.m., and on Sunday from 1 p.m. to 5 p.m. For more information, contact the Bronx County Historical Society, 3309 Bainbridge Ave., The Bronx, NY 10467. Tel. (718) 881-8900. On the Net: www.bronxhistorical society.org/about/poecottage.html. For details on Poe, see The Poe Museum under Virginia in the South Atlantic section of this book and the Edgar Allan Poe National Historic Site under Pennsylvania. ◮

SAGAMORE HILL

Home of Teddy Roosevelt, President and Author

In **Oyster Bay, N.Y.**, on Long Island, the Summer White House of 26th U.S. President and author Theodore Roosevelt welcomes visitors. Sagamore Hill ($), a three-story mansion, was Roosevelt's home from 1885 until his death in 1919.

Roosevelt was not only the president, vice president, diplomat, naval strategist, combat commander of a volunteer cavalry regiment, assistant secretary of the Navy, North Dakota deputy sheriff, governor of New York, ornithologist, expert big-game hunter, pioneering conservationist and winner of the Nobel Peace Prize and Congressional Medal of Honor, he also established himself as a noted historian, biographer, essayist, editor, columnist and critic. He wrote 36 books. These include: *Naval Operations of the War Between Great Britain and the United States* (1882); *Hunting Trips of a Ranchman* (1886); *Life of Thomas Hart Benton* (1887); *Essays on Practical Politics* (1888); *New York City: A History* (1895); a volume on the War of 1812; *Hero Tales from American History* (1895); *Winning of the West* (1896); and *Rough Riders* (1899).

Sagamore Hill, on Cove Neck Road, is open daily, except for Thanksgiving, Dec. 25 and Jan. 1, from 10 a.m. to 4 p.m. The site is closed on Monday and Tuesday off-season. The visitor center/bookstore hours are 9 a.m. to 4:50 p.m. Grounds are open daily without charge from dawn to dusk. For more information, contact Sagamore Hill, 20 Sagamore Hill Road, Oyster Bay, NY 11771-1809. Tel. (516) 922-4447. E-mail: sahi_information@nps.gov. On the Net: www.nps.gov/sahi/index.htm. ◭

ROBERT LOUIS STEVENSON COTTAGE
Where Ailing Scottish Author Stayed

The Upstate country cottage where Scottish writer Robert Louis Stevenson and his wife, Fanny, and his stepson stayed from October 1887 to April 1888 is open to the public as a museum in **Saranac Lake, N.Y.**, 45 miles west of Burlington, Vt. The former Baker Cottage, at 11 Stevenson Lane (reached via Routes 3 and 86), contains the original furniture from Stevenson's stay, books, childhood photographs, newspaper clippings, two of Fanny's scrapbooks of reviews, paintings, and Davos woodcuts.

Stevenson, author of *Treasure Island*, *Kidnapped*, and *The Strange Case of Dr. Jekyll and Mr. Hyde*, reportedly had come to Saranac Lake from England to be treated for tuberculosis at Dr. Edward Livingston Trudeau's progressive "Adirondack Cottage Sanatorium."

At the cottage, you'll also find the boots and beaver coat Stevenson wore at Saranac Lake, his velvet smoking jacket, ice skates, a yachting cap from the South Seas period, a lock of his hair, and a bronze plaque by Gutzon Borglum (1916). The famous sculptor called Stevenson "a sculptor of words." A mantelpiece still shows burn marks where Stevenson absentmindedly left lighted cigarettes.

While wintering at the quaint farmhouse in the Adirondack mountains, Stevenson wrote several essays for Scribner's Magazine. These include *A Chapter on Dreams*, *The Lantern Bearers*, *Beggars*, *Pulvis et Umbra*, *Gentlemen*, *Some Gentlemen in Fiction*, and *Popular Authors*. The essays were later part of the collection, *Across the Plains* (1892). He also began work on *The Master of Ballantrae* (1889). It was during his stay at Saranac Lake that Stevenson quarreled with his friend and collaborator, W.H. Henley.

The Robert Louis Stevenson Cottage and museum is open July 1 through mid-September, Tuesday through Sunday, from 9:30 a.m. to noon and 1 p.m. to 4:30 p.m. You can make an appointment for a guided tour year-round. For more information, contact The Stevenson Cottage, 11 Stevenson Lane, Saranac Lake, NY 12983. Tel. (518) 891-1462 or (518) 891-1990. On the Net: www.pennypiper.org. For more on Stevenson, see Silverado Museum under California in the Pacific section of this book. ◮

ELIZABETH CADY STANTON HOME

Women's Rights Architect, Feminist Writer

An important part of the **Women's Rights National Historical Park** in **Seneca Falls, N.Y.,** is the modest home of America's best known 19th-century feminist, Elizabeth Cady Stanton (1815-1902). The park's visitor center is located in downtown Seneca Falls on Route 5/20 East at 136 Fall St. Take I-90 (New York State Thruway) to Exit 41, then Rt. 414 South four miles to Rt. 5/20 East in Seneca Falls, 60 miles west of Syracuse. Access to the Elizabeth Cady Stanton House ($) is by guided tour only.

Stanton reared her three children in the modest 1 1/2-story, white clapboard house with green shutters and small front porch. In the house, she also helped create the movement for women's right to vote in the mid-1800s, on the heels of the anti-slavery movement. The thirtyish Stanton, with a group of friends, planned the historical Women's Rights Convention, held July 19-20, 1848, in Seneca Falls. The convention attracted 300 women and men, including abolitionist **Frederick Douglass**.

At the meeting in Wesleyan Chapel, the group boldly signed the Declaration of Sentiments, modeled on the U.S. Declaration of Independence signed 72 years earlier. "We hold these truths to be self evident: that all men *and women* are created equal...", the new Declaration read. This convention spawned the revolution we now know as the Women's Rights Movement.

Stanton helped compile the first three volumes (1881-86) of the six-volume *History of Woman Suffrage* (1881-1922). She also wrote her autobiography, *Eighty Years and More* (1898); *The Woman's Bible* (1892-98); and *Solitude of Self*. With Susan B. Anthony, co-founder of the Women's Rights Movement, Stanton wrote the feminist journal Revolution.

Women's Rights National Historical Park is open daily, except Thanksgiving, Dec. 25 and Jan. 1, from 9 a.m. to 5 p.m. with extended hours in summer. For more information, contact the Women's Rights NHP, 136 Fall St., Seneca Falls, NY 13148. Tel. (315) 568-2991. On the Net: www.nps .gov/wori.

FURTHER READING *Elizabeth Cady Stanton* by Harriet Sigerman (2001); *In Her Own Right* by Elizabeth Griffin (1985) ◮

TWAIN IN ELMIRA
Literary Lion's Study and Exhibit

The close association of Elmira College in **Elmira, N.Y.**, in the western part of the state, with American literary lion Samuel Langhorne Clemens (pen name Mark Twain) has established the private school as one of the leading centers for Mark Twain research in the world. Twain spent 20 summers in Elmira because his sister-in-law, Susan Crane, and her husband lived near the town on **Quarry Farm**. The farm was the family home of Twain's wife, Olivia Langdon, who was Susan Crane's younger sister.

For more than 20 summers the Clemens family lived with the Cranes at Quarry Farm. In 1874, the Cranes built a free-standing study for Twain on the top of a knoll near the main house. Twain dubbed the octagonal cabin with windows on all sides "The Cozy Nest." In the cabin, Twain wrote portions of his most famous works, including *The Adventures of Tom Sawyer* (1876) and The *Adventures of Huckleberry Finn* (1884). Elmira College moved the study from Quarry Farm to its campus in 1952.

Twain fans today can tour the **Mark Twain Study and Exhibit**, and researchers can avail themselves of the extensive **Mark Twain Archives**, both part of Elmira College's **Center for Mark Twain Studies**. In addition, you can view a 12-foot bronze **Mark Twain Statue** at the center, as well as the **Twain gravesite** in Woodlawn Cemetery at 1200 Walnut St. in Elmira.

Quarry Farm today serves as a home for visiting Mark Twain scholars. The college has adapted a 19th-century carriage barn and former housekeeper's cottage for use by visiting Twain scholars, many with fellowships from the college. Twain and Olivia were married in the parlor at Quarry Farm. The parlor was the same room where, 40 years later, Twain 's body lay in state after his death in 1910.

The Mark Twain Exhibit in Hamilton Hall on the campus houses photographs, furniture, clothing, stereoscopic views, and memorabilia from the summers Twain spent in Elmira.

The bronze Mark Twain Statue, a gift of the Elmira College Class of 1934, weighs 376 pounds. The statue of the seated author rises 12 feet from base to top. That is two fathoms, the depth riverboat pilots on the Missouri River near Twain's hometown of Hannibal sought for clear passage. They would yell out "mark twain," at 12 feet. Clemens took his pen name from that familiar sound from his boyhood. Gary Weisman of Roseville, Penn., created the statue.

The **Mark Twain Archive**, on the second floor of the Gannett-Tripp Library, welcomes serious students of Twain. The room of rich woodwork, period furnishings and marble accents features a relief above the mantel from the old Klapproth's Tavern. Twain was known to frequent the establishment during his summers in Elmira. For an appointment, contact the library at Tel. (607) 735-1869.

The **Mark Twain Study** (Cozy Nest) at the heart of the campus is open for student-led tours from mid-June through August, Monday through Saturday, from 9 a.m. to 5 p.m. and other times by appointment. The Twain statue and gravesite can be visited during daylight hours.

For more information, contact Elmira College, One Park Place, Elmira, NY 14901. Tel. (607) 735-1800 or 1-800-935-6472. E-mail: twaincenter@elmira .edu. On the Net: www.elmira.edu/MarkTwain/twainhom.htm. For more on Twain, see Hartford, Conn., in the New England section of this book and Hannibal, Mo., in the West North Central section.

HOT TIP The Mark Twain Room at the Buffalo and Erie County Public Library, 1 Lafayette Square (Court Street and Broadway) in Buffalo, N.Y., displays an original manuscript of *The Adventures of Huckleberry Finn*. Tel. (716) 858-8900.

> *It is the loveliest study you ever saw...octagonal with a peaked roof, each face filled with a spacious window...perched in complete isolation on the top of an elevation that commands leagues of valley and city and retreating ranges of distant blue hills. It is a cozy nest...*
>
> — TWAIN in an 1874 letter to William Dean Howells

'WHITMANLAND'

Exploring Roots of Poet Walt Whitman

Walt Whitman, America's greatest 19th-century poet, who wrote the seminal *Leaves of Grass* (1855), was born in 1819 in Suffolk County, N.Y. Young Whitman's contemplation of the grass on the high shores of Long Island Sound gave name to his poem. Whitman (1819-1892) was born along the sound and spent his childhood in the area where his ancestors had settled in the 1600s.

Today, you can visit the restored **Walt Whitman Birthplace State Historic Site and Interpretive Center** in **South Huntington, Long Island, N.Y.**, as well as several other sites related to the poet and the Whitman family. The birthplace is located at 246 Old Walt Whitman Road in West Hills. Reach the site via I-495 and Route 25 (Jericho Turnpike) or Northern State Turnpike to Route 110 on Long Island.

The Whitman family, mostly farmers, came to Long Island before the mid-17th century. "Whitmanland" covered more than 500 acres in what is now West Hills and South Huntington. The Whitmans either built or owned several homes in the area. The poet's father, Walter Whitman, Sr., built the birthplace home circa 1819. Ancestor Nathaniel Whitman built the original homestead on the site circa 1690. The barn here might have been owned by the poet's great-grandfather. Walt's favorite sister, Hannah Louisa Heyde, wrote a letter in 1905 describing the house. The state of New York owns and operates the site.

Other Whitman-related sites on the walking tour "over the paths that Walt Whitman trod" include: the Joseph Whitman House, built before 1692, at 365 West Hills Road; the Whitman-Carll House, a house that Isaiah Whitman sold to Capt. Timothy Carll, a Revolutionary soldier, in 1788, at 356 West Hills Road; the Whitman-White House, built by Samuel Whitman before 1700 and sold to the White family in 1772, at 349 West Hills Road; the 18th-century West Hills School House, 79 Sweet Hollow Road; Peace and Plenty Inn, the center of early West Hills social life, 107 Chichester Road; the Whitman-Rome House, built by Nathaniel Whitman and sold to the Rome family in 1822, at 85 Chichester Road; and the Whitman-Place House, built in 1810 by Jesse Whitman and sold by Tredwell Whitman in 1835, at 69 Chichester Road.

Many consider Whitman America's greatest poet. Books and poetry collections by Whitman include: *Leaves of Grass* (1855), which contained his famous poem *Song of Myself*; *Drum-Taps* (1865); *Sequel to Drum-Taps* (1866); *Democratic Vistas* (1871); *Memoranda during the War* (1875); *Specimen Days and Collect* (1882); *November Boughs* (1888); and *Good-Bye, My Fancy* (1891). Whitman was revising the ninth edition of Leaves of Grass when he died in 1892.

For more information on Whitmanland, contact the Walt Whitman Birthplace State Historic Site, 246 Old Walt Whitman Road, West Hills, South Huntington, Long Island, New York 11746. Tel. (631) 427-5240. Email: wwba@yahoo.com. On the Net: www.liglobal.com/walt/birthplace.shtml. For more on Whitman, see **Walt Whitman House** under New Jersey in this book. Whitman died in Camden, N.J. ◮

BIG APPLE, BY THE BOOK

Writers from around the globe have flocked to New York City to live and work since Colonial days. Some were actually born in The Big Apple, mega-magnet of culture, literature and inspiration. New York's literary reputation has been burnished by the famous and fabulous since publisher John Peter Zenger's trial for seditious libel in 1735. Throw in the likes of James Fenimore Cooper, William Dean Howells, Edith Wharton and Thomas Wolfe; Harlem Renaissance writers Langston Hughes and James Baldwin; F. Scott Fitzgerald, Mary McCarthy and Allen Ginzberg, as well as the thousands of current-day novelists, journalists, playwrights and publishing houses, and it's no wonder that the Big Apple is called America's literary capital.

Literature-loving travelers today might have to search for signs of famous writers from the past, but with some effort you can find their former homes, funky hang-outs, and fascinating hints of their New York days. Here is a sampling:

THE ALGONQUIN HOTEL, 59 W. 44th St., hosted the witty coterie of young writers known as **The Algonquin Round Table** for the better part of a decade, beginning in 1919. The influential literary group included Dorothy Parker (then a columnist at Vanity Fair), Harold Ross (founder of the New Yorker), Robert Benchley, Heywood Broun, Broun's wife Ruth Hale; critic Alexander Woollcott; comedian Harpo Marx; and playwrights George S. Kaufman, Marc Connelly, Edna Ferber, and Robert Sherwood. The fabulous quipsters lunched in the bar in the hotel's Rose Room, now the Round Table Room, skewering well-known personalities, including themselves. Agents, actors, artists and guests joined in the merriment. When William Faulkner won his Nobel Prize in 1949, he wrote his acceptance speech in the landmark hotel.

DOROTHY PARKER Sites include where she was born, lived, worked, went to school, hung out, and wrote about. She died in 1967 at home in the Volney; a residential hotel located at 23 East 74th Street between Fifth and Madison avenues on New York's fashionable Upper East Side. For more on Dorothy Parker's New York, go to the Dorothy Parker Society's Web site at www.dorothyparkernyc.com.

GRAMERCY PARK historic district. The neighborhood runs from 14th to 23rd streets along Manhattan's East Side and centers on Gramercy Park, a gated, private park on Irving Place between 21st & 20th streets. The exclusive area remains home to writers, artists and movie stars.

Commemorative plaques in the neighborhood are being installed to honor some of the interesting people who have worked and lived in the district. These include poet W. H. Auden at the Washington Hotel; homesites of poet Hart Crane at 44 Gramercy Park North and Stephen Crane at 145 East 23rd St.; Mary McCarthy and Edmund Wilson at the Gramercy Park Hotel, 2 Lexington Ave.; John Steinbeck home, 38 Gramercy Park East; Booth Tarkington, 26 Gramercy Park South; Edith Wharton, 14 West 23rd St.; Nathaniel West, Hotel Kenmore, 145 East 23rd St.; and Oscar Wilde, 47 Irving Place. On the Net: www.preserve2 .org/gramercy.

PETE'S TAVERN, 129 East 18th St., on Irving Place at Gramercy Park, bills itself as "the tavern O. Henry made famous." The watering hole, opened in 1864, is New York City's oldest tavern. O. Henry reportedly wrote his popular short story, *Gift of the Magi*, while sitting up near the front window in 1904. For more information, call (212) 473-7676. On the Net: www.petestavern.com.

CHUMLEY'S, 86 Bedford St., near Barrow Street in the West Village. Chumley's, a speakeasy in the Prohibition era, advertises its literary ties with dog-eared photos and jackets of famous books. The bar, with sawdust-covered floor, dim lighting and flowing brew, was a favorite hangout of Ernest Hemingway and F. Scott Fitzgerald. Tel. (212) 675-4449.

Former **HERMAN MELVILLE HOMESITE**, 104 East 26th St., where the New York native and author of *Moby-Dick* died;

LANGSTON HUGHES PLACE, where the Harlem Renaissance writer lived, 20 East 127th St. in Harlem, has been given landmark status by the New York City Preservation Commission.

JAMES WELDON JOHNSON HOMESITE, 187 W 135th St. near Adam Clayton Powell Boulevard. Weldon, who wrote *Lift Every Voice and Sing*, lived at the site from 1925 to 1938.

HENRY JAMES was born in 1843 in Washington Place.

Children's book writer Margaret Wise Brown enrolled as a graduate teacher trainee at the progressive **BANK STREET COLLEGE OF EDUCATION**, 610 West 112th St. on Manhattan's Upper West Side, one block from the Cathedral of St. John the Divine.

HOT TIPS For a good overview of New York's literary legacy, go online to Joan Brodsky Schur's article *A Magnet for Wordsmiths* at www.ncte americancollection.org/litmap/new_york.htm.

The writer some call "America's Shakespeare," Edgar Allan Poe, lived in a small wooden farmhouse in the **Bronx, N.Y.**, from the summer of 1846 to January 1847. Poe had brought his ailing wife, Virginia, to the cottage hoping the country air would revive her, but she died of tuberculosis at age 26. Poe, deeply saddened, left the cottage. The Edgar Allan Poe Cottage ($), located at East Kingsbridge Road and Grand Concourse, is open on weekends for guided tours by reservation. ⏏

GREEN HILLS FARM
Home of Pearl S. Buck

LOCATION Bucks County, Penn., in Perkasie, 30 miles north of Philadelphia, at 520 Dublin Road.

The **Pearl S. Buck House** ($) is open March through December, Tuesday through Saturday, for guided tours at 11 a.m., 1 p.m. and 2 p.m.; and Sunday at 1 p.m. and 2 p.m. Closed major holidays. For more information, contact The Pearl S. Buck House, P.O. Box 181, Perkasie, PA 18944-0181. Tel. (215) 249-0100. On the Net: www.pearl-s-buck.org/psbi/PSBHouse /visiting.asp.

FRAME OF REFERENCE Pearl Comfort Sydenstricker Buck lived at this farm after returning from Japan in 1934. She and husband, Richard Walsh, bought the 60-acre homestead in 1935. Buck lived in the farmhouse, built in 1835, for the last 38 years of her life. She was buried on the grounds after her death in 1973.

SIGNIFICANCE Buck is the only American woman to have received both a Pulitzer Prize and the Nobel Prize for Literature. She was one of the most popular American authors of her day, winning acclaim for her novels about life in China, especially *The Good Earth*, (1931), later a popular motion picture. The novel sold 1,800,000 copies in its first year and was awarded the Pulitzer Prize for fiction in 1932. It has been translated into more than 30 languages. Other film adaptations of Buck's works: *China Sky* (1945) and *The Devil Never Sleeps/Satan Never Sleeps* (1962). Buck was a humanitarian, crusader for women's rights, editor of Asia magazine and philanthropist.

During her 40-year career Buck published 80 works, including novels, plays, short-story collections, poems, children's books and biographies. She also wrote five novels under the pseudonym John Sedges and translated Lo Guangzhong's (1330-1400) *The Water Margin / Men of the Marshes*, which appeared in 1933 under the title *All Men Are Brothers*.

Buck was awarded the Nobel Price for Literature in 1938, the third American winner, following Sinclair Lewis and Eugene O'Neill. Only nine women have received the Nobel Prize for Literature, including American writer Toni Morrison. At Green Hills, Buck wrote many of her books, including *The Proud Heart* (1938), and a short story, *Christmas Ghost* (1960), woven around a legend of Green Hill Farm.

ABOUT THE SITE The stone house was already 100 years old when Buck moved in with Walsh, who also was her publisher and the president of John Day Company, and their eight children. The Walshes renovated and expanded the two-story house with white trim and green shutters, preserving its typical 19th-century Pennsylvania architecture. Today, you can tour 12 rooms of the house where Buck wrote, reared her brood of natural and adopted Asian children, gardened and entertained friends, including writer James Mitchener.

The house melds Chinese and 19th-century Pennsylvanian traditions of art and architecture with influences of the Orient, where Buck grew up and lived much of her adult life. Pennsylvania country furniture sits next to exotic Chinese screens, artwork and rare Peking Fetti carpets. You'll also find the author's personal mementos collected in China and Buck's literary and humanitarian awards, including the Nobel and Pulitzer Prizes in the house.

Visitors also can tour a pre-Revolutionary War cottage on the grounds, a barn built in 1827, and Buck's greenhouse. In the greenhouse, you'll see more than 20 varieties of camellias, Buck's favorite flower.

HOT TIPS Reservations are required for groups of more than 10. The site offers several special events, including spring flower and art shows, and a December holiday festival. Picnicking is permitted. Groups of 25 or more may order a catered gourmet Chinese luncheon or dinner in the site's Cultural Center, where you'll find the International Gift Shop.

THE BEST STUFF You can view the Chinese hardwood desk where Buck wrote *The Good Earth* in her library. Two lamps, fashioned from Pennsylvania jugs, sit on her desk.

THE WRITER AND HER WORK
BORN: June 26, 1892, in Hillsboro, W. Va., to missionaries to China
DIED: March 6, 1973, in Danby, Vt.
EDUCATED: Boarding school in Shanghai; Randolph-Macon Woman's College, 1914; M.A. literature, Cornell, 1926
MARRIED: John Lossing Buck, divorced 1935; Richard Walsh; two daughters
IMPORTANT WORKS: *East Wind, West Wind*, 1930; *The Good Earth*, 1931; *Sons*, 1932; *The Young Revolutionist*, 1932; *This Proud Heart*, 1938; *The Patriot*, 1939; *Of Men and Women,* 1941; *Dragon Seed*, 1942; *The Story of Dragon Seed*, 1944; *Portrait of a Marriage,* 1945; *The First Wife* (play),

1945; *The Angry Wife*, 1949; *The Child Who Never Grew*, 1950; *The Hidden Flower*, 1952; *Come My Beloved*, 1953; *Christine* (play), 1960; *The Christmas Ghost*, 1960; *Satan Never Sleeps*, 1961; *Fourteen Stories*, 1961; and *Hearts Come Home*, 1962; *Stories of China*, 1964; *Escape at Midnight and Other Stories*, 1964; *Fairy Tales of the Orient* (edited), 1965; *To My Daughters With Love*, 1967; *The New Year*, 1968; *The People of China*, 1968; *The Good Deed*, 1969; *Mandala*, 1970; *China As I See It*, 1970; *Pearl Buck's America*, 1971; *China Past and Present*, 1972; *All Under Heaven* (1974); *The Rainbow*, 1974; *Pearl S. Buck's Book of Christmas* (edited), 1974; *Words of Love*, 1974; *East and West*, 1975; and *The Woman Who Was Changed*, 1979.

ACCOLADES: Nobel Prize in Literature, 1938; Pulitzer Prize for fiction, 1932; National Institute of Arts and Letters, 1936; American Academy of Arts and Letters, 1951

INTERESTING BIO FACT: Buck returned to America in 1934 after living in China and Japan for the first 40 years of her life. Buck and her husband were active in humanitarian causes through the East and West Association, which was devoted to mutual understanding between the peoples of Asia and the United States, Welcome House, and The Pearl Buck Foundation. Buck was a friend of Eleanor Roosevelt and anthropologist Margaret Mead, and advocated the rights of women and racial equality. Because of these activities, the FBI kept detailed files on her for years.

Buck later focused her activities on children, raising millions of dollars for the adoption and fostering of Asian children abandoned by their American fathers stationed in the Far East. She coined the word "Amerasian" to describe these children.

FURTHER READING *Pearl S. Buck* by Kang Liao (1997); *Pearl S. Buck: A Cultural Biography* by Peter Conn (1996); *Pearl S. Buck: Good Earth Mother* by W. Sherk (1992); *Pearl S. Buck: The Final Chapter* by Beverly E. Rizzon (1988)

ELSEWHERE IN THE AREA Moravian Pottery and Tile Works, James A. Mitchener Art Museum, Fonthill Museum-Henry Mercer Castle, all in Doylestown, Penn. ◬

RACHEL CARSON HOMESTEAD

Childhood Home of 'Silent Spring' Author

Location Southwestern Pennsylvania, in Springdale, 30 miles northeast of Pittsburgh, at 613 Marion Ave., on the banks of the Allegheny River. The site is just north of the intersection of the Pennsylvania Turnpike (I-76) and Route 28. From Exit 5 on the turnpike, go north along Freeport Road/Pittsburgh Street for 2.5 miles. Turn left onto Colfax Street, then right onto Marion Avenue. From north, take Exit 11 on Route 28 to Route 910 to Freeport Road.

The Rachel Carson Homestead ($) is open from early March through late November, on Saturday from noon to 4 p.m. and on Sunday from 1 p.m. to 5 p.m. Tours available other times by appointment. The Nature trail is open daily from dawn to dusk.

For more information, contact the site at P.O. Box 46, Springdale, PA 15144-0046. Tel. (724) 274-5459. E-mail: rcarson@salsgiver.com. On the Net: www.rachelcarsonhomestead.org.

FRAME OF REFERENCE Rachel Louise Carson was born in this circa mid-1800s house in 1907 and lived on a 65-acre farm until age 22. The Rachel Carson Homestead Association was formed in 1975 and restored the National Register historic site.

SIGNIFICANCE Through her best-selling, landmark book *Silent Spring* (1962), writer-scientist-teacher-ecologist Carson alerted the world to the hazards of widespread, indiscriminate and prolonged pesticide use. The firestorm of awareness inspired by the book helped bring about the formation of the U.S. Environmental Protection Agency in 1970 and the banning of DDT in America in 1972.

Carson also wrote *The Sea Around Us* (1951) and *Edge of the Sea* (1955), both influential bestsellers. These books constituted a biography of the ocean and brought Carson fame as a naturalist and science writer. She is considered one of the greatest forces for environmental protection in the early 20th century.

ABOUT THE SITE Guides bill the rectangular, clapboard five-room farmhouse on a patch of rural land as "the birthplace of a healthier planet." The modest house, restored to Carson's childhood era, features family artifacts and an exhibit titled "A Reverence for Life." The exhibit traces Carson's life from her days as a slim, quiet girl in Springdale through her influential career as a reluctant crusader.

In the writer's tiny bedroom, you'll find copies of St. Nicholas, a magazine that published several of young Carson's articles. Her first article was published at age 8. The pieces reflected Carson's love of nature, honed by her mother, and exploration of the hills and river. On the 1-acre grounds, you can view an organic Butterfly Garden, the new Sense of Wonder Garden, and the old spring house.

HOT TIPS Parking is on-street along Marion Avenue. Allow 1 hour for a guided tour of the house and grounds and a visit to the gift shop/bookstore. Dress for the weather. Photography is permitted. The site offers many educational events and programs, especially for children. The site hosts an annual Rachel Carson Day on the writer's birthday in May.

Carson's last home in Silver Spring, Md., a private residence, is headquarters for the Rachel Carson Council.

THE BEST STUFF The self-guided, quarter-mile **Wild Creatures Nature Trail** meanders through the woods and fields around the homestead. The trail features interpretive signs and historical information about Carson's childhood. The nearby, 34-mile **Rachel Carson Trail** offers scenic views of the Allegheny River.

THE WRITER AND HER WORK

BORN: May 27, 1907, in Springdale

DIED: April 14, 1964, in Silver Spring, Md.

EDUCATED: Pennsylvania College for Women (Chatham College), 1929; MA zoology, Johns Hopkins University, 1932; studied at the Woods Hole Marine Biological Laboratory

IMPORTANT WORKS: *Under the Sea-Wind* (1941); *The Sea Around Us* (1951); *The Edge of the Sea* (1955); *Silent Spring* (1962); *The Sense of Wonder* (1965). Articles include: *Undersea* (1937); *Help Your Child to Wonder* (1956); *Our Ever-Changing Shore* (1957)

ACCOLADES: National Book Award for *Silent Spring*; John Burroughs Medal; Schweitzer Medal of the Animal Welfare Institutes; National Wildlife Federation's Conservationist of the Year award; National Audubon Society medal, the first awarded to a woman

INTERESTING BIO FACT: Carson had a career in federal service as a scientist, editor, and writer of radio scripts and articles on natural sciences and conservation before she turned to writing full-time.

Disturbed by the profligate use of synthetic chemical pesticides after World War II, Carson changed her focus in order to warn the public about the long-term effects of pesticide misuse. In *Silent Spring*, she challenged the practices of agricultural scientists and the government and sounded a clarion call for change in the way we view the natural world. Many — especially those in the chemical industry — branded her a hysterical woman, but she stood her ground. The book prompted President John F. Kennedy to call for an investigation of pesticide use and controls. She testified before Congress in 1963 and called for new policies to protect human health and the environment. Her contributions to heightened awareness helped bring about the U.S. Environmental Protection Agency in 1970 and the banning of DDT in 1972.

FURTHER READING *Rachel Carson: Witness for Nature* by Linda J. Lear (1997)

ELSEWHERE IN THE AREA Hartwood Acres in Hampton Township; Burtner House in Freeport; Tour-Ed Mine and Museum ⬠

ZANE GREY MUSEUM
Western Writer's East Coast Home

LOCATION Eastern Pennsylvania, at the New York border, in Lackawaxen, 35 miles east of Scranton, Penn. Reach the park, at the junction of the Lackawaxen and Delaware Rivers, via I-84, NY 17 to US 6. Lackawaxen is located along Highway 4006 at Highway 590 and across the Delaware River from Highway 97. The museum is part of the National Park Service's 73-mile Upper Delaware Scenic and Recreational River. The park's information center is located in Narrowsburg, N.Y.

The Zane Grey Museum ($) is open seasonally, usually Memorial Day weekend through Labor Day weekend. Closed some weekends. For more information, contact the museum at RR 2, Box 2428, Beach Lake, PA 18405-9737. Tel. (570) 685-4871. On the Net: www.nps.gov/upde.

FRAME OF REFERENCE Pearl Zane Grey lived in Lackawaxen from 1905 through 1918. He first settled into a farmhouse near the museum house with his bride, and they moved next door in 1914. Grey moved his family to California in 1918 to be near the budding movie industry, but he retained the Lackawaxen house. Grey stayed in this enlarged house when on the East Coast until his death in 1939. His widow sold the property in 1945 to a family friend, Helen James.

James operated the house as an inn for 25 years, beginning in 1938. James and her husband opened the house as a museum in 1973 and sold it to the National Park Service in 1989.

SIGNIFICANCE Grey — dentist, amateur baseball player, sport fisherman, and the "Father of the Western Novel" — began his writing career in Lackawaxen at the urging of his wife, Dolly. He eventually authored 89 books, including more than 50 novels, nearly all bestsellers. He was best known for his 1912 novel, *Riders of the Purple Sage*. Several of Grey's novels were turned into popular movies, and millions enjoyed his stories on the television series, Zane Grey Theater, which ran from 1956 to 1961.

Most of Grey's works were tales of adventure on the plains of the Old West. They sold more than 13 million copies during his lifetime. When Grey died in 1939, the prolific, wildly successful and popular author left behind more than 20 unpublished manuscripts. All were published after his death.

155

ABOUT THE SITE Grey bought the three-story, blue-green wood house with basement from his brother, Romer, and then expanded it several times. The house sits on the banks of the Upper Delaware River, a place of natural beauty that made a lasting impression on the budding writer. Grey often came to Lackawaxen to escape from his New York City dental practice. He fished and soaked up nature with his brothers, as they had done on visits in their youth. Grey's first published article, *A Day on the Delaware* in Recreation magazine in 1902, reflected his Lackawaxen days.

Museum visitors today can tour the three rooms that served as Grey's office and study. In the rooms you'll see a frieze of Navajo sandpainting and Hopi kachina doll designs, painted by Dolly Grey's cousin. You'll also find plenty of Grey memorabilia, photographs and books.

HOT TIPS Park rangers conduct 20-minute tours of the rooms that were Zane Grey's study and office. Tours are limited to 10 persons, so be prepared to wait. Large groups should make reservations. Plan to spend 1 hour at the museum and nearby historic Roebling Bridge. The museum annually celebrates Grey's birthday with a special opening the last weekend in January. Picnicking sites are available in nearby Minisink Battleground Park.

Zane Grey's West Society offers a bi-monthly newsletter. Contact the society at 708 Warwick Ave., Fort Wayne, IN 46825. Tel (219) 484-2904. On the Net: www.zanegreysws.org. You can access a large collection of Grey works, letter and the family Bible at Northern Arizona University's Special Collections Department in the Cline Library in Flagstaff, AZ 86001-6022. Tel. (520) 523-5551.

THE WRITER AND HIS WORK

BORN: Jan. 31, 1872, in Zanesville, Ohio

DIED: Oct. 23, 1939, in California; ashes buried in Union Cemetery, Lackawaxen

EDUCATED: University of Pennsylvania, 1896, dentistry degree

MARRIED: Lina Elise "Dolly" Roth, 1905; three children

IMPORTANT WORKS: *Betty Zane* (1903); *Spirit of the Border* (1906); *The Last Trail* (1909); *The Heritage of the Desert* (1910); *Twin Sombreros* (1911); *Riders of the Purple Sage* (1912); *Maverick Queen* (1912); *Desert Gold* (1913); *Rustlers of Pecos County* (1914); *Light of Western Stars* (1914); *Rainbow Trail* (1915); *Lone Star Ranger* (1915); *Border Legion* (1916); *Wildfire* (1916); *Man of the Forest* (1917); *U.P. Trail* (1918); *Mysterious Rider* (1921); *Day of the Beast* (1922); *To the Last Man* (1922); *Tappan's*

Burro (1923); *Wanderer of the Wasteland* (1923); *Wild Horse Mesa* (1924); *Call of the Canyon* (1924); *Buffalo Hunter* (1925); *Vanishing American* (1925); *Thundering Herd* (1925); *Deer Stalker* (1925); *Under the Tonto Rim* (1926); *Nevada* (1926); *Valley of Wild Horses* (1927); *Forlorn River* (1927); *Avalanche* (1928); *Ranger* (1928); *Stairs of Sand* (1928); *Sunset Pass* (1928); *Fighting Caravans* (1929); *Drift Fence* (1929); *Shepherd of Guadaloupe* (1930); *Arizona Ames* (1930); *Dude Ranger* (1930); *Wolf Tracker* (1930); *Robber's Roost* (1930); *Raiders of Spanish Peaks* (1931); *West of the Pecos* (1931); *Wyoming* (1932); *Lost Wagon Train* (1932); *Thunder Mountain* (1932); *Hash Knife Outfit* (1933); *Code of the West* (1934); *Trail Driver* (1936); *Knights of the Range* (1936); *Majesty's Rancho* (1938); *Western Union* (1939); *Woman of the Frontier* (1940); *30,000 on the Hoof* (1940); *Wilderness Trek* (1944); *Shadow on the Trail* (1946); *Rogue River Feud* (1948); *Captives of the Desert* (1952); *Lost Pueblo* (1954); *Black Mesa* (1955); *Stranger from the Tonto* (1956); *Fugitive Trail* (1957); *Arizona Clan* (1958); *Horse Heaven Hill* (1959); *Tenderfoot* (1977); *Westerner* (1977)

INTERESTING BIO FACT: Grey spent the wealth from his books on traveling the world in pursuit of his favorite sport, fishing. In addition to cabins in the western U.S., he owned fishing camps in New Zealand, Australia and Tahiti, and he sailed his yachts to many prime fishing sites around the globe. Grey held 10 world records for large game fish. In 1930, he became the first person to catch a fish of more than 1,000 pounds on a rod and reel. Grey's nonfiction works include *Tales of Fishing* and *Tales of Swordfish and Tuna*.

FURTHER READING *Zane Grey on Fishing* by Tery Mort (2003); *Maverick Heart: The Further Adventure of Zane Grey* by Stephen J. May (2000)

ELSEWHERE IN THE AREA Delaware Aqueduct; Fort Delaware Museum of Colonial History along the Delaware River in Narrowsburg, N.Y. ◭

PHILADELPHIA, BY THE BOOK

People from around the globe flock to Philadelphia to see the historic sites connected to the birth of America. But beyond Independence Hall, the Liberty Bell and Washington Square, William Penn's City of Brotherly Love offers several literary treasures. This was the Colonial city where Thomas Jefferson drafted the Declaration of Independence, adopted by the Second Continental Congress in 1776. Political celebrity Benjamin Franklin lived, wrote and was buried in the city, America's capital from 1790 through 1800.

In Philadelphia, you'll find reminders of Jefferson, Franklin and Thomas Paine, the Revolutionary War leader who wrote the famous call for independence, *Common Sense* (1776). You'll discover other literary landmarks, too. These include:

DECLARATION HOUSE, or Graff House, at 7th and Market streets, which recreates the two second-floor rooms where Jefferson drafted the Declaration of Independence in 1776. You'll see the future president's bed, writing desk and boots. Tel. (215) 597-8974

FACETS OF FRANKLIN, include Franklin Court, site of Franklin's home, now marked by a sculpture resembling his house; Franklin's grave; the Ben Franklin Memorial, a 20-foot marble statue in the rotunda of the Franklin Institute science museum ; and Philosophical Hall, the learned society he founded in 1743. Franklin's best-known works include *Experiments and Observations in Electricity* (1751); *A Dissertation on Liberty* (1725); *Poor Richard's Almanac* (1733) and his *Autobiography* (1868). Most of the Franklin sites stand near Independence Hall. The Franklin Memorial exhibits some of Franklin's personal possessions, including his writing table.

THE LIBRARY COMPANY OF PHILADELPHIA, 1314 Locust St. Franklin founded the subscription library when he was 25 years old, and today interested individuals can still buy a "share" of the library. When Franklin founded the institution in 1731, subscription libraries were the first of his many innovations. When Philadelphia was the U.S. capital, the Franklin library effectively functioned as the Library of Congress.

The library welcomes visitors without charge to view exhibits. Tel. (215) 546-3181. On the Net: www.librarycompany.org

ROSENBACH MUSEUM AND LIBRARY, 2008-2010 Delancey Place. The library/museum collection includes such treasures as the original manuscript of James Joyce's *Ulysses*, first editions of **Henry Melville**'s novels, drawings by Maurice Sendak, and a reproduction of poet Marianne Moore's Greenwich Village study. Tel: (215) 732-1600. On the Net: www.rosenbach.org/main.html. ◭

POE NATIONAL HISTORIC SITE

Writer's Only Surviving Philadelphia Home

LOCATION Philadelphia, Penn., at 7th and Spring Garden Streets downtown, a few blocks north of Independence Hall. The row house is connected to the rear of a structure at 530 N. 7th St.

The Edgar Allan Poe National Historic Site is open Wednesday through Sunday, except for Thanksgiving, Dec. 25, and Jan. 1, from 9 a.m. to 5 p.m. For more information, contact the site at 532 North 7th St., Philadelphia, PA 19123. Tel. (215) 597-8780. The park is administered through the Independence National Historical Park. On the Net: www.nps.gov/edal.

FRAME OF REFERENCE Poe lived in Philadelphia, then a great literary center, for six years in several homes. He moved to this house with his wife, Virginia, his mother-in-law, and a tortoise-shell tabby named Catterina between the fall of 1842 and June of 1843, renting it until April 1844. The National Park system obtained the house in 1980.

SIGNIFICANCE Poe is often called the "America's Shakespeare" because the 19-century writer exerted such a profound influence on literature, not only in America but worldwide. Poe created or mastered five literary genres: short story, detective fiction, science fiction, lyric poetry and the horror story. Best known for his poetry (especially the lyrical poem *The Raven*) and short fiction, Poe helped transform the short story from anecdote to art and more or less created the detective story. He perfected the psychological thriller. Poe also produced some of the most influential literary criticism of his time, much written in Richmond, Va., as editor of the Southern Literary Messenger from 1835 to 1837.

Since the 1880's, scholars have been trying to establish a complete list of Poe's writings. Most of Poe's works appeared in magazines and newspapers, many of which are lost. Poe's works have remained in print for 150 years and have fascinated movie audiences through the years. The memorable film *The Pit and the Pendulum*, starring spook-master Vincent Price, horrified viewers throughout America in 1961.

160

ABOUT THE SITE The park comprises three buildings: the Poe house, the three-story brick house with white shutters connected to the Poe house, and a visitor center. You enter at the visitor center, where you'll find Poe exhibits, a library, small gift shop, and an 8-minute audio-visual presentation. Park rangers conduct tours of the home where Poe apparently spent the happiest, most productive years of his life. In Philadelphia, he published more than 30 short stories and three volumes of work. Critics gave him positive reviews and he invented the detective story.

Poe penned many of his most famous works in this row house, including *The Gold Bug, Fall of the House of Usher*, *The Tell-Tale Heart* and *The Murders in the Rue Morgue*. He likely began work on *The Raven*.

In Philly, the master storyteller also achieved his greatest successes as an editor and critic. After freelancing for a year, he became editorial assistant at Burton's Gentleman's Magazine. William Burton, a popular stage actor in Philadelphia, ran the magazine and introduced Poe to Philadelphia's artistic circles. Burton's Magazine was bought by George Graham, who renamed it Graham's Magazine. Both magazines first published a number of Poe's books in serial form.

HOT TIPS Parking in the area is tight, so consider taking mass transit. Watch your step in the house; floors are uneven and stairways are narrow and steep. Picnicking is allowed on the grounds. The park offers events and programs, including a Junior Ranger program and Halloween activities. For other Poe sites, look under Maryland, Virginia and New York in this book.

THE BEST STUFF Of Poe's several Philadelphia homes, only this one survives. Poe's furnishings in the house disappeared without a trace, a mystery befitting the pioneer of the detective story. The house's rooms today stand bare, provocatively filled only by echoes of the dark genius's past.

THE WRITER AND HIS WORK For details on Poe, see **Edgar Allan Poe Museum** under Virginia in the South Atlantic section of this book.

FURTHER READING *Edgar Allan Poe, His Life and Legacy* by Jeffrey Meyers (1992); *Edgar Allan Poe, Mournful and Never-ending Remembrance* by Kenneth Silverman (1991); *The Poe Log* by Dwight Thomas (1987); *The Tales of Poe - Modern Critical Interpretations* (1987) by Harold Bloom; *Edgar Allan Poe, The Creation of a Reputation* by Miller Robbins (1983)

ELSEWHERE IN THE AREA The nearby Independence National Historical Park has 24 sites, including Independence Hall, Liberty Bell Pavilion, Old City Hall, Congress Hall and Declaration House.

• Peripatetic Poe •

Poe lived and worked in numerous homes in the eastern United States and many are extant. Sites open to the public in addition to the Poe National Historic Site include:

THE EDGAR ALLAN POE MUSEUM in Richmond, Va., the city where he grew up;

EDGAR ALLAN POE ROOM at the University of Virginia, in Charlottesville, Va., where Poe studied one year. You can take a virtual tour by logging on to www.student.virginia.edu/ ~ravens/poe-rm.html.

THE EDGAR ALLAN POE HOUSE and Museum, Baltimore, Md., where he resided for three years, beginning in 1833;

THE POE COTTAGE in The Bronx, N.Y., in Poe Park at Concourse and Kingbridge Road, where Poe took his sickly wife in 1846. The couple lived there until 1849. This was Poe's last home. ◣

Erskin Caldwell Birthplace

CEDAR HILL

Home of Frederick Douglass

LOCATION The southeast area of the nation's capital, Washington, D.C., at 1411 W St. SE, at 14th Street in the Anacostia area several blocks east of I-295. Take Martin Luther King Avenue to W Street. Follow W Street 4 blocks to the visitor center parking lot on right.

The **Frederick Douglass National Historic Site** ($) is open daily, except for Jan. 1, Thanksgiving, and Dec. 25, 9 a.m. to 4 p.m. in fall and winter, and from 9 a.m. to 5 p.m. in spring and summer. Tours begin at the visitor center.

For more information, contact Frederick Douglass National Historic Site, 1411 W St. SE, Washington, D.C. 20020. Tel.: (202) 426-5961. On the Net: www.nps.gov/frdo/cedar.htm.

FRAME OF REFERENCE Frederick Augustus Washington Bailey (christened after his mother, Harriet Bailey) Douglass moved to Washington in 1892. In 1877 at age 60, he bought this house and named it Cedar Hill. He lived in the hilltop house the last 17 years of his life, until his death in 1895. The site opened to the public in 1972 and became a National Historic Site in 1988.

SIGNIFICANCE The famous abolitionist, writer, lecturer, statesman, and Underground Railroad conductor was one of most effective and respected black leaders of the 19th century and one of the greatest orators of his day. Douglass escaped slavery in New York at age 20 after several attempts, for which he was severely punished. He took the surname Douglass after Sir Walter Scott's poem *Lady of the Lake*.

Renowned for his eloquence, Douglass lectured throughout America and England on the brutality and immorality of slavery and advocated for the 15th Amendment to the U.S. Constitution, guaranteeing freed slaves the right to vote. Later, the tall and dignified "Sage of Anacostia" fought for suffrage and equal rights for women. He has become a symbol for the fight for human, civil and equal rights and a hero for oppressed people.

As Douglass' speeches became more polished with his personal and intellectual growth, many doubted he had been reared in the deprivations of slavery. In answer, he wrote his best-known work, *Narrative of the Life of Frederick Douglass: An American Slave* (1845), later titled *Life and Times* of *Frederick Douglass*, which told his story. Douglass refined and reissued the biography twice after the *Narrative*. Douglass also published the newspapers North Star and Frederick Douglass' Paper, which brought news of the anti-slavery movement to thousands. As part of the Underground Railroad in Upstate New York, he personally helped hundreds of slaves escape to freedom. His confident and radical accounts stand out among the fugitive-slave narratives popular in the pre-Civil War North.

ABOUT THE SITE The restored two-story, white brick and green-shuttered house sits atop a 50-foot-high, grassy hill surrounded by a wrought-iron fence. The 8.5-acre site is shaded by old oaks, cedars and a magnolia and commands views of the Washington Monument and the Anacostia River. Two chimneys stand watch at each end of the tin roof of the large, handsome house, which Douglass expanded from 14 to 21 rooms, including a spacious china closet.

Nearly everything at Cedar Hill belonged to Douglass. Wall, floor and window coverings have been reproduced. Many of Douglass' personal possessions are displayed, including his barbells. A large, ornately framed oil painting of Douglass, made when he was age 65 and living at Cedar Hill, hangs in the east parlor. Other treasures include a German clock from German-American journalist Ottilia Assing. Assing was Douglass' longtime intellectual collaborator and lover.

The first floor features east and west parlors, dining room, kitchen and Douglass' study. The second floor has six bedrooms, including Douglass' and two guest rooms. On the main floor, a painting of the storming of Fort Wagner in South Carolina hangs in the hallway. During the Civil War, Douglass' sons served in the 54th Massachusetts Regiment, composed entirely of African-American volunteers.

The regiment's famous attack was portrayed in the 1989 film *Glory!*

HOT TIPS Begin your visit with the 17-minute presentation, *The Life and Times of Frederick Douglass,* and the Douglass exhibits in the visitor center. The center is handicapped accessible, as well as the first floor of house. The site tour includes the house, grounds and the outdoor "Growlery," where Douglass read. A ramp from the visitor center winds up to the house and a van is available on request. A bookstore offers books on Douglass. Group reservations required.

The Anacostia Metro Station on the Green Line is the closest stop. Connect to a B-2 (Mt. Rainer) bus. A bus stop is in front of site. Special programs offered year-round, including oratorical contest, Douglass' birthday wreath-laying ceremony, Easter egg hunt, Victorian Christmas programs and a January film festival.

THE BEST STUFF In Douglass' intriguing study, you'll find his roll top desk; sunglasses; walking cane collection — including one President Lincoln's widow gave him after the president's assassination; and a glass-fronted bookcase filled with books in many languages. Douglass taught himself French, Spanish, German and Italian, and he could speak several languages fluently. Among the heavy-famed wall portraits hangs one of abolitionist John Brown touching a black child's head. Douglass was an advisor to Brown, famous for his ill-fated raid on the federal arsenal at Harper's Ferry, W. Va., before the Civil War. Although he had no part in the plot, Douglass, fearing arrest, fled briefly to Europe after Brown's raid.

His wall of books — his most beloved treasures — and personal documents remain in the comfortable study as Douglass left them. His widow carefully preserved Cedar Hill as a memorial. The Park Service acquired the site in 1962.

THE WRITER AND HIS WORK

BORN: Feb. 1818, in area once called "Tuckahoe" along the Tuckahoe River in Talbot County, Md., near Easton

DIED: Feb. 20, 1895, in Washington, D.C.

EDUCATED: Self-educated with some tutoring; traded bread for reading lessons as child

MARRIED: Anna Murray, five children, died 1882; Helen Pitts, 1884

IMPORTANT WORKS: *The Narrative of the Life of Frederick Douglass, An American Slave by Himself* (1845); *My Bondage and My Freedom* (1855); *The Life and Times of Frederick Douglass* (1881)

INTERESTING BIO FACT: Douglass' early activism brought him into contact with many abolitionists and social reformers, including William Lloyd Garrison, **Elizabeth Cady Stanton** (see Middle Atlantic section of this book), John Brown and Gerrit Smith. During the Civil War, he helped recruit African-American troops for the Union Army, and he helped persuade President Lincoln to make emancipation a war cause. Douglass later served as assistant secretary of the Santo Domingo Commission, marshal and deed recorder for Washington and U.S. minister to Haiti.

FURTHER READING *The Life and Writings of Frederick Douglass* series by Philip S. Foner (1950, 1952, 1955); *Slave and Citizen: The Life of Frederick Douglass* by Nathan Irvin Huggins (1980); *Radical Passion: Ottilie Assing's Reports From America and Letters to Frederick Douglass* edited by Christoph Lohmann (2000)

ELSEWHERE IN THE AREA Congressional Cemetery, 1801 E. St., SE, and Anacostia Museum, 1901 Fort Pl. SE, both in Anacostia. America's capital teems with museums, historic sites, parks, gardens and monuments, including those to literary/historic figures Thomas Jefferson and Abraham Lincoln. For information, contact the Washington Convention and Visitors Corp., 1212 New York Ave. NW, Suite 600, Washington, S.C. 20005. Tel. (202) 789-7000. On the Net: www.washington.org. △

SOUTH ATLANTIC *DC*

VESTIGES OF STEPHEN CRANE

Florida Lighthouse Illuminates Famous Story

Journalist, poet and novelist Stephen Crane brought America its first naturalistic novel, *Maggie: A Girl of the Streets* (1893), as well as the seminal masterpiece of imagined realism that made him famous, *Red Badge of Courage* (1895). But it is his 1897 short story, *The Open Boat*, that provides a physical link between Crane and his literary fans today.

It was the Ponce Inlet Lighthouse near **Daytona Beach, Fla.**, that Crane and other survivors in a small dingy steered toward after their steamship, the Commodore, sank. The 1887 lighthouse, built of 1.25 million bricks with 8-foot thick walls at the bottom and 2 feet thick at the top, is located on Ponce Inlet, off Fla. A1A, 16 miles south of Daytona Beach. The lighthouse was declared a National Historic Landmark in 1998.

Crane's boat went down in the early morning hours of Jan. 2, 1897, 18 miles off the Florida coast. Crane, already a celebrity after the success of *Red Badge*, was on his way to cover the Cuban Revolution for the New York Press newspaper. He enlisted as a seaman on the Commodore, which was loaded with illegal arms and ammunition for Cuban rebels.

Crane and a few other surviving passengers drifted several days in the open boat before they were rescued. His story frankly tells of their hopes and fears after the shipwreck. Crane's ordeal in the cold waters impaired his health permanently.

The red brick lighthouse, completed in 1887, was named the Mosquito Inlet Lighthouse when construction began in 1883. The inlet's name was changed to Ponce de Leon Inlet in 1926 and the lighthouse name changed, too. The structure had a kerosene lamp in a fixed 2,000-pound lens made in Paris in 1867 for $50,000 and was visible for 20 miles at sea. Drapes were drawn around the Fresnel lens during the day to prevent the sun from cracking its prisms or starting fires on the ground. In 1953, the lighthouse was automated, making keepers unnecessary. In 1970, the Coast Guard abandoned it and its 10-acre grounds.

Visitors today can climb the 230 spiraling iron steps to the gallery at the top of the 175-foot lighthouse, the second tallest in America, after the one at Cape Hatteras, N.C. At the Lighthouse museum on the site, you can see a model of the oak and yellow pine, coal-fired Commodore and related artifacts. Divers located the wreckage of the 123-foot long, 178-ton Commodore in 1960 in 80 feet of water, 12 miles off Daytona Beach and removed some artifacts. Archaeologists continue to study the 200-year old wreckage. The museum occupies former quarters of the lighthouse keeper and assistants.

It is open daily except Dec. 25., from Memorial Day through Labor Day, 10 a.m. to 9 p.m., and in fall and winter from 10 a.m. to 5 p.m. For more information, contact Ponce Inlet Lighthouse, 4931 S. Peninsula Drive, Ponce Inlet, FL 32127. Tel. (386) 761-1821. On the Net: www.ponceinlet.org.

Crane was born Nov. 1, 1871, in Newark, N.J., youngest of 14 children of a Methodist minister. He died of tuberculosis at a spa in Germany, on June 5, 1900. He is buried in Hillside, N.J.

Crane's novels include *The Little Regiment and Other Episodes in the Civil War* (1896); *George's Mother* (1896); and *The Monster* (1899). He recorded his war correspondent experiences in Greece, Cuba, Texas and Mexico in *Active Service* (1899) and *Wounds in the Rain: War Stories* (1900). Short stories include: *The Bride Comes to Yellow Sky*; *The Blue Hotel*; *Virtue in War*; *The Second Generation*; *A Self-Made Man*; *A Fishing Village*; *The Upturned Face* and the Whilomville stories. Crane's collection of poems, *Black Riders and Other Lines* (1895) has been compared to Emily Dickinson's stark style.

The dark *Maggie,* the story of a slum girl's descent into prostitution, was such a complete break with tradition that no publisher would touch it, forcing the 22-year-old Crane to borrow money from his brother and print it himself under a pseudonym. Literary naturalism, as embodied in *Maggie,* focuses on the amorality of the universe; morals matter less than circumstance. *The Red Badge of Courage*, in which an ordinary soldier tells of the Civil War, is considered America's first modern war novel.

FURTHER READING: *Stephen Crane's Career: Perspectives and Evaluations* by Thomas A. Gullason (1972) ⌂

ERNEST HEMINGWAY HOME

Writer's Personal Paradise in Key West

LOCATION Island of Key West, Fla., 150 miles southwest of Miami at the tip of the Florida Keys, at 907 Whitehead St. in the Old Town area. From Miami, take US 1 into Key West (I-95 South turns into US 1). Follow US 1 (Oversea Highway) to Key West. US 1 continues to the right fork in Key West and becomes North Roosevelt. North Roosevelt becomes Truman Avenue. Stay on Truman to Whitehead Street and turn right. The site is on right 1 block ahead.

The Ernest Hemingway Home and Museum ($) is open daily from 9 a.m. to 5 p.m. Tours available; group tours require reservations. For more information, contact the museum at 907 Whitehead St., Key West, FL 33040. Tel. (305) 294-1136. On the Net: www.hemingwayhome.com.

FRAME OF REFERENCE Ernest Miller Hemingway lived and wrote in this 1851 mansion from 1931 until 1940, when he and his second wife, Pauline, divorced and Hemingway went to Cuba. Pauline and their two sons remained in the house until her death in 1951. Hemingway owned the house and used it as a retreat until his death in 1961.

SIGNIFICANCE The novelist, journalist and short-story writer's years in Key West were his most productive. At this site, Hemingway wrote *For Whom the Bell Tolls*, *Death in the Afternoon*, *Green Hills of Africa*, *To Have and Have Not*, *The Snows of Kilimanjaro* and numerous stories, including *The Short Happy Life of Francis Mancomber*. Hemingway, one of America's most important and influential writers, helped change the style of English prose with his short, declarative sentences and his tough, terse style. The Nobel Prize and Pulitzer Prize-winning writer still enjoys an international reputation.

Several of Hemingway's books, including *The Sun Also Rises*, *For Whom The Bell Tolls*, and *To Have and Have Not* were made into successful motion pictures. **William Faulkner** co-scripted the screenplay for *To Have and Have Not* in 1944. While in Paris, fellow writer **John Dos Passos** advised Hemingway to visit Key West, where this house later became Hemingway's personal paradise.

ABOUT THE SITE The 1851, two-story Spanish Colonial-style house is built of coral and native rock, hewn from the site's grounds. Wide verandahs surround both levels of the airy eight-room house and floor-to-ceiling glass doors and windows open to the balconies and sea breezes.

Hemingway wrote in his studio behind the main house, located over the pool house, beginning work at 6 a.m. He often spent afternoons fishing with pals. He accessed the studio via a catwalk from the main house, but visitors today enter the white-walled room by an outside staircase. The round table supporting Hemingway's Royal portable typewriter is the room's centerpiece. Hemingway's rattan lounge chair where he rested is nearby.

European antiques from Hemingway's many trips, personal treasures and gifts from famous friends fill the mansion. You'll find a replica of a ceramic cat that artist Pablo Picasso gave Hemingway, a cardinal's chair used as a set for Hemingway's play *The Fifth Column*, a 17th-century carved bench in the entrance hall, and a Venetian glass chandelier over the 18th-century Spanish walnut dining room table. A Spanish gate functions as a headboard in the master bedroom. The trophy mounts and skins are souvenirs of Hemingway's African safaris and hunting expeditions.

Palm trees and lush tropical plants fill the landscaped yards, surrounded by a privacy wall of Baltimore block, once used as ship ballast. Pauline Hemingway had the large pool behind the house built for her husband in 1937 while he was away covering the Spanish Civil War. It was the first in Key West. When Hemingway returned and discovered the pool's cost was $20,000, he reportedly took a penny, pressed it into the wet cement of the patio and said to Pauline, "Here, take the last penny I've got." You can see that penny today, sealed under an acrylic cover.

HOT TIPS The house is handicapped accessible. A small parking area on Whitehead Street next to house accommodates only seven cars. Be sure to buy a Hemingway book in the Home and Museum Book and Gift Shop, where your purchase will be embossed with a seal and Hemingway Home decal.

Hemingway wrote *A Farewell to Arms* in his first Key West residence, Casa Antigua, at 314 Simonton St. The house and exotic atrium garden ($) are open for tours ($); call (305) 292-9955.

THE BEST STUFF More than 60 cats, some the six-toed descendants of Hemingway's tomcat, roam the grounds. The writer's six-toed cat was a gift from a sea captain Hemingway had befriended.

THE WRITER AND HIS WORK

BORN: July 21, 1898, in Oak Park, Ill.

DIED: July 2, 1961, of suicide, in Ketchum, Idaho

EDUCATED: Public schools in Illinois

MARRIED: Four times; three sons

IMPORTANT WORKS: *Three Stories and Three Poems* (1923); *In Our Time* (1924); *The Sun Also Rises* (1926); *Men Without Women* (1927); *A Farewell To Arms* (1929); *Death In The Afternoon* (1932); *Winner Take Nothing* (1933); *The Green Hills of Africa* (1935); *To Have And Have Not* (1937); *The Spanish War* (1938); *The Short Stories of Ernest Hemingway* (1938); *Fifth Column* (1938); *The Spanish Earth* (1938); *For Whom The Bell Tolls* (1940); *Across The River And Into The Trees* (1950); *The Old Man And The Sea* (1952); *Complete Stories* (1954); *Two Christmas Tales* (1958); *The Wild Years* (1962); *The Short Happy Life of Francis Macomber* (1963); *A Moveable Feast* (1964); *By-Line* (1967); *The Fifth Column* (1969); *Hemingway's African Stories* (1969); *Islands In The Stream* (1970); *The Nick Adams Stories* (1972); *88 Poems* (1979); *The Dangerous Summer* (1983); *Dateline: Toronto* (1985); *The Garden Of Eden* (1986)

ACCOLADES: Nobel Prize for Literature, 1954; Pulitzer Prize for fiction, 1953 for *Old Man And The Sea*

INTERESTING BIO FACT: Bad eyesight kept Hemingway out of the armed forces during World War I, but he volunteered as an ambulance driver in Italy. In July 1918, he was severely wounded by shrapnel, an event later the basis for one of his most successful novels, *A Farewell to Arms*. Hemingway's adventures as a foreign correspondent, exploits in Cuba, and his big-game safaris in Africa all set the stage for his future writings. He was unable to personally accept his Nobel Prize in 1954 because of injuries after an airplane crash in Uganda.

FURTHER READING *Papa: Hemingway in Key West* by J. McLendon (1972, 1990); *Hemingway vs. Fitzgerald: The Rise and Fall of a Literary Friendship* by Scott Donaldson (1999); *Hemingway: A Life Without Consequences* by James R. Mellow (1993); *Ernest Hemingway* by R.B. Lyttle (1992); *Ernest Hemingway* by P.L. Hays (1990); *Hemingway's Art of Nonfiction* by R. Weber (1990); *My Brother, Ernest Hemingway* by L. Hemingway (1962)

ELSEWHERE IN THE AREA Casa Antigua, 314 Simonton St., Hemingway's first Key West residence; Heritage House Museum and **Robert Frost Cottage**, 410 Caroline St. You may sit in the garden at the Frost cottage and view it from outside. The Heritage House Museum at the site displays Frost memorabilia and photographs. **Tennessee Williams** also had a home in Key West. It is now a private residence.

• More Hemingway •

Want more of Ernest Hemingway? Check out these other sites under the appropriate states in this book: The **Ernest Hemingway Birthplace** in Oak Park, Ill.; The **Hemingway-Pfeiffer Museum** in Piggot, Ark.; The **Kennedy Library**, Boston, Mass.; and the **Hemingway House**, Ketchum, Idaho.

• What Is The Lost Generation? •

When we think of The Lost Generation of American writers who relocated to Paris after World War I, **Ernest Hemingway** comes to mind. Among this famous circle of 20th-century literary luminaries, he best epitomized the adaptation of naturalistic technique, focusing on the amorality in a world where morals matters less than circumstance. His war experiences on the Italian front left him disillusioned and laid the groundwork for his novels *A Farewell to Arms* and *The Sun Also Rises*.

Gertrude Stein coined the term "Lost Generation" in her epigraph to *The Sun Also Rises:* "...you are all a lost generation".

Hemingway, as did youthful Lost Generation writers F. Scott and Zelda Fitzgerald and John Dos Passos, took up residence in France in the post-war years to find new meaning in life. They lived a bohemian lifestyle, rejecting materialism, drinking and loving excessively as they created great literature. Their themes of spiritual alienation, self-exile and cultural criticism, their new way of writing, and their bigger-than-life reputations live on. ◮

HINTS OF ZORA NEALE HURSTON

Celebrating Harlem Renaissance Writer

After long obscurity, interest in Harlem Renaissance luminary Zora Neale Hurston has been on the rise for several decades. Her works have become part of literary anthologies and high school curricula around the United States. Those who want to learn more about the writer can visit two sites in Florida: her hometown of **Eatonville** and the city where she died, **Fort Pierce**.

Every year during the last weekend in January, Eatonville celebrates Hurston and the town's history with the Annual Zora Neale Hurston Festival of the Arts and Humanities. The event's speeches, street festival, educational presentations, artistic competitions and awards banquets draw tens of thousands of people to tiny Eatonville to celebrate African-American pride and culture.

You'll find historic Eatonville, the first incorporated African-American municipality in America, 10 miles northeast of Orlando via I-4. The town also is home to The Zora Neale Hurston Museum of Fine Arts and the Zora Neale Hurston Youth Institute, a year-round arts and humanities program for students. The museum features exhibitions of artists of African descent.

In Fort Pierce, Hurston lived in a little mint-green, cinder block house while working as a reporter and columnist for the Fort Pierce Chronicle. She spent the last years of her life in the simple house in the Benton Quarters neighborhood. It is privately owned and not open to the public. A small plaque next to the home's front door documents it as a national and state historic landmark.

Hurston died alone in the St. Lucie County Welfare Home in Fort Pierce on Jan. 28, 1960, and was buried in an unmarked grave. The grave remained obscure until author Alice Walker visited it in 1973. Walker placed a memorial stone at the burial site in The Garden of Heavenly Rest and sparked a renewed interest in Hurston.

The Fort Pierce school where Hurston worked as a substitute teacher, Lincoln Park Academy, also salutes the author with several plaques. Visitors, however, are not allowed on campus near Hurston's former house.

174

Hurston wrote four novels, two books of folklore, an award-winning autobiography, *Dust Tracks on a Road (1942),* and more than 50 short stories. Hurston's 1937 novel, *Their Eyes Were Watching God,* stands as her greatest literary achievement. Her work, brimming with dialect, neither romanticizes African-American life nor condemns it. Hurston held controversial views on race, which led her to write an article against school desegregation in 1955.

Hurston's works include: *Jonah's Gourd Vine* (1934); *Mules and Men* (1935); *Tell My Horse* (1937); *Moses, Man of the Mountain* (1939); *Seraph on the Suwanee* (1948); *Sanctified Church* (1981); *Mule Bone* (a play written with Harlem Renaissance star Langston Hughes in 1996); *Spunk* (1985); *The Complete Stories* (1995) and *Barracoon* (1999).

Hurston, born circa 1891, earned degrees at Howard University and Barnard College. She won literary recognition during the Harlem Renaissance of 1920s, but she returned to Eatonville during the Depression, her career on hold. Eventually, she returned to writing. Today many of her books are again in print.

For more information about the Hurston Festival , contact The Association to Preserve the Eatonville Community, Inc., 227 E. Kennedy Blvd. Eatonville, FL 32751. Tel. (407) 647-3307. E-mail: zora@cs.ucf.edu. On the Net: pec@zoranealehurstonfestival.com.

FURTHER READING *Wrapped in Rainbows: The Life of Zora Neale Hurston* by Valerie Boyd (2002); *Women, Violence and Testimony in the Works of Zora Neale Hurston* (African-American Literature and Culture, Vol. 3) by Diana Miles (2003) ◮

LAURA RIDING JACKSON HOME
Honoring 1920s Avant-Garde Poet

Avant-garde poet Laura Riding Jackson lived in **Vero Beach, Fla.**, in a house at 255 Live Oak Drive, now located on the grounds of the Environmental Learning Center. The small, frame house was originally located in Wabasso, Fla. In 1994, a nonprofit group moved the home to the grounds on an island in the Indian River Lagoon in Indian River County. The home, open by appointment, serves as a haven for the study of literature, philosophy and history. It endures as an example of a disappearing architectural style and a symbol of an older, more environmentally sensitive way of life.

Jackson's work was widely noted in the 1920s and 1930s, a period when she lived and collaborated with novelist Robert Graves. She and Graves operated a small publishing firm in Majorca and published such writers as Gertrude Stein. Riding was a member of Vanderbilt University's Fugitives Group with **Robert Penn Warren,** John Crowe Ransom and Allen Tate. About 1940, she renounced poetry. She married Time Magazine critic and poetry editor Schuyler B. Jackson and moved to her house in Indian River County when the area was wilderness.

The couple lived simply, raising citrus and working on a comprehensive study of language. After Schuyler's death in 1968, Laura finished that project with the assistance of a Guggenheim fellowship. The resulting book, *A New Foundation for the Definition of Words and Supplementary Essays,* was published posthumously in 1997.

The two-story, 1,400-square-foot house was built circa 1910 of locally milled Florida pine in Florida's historic "Cracker" style of vernacular architecture. Jackson's personal furnishings remain in the house. The site is open Saturdays from 9 a.m. to noon by appointment only.

For more information, contact the Laura Riding Jackson Home Preservation Foundation, P.O. Box 3233, Vero Beach, FL 32964. Tel.: (772) 589-6711. E-mail: charterry@aol.com. On the Net: info@lauraridingjackson.org. Reach the Environmental Learning Center at 255 Live Oak Drive, Vero Beach, FL 32963. Tel. (772) 589-5050. ◢

SAN CARLOS INSTITUTE
Honoring Poet José Martí

In **Key West**, **Fla.,** the legendary Cuban political activist, poet, journalist and teacher José Julián Martí is memorialized at the San Carlos Institute, 516 Duval St. Cuban exiles founded the institute in 1871 as a place to help preserve the language, cultural value and democratic ideals of the Cuban people in America. The white, two-story institute stands near the place where Martí (1853-1895) once assembled Cuban exiles and the school originally stood. Martí dubbed the original institute "La Casa Cuba," home of the Cuban people.

Today's institute, considered a patriotic shrine, serves as a school, museum, theater, library, conference center and gallery. The library contains Martí's complete writings, and displays tell the story of Martí and the Cuban Revolution. The institute is of Cuban architecture and has three grand arches at the entrance and an intricate wrought-iron enclosed balcony. The building's features include mosaic tiles used as wainscoting above the white marble staircase, high ceilings, wrought-iron balustrades and Cuban tile floors. The renovated school reopened in 1992 after 20 years of deterioration. In that time, valuable books, paintings, and other historical material had been lost and damaged.

The San Carlos Institute began as a small wooden school on nearby Anne Street. The school was rebuilt several times at different locations, following the 1885 great fire of Key West and then after a hurricane in the 1920s. The Cuban community built the present institute on Duval Street, in the heart of Key West. Martí, a native of Havana, went to prison for renouncing a pro-Spanish classmate. He spent most of his life in exile. In Spain, he wrote *El presidio político en Cuba*, a fierce attack on Cuban prisons. He then returned to New York and reported on life in America for Latin American newspapers and magazines. Seventeen of his 74 volumes of written works described life in America. Among his many poems, *Cultivo una Rosa Blanca* (I Cultivate A White Rose) stands as his most celebrated.

While in exile, Martí plotted a second struggle for Cuban independence from Spain, and in 1892 he founded the Cuban Revolutionary Party. In 1895, he sailed for Cuba with fighters and supplies from Florida. He was killed in a skirmish two weeks after his arrival. A statue of Martí in Havana honors him.

The San Carlos is open daily except Mondays. Guided tours and film presentations are offered hourly in English and Spanish. For more information, contact San Carlos Institute, 516 Duval St., Key West, FL 33040. Tel.: (305) 294-3887. On the Net: www.cubanfest.com/sancarlos.htm.

FURTHER READING: *José Martí and the Emigré Colony in Key West* by C. Neale Ronning (1990); *José Martí: Mentor of the Cuban Nation* by John M. Kirk (1983) ◪

SOUTH ATLANTIC *Florida*

MARJORIE KINNAN RAWLINGS HOUSE

Where 'The Yearling' Was Born

LOCATION North central Florida, just south of Cross Creek, Fla., between Orange and Lochloosa Lakes on Country Road 325. From U.S. 441 at Ocala, take C 235 to C 346 to C 325 to the site. From U.S. 441 in Gainesville, take C 346 to C 325 to the site.

The yard, citrus grove and nature trails of the **Marjorie Kinnan Rawlings Historic State Park** ($) are open daily from 9 a.m. to 5 p.m. for self-guided tours. The house is open for guided tours on the hour Thursday through Sunday, except for August and September and Thanksgiving and Dec. 25, 10 a.m. to 11 a.m., and 1 p.m. to 4 p.m. For more information contact Marjorie Kinnan Rawlings Historic State Park, 18700 S. CR. 325, Hawthorne, FL 32640. Tel. (352) 466-3672. On the Net: www.Florida StateParks.org.

FRAME OF REFERENCE Rawlings purchased this 72-acre farm (along with two mules, 150 chicken coops and 3,000 citrus trees) in 1928 after a spring vacation in the area. After divorcing her first husband in 1933, Rawlings stayed in Cross Creek until 1941. After her second marriage in 1941, she lived here intermittently until her death in 1953. The site opened to the public in 1996.

SIGNIFICANCE Rawlings wrote six novels in her Florida home, including *Cross Creek* and *The Yearling*, for which she won the Pulitzer Prize in 1939. She also wrote a volume of short stories and a collection of essays in Cross Creek, which was the place where she wrote as well as what she wrote about. *The Yearling*, a tale of a boy, his pet deer, and his sad passage to adulthood, was made into a motion picture in 1946 and has been published in more than 20 languages. Rawling's works explore the need for people to live in harmony with nature. Her books were inspired by rural Florida's beauty and the spirit of its people.

ABOUT THE SITE Rawlings restored the farm to working condition and her house remains almost as she left it. The eight-room, Florida Cracker-style farmhouse sits snugly among 110 orange, tangerine and grapefruit trees surviving from Rawlings' grove. The white, old board and batten, one-story house is built of heart pine and cypress and has a raised floor, high ceilings, and many windows and doors for cross-ventilation. Rawlings enlarged the front porch with its green screen door and added screens.

When updating the house, Rawlings installed French doors in the living room, built a hidden liquor cabinet in the room's southeast corner and added an indoor bathroom. (In the yard stands a replica of the outhouse with screen door and signal flag.) Other structures on the grounds include a reconstructed barn, an original pump house and a tenant house. The two-bedroom wing in back was once a tenant house and was connected to the main house in 1925. The dining room, where Rawlings elegantly entertained, displays her antique Hitchcock chairs, fine crystal and Wedgwood china. Rawlings dined and corresponded with many literary friends, including **Ernest Hemingway, Thomas Wolfe, F. Scott Fitzgerald, Robert Frost, Zora Neale Hurston** and **Margaret Mitchell.**

Visitors today can stroll through a small restored patch of the orange grove or hike the old East Grove Trail loop. Beyond the orange grove you can glimpse the old cow pasture where Dora, Rawlings' "evil-tempered" Jersey cow, grazed.

The house brims with Rawlings' furniture, including the spool-top bed given her by a neighbor, a red velvet chair and matching fainting couch in the living room, paintings and books. In the refurbished kitchen, a wood stove — like the one Rawlings used to cook meals with veggies and herbs from her garden — and authentic pots and pans reflect the 1930s. New jars of her favorite jams and jellies made during living history demonstrations at the site line the shelves.

HOT TIPS Pick up the brochure "Self-Guided Walk Around the House and Grounds" before starting your visit. Tours are limited to 10. The house is wheelchair accessible. Parking available at entrance. Bathrooms are located near tenant house. Before visiting, orient yourself with the terrific 1983 video, *Cross Creek.*

THE BEST STUFF On the front porch, where Rawlings often wrote, you'll find the cypress table with palmetto palm post, made by husband Norton Baskin, deerhide chairs, her daybed, and a portable Royal typewriter like the one Rawlings used. Here, she enjoyed the breeze, kept an eye on her farm and watched the road for visitors.

Although the writer used the last name Rawlings professionally, she liked to be known as Mrs. Norton Baskin. Her gravestone in Antioch Cemetery northeast of Cross Creek on SE 189, reads: "Marjorie Kinnan

Rawlings, 1896-1953, Wife of Norton Baskin. Through Her Writings She Endeared Herself To The People Of The World."

THE WRITER AND HER WORK

BORN: Aug. 8, 1896, in Washington, D.C.

DIED: Dec. 14, 1953, in a St. Augustine, Fla. hospital

EDUCATED: University of Wisconsin, 1918

MARRIED: Charles A. Rawlings, Jr., 1919; Norton S. Baskin, 1941

ACCOLADES: Pulitzer Prize 1939 for *The Yearling*

IMPORTANT WORKS: *Jacob's Ladder* (1931); *South Moon Under* (1933); and the semi-autobiographical *Cross Creek* (1942, film 1983); *The Sojourner* (1953); *Golden Apples* (1935); *Mountain Prelude* (1947); *The Secret River* (1955); *The Marjorie Rawlings Reader* (1956). Rawlings also wrote short stories, poems, nonfiction articles and a cookbook, *Cross Creek Cookery* (1942). Check out *Short Stories by Marjorie Kinnan Rawlings*, edited by Rodger Tarr (1994); and *Poems by Marjorie Kinnan Rawlings, Songs of a Housewife*, also edited by Tarr (1996).

INTERESTING BIO FACT: Among the letters, original manuscripts and memorabilia housed at the George A. Smathers Library at the University of Florida, Gainesville, are materials Rawlings gathered for an intended biography of writer **Ellen Glasgow**. (Look under Virginia and the Southeast section of this book.)

FURTHER READING *Marjorie Kinnan Rawlings: a Descriptive Bibliography* by Rodger L. Tarr (1996); *Invasion of Privacy: The Cross Creek Trail of Marjorie Kinnan Rawlings* by Patricia Nassif Acton (1988); *Marjorie Kinnan Rawlings: Sojourner at Cross Creek* by Elizabeth Silverthorne (1988); *Frontier Eden: The Literary Career of Marjorie Kinnan Rawlings* by Gordon Bigelow (1966)

ELSEWHERE IN THE AREA Paynes Prairie Preserve State Park on US 441 ◢

STEPHEN VINCENT BENÉT HOUSE

Wrote Poem 'John's Brown's Body'

You can track the prolific poet, novelist and short-story writer Stephen Vincent Benét to the campus of Augusta College in **Augusta, Ga**., on Walton Way. The Pulitzer Prize winner who penned the epic Civil War poem, *John Brown's Body*, lived in a two-story, Federal-style house completed in 1829 in Augusta, where his army family moved in 1911, when the site was the Augusta Arsenal. The arsenal closed in 1955.

The two-story, yellow brick house today functions as the Augusta College Admissions Office. The house has a two-tiered portico supported by Tuscan pillars, and dentiled cornices nearly encircle the three-bay facade. An arched transom tops the main door. It was placed on the National Register of Historic Places in 1971.

Benét won the Pulitzer Prize for Poetry in 1929 for *John Brown's Body*, penned while he was living in France. The title of the 1928 poem was that of a song written by William Steffe in 1852, and the tune was used by Julia Ward Howe in her *Battle Hymn of the Republic* in 1862.

Benét graduated from Yale in 1919, submitting his third volume of poems instead of a thesis. Benét's popular poem, *American Names*, which ends with the line "bury my heart at Wounded Knee," later the title of a popular book, appeared in 1931. He died in 1943.

Augusta, population 195,000, has many historic buildings. The First Presbyterian Church, organized in 1804, was designed by Robert Mills, the designer of the Washington Monument. The old Medical College building on the Augusta College campus, built in 1835, was one of the first in America.

The admissions office is open Monday through Friday from 8 a.m. to 6 p.m. For a guided tour, contact Public Relations Department, Augusta State University, 2500 Walton Way, Augusta, GA 30904. Tel.: (706) 737-1878. E-mail: kschofe@aug.edu. On the Net: www.aug.edu. Click on P for public relations.

FURTHER READING *Stephen Vincent Benét: Essays on His Life and Work*, ed. by David Garrett Izzo (2002); *Stephen Vincent Benét* by Parry Stroud (1962); *Stephen Vincent Benét* by William Rose Benét (1943) ◮

ERSKINE CALDWELL BIRTHPLACE
Childhood Home of 'Tobacco Road' Author

LOCATION West Central Georgia in Moreland, 40 miles southwest of Atlanta. From I-85, take Exit 8 to Highway 29 south to the Moreland Town Square. Turn right on Camp Street. The house is two blocks ahead on the left just before the railroad tracks.

The Erskine Caldwell Birthplace Museum ($) is usually open Saturday and Sunday from 1 p.m. to 4 p.m. and by appointment. For more information, contact Caldwell Birthplace, P.O. Box 207, Moreland, GA 30259. Tel.: (404) 254-8657. E-mail: winston@newnan.com. On the Net: www.newnam.com/ec.

FRAME OF REFERENCE Erskine Caldwell was born in this house, called "The Little Manse," in 1903. The White Oak Associated Reformed Presbyterian Church that year provided the house for his father, Sylvester, who was the church's itinerant pastor. Caldwell lived in the house until 1906. The house was built circa 1890.

SIGNIFICANCE Caldwell authored 25 novels, 150 short stories, and 12 nonfiction books and was one of the most widely read writers of the 20th century. With the publication of his first book, *God's Little Acre* (1933), which sold 14 million copies and became one of the best-selling novels of all time, he also became one of the most controversial and censored writers of his era. Caldwell went to court to fight a ban of the novel, winning his case in landmark First Amendment litigation.

Caldwell was one of America's first authors whose works were published in mass-market paperback editions. By the late 1940s, he had sold more books than any writer in U.S. history to that time, eventually selling 80 million books in 43 languages. His novel *Tobacco Road* made theater history when it ran for 7 1/2 years on Broadway. It then became a popular movie, as did three of his other novels. **William Faulkner** called Caldwell "one of the greatest U.S. writers, ahead of Hemingway."

ABOUT THE SITE This humble, one-story house had long been abandoned and neglected in Coweta County when the town of Moreland, population 400, and the Moreland Community Historical Society decided to save it from demolition. After years of fund-raising, the five-room, white clapboard house was moved 3 miles to Moreland's town square in 1990. It was restored to its 1903 appearance — minus the outdoor privy — and faces the same direction as on the original site. The house's "saddlebag" design has two front porches and two doors on the street side. An old well dominates one porch. Its cedar roof is sun-bleached and its paint is peeling.

Except for a small office, the house is unfurnished. Glass showcases display some of Caldwell's personal belongings, including his blue, portable Smith-Corona typewriter, jacket, watch, ashtray, passport, red leather pocket dictionary, childhood books and a set of vases from his Tucson home. Photos, movie posters and other items depicting the turn-of-the-century rural South decorate the walls.

HOT TIPS Call ahead and arrange your visit, since volunteers who run the site are not always on the premises. Park in front of the house, which is handicapped accessible. Caldwell books and souvenirs are sold from a corner table in one room. Check out vintage videos of *Tobacco Road* and *God's Little Acre* if you can get your hands on them before your visit. Actor Burt Reynolds narrates an audio book of *God's Little Acre* (1997). The house is open for small events by reservation.

THE BEST STUFF People flocked to see *Tobacco Road* on Broadway and in theaters across America, but the movie poster promoting the movie didn't mention Caldwell, its creator. A bright red movie poster displayed here does. In his own hand, the writer playfully penned *by ? Erskine Caldwell?* beneath the movie title.

THE WRITER AND HIS WORK

BORN: Dec. 17, 1903, in the White Oak community of Coweta County near Moreland

DIED: April 11, 1987, in Paradise Valley, Ariz.

MARRIED: Four times, three ending in divorce

EDUCATION: Home-schooled; briefly attended Erskine College and Universities of Virginia and Pennsylvania

IMPORTANT WORKS: Caldwell was most productive while living in Maine from 1932 to 1944. During that time he wrote *Tobacco Road* (1932), *God's Little Acre* (1933), *Journeyman* (1935), *The Sacrilege of Alan Kent* (1936), *Trouble in July* (1940) and *Georgia Boy* (1943). Later came *Claudell Inglish* (1961). His 1937 *You Have Seen Their Faces* was a collaboration about tenant farmers with his second wife, photographer

Margaret Bourke-White. This book drew national attention to the plight of the rural poor during the Depression and helped validate Caldwell's earlier works, which some had criticized as exaggerated or downright false.

INTERESTING BIO FACT: Caldwell's father moved from church to church all over the South. The family rarely lived for more than six months in the same place. In 1919, when the family had moved to Wrens in east Georgia's Jefferson County, Caldwell began his literary career writing for the local newspaper and worked as a baseball correspondent for The Augusta Chronicle. The future author explored the farming country of the Georgia Sand Hills, learning first-hand about the abject poverty, squalor and despair of sharecroppers and day laborers. Caldwell also worked as a gun runner to South America, cotton picker, stage hand, pro football player, book reviewer and screen writer.

FURTHER READING *Erskine Caldwell: the Journey from Tobacco Road* by Dan B. Miller (1995); *The People's Writer* by Wayne Mixon (1995); *Erskine Caldwell and the Fiction of Poverty* (1991) by Sylvia Jankins Cook

ELSEWHERE IN THE AREA Interesting Moreland sites include the tiny 1876 Old Moreland Post Office, the 1899 Cureton-Cole General Store and the Town Museum, all on Main Street; the 1840 Stagecoach Stop on Henry Camp Road; 1850 Founder's Cemetery on East Camp Street, burial ground for town founders and Confederate soldiers.

• TOBACCO ROAD TODAY •

You can still find the Tobacco Road made famous in Erskine Caldwell's 1932 novel by that name, in **Augusta, Ga.** But don't expect anything like the ribbon of hard-packed dirt that for decades linked farmers to a small port on the Savannah River. Today the legendary road is a busy, five-lane asphalt thoroughfare lined with shopping centers. You have to look carefully to find reminders of the area's tobacco-growing history.

Beginning in the late 1700s, tobacco farmers packed their valuable crops in hogshead barrels, then rolled the barrels along crests of the river bluff ridges to the river. There, boats waited to ship them to Savannah, a major coastal port. The repeated parade of wooden barrels flattened the ridge tops into crude industrial highways. From the air, these tobacco roads looked like fronds of a giant palm leaf, its stem springing from the Savannah River's muddy waters. In Caldwell's dark-humored *Tobacco Road,* sharecropper Jeeter Lester and his desperate, depraved, depression-era family inhabit a tumbledown shack facing one of these sand-packed highways.

Now, reflective green highway signs with Tobacco Road in bold white letters testify to the past Caldwell documented. The signs sway in Southern winds over five lanes of paved highway linking Gate 5 of the 56,000-acre Fort Gordon military base to Bush Field airport along the Savannah River's west bank. Gone are the farming shanties of the 1920s and 30s, once as much a part of the Sandhills rural landscape as poverty, sharecroppers and tobacco roads. Instead you'll find strip malls, stoplights, a prison, a sewage plant and several schools, including the Tobacco Road Elementary School. It's a typical urban scene found all over modern America.

To find the road, take exit 10 from I-520 to Bush Field, two miles ahead on the left. Turn right onto Tobacco Road. ◭

> *Tobacco Road is a thoroughfare of indeterminable length through every state in the union. Sometimes it is an alley, sometimes it is a paved highway; now it is a dirt road through Arkansas, now it's a boulevard through Massachusetts.*
>
> — From *You Have Seen Their Faces*

MARY GAY HOUSE
Home of Civil War Diarist

As the Civil War exploded around her, Georgia poet Mary Ann Harris Gay, like South Carolina's more famous **Mary Chesnut**, kept a diary. She later organized it into a book, *Life In Dixie During The War* (1892). **Margaret Mitchell** used Gay's book, one of only a few eyewitness accounts written by a woman, as a reference when writing her epic novel *Gone With The Wind*. **Mark Twain** made fun of Gay's flowery poetry in *Tom Sawyer*.

The Southern aristocrat, born circa 1828 in Jones County, is memorialized in **Decatur, Ga.**, northeast of downtown Atlanta. The 1820 house, where Gay lived most of her life, is part of Adair Park on Adair Street. It was moved from its first location on nearby Marshall Street. The house's original front three rooms are authentically restored and furnished in keeping with the Federal period of 1815-1825. The home exterior mirrors an 1850s photograph. The house, on the National Register of Historic Places, is owned and operated by the DeKalb County Junior League. It is open for community events by reservation.

During the Civil War, Gay's brother, Thomie, asked her to hide Confederate winter uniforms until they were needed. Gay knocked a hole in the parlor ceiling, stored the uniforms in the attic, and later claimed that a cannonball was responsible for the ceiling damage. When summer ended, she said she wanted to transport bedding to a sick relative and tricked a Union general into providing gunny sacks, horse, wagon and driver for the journey to deliver the uniforms. After the war, she was active in civic, club and church work.

"Miss Mary" Gay's poems include: *Tallassee Falls, My Childhood Home, To My Love, The Busy Body* and *A Vision*. Some of her poetry was published in 1859 in *Prose and Poetry*, written in Decatur. The 11th edition of the book was published in 1881. Gay died in 1918 and is buried in Decatur Cemetery in Old Cemetery Lot 159.

For more information, contact the DeKalb Junior League, P.O. Box 183, Decatur, GA 30031. Tel.: (404) 378-4536 or the DeKalb Historical Society, 101 E. Court Square, Decatur, GA 30030. Tel. (404) 373-1088. On the Net: www.jldekalb.org/Pages/marygay/history.html. ◿

THE WREN'S NEST

Home of Joel Chandler Harris

LOCATION Atlanta, Ga., southwest of downtown, at 1050 Ralph David Abernathy Blvd., S.W. From north and south, take I 75/85 to Abernathy Boulevard exit west, or I-285 to Boulevard exit east. From east and west, take I-20 to Exit 55A on to Ashby Street/West End to Abernathy Boulevard.

The Wren's Nest House Museum ($) is located next to the West Hunter Street Baptist Church. It is open for guided tours Tuesday through Saturday, except for major holidays, 10 a.m. to 2:30 p.m.

For more information, contact Director, The Wren's Nest House Museum, 1050 Ralph David Abernathy Blvd., S.W., Atlanta, GA 30310-1812. Tel. (404) 753-7735. E-mail wrensnest@mindspring.com. On the Net: www.123atlanta.net/attractions/wrens-nest.html.

FRAME OF REFERENCE Joel Chandler Harris lived and wrote in this house from 1881, the year his first book was published, to his death in 1908.

SIGNIFICANCE This ornate, Victorian-era house was the long-time home to the 19th-century author, journalist and pioneer folklorist. Harris, a shy, red-haired man with freckles, is famous for recording the dialect tales told to him by slaves in his childhood in his newspaper columns and books. He wrote 30 books, including nine volumes of the Uncle Remus tales.

The Uncle Remus tales, rooted in Africa, preserve slave stories about cunning animals, revealing moral lessons and also addressing the slaves' submissive situation.

The tales, written true to the basic patterns and rhythms of African-American speech in the South at the time, still sell worldwide and have been translated into 27 languages. The books ushered in a new tradition in American literature.

ABOUT THE SITE When Harris, an editor at The Atlanta Constitution, bought the 1870 farmhouse and 5 acres of land in 1881, he named his new home Snap Bean Farm. When a family of wrens nested in the Harris mailbox, friends gave directions to the house by saying it was the "house with the wren's nest." The name caught on. To accommodate his large and growing family, Harris expanded and updated the original, five-room farmhouse to its present two stories with a dozen large rooms. The charming site opened to the public in 1913.

Located in Atlanta's historic West End District, once separate from the city, the spacious, gingerbread house with a bright, Queen Anne-style, gold and brown exterior, now occupies 3 1/2 acres of towering trees and flowering azaleas. The grounds include a small amphitheater, picnic area and a wisteria-draped storytelling shelter. The Wren's Nest offers a popular, year-round storytelling program for visitors of all ages.

The house not only reveals details of Harris' life, but with its meticulous restoration and original Harris family furnishings, offers a rare Victorian-era experience. The site has a small museum store. A 13-minute video, shown in the East Parlor, tells of the home and Harris' life.

HOT TIPS A small parking lot behind the house has a few parking spaces and on-street parking is sparse. A MARTA bus stop is located in front of the house. Allow an hour for the introductory video and guided tour. Food outlets are limited in the immediate area, but a nearby Krispy Kreme donut shop lets hungry customers view the donut-making process through glass walls.

THE BEST STUFF This is a great guided tour, if you're patient. Storytelling guides take visitors through the rooms, painstakingly pointing out photographs, family memorabilia, gifts, books and original Victorian-era furniture, including Mrs. Harris' upright parlor grand piano and bustle chair. You can hear about Harris' roll top desk from the Atlanta Constitution office, where he coined the name Uncle Remus in his column, and his public shyness (despite good friend **Mark Twain**'s urging him to go on the lecture circuit) as revealed by the photograph of Harris in the front hall. It was the only portrait he ever allowed.

As you peer into the master bedroom — preserved exactly as it was when Harris lived there right down to toiletries on the dresser — you'll hear about the four sketches of black children, each reading a book, hung over the mantel. Harris believed blacks were intelligent and should read, a radical idea at the time.

A stuffed owl perched high in a corner of the family room was a gift to Harris from an admirer, President **Teddy Roosevelt**. In the East Parlor you'll find large wood carvings of Remus tales characters and the home's original blue mailbox, complete with fake wren's nest inside.

THE WRITER AND HIS WORK

BORN: Dec. 9, 1845 or 1848 in Eatonton, Ga., to unwed Mary Harris, in Billy Barne's Tavern

DIED: July 3, 1908, at The Wren's Nest

EDUCATED: Self-educated

MARRIED: Ester LaRose in 1873; nine children

IMPORTANT WORKS: *On the Plantation* (1892); *The Story of Reconstruction* (1902); *Other Georgia Sketches* (1887) The series of Uncle Remus tales, which began in 1880 with *Uncle Remus: His Songs & Sayings* ended in 1918 with *Uncle Remus Returns. The Complete Tales of Uncle Remus* (1955). Works that show the dark side of slavery include: *Mingo and Other Sketches in Black and White* (1884); *Free Joe* (1887); *Daddy Jake the Runaway* (1889)

THE BEST STUFF When Disney's movie based on Harris' tale, *Song of The South*, came out in 1946, it was enormously and enduringly popular. During the turbulent civil rights era of the 1960s, many African-Americans voiced loud objections to the stereotypical portrayal of slaves, as embodied in the obsequious Uncle Remus. They also claimed the film made slavery seem pleasant. Disney took the film out of circulation. The studio, however, re-released it in 1972, 1981 and 1986. The movie again is out of circulation and Disney has never released a video of the film in the United States. But you can buy copies of a video released in Britain on the Internet for $165.

According to site director Sharon Crutchfield, an African-American, many blacks see Harris as the inventor of a damaging myth, not as a writer who wanted to close the deep racial divide in the South and who preserved an important African-American legacy. Harris is "the most vilified author they never read," she said.

FURTHER READING *Joel Chandler Harris* by R. Bruce Bickley (1987)

ELSEWHERE IN THE AREA Underground Atlanta, CNN studios and Coca-Cola World downtown; Stone Mountain Park, 16 miles east of the city; Atlanta History Center at 130 West Paces Ferry Road, NW

• Uncle Remus Museum •

If you have more than a passing interest in Joel Chandler Harris' stories and the pre-Civil War period of his childhood, then you'll want to visit the Uncle Remus Museum ($). This quaint museum is located in the small town of **Eatonton, Ga.**, "Dairy Capital of Georgia," 120 miles southeast of Atlanta in Putnam County near Lake Oconee. Writer Alice Walker was born in Eatonton in 1944.

Harris was born in Eatonton in 1848. As a youth, this son of an unwed mother worked for Joseph Addison Turner, publisher of a newspaper at Turnwold Plantation. At Turnwold, Harris listened to the dialect tales told by slaves, stories he eventually preserved in the *Tales of Uncle Remus*.

The 17- by 24-foot museum is fashioned from two, 1880s slave houses that once stood on the plantation. The plantation was home to "the Little Boy" depicted in *The Tales*, Joseph Sidney Turner. The walls of the recon-structed log cabin, opened in 1963, now display pottery, pots, pans and other wares from the era, as well as authentic antebellum furniture. You'll also find large paintings of antebellum scenes, shadow boxes, delicate wood carvings of "de critters," and first editions of Harris' books. Colorful window scenes depict a Southern plantation.

The museum centerpiece is a large portrait of "Uncle Remus" and "the Little Boy" presented to the site by Walt Disney, whose company produced the 1950s movie *Song of the South*, based on the Remus tales. (Harris de-scendants sold the rights to the stories to Disney for $10,000. The movie garnered more than $300 million.)

Near the shady yard, surrounded by a picket fence, a painted cast iron statue of Brer Rabbit reigns near the parking lot. A statue of the wily hare in red jacket also stands in Eatonton's courthouse square, 3 blocks north. The museum, at the corner of Jefferson Street and Washington Avenue, also has a blacksmith shop and restrooms. You can glimpse privately owned Turnwold Plantation, about 15 miles east, from Old Phoenix Road. A plaque stands out front.

The museum is open daily, September through May, from 10 a.m. to noon and 1 p.m. to 5 p.m., excluding Tuesdays. Sunday hours are 2 p.m. to 5 p.m. For more information, contact Uncle Remus Museum, 441 Jef-ferson St., Eatonton, GA 31024. Tel. (708) 485-6856. On the Net: www .gsu.edu/~jma/edres/uncleremusmuseum.htm.

• From *The Tar Baby Story* •

One day atter Brer Rabbit fool 'im wid dat calamus root, Brer Fox went ter wuk en got 'im some tar, en mix it wid some turkentime, en fix up a contrapshun w'at he call a Tar-Baby, en he tuck dish yer Tar-Baby en he sot 'er in de big road, en den he lay off in de bushes fer to see what de news wuz gwine ter be. En he didn't hatter wait long, nudder, kaze bimeby here come Brer Rabbit pacin' down de road—lippity-clippity, clippity -lippity—dez ez sassy ez a jay-bird. Brer Fox, he lay low.

> — Excerpt from *The Wonderful Tar Baby Story*
> A tale of Uncle Remus

SOUTH ATLANTIC *Georgia*

MARTIN LUTHER KING JR. NEIGHBORHOOD

Writings Embodied Civil Rights Leader's Ideals

LOCATION Atlanta, Ga., east of the downtown business district. From I-75/I-85 southbound, take Exit 95 at Piedmont/Butler/John Wesley Dobbs. At second light, turn left onto Auburn Avenue. Follow signs .6 mile to Park. From I-85 north, take Exit 94 at Edgewood/Auburn Ave and proceed to second light. Turn right at light onto Auburn Avenue and follow signs .5 mile to park. The Visitor Center is located at 450 Auburn Ave., NE.

The visitor center at the **Martin Luther King Jr. National Historic Site** is open daily, except Dec. 25 and Jan. 1, from 9 a.m. to 5 p.m. Park closes at 6 p.m. Memorial Day through Labor Day. Guided tours of the King birth home are limited to 15. Private organizations conduct tours of other important King sites in "Sweet Auburn," the neighborhood of King's youth. Days and times vary. Both the Park Service and private organizations schedule events.

For more information, contact Martin Luther King, Jr. National Historic Site, 450 Auburn Ave, NE, Atlanta, GA 30312. Tel. (404) 331-3920. On the Net: www.nps.gov/malu.

FRAME OF REFERENCE Martin Luther King, Jr. was born in an 1895 Victorian house in "Sweet Auburn" in 1929. He grew up in this Atlanta neighborhood, preached here, and helped organize civil rights activities here from the mid-1950s to his death in 1968.

SIGNIFICANCE King, recipient of the Nobel Prize for peace in 1964, is the recognized leader of the Civil Rights Movement. His historic speeches and writings, including his famous *Letter From Birmingham Jail*, reveal as no other literature this turbulent period in the 1960s. The Civil Rights Movement began as nonviolent protests for racial equality — an activist approach King embraced — and later saw race riots, which King disdained. The Baptist minister and author, who followed the teachings of the Bible and Gandhi, never veered from his passionate commitment to peaceful protests as the way to freedom.

History holds King the most eloquent spokesman for racial justice of the time. His teachings, dignified example and leadership in the Montgomery bus boycott, the 1962 protest in Birmingham, Ala., (where he ended up in jail) and the 1965 Selma-to-Montgomery march inspired the Civil Rights Movement.

This site, a combination of exhibits, King's grave, historically significant buildings and the Martin Luther King Jr. Center for Nonviolent Change, memorializes the slain civil rights leader. It celebrates his ideals of justice, equality and freedom.

ABOUT THE SITE The park comprises the Martin Luther King, Jr. National Historic Site and the Preservation District that helps maintain the historic atmosphere of King's "Sweet Auburn" boyhood community. Sweet Auburn is still an active "town within a city" and straddles Auburn Avenue in east Atlanta.

The National Park Service owns 22 restored historical structures, some rented as private residences. The Historic Site includes King's birth home, a Queen Anne-style house at 501 Auburn Ave.; the 1922 brick Ebenezer Baptist Church, where King and his father were co-pastors from 1960-1968; the Freedom Hall Complex, which includes King's marble tomb and the Martin Luther King, Jr. Center for Nonviolent Social Change, Inc. (referred to as "The King Center" and operated by the King Family); and several important "Sweet Auburn" buildings. The visitor center houses exhibits and a theater, where you can see a riveting 30-minute documentary on King and the Civil Rights movement.

The Preservation District includes about a dozen Sweet Auburn buildings, such as the Wheat Street Baptist Church, Royal Peacock Club, Sweet Auburn Curb Market, Butler Street YMCA, the *Atlanta Daily World* and radio station WERD. The 100 businesses and public services along Auburn Avenue at the time of King's boyhood were all owned and/or operated by African-Americans. Morehouse College, King's alma mater, is located outside the district but nearby.

HOT TIPS Allow at least a half day for your visit. Better still, a whole day and enjoy lunch in the neighborhood. Stop first at the visitor center. Here you can get maps, schedules of activities and free tickets for guided tours *that day* of the boyhood home and neighborhood. Tours are daily, except for Dec. 25 and Jan. 1, and begin at 10 a.m. You also can pick up guide booklets for self-guided tours of Sweet Auburn. Cassette and Braille guides are available.

Park on street or in a parking lot just north of the visitor center on John Wesley Dobbs Avenue. Allow 1 to 2 hours at the visitor center to see the movie and exhibits. Birth home tours take about 20 minutes. Allow 1 to 2 hours to visit the Center for Nonviolent Social Change, King gravesite and Ebenezer Church. The pavilion at the gravesite teems with activity, such as singing youth groups, so set aside time to enjoy.

The extensive gift shop at The King Center is full of wonderful books and theme items. Shirts or sweatshirts bearing King quotes make great gifts. The center's Freedom Hall Auditorium offers a full list of performances ($).

Sidewalks and busy paved roads connect sites. Be prepared to walk. Take precautions against Atlanta's infamous heat and humidity in the summer. Food and beverages are available at the site. Two documentaries may help prepare you for your visit: *Eyes On The Prize* and *King: Montgomery to Memphis*.

THE BEST STUFF The movie, *A New Time, A New Voice.*, shown in the Visitor Center theater is a top-drawer, three-hanky documentary on King and the Civil Rights Movement. You won't forget Coretta Scott King talking about the first time she saw her future husband. "He's so short," she admits to thinking.

Footage of King exhorting the crowds and behind-the-scenes encounters bring tears to the eye. As Sixties race riots broke out across the land, King, criticized for remaining nonviolent, passionately tells other leaders: "I'm sick and tired of violence! I'm not going to use violence!"

The walk-through exhibit hall weaves King's story into that of the Civil Rights Movement through photographs, videos and audio presentations, art (some life-sized) and memorabilia. You can walk down a "highway" in Alabama amid statues of other civil rights marchers and their songs of freedom.

At the King Center museum, you'll find King's Nobel medal, his black robe with crimson sash, the suit he was wearing when he was stabbed by a mentally ill woman in New York in 1958, his personal Bible and handwritten speeches and a "To Do List." There's also a tribute to Indian leader Mohandas Gandhi, whose belief in civil disobedience — gleaned from writings of American philosopher **Henry David Thoreau** — influenced King.

The key attached to a green plastic diamond with the words, *Room 301, Lorraine Motel and Hotel, Memphis*, dominates one display case. This is the room where King was staying when he was assassinated in 1968.

King's Georgia-marble crypt sits within a brick circular pod set in a bright blue Reflecting Pool. The inscription is a variation of a famous phrase from his "I Have A Dream" speech, delivered on the steps of the

Lincoln Memorial: *Free at last! Free at last! Thank God Almighty, I'm free at last!*

THE WRITER AND HIS WORK
BORN: Jan. 15, 1929, in Atlanta
DIED: April 4, 1968, in Memphis, Tenn., assassinated at age 37 by James Earl Ray
MARRIED: Coretta Scott, 1953; four children
EDUCATION: Morehouse College 1948; Crozer Theological Seminary, 1951; Boston University, Ph.D. 1955
IMPORTANT WORKS: *The Measure of a Man* (1959); *The Strength to Love* (1963); *Why We Can't Wait* (1964); *Where Do We Go from Here?* (1967); *A Call to Conscience* (1967); *I've Been To The Mountaintop* (1969); *Letter From Birmingham Jail* (1968); *The Triumph of Conscience* (1968); *Autobiography of Martin Luther King Jr*, edited by Clayborne Carson (1998) *A Testament of Hope: The Essential Writings and Speeches of Martin Luther King Jr.* (2003)
ACCOLADES: Nobel Peace Prize, 1964

FURTHER READING *Martin Luther King, Jr.* by Marshall Frady (2002); *Martin's Big Words* by Doreen Rappaport (2001); *He Had A Dream* by Flip Schulke (1995)

ELSEWHERE IN THE AREA The Wren's Nest, 1050 Ralph David Abernathy Blvd., S.W.; Margaret Mitchell House, 990 Peachtree St.; The Civil War Cyclorama in Grant Park; Stone Mountain, the "Confederate Mount Rushmore," 16 miles east of Atlanta ◭

SIDNEY LANIER COTTAGE
Birthplace of 19th-Century Poet

LOCATION Central Georgia, in Macon, near the downtown business area, at 935 High Street. From I-75 east and west, exit Hardeman Avenue, which turns into Washington Avenue. Turn right on Orange Street, left onto High Street. From north and south on US 16, exit 1A onto Spring street west, right on Washington Street, left on Orange Street, left onto High Street to site.

The Sidney Lanier Cottage ($) is open Monday through Friday, 9 a.m. to 1 p.m. and 2 p.m. to 4 p.m., and on Saturday from 9:30 a.m. to 12:30 p.m. Closed major holidays.

For more information, contact the Middle Georgia Historical Society, P.O. Box 13358, Macon, GA 31208. Tel. (478) 743-3851; E-mail: sidneylanier@bellsouth.net. On the Net: www.cityofmacon.net/Living/slcottage.htm.

FRAME OF REFERENCE Sidney Clopton Lanier was born in a back room of this cottage in 1842, staying here only briefly as an infant. He returned to Macon as an adult. The house, built circa 1840, opened to the public in 1973.

SIGNIFICANCE This charming cottage, owned by Lanier's grandparents at the time of his birth, today is revered as a shrine to "the South's most famous poet." A lover of his native Georgia, Lanier penned the highly regarded poems *The Song of the Chattahoochee*, about a river in the northern part of the state, and *The Marshes of Glynn*, located in Georgia's coastal region. As a poet in the age of realism following the atrocities of the Civil War, he also was an accomplished musician, linguist, mathematician and lawyer.

ABOUT THE SITE The white, wood house with wide front porch, gabled roof, white brick chimneys and black shutters, originally had four rooms. Through the years, a kitchen, back rooms and second story were added. Although furnishings are not original to the house, everything reflects the Victorian era. Wall covering and carpets were authentically reproduced. Four original fireplaces and the heart-of-pine floors are original. The house sits among other historic houses on a shaded, brick street.

Lanier memorabilia are lovingly displayed in the back room, where Lanier was born more than 160 years ago. In a glass-fronted cabinet, you'll find the family's silver tea service, knife and bread board, Lanier's alligator slippers and even a whisk broom. The cabinet also protects Lanier's alto flute. The poet was first flutist in the Peabody Orchestra in Baltimore, Md.

HOT TIPS Finding the cottage is no easy task because of one-way and merging streets, so map your way to the site before you visit. Parking is on-street in front of the cottage. Visits are by guided tour only; ring front bell for access. Allow a half-hour to tour. Other Lanier-related sites in Macon include: John Hill Lamar House (c. 1830), 544 Orange St., where Lanier met and courted his future wife; law office of Sidney Lanier, 336-48 2nd St.; First Presbyterian Church (c. 1858), where the poet was a member; Clifford Anderson-Dickey House (c. 1859), home of Lanier's uncle.

THE BEST STUFF In the back room, you'll find the double-wide, hand-made rocking chair of Lanier's uncle, donated by descendants, and the tiny-waisted wedding dress worn by Lanier's bride, Mary Day, in 1867.

THE WRITER AND HIS WORK

BORN: Feb. 3, 1842, in Macon

DIED: Sept. 7, 1881, in Lynn, N.C.; buried in Greenmount Cemetery, Baltimore, Md.

EDUCATED: Ogelthorpe College, Milledgeville, Ga., 1860

MARRIED: Mary Day, 1867; four sons

IMPORTANT WORKS: *Poems of Sidney Lanier* (1884, 2002); *The English Novel and Principle of its Development* (1883); and *Shakespeare and His Forerunners* (two volumes, 1902); *Boys King Arthur* (1989); *Music and Poetry* (2001). Lanier's wife edited a book of his poems in 1884 titled *The Poems of Sidney Lanier*. Poems include *The Dying Words of Stonewall Jackson*.

INTERESTING BIO FACT: Lanier served as a Confederate soldier in the Macon Volunteers and was imprisoned in 1864 for four months in Maryland. After his release, he walked home, arriving in Macon on March 15, 1865, desperately ill. As a prisoner, he had contracted tuberculosis, which ravaged his health the rest of his life.

FURTHER READING *Sidney Lanier* by Edwin Mims (2002); *Sidney Lanier: Poet of the Marshes* by Jack Debellis (1991)

ELSEWHERE IN THE AREA Grand Opera House (1883), 651 Mulberry St.; Georgia Music Hall of Fame at MLK Jr. Boulevard and 5th Street; Tubman African American Museum, 340 Walnut St.; Ocmulgee National Monument (prehistoric Indian ceremonial center) on U.S. 80. Macon boasts about 5,500 registered historic sites. ⚲

CARSON MCCULLERS' COLUMBUS

Where Novelist Grew Up, Set Novels

LOCATION West central Georgia at the Alabama state line, in and around Columbus. The city is reached via I-185 from the north, U.S. 27/280 from east and south, and U.S. 80 from the west.

For information on the self-guided Carson McCullers Columbus Tour, contact the Historic Columbus Foundation, Inc, P.O. Box 5312, Columbus, GA 31906. Tel. (706) 322-1756, or the Columbus Convention and Visitors Bureau, P.O .Box 2768, Columbus, GA 31902. Tel. (760) 322-1613 or 1-800-999-1613.

FRAME OF REFERENCE Lula Carson Smith was born in Columbus in 1917 and lived in her hometown until age 17, when she left in 1934 to study in New York City.

SIGNIFICANCE By the time of her death in 1967, McCullers — novelist, short-story writer, poet and essayist — had achieved international fame as one of the finest writers in American literature. In the 1940s she was more widely read than literary heavyweight William Faulkner.

Her four major novels all reached the New York stage, the movie screen and television featuring big stars and major directors. *Reflections in a Golden Eye,* directed by John Huston and starring Marlon Brando and Elizabeth Taylor, hit the theaters in 1967. The highly successful *The Heart Is A Lonely Hunter* premiered in 1968. Playwright Edward Albee adapted *The Ballad of Sad Cafe* for Broadway in 1963. It ran for 123 performances and later was made into a TV movie. *The Member of the Wedding*, staring Julie Harris and Ethel Waters, ran for 501 Broadway performances from 1950 to 1951, and was filmed in 1997. *The Square Root of Wonderful* closed after 45 Broadway performances in 1957.

In her family home, McCullers wrote *The Heart is a Lonely Hunter,* set in a town suspiciously like Columbus, at age 22. The novels *Reflections in a Golden Eye, A Member of the Wedding, Clock Without Hands*, and *Ballad of Sad Cafe*, also were drawn from her life in Columbus.

ABOUT THE SITE It is said that McCullers, whose psychological novels and stories examined the heart's secrets and told of spiritual isolation, once remarked she returned to the South for visits "to renew my sense of horror." Once scorned by her hometown, Columbus now honors her with "A Journey Through the Heart," a 31-site driving/walking tour of places tied to the author and the settings for three of her novels. Sites include McCullers' childhood home, 423 Thirteenth St., now a parking lot; and the Smith-McCullers family home, at 1519 Stark Ave., purchased by McCullers' parents in 1926 when Carson was 10. The home is now part of Columbus State University and is the Carson McCullers Center for Writers and Musicians. A historic marker stands out front. McCullers married her husband, Reeves, in the parlor. She later returned to Columbus several times to recuperate from illness and wrote parts of several novels in the city.

Stop 25 on the tour is the Wynnton School, which Carson attended from 1925 to 1929; Stop 30 is Columbus High School where Carson graduated in 1933. Also, the Bradley Library (stop 23 on the tour), at 1120 Bradley Drive in the Wynnton community, exhibits McCullers' first editions, as well as reviews of her works.

HOT TIPS The "Journey Through The Heart" tour is a combination driving/walking tour, so keep weather conditions in mind. Get the tour brochure in advance by calling or dropping by the Historic Columbus Foundation, 700 Broadway. Begin your tour at McCullers' childhood homesite in downtown Columbus and conclude in Wynnton, east of downtown. Parking is on-street. Allow several hours for the tour.

Carson McCullers lived in a Victorian house in **Nyack, N.Y.**, within the New York City metropolitan area, for about 25 of her 50 years. She also briefly lived in a house in Brooklyn Heights. See New York in the Middle Atlantic region of this book.

THE BEST STUFF McCullers fans most likely will find the sites that served as novel settings the most interesting part of the tour. Her masterpiece, *The Heart Is a Lonely Hunter,* features these Columbus sites: the former Springer Opera House (now State Theater of Georgia), where "Baby Wilson" was to perform; the Columbus Stockade, where "Antonapoulos" was jailed; and the former Union Station, now home for the local chamber of commerce, where "Mr. Singers" boarded a train to visit Antonapoulos.

THE WRITER AND HER WORK
BORN: Feb. 19, 1917, in Columbus
DIED: Aug. 15, 1967, in Nyack, N.Y.; buried in Nyack's Oak Hill Cemetery
MARRIED: James Reeves McCullers, Jr., 1937; divorced 1941, remarried

1945. Reeves, who killed himself in 1953, tried to convince McCullers to commit suicide with him.

EDUCATION: Studied piano at Julliard School of Music and creative writing at Columbia and New York University

IMPORTANT WORKS: *The Heart is a Lonely Hunter* (1940); *Reflections in a Golden Eye* (1941); *The Member of the Wedding* (1946); *The Ballad of the Sad Cafe* (1951); *The Novels and Stories* (1951); *The Square Root of Wonderful* (1958); *The Clocks Without Hands* (1961); *The Mortgaged Heart* (1971) and *Illumination and Night Glare* (1999)

INTERESTING BIO FACT: McCullers was debilitated by rheumatic fever in childhood and suffered a series of strokes in her twenties that left her partially paralyzed. She was confined to a wheelchair in her last years. When the young McCullers moved to New York to attend Julliard, she lost the tuition money for which her family had made enormous sacrifices. She didn't tell and took odd jobs and writing classes instead.

FURTHER READING *Carson McCullers: A Life* by Josyane Savigneau (2001); *Critical Essays on Carson McCullers,* edited by Beverly Lyon Clark (1996); *Wunderkind: The Reputation of Carson McCullers,* 1940-1990 by Judith Giblin James (1995); *Understanding Carson McCullers* By V.S. Carr (1989)

ELSEWHERE IN THE AREA The Woodruff Farm House (1870), 708 Broadway, and The Log Cabin next door; Chattahoochee Promenade, an outdoor history museum on Front Avenue between Fifth and Seventh streets; 700 Broadway, a formal 1870 brick town house housing the Historic Columbus Foundation offices ◭

MARGARET MITCHELL HOUSE

Where 'Gone With The Wind' Was Born

LOCATION Midtown Atlanta, Ga., at 990 Peachtree St., three blocks east of I-75/85. From east and west, take I-20 to I-85 north/south to the 10th Street exit. Site is at the corner of Peachtree Street and 10th Street at Crescent Avenue.

The Margaret Mitchell House and Museum ($) is open for guided tours daily 9 a.m. to 5 p.m. except for Thanksgiving, Dec. 25 and Jan. 1. Last tour begins at 4:30 p.m. Group tours available by appointment only. For more information, contact The Margaret Mitchell House and Museum, 990 Peachtree St., Atlanta, GA 30309. Telephone (404) 249-7015. On the Net: www.gwtw.org.

FRAME OF REFERENCE In a tiny, first-floor apartment in this house, former newspaper reporter Margaret "Peggy" Mitchell wrote most of her epic Civil War novel, *Gone With The Wind*, from 1925 to 1932. After a long struggle to raise funds for restoration and two damaging fires, the house opened to the public in 1997. The adjacent museum opened in 1999.

SIGNIFICANCE *Gone With The Wind*, which Mitchell originally titled *The Road To Tara*, is second only to the Bible as the world's best-selling book. Every year the novel sells 250,000 copies in a host of languages. Mitchell's 1000-page book was published in 1936 and was awarded the Pulitzer Prize in 1937. The only novel she ever wrote was made famous by the 1939 blockbuster movie of the same name.

The film, which grandly premiered Dec. 15, 1939, at Loew's Grand Theatre in Atlanta, won eight Academy Awards, including Best Picture. Hattie McDaniel, who played the house servant, Mammy, in the movie, was the first African-American to win an Oscar. The American Film Institute named it in the Top 10 of their 100 Greatest American Movies of All Time. Around the globe, *Gone With The Wind* is considered the definitive story of the Old South.

ABOUT THE SITE Mitchell, known for her wit, dubbed the three-room apartment where she and second husband, John Marsh, set up housekeeping "the dump." Friends, however, claimed her home was usually tidy and clean. Mitchell's apartment #1 occupies the east side of the three-story, red brick Tudor Revival house, built in 1899. The house was converted to 10 apartments in 1919. Visitors now enter from a new front porch, but the Marshes accessed the Crescent Apartments from the rear, where the old entrance hall still has original tiles.

Although nothing but the walls is original in "the dump," it has been restored and furnished to 1920s perfection. The living room, the bedroom and kitchen are square and small. Mitchell could have stood in the middle of the 6- by 6-foot galley kitchen and reached the sink, gas stove and cabinets. The ice box was kept on the porch. The Marshes ate at a little table in front of a blue-curtained window in the bedroom. It was a tiny place for a tiny woman; Mitchell was 4 feet 9 inches tall.

The visitor center houses an airy gallery with photographs and an exhibit about Mitchell's young life titled *Before Scarlett: Girlhood Writings of Margaret Mitchell - 1907-1908*. A 15-minute introductory video, *It May Not Be Tara*, begins your guided tour. The house itself also displays family photographs and memorabilia and letters written by Mitchell and her husband to family members describing their hectic lives after fame. "My Dear Mother," Marsh writes, "Poor Peggy is about worn to a frazzle with all the duties of being a celebrity..."

The two-block site, still surrounded by several buildings that Mitchell gazed upon from "the dump," is on the National Register of Historic Places. It dominates a fashionable area where Mitchell was born, grew up, was introduced to society, worked, married, wrote, attended the glittering premier of the movie based on her book — and tragically died.

HOT TIPS Free parking is available behind the site in a lot on Crescent Street. The home is adjacent to the Midtown MARTA station. Allow an hour for the video, a look at the galleries and the tour, plus a half hour at the *Gone With The Wind* museum.

The site has a small gift shop but no food is sold.

THE BEST STUFF If Mitchell's massive manuscript had survived, undoubtedly it would be the centerpiece of the home. But the very private author directed her husband to destroy her writings and personal letters after her death, which he dutifully did. Marsh did spare a few sheets of the *GWTW* manuscript as proof of authorship. Those rare sheets remain in an Atlanta bank vault, site personnel say.

In the apartment, you see a Remington typewriter similar to the one Mitchell used to hammer out as many as 60 versions of a single *GWTW* chapter. The typewriter sits on a small table that faces a window. You'll also see a Victorian love seat, Marsh's favorite photo of his wife perched on the bed and a cat dish, a reminder of Mitchell's beloved pet. Guides pepper visitors with anecdotes giving an up-close-and-personal side of the Mitchell family: Mitchell was laid up with a leg injury when she began her epic novel, at her husband's urging. Mitchell might have based the character of sweet Melanie on an aunt, a Catholic nun in love with the infamous criminal Doc Holliday.

Among the tantalizing movie memorabilia you'll find in the museum are trousers Clark Gable wore in *Gone With The Wind*, the green bonnet he brought to "Scarlett" from Paris, and the grand front door to Tara from the movie set.

THE WRITER AND HER WORK

BORN: Nov. 8, 1900, in Atlanta

DIED: Aug. 14, 1949, in Atlanta; struck by a speeding car while crossing Peachtree Street; buried in a nearby cemetery at Memorial Drive and Oakland Street

EDUCATION: Smith College, studied medicine one year

MARRIED: Berrien "Red" Kinnard Upshaw, 1922; annulled; John Robert Marsh, 1925

OTHER WORKS: *Lost Laysen*, a lost novella written at age 16, published 1995

INTERESTING BIO FACTS: Although Mitchell was born into one of Atlanta's wealthiest families, she refused to return to daddy's mansion after her first abusive marriage to "Red" ended. The former debutante took a job at the Atlanta Journal newspaper, writing for the Sunday section. Some say Mitchell based *GWTW's* dashing Rhett Butler on ex-husband Red and much of Scarlett's sweet Ashley Wilkes on second husband, John.

Ever the activist, Mitchell worked diligently for the American Red Cross and anonymously funded 50 medical school scholarships to African-American students at Morehouse College in Atlanta.

FURTHER READING *Margaret Mitchell and John Marsh: The Love Story behind Gone with the Wind* by Maryianne Walker (1993); *Southern Daughter: The Life of Margaret Mitchell* by Darden Asbury Pyron (1991); *Margaret Mitchell of Atlanta: The Author of 'Gone With the Wind'* by Finis Farr (1965). *The Wind Done Gone* by Alice Randall (2001), tells the Gone With the Wind story from a slave's point of view.

ELSEWHERE IN THE AREA Martin Luther King Jr. National Historic Site; Atlanta History Center, 130 West Paces Ferry Road, NW

• MUSEUMS ABOUT THE MOVIE •

GWTW STILL RULES IN GEORGIA Can't get enough of *Gone With The Wind* in Atlanta? Then travel 15 miles south to the **Road To Tara Museum** ($) in **Jonesboro, Ga.**, a small town in Clayton County. Here, Mitchell's 1936 book and David O. Selznick's 1939 movie, as well as remnants of the antebellum South, remain alive and well. Or you can go to **Marietta, Ga.**, just northwest of Atlanta off I-75, where you find the **Gone With The Wind Museum** ($).

In Jonesboro, your first stop should be the Jonesboro Depot Welcome Center on Main Street. In this 1867 depot, you'll find possibly the world's largest permanent *Gone With The Wind* exhibit, amassed by historian Herb Bridges in the Road To Tara Museum. The museum opened in 2001. Bridges' collection includes original movie props, posters and souvenirs; costumes, including Scarlett's flowered ball gown; stage play marquees from around the globe; collectible plate and doll collections; a foreign edition library; and a rare display of behind-the-scenes photographs made during movie production.

To get to the museum, take I-75 south from Atlanta to exit 228. Go west 4 miles to the museum. For more information, contact Road To Tara Museum, 104 N. Main St., Jonesboro, GA 30236. Telephone: toll free 1-800-662-7829 or (770) 478-4800. On the Net: www.visitscarlett.com.

Also in Jonesboro, a **Gone With The Wind Tour** gives a glimpse of a Southern plantation more like the Hollywood version than the one Mitchell actually wrote about in her novel: "a clumsy, sprawling building ... built according to no architectural plan whatever." In Jonesboro, you'll find the 1839 Greek Revival mansion Stately Oats and the authentic community that surrounded it. A Confederate cemetery where 600 are buried is laid out in the shape of a Confederate flag.

For information on the Gone With The Wind Tour, call (770) 477-8864. The tour begins at the Jonesboro Depot Welcome Center, Monday through Saturday at 1 p.m. or by appointment.

• More in Marietta •

You will find a 250,000-item collection of memorabilia from Mitchell's movie in Marietta at The Gone With The Wind Museum. The museum is located downtown, just off Glover Park, commonly called Marietta Square, at 18 Whitlock Ave. The private Shaw-Tumblin Collection includes Vivien Leigh's (Scarlett) Best Actress Oscar, Clark Gable's (Rhett) signed movie contract, and 39 costumes worn by main cast members. You'll find the hat Leigh wore in the barbecue scene at Twelve Oaks, Belle Whatley's dress, Gable's waist coat, and Leslie Howard's tattered uniform. An exhibit on Margaret Mitchell displays personal papers and quotes.

The museum is open Monday through Saturday 10 a.m. to 5 p.m. and noon to 5 p.m. on Sunday. For more information, call (770) 429-1115. On the Net: http://roadsidegeorgia.com/site/gwtw.html.

• And In Texas... •

You'll find more *GWTW* items at the LBJ Library and Museum at the University of Texas, Austin campus. The exhibit, titled, *From Gutenberg to Gone With The Wind*, includes pages written by F. Scott Fitzgerald for the screenplay; a storyboard for the "Burning of Atlanta" sequence; Technicolor makeup and wardrobe tests of Vivien Leigh, Clark Gable, Olivia de Havilland and Leslie Howard; and screen tests of actresses trying for the role of Scarlett O'Hara. The collection is part of the Harry Ransom Humanities Research Center, located at 21st at Guadalupe St.

For more information, call (512) 471-8944. On the Net: www.hrc .utexas.edu.

FURTHER READING *Frankly, My Dear...: Gone With the Wind Memorabilia* by Herb Bridges (1995) △

FLANNERY O'CONNOR CHILDHOOD HOME

Where Writer's Unusual Career Began

LOCATION Coastal Savannah, Ga., at 207 East Charlton St. at Lincoln Street, on the south side of Lafayette Square. From north and south, take I-95 to I-16 east and west into downtown Savannah.

The Flannery O'Connor Childhood Home ($) is open Saturday and Sunday from 1 p.m. to 4 p.m. and by special arrangement at other times. Literary activities are held from October through May. The home presents special readings for the Georgia Heritage celebration and for Saint Patrick's Day.

For more information, contact the Flannery O'Connor Childhood Home Foundation, 207 E. Charlton St., Savannah, GA 31419. Tel. (912) 233-6014. On the Net: www.ils.edu/flannery.

FRAME OF REFERENCE Mary Flannery O'Connor was born in Savannah in 1925 and lived in this house, built in 1856, until she was 13, when her family moved to Atlanta. The O'Connor home foundation bought the house in 1989 to preserve the place where O'Connor began writing as a child.

SIGNIFICANCE O'Connor wrote about life in the South in two novels, *Wise Blood* (1952) and *The Violent Bear It Away* (1960), as well as 32 short stories, seven of which were made into movies. She also authored commentaries and literature reviews between 1956 and 1964 for two publications of the Catholic Diocese of Savannah, The Bulletin, and its successor, The Southern Cross.

In her writings, often described as grotesque, O'Connor pits her characters against a violent, ultimately inexplicable world as they search for God. Her combination of gothic eeriness with a feeling for the power of redemption made a significant contribution to American literature.

ABOUT THE SITE The three-story house, built of Savannah gray brick, is maintained as a memorial to O'Connor and as a literary center for Savannah, America's oldest planned city. Currently only the first floor, the parlor level, is open to the public. Here visitors will find a large living room, refurbished in the style of a middle-class home in the 1930s, complete with twin fireplaces, shiny heart-of-pine floors, chandeliers, heavy furniture and lace curtains. The entry level also has a dining room, kitchen and sun room.

The two top floors, where the O'Connor family had bedrooms and a bathroom, are now apartments, as is the basement, which the O'Connors used for storage. Rental income helps the foundation pay the house mortgage as refurbishing continues. The house is a National Historic Landmark. The backyard, where five-year-old Mary taught a chicken to walk backwards, became a walled garden in 1993.

HOT TIPS Park on street. The Cathedral of St. John The Baptist, where Flannery was baptized and attended Mass, is located across Lafayette Square from the site.

THE WRITER AND HER WORK
BORN: March 25, 1925, in Savannah
DIED: Aug. 3, 1964, at age 39 of lupus in Milledgeville, Ga.; buried beside her parents in Memory Hill Cemetery, Milledgeville
EDUCATED: Georgia State College for Women (now Georgia College), 1945; State University of Iowa, M.F.A., 1947
ACCOLADES: Include three O. Henry Awards (1957, 1963, 1965); National Book Award, 1972
IMPORTANT WORKS: *Wise Blood* (1952), *A Good Man Is Hard To Find* (1955), *The Violent Bear It Away* (1960); *Everything That Rises Must Converge* (1965), *Mystery and Manners* (essays, 1969); *The Complete Short Stories* (1971), *The Habit of Being: Letters*, edited by Sally Fitzgerald (1979); *The Presence of Grace and Other Book Reviews*, edited by Carter W. Martin (1983)

FURTHER READING *Flannery O'Connor: A Descriptive Bibliography* by David Farmer (1981); *Mystery and Manners: Occasional Prose* by Flannery O'Connor, selected and edited by Sally and Robert Fitzgerald (1969)

ELSEWHERE IN THE AREA Fort Pulaski National Monument, US-80 East; Juliette Gordon Low Birthplace (founder of Girl Scouts U.S.A.), 10 E. Oglethorpe Ave.; Roundhouse Railroad Museum, 601 W. Harris St.; Savannah History Museum 303 Martin L. King, Jr. Blvd.; Savannah Ogeechee Canal Museum, 681 Fort Argyle Road; Ships of the Sea Maritime Museum, 41 M.L. King, Jr. Blvd.

• ANDALUSIA •

Flannery O'Connor wrote the bulk of her fiction on a farm in **Milledge-ville, Ga.,** where she moved in 1951 with her mother. O'Connor's uncle, Dr. Bernard M. Cline, purchased the Grey Quail Farm, about 25 miles northeast of Macon in central Georgia, in 1941. He renamed it Red Sorrel Farm after a favorite horse. O'Connor later discovered an earlier name for the farm, Andalusia, and persuaded her family to change it again. The site on US 441 is now owned and operated by the Flannery O'Connor Andalusia Foundation and is open to the public.

Trolley tours of the farm are available on the third Saturday of each month by reservation. Some rooms of the house are open for tours. For information, contact the Andalusia Foundation at (478) 454-4029 or the Milledgeville Convention and Visitors Bureau at 1-800-653-1804. ◮

RACHEL CARSON HOUSE

Writer Who Fueled Environmental Movement

A house near **Silver Spring, Md.**, in Montgomery County once belonged to Rachel Carson, the biologist, naturalist and writer who is credited with beginning the modern environmental movement. The house at 11701 Berwick Road is a private residence and, since 2003, headquarters of the Rachel Carson Council. The house currently is not open to the public.

Through her best-selling book *Silent Spring* (1962), Carson alerted the world to the hazards of widespread pesticide usage. This heightened awareness helped bring about the eventual formation of the U.S. Environmental Protection Agency in 1970 and the banning of DDT in the US in 1972. Carson also wrote *The Sea Around Us* (1951) and *Edge of the Sea* (1955), both bestsellers.

The Rachel Carson House, designated a National Historic Landmark in 1991, is a simple, post-World War II ranch house, designed by Carson and built in 1956. It is situated in a naturalistic landscape. The one-story house is asymmetrical with a low-pitched asphalt shingle roof and wide eaves. The walls are brick except in the attic gables. The front of the building has two large single-paned windows with smaller sash windows on either side.

Much of Carson's thoughtful landscaping remains intact. The front yard has evergreens, including a spruce, hemlock and white pine trees as well as flowering shrubs. Carson died in the house in 1964.

For more information, contact the Rachel Carson Council, P.O. Box 10779, Silver Spring, MD 20914. E-mail: rccouncil@ aol.com. On the Net: www.cr.nps.gov/nr/feature/wom/2001/features.htm. For more on Carson, look under Pennsylvania in the Middle Atlantic section of this book. ◭

FORT McHENRY

Inspiration For Poet Francis Scott Key

LOCATION Baltimore, Md., at the tip of Locust Point, just south of the city's Inner Harbor. From I-95 South, take the Fort McHenry Tunnel. Bear right from tunnel and take Exit 55 to Key Highway, following signs to Fort Avenue, which dead-ends at the fort. From I-95 North, take the Key Highway exit. Follow signs to Lawrence Street. Take left on Lawrence to Fort Avenue and take another left to monument entrance.

Fort McHenry National Monument and Historic Shrine ($) is open daily except Dec. 25 and Jan. 1, from 8 a.m. to 5 p.m. Extended summer hours. Group tours require three-day notice. For more information, contact the National Park Service, Fort McHenry National Monument, Baltimore, MD 21230-5393. Tel. (410) 962-4299. On the Net: www.nps.gov/fomc.

FRAME OF REFERENCE Francis Scott Key, a young Washington lawyer, penned the poem that later became America's national anthem during the War of 1812, called America's "Second War of Independence." The battle Key witnessed unfolded Sept. 13 - 14, 1814.

SIGNIFICANCE Fort McHenry, a key defense of Baltimore, came under a fiery British bombardment during the Battle of Baltimore. Key, who witnessed the battle from a boat in the Chesapeake Bay, was awed by the sound and light effects of the newfangled Concreve rockets. British ships in the Patapsco River pummeled the fort with 1,500 to 1,800 shrieking rockets for 25 hours. Hence the "rockets' red glare" that Key described in his poem. Key titled his poem *Defense of Fort McHenry*. It was later set to music and became *The Star-Spangled Banner*.

ABOUT THE SITE Fort McHenry today looks much the way it did in 1814. The brick fort, completed in 1805, is star-shaped, with five bastions along 15-foot-high walls, following an old French design. It sits on a 53-acre site jutting into the Patapsco River below Baltimore's Northwest Harbor. The fort's visitor center houses a small gift shop and a theater, where you can see a 16-minute orientation film, *The Defense of Fort McHenry*.

The fort has endured few alterations during its 100 years of military use, as a key defense site in War of 1812 through a final stint as an Army hospital during World War I. You still can see remnants of the "dry moat"

212

encircling the castle-like fort. U.S. infantry troops were stationed in the moat in 1814. Then about 1,000 military men gathered to defend Baltimore from a British naval onslaught.

The 15 United States had declared war against England on June 18, 1812, after the British confiscated American merchant ships and cargo and "impressed" U.S. seamen, making them serve with the English in the fight with Napoleon's France.

British soldiers also advanced toward the fort by land. But the British ships withdrew after their land invasion failed to materialize, and they realized the exchange of fire from ship to fort was a standoff. Major Armistead ordered the smaller flag that had flown during the battle lowered and his giant cotton flag hoisted. The custom-made flag and the "rockets' red glare" inspired Key.

Today a walk through the sally port (entrance), Ravelin (a wedge-shaped outwork designed to protect the entrance), and "bombproofs" (underground, arched chambers to protect men and artillery from shelling) take visitors back 180 years. Exhibits in the fort illustrate the site's various uses. Despite the intrusions of modern life — which are everywhere at the watery edges of the park — ships, barges, cranes and smokestacks, the most prominent with big blue letters reading *Lehigh Cement*, yesterday stubbornly endures.

HOT TIPS Finding Fort McHenry can be difficult if approaching from the West. You'll be driving through the busy downtown area, and signs to the fort are nearly impossible to see. It's worth the extra time to bypass the city on I-695 until reaching I-95 and proceed to the site. A water taxi service operates daily around the Inner Harbor. Call (410) 563-3901 for water taxi information.

Park at the visitor center for a walking tour. Allow two hours. Do not touch cannons, statutes or exhibits and do not walk on the seawall. Site hosts special events and living history encampments.

THE BEST STUFF The big attraction at Fort McHenry is the exact replica of the flag sewn by a Baltimore woman, Mary Pickersgill, at the request of fort Commander Maj. George Armistead. (You can visit Mary Pickersgill's "Flag House" and 1812 Museum at 844 East Pratt St. in Baltimore.) Major Armistead wanted to make sure that the invading British had no trouble seeing the 30-by 42-foot flag from a distance.

Bad weather, however, often prohibits the flying of the giant, 15-star flag replica above the fort. High winds can whip the flag around so badly the 89-foot flagpole could snap. To see the original tattered flag, with 15 stars and stripes, visit the Smithsonian Institution's Museum of American History in Washington, D.C.

The original flag was preserved by Armistead's descendants, one of whom was nephew Lewis Armistead. He died leading a Confederate charge at Gettysburg. The rainy night in 1814 before Key wrote his poem, Armistead flew a smaller flag. With the morning's calmer weather, he ordered his huge flag raised. That's the one Key saw "by the dawn's early light."

Smaller flag or not, after you watch the orientation film at the Visitor Center and the last strains of the *Star-Spangled Banner* ring out, the curtain on a large picture window slowly draws back to reveal *The Flag* waving over Fort McHenry. Almost everyone gets teary-eyed.

THE WRITER AND HIS WORK

BORN: Aug. 1, 1779, in Frederick, Md., on the family estate, "**Terra Rubra**."
    A U.S. flag flies continually at the birth site, by order of Congress.

DIED: Jan. 11, 1843, in Baltimore; buried in Mt. Olivet Cemetery in Frederick, where a large monument bearing a sculpture of Key honors him

MARRIED: Mary Tayloe Lloyd in 1802; 11 children

EDUCATED: Home-schooled, prep school; graduated from St. Johns College, Annapolis; studied law

IMPORTANT WORK: Key, an amateur poet, wrote enough songs and verse for a collection, *Poems of the late Francis S. Key, Esq.*, printed in 1857. He also wrote a study, *The Power of Literature and Its Connection with Religions* in 1834. But it's the *Star-Spangled Banner* that made him famous, a poem with an interesting tale.

Key was watching safely from the deck of an American truce ship nearly 2 miles away in the Chesapeake Bay during the attack. The British had detained him while on a mission with the U.S. Commissioner of Prisoners to secure the release of an American prisoner, Dr. William Beanes. The mission succeeded, but the British kept Key and the commissioner overnight, fearing that the Americans had learned of their battle plans. (The British let them go the next day.)

At dawn, Key saw Gen. Armistead's great flag above the fort, and wrote out his emotions on the back of a letter he had in his pocket. After the British released him and Beanes, Key wrote more lines while sailing back to Baltimore. He added to the poem in his lodging at the Indian Queen Hotel.

Judge J. H. Nicholson, Key's brother-in-law, took the copy that Key finished in his hotel on Sept. 14, 1814, to a local printer. Copies were circulated around Baltimore under the title *Defence of Fort M'Henry*. Two of these copies survive. Key's poem was printed in a newspaper for the first time in the Baltimore Patriot on Sept. 20, 1814, then in papers as far away as Georgia and New Hampshire. To the verses was added a note "Tune - Anacreon in Heaven," a popular English drinking song.

The first musical edition was published by Benjamin Carr of Baltimore and titled *The Star-Spangled Banner*. In time, the song's popularity grew. Congress adopted Key's poem as our national anthem on March 3, 1931.

Key's original manuscript remained in the Nicholson family for 93 years. In 1907, it was sold to Henry Walters of Baltimore. In 1934 it was bought at auction in New York from the Walters estate by the Walters Art Gallery, Baltimore for $26,400, then resold in 1953 to the Maryland Historical Society. The original manuscript has been stored at the Maryland Historical Society Museum & Library, 201 W. Monument St. in downtown Baltimore. Plans called for its display beginning in late fall of 2003 in an overview of Maryland history titled "Looking for Liberty." Another copy that Key made remains in the Library of Congress.

At the Fort McHenry visitor center you can see the framed act signed by President Herbert Hoover declaring Key's poem our national anthem. A glass case protects a fragment from one of the "bombs bursting in air" that Key saw.

INTERESTING BIO FACT: Key was active in the American Colonization Society, which helped freed slaves settle in Liberia, Africa.

ELSEWHERE IN THE AREA Flag House and 1812 Museum, the U.S.S. Constellation (launched in 1797), Babe Ruth Birthplace and Baseball Center, Baltimore Maritime Museum, National Aquarium, all in Baltimore. The Inner Harbor waterfront offers interesting shops, places to eat. ◮

H. L. MENCKEN HOUSE
Tribute to Influential Social Critic

The **Baltimore, Md.**, row house where the influential journalist, social critic and literary figure Henry Louis Mencken lived most of his life should again be open to the public in the near future. An ambitious plan to renovate the 1883 Italianate-style brick house at 1524 Hollins St. on Union Square is being hammered out as fund-raising continues. The plan includes installation of a museum-quality environmental control system to protect Mencken artifacts.

The H. L. Mencken House, owned by the city of Baltimore, became a National Historic Landmark in 1983 and opened to the public in 1984 as part of Baltimore's City Life Museum. The house closed in 1997 with the impending failure of City Life. A historic marker is mounted next to its double front doors.

Mencken lived in the three-story house, with arched doorway and front steps to the sidewalk, from age 2 until his death on Jan. 29, 1956, except for the five years of his happy marriage at age 50 to Sara Haardt. From 1930 to 1935 the couple lived on Cathedral Street in Baltimore. After Sara's death from tuberculosis in 1935, Mencken moved back into the house and shared it with his brother, August. Mencken did much of his writing in his second-floor study.

Mencken, born in Baltimore on Sept. 12, 1880, was the most influential editor, essayist and social critic in America - "The Voltaire of His Time" - during the first half of the 20th century. As co-editor of the Smart Set magazine from 1914-1924 and the American Mercury from 1924 to 1933, he attacked American culture, educational system, religion, politics and the "booboisie," his word for the great American public. He marshaled his great influence in the 1920s behind such bold new writers as James Branch Cabell, **Theodore Dreiser** and **Sinclair Lewis**.

The often-quoted Mencken's best and most influential essays include *Puritanism as a Literary Force* (1917), in which he labeled Puritanism as the root of America's problems; and *The Sahara of the Bozart* (1920), a biting criticism of Southern culture. Important works include *Prejudices*, a collection of essays (1919-1927); book-length studies of George Bernard Shaw (1905), Friedrich Nietzsche (1908), women (1917), democracy (1926), and religion (1930); the autobiographical trilogy *Happy Days* (1940), *Newspaper Days* (1941) and *Heathen Days* (1943); *The American Language* (1919,

1945, 1948) and *The Diary of H. L. Mencken*, recorded from 1930 to 1948 and published in 1990.

Mencken's books remain in print. He still attracts literary and biographic controversy and reigns as one of the most quoted — and misquoted — American writers.

For more information, contact Friends of the H. L. Mencken House by e-mail at secretary@menckenhouse.org. Tel. (803) 732-7063. On the Net: Mencken Society at www.mencken.org. ◮

DOROTHY PARKER MEMORIAL GARDEN
Writer's Ashes Buried at NAACP Site

Writer Dorothy Rothschild Parker was born in New York City, lived most of her life there, and died there at age 73 in June 1967. But in a convoluted tale befitting the literary giant, her ashes were buried 21 years after her death in the yard of the headquarters of the NAACP in **Baltimore, Md.** In the Dorothy Parker Memorial Garden at the organization's national headquarters, 4805 Mount Hope Drive, you will find a circular brick memorial and plaque where the urn of Parker's ashes is buried in a small stand of pines.

An epitaph inscribed atop the urn's lid reads: "Here lie the ashes of Dorothy Parker (1893-1967) Humorist, writer, critic, defender of human and civil rights. For her epitaph she suggested 'Excuse My Dust'. This memorial garden is dedicated to her noble spirit which celebrated the oneness of humankind, and to the bonds of everlasting friendship between black and Jewish people."

Parker was drama critic at Vanity Fair magazine and member of New York's famous Alqonquin Round Table, a group of witty young writers in the 1920s. (See Big Apple, By The Book in the Middle Atlantic section of this book.) Her works include her best-selling book of poems, *Enough Rope* (1926); was well as *Sunset Gun* (1928); *After Such Pleasures* (1933); *Death and Taxes* (1931); *Here Lies* (1939); *Laments for the Living* (1930); *Not So Deep as a Well* (1936); *The Portable Dorothy Parker* (1976); *Sunset Gun* (1928); and the screenplay, *A Star Is Born* (1939), written with second husband Alan Campbell. Her acclaimed story, *Big Blond*, won the O. Henry Prize in 1929.

How Parker's ashes finally arrived Baltimore in October 1988 is a strange tale.

When the writer died in 1967 she left no heirs. She willed her literary estate to Martin Luther King, Jr., although she'd never met the civil rights leader. Parker also named the author **Lillian Hellman**, her on-again-off-again friend, as her executor. Hellman arranged for Parker's funeral, but never told the crematory what to do with her ashes. The box with Parker's remains sat on a shelf at the crematory for 6 years, then was sent to the offices of Parker's lawyers, where they sat for 15 years in a filing cabinet.

In 1988, word about the ashes' fate somehow got out and New York tabloids publicized the story. The NAACP retrieved the ashes, then built a memorial garden at its headquarters for Parker's remains. On Oct. 20, NAACP president Benjamin Hooks dedicated the memorial garden on the office property. The brown brick memorial is circular, recalling The Round Table that Parker helped make famous.

For more information, go to the Dorothy Parker Society of New York's Web site at www.dorothyparkernyc.com, or the NAACP's Web site at www .NAACPorg.net. To arrange a tour of the Parker Memorial, call the NAACP headquarters at (410) 580-5767. ◭

EDGAR ALLAN POE HOUSE AND MUSEUM

Documenting Writer's Years In Baltimore

LOCATION Downtown Baltimore at 203 N. Amity St., between Saratoga and Lexington Streets. Look for an antique black street lamp and two historical markers at the site. From north, south and east, take I-95 to Baltimore, then I-395 into the downtown area. From Baltimore Street turn right on to Amity. From west, take I-40, turn south on Carey Street, left on Saratoga then right on Amity.

The Edgar Allan Poe House and Museum ($) is open Wednesday through Saturday from noon to 3:45 p.m. Call ahead to verify seasonal days and hours.

For more information, contact the Edgar Allan Poe House and Museum, 203 N. Amity St., Baltimore, MD 21223-2501. Tel. (410) 396-7932. On the Net: www.eapoe.org/index.htm.

FRAME OF REFERENCE The young Poe lived for three years in this 1830 brick row house, beginning in 1833, with his aunt, Maria Clemm, and her daughter, Virginia Eliza Clemm. Virginia later became Poe's wife at age 14. Poe left the house in August or September of 1835, moving to back to Richmond, Va., to edit the Southern Literary Messenger. The house was a private home until 1939 when the city of Baltimore acquired it. The Edgar Allan Poe Society of Baltimore saved the house from demolition in 1941.

SIGNIFICANCE In Baltimore, where Poe claimed he was born (although it actually was Boston) and where he died, Poe wrote several short stories, including his first published horror tale, *Berenice*, and *MS Found in a Bottle*. In this house he also wrote poems, including *Latin Hymn* and *Fanny*, as well as reviews and editorials.

This was but one of many homes for Poe, who profoundly influenced literature not only in America but worldwide. Poe created or mastered five literary genres: short story, detective fiction, science fiction, lyric poetry and the horror story. Best known for his poems and short fiction, Poe helped transform the short story from anecdote to art and practically created the detective story. He perfected the psychological thriller. Poe also produced some of the most influential literary criticism of his time.

Poe's work has remained in print for 150 years and has fascinated movie audiences through the years. Many can't forget *The Pit and the Pendulum* starring Vincent Price, which scared viewers throughout America in 1961. Since the 1880's, scholars have been trying to establish a complete listing of Poe's writings. Most of Poe's works appeared in magazines and newspapers, many of which are very rare or entirely lost.

When Maria Clemm was unable to pay the rent for the house after the death of her aging mother, who also lived in the house, Edgar decided to propose to Virginia in an emotional letter. She accepted. Both Clemms moved with Poe to Richmond.

ABOUT THE SITE The brick house, once the southern part of a duplex, is a five-room, 2 1/2 story duplex with tin gable roof and simple wooden stoop. The city tore down the northern half of the structure years ago. Poe, most biographers say, slept in the tiny attic bedroom, reached by a very narrow, winding staircase. The first floor has a parlor at the front and kitchen at the rear, both with fireplaces; the second floor comprises two bedrooms. The front bedroom also has a fireplace. The two-bay house has uneven plank flooring and walls, and ceilings are horsehair plaster, probably whitewashed when Poe lived here but now off-white. Doors, baseboards and trim work are wood painted brown and the wooden mantel is off-white.

Sometime after Poe left, the house was extended 4 feet at the back and this extension, with slanted roof and interior chimney, remains. You can detect the original size by the change in floorboard pattern.

Displayed are Poe's telescope, a lap desk (possibly used in his student days at the University of Virginia), Poe's sextant, glassware and china belonging to Poe's foster father, John Allen, and several lavishly illustrated volumes. You'll also see a full-sized, color reproduction of the only known portrait of Virginia Poe, painted at her death in 1847.

On the second floor, visitors will find a set of Gustave Dore's 1884 illustrations for Poe's *The Raven*, a reprint of Poe's 1849 obituary in the Philadelphia Dollar Newspaper, and videos and displays about Poe's gloomy life and mysterious death. Period furniture in the house is similar to that the Clemms and Poe might have used.

HOT TIPS Free on-street parking is available on Amity Street. Knock on the front door of the Poe House for admittance. Allow at least an hour for your visit. Site events include Halloween at the Poe House and the Edgar Allan Poe Birthday Celebration, the world's largest, on the weekend nearest January 19.

You can tour the Westminster Burying Grounds and Catacombs ($), **Poe's gravesite**, in spring and summer by reservation; call (410) 706-2072. The Baltimore cemetery gates at Fayette and Greene streets are open to the public daily from 8 a.m. to dusk. Metered, on-street parking available. Poe, wife Virginia, and Maria Clemm are buried in lot 27.

THE BEST STUFF Quite simply, is the house itself: the wood floors where Poe paced; the windows through which he gazed and pondered; the bedroom where he slept.

THE WRITER AND HIS WORK For more facts about Poe, look under Virginia in the South Atlantic section of this book. For other Poe sites, see Pennsylvania, Arkansas and New York.

ELSEWHERE IN THE AREA Poe-related sites in Baltimore include: Church Hospital, 100 N. Broadway, where Poe was hospitalized with a mysterious illness and died; Sir Moses Ezekiel statue of Poe at University of Baltimore Law Center Plaza at Maryland and Mt. Royal Avenues; John H. B. Latrobe House, 11 E. Mulberry St., a key place in Poe's life. The Latrobe House is not open to the public. The Great Baltimore Fire (1904) destroyed most Poe sites; urban growth has claimed others. ◢

CHARLES KURALT OFFICE
UNC Recreates Journalist's Workplace

After his death in 1997, every piece of television journalist Charles Bishop Kuralt's penthouse office in Manhattan, N.Y., was moved to his alma mater, the University of North Carolina at **Chapel Hill, N.C**. (Like Thomas Wolfe, Kuralt, born in 1934, was editor of the Daily Tar Heel student newspaper.) You can view the office of the native North Carolinian, famous for his *On The Road* series that aired on the CBS television network, in the School of Journalism and Mass Communications. The school is housed in Carroll Hall near Franklin Street.

The office furnishings, in what is now the Charles Kuralt Learning Center, were a gift of Kuralt's widow, Suzanna. The recreated office is masculine, yet elegant, with Oriental rugs, paneled walls, mahogany bookshelves and a brick fireplace. Photographs and awards cover the walls. In the office you can see Kuralt's glasses, videos, his travel books of America (arranged in alphabetical order), 12 of his 13 Emmys, two of his three Peabody Awards, his program from the National Medal of Arts awards signed by President Bill Clinton, his membership certificate in the Kansas Barbed Wire Association and a bust of Kuralt, a gift from his brother. The journalist thought the bust was too imposing and topped it with a UNC baseball cap.

Kuralt, who worked for CBS News nearly 40 years, was the youngest correspondent the network had ever hired. That record still stands. The newsman and Suzanna are buried in the Old Chapel Hill Cemetery on campus.

Kuralt's literary works include: *Dateline America* (1982); *Southerners* (1989); *A Life on the Road* (1990); *From Sea to Shining Sea* (1992); *Charles Kuralt's America* (1995); *Charles Kuralt's Seasons* (1997); *To the Top of the World* (1998); *American Moments (1998); North Carolina is My Home* (1998); *The Charles Kuralt Collection* (1998); *On the Road with Charles Kuralt* (2000). Kuralt also narrated many books, including a *Winnie the Pooh* series for author A. A. Milne.

You can visit the Kuralt Learning Center on Tuesdays and Thursdays from 1 p.m. to 4 p.m. Call UNC at (919) 962-1204 to arrange a tour for other times. On the Net: www.jomc.unc.edu/jomcataglance/facilities/center.html.

FURTHER READING *Remembering Charles Kuralt* by Ralph Grizzle (2001)

SOUTH ATLANTIC *North Carolina*

• PAUL GREEN EXHIBIT •

MUSEUM TELLS STORY OF PLAYWRIGHT Rural North Carolina native Paul Eliot Green won the Pulitizer Prize for drama in 1927 for his Broadway play, *In Abraham's Bosom*. He also wrote 16 outdoor dramas, including America's oldest, *The Lost Colony* (1937), which still plays every summer at Manteo on the state's Outer Banks. You can view a permanent exhibit on Green at the **Chapel Hill Museum**, at 523 E. Franklin St., at the intersection with North Boundary Street.

The museum, which "exhibits the character and characters of Chapel Hill," is open Wednesday through Saturday from 10 a.m. to 4 p.m., and on Sunday from 1 p.m. to 4 p.m. The Paul Green Legacy exhibition highlights the writer's life and legacies through text, photographs, and a recreation of his office, where you'll find some of Green's personal books.

Green, a UNC graduate, went on to teach in the university's philosophy and drama departments. He also wrote movies, plays, novels, poems and essays.UNC's fine arts theater is named after him.

For more information, contact the museum at 523 East Franklin St., Chapel Hill, NC 27514. Tel. (919) 967-1400. E-mail: info@chapelhillmuseum .org. On the Net: www.chapelhillmuseum.org. ◳

O. HENRY'S HOMETOWN
Short-Story Writer Remembered

Visitors to **Greensboro, N.C.**, will find a monument to the city's best-known writer, O. Henry, master of the short story, in the heart of its downtown area. At the corner of North Elm and Bellemeade Streets stands a three-piece bronze likeness of William Sydney Porter (1862-1910), nom de plume, O. Henry, and a 7- by 14-foot open book of his short stories. The author's dog, Lovey, shares the limelight.

O. Henry 's famous story, *Gift of the Magi*, enjoys widespread popularity today. O. Henry's important works include his first collection of short stories, *Cabbages and Kings* (1904); and a second collection, *The Four Million* (1906), followed by eight more collections between 1907 and 1910. Three more collections were published posthumously.

At the **Greensboro Historical Museum**, 130 Summit Ave., you'll find an exhibit about the life and times of O. Henry. The exhibit, titled "O. Henry's Greensboro," represents the town Porter probably knew as a young man and offers a look at O. Henry's life from his childhood through his successful days in New York. The exhibit features O. Henry's family cradle, a school desk from the one-room schoolhouse that his aunt ran and he attended, family photographs, sketches he made of Greensboro people when he worked as a clerk in his uncle's drugstore, and a doctor's office (Porter's father was a doctor). The recreated uncle's drugstore is also part of the exhibit.

Other O. Henry items include first editions, a portrait, letters he wrote to his daughter, Margaret, while he was in prison in Texas for embezzling from a bank, his top hat, wedding cups from his second marriage and photographs.

The museum is open Tuesday through Saturday, 10 a.m. to 5 p.m., and Sunday from 2 p.m. to 5 p.m. From I-85/I-40, take the S. Elm/Eugene Street Exit to downtown. Turn right on Bellemeade Street. The museum is three blocks ahead. Park on Lindsay Street.

For more information, contact the Greensboro Historical Museum, 130 Summit Ave., Greensboro, NC 27401-3016. Tel.: (336) 373-2610 or (366) 373-2043. E-mail: linda.evans@ci.greensboro.nc.us. On the Net: www.greensborohistory.org. For more about O. Henry, look under Texas in the West South Central section of this book.

O. Henry is buried in Riverside Cemetery in Asheville, N.C., near the grave of novelist Thomas Wolfe. ◪

CONNEMARA

Carl Sandburg's Mountain Home

LOCATION Western North Carolina, in Flat Rock, 42 miles south of Asheville, N.C. From I-26, take Exit 22 and turn west onto US 25 (Upland/Highland River Road). Follow signs; go south to Little River Road. Visitor parking lot is off Little River Road. The **Carl Sandburg Home National Historic Site ($)** is open daily, except Dec. 25, from 9 a.m. to 5 p.m. For more information, contact Carl Sandburg Home National Historic Site, 1928 Little River Rd., Flat Rock, NC 28731. Tel. (704) 693-4178. E-Mail: CARL_Administration@nps.gov. On the Net: www.Sandburg.org.

FRAME OF REFERENCE Charles August Sandburg lived at Connemara from 1945 until his death on July 22, 1967, at age 89. The farm became a National Historic Site in 1968.

SIGNIFICANCE During the 22 years the two-time Pulitzer Prize-winning poet, biographer, historian, social thinker, musician, novelist and social activist lived at Connemara, he produced more than one-third of his literary works. Sandburg authored 40 books, including his only novel, *Remembrance Rock*; his autobiography, *Always the Young Strangers*; and *The Complete Poems*. Sandburg and his wife, Lilian (Steichen), whom he called Paula, reared their three daughters (Margaret, Janet and Helga) at Connemara, along with Lilian's prize-winning, 300-head herd of Chiming goats.

In his poems, Sandburg commemorated ordinary American people, telling of their hopes, common wisdom, heroes, ballads and worth. He reflected upon the times in which he lived, when America was changing from the agrarian society of his youth into a hurried nation of industry and cities.

ABOUT THE SITE The rolling 264-acre farm comprises 25 structures, ponds, lakes, five miles of walking trails and a dramatic view of the Blue Ridge mountains. Two floors of the 22-room, white wood main house with tin roof and the basement are open for guided tours. You can visit Lilian's office, the dining room with vintage TV (Sandburg called it "the idiot box"), Sandburg's formal office downstairs with his typewriter amid the books and clutter, his upstairs "cozy corner" office with desk and book shelves made of orange crates, and the downstairs bedroom where he died. The basement houses the site's Information Center and bookstore.

Areas of interest include a family garage converted from the old kitchen, chicken house, pump house, spring house (where Lilian cured goat cheese), woodshed, Swedish House (where Sandburg stored important documents), tenant house, gazebo, goat house, remains of ice house, farm manager's house, greenhouse, barn pump house, sick-goat isolation quarters, barn garage, vegetable garden, barnyard and corncrib, buck kid quarters, main goat barn, horse barn, cowhide storage shed, silo and milk house. Sandburg's Jeep and some farm equipment also are on display.

Ironically, the Lincoln biographer's farm once served as the summer home of the first Secretary of the Confederate Treasury, Christopher Gustavus Memminger of Charleston, S.C. The Sandburgs bought Connemara from the heirs of textile tycoon Ellison Smyth.

HOT TIPS A small information center at the parking lot has restrooms and an exhibit about the Sandburgs. Visitors must take a .3 mile gravel path that rises 100 feet from the center to the main house. If you are unable to make the hike, call for transportation at the house phone in the center. Visitors can roam the farm to their hearts' content, but stay on established walks and paths. Don't climb fences. Wear sturdy shoes and dress for the weather; winter can bring snow and ice. No smoking.

Other restrooms are near the main house. Kids will love to watch the goat herd being fed in the red barn. The 20 or so goats are all descendants of Lilian's original herd.

Sandburg events include the Folk Music Festival in May and the Sandburg-Lincoln Festival and Poetry Celebration every summer. The Poetry Celebration offers a forum for student writers, grade 7 through college. Nearby Asheville celebrates The World of Carl Sandburg and Rootabaga Stories each summer. For information, contact Connemara. For more on Sandburg, check out the Carl Sandburg birthplace under Illinois in the East North Central region of this book.

THE BEST STUFF Inside the white clapboard main house, you'll think Sandburg had just returned from one of his rejuvenating strolls around the farm. Did he actually place those colorful fall leaves on his desk in the downstairs study? It seems he just finished reading the magazines, catalogues and research materials cluttering his workspace. The ever-ready guitar and walking canes wait nearby.

The Sandburgs remodeled the nearly 175-year-old house before moving in, building bookshelves in nearly every room — even around and over the doors — to house their 10,000-volume library. They arranged books by subject; poetry in the dining room. In most rooms, Sandburg kept stacks of research literature, a fire extinguisher, his green eye shades, and a guitar, just in case. A recording of Sandburg singing folk songs and playing his guitar might fill the house. Lilian refused to put curtains on Connemara's windows, saying the view was too grand. But today fringed white shades help protect the undisturbed house furnishings from damaging sun.

In the house, it's easy to imagine Carl, Lilian, daughters and grandchildren gathered for Sunday night dinner. Jackson, the resident cocker spaniel, and Chula, the Siamese cat, rest sleepily in their respective corners. Sandburg reads an after-dessert poem then strums and sings a favorite folksong. Then the poet retires to his upstairs office, dubbed his "cozy corner" for a night of writing.

Park rangers regale visitors with appealing tales of this famous man. He worked late into the night writing, puffing a stogy. He arose late in the morning, well after the rest of the family had gone about their chores. Later he would read new lines of poetry to Lilian, eat a light lunch, usually including goat cheese, then go for a walk.

One park ranger tells the story of the famous television journalist Edward R. Murrow's interview with Sandburg on Connemara's front porch. When asked what word in all of the English language he liked least, Sandburg emphatically replied, *Exclusive*! He was, after all, "our nation's poet."

THE WRITER AND HIS WORK

BIRTH: Jan. 6, 1878, in Galesburg, Ill.

DEATH: July 22, 1967, in Flat Rock; ashes buried in Galesburg

EDUCATION: Self-educated; awarded a degree from Lombard College, Galesburg

ACCOLADES: Two Pulitzer Prizes: for history for his four-volume *Abraham Lincoln: The War Years* and for poetry in 1951 for *Complete Poems*; American Academy of Arts and Letters Gold Medal for History and Biography, the Poetry Society of America's gold medal for distinguished achievement, and the Boston Arts Festival Award for his contribution to the art of American poetry.

IMPORTANT WORKS: *Abraham Lincoln: The Prairie Years* (1926); *Abraham Lincoln: The War Years* (1939); *The American Songbag* (1927); *Steichen The Photographer* (1929); *Potato Face* (1930); *Home Front Memo* (1943);

Always The Young Strangers (1952); *Remembrance Rock* (1948); *Mary Lincoln* (1932); *Lincoln Collector* (1949); *The Chicago Race Riots* (1919); *The Sandburg Range* (1957). For children - *Rootabaga Stories* (1922); *Abe Lincoln Grows Up* (1928); *Prairie-Town Boy* (1955) *Wind Song* (1960); *The Wedding Procession Of The Rag Doll And The Broom Handle And Who Was In It* (1978); *Rainbows Are Made* (1982). Poetry includes – *Chicago Poems (1916); Cornhuskers* (1918); *Smoke and Steel* (1920); *Slabs of the Sunburnt West* (1922); *Selected Poems* (1926); *Good Morning, America* (1928); *The People, Yes* (1936); *Complete Poems* (1950, 1970); *Harvest Poems* (1960); *Honey and Salt* (1963); *Breathing Tokens* (1978)

FURTHER READING *The Letters of Carl Sandburg* by Herbert Mitgang (2002); *Carl Sandburg: A Biography* by Milton Meltzer (1999); *Carl Sandburg* by Harry Golden, et. al. (1998); *The Other Carl Sandburg* by Philip R. Yanella (1996)

ELSEWHERE IN THE AREA Historic Flat Rock Playhouse; Thomas Wolfe House and Museum in Asheville ◮

> *Even when everyone was in town and Connemara was peopleless, she never seemed empty — but like a strong, gentle creature in the sun and perfectly content.*
>
> — Granddaughter PAULA STEICHEN
> In her Book, *My Connemara*

THOMAS WOLFE MEMORIAL

Autobiographical Writer's Boyhood Home

LOCATION Western North Carolina, in downtown Asheville, at 52 N. Market St. From east and west, take I-240 to the Charlotte Street exit. Go right on College Street, left on Market. From north and south, reach I-240 from I-85. The Thomas Wolfe Memorial ($) is open April through October, except Mondays. Hours are 9 a.m. to 5 p.m. Tuesday through Saturday; 1 p.m. to 5 p.m. on Sunday. From November through March, hours are 10 a.m. to 4 p.m. Tuesday through Saturday and from 1 p.m. to 4 p.m. on Sunday. Guided tours of the **Old Kentucky Home** leave the visitor center/museum hourly at the bottom of the hour with the last tour at 4:30 p.m. Museum exhibits are self-guided.

For more information, contact Thomas Wolfe Memorial, 52 N. Market St., Asheville, NC 28801. Telephone (828) 253-8304. E-mail: contactus@wolfememorial.com. On the Net: www.wolfememorial.com.

FRAME OF REFERENCE Thomas Clayton Wolfe, possibly America's most autobiographical major writer, grew up in this boarding house run by his mother, Julia Wolfe. He lived here from 1906 to 1916 (age 6 to age 15), when he left to attend the University of North Carolina at Chapel Hill. The house was built in 1883. In 1916 Wolfe's mother enlarged and modernized the house, adding 11 rooms. The house closed in 1998 after a suspicious fire that nearly destroyed it. After extensive reconstruction the Wolfe house reopened in May 2004.

SIGNIFICANCE Wolfe, one of America's greatest 20th-century novelists, called this rambling former boardinghouse Dixieland in his famous epic novel, *Look Homeward, Angel*. The book, Wolfe's first, published in 1929 when Wolfe was 28, has never gone out of print. It also became a successful Broadway play. Wolfe, known for his opulent language and unique style, spent his formative years in this house, observing a wealth of colorful boarders from around the country. They became fodder for his literary works. Wolfe's boyhood home not only colored his work but influenced the rest of his life. His reminiscences were so brutally honest and realistic that *Look Homeward, Angel* was banned from Asheville's public library for seven years. Today, Asheville celebrates its native son.

ABOUT THE SITE Julia Wolfe, a hard-nosed businesswoman, opened her boarding house in 1906, when Asheville was basking in its newfound reputation as a health resort. By 1910 the mountain town boasted 100 boarding houses. Julia's place, named Old Kentucky Home by a previous owner, could host up to 35 boarders. Although she took great pride in her business, young Thomas hated the drafty place and wished he could have lived with his siblings in his father's house down on Woodfin Street. In *Look Homeward, Angel*, Wolfe recalled the house as a "big cheaply constructed frame house of eighteen or twenty drafty, high-ceilinged rooms."

The Old Kentucky Home closed after an apparent arsonist set a fire on a night in July 1998. The fire started beneath the front window of the dining room, which suffered the most damage of any room in the rambling two-story house. The fire destroyed much of the house as well as 200 Wolfe artifacts, but firefighters and volunteers who rushed to the scene managed to save more than 600 items. Today the dining room's ornate Eastlake mantelpiece is a reproduction of the destroyed original. The 29-room, 6,000 square foot, Queen Anne-style home facing Spruce Street again displays most of the 300,000 artifacts as well as the rescued family heirlooms that had been stored during reconstruction.

The visitor center features an introductory movie, *Thomas Wolfe, Carving Literature from Life*, and interesting exhibits that you shouldn't overlook. You'll find items that Wolfe had with him in the Chelsea Hotel in New York, where he lived and wrote. They include his tux, luggage, desk and chair, bed, size 13 slippers, and even his pencils and a drinking glass. He didn't actually use the Remington typewriter, but the one on display was used by Wolfe's secretary, who retyped his handwritten manuscripts and took his dictation.

Other displayed items include the Wolfe family Bible, the boardinghouse guest register, stone-cutting tools of W.O. Wolfe (the writer's father), and the peeling white door from Julia's room. Old-fashioned telephones have recorded voices of Wolfe's mother and two siblings. Mother Julia, whom Wolfe recreated as Eliza in *Look Homeward, Angel* says: "I didn't think I was Eliza in the book. . . Eliza's a good character!"

HOT TIPS Limited parking is available at the south side of the visitor center. A large lot on the north side is privately owned; towing is enforced. Parking decks are nearby.

Be sure to pick up a copy of *A Literary Journey: A guide to the principal sites in Asheville closely identified with the life and writings of Thomas Wolfe* for $1 at the visitor center. Sites include: the author's grave at Riverside Cemetery, 53 Birch St.; First Presbyterian Church, where his funeral services were held; 92 Woodfin St., site of the Wolfe home where Thomas was born, now a YMCA parking lot; North State School for Boys, which Wolfe attended; and novel settings around Asheville. The marble angel immortalized in *Look Homeward, Angel* stands in Oakdale Cemetery in Hendersonville, 24 miles south of Asheville. The cemetery on W. 6th Avenue is marked with a historical plaque directing you to the graveyard statue, "Wolfe's Angel." Wolfe's father imported the statue from Carrara, Italy.

Allow an hour to take in the Exhibit Hall and the excellent introductory movie and 45 minutes for a tour of the house.

THE BEST STUFF The house showcases the rooms Wolfe recreated in his novel. The bright sun parlor, where Wolfe wrote about boarders gathering to listen or dance to records on the phonograph, features furniture from the demolished family home on Woodfin Street. The tables of the spacious dining room are spread with white tablecloths, family china, silverware and crystal. The kitchen's cast-iron coal range and original utensils round out the room where guests' meals were prepared, much as Julia Wolfe might have left them. Visitors can view the upstairs bedroom, with a lovely bay window of stained glass, where Wolfe's brother Ben died in 1918. Wolfe made the scene famous in *Look Homeward, Angel*.

THE WRITER AND HIS WORK

BORN: Oct. 3, 1900, in Asheville

DIED: Sept. 15, 1938, in Baltimore, Md., at age 37; buried Riverside Cemetery in Asheville

EDUCATION: UNC at Chapel Hill, edited school newspaper; M.A. Literature, Harvard

IMPORTANT WORKS: *Look Homeward, Angel* (1929); *Of Time and the River* (1935); *From Death To Morning* (1935); *The Web and the Rock* (1939); *You Can't Go Home Again* (1940); *The Hills Beyond* (1941); *The Complete Short Stories of Thomas Wolfe* (1987) edited by Francis E. Skipp (1987); plus numerous plays, essays, poetic passages and letters.

INTERESTING BIO FACTS: The 6-foot-2 1/2-inch Wolfe's *Look Homeward, Angel* proved too frank for the good citizens of Asheville, Wolfe's fictional "Altamont." The town banned the book. Always restless, Wolfe traveled by steamship to Europe seven times, meeting on one trip the love of his life, a married Jewish costume designer named Aline

Bernstein. She supported Thomas emotionally and financially in New York, but refused to leave her husband for him. Wolfe likely depicted her as Mrs. Jack in *You Can't Go Home Again*.

As Wolfe lay dying in a Baltimore hospital, after suffering tubercular meningitis and pneumonia on a cross-country trip, his family wouldn't allow Bernstein to visit him because they feared her visit would have upset him too much.

FURTHER READING *Thomas Wolfe* by Ted Mitchell et. al. (1999); *The Autobiographical Outline for Look Homeward, Angel* edited by Lucy Conniff and Richard S. Kennedy (1991); *My Other Loneliness: Letters of Thomas Wolfe and Aline Bernstein* edited by Suzanne Stutman (1983); *The Letters of Thomas Wolfe to His Mother* edited by C. Hugh Holman and Sue Fields Ross (1968)

ELSEWHERE IN THE AREA Biltmore Estate and Village, US 25; Colburn Gem and Mineral Museum , 2 South Pack Square; Smith-McDowell House (circa 1840) 283 Victoria Road; historic Grove Park Inn; Cradle of Forestry, US 276; Mineral Museum, Blue Ridge Parkway milepost 331; Mountain Farm Museum, US 441. For information on Asheville trolley tours, call (888) 667-3600. E-mail: www.ashevilletrolleytours.com

> *In the old house I feel beneath my tread the creak of the old stair, the worn rail, the whitewashed walls, the feel of darkness and the house asleep, and think, "I was a child here; here the stairs, and here was darkness; this was I, and here is Time."*
>
> — THOMAS WOLFE
> *Return*, a short piece written for *The Asheville Citizen* in 1937

WOODLANDS PLANTATION
Site of Poet William Gilmore Simms' Home

LOCATION Bamberg County, S.C., along the Edisto River, halfway between Charleston and Augusta, Ga. The site of the now privately owned former plantation is located in the community of Midway on US 78. From east and west, take US 78. From north and south, take US 301 to US 78. The locked entrance is just north of US 78. An S.C. historic marker locates the site. Woodlands is not open to visitors except by special arrangement. For information contact Felicia Dryden, Tel. (303) 440-4029; E-mail: fdryden@ecentral.com.

FRAME OF REFERENCE William Gilmore Simms lived, entertained many illustrious guests, and wrote at Woodlands Plantation from the time of his marriage in 1836 through the 1860s.

SIGNIFICANCE Simms was an acclaimed poet and the most prolific and widely known novelist of the antebellum South. Simms published 18 volumes of poetry, 30 volumes of fiction, biographies (telling the world of "The Swamp Fox," Francis Marion), essays, histories and articles before the Civil War. He often is compared to James Fenimore Cooper, though some scholars consider Simms' work less important.

In the 1850s, Simms, who briefly practiced law, edited journals, including the Southern Literary Journal and the pro-slavery Southern Quarterly, edited several newspapers, and served in the S.C. legislature and as the state's poet laureate. He defended slavery as "a wisely devised institution of heaven." His strong anti-abolition stand and ardent backing of states' rights ignited criticism. The upheaval of the Civil War (1860-1865) ended his illustrious career.

Woodlands was owned by Simms' father-in-law, Nash Roach, a wealthy planter from Charleston. Simms himself was not born to the Southern aristocracy, which dominated S.C. politics and social life in the 19th century. At Woodlands Simms lived with his large family and 70 African-American slaves, who worked in the fields and in the house. Simms wrote his historic romance novels at Woodlands. His first, *The Yemassee* (1835), told of Indian warfare in Colonial and Revolutionary South Carolina. The novel was especially popular with Northern readers, greatly curious about the South.

Simms' books are vivid tales of frontier adventure in the wilderness and swamps in the Southwest and South Carolina during the American Revolution. They brim with heroics of common, unlettered men in uncommon times.

ABOUT THE SITE The comfortable brick house that dominated Simms' plantation was large, with an expansive front portico reached by many front steps, according to written descriptions. Simms' large library/study on the lower floor housed about 10,000 volumes. T his is where the author wrote. Near the study was a well-appointed dining room where the outgoing Simms regaled his many guests with anecdotes. The plantation grounds boasted landscaped gardens and a grapevine swing, where guests often read. Oak and pine forests flourished. The first house burned down in April 1862 in a fire of unknown origin.

In 1865 as Sherman marched toward Columbia, South Carolina's capital, Union soldiers burned down the new mansion, slave cabins and other structures, sparing only two outhouses, which still stand. Simms wrote in one of them after the war. Another house that replaced the original plantation house was constructed from the rubble Sherman left behind. The ground floor was completed about 1868 with additions up to about 1925. Tenant houses on "the Simms place" stood on the property until about 1970 but fell to fire or neglect.

The 49-acre site, now owned by The William Gilmore Simms Literary Society, Inc., is a National Historic Landmark. Simms descendants gather there for family retreats and hunting parties. Some own contiguous property and raise trees for lumber sales. Many descendants of the enslaved people at Woodlands also live on or near original parts of the plantation. The Rumph family bought part of the property in 1917 and continues to farm the land. Slave descendants use the original cemetery on the plantation property that was the burial ground of their ancestors.

HOT TIPS For a drawing of 19th-century Woodlands, go to the William Gilmore Simms Society Web site at www.westga.edu/~simms/

THE WRITER AND HIS WORK
BORN: April 17, 1806, in Charleston, S.C.
DIED: June 11, 1870, at Woodlands; buried at Magnolia Cemetery, Charleston
EDUCATED: Schooling sporadic; once apprenticed as a druggist

MARRIED: Anna Malcolm Giles, 1826; Chevillette Roach, 1836; 16 children (15 by Roach)

INTERESTING BIO FACT: The poet and staunch abolitionist from Massachusetts, **William Cullen Bryant**, once visited Woodlands. Although he found the slaves on the plantation well-treated, this did not change his anti-slavery views.

IMPORTANT WORKS: *Martin Faber: The Story of a Criminal* (1833); *The Yemassee: A Romance of Carolina* (1835); *Richard Hurdis* (1838); *Beauchampe* (1842); *The Life of Francis Marion* (1845); *The Wigwam and the Cabin* (1845); *The Sword and the Distaff* (1852); *The Golden Christmas* (1852); *Woodcraft* (1854); *The Partisan: A Romance of the Revolution* (1856;) *Paddy McGann* (1863). Poems include *The Grape-Vine Swing*; *Song in March*; *The Decay of a People*; *The Swamp Fox*

FURTHER READING *Long Years of Neglect: The Work and Reputation of William Gilmore Simms* edited by John C. Guilds, 1988; *William Gilmore Simms* by William Peterfield Trent, 1892; *The Poetry of William Gilmore Simms* by James E. Kibler, Jr., 1978; *The Letters of William Gilmore Simms,* edited by Mary C. Simms Oliphant et al. (1952-1956)

ELSEWHERE IN THE AREA Edisto Gardens and Orangeburg Massacre Monument (Civil Rights statue) 15 miles north in Orangeburg ⏃

MULBERRY PLANTATION

Home of Mary Chesnut, the 'Dixie Diarist'

LOCATION Central South Carolina, southeast of downtown Camden, at 559 Sumter Highway (US 521) next to I-20 (exit 98 east) at the Wateree River. The Mulberry House is privately owned and not open to the public. For an online photograph go to http://users.arczip/com/chesnut/SCCH-ES/WEBPG/mulberry.html.

FRAME OF REFERENCE At Mulberry Plantation, Mary Chesnut, who had a ringside seat for the exciting rise and miserable fall of the Confederacy, penned a famous series of diaries from February 1861 to July 1865. Chesnut lived mainly at Mulberry, owned by her husband James Chesnut's wealthy planter family, during the tumultuous years of the Civil War. The house became a National Historic Landmark in 2000.

SIGNIFICANCE Historians consider Chesnut's diaries, first edited and published in 1905, then again in 1949 under the title *A Diary from Dixie*, the most intelligent and telling record of the Confederacy and of the South during the war years. In 1981, the complete diaries were published as *Mary Chesnut's Civil War*. Chesnut's candid, first-hand look at the Confederate experience — from Camden to Charleston to Columbia to Richmond to Montgomery — remains unsurpassed. She wrote much of her diary at Mulberry.

ABOUT THE SITE The brick, three-story main house at Mulberry, which had been in Chesnut family hands since the 1700s, had 2-foot thick walls, a grand, white-columned front porch, marble steps and slate roof. The antebellum plantation, a small and independent community, was designed with an eye to utility as well as beauty. A mile-long, live oak-tree lined road led from the Wateree River dock to the house. Paved paths connecting the manor house to the kitchen, smokehouse, dairy and icehouse, were bordered by lilacs and roses.

The plantation also had stables, barns, wheelwright's shop, cotton gin, blacksmith's shop and quarters for the 500 slaves who lived at Mulberry. In addition to vast cotton fields, slaves tended a large flower garden, strawberry and raspberry patches, and groves of fruit trees.

The Chesnut house, Sarsfield, and Mary and James Chesnut's burial sites at Knight's Hill in Camden are all private property and not open to the public.

HOT TIPS On the Net, http://users.arczip.com/chesnut/SCCHES/WEB PG/clinks.html connects you with Civil War sites in S.C. and Confederate glitterati about which Mary wrote and other Chesnut-related items: a photograph of Sarsfield, her and James' private home where she died; a facsimile of page 22 of Mary's handwritten diary; Civil War views of Charleston and Columbia; Confederate military leaders and the Chesnut commemorative stamp (1994).

There's also a photo of the two-story cottage in Columbia where Mary entertained Confederate President Jeff Davis in 1864, but you actually can visit this site — with an overnight reservation. It now is a bed and breakfast at 1718 Hampton St. For more information, contact The Chesnut Cottage Bed and Breakfast at (803) 256-1718. On the Net: www.bbonline.com/sc/chesnut

THE BEST STUFF Mary Chesnut's descriptions of life at Mulberry and "weary, dreary Camden" (population 1,000 at the time) are seen best in her published diaries. Her handwritten manuscripts, which originally total 400,000 words and 50 volumes, and Chesnut family papers, now reside on the main campus of the University of South Carolina in downtown Columbia, at the South Caroliniana Library.

THE WRITER AND HER WORK

BORN: March 31, 1823, in Stateburg, S.C, eldest child of wealthy Philadelphian Mary Boykin and Stephen D. Miller, U.S. congressman and senator and S.C. governor

DIED: Nov. 22, 1886, at Mulberry, possibly in the home's library

MARRIED: James Chesnut, Jr., April 23, 1840

EDUCATED: In her younger years, Chestnut was taught at home, as were most children of the South's planter elite. Later she attended an exclusive boarding school for girls in Charleston, where she learned to speak fluent French and German.

IMPORTANT WORKS: Chesnut began three unfinished novels including *The Captain and the Colonel*, and *Two Years*. The slim novels were published in 2002 under the title *Two Novels By Mary Chesnut*.

FURTHER READING *Mary Boykin Chesnut, A Biography* by Elisabeth Muhlenfeld (1981); *The Private Mary Chesnut: The Unpublished Civil War Diaries* (1984) by C. Van Woodward, Elisabeth Muhlenfeld, et al.

ELSEWHERE IN THE AREA Historic Camden Revolutionary War Site on U.S. 521 near I-20; Camden Archives and Museum, 1314 Broad St.; Historic Boykin 12 miles south of Camden

• FROM MARY CHESNUT'S DIARY •

ON SLAVERY :

I wonder if it is a sin to think slavery a curse to any land. (U. S. Senator from Massachusetts Charles) *Sumner said not one word of this hated institution which is not true. Men & women are punished when their masters & mistresses are brutes & not when they do wrong — & then we live surrounded by prostitutes.*

The Bible authorized marriage & slavery — poor women! poor slaves!

ON THE WAR:

Half the people that we know in the world are under the enemy's guns.

ON LIFE AFTER THE WAR, WHILE TRAVELING BACK TO MULBERRY FROM EXILE:

(I)...did not see one living thing — man, woman, or animal.

AND LATER:

I am so utterly heartbroken......I can not bear to write the horrible details of our degradation. I am sick at heart.....I was ill enough and wish I had died. ◮

WESTOVER

Colonial Estate of Diarist William Byrd II

LOCATION Charles City County in eastern Virginia off VA 5 between Richmond and Williamsburg. From I-295, take exit 22 east on VA 5 to the site overlooking the James River. The grounds and gardens ($) are open for self-guided tours from 9 a.m. to 6 p.m. daily. The house is not open to the public except for a spring garden festival.

For more information, contact Westover, 7000 Westover Road, Charles City, VA 23030. Telephone (804) 829-2882. On the Net: www .jamesriverplantations.org Note: There is no "city" in Charles City County; the heart of the locale, established in 1616, is the 250-year-old Charles City Courthouse.

FRAME OF REFERENCE William Evelyn Byrd II, founder of Richmond, built Westover circa 1730 and lived here until his death in 1744.

SIGNIFICANCE Byrd was one of Colonial America's richest planters with an estate of 200,000 acres worked by thousands of slaves. His lifestyle was independent, gracious, genteel, cultured and full of reading and writing. Planters like Byrd practically controlled the governments of Virginia and the other southern colonies. Byrd served in the House of Burgesses, represented the colony in England and was appointed a member of the Supreme Council.

Byrd's rarefied lifestyle shaped the writings for which he is best remembered:

The Secret History; The History of the Dividing Line; A Progress to the Mines; and A Journey to the Land of Eden. None of these works were published until 1841, nearly 100 years after Byrd's death. Byrd's *Secret Diary* provides vignettes of his life, exemplifying the colonial Southern aristocracy. He was one of few colonists who advocated marriage with Indians. Byrd's extensive secret journals, written in a personal shorthand, were decoded and published in the early 1940s. The Virginian recorded historical episodes with great wit, even giving characters names used in comedy of the period.

Byrd reportedly read Hebrew, Greek, Latin, Italian and French. His library of 4,000 volumes, imported from abroad, was one of the finest in the colonies. The east wing containing the library was burned down during the

Civil War, which also ended the South's plantation system and Westover's heyday. The east wing visible today was rebuilt in 1900.

ABOUT THE SITE Westover, named for Henry West — the fourth Lord Delaware and son of Thomas West, Governor of Virginia — reigns as a supreme example of Colonial American Georgian architecture, a style named after England's King George. The elegant three-story mansion was built of brick with steep roof, tall chimneys at both ends, two wings and elaborate, often later copied, doorway. A row of towering tulip poplars, now more than 150 years old, shade the mansion's entrance. Westover's grandeur and artistic details represented Byrd's political and social aspirations.

Just east of the mansion is the ice house and a small structure containing a dry well. From the well, residents fleeing attacking Indians could enter passageways going under the house to the river.

HOT TIPS During Historic Garden Week in Virginia each spring, many of the James River Plantations, including Westover, open their magnificent gardens and private homes for tours ($). For information, contact Historic Garden Week in Virginia, 12 E. Franklin St., Richmond, VA 23219, or go to www.VAGardenweek.org. Wear comfortable shoes and dress for the weather.

THE BEST STUFF The famous wrought iron Westover gates, with Byrd's initials embedded in the delicate ironwork, grace the north side of the mansion facing the river.

In a play on the name Byrd, a pair of lead eagles keep sentry atop massive gateposts flanking the gate. The fence has supporting columns topped by stone finials cut to resemble an acorn for perseverance, a pineapple for hospitality, a Greek Key to the World for knowledge, a cornucopia for abundance, a beehive for industry and an urn of flowers for beauty.

THE WRITER AND HIS WORK
BORN: March 28, 1674, on a Tidewater, Va., plantation to Mary Horsmanden Byrd and William Byrd I
DIED: August 26, 1744; buried at Westover amid the estate's formal gardens
MARRIED: Lucy Parke, 1706, died in 1716; married Maria Taylor 1724
EDUCATED: Studied business and law in the colonies and abroad
IMPORTANT WORKS: *The History of the Dividing Line betwixt Virginia and*

North Carolina' Run in the Year of Our Lord 1728 (1841); *The Secret Diary of William Byrd of Westover, 1739-1741* (1941) edited by Louis B. Wright and Marion Tinling; *A Journey to the Land of Eden, A.D. 1733; A Progress to the Mines* (1841), edited by Edmund Ruffin (Byrd's writings were first published in this volume.); *Another Secret Diary of William Byrd of Westover for the Years 1739-1741* (1942), edited by Maude H. Woodfin and decoded by Marion Tinling (Includes *Letters and Literary Exercises of William Byrd, 1696-1726); A Discourse Concerning the Plague* and *The Female Creed* (1721); *The London Diary, 1717-1721,* (1958) edited by Louis B. Wright and Marion Tinling; *The Prose Works of William Byrd of Westover* (1966)

FURTHER READING *The Diary and Life of William Byrd II of Virginia, 1674-1744* (1987) by Kenneth A. Lockridge; *William Byrd of Westover* (1971) by Pierre Marambaud

ELSEWHERE IN THE AREA Four other privately owned James River plantations in the Charles City County area welcome visitors: Belle Air Plantation, 11800 John Tyler Highway; Berkeley Plantation, 12602 Harrison Landing Road; Evelynton Plantation, 6701 John Tyler Highway; Sherwood Forest Plantation, 14501 John Tyler Highway; and Shirley Plantation (1613), the oldest plantation in Virginia, 501 Shirley Plantation Road. For more information, contact James River Plantations, P.O. Box 218, Charles City, VA 23030 or go to www.jamesriverplantations.org. Other area plantations have been transformed into bed and breakfast inns. ▲

SPENCE'S POINT

John Dos Passos' Farm

The farm where writer John Roderigo Dos Passos lived and wrote for much of his life survives as a historic landmark on Sandy Point Neck in **Westmoreland County, Va.** It is a private residence and not open to the public. The house, along VA 749, was placed on the National Register of Historic Places in 1971 following Dos Passos' death in 1970.

Dos Passos, acclaimed as one of the major and most influential of modern American writers, wrote much of his fiction from 1949 to 1970 at Spence's Point, which he renovated in 1949 as his country home. Dos Passos' father bought the house, built in 1806 in the Federal style, in the late 19th century. The younger Dos Passos added a west wing to the brick, three-bay house. The wing, which commands a view of the Potomac River, contains a large library and dining room. The house has two full floors over a raised basement.

Dos Passos (1896 -1970) wrote books as bitter indictments of America. The Harvard graduate's works attack the materialism and hypocrisy of his country, especially the period between the two world wars. His trilogy, *U.S.A.*, collected in 1938, covers the years 1900 through 1930 and comprises *The 42nd Parallel* (1930), *1919* (1932), and *The Big Money* (1936). In the trilogy Dos Passos created a new form of storytelling, one driven by social history.

After *U.S.A.*, the radical left-wing views imbued in earlier works succumbed to a conservative social philosophy. In his second trilogy, *District of Columbia* (1952), which includes *Adventures of a Young Man* (1939), *Number One* (1943), and *The Grand Design* (1949), Dos Passos defends many of the principles he had previously skewered.

Other notable works include *Three Soldiers* (1921), *Manhattan Transfer* (1925), and *Midcentury* (1961), his best-received work. In this novel, Dos Passos returned to the kaleidoscopic technique of his earlier successes to depict a panoramic view of postwar America. Nonfiction works include *Tour of Duty* (1946), *Men Who Made the Nation* (1957), *Mr. Wilson's War* (1963), and his autobiographical *The Best Times* (1967). Posthumously published were *Easter Island* (1971), a travel book, and *The Fourteenth Chronicle* (1973), his diaries and letters.

For more information about Spence's Point, contact the Westmoreland County Museum at (804) 493-8440.

SOUTH ATLANTIC *Virginia*

243

FURTHER READING *John Dos Passos* by Lisa Nanney (1998) ◢

JOHN FOX, JR. MUSEUM

Home of Chronicler of Appalachia

LOCATION Southwest Virginia in the Cumberland Mountain range near the Kentucky border, in Big Stone Gap, at 117 E. Shawnee Ave.

The John Fox, Jr. Museum ($) is open for guided tours Tuesday through Sunday from 2 p.m. to 5 p.m. beginning the Wednesday after Memorial Day through the Sunday before Labor Day. Closed all holidays. Tours for 20 or more can be scheduled any time. For more information contact The John Fox, Jr. Museum. P.O Box 1976, Big Stone Gap VA 24219. Telephone (276) 523-1235 or (276) 523-2747. E-mail: info@bigstonegap.org. On the Net: www.bigstonegap.org/attract/johnfox,.htm.

FRAME OF REFERENCE John Fox, Jr. moved to Big Stone Gap in 1890. The house was built in 1888. It is a Virginia and National Historic Landmark.

SIGNIFICANCE In this house, Fox wrote *The Trail of the Lonesome Pine*, the novel on which the official state play of Virginia is based; 14 other novels; and more than 500 short stories. *The Little Shepherd of Kingdom Come* (1903), a 322-page Civil War novel, was Fox's best-known and best-selling book, although *The Trail of the Lonesome Pine* was better accepted among critics. *The Trail* deals with the results of progress, both good and bad, upon mountain culture and helped put this Appalachian region on the literary map. Fox traveled widely and worked as a war correspondent in Cuba in 1898 and in the Orient in 1904.

ABOUT THE SITE The Fox family may have modeled this fabulous home after Sir Walter Scott's Abbotsford. The rambling, 20-room house, often expanded to accommodate a growing family, has a rustic exterior of cedar shakes and an L-shaped stone porch on two sides. To tour, enter the front gate and go to the right side porch. Twelve rooms are open to the public.

The house is much as the Fox family left it, and furnishings are original right down to the pots and pans in the kitchen, where today chefs prepare catered luncheons and dinners. The most unusual furnishings include Fox's desk and Remington typewriter (although he usually wrote in long-hand and refused to dictate), a bedroom table featuring hand-carved dogs, a decorated porcelain chamber pot, the family's unusual rose medallion china and a dining room sideboard that Fox family ancestors brought from England when they arrived in the 1700s. This is the oldest piece in the house.

In the downstairs bedroom, you can view the rosewood bed in which the writer, as well has his nine siblings, were born. The bedroom has a matching dresser with marble top. In the upstairs hallway, look for the framed "peacock chart" outlining family ancestry. Fox was a descendant of 16 signers of the Magna Carta (1215) and his family was considered British royalty. The Fox home was a stop for many distinguished visitors from England.

HOT TIPS The Fox Museum is open for private functions by reservation. Park free on-street in front of the house, which is handicapped-accessible on the first floor.

If you visit Big Stone Gap during late June, and July and August, be sure to catch the ***Trail of the Lonesome Pine* outdoor drama** ($) at the June Tolliver Playhouse, 6 blocks from the museum on Clinton Avenue. The play, the official outdoor drama of Virginia, opened in 1964. Based on Fox's best-selling novel of the same name, the musical drama weaves a tale of love, feuding and defiance after the discovery of coal in the Virginia mountains in the early 1890s. It features original folk music and a 72-foot panoramic painting of Powell Valley.

For information, contact the Lonesome Pines Arts & Crafts Association at (276) 523-1235 or toll free 1-800-362-0149, or write the Fox Museum.

THE BEST STUFF Staff say visitors are enamored with the embossed suede leather-bound program from a welcome home dinner for Theodore Roosevelt after the Spanish-American War (1898). Fox attended the gentlemen-only event in New York for the future president, a close friend of Fox's. You'll also see the beaver top hat Fox wore on formal occasions, still stored in a satin-lined, leather hat box.

THE WRITER AND HIS WORK
BORN: Dec. 6, 1862, in Stony Point, Va.
DIED: July 8, 1919, in a Knoxville, Tenn., hospital
MARRIED: Fritzie Scheff, 1908; divorced 1913
EDUCATED: Transylvania College; Harvard University, graduating cum laude in 1883 as the youngest member of his class; attended Columbia University Law School
IMPORTANT WORKS: *A Cumberland Vendetta and Other Stories* (1895);

Hell-Fer-Sartain and Other Stories (1897); *The Kentuckians* (1897); *A Mountain Europa* (1899); *Crittenden* (1900); *Blue-Grass and Rhododendron* (1901), a collection of essays; *The Little Shepherd of Kingdom Come* (1903); *Christmas Eve on Lonesome and Other Stories* (1904); *Following the Sun Flag: A Vain Pursuit Through Manchuria* (1905); *A Knight of the Cumberland* (1906); *The Trail of the Lonesome Pine* (1908); *The Heart of the Hills* (1913); *In Happy Valley* (1917); *Erskine Dale, Pioneer* (1920); and *The Purple Rhododendron* (posthumously in 1967).

INTERESTING BIO FACT: Fox's wife, Fritzie Scheff, a flamboyant Austrian prima donna, brought her 11-trunk fabulous wardrobe — reportedly with more than 100 pairs of shoes — and her colorful lifestyle to little Big Stone Gap. The house displays a few pictures of her. In his five years of their marriage, Fox did not publish a single book. Two later books received little recognition.

FURTHER READING *John Fox, Jr.: Appalachian Author* by Bill York (2002); *John Fox Jr* by Warren Titus (1971)

ELSEWHERE IN THE AREA H.W. Meador Coal Museum at East Third and Shawnee Avenue; June Tolliver House, once home of the heroine of *The Trail of the Lonesome Pine,* on Clinton Avenue East; and the Southwest Virginia Museum downtown. ⬖

ELLEN GLASGOW HOUSE

Home of Southern Novelist

After years of varied uses, the nearly 170-year-old former home of Pulitzer Prize-winning author Ellen Anderson Gholson Glasgow in **Richmond, Va.**, is now a private residence and business offices. A small plaque to the right of the front door marks the site. The stately, Greek Revival-style house at One West Main Street in downtown Richmond, former capital of the Confederacy, was the social historian's home for 50 years. The residence portion of the site is not open to the public, but the owners do open their doors to serious students and college classes on occasion.

Glasgow typed all but one of her 21 novels in her study, surrounded by exotic, imported wallpaper that she asked in her will to be preserved. She also wrote a collection of poems, a collection of stories and a book of literary criticism.

Her penetrating novels tell of the customs, mores and hardships following Reconstruction in the South. They weave a social history of her native Virginia. Glasgow's novels include *The Descendant* (1897); *The Deliverance* (1904); *Virginia* (1913); *Life and Gabriella* (1916); and *Barren Ground* (1925); *The Romantic Comedians* (1926); *They Stooped to Folly* (1929) and *The Sheltered Life* (1932), for which she was awarded the Pulitzer Prize in 1941. In 1942 she also received the Pulitzer Prize for her last published novel, *In This Our Life*.

At age 13, Glasgow moved into the 1841 Richmond house that her father, Francis Thomas Glasgow, superintendent of an iron works factory, bought in 1887. She was born in a nearby house on April 22, 1873, the eighth of 13 children, and lived at One Main Street until her death in 1945. Glasgow received no formal schooling but was extremely well-read and knowledgeable in the areas of philosophy, science and literature. As a popular writer of her time (she made the bestseller list five times), she entertained many contemporary literary figures, including **Gertrude Stein** and **Margaret Mitchell**.

A Richmond family bought the Glasgow House in 1986, returning the main portion of the house to a private residence for the first time since Glasgow's death. The house retains its massive tree-trunk columned back porch, carved interior moldings and three original items: a crystal chandelier, a front-hall light fixture and a mirror over the front parlor mantel. Some say the mirror was bought from fourth president James Madison, a Virginian. The two-story house with basement and carriage house has been painted a tan color to reflect the original color of stucco that covers the thick brick walls. The house had been painted gray for nearly 100 years. Glasgow referred to her home as "The Old Gray House."

Ghost stories about the house abound. Some visitors to the house have heard eerie sounds and seen other-worldly presences. Glasgow herself wrote that during her many years alone in the house "ghosts were my only companions." In her autobiography, *The Woman Within*, published posthumously, Glasgow describes a frightening encounter with a malevolent force.

Glasgow died of heart disease on Nov. 21, 1945, while sleeping in her second-floor bedroom of her beloved home. She is buried in Hollywood Cemetery in Richmond next to a gravesite believed to be that of Confederate Gen. J.E.B. Stuart.

FURTHER READING *Ellen Glasgow: A Biography* by Susan Goodman (1998) ◢

THOMAS JEFFERSON'S MONTICELLO

Home of Author of Declaration of Independence

LOCATION Central Virginia, 3 miles southeast of Charlottesville. From I-64 traveling east, take Exit 121A; from I-64 traveling west, take Exit 121. Take VA 20 south. Turn left onto VA 53 and follow signs to parking area.

Monticello ($) is open for guided tours daily March 1 through Oct. 31, 8 a.m. to 5 p.m. except Dec. 25; and Nov. 1 to Feb. 28 from 9 a.m. to 4:30 p.m. The nearby Monticello Visitor Center ($) on VA 20 is open daily March 1 to Oct. 31 from 9 a.m. to 5:30 p.m. It closes at 5 p.m. November through February. The Thomas Jefferson Memorial Foundation, Inc. owns and operates Monticello.

For information contact Development and Public Affairs Dept., Monticello, Box 217, Charlottesville, VA 22902. Tel. (804) 984-9800/9822. On the Net: www.monticello.org.

FRAME OF REFERENCE Monticello was Thomas Jefferson's mountaintop home from 1768, when he began construction, to his death in the house on July 4, 1826.

SIGNIFICANCE Monticello was the center of Jefferson's private life and stands as an autobiographical monument to his varied interests and ingenuity. Jefferson, in addition to being third president of the United States, vice president, governor of Virginia, minister to the Court of Louis XVI of France, U.S. secretary of state and founder of the University of Virginia, also was a prolific writer.

Although Jefferson is remembered as author of the Declaration of Independence, his 20,000 letters, his addresses, and his public and private papers document history and record this founding father's firm belief in democracy, the common man and natural rights. His writings continue to mold the American spirit.

Jefferson worked for freedom of speech, press, religion, and other civil liberties. He also compiled a *Manual of Parliamentary Practice* and prepared written vocabularies of Indian languages. He zealously supported the addition of the Bill of Rights to the U.S. Constitution. A consummate reader, Jefferson's vast book collection became the nucleus for the modern Library of Congress in Washington, D.C.

Jefferson designed Monticello and filled it with items that uniquely describe his varied life and many accomplishments. Jefferson's family and descendants are buried on the grounds. Monticello speaks volumes about the author of the Declaration of Independence, a man well-read enough and thoughtful enough to pen the document that framed enduring American ideals and lay the foundation for a land of idealized freedom. Monticello is considered one of America's architectural masterpieces.

ABOUT THE SITE Jefferson described Monticello, which means "little mountain," as his "essay in architecture." He built, remodeled and rebuilt the brick three-story, 21-room home over 40 years, reflecting The Father of American Architecture's pleasure in "putting up and pulling down."

The thrill of visiting the mansion, once the center of a 5,000-acre plantation, is savoring Jefferson's ingenious adaptation of inventions, the delightful twists and turns of Roman neoclassic architecture and decor of his custom-built home, and beholding the gardens, orchards and mountain beauty surrounding it. The house is 100 percent original. Visiting Monticello is like conversing with the man who contributed so much to America.

Beneath the main house, you can peer into the refurbished kitchen and "bottling room," where slaves Ursula and Jupiter transferred cider from 126-gallon kegs to bottles. Dusty bottles line the shelves in the wine cellar today.

In Monticello itself, modern machines measure heat and humidity. Today, instead of important guests (many uninvited and staying for weeks) and the houseful of extended family and 12 grandchildren, tourists from around world roam the estate.

A short walk takes you to the family cemetery, where Jefferson and many of his 2,000 descendants are buried, some recently. The inscription on the marble obelisk marking Jefferson's grave are as he instructed: *Here was buried Thomas Jefferson, Author of the Declaration of American Independence, Of the Statute of Virginia for Religious Freedom, and the Father of the University of Virginia.* Jefferson made no mention of his political positions, which he called "his duty."

Near the site entrance at the intersection of I-64 and Rt. 20, the Monticello Visitor Center offers fascinating exhibits that chronicle the life of this extraordinary man. More than 400 personal possessions and artifacts from Monticello are on display. The Visitor Center houses a gift shop and theater, where you can see a 1/2-hour film, *Thomas Jefferson: The Pursuit of Liberty.* The film runs daily at 11 a.m. and 2 p.m.

Monticello and its grounds continually undergo study and restoration. The search for additional original Monticello items never ceases.

HOT TIPS Guided tours include only the first floor of the home, although guides are available for scheduled tours of the gardens. A short shuttlebus ride takes visitors from the Monticello parking lot to the house. Allow two hours to visit Monticello. In season, long lines for guided tours may require additional time. Add another 1 1/2 hours for the museum and movie at the visitor center.

At the visitor center, you can purchase Resource Packets geared to the classroom or for use during visits with kids. For information on school programs, contact: Monticello Education Dept. P.O. Box 316, Charlottesville, VA 22902. Tel. (804) 984-9853. Snacks are available at the Monticello ticket booth on the grounds. Picnic facilities and a greenhouse offering Monticello plants stand nearby. For a culinary trip into history, catch the luncheon buffet at 1784 Michie Tavern near Monticello.

The ticket booth gives $2 bills as change. The bill features Jefferson's portrait and an engraving of the signing of the Declaration of Independence and is a great souvenir.

THE BEST STUFF The moment you step into Monticello's entrance hall, you experience Jefferson's thoughtful, ingenious personality. The airy, two-story room functioned as a greeting hall for guests and as Jefferson's private museum. The room houses paintings, sculptures, 350 maps and globes and Native American artifacts. Here, Jefferson hung moose, deer and elk antlers from the western expeditions of **Lewis and Clark** (directed by President Jefferson) according to size so that guests could make comparisons.

A glass exhibit case protects bones of a woolly mammoth, extinct for 10,000 years, brought from Kentucky by William Clark. The Jefferson-designed seven-day clock towers next to the arched front door. A network of weights and cables shows the day of week on this unique timepiece. You have to go into the basement to see the bottom of the clock (Friday and Saturday). Jefferson designed the clock for his Philadelphia home during his days at the Continental Congress. It didn't quite fit Monticello's wall, so Jefferson solved the problem with a hole in the foyer floor.

The best stuff also includes:

JEFFERSON'S "CABINET," or personal study. Between the library of 10,000 volumes and the master bedroom, this many-sided room was where

Jefferson read (in seven languages), wrote letters and conducted scientific experiments. A five-sided revolving bookstand Jefferson designed allowed him to read five books at once. Here, Jefferson received word the Louisiana Purchase was completed.

JEFFERSON'S BEDROOM. The bed rests in an alcove between the bedroom and cabinet so that Jefferson could retire from either room. The bedroom features a skylight (Monticello boasted 13 of these, which were rare at the time.), a walk-up closet over the bed and a wooden medicine chest. Jefferson served as his own physician, studying and experimenting with herbs. The polished chest has 150 glass bottles filled with homegrown herbs. The library had 150 medical books. The 6-foot, 3-inch bed is where Jefferson died.

MULBERRY ROW. Here is where you can learn about the complex African-American community at Monticello. This 1,000-foot long dirt road was the center of activity to support Monticello for the 60 years of Jefferson's residency. Along the road, named for the mulberry trees that lined it, stood 17 structures. They include slave cabins, a stable, wood- and iron-working shops and a smokehouse. Only three partial stone buildings survive today. An orchard and two-acre vegetable garden, recreated from Jefferson's extensive records, spread over land next to Mulberry Row.

EXHIBITS: Don't pass up the extensive exhibit of Jefferson possessions and Monticello artifacts at the visitors center. Note especially the display of the contents of Jefferson's pockets, including a red leather pocketbook, the knife he used to scrape mud from his boots, and the "ivory notebook", small strips of ivory that spread out like a fan. Jefferson carried these notebooks for his copious notes on subjects such as his observations on weather. He was one of the first systematic observers of American climate and made daily notations of temperature. Jefferson also attached an odometer to the carriage he designed and recorded its mileage.

Young people will be interested in copies of letters Jefferson wrote to his daughter, instructing her on use of time. He suggested she read French from 3 p.m. to 4 p.m. and "exercise yourself in music" from 4 p.m. to 5 p.m. Jefferson himself was an accomplished violinist.

252   **THE WRITER AND HIS WORK**

BORN: April 13, 1743, at Shadwell, the family farm in Goochland (now Albemarle) County, Va.

DIED: July 4, 1826, the 50th anniversary of Declaration of Independence, at Monticello

MARRIED: Martha Wayles Skelton, 1772; six children (Two survived to adulthood.)

EDUCATED: The College of William and Mary, 1760-1762; studied law

IMPORTANT WORKS: *Summary of the Rights of British America* (1774); *Declaration of Independence* (1776); "Autobiography" an account of Jefferson's life up to 1790, edited by his grandson T.J. Randolph and first printed in *Memoirs, Correspondence, and Miscellanies* (1829); *Notes on the State of Virginia* (1781)

INTERESTING BIO FACT: Jefferson was 33 when he wrote the first draft of the Declaration of Independence in Philadelphia.

FURTHER READING *The Worlds of Thomas Jefferson* (2002) by Susan R. Stein; *Restoration of the Republic: The Jeffersonian Ideal in 21st Century America* (2002) by Cary Hart; *American Sphinx: The Character of Thomas Jefferson* (1998) by Joseph J. Ellis; *The Adams-Jefferson Letters: The Complete Correspondence Between Thomas Jefferson and Abigail and John Adams* (1998) edited by Lester J. Cappon

ELSEWHERE IN THE AREA Historic Michie Tavern (1784), one of the oldest homesteads in America, on VA 53 near Monticello; The University of Virginia, the "academic village" Jefferson designed; and James Monroe's 535-acre estate, Ash Lawn-Highland, south of Monticello on VA 53. ◮

EDGAR ALLAN POE MUSEUM

Documenting Dark Genius' Life in Richmond

LOCATION Richmond, Va., in the heart of the city's Historic Shockoe Bottom district east of downtown, in The Old Stone House at 1914-16 E. Main Street. From I-95 north, take Exit 74-B to Franklin Street at left. Take next right onto 15th Street, then next left at traffic light onto East Main Street. Museum ($) is 4 blocks east on left. From I-95 south, take Exit 74-C (Broad Street) and bear right (Route 33) as exit ramp splits to 17th Street. Turn left onto Broad Street at next traffic light to 18th Street and turn right onto 20th Street. Museum is 2 blocks ahead on right at East Main and 20th streets. From east and west via I-64, go to I-95 south.

The museum is open Tuesday through Saturday, 10 a.m. to 5 p.m., and Sunday 11 a.m. to 5 p.m. Museum shop closes 4:30 p.m. Holiday hours vary. Guided tours begin on the hour with last at 4 p.m. Group tours by reservation.

For more information, contact the Edgar Allan Poe Museum, 1914 East Main St., Richmond, VA 23223. Telephone (804) 648-5523 or toll-free at 1-888-21E-APOE. E-mail: info@poemuseum.org. On the Net: www.poemuseum.org.

FRAME OF REFERENCE Edgar Allan Poe lived and wrote in Richmond, where he moved with his parents at age 2, throughout his adult life. Although he never lived in the Old Stone House, he lived in five other houses in the area and worked at several nearby sites until his death in 1849. Poe, however, would have been familiar with the house, more than 100 years old at Poe's birth.

SIGNIFICANCE Poe has profoundly influenced literature not only in America but worldwide. Poe created or mastered five literary genres: short story, detective fiction, science fiction, lyric poetry and the horror story. Best known for his poems (especially the lyrical poem *The Raven*) and short fiction, Poe helped transform the short story from anecdote to art and practically created the detective story. He perfected the psychological thriller. Poe also produced some of the most influential literary criticism of his time, much written in Richmond as editor of the Southern Literary Messenger from 1835 to 1837.

Since the 1880's, scholars have been trying to establish a complete listing of Poe's writings. Most of Poe's works appeared in magazines and newspapers, many of which are lost. Poe's creations have remained in print for 150 years and have fascinated modern movie audiences. The 1961 film *The Pit and the Pendulum*, starring spook-master Vincent Price, ushered in a new age of horror movies.

The museum tells the story of the man called "America's Shakespeare," who spent most of his life in the town where his natural parents married. His actress mother also died in a theater fire in Richmond. The museum documents Poe's life, works and career, focusing on his accomplishments in Richmond.

ABOUT THE SITE The two-story Old Stone House, circa 1754, is the oldest structure within the original boundaries of Richmond. The museum, opened in 1922, displays much of the largest collection of Poe memorabilia in the world. Here, you'll find original Poe manuscripts, letters, reviews and rare first editions. The museum maintains a Poe library open by appointment and a museum shop full of "Poeana."

The five-building complex, surrounded by a wrought-iron fence, includes the Memorial Building, a converted carriage house, and the Enchanted Garden. The formal garden memorializes Poe's romantic poetry and enshrines a Poe bust. Also on display: Poe's desk and feather pen; five portraits of Poe, including the famous 1848 daguerreotype; Poe's embroidered cream-colored silk vest; and a large marble memorial to Poe once housed at the Metropolitan Museum of Art in New York.

At the museum you also can see:

THE WALKING STICK Poe accidentally left in Richmond just before his mysterious death, the key found in his pocket during his final delirious days that opened the trunk in which he packed his few possessions, and the lock of hair a friend clipped from the poet's famously lofty brow after he died.

AN EXHIBIT OF POE FIRST EDITIONS includes the expected — an 1845 copy of *The Raven and other Poems,* and the unexpected — a rare textbook on conchology (shell collecting). When the book became a bestseller, Poe was accused of plagiarism when it was discovered he wrote only the introduction.

POE'S FIRST BOOK, *Tamerlane,* the 1827 publishing flop that is now the one of the rarest and most valuable pieces of American literature. You'll also see an original manuscript of the mysterious prose-poem *Siope* written in Poe's fastidious hand and the edition of *Godey's Lady's* Book containing Poe's scandalous and highly popular *Literati of New York City*. This is the gleefully opinionated piece of literary gossip that made Poe unwelcome in the drawing rooms of successful New York writers while ensuring his East Coast notoriety.

FORTY-THREE ILLUSTRATIONS by James William Carling in the Raven Room. Carling submitted these drawings to Harper and Brothers Publishers in 1882 for its edition of *The Raven*. Gustave Dore submitted illustrations that the magazine used.

HOT TIPS Plan to spend 1 1/2 hours at the site if you take the guided tour. Parking is in a small lot off 20th Street. Time-limited parking is available on 20th Street. Site restroom is unisex. To view the Edgar Allan Poe Room at the University of Virginia, where Poe studied a year, go online to www.student.virginia.edu/ ~ravens/poe-rm.html. For other Poe sites, see Pennsylvania and Maryland in the book.

THE BEST STUFF Poe's father abandoned him, and after his mother died he became the ward of the prominent John Allen family of Richmond. Although Poe led a pampered life, Allen never liked Poe. In keeping with the gloomy persona of Poe, known for his drinking sprees and the mystery surrounding his death at age 40, the museum features a Death Room detailing 12 of the 26 theories about how he died. They include severe beating, diabetes, rabies, epilepsy, carbon monoxide poisoning and alcohol dehydrogenase.

THE WRITER AND HIS WORK

BORN: Jan. 19, 1809, Boston, to actor parents

DIED: Oct. 7, 1849, in Baltimore, Md.; buried in Presbyterian Cemetery, Baltimore

EDUCATED: London boarding school; William Burke Academy, Richmond; University of Virginia and West Point, from which he was dismissed

MARRIED: Virginia Clemm, Poe's 14-year-old cousin, 1836; died age 26

IMPORTANT WORKS: Poems — *Tamerlane* (1827); *To The River* (1829); *The City In The Sea* (1831); *Lenore* (1831); *To One In Paradise* (1834); *The Conqueror Worm* (1843); *The Raven* (1845), *The Bells* (1848); *To Helen* (1848); *Eldorado* (1849); *Annabelle Lee* (1849). Long tales — *The Gold Bug* (1843), *The Murders In The Rue Morgue* (1841); *The Mystery of Marie Roget* (1850); *The Narrative of Arthur Gordon Pym Of Nantucket* (1850).

Stories — *Ms. Found In A Bottle* (1833); *Berenice* (1835); *King Pest* (1835); *The Fall of The House of Usher* (1839); *William Wilson* (1839); *A Descent Into The Maelstrom* (1841); *The Pit and The Pendulum* (1842); *The Masque of the Red Death* (1842); *The Tell-Tale Heart* (1843), *The Purloined Letter* (1845); *The Cask of Amontillado* (1846); *Some Words With A Mummy* (1850); *The Premature Burial* (1850); *Hop Frog* (1850); *Serenade* (1850); *The Man That Was Used Up* (1850); *The System Of Dr. Tarr And Prof. Fether* (1850); *Diddling* (1850); *The Imp Of The Perverse* (1850); *The Domain Of Arnheim* (1850); *The Landscape Garden* (1850)

INTERESTING BIO FACT: The cause of Poe's death remains an intriguing mystery. On Sept. 28, 1849, the newly engaged Poe got off a train in Baltimore drunk and feverish. He went to the house of a friend, Dr. Nathan C. Brooks, who was not home. Poe wandered for five days. On Oct. 3, another doctor friend, J.E. Snodgrass, went to Ryan's Saloon, where he found Poe semi-conscious and lying on a plank suspended between two barrels on the sidewalk. Poe was rushed to a nearby hospital, arriving in a coma. He awoke delirious and ranted for two days. On Sunday, Oct. 7, he spoke his last words, "Lord help my poor soul."

FURTHER READING *Edgar Allan Poe, His Life and Legacy* by Jeffrey Meyers (1992); *Edgar Allan Poe, Mournful and Never-ending Remembrance* by Kenneth Silverman (1991); *The Poe Log* by Dwight Thomas (1987); *The Tales of Poe - Modern Critical Interpretations* (1987) by Harold Bloom; *Edgar Allan Poe, The Creation of a Reputation* by Miller Robbins (1983)

ELSEWHERE IN THE AREA Poe fans can visit the sites of five homes where the writer lived while in Richmond, as well as the site of the Southern Literary Messenger. None of the structures remain, all victims of urban growth. Ask for directions to the sites at the Poe museum. ⌂

FINDING JOHN SMITH

America's Earliest Historian at Jamestown

If literature doesn't pop into your mind when you think of **Jamestown Va.**, site of the first permanent English colony in North America, think again. According to some historians, American literature began with Capt. John Smith. He was the leader of the band of fortune-seeking English men and boys who sailed to coastal Virginia nearly 400 years ago, and he penned an important history of the New World during his stay from May 1607 through October 1609.

Smith's first book, *A True Relation of Such Occurences and Accidents of Note as Hath Happened in Virginia* (1609), picturesquely told of clashes with red men. Some scholars claim this was the first American work of literature. (Others, however, say no, since it was written by an Englishman and published in London.)

Smith also wrote *Map of Virginia with a Description of the Country* (1612); *A Description of New England* (1616 and reprinted 8 years later in *The Generall Historie*); and *New England Trials* (1620, 1622). *The Generall Historie of Virginia, New England, and the Summer Isles* (1624) told of the New World's economic promise. The book gave heroic accounts of non-Puritans and American Indians, especially Pocahontas, princess daughter of Chief Powhatan.

Smith also penned *The True Travels, Adventures, and Observations of Captaine John Smith* (1630); and *Advertisements for the Unexperienced Plant-ers of New England, or Anywhere* (1631). In short, the writings of Smith, born circa 1579, were advertisements for colonization. They glorified Smith himself, the blustering soldier of fortune whose exploits, valor and background survive only in his stories.

Jamestown, named for King James I, was the first permanent English settlement in North America, 13 years before the Pilgrims landed at Plymouth Rock and 42 years after the Spanish settled St. Augustine, Fla. Jamestown was the capital of Virginia for 92 years before the last of a series of disastrous fires sent the capital upriver to Williamsburg. The Virginia Company of London sponsored the settlement in search of fortune. This was the first center of religious, social, economic and political life in England's New World.

When the governor of Jamestown was executed for treason in December 1607, Smith was elected president of Jamestown. He began to organize trade with the natives and was captured by Chief Powhatan. Smith barely escaped death when Pocahontas pleaded for his life.

A visit to Jamestown today offers a palpable vista into what Smith experienced and wrote about during his stay in Virginia. After Smith's 2-year stay at the colony, he lived in England until 1614, then returned to America to explore the area from the Penobscot River to Cape Cod. He christened the area New England, thinking that the vast area deserved its own name. Smith made a map of the coast, bestowing English names like Cape Ann, Charles River and Plymouth. Smith died in London on June 21, 1631.

Today's Jamestown consists of two parts: 1,500-acre Jamestown Island, the archaeological site where the English colony began, and Jamestown Settlement, the 20-acre re-creation of that colony adjacent to the island. Both are part of the Colonial National Historical Park, which also includes Yorktown, 8 miles northeast on Colonial Parkway, and the Cape Henry Memorial.

Jamestown Settlement, operated by the Commonwealth of Virginia's Jamestown-Yorktown Foundation, is open daily, except Dec. 25 and Jan. 1, from 9 a.m. to 5 p.m. The National Park Service operates James Island ($) along with the Virginia Society of Antiquities. The site is open daily, except Dec. 25, from 8:30 a.m. to 4:30 p.m., with extended hours April through October.

For more information about both sites, contact Colonial National Historical Park. P.O. Box 210, Yorktown, VA 23690 Tel. (757) 898-3400. On the Net: www.nps.gov/colo. For more on John Smith, go to http://guweb2 .gonzaga.edu/faculty/campbell/en1310/smith.

Further Reading *Captain John Smith, Works, 1608-1631*, edited by Edward Arber (1884, re-edited by A.G. Bradley 1910); *Captain John Smith, His Life & Legend* by Bradford Smith (1953); *Captain John Smith* by Everett Emerson (1993) ◪

ANNE SPENCER HOUSE AND GARDEN

Where Harlem Renaissance Poet Drew Inspiration

LOCATION Central Virginia, in Lynchburg, at 1313 Pierce St. Take I-29 to the Kemper Street/VA 501 business exit. Go west on Kemper Street and take right on 12th Street. Go two blocks and turn right onto Pierce Street. The site is two blocks ahead.

The Anne Spencer House and Garden ($), operated by Anne Spencer Memorial Foundation, is open for tours Monday through Saturday, 10 a.m. to 4 p.m., by appointment only. Closed Dec. 25 and Jan. 1. Call for tours as far as possible in advance at (804) 845-1313 or (804) 845-2211.

For more information contact The Anne Bethel Spencer House and Garden, P.O. Box 168, Lynchburg, VA 24501. Telephone (804) 845-0517. On the Net: www.lynchburgbiz.com/Anne_Spencer/gallery.html.

FRAME OF REFERENCE Anne Bethel Scales Spencer lived in this house from 1908 until her death in 1975. Her husband, Edward Spencer, built the house, now a National Historic Landmark, in 1903. It opened to the public in 1977.

SIGNIFICANCE Spencer was an internationally acclaimed poet who was part of the Harlem Renaissance, the Black literary movement of the 1920s that charted a new course in American literature. The movement included Langston Hughes, Jean Toomer and **Zora Neale Hurston**. Spencer published extensively from 1920 through 1935. Her poems appeared in the era's most prestigious collections, including *The Book of American Negro Poetry* by **James Weldon Johnson** (1922). Many of her later writings were lost.

Spencer filled her poems with themes of friendship, human relations, personal rights of women and contempt for racial discrimination. Her 50 complete poems often reflect a search for beauty and meaning in a dark world.

For 70 years, Spencer drew inspiration for her writing from the formal garden behind her house. She fashioned metaphors for human life by using images of birds, flowers and insects. She often sought sanctuary in her garden after a day working as the librarian at nearby **Paul Laurence Dunbar** High School (named for the Ohio poet), Lynchburg's segregation-era African-American high school. The school, once a proud symbol of black achievement, was demolished in 1970.

ABOUT THE SITE The rambling, two-story house with brown shingles, slate roof and mint green shutters stands inconspicuously one door down from the Wayside Gospel Temple in a quiet residential neighborhood. Edward Spencer built a small cottage of similar materials in the garden for his writer wife, which she filled with pictures, books and things she loved. Edward named the garden Edankrall. To get the garden's name, he combined his and his wife's first names (Ed, Ann) and grafted the African word "krall," meaning dwelling, to them.

The home's first floor includes living and dining rooms, sunroom, kitchen and library, where Edward built a phone booth to ensure his busy wife's privacy. Upstairs are three bedrooms, a second sunroom and a walk-in linen closet, once son Chauncey's bedroom. The Spencers fashioned the attic into a dormitory for grandchildren.

Spencer's warm home attracted friends and neighbors, as well as such American luminaries as George Washington Carver, **Martin Luther King Jr.** and Thurgood Marshall. The house remains almost exactly as Spencer left it.

HOT TIPS Volunteers operate the site, so it's wise to arrange tours as far in advance as possible. Parking is on-street. If you can get your hands on it, the 1980 documentary, *Echoes from the Garden: The Anne Spencer Story*, will aid your visit. For information on the Annual Anne Spencer Foundation Poetry Contest, contact the museum.

THE BEST STUFF The gates of Edankrall, the garden and cottage where Spencer found solitude and inspiration, usually stand open to curious visitors at any time. The poet made Edankrall and her little study in the garden her refuge. From the neat rows of roses, tulips and flowering trees, she drew inspiration for the poems that would establish and secure her reputation as a thinker and writer of national significance.

The garden, the width of the house and the depth of the block, has three sections. Spencer's prized roses, the oldest dating back to 1910, occupy the area next to the house. The cottage/study dominates the second section. Inside, photos and framed mementos cover the walls. Spencer's simple desk, amid plain, functional furniture and with a wood stove nearby, looks out windows to her garden. In front, a vine-covered pergola, replaced by a local boy scout troop, blooms in spring. Brick-lined gravel paths lead visitors through to a goldfish pond in the back area. A cast head of an Ibo tribesman, given to Spencer by the founder of the NAACP, **W.E.B. Dubois** (see Massachusetts in this book), watches over the pond.

THE WRITER AND HER WORK

BORN: Feb. 6, 1882, in Henry County, Va., an only child

DIED: 1975 in Lynchburg

EDUCATED: Virginia Theological Seminary and College, valedictorian

MARRIED: Edward A. Spencer, 1901; two daughters, one son

IMPORTANT WORKS: *Before the Feast at Shushan*; *At the Carnival*; *Dunbar*; *Change*; *Black Man O' Mine*; *The Wife-Woman*; *Translation*; *White Things*; *Substitution*; *Innocence*; *Neighbors*; *Questing*; *Life-Long*; *Poor Browning*; *I Have a Friend*; *Creed*; *Letter to My Sister*; *For Jim, Easter Eve*; *Lady, Lady*; *Lines to a Nasturtium (A Lover Muses)*; *Rime for the Christmas Baby*; *Grapes: Still-Life*; *Requiem.*

BIO FACTS: Spencer, daughter of civil rights activist parents, worked to establish the Lynchburg chapter of the NAACP in 1918. She became a black feminist voice, as well as one in love with earth's beauty. Harlem Renaissance writer **James Weldon Johnson** "discovered" her and selected her pen name, simply Anne Spencer. Johnson introduced her to influential social critic **H. L. Mencken**, who helped Spencer publish her first poem. Spencer later declined his patronage.

ELSEWHERE IN THE AREA The Legacy Museum of African-American History, 403 Monroe St.; Miller-Claytor House, on James Riverfront; Walton's Mountain Museum; Appomattox Court House National Historical Park, 18 miles east of Lynchburg off US 460 on VA 24.

ADDITIONAL READING *Time's Unfading Garden: Anne Spencer's Life and Poetry* by J. Lee Greene (1977); *Anne Spencer: Poet, Librarian* by Keith Clark ◭

SOUTH ATLANTIC *Virginia*

This small garden is half my world
I am nothing to it — when all is said,
I plant the thorn and kiss the rose
but they will grow when I am dead.

— ANNE SPENCER

BOOKER T. WASHINGTON MONUMENT

First Chapter of 'Up From Slavery'

LOCATION Central Virginia, in rural Franklin County near the small town of Hardy. The site is about 22 miles southeast of Roanoke and 45 miles southwest of Lynchburg. From north, south and west, take VA 220 to Highway 697, which turns into VA 122, to site. From east, take VA 24 to Va. 122 south to site.

The Booker T. Washington National Monument ($) is open daily except Jan. 1, Thanksgiving, and Dec. 25 from 9 a.m. to 5 p.m. For more information, contact Booker T. Washington National Monument, 21230 Booker T. Washington Highway, Hardy, VA 24101. Telephone (540) 721-2094. On the Net: www.nps.gov/bowa.

FRAME OF REFERENCE Booker Taliaferro Washington was born a slave on this tobacco farm in 1856 and left in 1865 at age 9, when he was set free after the Civil War. Despite the farm's small size, Washington always referred to the farm as a plantation.

SIGNIFICANCE Washington, author, statesman and leading educator of African-Americans at the end of the 19th century, is known for his autobiography, *Up From Slavery*. He founded Tuskegee Institute in Alabama in 1881 and later became an important and controversial leader of his race at a time when increasing racism in America had created an era of legalized oppression. Washington saw education as the true emancipator for ex-slaves.

From 1895 to 1915, Washington was the most powerful and influential African-American in the United States. Although in his time many black intellectuals maligned him for accommodating whites, today he is regarded as a major leader in the struggle for civil rights.

ABOUT THE SITE The 224-acre park encompasses most of the original 207-acre farm owned by the James Burroughs family. The site includes a reconstructed one-room log cabin like the one where Washington was born and lived as a boy, a smokehouse, blacksmith shed, corn crib tobacco barn and farm animal structures. The original sites of Washington's boyhood cabin, which served as the plantation kitchen, and the Burrough's five-room "big house" are outlined by stone slabs on the hill behind the visitor center.

Visitors can walk the 1.5 mile Jack-O-Lantern Branch Heritage Trail loop through much of the original Burroughs property. Along the way, informational kiosks tell about slave life and the ecosystem of the 19th-century farm. A 15-minute documentary, *Longing To Learn: The Booker T. Washington Story*, is shown on request in the visitor center, where you will find displays telling of the educator's life and a small bookstore.

HOT TIPS Plan to spend an hour at the site if you do not take the Jack-O-Lantern trail, which might be difficult for young children and adds another hour to the visit. Be prepared to walk and wear comfortable shoes; the land is hilly and often muddy. Some paths are paved but others are made of gravel. Dress for the weather. Do not pet or feed the animals. No food is available at the site, but small shopping plazas in the area have food outlets and the park has several picnic tables. The site is partially wheelchair accessible. Restrooms are located in the visitor center.

To make the most of your visit, read *Up From Slavery*, before visiting the site. The park offers many events geared toward young people and a Junior Ranger program for children 8 through 12.

THE BEST STUFF Costumed interpreters in summer take visitors around the recreated farm with its pigs, chickens and free-roaming ducks. Washington's 14- by 16-foot birth cabin has dirt floors which also served as beds, a big fireplace and crude furnishings and offers a hands-on lesson about the life of slaves when slavery was an integral part of American life. Teens and older visitors might enjoy the hiking trail, which notes places where the 20 Burroughs slaves might have mourned and buried their dead, courted, married, played and secretly hunted for food.

The visitor center displays a replica of an 1861 inventory of proprietor James Burroughs' belongings. It lists the value of "1 negro boy (Booker)" as $400. A man named Lee was valued at $1,000.

THE WRITER AND HIS WORKS
For details about Washington, look under Alabama in the East South Central section of this book.

INTERESTING BIO FACT: Washington walked to school in Franklin County — not as a student, but to carry books for one of James Burroughs' daughters. It was illegal to educate slaves. "I had the feeling that to get into a schoolhouse and study would be about the same as getting into paradise," he later wrote.

At age 16, he walked much of the 500 miles from West Virginia, where he lived after leaving the plantation, to tidewater Virginia. There, he enrolled in an ambitious, new school for black students, the Hampton Institute. The head teacher was suspicious of his rural ways and ragged clothes. She admitted young Washington only after he had cleaned a room to her satisfaction. ⌂

I was born in a typical log cabin, about fourteen by sixteen feet square. In this cabin I lived with my mother and a brother and sister till after the Civil War, when we were all declared free.

— BOOKER T. WASHINGTON
in *Up From Slavery*

PEARL S. BUCK BIRTHPLACE

Where East Meets West

LOCATION East central West Virginia, in Hillsboro, in the Little Levels of Pocahontas County, 10 miles south of Marlinton, on US 219. From north take I-81 to Highway 42/39 in Virginia, to Highway 39 west to US 219 south in West Virginia to the site. From south take I-81 north to I-64 west to US 219 north. From east and west take I-64. to US 219. The site is 30 miles north.

The Pearl S. Buck Birthplace ($) is open for guided tours from May 1 through Nov. 1, Monday through Saturday, from 9 a.m. to 4: 30 p.m. Reservations suggested. Open holidays except for Thanksgiving, Dec. 25 and Jan. 1. For more information contact Pearl S. Buck Birthplace Foundation, Inc., Box 126, Hillsboro, W. VA 24946. Telephone (304) 653-4430. On the Net: www.wvnet.edu:80omb00996/

FRAME OF REFERENCE Pearl Comfort Sydenstricker Buck was born in 1892 in this house, owned by Pearl's maternal grandparents, while her missionary parents were on furlough from the Orient. The family returned to China 6 months later.

SIGNIFICANCE Buck is the only American woman to have won both a Pulitzer Prize and the Nobel Prize for literature. She was one of the most popular American authors of her day, winning acclaim for her novels about life in China, especially *The Good Earth,* later a popular motion picture. The novel sold 1,800,000 copies in its first year and was awarded the Pulitzer Prize for fiction in 1932. It has been translated into more than 30 languages. Other film adaptations of Buck's works include *China Sky*, 1945 and *The Devil Never Sleeps / Satan Never Sleeps*, 1962.

Buck was a humanitarian, crusader for women's rights, editor of Asia magazine and philanthropist. During her 40-year career she published 80 works, including novels, plays, short story collections, poems, children's books and biographies. She also wrote five novels under the pseudonym John Sedges and translated Lo Guangzhong's (1330-1400) *The Water Margin / Men of the Marshes*, which appeared in 1933 under the title *All Men Are Brothers*.

Buck's Nobel Prize in 1938 made her the third American winner, following **Sinclair Lewis** and **Eugene O'Neill**. Only nine women have received the Nobel Prize for literature, including American writer Toni Morrison.

ABOUT THE SITE The rambling frame house is one of three main structures on 13 acres of the former 16-acre farm. The white house, with double front portico and chimneys at each end, was built by the Stultings, Buck's maternal family who emigrated from Holland in 1847. The house design was based on the grandparents' former home in Holland. The house has been restored to look as it did at the time of Pearl's birth.

Period rooms have some original family furnishings, including the Stulting family bed in grandfather's bedroom, hewn from cherrywood fence posts. Rooms also display Buck memorabilia, including her milk glass hand dish, a Chinese dress and her father's Chinese translation of the Bible. Pearl's father, a serious, scholarly man, spent years translating the Bible from Greek to Chinese. Visitors also will find mementos of the family's stay in the Orient throughout the house, including a Chinese vendor's drum, a black lacquer box, an embroidered silk belt purse and Chinese shoes.

You will find two other structures at the site: the Stulting Barn, housing farm implements of the late 1800s, and the Sydenstricker House, birthplace of Pearl's father. This two-room log house was dismantled and brought to the site from its original location 40 miles away. It has period furnishings. The historic house- museum opened to the public in 1974.

HOT TIPS Park in lot at site. Two floors of the three-story house are wheelchair accessible. Lunch can be provided for groups of 10 or more with advance notice.

THE BEST STUFF The upstairs bedroom where Pearl was born features a closet with wooden doors carved into an Oriental dragon and leaf design. Visitors are fascinated by the spindle bed in which Pearl's mother gave birth in her own childhood bedroom. A mold depicting the actual size of a woman's foot drives home the ancient Chinese practice of binding girl's feet.

THE WRITER AND HER WORK
BORN: June 26, 1892, in Hillsboro, to missionaries in China
DIED: March 6, 1973, Danby, Vt.
EDUCATED: Boarding school in Shanghai; Randolph-Macon Woman's College, 1914; M.A. in literature, Cornell University, 1926

MARRIED: John L. Buck, 1917, divorced 1935; Richard Walsh, 1935; nine adopted Asian children and one biological daughter

IMPORTANT WORKS: *East Wind, West Wind*, 1930; *The Good Earth*, 1931; *Sons*, 1932; *The Young Revolutionist*, 1932; *This Proud Heart*, 1938; *The Patriot*, 1939; *Of Men and Women*, 1941; *Dragon Seed*, 1942; *The Story of Dragon Seed*, 1944; *Portrait of a Marriage*, 1945; *The First Wife* (play), 1945; *The Angry Wife*, 1949; *The Child Who Never Grew*, 1950; *The Hidden Flower*, 1952; *Come My Beloved*, 1953; *Christine* (play), 1960; *The Christmas Ghost*, 1960; *Satan Never Sleeps*, 1961; *Fourteen Stories*, 1961; and *Hearts Come Home*, 1962; *Stories of China*, 1964; *Escape at Midnight and Other Stories*, 1964; *Fairy Tales of the Orient* (edited), 1965; *To My Daughters With Love*, 1967; *The New Year*, 1968; *The People of China*, 1968; *The Good Deed*, 1969; *Mandala*, 1970; *China As I See It*, 1970; *Pearl Buck's America*, 1971; *China Past and Present*, 1972; *All Under Heaven* (1974); *The Rainbow*, 1974; *Pearl S. Buck's Book of Christmas* (edited), 1974; *Words of Love*, 1974; *East and West*, 1975; and *The Woman Who Was Changed*, 1979.

ACCOLADES: Nobel Prize in Literature (1938); Pulitzer Prize for fiction (1932); National Institute of Arts and Letters (1936); American Academy of Arts and Letters (1951)

INTERESTING BIO FACT: Buck returned to America in 1934 after living in China and Japan for the first 40 years of her life. Buck and second husband Walsh bought a farm in Pennsylvania (see Pennsylvania in the Middle Atlantic region of this book) and were active in humanitarian causes through the East and West Association. The association worked for mutual understanding between the peoples of Asia and the United States. Buck also established Welcome House and The Pearl Buck Foundation to this end. Buck was a friend of Eleanor Roosevelt and anthropologist Margaret Mead and advocated the rights of women and racial equality. Because of these activities, the FBI kept detailed files on her for years.

Buck later focused her activities on children, raising millions of dollars for the adoption and fostering of Asian children often abandoned by their American fathers stationed in the Far East. She coined the word "Amerasian" to describe these children.

268   **FURTHER READING** *Pearl S. Buck* by Kang Liao (1997); *Pearl S. Buck: A Cultural Biography* by Peter Conn (1996); *The Several Worlds of Pearl S. Buck*, edited by Elizabeth J. Lipscomb (1994); *Pearl S. Buck: Good Earth*

Mother by Warren Sherk (1992); *Pearl S. Buck: The Final Chapter* by Beverly E. Rizzon (1988)

ELSEWHERE IN THE AREA Droop Mountain Battlefield State Park (Civil War) 5 miles south in Droop; Cass Scenic Railroad about 40 miles north in Cass, Cranberry Glades Botanical Area at Cranberry Mountain Visitor Center and Lost World Caverns 10 miles north ◬

Lew Wallace Study

ROBERT S. ABBOTT HOUSE

Faint Reminder of African-American Journalist

From 1926 until his death in 1940, Robert Sengstacke Abbott lived in a large house on the South Side of **Chicago, Ill.** Abbott was the most successful African-American publisher of his era. His newspaper, the Chicago Defender, which he established in 1905, encouraged southern blacks to leave the South and seek haven in the northern cities, particularly Chicago. Today, the deteriorated house, in the heart of Chicago's "Black belt," is a privately owned apartment building.

The Robert S. Abbott House, located at 4742 Martin Luther King Drive, became a National Historic Landmark in 1976. The Queen Anne-style structure with Greek neoclassical elements, has a Dutch-gable roof, stone parapet, dormers, portico and stunning interior staircase. The three-story building was a duplex when Abbott lived in one half of it, and the South Side was a Mecca of Black opulence.

Abbott was born in 1870 to slave parents in a cabin on St. Simons Island, Ga.

He graduated from Hampton Institute in Virginia, the same post-Civil War school from which **Booker T. Washington** graduated. He later earned a law degree from Kent State. But because he was black, Abbott could not find a job as a lawyer. He then founded The Chicago Defender with an initial investment of 25 cents. Abbott wrote the first four-page edition on his kitchen table and it was hand-delivered. By 1920, the newspaper had a paid circulation of 230,000.

The Defender soon became the most widely circulated black newspaper in the country and made Abbott one of America's first black self-made millionaires. The newspaper was a 20th-century pioneer, intelligently exploring the political and social condition of African-Americans and using red headlines on articles about the lynching of blacks in the South.

Abbott, considered the founder of the modern Black press, also published a short-lived paper called Abbott's Monthly. He died of Bright's disease on Feb. 29, 1940. He left the newspaper to his nephew and the Defender continued circulation as part of a newspaper chain called Sengstacke Enterprises, Inc. In 2003, multimedia company Real Times Inc. bought Sengstacke Enterprises.

For more information, contact the Chicago Commission on Landmarks, 33 North LaSalle St., Suite 1600, Chicago, IL 60602. Tel: (312) 744-3200.

E-mail: landmarks@cityofchicago.org. On the Net: www.ci.chi.il.us/land marks.

FURTHER READING *The Lonely Warrior: The Life and Times of Robert S. Abbott* by Roi Ottley (1955) ◮

EAST NORTH CENTRAL *Illinois*

ERNEST HEMINGWAY BIRTHPLACE

Documenting Novelist's Early Years

LOCATION Northern Illinois, in Oak Park, 10 miles west of downtown Chicago, at 339 N. Oak Park Ave. Reach Oak Park via I-290.

The Ernest Hemingway Birthplace ($) is open year-round, except Dec. 25 and Jan. 1, Monday through Friday, from 1 p.m. to 5 p.m., on Saturday from 10 a.m. to 5 p.m. and on Sunday 1 p.m. to 5 p.m. Tours available.

For more information, contact Ernest Hemingway Foundation of Oak Park, 339 N. Oak Park Ave., Oak Park, IL 00302. Tel. (708) 848-2222. E-Mail: EHFOP@sbcglobal.net. On the Net: www.ehfop.org.

FRAME OF REFERENCE Ernest Miller Hemingway was born in 1899 in this house, built in 1890. He lived here until his grandfather, who owned the house, died in 1905. The family then rented a nearby house and later built a home at 600 N. Kenilworth Ave. After graduating from high school, Hemingway left Oak Park in 1917 to become a reporter for the Kansas City Star. The house opened to the public in 1993.

SIGNIFICANCE The youth who would become a major American literary figure and win both the Nobel Prize in literature and the Pulitzer Prize spent his formative years in Oak Park. Hemingway, son of Clarence "Ed" Hemingway, a physician, and Clara Hall, was the second of six children. The writer grew up in a strict religious environment full of culture (his mother's pursuits) and church choir practice, as well as sports, hunting and fishing (his father's passions). In Oak Park, Hemingway received his only formal education at Oak Park and River Forest High School, where he wrote for the school newspaper and literary magazine. Here, the future novelist, journalist and short-story writer assimilated the Midwestern, small-town life that imbued his later work.

ABOUT THE SITE The three-story, white clapboard house with turret and full front porch has 12 rooms. These include Grace Hemingway's upstairs bedroom, where Ernest was born on July 21, 1899. The decidedly feminine bedroom has been refurbished according to historic photographs, complete with a dressing table draped in frilly white organdy and an iron bed.

Visitors enter the Victorian, Queen Anne-style house via a hallway with staircase to the right and library ahead. A spacious parlor opens to the left and leads into the dining room. In the parlor, Ernest's grandfather, "Abba," held daily devotions for the family. The sitting area in the parlor's front bay has been restored to show how the home looked during the Hemingways' residence, with flowered carpeting, pink and green striped wall covering, and Nottingham lace curtains. A fireplace with carved oak mantle dominates the south wall. A white plaster cornice with a bas-relief rose pattern encircles the room.

A living-room area, between the parlor and dining room, displays a piano, always a permanent fixture in the Hemingway household. Grace Hemingway, an opera singer early in her career, became a prominent music and voice instructor. The children all played musical instruments. Young Ernest played the cello.

Beyond double-pocket doors, you enter the dining room, then the kitchen, once described as a "dark room." A large black coal stove stood along one wall. Here hangs an original picture of Grace on the far wall near a butler's pantry.

A long hall runs the length of the house on the second floor, with entries to six bedrooms and one bathroom. Grandfather Hall slept in the turret bedroom, next to Dr. Hemingway's room. Little Ernest and Marcelline's nursery is right of Grace Hemingway's bedroom. The small stuffed dog with red tongue and shiny, shoe button eyes that sits on Ernest's white iron bed represents Carlo, his special toy that older sister Marcelline wrote about years later.

HOT TIPS You'll find photographs of Hemingway, his childhood diary, letters, early writings, videos, programs and a collection of other Hemingway artifacts at the **Ernest Hemingway Museum** ($), part of The Arts Center at 200 N. Oak Park Ave. in Oak Park. For details, contact the Ernest Hemingway Foundation of Oak Park.

The foundation also offers tours of Hemingway-related sites. Included are: Oak Park and River Forest War Memorial, inscribed with Hemingway's name; his alma mater, Oak Park and River Forest High School, First United Church of Oak Park, where he was baptized; as well as the Historical Society of Oak Park and River Forest, displaying memorabilia.

THE BEST STUFF The great writer's "first book," written when he was 2 1/2 years old, claims an important spot on a kitchen wall. Little Ernest drew pictures for his story and his mother wrote captions beneath them.

Grace kept extensive scrapbooks to record each of her children's lives, preserving this gem from the novelist's young life.

THE WRITER AND HIS WORK For details about Hemingway, see Florida in the South Atlantic section of this book.

FURTHER READING *Hemingway* by Kenneth Lynn (1987); *Hemingway, Life and Works* by G.B. Nelson and G. Jones (1985); *Ernest Hemingway* by K. Ferrell (1984)

ELSEWHERE IN THE AREA Frank Lloyd Wright Home and Studio, 951 Chicago Ave.; Cheney Mansion (1913), 220 N. Euclid Ave., both in Oak Park

• HEMINGWAY HOMES •

Other Hemingway homes include The Ernest Hemingway Home and Museum in Key West, Fla., and The Hemingway-Pfeiffer Museum and Educational Center in Piggott, Ark. ◢

LAND OF LINCOLN

Illinois Honors Man Whose Words Galvanized Nation

LOCATION The Illinois capital, **Springfield**, where you'll find the Lincoln Home, is located in the central part of the state. **Lincoln's New Salem** is 20 miles northwest of Springfield. The Lincoln Home Visitor Center is located in downtown Springfield at 426 S. 7th Street. From north and south, take US 55 to downtown exits. Follow brown signs to Lincoln Home Area, several blocks east of the State Capitol. From east and west, take US 36 to downtown exits. Park $ at the visitor center on 7th Street.

To reach New Salem, leave Springfield via Jefferson Street, which becomes Rt. 97. Follow Rt. 97 to the New Salem park entrance, seven miles northwest of Salisbury and two miles southeast of Petersburg.

The Lincoln Home National Historic Site is open daily, except Thanksgiving, Dec. 25 and Jan. 1, from 8:30 a.m. to 5 p.m., with hours extended spring through fall. For more information, contact Lincoln Home NHS, 413 S. 8th St., Springfield, IL 62703. Tel. (217) 492-4241. E-mail: -liho_information@nps.gov. On the Net: www.nps.gov/liho.

In addition, 10 Lincoln-related sites in Springfield welcome the public. They are owned and operated by federal, state and local governments, as well as private entities. Days and hours of operation vary. For more information, contact Springfield Illinois Convention and Visitors Bureau, 109 N. 7th St., Springfield, IL 62701. Tel. 1-800-545-7300 or (217) 789-2360.

Lincoln's New Salem is open March through October, Wednesday through Sunday, from 9 a.m. to 5 p.m. Closes 4 p.m. November through February. Closed state holidays. For information, contact Lincoln's New Salem, R.R. 1, Box 244A, Petersburg, IL 62675. Tel. (217) 632-4000. On the Net: www.lincolnnewsalem.com.

FRAME OF REFERENCE Lincoln, America's 16th president, lived in New Salem for six years, from 1831-1837, when he was elected to the Illinois State Legislature at age 28. He lived in Springfield for 24 years, from 1837 to 1861, when he left for Washington, D.C., as president-elect at age 52.

SIGNIFICANCE In the heart of today's Land of Lincoln, the future president matured from an aimless young man into a purposeful lawyer and politician. Lincoln's writings and world-famous speeches, especially *The Gettysburg Address* (1863), helped steer America though the Civil War.

Lincoln's words not only changed the course of U.S. history, but resonate today with enduring truths.

Lincoln spent 30 years in Illinois, almost all of his adult life. Visits to Lincoln's New Salem Village and the Springfield he loved open a treasure chest of history. In Illinois, you'll find tangible reminders and unique insights into the man who played a leading role in America's story and whose words galvanized a country torn apart. You can literally walk in the footsteps of Abraham Lincoln.

ABOUT THE SITES You can visit Springfield and Lincoln's New Salem separately or together as a full-day adventure.

LINCOLN'S NEW SALEM Lincoln's New Salem is where twenty-something Lincoln spent six years working odd jobs and studying law in the shade of oak trees. In New Salem, the young man earned the nickname "Honest Abe," for repaying a loan he and a friend had taken out to buy a general store that failed.

New Salem is an authentic log-cabin village, reconstructed on the actual site of the 160-year-old settlement where Lincoln lived. The village, within a 700-acre park, includes 23 reconstructed buildings. Visitors walk dirt roads among homes, stores, a blacksmith shop, the Rutledge Tavern, a grist mill, schoolhouse, barns, woodsheds and even outhouses. The cooper shop is original. Each log structure features period furnishings.

You can go inside some of the small buildings, including the schoolhouse, and experience what life was like for Lincoln and his frontier neighbors. Chatty costumed interpreters pepper their tales of New Salem life with stories of Honest Abe.

A grand visitor center houses an intriguing museum, gift shop and theater, where you can see an excellent 18-minute orientation film, *The Turning Point*. A souvenir shop and bookstore are located next door. The site has a seasonal campground, picnic area and amphitheater, offering a variety of productions in summer months. Also in summer, visitors can learn about steamboat travel on the Sangamon River via hourly boat trips aboard the *Talisman*.

SPRINGFIELD The centerpiece of The City Lincoln Loved is the two-story house where the Lincolns lived for 17 years. The beige clapboard house with green shutters is the only home they ever owned. The site includes four blocks of Lincoln's neighborhood, most of which has been restored. Interpretive signs along the wooded boardwalks mark 13 houses of

Lincoln's neighbors. The lovely neighborhood of graveled streets and high prestige is only a short walk from the law offices and the Old State Capitol where Lincoln worked.

The Lincoln Home Visitor Center houses a bookstore and two theaters, where you can see a movie on Springfield and a filmed tour of the Lincoln home. Scheduled visits to the home are by ranger-guided tour only. Tour size is limited. Pick up tickets for the free tour at the Information Desk.

OTHER LINCOLN-RELATED SITES IN SPRINGFIELD ARE:

LINCOLN-HERNDON LAW OFFICES ($): Corner of Adams and 6th Street across mall from Old State Capitol. Guided tour only. This is the only survivor of several buildings in the immediate area where Lincoln practiced law for 23 years. The offices are furnished much as they were when the future president and his third law partner, William H. Herndon, rented space on the brick building's third floor.

LINCOLN FAMILY PEW: First Presbyterian Church at 7th Street and Capitol Avenue

LINCOLN LEDGER: Lincoln's original account at Marine Bank, on display at the Bank One lobby across 6th Street from Old Capitol

THE OLD CAPITOL: This stately, columned building was reconstructed in the mid-1960s with its original exterior sandstone blocks. First built in 1839, the capitol has been restored inside and out to its 1850s appearance. Here, the future president's political career took shape. Lincoln gave his famous "House Divided" speech in the semi-circular House of Representatives chamber in 1858. Costumed actors offer a program *Mr. Lincoln's World* at the Old Capitol on Fridays and Saturdays, except in May.

LINCOLN TOMB: Oak Ridge Cemetery, north of downtown. Entrance at 1500 Monument Ave. or N. Walnut St. The graves of Lincoln and his family lie within the white granite monument with an obelisk towering 117 feet. A statue of Lincoln, the US Coat of Arms, and four military groupings grace the exterior. A bronze Lincoln Head at the entrance is a replica of the carving by Gutzon Borglum, which resides in the U.S. Capitol. Visitors enter the tomb by a bronze front door into a stately rotunda, then pass through a circular walkway to the red marble monument marking Lincoln's burial site.

Statuary along the walkway depict Lincoln's career. His wife and three sons are buried nearby in the tomb. A phalanx of flags flank

Lincoln's gravestone. The words *Now He Belongs To The Ages* are inscribed on the marble wall.

Young people especially will enjoy the solemn ceremonies held some evenings, June through August. Soldiers in Civil War costumes lower the American flag, somberly fold it, and present it to someone in the crowd.

HOT TIPS Most of Springfield's Lincoln-related sites can be reached by a self-guided walking tour from the Lincoln Home Visitor Center. Plan to drive to Lincoln's tomb north of the downtown area. Trolley and carriage tours are available downtown.

Set aside a full day to visit all the sites; pick up maps and detailed guide of Mr. Lincoln's Neighborhood ($). Walking is on boardwalks, bricks and city sidewalks. Surfaces near the Lincoln Home are uneven. Watch for heavy traffic. Dress for the weather at New Salem; Village "streets" can be dusty or muddy. Food available at the site.

THE BEST STUFF Springfield treasures include: The Lincoln Home Victorian parlor where Lincoln learned of his nomination for the presidency; the front bedroom where Lincoln paced away sleepless nights as the country divided; the black horsehair sofa in the law office where Lincoln read the morning newspaper out loud, driving his law partner crazy; the somber Lincoln Tomb, evoking a wave of patriotism and reverence.

New Salem activities include a steamboat ride, a visit to the tavern, a walk to the outhouse. The village offers an exciting, hands-on way to study, as the orientation movie put it, *this place that changed the man and changed the course of history*.

THE PRESIDENT AS WRITER

BORN: Feb. 12, 1809, in a cabin in Hodgenville, Ky.

DIED: April 15, 1865, in Washington D.C., after being shot in Ford's Theater

MARRIED: Mary Todd, 1842, four sons (Only one survived to adulthood.)

EDUCATED: Largely self-educated; studied law

IMPORTANT SPEECHES: Speech in the U.S. House of Representatives, July 27, 1848; *A House Divided* speech, delivered in Springfield at close of the Republican State Convention, June 16, 1858; *Emancipation Proclamation*, Jan. 1, 1863; *The Gettysburg Address*, Nov. 19, 1863; *Second Inaugural Address*, March 4, 1865

INTERESTING BIO FACT: Before he left Springfield on Feb. 11, 1861,

Lincoln told his law partner to keep their firm's sign board up. When he left Washington, he would return to practice law in Springfield. Herndon later wrote that the President-elect clasped his hand warmly, "and with a fervent 'Good-by,' he disappeared down the street, and never came back to the office again."

ELSEWHERE IN THE AREA Governor's Mansion, nation's third oldest; Oliver P. Parks Telephone Museum, 529 7th St.; 1850s Clayville Stagecoach Stop, 12.5 miles west of Springfield on IL 125

• PRESIDENTIAL WRITINGS •

You can find a 20,000-document collection of Abraham Lincoln Papers at the Library of Congress, much of which is available online. The collection includes correspondence and enclosures to and from Lincoln, drafts of speeches, notes and other printed materials, mostly from the 1850s through Lincoln's presidential years, 1860 to 1865.

On the Net you'll find Lincoln's draft of the Emancipation Proclamation, the March 4, 1865, draft of his second Inaugural Address, and his Aug. 23, 1864, memorandum expressing his expectation of being defeated for re-election as president. Online presentations comprise about 61,000 images and 10,000 transcriptions. Go to the Library of Congress Web site at www.loc.gov. Click on America Memory, then type Abraham Lincoln Papers in the search box. Type the words Gettysburg Address in the search box to view a reproduction of Lincoln's handwritten draft of the world-famous 1863 speech.

• LINCOLN HERITAGE TRAIL •

The most interesting way to learn about Abraham Lincoln is to follow the Lincoln Heritage Trail. This self-guided auto tour begins at Lincoln's birthplace near Hodgenville, Ky. It wends hundreds of miles through rural areas and cities in Kentucky, Indiana and Illinois, where Lincoln is buried in Springfield. Among the two dozen sites along the trail are:

ABRAHAM LINCOLN BIRTHPLACE NATIONAL HISTORIC SITE, 3 miles south of Hodgenville, on US 31E. Here you'll find the 345-acre Sinking Spring Farm that Abraham Lincoln's father Thomas bought in 1807 for $200. A

19th-century log cabin, symbolizing the tiny, dirt-floored home where Lincoln was born, stands enshrined in a granite, neo-classical temple. Fifty-six granite steps, one for each year the 16th U.S. President lived, take you up to the grandiose structure. The original "sinking spring," where the Lincolns drew water, still bubbles next to the six-columned temple. Historic hiking trails and picnic tables are located at the site.

The visitor center houses a museum and theater, where you can see an 18-minute orientation film, *Lincoln: The Kentucky Years.* A private gift shop is located on the premises. The museum displays a preserved cross-section of the huge Boundary Oak that marked a corner of the Lincoln farm in the lobby. The oak died in 1976.

The site is open Memorial Day through Labor Day at 8 a.m. Closing times vary. For information contact Abraham Lincoln Birthplace NHS, 2995 Lincoln Farm Rd., Hodgenville, KY 42748. Tel. (270) 358-3137. The Lincoln Museum is located nearby in the Hodgenville town square.

THE KNOB CREEK FARM, Ky., 6 miles east of Hodgenville on US 31E: An 1800s log cabin recreates the Lincoln family farm where they lived from 1811 through 1816. Cabin is open April 1 to Nov. 1. The site became part of the National Park Service in 2001. For information contact Lincoln Boyhood Home - Knob Creek, 7120 Bardstown Road, Hodgenville, KY 42728. Tel. (270) 358-3137.

LINCOLN BOYHOOD NATIONAL MEMORIAL, Lincoln City, Ind.

LINCOLN'S NEW SALEM STATE HISTORIC SITE IL, 20 miles north of Springfield.

LINCOLN HOME NATIONAL HISTORIC SITE, 413 S. Eighth St., Springfield, IL.

For more information on the Lincoln Heritage Trail, contact the Indiana Tourism Development Division (Tel. 1-800-289-6646), Kentucky Department of Travel Development (Tel. 1-800-225-TRIP), the Illinois Bureau of Tourism (Tel. 1-800-223-0121), or the individual sites. Also, **The Lincoln Museum**, 200 E. Berry St., P.O. Box 7838, Fort Wayne, IN 46802-7838. Tel. (219) 455-3864 also has information.

Other Lincoln sites include: Mount Rushmore in South Dakota; Ford's Theater and The Lincoln Memorial, both in Washington, D C; and the memorial where Lincoln delivered the Gettysburg Address at Gettysburg Battlefield in Pennsylvania. ⌑

VACHEL LINDSAY HOME

Prairie Troubadour's 'Spiritual Center'

LOCATION Central Illinois, in the capital, Springfield, at 603 S. 5th St., corner of 5th and Edwards streets, next to the Governor's Mansion. The house is part of the Old State Capitol Complex downtown.

The Vachel Lindsay Home State Historic Site is open Tuesday and Saturday from noon to 4 p.m. For more information, contact the Vachel Lindsay Home, 603 S. 5th St., Springfield, IL 62701. Tel.: (217) 524-0901. On the Net: www.springfield.k12.il.us/schools/lamphier/projects/lindsay.

FRAME OF REFERENCE Nicholas Vachel Lindsay was born in 1879 in this circa 1846 house, a year after his parents bought it. Lindsay grew up here, and in 1929 he brought his young wife and two children to the home to live. He ended his life here in 1931. The site first opened to the public in the early 1960s. It closed in 1994 for renovations then reopened in 2001.

SIGNIFICANCE Vachel Lindsay — poet, idealist, troubadour — was one of America's most popular poets during the 1920s, largely because of his "tramps" around the country between 1906 and 1912. Walking thousands of miles, he dramatically read his poetry in exchange for room and board, earning him the appellation "prairie troubadour." He was one of the trio of Prairie Poets with **Edgar Lee Masters** and **Carl Sandburg**, his close friend. Lindsay illustrated many of his verses with beautiful artwork.

Lindsay is called Springfield's "second most famous" son, the first being Abraham Lincoln, whose home and law office were located nearby. Lincoln also was a frequent visitor of the first owners of the house.

Lindsay grew up in this well-located house, and at the height of his career wrote much of his strongly rhythmical poetry in the upstairs bedroom as he gazed out onto the lawn of the Illinois Governor's Mansion. Later, as his career declined and his marriage crumbled, Lindsay killed himself in the house at age 52.

ABOUT THE SITE The architect who designed Lincoln's Springfield home also built Lindsay's two-story, 12-room Greek Revival-style house with four porches. The exterior pine siding has been painted light gray and the shutters black. The elaborate front porch with columns and intricate detailing looks as it did in 1917, when the Lindsays lived in the house. Landscaping has even been restored in keeping with details written by Mrs. Lindsay.

The poet's mother was an artist who often painted on an easel in the parlor. She also designed the striking cut glass window on the front door as well as the East Lake honey oak staircase. The downstairs parlor, parents' bedroom, kitchen with five doors, and dining room, where Dr. Lindsay sometimes saw patients, have most of their original furnishings. Eight upstairs bedrooms include the poet's bedroom. In the entry hall, the 1929 bust of Vachel Lindsay, which once stood at the Vachel Lindsay bridge in Springfield, greets visitors.

Lindsay called this house his "Heart's Home," his spiritual center, where "everything begins and ends there for me."

HOT TIPS Lindsay-related sites in Springfield include: 1912 YWCA, 421 E. Jackson, where Lindsay lectured; 1917 Springfield High School, 101 S. Lewis, where the poet graduated; Lindsay's Restaurant, 701 E. Adams, where Lindsay art reproductions are displayed; 1912 First Christian Church, with the Lindsay family pew.

THE BEST STUFF During restoration of the Lindsay home, workers found 15 coats of exterior house paint and 10 coats on an 1893 addition to the house. Wallpaper and carpeting were commissioned to match original swatches discovered in the house.

THE WRITER AND HIS WORK

BORN: Nov. 10, 1879, in Springfield

DIED: Dec. 5, 1931, in Springfield; buried Oak Ridge Cemetery in Springfield

EDUCATED: Hiram College, Hiram, Ohio; studied art in Chicago and New York City

MARRIED: Elizabeth Connor, 1925; two children

IMPORTANT WORKS: *Rhymes To Be Traded For Bread* (1912); *General William Booth Enters into Heaven and Other Poems* (1913); *The Congo and Other Poems* (1914); *Adventures While Preaching the Gospel of Beauty* (1914); *The Art of Moving Picture* (1915, 2002); *A Handy Guide for Beggars* (1916); *The Chinese Nightingale and Other Poems* (1917, 2002); *The Daniel Jazz and Other Poems* (1920); *The Golden Whales of California* (1920); *Every Soul Is a Circus* (1929); *Adventures, Rhymes & Designs* (1968); *Johnny Appleseed and Other Poems* (1981); *The Golden Book of*

Springfield (1920, 1999); *Tramping Across America: Travel Writings of Vachel Lindsay* (1999); The *Amazing Genius of O. Henry* (2001). Poems include - *Abraham Lincoln Walks at Midnight*; *An Indian Summer Day on the Prarie*; *The Flower-Fed Buffaloes*; *Love and Law*; *The Prarie Battlements*; *To Gloriana*

INTERESTING BIO FACT: In his day, people considered Lindsay an eccentric, but he considered himself a messenger of God. To him, his poetry and his art were gospel.

Living the "vagabond" life, he reportedly walked more than 2,800 miles, carrying a knapsack and books of poetry. Across America he powerfully performed his poetry for the people. In the late 1920s, he became severely depressed as his popularity waned, debts mounted and his marriage floundered. In 1931 he killed himself by drinking a household cleanser, dying in his wife's arms. Newspapers reported his death was due to heart disease. The truth was not revealed until 1935 when Elizabeth Lindsay told the facts about her husband's suicide to his biographer, **Edgar Lee Masters**. (See Edgar Lee Masters Home under Illinois in this book.)

FURTHER READING *Vachel Lindsay: A Poet In America* by Edgar Lee Masters (1969); *Vachel Lindsay: The Poet As Film Theorist* by Glenn Joseph (1973); *Vachel Lindsay: Poet in Exile* by Mildred Weston (1987)

ELSEWHERE IN THE AREA Lincoln Home National Historic Site, 413 S. 8th St.; Lincoln-Herndon Law Offices, Adams and 6th Streets; Lincoln Tomb, Oak Ridge Cemetery, 1441 Monument Ave.; The Old Capitol downtown ⌂

HENRY DEMAREST LLOYD HOUSE

Home of Muckraking Journalist

Among the many structures the Landmarks Preservation Council of Illinois has saved is the house once occupied by the pioneer muckraking journalist Henry Demarest Lloyd. The house, called Wayside, is located in **Winnetka, Ill.**, on a bluff along Chicago's North Shore, at 830 Sheridan Road. It is a private residence and not open to the public on a regular basis.

When the rambling, three-story brick house was added to the National Register in 1966, it was the first building designated as an historic landmark in Winnetka. The Lloyd family had occupied the house for at least 90 years until 1976. The core of Wayside dates back to the 1850s.

Lloyd (1847-1903) — lawyer, social reformer and journalist — is best known for his book, *Wealth Against Commonwealth* (1894), a major denunciation of big business. Lloyd moved to Winnetka in 1878, from his native New York City with his wife, Jessie. While editor of the newspaper of the American Free Trade League in New York, he earned a national reputation as a leading 19th-century "muckraking" journalist. At the newspaper, the Free-Trader, he helped bring down Boss Tweed in the 1870s Tammany Hall corruption scandals. In 1872, he joined the staff of the Chicago Tribune, then a leading progressive newspaper.

President Theodore Roosevelt coined the term "muckraking" in 1906 to describe writers who were uncovering political and business corruption in America. Roosevelt compared the journalists to the *Pilgrim's Progress* character who raked up filth on the floor with his muck-rake. (John Bunyan wrote *Pilgrim's Progress* (1678), probably literature's best example of allegory in which characters represent deeper truth)

The Lloyds first moved into a house known as Keflawn overlooking Lake Michigan. The Lloyds converted a china closet to a study, where Lloyd wrote articles for the Chicago Tribune and various magazines. His 1881 exposé of Standard Oil Co.'s monopolistic business practices was explosive.

In 1884, Keflawn was moved several hundred feet west and joined to the 1855 John Garland home, which had years before been moved from the east to the west side of Sheridan Road. Lloyd's newly created home was faced with red brick and dubbed Wayside, after the Wayside Inn once owned by Garland. In his third-floor study, which his wife added to the house as a surprise, Lloyd wrote seven books, including *Wealth Against Commonwealth*. Other reform tracts include *Labor Copartnership* (1898), *A*

Country without Strikes (1900) and *Newest England* (1900). The study was Lloyd's retreat, with a fireplace, skylight and private porch.

Famous visitors and lecturers gave "parlor talks" at Wayside, making it a haven for all people and a cultural center in Winnetka. Lloyd, ever promoting democratic self-governance and social reform, also was active in the village's political and social affairs.

Lloyd is buried in the cemetery of Christ Church across the street from Wayside. His grave lies beneath a bronze plaque and a piece of granite from Rhode Island, where he had a summer home.

For more information about the Lloyd House, contact the Landmarks Preservation Council of Illinois, 53 W. Jackson Blvd., Suite 752, Chicago, IL 60604. Tel.: (312) 922-1742. E-mail: fund@lpci.org. On the Net: www.landmarks.org.

FURTHER READING *The Journalist As Reformer: Henry Demarest Lloyd and Wealth Against Commonwealth* by Richard Digby-Junger (1996); *Henry Demarest Lloyd* by E. Jay Jernigan (1976)

EDGAR LEE MASTERS HOME

Poet Who Created 'Spoon River Anthology'

LOCATION Central Illinois, in Petersburg, 20 miles northwest of Springfield, at the intersection of IL 97 and IL 123, 8th and Jackson streets. From I-55 north and south, take IL 136 to IL 97 south or IL 125 to IL 97 north to the site.

The **Edgar Lee Masters Memorial Museum** is open Memorial Day through Labor Day, Tuesday through Saturday, from 10 a.m. to noon and 1 p.m. to 3 p.m., and on Sundays 1 p.m. to 4 p.m. Tours year-round by appointment. For more information, contact the Edgar Lee Masters Museum at P.O. Box 115, Petersburg, IL 62675. Tel.: (217) 632-7063 (Petersburg Chamber of Commerce). E-mail: Petersburg2@myrealbox.com. On the Net: www.petersburgil.com/edgar_lee_masters.html.

FRAME OF REFERENCE Edgar Lee Masters lived in this house from age 1 to age 11 (1869 to 1881), when the family moved to Lewiston, Ill. The home opened to the public in 1966.

SIGNIFICANCE Masters, who practiced law 30 years in Chicago, published 53 volumes of poetry, plays, novels and biographies, including the lives of **Vachel Lindsay** (1935), **Walt Whitman** (1937) and **Mark Twain** (1938). (See entries in this book.) His *Lincoln the Man* (1931) was a bitter attack on the 16th president. Masters is famous for his best-selling *Spoon River Anthology* (1915). The landmark work comprises 244 free-verse poems spoken by deceased residents of Spoon River, an imaginary rural Illinois village, from their graves on "the hill". The modern literary classic created controversy because many of the supposedly fictional speakers, with distinct personalities and direct dialogue, were recognizable as real people. Masters was a master at portraying small-town, Midwestern life and is recognized as a pioneer of New Poetry.

ABOUT THE SITE The 1 1/2-story, white wood house with small, open front porch is plain and modest. It was moved from nearby West Monroe Street to its current site in 1960 and restored. The four small rooms on the main floor and the two, upper-level rooms are furnished with period pieces, including the desk from Masters' room in New York's Chelsea Hotel, where he wrote many of his later works.

Visitors also will see the death mask of Master's father, Harden, and several pieces from his beloved grandparents, Squire Davis and Lucinda Masters. Also displayed are Edgar Masters' top hat, necktie, pipe, family photos and his great-great grandfather's clock that was brought from Tennessee.

HOT TIPS Park on street free. Picnic table located in yard. The site is not handicapped accessible. Be sure to view the award-winning video *The Valley of the Spoon* before beginning your tour. The site has a small gift shop.

THE BEST STUFF Copies of Reedy's Mirror magazine, which first serialized *Spoon River Anthology*, are displayed, as well as copies of some of his galley proofs. The originals reside in a safe. Masters used the pseudonym Webster Ford on his early publications in Reedy's Mirror. After a public outcry demanding Webster Ford's true identity, he began using his real name. Masters eventually wrote a verse-play titled *Manila*, based upon the *Spoon River* poems.

THE WRITER AND HIS WORK
BORN: Aug. 23, 1868, Garnett, Kan.
DIED: March 5, 1950, Melrose Park, Penn.
EDUCATED: Knox College, 1 year; studied law
MARRIED: Helen Jenkins, three children; Ellen Coyne, one son
IMPORTANT WORKS: *Maximilian* (1902, poetry and essays); *The New Star Chamber and Other Essays* (1904); *The Blood of the Prophets* (1905, poems); *Starved Rock* (1919), *Domesday Book* (1920); *Poems of People* (1936); *Illinois Poems* (1941). Collections of Masters' works are available in multiple-volume editions.
INTERESTING BIO FACT: Although Masters' law partner was famed attorney Clarence Darrow, it was *Spoon River* that brought Masters himself national recognition. After the huge success of the anthology, Masters quit his law practice and moved in 1923 to New York City to write. From 1923 to 1944, he lived in the Chelsea Hotel, then in convalescent homes until shortly before his death.

FURTHER READING *Edgar Lee Masters: A Biography* by Herbert R. Russell (2001); *Beyond Spoon River: The Legacy of Edgar Lee Masters* by Ronald Primeau (1981)

ELSEWHERE IN THE AREA Lincoln's New Salem State Historic Site, 2 miles southeast of Petersburg along IL 97; Abraham Lincoln Drama near New Salem ♙

CARL SANDBURG COTTAGE
Where Prairie Poet Was Born, Buried

LOCATION Northwestern Illinois on the south side of Galesburg, 45 northwest of Peoria, at 331 E. Third St. From I-74 take US 34 west to the site.

The **Carl Sandburg State Historic Site** is open Wednesday through Sunday from 9 a.m. to 5 p.m. except for Thanksgiving, Dec. 25 and Jan. 1 For more information, contact the site at 313 E. Third St., Galesburg, IL 61401. Tel.: (309) 342-2361. E-mail: carl@sandburg.org. On the Net: @sandburg@misslink.net or http://home.crics.net/~sandburgsite or www.sandburg.org

FRAME OF REFERENCE Carl August Sandburg was born in this humble cottage on Jan. 6, 1878, and lived here with his Swedish immigrant parents one year. The Sandburgs bought the little house in 1874 . After the future poet's birth they moved to a larger house in Galesburg. The Carl Sandburg Historic Site Association restored the site and first opened it to the public in 1946.

SIGNIFICANCE Sandburg — poet, biographer, historian, social thinker, musician, novelist, social activist and winner of Pulitzer Prizes in both history and literature — changed the course of American poetry. In Galesburg, he put down the Midwestern, working-class roots that greatly influenced his work.

Sandburg was the second of seven children of August and Clara Anderson Sandburg. The Prairie Poet, as Sandburg later was known, was called Charlie as a boy, because it sounded less Swedish and more American.

In his autobiography, *Always The Young Strangers* (published at age 75), Sandburg tells simple but richly textured stories of the first 21 years of his life as a child and teen in Galesburg during the late 1800s and early 1900s. Young Charlie left school in eighth grade and later became a hobo, out to see and learn about the country.

Sandburg, the biographer of Abraham Lincoln, writes of attending a funeral procession for Gen. Ulysses S. Grant, watching from atop his father's shoulders as American history was being made. Sandburg's stories give a nostalgic view of small-town life and a valuable perspective on U.S. history.

ABOUT THE SITE The tiny, three-room cottage, owned and operated by the state of Illinois since 1970, measures only 20 by 22 feet. A white picket fence surrounds the cottage and visitor center next door. The cottage's cozy kitchen, parlor and bedroom have been restored to reflect the Sandburg's simple, 19th-century life. Sandburg's parents owned some of the site's furnishings, including the ash kitchen table and chairs and the gold tealeaf ironstone dishes.

In the tiny bedroom, with cream walls, pine floors and white, lace curtains, you'll find the Sandburg family's Singer sewing machine, as well as a spindle bed and cradle, both period pieces.

Outside the white, wood-frame cottage with green shutters, The Sandburg Association has restored a perennial garden surrounding Remembrance Rock, a red granite boulder named after Sandburg's only novel. The ashes of Sandburg and his wife, Lilian, are buried beneath it, as the writer requested before his death in 1967.

A visitor center in a two-story house next to the cottage offers a museum, gift shop and small theater, where you can view videos about Sandburg. A renovated barn on the site hosts poetry readings and other events.

HOT TIPS The Carl Sandburg Historic Site Association sponsors many free activities throughout the year to honor and remember Sandburg, including poetry readings, concerts, a fund-raising Penny Parade, and the Sandburg Days Festival each spring. The group also hosts band and folk music concerts held on the grounds in warm weather and inside the barn in cool weather. For details, contact the association.

Reservations for groups of 25 or more are required. The grounds are handicapped accessible but the cottage is not.

THE WRITER AND HIS WORK For details about Sandburg, look under North Carolina in the South Atlantic section of this book.

THE BEST STUFF The museum tells the story of Sandburg's life and accomplishments with photographs, posters and memorabilia. Visitors will find a guitar Sandburg once played and his Remington typewriter from the Chicago Daily News. In the tranquil park surrounding Remembrance Rock, a **Quotation Walk** features Sandburg quotes on flagstones that wind past benches and flowerbeds. Four evergreens guard the rock.

FURTHER READING *The Great and Glorius Romance: The Story of Carl*

Sandburg and Lilian Steichen by Helga Steichen (2002); *The America of Carl Sandburg* by Hazel B. Durnell (1997); *The Poet and the Dream Girl: The Love Letters of Lilian Steichen and Carl Sandburg* by Margaret Sandburg (photographer) and Carl Sandburg (photographer)

ELSEWHERE IN THE AREA Other Sandburg family homes in Galesburg, all private residences and not open to the public, are located at 641 E. South St., 806-810 E. Berrien St., and 809 Berrien St. Additional Sandburg-related sites include: Old Seventh Ward School that Sandburg attended; Brooks Street Fire Station, where Sandburg groomed horses as a student; Old Main building at Knox College, where Lincoln and Douglas debated in 1858, on South Street. Also: Galesburg Railroad Museum, Seminary and Mulberry streets, and historic mansions along Prairie Street. ◮

VIRTUAL DREISER

Visiting Writer's Life, Landmarks

Theodore Dreiser, best known for his novels *Sister Carrie* (1900) and *An American Tragedy* (1925), was born in the industrial slums of **Terre Haute, Ind.**, in 1871, the ninth of 10 children. You can't visit the Dreiser house today; it was demolished long ago. But you can view photographs of it online, courtesy of the University of Pennsylvania's Rare Book and Manuscript Library. The collection also shows a vast series of other Dreiser-related photographs, including his New York City studio, Chicago apartment house and his Upstate New York estate, Iroki.

To see Drieser's Terre Haute birthplace, go to http://oldsite.library .upenn.edu/special/photos/dreiser/440-1.html; http://oldsite.library.upenn .edu/special/photos/dreiser/440-2.html; and http://oldsite.library.upenn .edu/special/photos/dreiser/440-3.html. Two different photographs are labeled as Dreiser's birthplace in Terre Haute. This is because Dreiser biographers have given two addresses of the humble house: S. 9th St. and 12th and Walnut. Both sites are pictured, as well as Dreiser's home in Sullivan, Ind.

Drieser, considered one of America's most important novelists, was a Naturalist writer concerned with the effects of the industrial revolution and urbanization. Other works by the former newspaper reporter and women's magazine editor include: *Jennie Gerhardt* (1911); *The Financier* (1912); *The Titan* (1914), two volumes in a projected trilogy based on the life of the transportation magnate Charles T. Yerkes. *The Genius* (1915), a sprawling semi-autobiographical chronicle of Dreiser's numerous love affairs, was censured by the New York Society for the Suppression of Vice. Its sequel, *The Bulwark*, appeared posthumously in 1946.

Dreiser's autobiographical *Dawn* (1931) stands among the most candid self-revelations by any major writer. He completed most of *The Stoic*, the long-postponed third volume of his trilogy on Yerkes, just before his death in 1945 in Hollywood, Calif. His other works include short stories, plays and essays.

Dreiser is buried in the Whispering Pines section of Forest Lawn Memorial Park in Glendale, Calif.

FURTHER READING *A Theodore Dreiser Encyclopedia* by Keith Newlin (2003); *Theodore Dreiser: Beyond Naturalism* edited by Mariam Gogol (1995); *Theodore Dreiser: An American Journey 1908-1945* by Richard Lingeman (1990) ◬

GENE STRATTON-PORTER STATE HISTORIC SITE

Naturalist Writer's Estate from 1914 to 1920

LOCATION The Gene Stratton-Porter State Historic Site, called **Limberlost North**, is located in northeastern Indiana, in **Rome City**, along Sylvan Lake, 30 miles south of the Michigan and Ohio border. From I-90/80 or US 6, take IN 9 to the site.

The site is open April 1 through mid-November, except for Easter, Tuesday through Saturday from 9 a.m. to 5 p.m., and on Sunday from 1 p.m. to 5 p.m. Guided cabin tours begin on the hour, ending at 4 p.m. Grounds are open dawn to dusk.

For more information, contact the Gene Stratton-Porter State Historic Site, 1205 Pleasant Point, Box 639, Rome City, IN 46784. Tel.: (260) 854-3790. E-mail: gsporter@kuntrynet.com. On the Net: www.genestratton-porter.com.

FRAME OF REFERENCE Geneva (Gene) Grace Stratton-Porter and her husband, Charles, moved into this grand "cabin" in 1914, after moving from Geneva, Ind., where they had lived next to the Limberlost Swamp. The writer was appalled that logging, farming and inept lake management had drained the Geneva wetland. She lived in Rome City until 1920, when she moved to California. The house opened to public in 1947.

SIGNIFICANCE On this wooded estate, known as Wildflower Wood, Stratton-Porter, — novelist, poet, essayist, illustrator and one of America's first naturalist photographers — lived and wrote for nearly a decade. The undeveloped forests and swamp lands of Limberlost North, as well as the formal gardens she designed and tended, provided her a laboratory, inspiration and oftentimes, her subject.

Although other authors such as **John Burroughs** and **John Muir** had already established nature writing as a successful genre, Stratton-Porter's prolific output of best-selling, romance-spiced nature writings found an enthusiastic audience with middle-class Americans in the early 1900s.

Stratton-Porter's 26 books have been through multiple editions and translated into foreign languages. The most popular of these sold millions of copies through WWI and her readers were estimated at 50 million. Eight of her books were made into motion pictures.

ABOUT THE SITE The two-story, 16-room cabin, designed by Porter, rests in the heart of 123 acres of fields, woods, and formal gardens, and has an exterior of Wisconsin cedar logs. Paneling throughout the first floor is of local wild cherry. Three extraordinary fireplaces adorn the first floor: one of polished English brick, one of stone and Indian artifacts and one of multicolored "puddin'" stone. Many of Stratton-Porter's furnishings and personal memorabilia, including her personal library, are preserved in the home. In the living room, you'll find original family portraits and furniture, as well as the family's Emerson piano.

In the entrance hall, there's a newel post light that reminded the writer of an Indian torch on the solid wild cherry banister. Many of Stratton-Porter's nature photos hang above the rich wild cherry paneling in the dining room. The Carriage House Visitors Center is erected over the foundations of Stratton-Porter's original carriage house. Here you'll find exhibits about Stratton-Porter's life, several documentaries, and five movies based on her novels, including the versions of *Freckles*. The stone mausoleum of Stratton-Porter and her daughter, Jeannette, is near the orchard.

HOT TIPS Call or write ahead for handicapped assistance, group reservations and pontoon rides. Pets must be leashed and kept in parking area. A picnic pavilion is located on the grounds. Gift shop offers author's books. The site offers many activities and event, including Spring Family Fun Day, bird-watching and wildflower walks. Contact the site for details.

THE BEST STUFF The imagination Stratton-Porter called on to design her cabin is evident in the grounds at Limberlost North. A flagstone path through a wisteria-laden arbor leads up to the house through her formal garden, encompassing an acre and comprising 35 individual garden plots. Shrubs and flowering plants abound in the Wildflower Wood around the cabin. Stratton-Porter transplanted thousands of trees, shrubs and wildflowers to this Rome City site from local swamps and many remain today.

THE WRITER AND HER WORK
BORN: Aug. 17, 1863, in Wabash County, Ind.
DIED: Dec. 6, 1924, in Los Angeles; buried in Hollywood Cemetery; remains relocated to Limberlost North in 1999
EDUCATED: Largely self-educated
MARRIED: Charles Darwin Porter, 1886
IMPORTANT WORKS: Novels - *The Song of the Cardinal* (1903); *At the Foot*

of the Rainbow (1907); *Freckles, A Girl of the Limberlost* (1909); *The Harvester* (1911); *Laddie* (1913); *Her Father's Daughter* (1921); *Michael O'Halloran* (1915); *A Daughter of the Land* (1918); *The White Flag* (1923); *The Keeper of Bees* (1925); *The Magic Garden* (1927); nonfiction - *What I Have Done with Birds* (1907); *Music of the Wild* (1910); *Moths of the Limberlost* (1912); *Tales You Won't Believe* (1925)

INTERESTING BIO FACT: In 1920, Stratton-Porter left Indiana for California, where she organized her own movie company and based a number of films on her books. She died in Los Angeles after a traffic accident.

FURTHER READING *Coming Through The Swamp: The Nature Writings of Gene Stratton-Porter,* edited by Sydney L. Plum (1996); *Gene Stratton-Porter* by Judith Reick Long (1990); *Lady of Limberlost* by Jeannette Porter Meehan, Gene's daughter (1927) for sale at site

ELSEWHERE IN THE AREA Rome City hosts the annual Gene Stratton-Porter Chautauqua Days Festival, featuring family activities, music and pontoon rides. The writer met her future husband at the festival in the late 1800s after a year of correspondence. ◬

LIMBERLOST

Stratton-Porter's 1895 Home

About 100 miles southeast of Gene Stratton-Porter's house in Rome City you can visit Limberlost, the rustic house where the writer lived from 1895 to 1913. The **Limberlost State Historic Site** in **Geneva, Ind.**, is located at the edge of what was Limberlost Swamp, a nearly lost wetlands now undergoing restoration. In the 18 years Stratton-Porter lived in Geneva, she wrote six novels, including her best-selling *Freckles*, and five nature books.

Stratton-Porter used money from sales of oil found on land her husband owned to build the 14-room Limberlost, which she designed in the Queen Anne style. Cedar logs shipped from Wisconsin and redwood shingles form the cabin's rustic exterior. The downstairs rooms of the large, two-story house, which boasted such modern conveniences as gas fireplaces and running water, have custom-made, red oak paneling and stenciled ceilings. The house reflects a mix of the "arts and crafts" style and the Victorian style of the day. The house brims with original furniture and Stratton-Porter's personal memorabilia. These include original paintings, photographic backdrops, jewelry, easel and in her bedroom, her moth collection.

The swamp — and hence the cabin — got its name from the fate of Limber Jim Corbus, who never returned from a hunting trip in the swamp. When folks asked about his fate, the reply was "Limber's lost!"

The young writer first moved to Geneva in 1890 with her family. Later, seeking to relieve the boredom of being a small-town housewife, Stratton-Porter began photographing and listing swamp animals and birds. She became known as the "Bird Woman," wading in the wetland and packing a revolver to ward off snakes.

Unsolicited, she sent her wildlife photos to a magazine, which asked for more of her work. This led to assignments with other magazines, as well as her novels and nature books, which she wrote in longhand.

Limberlost State Historic Site is located 12 miles west of the Ohio border, at the intersection of US 27 and IN 116. The site, open to the public since 1947, offers tours daily from mid-March to mid-December except for Mondays. For more information, contact Limberlost, P.O. Box 256, Geneva, IN 46740. Tel.: (219) 368-7251. On the Net: www.genevapl.lib.in.us

The Limberlost Swamp Project is restoring a portion of the wetlands that Stratton-Porter explored and kept alive in her writings. For details, contact Limberlost Swamp Remembered, P.O. Box 603, Geneva, IN 46740. ◣

ERNIE PYLE BIRTHPLACE
Tribute to Famous WWII Correspondent

LOCATION West central Indiana, in Dana, 5 miles east of the Illinois border, at 120 W. Briarwood Ave. The site is 1 mile north of US 36 on IN 71.

The Ernie Pyle State Historic Site ($) is open April 1 through Nov., except for Easter, Wednesday through Saturday, from 9 a.m. to 5 p.m., and on Sunday from 1 p.m. to 5 p.m.

For more information, contact the Ernie Pyle State Historic Site, P.O. Box 338, Dana, IN 47847-0338. Tel.: (765) 665-3633. E-mail: erniepyle@abcs .com. On the Net: www.indianamuseum.org and click "historic sites", then click "Ernie Pyle," then click "photo gallery."

FRAME OF REFERENCE Ernest Taylor Pyle was born on a farm near Dana in 1900. The birthplace home was moved to the current location in 1976 and became a State Historic Site. The visitor center opened in 1995.

SIGNIFICANCE Ernie Pyle was probably the most famous war correspondent in World War II and was celebrated for his intimate accounts of soldiers on the front line. The Pulitizer Prize winner went to England in 1940 to report on the Battle of Britain and two years later he was covering U.S. involvement in the war. During the next three years, the fighting took Pyle to North Africa, Italy and the Normandy Beaches in France.

Pyle wrote "Pyle upon Pyle" of news columns giving a foxhole view of average soldiers on the front line to the people back home. When he died in 1945 in Japanese machine gunfire while covering the Okinawa campaign on the island of Ie Shima, Pyle's readership was worldwide, with his column printed in 400 daily and 300 weekly newspapers.

Many of Pyle's columns were published in book form, including *Here Is Your War* (1943). The movie *G.I. Joe* (1945) was about Pyle's coverage of the Italian campaign.

ABOUT THE SITE Pyle's plain, two-story wood house sits in an open area, along with a military Jeep and two authentic World War II Quonset huts that serve as a visitor center. In the center, life-size exhibits with mannequins spotlight individual Pyle columns and bring each story to life with murals and WWII artifacts. You'll learn about survival on the front lines, living in a dug out, and the fight at Omaha Beach in France. Displays include Pyle's portable typewriter in a glass case, as well as his military knapsack and cap.

Audio stations allow visitors to hear selections from Pyle's newspaper writings, read by actor William Windom. The center also houses a video theater, research library and gift shop.

HOT TIPS The visitor center and house exhibits are handicapped accessible but restrooms are not. Call the site to schedule group tours, community room rentals, and education outreach programs in the regular season or off-season. Call in advance for teacher packets.

The Dana Community Volunteer Fire Department hosts an annual **Ernie Pyle Festival** the second weekend in August. The family event takes place near the Pyle historic site. Check the museum shop for the Ernie Pyle GI Joe. To learn about the only home Pyle ever owned, see New Mexico in the Mountain section of this book.

THE BEST STUFF Site managers say the most moving exhibit features Pyle's Pulitzer Prize-winning column about the death of Captain Waskow, a beloved officer. Also, a life-size vignette recreates the spot on Ie Shima where Japanese gunfire cut down Pyle. Admiring soldiers erected a temporary, handmade memorial to him at that spot.

THE WRITER AND HIS WORK

BORN: August 3, 1900, on the Sam Elder farm near Dana
DIED: April 18, 1945, Ie Shima, Ryukyu Islands in the Pacific
EDUCATED: Indiana University (journalism)
MARRIED: Geraldine (Jerry) Siebold, 1925
IMPORTANT WORKS: *Ernie Pyle in England* (1941), *Here Is Your War* (1943), *Brave Men* (1944), *Last Chapter* (1946); a posthumous anthology, *Ernie's War: The Best of Ernie Pyle's World War II Dispatches* (1986) edited by David Nichols
ACCOLADES: Pulitzer Prize for reporting, 1944
INTERESTING BIO FACT: Pyle, who loved to travel, persuaded executives at Scripps-Howard, which owned the Washington Daily News where he was managing editor, to make him a roving reporter. In a nearly 6-year odyssey, Pyle and wife Jerry criss-crossed America 35 times. They also visited Central and South America. Pyle wrote about ordinary people in everyday situations. His unpretentious pieces gained a loyal national following.

In 1927, Pyle began the country's first-ever daily aviation column at the Daily News. He was the newspaper's managing editor for three years before becoming a roving columnist for Scripps-Howard.

During WWII, in a column from Italy, Pyle proposed "fight pay" for combat soldiers. In May of 1944, Congress acted on Pyle's suggestion, giving soldiers 50 percent extra pay for combat service in legislation nicknamed "the Ernie Pyle bill."

FURTHER READING *Ernie Pyle's War: America's Eyewitness to World War II* (1997) by James Tobin; *The Story of Ernie Pyle* (1950, re-issued 1970) by Lee G. Miller

ELSEWHERE IN THE AREA Culbertson Mansion; Angel Mounds, 700-year-old Mississippian Indian town, in Evansville

• ERNIE PYLE'S GRAVE •

When Ernie Pyle's Jeep was fired on, the war correspondent took cover in a nearby ditch. When he peered over the edge, a bullet struck him in the temple, killing him instantly. The U.S. soldiers of the 77th Infantry Division made Pyle a wooden coffin and buried him wearing his helmet at the site. Pyle was reburied at the Army cemetery on Okinawa. His remains were later moved to the National Memorial Cemetery of the Pacific, Punchbowl Crater, in Honolulu. A wooden cross on Ie Shima was replaced by a permanent stone monument. Its inscription reads: "At this spot the 77th Infantry Division lost a buddy Ernie Pyle 18 April 1945."

On the Net: www.findagrave.com/cgi-bin/fg.cgi?page+gr&GRID=2143 and type in the name Ernie Pyle. ◭

JAMES WHITCOMB RILEY HOME

Celebrating 'America's Children's Poet'

LOCATION Central Indiana, in the state capital, Indianapolis, at 528 Lockerbie St., 3 blocks north of Monument Circle downtown.

The James Whitcomb Riley Museum Home ($) is open Tuesday through Saturday from 10 a.m. to 3:30 p.m., and on Sunday from noon to 3:30 p.m. Closed holidays and first two weeks of January. For more information, contact the James Whitcomb Riley Museum Home, 528 Lockerbie St., Indianapolis, Ind. 46202. Tel.: (317) 631-5885. E-mail: rileyhome@rileymem.org. On the Net: www.rileykids.org.

FRAME OF REFERENCE James Whitcomb Riley lived in this house, built in 1872, from 1893 until his death in 1916. The Riley Memorial Association opened it to the public in 1922.

SIGNIFICANCE Riley wrote and published nearly 1,050 poems in his lifetime, the best of which recalled people and events from his Indiana boyhood. Riley had many homes in and around Indianapolis, where he wrote for the Indianapolis Journal until his first book of poetry was published in 1883. He lived in this two-story house the last 23 years of his life as a paying guest of friends.

The Hoosier poet's popularity rested on his whimsical humor, his quaint use of dialect, his clear understanding of rural Midwestern life, down-to-earth style and his lively and dramatic persona. He traveled the country widely, performing his poetry to packed houses, including New York's Carnegie Hall. His poems also appeared in newspapers nationwide. Riley's works later were reproduced in beautifully illustrated books which attracted national and international readership. Book royalties made Riley the wealthiest writer of his time. His tales for children were especially popular, earning him the title of "children's poet," as well as such literary fans as **Hamlin Garland** (see Wisconsin in this book).

ABOUT THE SITE The Italianate-style, brick house with stone trim and slate roof, nestled in the heart of Indianapolis' historic Lockerbie neighborhood, showcases many of the colorful poet's personal belongings. The late Victorian structure features dark, carved woodwork, Italian and faux marble fireplaces, and a rose window on the staircase landing. The estate brims with the same fine furnishings that were there when Riley died in 1916. These include the Apollo electric player piano where "Uncle Jim" Riley accompanied his niece as she played the violin.

In the downstairs library near the red, formal dining room, visitors will find Riley's tapestry-upholstered chair and a portrait of his friend **Joel Chandler Harris**. (See Georgia in the South Atlantic section of this book.) The museum was Indiana's first memorial to the popular children's poet.

HOT TIPS A parking lot is located at the site. Only the first floor is handicapped accessible. The Riley Memorial Association supports many endeavors for children. These included the Riley Hospital for Children, part of the Indiana University Medical School, and Camp Riley in Martinsville, Ind. The organization seeks donations for the home and its projects. Contact the RMA, 50 S. Meridian St., Suite 500, Indianapolis, IN 46204-3540. Tel. (317) 634-4474.

THE BEST STUFF Riley's bedroom, one of five upstairs, still has his writing desk, the painting of his beloved poodle, Lockerbie, and his signature top hat and cane displayed on his bed.

THE WRITER AND HIS WORK

BORN: Oct. 7, 1849, in a log cabin in Greenfield, Ind.

DIED: July 22, 1916, at his home in Indianapolis; buried Crown Hill Cemetery in Indianapolis, Lot 88

EDUCATED: Public schools and travel

IMPORTANT WORKS: Children's Poetry — *Little Orphant Annie*; *The Raggedy Man*; *Nine Little Goblins*; *A Nonsense Rhyme*; *A Fire at Night*; *A Boy's Mother*; *Farmer Whipple*; *The Fishin' Party*; *Hoosier Deutsch Lullaby*; *The Impetuous Resolve*; *A Life Lesson*; *Wrangdillion*. National Poetry — *A Peace Hymn of the Republic*; *An Old Sweetheart of Mine*; *The Silent Victors*; *A Monument for the Soldiers*; *Dead in Sight of Fame*. Nature poetry — *Knee-Deep in June*; *On the Banks of Deer Crick*. Kenotic poetry (poetry of humility, in which Riley excelled) — *The Old Swimmin' Hole*; *Out to Old Aunt Mary's*; *Nothin' to Say*; *When the Frost Is On the Punkin'*; *Hope*; *Old Fasioned Roses*; *Dot Leedle Boy of Mine*; *The Hoss*; *The Prayer Perfect*. Other poetry — *Advertising Doggerel*; *A Local Politician*; *The Old Band*; *On Quitting California*; *Since My Mother Died*. Prose — *The Bear Story*; *Little Red Riding Hood*; *Obituary of Nellie Cooley*; *An Old Soldier's Story*; *The Use and Abuse of Poetic Theme*

INTERESTING BIO FACT: Riley's parents worried their son "Bud," one of six children, wasn't going to amount to anything. The short, blonde, square-shouldered boy was bad at history and math. As a man, Riley attempted to study law, as his father wished, but gave up. He wandered the Midwest as a sign painter. He traveled with a "Miracle Medicine Show" and drew crowds with songs he played on a violin, banjo or guitar. He liked drama. Riley would act the roles of interesting characters he had seen in his travels and mimicked their speech. Entertaining was Riley's real talent.

FURTHER READING *James Whitcomb Riley: Young Poet* by Minnie Belle Mitchell (2002); *James Whitcomb Riley Cookbook* by Dorothy J. Williams et. al. (2001); *James Whitcomb Riley: A Life* by Elizabeth J. Van Allen (1999)

ELSEWHERE IN THE AREA Col. Eli Lily Civil War Museum, 431 N. Meridan St.; Morris Butler House Museum, 1204 N. Park Ave.; President Benjamin Harrison Home, 1230 N. Delaware St.; Indianapolis Zoo

• RILEY CHILDHOOD HOME •

About a 15-minute drive from Indianapolis, in **Greenfield, Ind.**, the house where James Whitcomb Riley spent his boyhood welcomes visitors. **The James Whitcomb Riley Old Home and Museum** ($) at 250 W. Main Street (US 40) displays some Riley family belongings. Visitors to the eight-room, Greek Revival-style frame house will find Mother Riley's blue satin cape, a portrait of Riley's parents and a rocking chair and inlaid sewing box made by Riley's father. Furnishings are period pieces and not original.

Riley's best poems recollect his childhood and youth in Greenfield, which Riley later called "the best town outside of heaven." Here, young "Bud" Riley swam in "The Old Swimmin' Hole," met traveling salesmen like "The Raggedy Man," and played with "Little Orphant Annie," who worked for the family in exchange for room and board.

Riley's father, Reuben, a successful lawyer, built the two-story, white wood house with bright green shutters in 1850. The house, with a 1 1/2-story rear wing, stands on the same plot where the Riley's first Greenfield home, a log cabin, was located. The cabin, where Riley was born in 1849, was demolished when the new house was built. The city of Greenfield bought the home in 1936 and the Riley Old Home Society was established.

The site has a gift shop, where you can find printed collections of Riley's poems. The Riley Museum, next to the house, displays Riley family memorabilia and other historic items. The **Riley Festival** is held the first weekend in October in downtown Greenfield. For details, call (317) 426-2141. E-mail: rileyfst@hccn.org.

The Riley Old Home and Museum is open April 1 through the first week of November, Monday through Saturday, from 10 a.m. to 4 p.m. Closed major holidays. For more information, contact Greenfield Parks and Recreation, 280 N. Apple St., Greenfield, IN 46140. Tel.: (317) 462-8539 or (317) 477-4340. E-mail: parks_rec@greenfieldin.org. On the Net: www .jameswhitcombriley.com. ◮

LEW WALLACE STUDY

Museum Honors Author of 'Ben-Hur'

Lew Wallace was a lawyer, Indiana state senator, a Union major general in the Civil War, vice president of the court-martial after the assassination of President Lincoln, New Mexico Territory governor, American minister to Turkey from 1881 to 1885, lawyer, violinist, inventor, artist, poet and novelist. Wallace is best remembered today, however, as author of the classic historical novel *Ben-Hur: A Tale of the Christ* (1880).

Wallace's house in **Crawfordsville, Ind.**, is now a private residence not open to the public. But his magnificent study, which Wallace dreamed about for years, designed and completed in 1898 as free-standing structure, welcomes visitors. **The Ben-Hur Museum and Gen. Lew Wallace Study** ($), at Pike Street and Wallace Ave., is accessible from US 136 or US 231 downtown. It is owned and operated by the city of Crawfordsville. The National Historic Landmark is open April through October; days and hours vary. It is open for limited days and hours in March and by special appointment December through February.

Wallace's hefty book became the best-selling novel of the 19th century and has not been out of print since it was first published. *Ben-Hur* was made into a popular Broadway play in 1899, running for 21 years, and later was made into several Hollywood movies. The 1959 film version, starring Charlton Heston, was the most expensive movie made until that time. It grossed more than $40 million. It also won 11 Oscars, a record number then.

The stately red-brick study/museum has a copper-domed roof and stained glass skylight reflecting a Turkish mosque, a columned entrance modeled on the abbey of the church of St. Pierre in France, and a 40-foot tower with arched windows designed from the Cathedral of Pisa. The study occupies a 3 1/3-acre wooded site behind a massive brick wall. Architect John G. Thurtle, working from Wallace's specifications for his "pleasure-house for my soul," produced what one newspaper called "the most beautiful author's study in the world . . . a dream of oriental beauty and luxury."

The study features an array of architectural styles and a limestone frieze with likenesses of characters from Wallace's novels that runs around the tower and study. Marking the location of the beech tree under which the Indiana native wrote much of Ben-Hur, visitors will find a bronze statue of Wallace. The statue is a duplicate of the one in the

U.S. Capitol in Washington, D.C. Nearby stands a monument to Wallace's father, David Wallace, Indiana's sixth governor.

The museum is packed with Wallace mementos, including the arms, shield and charm of an Apache chief killed by Wallace's bodyguards in New Mexico Territory; a sword presented to Wallace by his fellow Montgomery County citizens in honor of his gallantry at the Battle of Fort Donelson; a horseshoe from "Old John," Wallace's war horse; a Confederate cavalry flag captured during the Battle of Monocacy; and an outfit a "Roman soldier" used in the 1959 movie Ben-Hur. You'll also find 92 different editions of *Ben-Hur*. Experts estimate four times that number actually might have been printed. You should start your tour of the museum with the 15-minute video about Wallace.

Plans are under way to restore Wallace's original carriage house and turn it into a visitor center, gift shop and office space. Currently, the site is only partially handicapped-accessible. Wallace's home was sold in 1917 and was drastically remodeled in 1937. Much of the two-story Italianate structure was demolished and now it's a private, ranch-style home on the southeast corner of the block outside the wall that surrounds the study.

Wallace, born 1827, enjoyed his dream-come-true study for only a short time before he died in his Crawfordsville home in 1905. He left behind seven published novels. Two in addition to *Ben-Hur* also were popular historic novels: *The Fair God* (1873) and *The Prince of India* (1893). Other Wallace books include: *The Life of Ben Harrison* (1888); *The Boyhood of Christ* (1888) and *Lew Wallace: An autobiography* (1906), finished by his wife Susan, also a novelist. Three of Wallace's poems were set to music. Wallace also wrote an epic poem, *The Wooing of Malkatoon* (1898) and a play *Commodus* (1898).

For more information about the site, contact The Lew Wallace Study Preservation Society, 922 E. South Blvd., Crawfordsville, IN 47933. Tel.: (765) 362-5769. E-mail: study@wico.net. On the Net: www.ben-hur.com.

FURTHER READING *Lew Wallace: Boy Writer* by Martha E. Schaaf (2001); *Lew Wallace: Militant Romantic* by Robert Morsberger (1980) ◢

SOJOURNER TRUTH SCULPTURE
Adopted Home Town Honors Orator

After being freed under the New York Anti Slavery Law of 1827, a tall black woman with a booming voice named Isabella Van Wagenen began traveling America, preaching and singing in the name of freedom for slaves, equal rights for women and peace. We know her by the name the fiery itinerant orator assumed in 1843: Sojourner Truth.

Truth's adopted home town of **Battle Creek, Mich**., honors her today with a sculpture, plaque, Sojourner Truth Day and a museum display. Truth bought a home in Battle Creek in 1857 after delivering an anti-slavery speech at a Quaker convention. She spent the rest of her life there, when she wasn't away on extensive travels. She died in the southern Michigan city 1883 at age 84.

Although Sojourner Truth couldn't read or write, in addition to her oral literature she produced a memoir. *The Narrative of Sojourner Truth: A Northern Slave* (1850), written down by Olive Gilbert, a supporter, was reprinted five times in Truth's life. She sold the book to support her travels in the Northeast and Midwest. It remains in demand. More than 50 modern books and plays continue to tell her story, schoolchildren across the country learn about her famous "Ain't I A Woman" speech, delivered at a Women's Rights Convention in Ohio in 1851.

In Battle Creek, a 12-foot bronze sculpture, designed by Los Angeles sculptress Tina Allen depicts Truth as a bespectacled, grandmotherly woman with her hand on the Bible. The city also has the Sojourner Truth Memorial Highway (MI 66) and a Sojourner Truth plaque in the Hall of Justice among other tributes. The Kimball House Museum, at 196 Capital Ave., preserves a small piece of wood from Truth's home on what was 10 College St. The little house was torn town in 1915.

More than 1,000 people attended Truth's funeral in 1883. She was buried in Oak Hill Cemetery, lot #634, where Battle Creek groups care for her grave and have erected markers.

For more information, contact the Historical Society of Battle Creek/ Sojourner Truth Institute, 165 N. Washington Ave., Battle Creek, MI 49017 Tel.: (269) 965-2613. Truth is also honored with a memorial in **Northampton, Mass**., where she once lived, and one in **Ulster County, N.Y.**, where she was born.

FURTHER READING *Sojourner Truth: A Life, a Symbol* by Neil Irvin Painter (1996); *Glorying in Tribulation: The Lifework of Sojourner Truth* by Erlene Stetson and Linda David (1994) ◮

NOAH WEBSTER HOUSE

Defining Famous Lexicographer

You can find the house where Noah Webster lived his last 20 years in **Dearborn, Mich.**, at The Henry Ford Museum and Greenfield Village ($). Webster produced America's first dictionary. Henry Ford bought the Noah Webster House in 1936 and moved it to Greenfield Village from the campus of Yale University, which Webster attended, in New Haven, Conn.

Webster, with wife Rebecca, moved into this house when he was nearly 65 years old. In his home's study, the Connecticut native, author and lexicographer worked on his two-volume *An American Dictionary of the English Language*. The dictionary took him 25 years to complete, contained 70,000 definitions and required Webster to navigate 26 languages. It was published in 1828. His magnum opus followed Webster's *A Compendious Dictionary of the English Language*, the first truly American dictionary, published in 1806. Webster's dictionary first distinguished American usage from British.

Webster also wrote medical and scientific texts and composed political tracts, as well as the popular "blue-backed speller." This textbook, formally titled *A Grammatical Institute of the English Language* (1872), helped standardize American spelling. Other works by Webster include *A History of the United States*; a version of the Bible, which he saw as his most significant work; and a book of essays completed only weeks before he died on May 28, 1843, in his New Haven home.

In Dearborn, Webster's two-story, white wood house with columned entrance appears as it did in 1835. Furnishings are based on descriptions in family letters and an inventory found at Webster's death. The spacious, nearly square house was modestly furnished, with an unusually large library of more than 1,000 volumes. Webster's collection included works on language, religion, travel, natural history, the ancient world, and biographies of famous Americans. He also owned a number of dictionaries and nearly one hundred spellers and grammar books by various authors.

It's unclear where the kitchen was located in Webster's time; today's house is without one. The house is situated on a grassy hillside in Greenfield Village, built to look like a New England village around a traditional town green.

Among the authentic buildings at the 93-acre Greenfield Village are Thomas Edison's Menlo Park workshop, a **William McGuffey** (see entry under Ohio in this book) schoolhouse, and the Wright brothers' Ohio cycle shop. The village, where Ford began collecting American treasures in 1933, documents nearly 300 years of technological and cultural change in America.

Greenfield Village is open daily, except for Thanksgiving and Dec. 25, from 9 a.m. to 5 p.m. Interiors of village buildings are closed January through March.

For more information, contact Greenfield Village, 20900 Oakwood Blvd., P.O. Box 1979, Dearborn, MI 48121. Tel: (313) 271-1620. For more on Webster, see Connecticut in the New England section of this book.

ELSEWHERE IN THE AREA Henry Ford Estate; Dearborn Historical Museum; The Automotive Hall Of Fame **⌂**

SHERWOOD ANDERSON'S OHIO

Towns Preserve Writer's Small-town Roots

LOCATION The Ohio towns of **Camden**, **Clyde** and **Elyria** have Anderson-related sites. Camden is located in southwestern Ohio along US 127 at OH 725. Clyde, in northern Ohio, is 20 miles southwest of Sandusky, along US 20. Elyria is located just west of Cleveland along US 80/90. Anderson was born in Camden, grew up in Clyde, and put down roots as a businessman in Elyria before pursuing his writing career full-time. The Anderson-related sites are privately owned with varying hours of operation; residences are not open to the public. Some are businesses or libraries and as such, can be visited by the public.

For more information contact The Sherwood Anderson Literary Center, 509 Washington Ave., Elyria, OH 44035. Tel.: (440) 933-0865. E-mail: sherwoodanderson@winesburg.com. On the Net: www.sherwood anderson.org.

FRAME OF REFERENCE Sherwood Anderson was born in Camden in 1876. The family moved to Clyde in 1884 and Anderson left for Chicago about 1897. He also spent parts of 1898 and 1899 in Clyde. Anderson lived in Elyria from 1906 to 1913, when he returned to Chicago to write. (Anderson also briefly lived in Cleveland and Springfield, Ohio.)

SIGNIFICANCE Anderson, a leading Naturalistic writer, spent almost half of his life in Ohio towns. The state largely defined Anderson, a novelist, short-story writer, poet, playwright, newspaper editor (Marion, Va.), political journalist and critic who authored 27 works. His seven novels include his masterpiece, *Winesburg, Ohio* (1919), depicting life in a typical Midwestern town through the eyes of its repressed inhabitants. The town of Clyde served as the model for Winesburg.

Anderson ingeniously described small-town life and its vicissitudes, illuminating the harsh effects of industrialization on individual lives. He greatly influenced the short story, centering on mood and psychological insight rather than plot, and telling the story in prose derived from everyday speech. Anderson helped cement the Naturalism movement in literature of the late 19th century. Critic **H. L. Mencken** (see Maryland in the South Atlantic section of this book) in the 1920s dubbed him "America's most distinctive novelist."

ABOUT THE SITES

CAMDEN: Anderson's birthplace, a small wood house, is located at 142 S. Lafayette St. The site of his father's harness shop was 29 N. Main St.

CLYDE: The fictional Winesburg has 11 sites relating to Anderson's life and writings. They include: the family home at 129 Spring Ave., built circa 1880; the family house at 214 Race St., where they lived circa 1887; Clyde Museum, featuring a large Anderson display, at 124 W. Buckeye St.; Clyde Public Library, with an Anderson collection, at 222 W. Buckeye St.; site of 1876 Railroad Passenger Depot on Main Street; Empire House Hotel site (Willard House in *Winesburg*) at 118 W. Maple St.; historic Main Street; Presbyterian Church at 113 W. Forest St.; site of Fairgrounds, now a school and houses, on South Main; Waterworks Pond, now a park at Mulberry and South streets; grave of Anderson's mother, Emma Jane Anderson, Sec. 4, lot 23 in McPherson Cemetery.

Pick up *The Anderson Guide* to sites in Clyde at the Clyde Museum.

ELYRIA: From 1906 to 1913, Anderson, recently married, put down middle-class roots in Elyria. You can view three-story, brick Gray Apartments, then owned by Thomas Gray, at 401 Second St. at West Avenue, where he lived. The building today looks much as it did in Anderson's day, although the broad front porch now is missing.

You also can view Anderson's former home, a private, 1,500 square-foot frame colonial, at 229 Seventh St., where he moved in 1908. The simple, two-story home is painted pale yellow; the wide front porch Anderson knew is now enclosed. Anderson's three children were born here. He golfed at the Elyria Country Club, played billiards at Elks Hall and talked about literature at the Round Table Club in an unfulfilled life he later described in his later fiction.

In Elyria, Anderson was a prominent businessman. He owned Anderson Manufacturing Co., a mail-order paint and roofing products factory on Depot Street. The brick, two-story building stood at the site of present-day Englehard Chemical.

Anderson suffered a mental breakdown (some say largely fabricated) while living in Elyria. He walked out on his family and his job as president of his company on Nov. 28, 1912, for a full-time writing career — and an unconventional life of meaning — in Chicago. He had drafted his first two novels in Elyria, *Marching Men* and *Windy McPherson's Son*. Anderson might also have drafted the second chapter of *Winesburg* titled *Hands* in the town; some of the characters were based on Elyrians.

HOT TIPS The Sherwood Anderson Literary Center, a group of writers, readers and educators, offers a variety of writing and reading activities, including critique groups, seminars and networking. The center also presents a Sherwood Anderson Literary award for Ohio authors, playwrights, journalists and poets. The center is an affiliate of The Lorain County Historical Society, 509 Washington Ave., Elyria, OH 44035.For information about the Sherwood Anderson Short Story Contest, begun in Virginia in 1976 to honor Anderson, contact the Sherwood Anderson Association and Short Story Contest Committee, P.O. Box 1161, Marion, VA 24354. The committee also schedules an annual tour of **Ripshin,** Anderson's home in Marion, in conjunction with its awards banquet.

THE WRITER AND HIS WORK

BORN: Sept. 13, 1876, in Camden

DIED: March 8, 1941, in Panama Canal Zone, of peritonitis on a good-will tour to South America with fellow writers; buried Marion, Va., in Round Hill Cemetery

EDUCATED: Intermittent; one year at Wittenberg College, Springfield

MARRIED: Four marriages; three divorces; three children from first marriage

IMPORTANT WORKS: *Windy McPherson's Son* (1916); *Marching Men* (1917); *Mid-American Chants* (1918); *Poor White* (1920); *The Triumph of the Egg* (1921); *Horses and Men* (1921); *Many Marriages* (1923); *A Story Teller's Story* (1924); *Dark Laughter* (1925); *The Modern Writer* (1925); *Sherwood Anderson's Notebook* (1926); *Tar: A Midwest Childhood* (1926); *A New Testament* (1927); *Alice and the Lost Novel* (1929); *Hello Towns!* (1929); *Nearer the Grass Roots* (1929); *The American County Fair* (1930); *Perhaps Women* (1931); *Beyond Desire* (1932); *Death in the Woods* (1933); *No Swank* (1934); *Puzzled America* (1935); *Kit Brandon* (1936); *Plays, Winesburg and Others* (1937); *Home Town* (1940); *Sherwood Anderson's Memoirs* (1942)

ACCOLADES: Dial Award (first), 1921

INTERESTING BIO FACT: Although small-town born, Anderson lived in several big cities, including New York, New Orleans and Chicago. In Chicago, he took an advertising job and joined the Chicago Group, which included such writers as **Theodore Dreiser** and **Carl Sandburg.** After a trip to Europe in the 1920s, he shared an apartment in New Orleans with **William Faulkner,** whom he encouraged to write about his home state of Mississippi. Anderson's works influence many important writers of the next generation, including **Ernest Hemingway**.

FURTHER READING *Sherwood Anderson and the American Short Story* by P.A. Abraham (1994); *Winesburg, Ohio: An Exploration* by Ray Lewis White (1990); *A Story Teller and a City* by Kenny J. Williams (1988) ◬

MALABAR FARM

Home of Best-Seller Louis Bromfield

LOCATION Central Ohio, in Lucas, 12 miles southeast of Mansfield, at 4050 Bromfield Road. From US 71, take OH 39 east to OH 95 south to OH 603 north to Pleasant Valley Road west to Bromfield Road south to the site.

Malabar Farm State Park is open daily year-round. Contact the site for hours, which vary with activities. Tours of Bromfield's country home ($) are offered year-round. Farm Wagon Tours ($) are available May through October, weather permitting. For more information, contact Malabar Farm State Park, 4050 Bromfield Road, Lucas, OH 44843. Tel. (419) 892-2784. On the Net: www.malabarfarm.org or www.dnr.state .oh.us/parks/malabar.htm.

FRAME OF REFERENCE Louis Bromfield founded Malabar Farm in 1938 to turn his principles of grass-based, sustainable farming into reality. The writer lived at Malabar from 1939 until his death in 1956. The state of Ohio accepted ownership of the farm in 1972; it became a state park in 1976. Today the site operates as a working farm, as well as cultural, recreational and educational center.

SIGNIFICANCE Novelist, playwright, essayist, conservationist and scientific farmer Bromfield authored 30 books, all of them bestsellers. Some were made into popular movies. His novel, *Early Autumn,* won a Pulitzer Prize in 1927. Many of Bromfield's novels have rural settings and center on the contrast between city and country.

Bromfield was one of the first voices to advance the merits of soil conservation, founding Malabar Farm as a place for testing new farming techniques.

His fame as an author helped promote better agricultural methods through his demonstration farm and his nonfiction writing.

ABOUT THE SITE Malabar today is a major Midwestern attraction where visitors can enjoy nature while recreating and learning, just as visitors did in Bromfield's day. Then, the basement of the Bromfield house served as a meeting place for the Farm Bureau, the Junior Chamber of Commerce of Mansfield, the Farm Cooperative and other gatherings. Visitors can see the house and farm existing just as they did in Bromfield's time. The out-buildings and pastures still house chickens, goats and beef cattle. The hills are ribboned with strips of corn, wheat, oats and hay. Malabar also offers a variety of activities ranging from hands-on farming programs and nature hikes along 12 miles of scenic trails to horseback riding in the summer and cross-country skiing in the winter.

The centerpiece of the 914-acre park is the "Big House," the 32-room country mansion which Bromfield built in 1932. He and architect Louis Lamoreux designed the house, a blend of Western Reserve architectural styles. The home remains just as Bromfield left it when he died in 1956.

Bromfield, a large and gregarious man, named his dream-come-true farm Malabar, a name from India. The financial success of his book *The Rains Came*, set in India, which he and his wife visited in 1932, made the farm possible.

The Malabar Inn Restaurant, a restored "stagecoach" inn built in 1820 offers home-cooked meals to park visitors Tuesday through Sunday, May 1 through Oct. 31. The inn is also open on weekends in March and April. Group reservations are available April through December.

HOT TIPS The farm offers special hands-on kids programs about farm animals, agriculture and nature. Space for events is available. Dress for the weather and wear durable shoes for visits. A 15-site horseman's camp offers primitive camping. Fire rings, picnic tables, drinking water and latrines are available. Ski rentals at Big House gift shop. Ohio fishing license necessary to fish at site. Malabar Farm's Youth Hostel is nearby.

Be sure to visit the 1847 **Oak Hill Cottage** in Mansfield where Bromfield played as a child. The writer's memories of the seven-gabled house provided the basis for his books *Shane's Castle* and *The Green Bay Tree*. The cottage, said to be haunted by family ghosts, is located at 310 Springmill St.

THE BEST STUFF In Bromfield's day, Malabar was not merely a working farm; it was a Mecca for friends, including such celebrities as James Cagney, Errol Flynn, and Shirley Temple. Actors Humphrey Bogart and Lauren Bacall were married at Malabar in 1945, and Bromfield was best man.

THE WRITER AND HIS WORK

BORN: 1896, on a Mansfield, Ohio farm
DIED: March 18, 1956, in Columbus, Ohio

EDUCATED: Studied agriculture 2 years at Cornell; journalism degree, Columbia, 1916

MARRIED: Mary Appleton Wood, 1921; three daughters

IMPORTANT WORKS: *The Green Bay Tree* (1924); *Possession* (1925); *Early Autumn* (1926); *A Good Woman* (1927); *The House of Women* (1927); *24 Hours* (1930); *One Heavenly Night* (1930); *A Modern Hero* (1932); *The Farm* (1933); *The Rains Came* (1937); *It Takes All Kinds* (1939); *Brigham Young - Frontiersman* (1940); *Until Day Break* (1942); *Mrs. Parkington* (1943); *Pleasant Valley* (1945); *Wild Is The River* (1947); *Animals and Other People* (1955); *From My Experience* (1955)

ACCOLADES: Pulitzer Prize, 1927; decorated for service in WWII; numerous honorary degrees

INTERESTING BIO FACT: As a young man in New York, Bromfield worked as a contributing editor to Time Magazine before turning to writing novels. At age 29, Bromfield was regarded as one of America's most promising young novelists, compared to **Fitzgerald**, **Steinbeck** and **Hemingway**. Bromfield helped Hemingway first get published during the decade Bromfield lived in France. He also was a friend of **Edith Wharton**.

FURTHER READING *Yrs, Ever Affly: The Correspondence of Edith Wharton and Louis Bromfield*, edited by Daniel Bratton (1999); *Louis Bromfield, Novelist and Agrarian Reformer* by Ivan Scott (1998); *The Heritage: A Daughter's Memories of Louis Bromfield* by Ellen Bromfield Geld (1995); *Louis Bromfield and the Malabar Farm Experience* by John T. Carter (1995)

ELSEWHERE IN THE AREA In Mansfield-Brownella Cottage (1887); Heritage Center Museum; Kingwood Center, estate and French Provincial mansion; Lincoln Highway National Museum; The Living Bible Museum, 41 life-sized dioramas; 1886 Ohio State Reformatory, now abandoned but site of several films; Ohio Bird Sanctuary at headwater of Clearford River ◭

HART CRANE MEMORIALS
Recalling Poet Who Wrote 'The Bridge'

Two sites in Ohio memorialize Harold Hart Crane, the poet and novelist considered one of the most significant modernist American poets. The historic society in **Garrettsville, Ohio**, the town where Crane was born on July 21, 1899, recently erected a memorial marker in front of the birth house at 10688 Freedom St. The house is a private residence and not open to the public.

In **Cleveland, Ohio**, the city where Hart grew up, a bronze sculpture of Hart stands on the campus of Case Western Reserve University along East Boulevard at the Freiberger Library. The campus is just north of the Route 5 bypass on OH 45. The lighted Hart Crane Memorial, by artist William McVey (1985), depicts a thoughtful Crane, hat in hand, looking toward the horizon. In addition, the Kent State University library in **Kent, Ohio,** houses the **Hart Crane Papers**, 1917-23. The collection includes letters, manuscripts and artifacts, including Crane's christening gown and cup. On the Net: http://speccoll.library.Kent.edu/literature/poetry/crane .html.

Crane, a major influence on American poetry, is best known for his epic poem, *The Bridge* (1930), read on national television at a celebration of the Brooklyn Bridge. Crane had little formal education, but at age 16 published his first poem, *C 33*, titled for the prison cell number of Oscar Wilde. After publishing two books of poems, including *White Buildings* (1926), he was awarded a Guggenheim fellowship and began traveling widely, devoting himself to poetry. He became an important proponent of literary Naturalism, a deterministic perspective focusing on a world in which morals matter less than circumstance, along with **Ezra Pound** and **Carl Sandburg.** Crane often wrote of the positive aspects of urban industrial life. Other Crane works include: *The Complete Poems of Hart Crane*, published posthumously; *The Complete Poems and Selected Letters and Prose of Hart Crane* (1966); *Voyages* (1921-1926, poem series).

Crane, given to alcohol, a violent temper and homosexual exploits, committed suicide at age 32 by jumping from the oceanliner S.S. Orziba into the Gulf of Mexico on April 27,1932, after a heterosexual love affair went awry. Crane was the favorite poet of playwright, **Tennessee Williams** (see entry under Mississippi in the East South Central section of this book). Robert Lowell called him the Shelley of his age. For more information about the Garrettsville memorial, contact the Garrettsville Hiram Area Chamber of Commerce, P.O. Box 1, Garrettsville, OH 44231. Tel.: (330) 527-2411. E-mail: erika@hammerdata.com. For information on the Hart Crane Memorial at Case Western Reserve, go online to www.cwru.edu and type "Hart Crane Memorial" in the search box.

FURTHER READING *Hart Crane: A Life* by Clive Fisher (2002); *The Broken Tower: A Life of Hart Crane* by Paul Mariani (2000); *Hart Crane* by Herbert Leibowitz (1989); *Hart Crane: A Descriptive Bibliography* (1972) ◭

LAWRENCE DUNBAR MEMORIAL

Honoring 'Poet Laureate of African-Americans'

LOCATION In Dayton, Ohio, at 219 Paul Laurence Dunbar St., two blocks north of 3rd Street and four blocks east of US 35. The house is part of the Dayton Aviation Heritage National Historical Park honoring Orville and Wilbur Wright, as well as their childhood friend, Paul Lawrence Dunbar.

The Dunbar State Memorial ($) is open from Memorial Day weekend through Labor Day, Wednesday through Saturday, from noon to 5 p.m.; after Labor Day through October, from 9:30 a.m. to 5 p.m. and on Saturday from noon to 5 p.m. From November to Memorial Day the site is open on weekends from 9:30 a.m. to 5 p.m. and by appointment Monday through Friday.

For more information, contact Dunbar State Memorial, P.O. Box 1872, Dayton, OH 45401. Tel.: (937) 224-7061 or 1-800-860-0148, or The Ohio Historical Society at (614) 297-2332.

FRAME OF REFERENCE Paul Laurence Dunbar bought this house for his mother, Matilda, in 1903. The house was built between 1887 and 1888. Dunbar moved into the house in 1904, two years before he died there. Dunbar's mother, Matilda, continued to live in the house and kept vigil over Paul's belongings until her death in 1934. The Dunbar house became the first state memorial to honor an African-American in 1936 and opened to the public in 1938. It became part of the national park system in 1992.

SIGNIFICANCE Dunbar, a prolific writer, produced novels, plays, short stories, news articles, essays, lyrics, orations and more than 400 published poems before his death at age 33. The son of former slaves, Dunbar became popular for his folksy, possibly over-idyllic poems about slave life on Southern plantations. His contributed to a growing social consciousness and cultural identity for African-Americans.

An international figure in the Age of Realism after the atrocities of the Civil War, both Dunbar's life and work symbolized the African-American struggle for equality. Dunbar often wrote and spoke about civil rights issues, just as his friends **Booker T. Washington, W. E. B. DuBois**, and **Frederick Douglass** did.

The experiences of his parents, Joshua and Matilda, fueled Dunbar's imagination and passion in his writings, using vivid social and historical settings. Joshua Dunbar escaped slavery on the Underground Railroad and later served in the 55th Regiment Massachusetts Volunteers in the Civil War. The discrimination Dunbar suffered after high school graduation also contributed to his writing about the black experience. He wrote in both classical English and plantation dialect.

ABOUT THE SITE The Dunbar house is one of three houses in a row on the residential street that comprise the Dunbar State Memorial. One house serves as the Dunbar museum. The other is the site of offices and a Dunbar library. The Dunbar House is a two-story, Italianate turn-of-the-century brick house, recently restored to its turn-of-the-century elegance. Several original Dunbar furnishings are displayed in the rooms, including a five-piece parlor suite upholstered in green cotton velvet, and a dining room sideboard that converts into an extra bed. When the house was renovated, wall coverings were created to match those found in the 1907 Sears catalog, where middle-class families at the time would have ordered their wallpaper.

HOT TIPS The site hosts frequent programs on Dunbar, his legacy, and African-American history. Contact the site for details.

THE BEST STUFF Dunbar's second-floor library, which he called his "loafing holt," is furnished much as it was when the writer lived in the house. Here you'll find his desk and Morris-style chair, bookcases filled with his book collection, and day bed. In the Dunbar museum, you'll find Dunbar's bicycle — built by the Wright brothers — his American Indian art collection and the ceremonial sword that President Teddy Roosevelt presented to him.

THE WRITER AND HIS WORK

BORN: June 27, 1872, in Dayton
DIED: Feb. 9, 1906, in Dayton
EDUCATED: Dayton Central High School
MARRIED: Alice Ruth Moore, 1898; separated 1901
IMPORTANT WORKS: *Oak and Ivy* (1893); *Majors and Minors* (1895); *Lyrics of Lowly Life* (1896); *Lyrics of the Hearthside* (1899); *Lyrics of Love and Laughter* (1903); *The Complete Poems of Paul Lawrence Dunbar* (1913); novels — *The Uncalled* (1898); *The Love of Landry* (1900); *The Fanatics* (1901); *The Sport of the Gods* (1902). Short stories — *The Heart of Happy Hollow* (1904)

INTERESTING BIO FACT: Despite his excellent high school record, after graduation Dunbar had trouble finding work. He finally took a job as an elevator operator in the Callahan Building in Dayton while he freelanced stories and poetry for newspapers and magazines. In 1892, when he published his first book of poetry at age 20 to critical acclaim, he sold copies of it for $1 to elevator riders.

FURTHER READING *Paul Lawrence Dunbar* by Tony Gentry (1993); *Paul Lawrence Dunbar: Black Poet Laureate* by Pearl Henriksen Schultz (1974)

ELSEWHERE IN THE AREA Carillon Historical Park, 2001 S. Patterson Blvd., where you'll find the Wright Flyer III; U.S. Air Force Museum at Wright-Patterson Air Force Base; Wright Brothers Memorial, OH 444 at Kaufman Road; Old Court House Museum on Main Street ⚘

ZANE GREY STUDY

Museum Remembers 'Father of the Western'

The **National Road-Zane Grey Museum** ($) in **Norwich, Ohio**, has dedicated a section to Pearl Zane Grey that houses a re-creation of the Ohio native's study. The museum is located at 8850 East Pike/ US 40, at I-70 exit 164/Norwich, 10 miles east of Zanesville — named for an ancestor of the writer — in central Ohio. Grey, called the "Father of the Western," authored 80 books, most set in the Wild West. Grey was born in Zanesville in 1872 and lived there until he left for college in 1890.

In the Zane Grey section of the museum, visitors can see a complete replica of the writer's study from his home in Altadena, Calif., where he wrote most of his books. After Grey's death in 1839, his widow donated the study furnishings to the city of Zanesville. Zanesville later gave the items to the museum. In addition to rugs, lamps and western decorations, the study displays Grey's Underwood typewriter, his roll-top desk, his recliner, and the lapdesk where he wrote his books in longhand. You'll also find Grey manuscripts, books, movie posters, fishing items, baseball equipment from his college days at the University of Pennsylvania, dental tools from his New York dental practice, and his collection of American Indian artifacts.

The museum features two other main sections, one dedicated to The National Road and the other to Ohio pottery. The National Road, called the "Main Street of America," stretched 600 miles from Cumberland, Md., to Vandalia, Ill. Begun in 1806, the road was the only significant land link between east coast and western frontier in the early 19th century. The Continental Congress commissioned Zane Grey's ancestor, Col. Ebenezer Zane to develop the first federally subsidized post road, called Zane's Trace, between Wheeling, W. Va., and Maysville, Ky. Later, part of Zane's Trace was included in the National Road. Zanesville was built on land owned by Col. Zane, who founded the town in 1797.

The museum's days and hours of operation vary by season. For more information, contact National Road/Zane Grey Museum, 8850 East Pike, Norwich, OH 43767. Tel. (740) 872-3143 or toll free at 1-800-752-2602. On the Net: www.ohiohistory.org/places/natlroad. For details on Grey, see Pennsylvania in the Middle Atlantic section of this book. More Grey sites are listed under Arizona and California. ◢

WILLIAM HOLMES MCGUFFEY HOUSE

Museum Honors Man Behind 'Eclectic Reader'

In the late 19th and early 20th centuries, millions of American children learned reading, spelling and civics from William H. McGuffey's *Eclectic Reader*. Today, the **William Holmes McGuffey Museum** at Miami University in **Oxford, Ohio**, honors this influential writer/educator/minister. McGuffey was a professor of languages and moral philosophy at the university.

The museum occupies McGuffey's restored, two-story brick house at 410 E. Spring St. on the college campus. McGuffey built the house in 1833 and lived there while he compiled the first six editions of his famous reader series. The university bought the federal-style house in 1958 and it became a National Historic Landmark in 1966.

McGuffey (1800-1873), a Presbyterian minister and respected educator, defined the educational experience in 19th-century America. His lessons in civics emphasized personal respect, hard work, and thrift. McGuffey came to Miami University in 1826 and built the house in 1833, the year a Cincinnati publisher asked him to write a series of readers for the new public schools. By the time he left Oxford for Cincinnati in 1836, he was becoming famous for the series, published that year. In the museum, with light-yellow walls and white woodwork, visitors will see period antiques and artifacts owned by university leaders in the 1800s.

The house features one of the largest collections of McGuffey's works and some items he once owned, including two small chairs made in Oxford in 1830. In his study you'll find his wooden lectern, a three-part secretary, and an intriguing octagonal desk, personally designed by McGuffey and crafted by a local cabinetmaker. At this eight-sided desk, the professor compiled his first *Reader* edition.

McGuffey refined his *Reader* series by inviting neighborhood children to hear lessons on his front porch. Scholars say he wanted to write the readers because he found the "overwhelming pessimism" of the era's schoolbooks and their preoccupation with death disturbing.

The museum is open Tuesday through Sunday from 1 p.m. to 5 p.m. Call ahead to confirm hours. The first floor is handicapped accessible; a computer display shows the second floor. For more information, contact the William Holmes McGuffey Museum , 410 East Spring St., Oxford, OH 45056. Tel.: (513) 529-8380. E-mail: McGuffeyMuseum@MUOhio.edu. On the Net: www.units.muohio.edu/mcguffeymuseum.

You'll find a reproduction of McGuffey's birthplace log cabin at Henry Ford's historic Greenfield Village in **Dearborn Mich.**, near Detroit.

FURTHER READING *William H. McGuffey: Boy Reading Genius* by Barbara Williams (1968) ⌂

EAST NORTH CENTRAL *Ohio*

HARRIET BEECHER STOWE HOUSE
Antislavery Author's Ohio Residence

Although Harriet Beecher Stowe, the author of the popular antislavery novel *Uncle Tom's Cabin* (1852), spent most of her life in New England, she lived in **Cincinnati, Ohio**, from 1832 to 1836. Today, you can visit her renovated Cincinnati house at 2950 Gilbert Ave. (OH 3 and US 22). Stowe moved to the house at age 21 with her sister and father, Dr. Lyman Beecher, who had been named president of Lane Seminary. The seminary built the house in 1833 to serve as the residence of its president. The site now operates as a cultural and educational center promoting African-American history and is open for tours.

The white, two-story house with gabled roof and broad, columned front porch is furnished in period pieces and displays family pictures and a family desk.

Harriet lived in the house until her marriage in 1836 to Calvin Ellis Stowe. The Stowes moved nearby, but Harriet returned to her father's house often when fellow abolitionists met. Stowe witnessed the evils of slavery firsthand while touring neighboring Kentucky and observed Ohio abolitionists bravely at work along the Underground Railroad, a secret network of safe heavens for escaped slaves. Stowe interviewed ex-slaves, taking notes she used later to write *Uncle Tom's Cabin*. The book told wrenching stories Stowe had heard in Ohio, like that of slave mothers forcibly separated from their children. While in Cincinnati, Stowe and her sister taught at the Western Female Institute and published *Geography for Children* in 1833.

In Ohio, Stowe (1811-1896) also befriended Dr. Gamaliel Bailey, with the magazine Philanthropy and later editor of National Era, the antislavery weekly. The Era first published *Uncle Tom's Cabin* in serial format. In 1850, Stowe moved from Ohio to Brunswick, Maine, where she completed the landmark novel that her experiences in Ohio inspired her to write.

The Harriet Beecher Stowe House is open for tours Tuesday through Thursday from 10 a.m. to 4 p.m. by appointment. It is closed major holidays. For more information about the site, contact Harriet Beecher Stowe House, 2950 Gilbert Ave., Cincinnati, OH 45214. Tel: (513) 632-5120. On the Net: www.ohiohistory.org/places/stowe/index.html. For details about Stowe, look under Connecticut and Maine in the New England section of this book.

HOT TIP In Washington, Ky., about 60 miles southeast of Cincinnati, the **Harriet Beecher Stowe Slavery to Freedom Museum** tells of slavery and the Underground Railroad. For information, call (606) 759-0505. On the Net: www.washingtonkentucky.com/museums/beecherstowe.html.

JAMES THURBER HOUSE

Humorist's Home in College Years

LOCATION Central Ohio, in the state capital, Columbus, at 77 Jefferson Ave., one block west of intersection of I-71 and US 40 (East Broad Street). From East Broad Street, turn north on Jefferson Avenue to the site.

The **Thurber House and Museum**, a busy literary center, offers self-guided tours daily from noon to 4 p.m. For more information, contact The Thurber House and Museum, 77 Jefferson Ave., Columbus, OH 43215. Tel.: (614) 464-1032. On the Net: www.thurberhouse.org.

FRAME OF REFERENCE James Grover Thurber lived in this house with his family from 1913 to 1917, Thurber's college years. The house was built circa 1873 and opened to the public in 1984.

SIGNIFICANCE Thurber, considered by many the pre-eminent humorist of the 20th century, made his reputation as a cartoonist and essayist for The New Yorker magazine during the 1930s. Thurber is famous for his many short stories, including *The Catbird Seat* and *The Secret Life of Walter Mitty*, two of the most anthologized pieces of modern fiction. He also wrote 30 books, several of which became Broadway hits. Mitty, like other Thurber characters, became a permanent fixture in America's literary folklore.

Thurber published five children's books, 23 volumes of essays and stories, and two collections of fables. His three volumes of memoirs include *My Life and Hard Times* (1933), his most popular book; and *A Thurber Album* (1952), about his Columbus years. He also co-wrote plays, the most recognized of which is the Broadway hit *The Male Animal* (1940, 1952). The enormously successful play, *The Years with Ross* (1959), conjured a portrait of The New Yorker and its founding editor. It appeared serially in The Atlantic Monthly, and then as a book.

This house where the young Thurber lived while commuting by trolley to classes at Ohio State is featured in many of his most famous short stories, including *The Day the Dam Broke*. Thurber wrote that he had "an exasperated fondness" for Columbus, a town he called by name in his writings. That fondness is returned. Unlike Thomas Wolfe, Thurber could always go home — to celebrity treatment.

ABOUT THE SITE The two-story Victorian house's furnishings typify those of a middle-class Ohio family between 1910 and 1920, with Mission Oak-style pieces popularized by the Sears and Roebuck catalogue. Visitors can tour the first-floor parlor and living room and dining room, where Thurber first heard the footsteps of the ghost in *The Night the Ghost Got In.* Mame Thurber's former kitchen now serves as a work space for the museum bookstore. The spacious attic, where grandfather slept when he visited, has been renovated and furnished as an apartment for the center's writer-in-residence program. For information on the program, contact the site.

The parents' upstairs bedroom, one of four, is now the Thurber House Museum. Here, you'll find a collection of Thurber memorabilia, including many first editions, original drawings and manuscripts, family photographs and letters, as well as Thurber baseball drawings. Changing exhibitions cover such topics as appliances and the role of women in Thurber's time.

HOT TIPS The Thurber Center, next to the house, contains a gallery displaying book-related art. It also houses The Thurber Writing Academy for K-12 students. Contact The Thurber House for details about the academy.

Seeking literary laughter? Contact The Thurber Chamber Theater about private troupe performances that bring Thurber's work to life. To book performances ($), call the Thurber House or e-mail thurberhouse@thurberhouse.org.

THE BEST STUFF The upstairs bedroom where the budding writer "Jamie" Thurber, the middle of three sons, slept remains sparsely furnished with a small bureau, plain bed and a sturdy oak table. The Underwood #5 typewriter on display is the one Thurber used while working at The New Yorker.

THE WRITER AND HIS WORK
BORN: Dec. 8, 1894, in Columbus
DIED: Nov. 2, 1961, in New York City; ashes buried in Green Lawn Cemetery, Columbus
MARRIED: Althea Adams, 1922, divorced, 1935; Helen Marie Wisner, 1935
EDUCATED: Ohio State University; left 1918 without degree; worked on college newspaper
IMPORTANT WORKS: *The Owl in the Attic and Other Perplexities* (1931); *The Seal in the Bedroom & Other Predicaments* (1950); *The Middle-Aged Man on the Flying Trapeze* (1935); *Let Your Mind Alone!* (1960); *The Last*

EAST NORTH CENTRAL Ohio

330

Flower: A Parable in Pictures (1939); *Fables For Our Time, and Famous Poems Illustrated* (1940); *Further Fables For Our Time* (1956); *My World - and Welcome to It* (1942); *Thurber's Men, Women and Dogs* (1943); *The Thurber Carnival* (1945); *The White Deer* (1945); *The Beast in Me and Other Animals* (1948); *The 13 Clocks* (1950); *The Thurber Album* (1952); *Thurber Country* (1953); *Thurber's Dogs* (1955); *The Wonderful O* (1957); *Alarms and Diversions* (1957); *The Years with Ross* (1959); *Lanterns & Lances* (1961); *Credos and Curios* (1962); *The Fireside Book Of Dog Stories* (1943)

ACCOLADES: Ohioana Sesquicentennial Medal, 1953

INTERESTING BIO FACT: While in New York, Thurber met the writer **E. B. White**, who arranged a meeting for Thurber with Harold Ross, editor of a struggling new magazine, The New Yorker. Thurber was hired on as managing editor and "worked my way down" to writer.

With White, Thurber published his first book, *Is Sex Necessary?* (1929), a parody of the popular sex and psychology books of the day. They wrote alternate chapters, and Thurber provided quick pencil sketches that White inked. "It was, to be sure, E. B. White...who first began to look at my drawings critically," Thurber said. With White's encouragement, Thurber began to submit sketches to The New Yorker, where he would publish hundreds of cartoons and spot illustrations before blindness overtook him. (A childhood injury had left Thurber blind in one eye. Despite many operations, he was completely blind by 1951.)

FURTHER READING *James Thurber: His Life and Times* by Harrison Kinney, 1995; *Remember Laughter: A Life of James Thurber*, by Neil A. Grauer, 1994; *James Thurber* by Robert E. Long, 1988; *Of Thurber & Columbustown* by Rosemary O. Joyce, Michael J. Rosen and Donn F. Vickers, 1984

ELSEWHERE IN THE AREA Franklin Park Conservatory and Botanical Garden, 1771 E. Broad St.; Wexner Center for the Arts, 330 W. Spring St.; Jack Nicklaus Museum next to Ohio State campus ⌂

WALDEMAR AGER COTTAGE

Norwegian-American Journalist and Novelist

The home of the Norwegian-American who published and edited an influential turn-of-the-century Norwegian language weekly, The Reform, and authored novels and short stories is undergoing restoration in **Eau Claire, Wis**. Tours are by appointment. The Waldemar Ager Association has been restoring the late-Victorian cottage, which Ager bought in 1903, since it obtained the property in 1992. The house was moved from its original site on the Lutheran Hospital campus to its current location at 514 W. Madison St. Lutheran Hospital had owned the house since 1962, when it was sold by the Ager family.

The Ager Association has restored the Ager House's main floor and exterior to its early 1900s state while preserving historic details. The first floor, including the parlor and the study where he wrote all seven of his novels, looks much as it did during the writer's most productive years. The basement offers space for meetings and Norwegian language classes. The second story awaits reconditioning.

Ager moved to Eau Claire in 1892 when he was 23. He and wife, Gurolle, reared nine children in this house during a period when more than 1 million people spoke Norwegian in the American Midwest. Ager visualized a Norwegian subculture with political loyalty to the United States. Eventually, as succeeding generations became more Americanized, his dream failed.

In addition to his Norwegian-language novels, Ager published several collections of short stories about the lives and culture of Norwegians in America. His novels include *In the Stream* (1899) and *Sons of the Old Country* (1926).

Ager spent much of his time lecturing throughout America in support of prohibition and of the preservation of Norwegian culture and language. With his death in 1941, the crisply edited Reform — once controversial but popular among a large segment of the Midwest's immigrants — also died as circulation and the Norwegian language in America dwindled. The Ager house tells of his dream.

For more information about the Ager house and special events, contact The Waldemar Ager Association, P.O. Box 1742, Eau Claire, WI 54702 or association president Tom Tompkins by e-mail at twt48@aol.com; Tel. (715) 835-9791. On the Net: www.agerhouse.org. When a planned library opens at the site, regular hours of operation will be established. ◣

THE GARLAND HOMESTEAD

Honoring Wisconsin's Frontier Author

LOCATION West Salem, in west central Wisconsin near the Minnesota border, at 357 Garland St. Reach the site via I-90, West Salem exit, to US 16 (Garland Street).

The Hamlin Garland Homestead ($) is open for guided tours Memorial Day through Labor Day, Monday through Saturday, from 10 a.m. to 5 p.m., and on Sunday from 1 p.m. to 5 p.m. Tours at other times by appointment. For more information, contact West Salem Historical Society, Inc., 360 N. Leonard St., West Salem, WI 54669. Tel. (608) 786-1399. On the Net: www.westsalemwi.com or www.uncw.edu/garland.

FRAME OF REFERENCE Hamlin Garland bought the 1859 home and 4 acres of land in 1893 and used the site as a summer home for the next 20 years. A fire partially destroyed the house in 1912, and Garland rebuilt it. He sold the house in 1938. The house opened to the public in the 1976.

SIGNIFICANCE Garland — novelist, short-story writer, biographer, poet, and essayist — authored 52 books and about 500 pieces for periodicals. His works, often autobiographical, tell of the hardships of pioneer life and the colorful social practices of rural Wisconsin.

The "frontier author" is best known for his innovative collection of short stories, *Main-Travelled Roads* (1891), and his memoir, *A Son of the Middle Border* (1917). Garland was awarded the Pulitzer Prize for best biography in 1921 for *Daughter of the Middle Border,* part of his "Middle Border" series. In this house, Garland continued his successful writing career.

ABOUT THE SITE The wooden two-story house, now painted beige with tin roof, was called Maple Shade when Garland purchased it for his parents. Garland enlarged and remodeled the house until "the only part which remains unchanged is the stairway," he said in 1938. Garland added a formal dining room for entertaining literary friends. The house was the first in the area to boast indoor plumbing, a room-sized fireplace, and a tennis court on the lawn.

After Garland sold the house in 1938, it was altered for two-family occupancy. When the West Salem Historical Society bought the house in

1973, it restored the house interior to its pre-1915 appearance. Period furnishings are based on photographs of the house in Garland's time. Garland's daughters returned mementos which their father took with him when he moved to California. You'll find his Royal typewriter at a parlor desk, some of his clothing, and the gowns he wore to receive various honorary degrees.

HOT TIP The West Salem Historical Society sponsors Garland Days the second weekend in September to mark the writer's birthday and a Christmas Open House the first weekend in December. A historical marker honoring the author stands north of West Salem in Swarthout Park on WI 16.

THE BEST STUFF Garland wrote in his upstairs study, where visitors will see his long writing table amid his book- and magazine-filled shelves. You'll also find a sculpture of Garland by Loredo Taft, his brother-in-law; a buffalo sculpture; jewelry box; and his 8mm movie projector.

THE WRITER AND HIS WORK
BORN: Sept. 14, 1860 in a log cabin in West Salem
DIED: March 4, 1940 in Los Angeles; ashes buried in Neshonoc Cemetery a mile outside West Salem
MARRIED: Zulime Taft, 1899; two daughters
EDUCATED: Cedar Valley Seminary, Osage, Iowa
ACCOLADES: Pulitzer Prize, 1921
IMPORTANT WORKS: *Main Travelled Roads* (1891); *Prairie Folks* (1892) and *Wayside Courtships* (1897, short-story collections); *Crumbling Idols* (1894); *Jason Edwards* (1892), *A Member of the Third House* (1892); *A Spoil of Office* (1892); *Rose of Dutcher's Coolly* (1895); *The Captain of the Gray-Horse Troop* (1902); *A Son of the Middle Border* (1917); *A Daughter of the Middle Border* (1921); *Trailmakers of the Middle Border* (1926); *Back-Trailers of the Middle Border* (1928). Garland's *Book of the American Indian* (1923, re-issued 2002) was illustrated by Frederic Remington. In 1896, Garland was commissioned to write a biography of Ulysses S. Grant which, after two years of research, was serialized in McClure's magazine. It was published as a book, *Ulysses S. Grant: His Life and Character*, in 1892. Garland also recorded the results of his lifelong interest in psychic phenomena in *Forty Years of Psychic Research* (1936).
INTERESTING BIO FACT: After wandering about and working at odd jobs, Garland settled in Boston in 1884 and continued his education

by reading 14 hours a day in the Boston Public Library. He became a teacher at Moses True Brown's Boston School of Oratory, as well as a respected lecturer. He toured America for 40 years, giving talks on American, French and German authors. Garland also had homes in Chicago and the Hudson Valley.

Garland's acclaimed first book, *Main Travelled Roads*, offered a harsh view of farming. Garland dedicated the book to his parents "whose half-century pilgrimage on the main roads of life has brought them only toil and deprivation."

FURTHER READING At the University of Southern California's Doheny Memorial Library, more than 8000 other pieces of correspondence, largely unpublished, are part of the **Hamlin Garland Collection** kept in Rare Books and Manuscripts. The Garland papers came to USC in 1940-41 by arrangement with the Garland family. The collection includes letters from such famous correspondents as Walt Whitman, William Dean Howells, Stephen Crane, Gertrude Atherton and Willa Cather. The papers also include nearly 800 manuscripts of Garland's writings, dozens of his literary notebooks, hundreds of photographs and Garland's personal library.

ELSEWHERE IN THE AREA Palmer-Gullickson Octagon House, 1 mile north of West Salem ⌂

LAURA INGALLS WILDER'S PEPIN

'Little House' Novelist's Birthplace

Although the cabin 7 miles north of **Pepin, Wis**., where Laura Ingalls Wilder was born in 1867 is gone, you can visit a replica of the cabin, **Little House Wayside**, at its original site off Highway 35 on County Road CC. A historical plaque marks the site near Pepin, in western Wisconsin on the shore of the Mississippi River, 40 miles southwest of Eau Claire.

Wilder spent her early childhood in Wisconsin with Ma, Pa and her sisters. Wilder later recalled her Pepin years in her book, *Little House in the Big Woods* (1932), the first of nine in her autobiographical *Little House* series. The cabin, built to specifications from Wilder's book, stands on part of the land once owned and farmed by Wilder's father, Charles Ingalls.

In the heart of Pepin, population 900, you'll also find The **Laura Ingalls Wilder Museum** at 306 Third St. (Highway 35). The wood-fronted museum sports a huge sign shaped as young Laura, with blue-dotted bonnet. The museum displays Ingalls-related memorabilia and souvenirs, as well as pioneer-era antiques.

The museum is open daily from May 15 through Oct. 15, from 10 a.m. to 5 p.m. Hours vary other months. For more information, contact the Laura Ingalls Wilder Museum, 306 Third St., Pepin WI 54759. Tel. (715) 442-3011. E-mail: pepinwis@nelson-tel.net. On the Net: www.pepin wisconsin.com

• WILD ABOUT WILDER •

Can't get enough of Laura Ingalls Wilder? Then you'll want to know about the **Laura Ingalls Wilder Historic Highway**. Established in 1995 along Highway 14 across Minnesota, the historic route now snakes through five midwestern states where the popular author lived and which she described in her *Little House* series of books. At Rochester, Minn., the driving tour branches off to follow Highway 66 to the north and Highway 63 to the south.

The Wilder Historic Highway runs through the towns of Pepin, Wis., where Wilder was born, then on to Burr Oak, Iowa, Spring Valley, Minn., and Walnut Grove, Minn. The tour ends in De Smet, S.D. The five towns boast not only former Wilder homes, but many of the places the author later wrote about in her books.

HOT TIP The Herbert Hoover Presidential Library in West Branch, Iowa, contains Wilder's writings in the **Rose Wilder Lane Collection**. On the Net: www.hoover.hara.gov.

For more information on the Wilder Highway, go to http://webpages. marshall.edu/~irby1/laura/highway.html. You can find details about Wilder under Missouri, Minnesota, South Dakota, and Iowa in this book. ◮

Willa Cather Home

LAURA INGALLS WILDER CHILDHOOD HOME

Where 'Little House' Author Lived One Year

The former hotel where author Laura Ingalls Wilders briefly lived as a child is located in northeastern Iowa in the tiny town of **Burr Oak**. The hotel now welcomes the public as the **Laura Ingalls Wilder Park and Museum** ($) at 3603 236th Ave. (off US 52). Burr Oak is 12 miles north of Decorah, Iowa, and 3 miles south of the intersection of US 52 and Highway 44 in Minnesota.

Wilder, author of the popular *Little House* books, came to Iowa in the fall of 1876 at age 9 with her family, fleeing the disastrous grasshopper plagues in Minnesota. The family arrived in the frontier crossroads town, population 120, to manage the Masters Hotel, owned by their friend William Steadman. The Wilders lived in Burr Oak, along Silver Creek, for a year before moving back to Walnut Grove, Minn.

The small three-story hotel is the only remaining childhood home of Wilder's standing on its original site. The white, wood hotel with open front porch and single, center chimney, is one of the five Wilder sites along the **Laura Ingalls Wilder Historic Highway**. The highway, established in 1995, traverses Minnesota, South Dakota, Wisconsin (where she was born) and Iowa. For details on the highway, see South Dakota in this book.

The hotel home has a brick chimney, two front doors and two windows. The left door led to the hotel's bar room. The right door opened to the parlor. The home is furnished with donated time-period pieces.

The Ingalls family probably lived in a small room in the basement across from the kitchen. Mary and Laura waited tables and did dishes. The girls attended a brick schoolhouse in Burr Oak. The family moved out of the hotel soon after arriving because Pa did not want his girls living next to a bar. They moved to a nearby brick house, where sister Grace was born. That house no longer stands.

Across the street from the hotel, you can see the Pfeiffer house, which was standing when the Ingalls family lived in Iowa. Kimball's Grocery, the Congregational Church, and the school Laura and Mary attended are gone, but you can stroll through the cemetery on the hill where Laura and her friend Alice Ward walked.

A group of private citizens bought and renovated the hotel building and opened it to the public as a museum in 1976. The building is listed on the National Register of Historic Places.

Wilder's series of nine *Little House* stories, beginning in 1932 with *Little House In The Big Woods*, had a missing link of one year (1876-77) in her childhood. The year apparently was the one she spent in Burr and comes between her stories *On the Banks of Plum Creek* and *By the Shores of Silver Lake*. Wilder (1867-1957) began writing books at age 65.

The museum, which has a small gift shop, is open in June, July and August, Monday through Saturday, from 9 a.m. to 5 p.m.; and September through May, Monday through Saturday, from 10 a.m. to 4 p.m. The site is open on Sunday from noon to 4 p.m. Groups by appointment only. For more information about the site and special events, contact the Laura Ingalls Wilder Park and Museum, 3603 236th Ave., Burr Oak, IA 52101. Tel. (563) 735-5916. E-mail: museum@lauraingallswilder.us. On the Net: www.lauraingallswilder.us.

For more Wilder sites, see South Dakota, Minnesota and Missouri in this book.

HOT TIP The Herbert Hoover Presidential Library, 210 Parkside Drive in West Branch, Iowa 52358, Tel. (319) 643-5301, houses Wilder's manuscripts.

FURTHER READING *Old Town In The Green Groves: Laura Ingalls Wilder's Lost Little House Years* by Cynthia Rylant (2002) ◮

WILLIAM ALLEN WHITE HOUSE

Influential 20th-Century Newspaperman

LOCATION East central Kansas, in Emporia, at 927 N. Exchange St. Emporia is located along I-35 61 miles southwest of Topeka.

The house is open for guided tours on Saturdays and Sundays from 2 p.m. to 4 p.m. Group tours by appointment. For more information, contact the William Allen White House, 927 N. Exchange St., Emporia KS 66801-3040. Tel. (620) 342-1803. E-mail: wawhitehouse@kshs.org. On the Net: From:www.kshs.org/places/white.

FRAME OF REFERENCE William Allen White rented the mansion in 1899 until he purchased it in 1901. He completed construction on the house, begun in 1885, and lived there for 45 years until his death in 1944. The house, a National Historic Landmark, was given to the Kansas State Historical Society in 2001.

SIGNIFICANCE As owner of the Emporia Gazette, the journalist, statesman and author played an important role in the colorful politics of Kansas, as well as the nation. His sarcastic 1896 editorial in the Gazette, *What's The Matter With Kansas?*, a sweeping denunciation of Kansas Populism, catapulted him into the national limelight and he eventually became one of the most influential American journalists of the 20th century. The Gazette, which White bought for $3,000 in 1895, became one of the most respected small-town newspapers in America.

White won a Pulitzer Prize for his editorial, *To an Anxious Friend*, which ran in the Gazette in 1922. He also was awarded a Pulitzer in 1947 for his posthumously printed, best-selling autobiography. During his lifetime, White collected his influential editorials into several books. He also published a collection of short stories and a novel.

In later life, White was regarded as a statesman for the Republican Party. Only once in his long career did he swerve from his party loyalty. As a Bull Moose in 1912, he supported and advised his good friend, Theodore Roosevelt, for president. White later said that "Roosevelt bit me and I went mad."

In 1924, White ran independently for governor of Kansas. He put his hat in the ring because the Klu Klux Klan, which White had branded in editorials as un-American and cowardly, had endorsed two other candidates for the office. While he finished third in the race, the Klan faded. White again had made his mark.

Will Rogers had White in mind when he said, "Kansas has more real newspapermen than all the rest of the states combined." White was a small-town newspaperman with big-time influence.

ABOUT THE SITE The 2 1/2-story, 6,000-square-foot house is constructed of stone, brick and timber in the Tudor style. The red sandstone on the first floor exterior gives the house its name "Red Rocks." Frank Lloyd Wright designed the main staircase, part of White's expansion of his new home. Plans call for visitors to walk White's lush gardens, complete with reflecting pool, and view original furnishings, first-edition books, and White memorabilia in the house.

You also can view an adjacent house White built for his mother. A new visitor center will explore White's journalistic legacy.

HOT TIPS The Emporia Gazette today is operated by the fourth generation of the White family. You can visit The Emporia Gazette and Museum at 517 Merchant St. where a small museum houses old newspaper equipment.

Emporia is wild about White. Look for the William Allen White Bust and Memorial at Peter Pan Park at S. Rural St. and Randolph Ave., once part of White's property. White named the park for his beloved daughter, who never grew up. Former President Herbert Hoover dedicated the bust on July 11, 1950. It is flanked by his famous editorial "Mary White" in remembrance of his daughter. On the Net: http://www.williamallenwhite.org/peterpanpark.html.

Next to The Gazette offices at 517 Merchant St., you'll find the William Lindsay White Memorial Park. The park, commemorating White's son, features a bust of the younger White (1900-1973) and several selections of writings by the two men. A highway marker honors White at the south end of the Emporia Service Area on the Kansas Turnpike (I-335). It reads *W. A. White died January 29, 1944. His courage, conscience and intelligence, abetted by a keen sense of humor, made him highly respected. He helped mold the America of his day.* In 1952, Emporia State University established The William Allen White Children's Book Award to honor White's memory.

THE BEST STUFF White treasures run the gamut from the mundane to the exotic. In the house you might see such souvenirs from around the world as White's collection of Pompeii artifacts and helmets from Russian Czars. But his press passes, everyday objects on his desk, and his address book — containing the personal phone numbers of Theodore Roosevelt and Frank Lloyd Wright — should prove just as fascinating.

THE WRITER AND HIS WORK

BORN: Feb. 10, 1868, in Emporia

DIED: Jan. 29, 1944

EDUCATED: University of Kansas and College of Emporia; no degree

MARRIED: Sallie Lindsay, 1893; two children

IMPORTANT WORKS: *The Editor and His People* (1924) and *Forty Years on Mainstree*t (1937, editorials); *In Our Town* (1906, short stories); *A Certain Rich Man* (1909, novel); also *The Real Issue, and Other Stories*; *The Court of Boyville*; *Stratagems and Spoils*; *The Old Order Changeth*; *God's Puppets*; *In the Heart of a Fool*; *The Martial Adventures of Henry and Me*; *Mass Media in a Free Society*; *Boys-then and now*; *Woodrow Wilson*; *A Puritan in Babylon: The Story of Calvin Coolidge*

ACCOLADES: Pulitzer Prize, 1947, for autobiography; Pulitzer for editorial, 1922; honorary degrees from eight universities; namesakes include University of Kansas William Allen White School of Journalism; William Allen White Library and William Allen White Elementary School, both in Emporia

INTERESTING BIO FACT: White was a tough newspaperman but he also was supremely human. Around the Gazette office the portly White was affectionately called "The Boss." He referred to his employees as "The Gazette family."

White was a family man. In 1921, his sixteen-year-old daughter, Mary, was brushed from a horse by a low-hanging limb of a tree and died. Only a brief notice appeared in The Gazette that day but a few days later, White poured out his grief in a classic editorial simply titled *Mary White*. The newspaperman and author is as much remembered for that prose as for anything he ever wrote.

FURTHER READING *The Poetry of William Allen White* edited by Donald S. Pady (2002); *Hometown News: William Allen White and the Emporia Gazette* by Sally Griffith (1999); *William Allen White: Maverick on Main Street* by John DeWitt (1975)

ELSEWHERE IN THE AREA All Veterans Memorial, 933 S. Commercial St.; National Teachers Hall of Fame, 1320 C of E Drive; One-Room Schoolhouse Museum, 18th Avenue at Merchant; Schmidt Natural History Museum at Emporia State; Lyon County Historical Museum, 118 E. 6th Ave. ◢

FITZGERALD'S ST. PAUL

Walking Tour Of Writer's Hometown

Francis Scott Key Fitzgerald was born in St. Paul, Minn., in 1896 and returned to live in the Twin City several times during his life. Today, you can see his homes and haunts on the **F. Scott Fitzgerald Walking Tour** of the city. The landmarks are listed in several guides to St. Paul and can be found on the Net at http://home.att.net/~caudle/fscotwlk.htm. The walking tour includes a dozen sites. Most are private and are not open to the public, but you can view them from the street.

Fitzgerald was one of the leading American authors of the 1920s and '30s and is best remembered for his masterpiece, *The Great Gatsby* (1925). Other famous Fitzgerald novels include *This Side of Paradise* (1920) and *Tender Is the Night* (1934).

As a youth, Fitzgerald attended St. Paul Academy, where he wrote for the school newspaper. His family later sent him to a Catholic prep school in New Jersey. From age 15 on, Scott returned to St. Paul only for holidays. He also came back to the city from Alabama after his future wife, Zelda, rebuffed his marriage proposal due to his lack of success. In St. Paul, he begin work on his novel, *This Side of Paradise*. With its publication in 1920, his success and wealth turned Zelda's head and they married, settling in New York City. They returned to St. Paul in 1921 when Zelda became pregnant.

Start your tour of St. Paul by parking on Laurel Street, between MacKubin and Arundel streets. The first stop is **481 Laurel**, twin buildings on the north side of the street known as San Mateo Flats. Fitzgerald was born at his home here in the left building. The pedestrian tour route then follows Laurel east to Arundel; turn right onto Holly Street; stay on Holly to left at Dale and then turn left onto Summit; left onto Western Avenue and then walk down to Selby. Return to your car by turning left through the parking lot at Arundel and walking a block back to Laurel Street. In addition to 481 Laurel, stops include:

A BROWNSTONE AT 472 HOLLY ST. This was the house of Scott's rich grandmother, Louisa McQuillan. Grandmother provided the Fitzgerald family with money when Edward Fitzgerald's sales jobs failed. This house is one of McQuillan's smaller homes. Her largest house was in downtown St. Paul on 10th Street, where 500 guests could be entertained. Grandmother McQuillan also had a winter home in Washington D.C., and traveled regularly to Europe. Young Fitzgerald's parents also traveled in Europe, but Scott stayed with grandma.

509/514 HOLLY ST., where the future writer lived in three different houses on the block during a five-year period, thanks again to Grandmother McQuillan's generosity. One house has been torn down. Fitzgerald later wrote about his childhood on Holly Street in stories that he sold to Scribner's and the Saturday Evening Post magazines.

580 HOLLY on the south side of the street, was Mrs. Backus' Boarding School for girls. Scott's mother, Molly, was determined to have her son associate with the "right" young people. There were dancing classes for boys and girls here, and she enrolled Scott. With his grandmother's money, Scott also attended the St. Paul Academy, around the corner on Dale Street. The former school has recently functioned as a group home.

AT 623 SUMMIT AVE., across Dale Street, you can see the side of another of Grandma McQuillan's houses built soon after her husband died in 1877.

593/599 SUMMIT. Scott's family had moved to the Romanesque brownstone building at 593/599 Summit while Scott was away at prep school. They lived in two apartments here, **593** and **599**. His grandmother died, leaving an inheritance to pay for Scott's education at Princeton. Fitzgerald once described his parents' house in a letter as "A house below the average on a street above the average."

513 SUMMIT. A Queene Anne house at 513 Summit was Mrs. Porterfield's boarding house. Scott visited several other young authors here while he was revising his novel. One of them later wrote screen plays in Hollywood with Scott. Sinclair Lewis lived across the street at 516 Summit.

475 SUMMIT. This Queen Anne style home at 475 Summit was home to one of Scott's best friends, Marie Hersey. She was one of the girls in the dancing class.

AT 445 SUMMIT, the 1882 Queen Anne house belonged to real estate developer Herman Greve. Sandra Greve Kalman and her husband were friends of Scott and Zelda. Sandra helped the couple find houses in St. Paul when they returned from New York.

ON WESTERN AVENUE, you'll find the Commodore Hotel, Angus Hotel (now an arcade) and the former W.A. Frost Drugstore, now a restaurant. Scott and Zelda lived in the Commodore when daughter Scottie was born. Stories abound about the couple's drinking and partying at the hotel's bar during Prohibition. The family later moved to a rental house about 8 blocks away on Goodrich Avenue.

SCOTT'S MOTHER, Molly, lived at the Angus Hotel after her husband died. Both lived into their seventies, but Scott had little contact with them. The Blair Arcade, filled with shops and condos, now occupies the former hotel.

W.A. FROST DRUGSTORE on Western Avenue, which Scott probably frequented, is now a restaurant. The drugstore's tin ceilings have been preserved.

Also, the **Fitzgerald Theater**, at the corner of Wabasha Avenue and Exchange Street downtown, is named for the novelist. Built in 1910 as a Shubert theater and renamed for Fitzgerald in 1994, it is home today to Garrison Keillor's *A Prairie Home Companion* radio show.

For details on Fitzgerald, see Alabama in the East South Central section of this book.

FURTHER READING *F. Scott Fitzgerald in Minnesota* by David Page and Jack Koblas (1996) ◢

SINCLAIR LEWIS' SAUK CENTRE

Boyhood Home and 'Original Main Street'

LOCATION Sauk Centre is located in Central Minnesota, 100 miles north of Minneapolis/St. Paul, at I-94 and U.S. 71. The **Sinclair Lewis Boyhood Home** ($), 810 Sinclair Lewis Ave., is open for guided tours daily, Memorial Day through Labor Day, from 8:30 a.m. to 5 p.m. The home is 3 1/2 blocks west of Main Street. For more information, contact the Sinclair Lewis Boyhood Home, P.O. Box 222, Sauk Centre MN 56378. Tel. (320) 352-7539.

The **Sinclair Lewis Birthplace** is located across Lewis Avenue from the boyhood home. It is private residence and not open to open to the public.

The **Sinclair Lewis Interpretive Center**, in the Chamber of Commerce building at 1220 Main St. South (Highway 71), is open daily, Memorial Day through Labor Day, from 8:30 a.m. to 5 p.m.; weekdays only rest of year. For more information, contact Sauk Centre Chamber of Commerce, P.O. Box 222, Sauk Centre, MN 56378. Tel. (320) 352-5201.

For information about other Lewis sites in Sauk Centre, contact the St. Cloud Convention and Visitors Bureau, 525 Hwy 10 South, Suite One, St. Cloud, MN 56304 Tel. (320) 251-4170 or toll-free: 1-800-264-2940.

FRAME OF REFERENCE Sinclair Harry Lewis was born in Sauk Centre in 1885 and lived there until 1902, when he left to attend college. He moved with his family into his boyhood home, built in 1889 across the street from his birthplace, at age 4. The Sinclair Lewis Foundation acquired the home, a National Historic Landmark, in the 1960s.

SIGNIFICANCE American novelist, playwright and social critic Lewis was the first American author to be awarded the Nobel Prize for literature. Lewis, who wrote 23 novels, was one of the best-selling authors of the Jazz Age of the 1920s. His satirical portrayal of middle-class life in small midwestern towns and cities changed the course of American literature and earned him international acclaim. In his most famous work, *Main Street* (1920), Lewis created the nation's symbol of main street, a term now evoking a clear cultural and historical image. To write his modern classic, Lewis drew on his impressions and experiences growing up in Sauk Centre, a town he characterized as "narrow-minded and socially provincial."

Lewis' other classic works include *Babbitt* (1922), *Arrowsmith* (1925, dedicated to **Edith Wharton**), *Dodsworth* (1929) and *Elmer Gantry* (1927).

Arrowsmith won him a Pulitzer Prize, which he declined. Many of Lewis' 23 books have been made into popular movies. He also wrote three plays.

F. Scott Fitzgerald, a 23-year-old contemporary novelist and Minnesota native, wrote to Lewis: "I want to tell you that *Main Street* has displaced (*The Damnation of*) *Theron Ware* in my favor as the best American novel. The amount of sheer data is amazing! As a writer and a Minnesotan let me swell the chorus — after a third reading."

ABOUT THE SITE When *Main Street* was published in 1920, people in Sauk Centre were furious. It was bad enough that Lewis thinly disguised their town as Gopher Prairie, but some folks even recognized themselves as unsavory characters in the novel. The town library even banned the book.

Lewis might have been persona non grata in Sauk Centre then, but today he's a celebrity. The town has honored its native son by restoring his childhood home, renaming the street where it stands "Sinclair Lewis Avenue" and opening a museum to him. Local fans also pay tribute with Sinclair Lewis Park, Sinclair Lewis Days, Sinclair Lewis Writer's Conference, the Sinclair Lewis Arch, a plaque at the town's Bryant library, and oversized street signs proclaiming "Original Main Street." Athletic teams at Sauk Centre High School are called the "Main Streeters."

Other Lewis-related sites include the First United Church of Christ, which the Lewis family attended, and the Episcopal Church of the Good Samaritan, where young Lewis took Greek lessons. The downtown Palmer House, now a hotel/restaurant, where the teen-age Lewis worked as a night clerk, inspired his Minniemashie House in *Main Street*. The Bryant Library downtown became the Gopher Prairie Public Library. Dr. Edwin Lewis' former office stands at the corner of Original Main Street and Sinclair Lewis Avenue. The building is combination apartment house and business.

SINCLAIR LEWIS BOYHOOD HOME The authentically restored home is a plain, two-story, wood-frame house, a Victorian painted gray and green. The house has a cozy parlor, where Sinclair's stepmother hosted the ladies study group he recreated in *Main Street* as the Thanatopsis Society. The second-floor room where Dr. Lewis had a home medical office today is furnished with equipment that belonged to second son, Claude, also a physician. (It's said that young Sinclair once watched his father amputate an arm in this room and then bury it in the back yard.) Lewis' graphic descriptions of medical emergencies in *Arrowsmith* unfolded on the open front porch as patients rushed to see Dr. Lewis.

The home's furnishings are mostly donated or collected early 20th-century items, but some items owned by Sinclair and his family remain. These include family photographs; a rustic kerosene cookstove in the kitchen; blue willow china, glassware and engraved silver; an original buffet; chairs and an oak and metal-filigree side table, red velvet platform rocker, chess set and young Sinclair's small wooden bed.

You can also see the writer's roll-top desk, his wallet, a pewter vase he bought in Sweden after receiving his Nobel Prize, and the cigarette case his son gave him.

The original carriage house, where young Lewis often hid out and where he began writing a diary and short stories, has been restored but is not open to the public.

Lewis' home, which boasted the first modern heating system in Sauk Centre and a newfangled bathroom, was a center of the town's social life. For young Lewis, the house and small town provided fuel for his imagination.

SINCLAIR LEWIS INTERPRETIVE CENTER A bronze bust of Lewis, cast for the Sinclair Lewis Centennial in 1985, welcomes you to the Interpretive Center at the junction of I-94 and US 71. At the museum, you can learn a lot about the history of Sauk Centre, but displays about the town's famous author are its centerpiece. You'll find Lewis' Nobel Prize; his writing desk; his diplomas from Sauk Centre High and Yale; his yellow blanket, classical music list, wastebasket made from an old hat box; letters; his death certificate; a magazine featuring a short story by Lewis titled *Green Eyes: A Handbook of Jealousy*; and the metal urn in which his remains were sent to Sauk Centre. The burial urn has a story, long told in Sauk Centre.

After Lewis died of a heart attack in near Rome, Italy, his body was cremated. His ashes were put into this urn and flown to the United States, arriving in Sauk Centre on Jan. 21, 1951. The town's undertaker dutifully polished the urn and deposited it in the bank to await services seven days later.

At the family's cemetery plot, Lewis' brother Claude decided not to bury the urn. He obviously planned to display it as a memorial in the town, possibly at the Bryant Library. He opened the urn, peered into it, and slowly poured out his brother's ashes. A wind gust scattered them.

It was reported that the undertaker, Charles Corrigan, said, "Well, Lewis got away from this town after all."

HOT TIPS Write ahead for the brochure, *Explore World Famous Sauk Centre*, to locate Lewis sites. For information on the annual Sinclair Lewis Writers' Conference, contact Sinclair Lewis 2002 Writers' Conference, 13 7th Street South, Sauk Centre, MN 56378. Tel. (320) 352-2735. On the Net: www .english.ilstu.edu/separry/sinclairlewis.

THE BEST STUFF The museum's Birth of a Novel display reveals how Lewis' creative technique. First, he collected names for characters from telephone directories and tombstones. Lewis developed biographies for each character and maps and descriptions of his fictional locations.

Lewis developed scenes in three stages. The first was handwritten and skeletal. The second included more detail and was typed. The last step was a detailed description of scenes. An Oct. 8, 1945, edition of Time magazine features Lewis on the front cover and a review of *Cass Timberlane*.

THE WRITER AND HIS WORK

BORN: Feb. 7, 1885, in Sauk Centre

DIED: Jan. 10, 1951, near Rome, Italy

EDUCATED: Yale University, 1908

MARRIED: Grace Livingston Hegger, 1914, divorced 1926; Dorothy Thompson, 1928, divorced 1942; two sons

IMPORTANT WORKS: *Hike and the Aeroplane* (1912); *Our Mr. Wrenn* (1914); *The Trail of the Hawk* (1915); *The Job* (1917); *The Innocents* (1917); *Free Air* (1917); *Man Trap* (1915); *The Man Who Knew Coolidge* (1928); *Ann Vickers* (1933); *Work of Art* (1934); *It Can't Happen Here* (1935); *Prodigal Parents* (1938); *Bethal Merriday* (1940); *Gideon Planish* (1943); *Cass Timberlane* (1945); *Kingsblood Royal* (1947); *The God Seeker* (1949); *World So Wide* (1951)

ACCOLADES: Nobel Prize for literature, 1930; Pulitzer Prize, 1926, which he declined

INTERESTING BIO FACT: Red-haired, skinny and geeky with bad skin, Lewis, the youngest of three sons, never fit in. While he was supposed to be chopping wood in the back yard, he read a book propped up on shed. Or he hid in the carriage house loft writing plays. As a successful writer basking in the limelight, Lewis traveled, lived in beautiful homes and the best hotels in America and Europe, married twice, had affairs, drank and worked hard, and made and lost friends. He died in Italy alone.

FURTHER READING *Sinclair Lewis: Rebel From Main Street* by Richard Lingeman (2002); *The Rise of Sinclair Lewis, 1920-1930* by James Hutchisson (1996); *Sinclair Lewis' Arrowsmith* edited by H. Bloom (1988)

ELSEWHERE IN THE AREA Oliver H. Kelly Farm (1860s), Elk River; Charles A. Lindbergh Historic Home/Museum, Little Falls; Munsinger/Clemens Gardens, St. Cloud; The Christie House and Memorial Wall, Iwo Jima, both in Long Prairie; St. John's Abbey, Collegeville, world's largest stained glass window ◭

> *Why should that fiery, honest, impatient spirit have come of such a house. . .?*
>
> — Novelist PEARL BUCK,
> after a visit to Lewis' Boyhood Home

LAURA INGALLS WILDER'S WALNUT GROVE
Sites Tell of Homesteading Years

The frontier settlement of **Walnut Grove** in southwest Minnesota resonates with the life of the *Little House* books author, Laura Ingalls Wilder. Wilder's wildly popular series of nine autobiographical books about the pioneer West not only made her a best-selling author, but later provided the story lines for the television show, *Little House on the Prairie*. The popular series, named for Wilder's novel written in 1935, ran on NBC from 1974 to 1984. (The historic Hollywood set for the show burned to the ground during the California wildfires of 2003.)

In Walnut Grove, 150 miles southwest of Minneapolis, you'll find the remains of **Laura's Dugout Home** ($ honor system), where the author lived for two years as a child, and the **Laura Ingalls Wilder Museum** ($) downtown. The museum tells the story of Walnut Grove and features Wilder-related items. During July, you also can see the nightly outdoor **Wilder Pageant** ($) performed by local actors.

For details about Laura Ingalls Wilder, look under Missouri in the West North Central section of this book.

LAURA'S DUGOUT HOME The Ingalls family built a sod house when they moved to the banks of Plum Creek in 1874 with plans to homestead the property. They lived at Plum Creek until 1876, when a grasshopper infestation brought crop failures, forcing them to move to Iowa. The sod house no longer stands, but you can view the deep depression in the earth where the family's pioneer lodging stood. The dugout is located on private property along Highway 5, but you can visit the ruins and also view 30 acres of restored native grasses around the dugout during daylight hours, May through October, weather permitting.

Entrance to the dugout ruins is through a 1900-era farmstead. A sign marks the sod house sight. Visitors can still identify the plum thickets, table lands, big rock, spring, and other sites that Wilder describes in *On the Banks of Plum Creek*.

LAURA INGALLS WILDER MUSEUM The Laura Ingalls Wilder Museum ($), 330 8th St., is located just south of US 14 in downtown Walnut Grove. The museum's collections are housed in eight buildings, including an 1890s depot, a school house, a chapel, jail cells, and early settlers home. Also on display are farming equipment and memorabilia from stars of the Little House TV series who have visited the site. You'll also find a quilt made by Wilder and daughter Rose, a Bible from the church the Ingalls attended, and models of the Ingalls farm and homes used on the TV show. Plans call for a life-sized dugout structure like the one Wilder describes in her book.

The Kelton Doll Collection includes more than 250 dolls from the 1870s to modern times collected by a local resident. The gift shop features books, bonnets, aprons and locally hand-crafted items.

The Wilder Museum is open April through October, Monday through Saturday, beginning at 10 a.m. and Sunday at noon. Closing times vary but are extended to 6 p.m. June through August and later during the Wilder Pageant. Hours limited November and December. The museum gift shop is open year-round. For more information, contact the Wilder Museum, 330 8th St., Walnut Grove, MN 56180. Tel. 1-800-528-7280. On the Net: lauramuseum@walnutgrove.org or www.walnutgrove.org.

THE WILDER PAGEANT The Wilder Pageant is presented every July on the banks of Plum Creek west of Walnut Grove. The nightly outdoor drama features local actors and tells the story of the Ingalls in Walnut Grove during the 1870s through the adult Laura's eyes. For more information, contact Wilder Pageant, P.O. Box 313, Walnut Grove, MN 56180. Tel. 1-888-859-1670. You can buy supper at the nearby Walnut Grove Community Center before the 9 p.m. performance. The pageant is held in conjunction with the **Walnut Grove Wilder Festival**.

HOT TIPS Walnut Grove has a campground; lodging is available in nearby towns, including Tracy, 7 miles from Walnut Grove. No pets or video cameras at the pageant.

ELSEWHERE IN THE AREA Currie End-O-Line Railroad Museum, 440 N. Mill St. Currie; Gilfillan Estate, Highway 67 in Morgan; Jeffers Petroglyphs, Rt. 2 in Comfrey; McCone Sod House, 12598 Magnolia Ave. in Sanborn; Pipestone National Monument, Highways 75 and 23, in Pipestone; Wheels Across the Prairie Railroad Museum, Highway 14, Tracy ◬

EUGENE FIELD HOUSE

Boyhood Home of 'Children's Poet,' Columnist

LOCATION Downtown St. Louis, Mo., at 634 S. Broadway, just south of I-64, west of I-70 at 4th Street and two blocks south of Busch Stadium. The **Eugene Field House and St. Louis Toy Museum** ($) is open March through December, Wednesday through Saturday, from 10 a.m. to 4 p.m., and on Sunday from noon to 4 p.m. In January and February and on Monday and Tuesday, tours are by appointment only. Closed major holidays.

For more information, contact The Eugene Field House and St. Louis Toy Museum, 634 S. Broadway, St. Louis, Mo. 63102. Tel. (314) 421-4689. E-mail: info@eugenefieldhouse.org. On the Net: www.eugenefieldhouse .org.

FRAME OF REFERENCE In 1845, Edward Walsh leased land from the St. Louis school system and built 12 row houses known as Walsh's Row. In 1850, Eugene Field's parents, Roswell and Frances Field, leased the second unit from the south end. Eugene was born in the row house in 1850 and the family lived there until 1864. In 1934, when Walsh's Row was scheduled for demolition, a community effort spearheaded by the local newspaper saved the Field house. Despite the Great Depression, school children collected nearly $2,000 to rescue the house. The other Walsh Row units were torn down. The restored house opened as a museum in 1936.

SIGNIFICANCE A prodigious writer, Field wrote several books of poetry, such as *A Little Book of Western Verse* and *Love Songs of Childhood*; short stories; translations of Homer, and even bawdy poems for gentlemen's clubs (published surreptitiously). Although he wrote hundreds of poems, Field is remembered as the "Children's Poet" for his popular verse that appealed especially to the younger set. These include *Little Boy Blue*, *The Sugar Plum Tree*, *The Gingham Dog and the Calico Cat*, and *Wynken, Blynken, and Nod* (Dutch Lullaby). His first published children's poem, *Christmas Treasures*, was written in St. Louis.

The St. Louis native, who worked at several midwestern newspapers and co-founded the student newspaper at his alma mater, the University of Missouri, is also known as the "Father of the Personal Newspaper Column." When he landed a job as a columnist in 1883 at the Chicago Morning News (now Chicago Daily News), he said he was hired to write "exactly what I please on any subject I please." His witty column, *Sharps and Flats*, became a vehicle for Field's wild sense of humor, which was ahead of his time. Field also worked at newspapers in St. Joseph, Mo., Kansas City and Denver.

Field's father, Roswell, was a well-known St. Louis attorney. In 1853, Roswell Field represented the slaves Dred and Harriet Scott when they brought action in federal court for their freedom. Field's mother, Frances, died when the poet was 6 years old.

ABOUT THE SITE The Eugene Field House Foundation has restored this early Victorian survivor to reflect the time when the Fields lived in the row house. The brick house has seven rooms on three floors, plus a basement and attic, where little Eugene slept. After Field's death, his widow, Julia, gave many of Eugene's belongings to the museum, which opened soon after her death in 1936.

Today, 90 percent of the home's furnishings were Field's, including many from his last home in Chicago, Sabine Farm. In the house, you'll find Field's desk, bookcases, bed and shaving stand. Other family pieces include portraits; a dining room table in the formal, gold-walled dining room; the upright piano in the parlor; and a scalloped Monteith bowl from Italy. The bowl was a wedding gift to Field's great-grandmother in 1764.

The museum also houses a toy collection, in keeping with Field's love of children and dolls. The collection spans hundreds of years and includes an 1837 dollhouse with original furnishings, a French 1860 tricycle shaped like a horse, and an 1857 rocking horse named Ho Bob.

In 1902, **Mark Twain** dedicated a plaque to mark the Field House. The plaque remains mounted out front.

HOT TIPS Parking is free in a small lot at the rear of the house. The site's gift shop features books for and by Field.

Field's late-life home, **Sabine Farm**, in Buena Park, Ill., outside Chicago was destroyed by fire. At Sabine Farm, the poet wrote some of his most famous works, including *Wynken, Blynken and Nod* and *Little Boy Blue*. His experiences in remodeling Sabine Farm provided material for his series of sketches called *The House*.

A Field home in Buena Park also burned down.

THE BEST STUFF Eugene Field as an adult was more than six-feet tall, lean, balding and intelligent, but he freely admitted that he had always loved dolls and had played with them as a sickly, prankish child. He said he believed "in ghosts, in witches and in fairies"... and "I adore dolls." The toy museum in Field's former home now displays baby dolls, bride dolls and dolls big and small.

THE WRITER AND HIS WORK

BORN: Sept. 3, 1850, in St. Louis.

DIED: Nov. 4, 1895, near Chicago, at age 45; buried in churchyard of the Church of the Holy Comforter in Kenilworth, Ill.

EDUCATED: Williams College; Knox College; University of Missouri, no degree

MARRIED: Julia Sutherland, 1873; eight children

IMPORTANT WORKS: Books — *The Tribune Primer* (1882); *Culture's Garland* (1887); *A Little Book of Western Verse* (1890,1892); *A Little Book of Profitable Tales* (1889,1890); *With Trumpet and Drum* (1892); *Second Book of Verse* (1893); *Echoes from the Sabine Farm* (1893); *The Holy Cross and Other Tales* (1893,1896); *Love Songs of Childhood* (1894); *Love Affairs of a Bibliomaniac* (1895); *The House* (1896); *The Poems of Eugene Field* (1910). Poems of childhood include: *With Trumpet and Drum; The Sugar-Plum Tree; The Naughty Doll; Pittypat and Tippytoe; Grandma's Prayer; Gold and Love for Dearie (Cornish Lullaby); Lollyby, Lolly, Lollyby; Fairy and Child; The Night Wind; Kissing Time; The Shut-Eye Train; The Violet's Love Story; Ballad of the Jelly-Cake; The Death of Robin Hood; Mother and Child ;The Bow-Leg Boy*

INTERESTING BIO FACT: Field's personal library had more than 3,500 volumes, including a collection of rare books. He said he was "fond of the quaint and curious in every line." His passion was detailed in his book, *Love Affairs of a Bibliomaniac* (re-issued 2003).

FURTHER READING *Eugene Field: An Anthology in Memoriam, 1850-1895* (1995)

ELSEWHERE IN THE AREA Jefferson National Expansion Memorial/ Gateway Arch on river front; The Old Courthouse, site of the Dred Scott slavery case of 1847; Scott Joplin House, 2658 Delmar Blvd.; Chatillon-DeMenil Mansion (1848), 3352 DeMenil Place; Tower Grove House (1849), 4344 Shaw; Robert Campbell House (1851), 1508 Locust St.; Samuel Cupple House at St. Louis University ◮

ST. LOUIS, BY THE BOOK
Walk of Fame Showcases Authors

The east central Missouri city known as the Gateway to the West, St. Louis, was the launching point for many literary luminaries. Nobel Prize-winning poet, playwright, editor and critic **T.S. Eliot** was born in the Mississippi River city. **Eugene Field**, known as The Children's Poet, also was born in St. Louis and lived there much of his life. Other literary notables include poet Marianne Moore, William Burroughs, Maya Angelou and **Tennessee Williams**, who is buried in Calvary Cemetery in St. Louis.

Since 1988 the city has showcased its cultural heritage with the St. Louis Walk of Fame, a walking tour. About 90 brass stars and plaques honoring nationally acclaimed individuals are permanently set into the sidewalks of the University City Loop downtown. In addition to stars for Moore, Burroughs and Williams, you'll find tributes to Scott Joplin, Ulysses S. Grant, Joseph Pulitzer and Dred and Harriet Scott. The Walk of Fame, along **Delmar Boulevard,** is free and accessible year-round. The stars are located between 6200 and 6600 Delmar, east of I-170 and west of I-70. Parking decks are nearby.

A plaque honoring Thomas Sterns (T.S.) Eliot (1888-1965) as a major innovator of modern English poetry was dedicated as the **T.S. Eliot Memorial** in 1998 at Christ Church Cathedral at 13th and Locust streets. Eliot's bronze star at 6525 Delmar gives biographical facts. The poet, grandson of the founder of Washington University in St. Louis, attended Smith Academy in the city.

Eliot's poem, *The Waste Land* (1922), is one of the most influential works of the 20th century. His other famous poems include *The Love Song of J. Alfred Prufock* (1911); *Portrait of a Lady* (1915); *Ash Wednesday* (1930) and *Four Quartets* (1943). The long-running Broadway musical *Cats* was inspired by his book, *Old Possum's Book of Cats*. Eliot, who lived in England, also wrote the plays *The Rock* (1934), and *Murder in the Cathedral* (1935), a play about the assassination of Archbishop Thomas Becket. Eliot received the Nobel Prize for Literature in 1948 and the American Medal of Freedom in 1965.

For more information on the Walk of Fame, contact The St. Louis Walk of Fame, 6504 Delmar, St. Louis, MO 63130 Tel. (314) 727-7827. On the Net: http://www.stlouiswalkoffame.org. ◮

WEST NORTH CENTRAL *Missouri*

MARK TWAIN'S HANNIBAL

River Town of 'Huck', 'Tom' and Young Sam Clemens

LOCATION Northeastern Missouri at the Illinois border, 85 miles west of Springfield, Ill. To reach the **Hannibal Historic Area**, take US 36 (Mark Twain Avenue) to the downtown area at the Mississippi river front. The **Mark Twain Boyhood Home and Museum** ($) and most related sites are located in or near the pedestrian mall between Main and 3rd streets at Hill Street, one block south of US 36. Follow the signs.

Historic Hannibal sites are privately operated. Days and hours of operation vary. The Mark Twain Boyhood Home and Museum is open daily, except Thanksgiving, Dec. 25, and Jan. 1. Summer hours are 8 a.m. to 6 p.m.; in spring and fall, from 8 a.m. to 5 p.m.; from November through December, on Sunday from 10 a.m. to 4 p.m.; December through February, from noon to 4 p.m.; and in March from 9 a.m. to 4 p.m.

For information, contact Mark Twain Boyhood Home and Museum, 208 Hill St., Hannibal, MO 63401. Tel. (573) 221-9010. On the Net: http://www.marktwainmuseum.org/

The **Mark Twain Cave** ($) is open daily in summer from 9 a.m. to 8 p.m.; from April through early October from 9 a.m. to 6 p.m.; and from November through early March, 9 a.m. to 4 p.m. For more information, contact the Mark Twain Cave, P.O. Box 913, Hannibal, MO 63401. Tel. (573) 221-1656.

For information on other Hannibal historic sites, contact the Hannibal Visitors and Convention Bureau, 505 North 3rd St., Hannibal, MO 63401. Tel. (573) 221-1656.

FRAME OF REFERENCE Hannibal was the boyhood home of Samuel Langhorne Clemens, a.k.a. Mark Twain, from 1839, when he was 4 years old, to the outbreak of the Civil War, when Twain left his hometown to travel. Twain grew up in Hannibal during the era when steamboats dominated the Mississippi River and slavery inflamed the nation.

SIGNIFICANCE This quaint, Mississippi River town claims fame as the place where the first great American writer born and reared west of the Appalachian Mountains — and the first to write in the American vernacular — grew up.

Sleepy Hannibal, a frontier village of 2,000 people in Twain's youth, provided the setting of his greatest books, including *The Adventures of Tom Sawyer* (1876) and The *Adventures of Huckleberry Finn* (1884), considered his masterpiece. Twain's characters and much of what he wrote about were taken directly from his youth here.

During a late-life interview in India, Twain was quoted as saying, *All that goes to make the me in me is a small Missouri village on the other side of the globe.*

Twain's works raised the level of humor to high art. His book and lectures made him a world celebrity. Twain's works have been translated into more than 60 languages. Twain is generally considered the greatest American writer of the 19th century and possibly of all time.

ABOUT THE SITE Several blocks of the riverfront are dedicated to Twain's boyhood.

The town has transformed a brick section of Hill Street between Main and Third Streets into a pedestrian mall. Twain sites here include: Twain's quaint, two-story, clapboard boyhood home, fully restored; the Mark Twain Museum in a next-door, historic stone building; the Mark Twain Museum Annex behind the Twain home; the J. M. Clemens law Office, where his father presided as Justice of the Peace in 1841; the 1830s Pilaster House/Grant's Drug Store, where the Clemens family once lived upstairs and the drug store operated downstairs; and a whitewashed replica of "Tom Sawyer's Fence."

The museum houses Twain memorabilia, first editions of Twain's works, one of the writer's famous white suits, and a series of Norman Rockwell paintings used for editions of *Tom Sawyer* and *Huck Finn*. The Annex offers an orientation slide show.

Also in the pedestrian mall area: **"Becky Thatcher's House,"** the 1840s home of Twain's childhood sweetheart Laura Hawkins, immortalized as Tom Sawyer's love, Becky Thatcher ($ upstairs tours); The Haunted House on Hill Street Wax Museum ($); the bronze **Tom and Huck Statue** by Frederick Hibbard at the foot of Cardiff Hill; the sites of "Muff Potter's Jail" and "Huck's house"; and the **Mark Twain Memorial Lighthouse** atop Cardiff Hill. The white, wooden lighthouse was first dedicated in 1935 in celebration of the 100th anniversary of Twain's birth.

The entire historic area teems with restored, Victorian buildings now housing candy stores, ice cream parlors, antique shops, souvenir stores, theme restaurants, and exhibits. Private companies offer tours ($) by trolley, train and riverboat.

The **Mark Twain Cave** ($) (Cameron Cave) one mile south of Hannibal on Hwy. 79, offers guided tours, restaurants, a large gift shop and camping. Here, "Tom, Becky and Huck" explored the far reaches of the cave, as did the young Clemens. Hannibal offers a variety of entertainment with Mark Twain themes.

A historic area at the town's waterfront, where the Mississippi yawns half-a-mile wide, protects the writer's boyhood home. The small area also includes a handful of surviving homes and buildings that played important roles in Twain's formative years and later in his books.

Riverboats still roam the river near Hannibal (population nearing 20,000 today), blowing their whistles for show. Tour guides point out *Jackson Island* and *Lovers' Leap* to camera-clicking tourists. Floods have wiped out much of the riverfront. Today, a low flood wall built in 1993 protects the historic district from Mississippi flood waters. It's hard to even see the river. A booming tourist industry has replaced the town's past glory as an important shoe manufacturing center.

So securely are Twain's boyhood adventures etched into our collective memory that nearly 200-year-old Hannibal bills itself as "America's Hometown."

HOT TIPS The *entire* family should enjoy this site. Allow a half day. Plan to spend more time if you are interested in the tours and related attractions. Guided tours ($) of the home and nearby related sites are available seasonally and begin at the Museum Annex.

Begin your self-guided tour at the Twain Boyhood Home near the US 36 bridge over the river. Park on the street or in small, nearby parking lots. Pick up information and maps at the Visitor Center at the site. Dress for the weather. Wear a light wrap in the cave, where the year-round temperature is 52 degrees.

SOUVENIR TIP: A copy of *Tom Sawyer* or *Huckleberry Finn* purchased at a local gift shop makes a meaningful memento of the visit. Ditto the post card with a photograph of Twain — with his shock of white hair, heavy mustache and trademark white suit — standing before his boyhood home. The photo was taken in 1902 during his last visit here. Twain was quoted as saying that each time he came back, *the house seemed to grow smaller than his memory of it, and that if he came back often enough it would look like a doll house.* Campgrounds are nearby and at the **Mark Twain State Park** in Florida, Mo., Twain's birthplace, 40 miles southwest.

THE BEST STUFF Shuffling around this picturesque "Hometown," eating ice cream and gawking at the Twain sites is delightful. Older kids who've read *Tom* and *Huck* will enjoy this trip back in time, as will their parents. Haven't we *all* read these great American literary works? The quaint shops, the brick street, the mighty Mississippi riverfront, the riverboat ... together they evoke bygone days of paddleboats, pirates, childhood and dreams.

The **Mark Twain Cave** will delight young visitors. Walk inside the cave's mouth, shaped like the letter "A", and experience the excitement Tom and his buddies found. The 55-minute tour loop reveals fantastic limestone formations like *Alligator Rock, Injun Joe's Canoe* and *Hanging Shoe*.

Twain described the cave, once a prehistoric Indian shelter and later a stop on the Underground Railroad, in *The Adventures of Tom Sawyer* this way: *McDougal's Cave was but a labyrinth of crooked aisles that ran into each other and out again and led nowhere. It was said that one might wander days and nights together through its intricate tangle of rifts and chasms and never find the end of the cave. No man 'knew' the cave. That was an impossible thing.*

THE WRITER AND HIS TIMES

BORN: Nov. 30, 1835, in Florida, Mo.

DIED: April 21, 1910, at his home, Stormfield, in Redding, Conn.; buried Elmira, N.Y.

EDUCATED: Largely self-educated

MARRIED: Olivia Langdon; 1870; three daughters, one son

ACCOLADES: Honorary degrees from Yale, University of Missouri, Oxford

IMPORTANT WORKS: *The Celebrated Jumping Frog of Calaveras County* (1867); *The Innocents Abroad* (1869); *Roughing It* (1872); *The Adventures of Tom Sawyer* (1876); *A Tramp Abroad* (1880); *The Prince and the Pauper* (1882); *Life on the Mississippi* (1883); *The Adventures of Huckleberry Finn* (1885); *A Connecticut Yankee in King Arthur's Court* (1889); *The Tragedy of Pudd'nhead Wilson and the Comedy of Those Extraordinary Twins* (1894); *Personal Recollections of Joan of Arc* (1896); *Following the Equator* (1897); *Autobiography* (1924); *The Mysterious Stranger Manuscripts* (1969); *What is Man? and Other Philosophical Writings* (1973)

Twain's works also include five travelogues, detailing his experiences in the western United States, along the Mississippi, in Europe, the Middle East and Asia. Twain wrote his last work, *The Death of Jean*, following the death of his youngest daughter, Jean, in 1909. He vowed never to write again.

FURTHER READING *River Boy: The Story of Mark Twain* by William Anderson (2003); *Mark Twain and Me* by Dorothy Quick (1999); *Mark Twain's America* by B.A. Devoto, et. al. (1997)

ELSEWHERE IN THE AREA The Molly Brown Dinner Theater, 200 N. Main, stages theme musicals. Also: 1878 Old Jail Museum, 201 S. Fourth St.; Mark Twain Outdoor Theater at Clemens Landing, US 61 south; and the Mississippi Riverboat *Mark Twain* river tours from the foot of Center Street. Mark Twain's modest birthplace welcomes visitors at the Mark Twain State Park in Florida, Mo.

• WHAT'S IN A NAME? •

When Samuel Langhorne Clemens became a writer, he used a term familiar to his boyhood on the shores of the Mississippi River as his pseudonym. When the riverboats huffed into Hannibal, a leadsman in the bows would constantly heave a line into the river waters and call out the depths. When he saw that the river's depth was two fathoms deep, the leadsman cried out "By the mark, twain!" This meant the boat was safe, with 12 feet of water beneath her. The exclamation "mark, twain" was a welcome sound in Hannibal.

It must have been especially pleasant for young Sam Clemens, who later took Mark Twain as his pen name.

• A TWAIN RIDE •

Mark Twain traveled throughout America, absorbing the places, people and experiences that became fodder for his writing. Other Twain sites in this book include Hartford, Conn.; Redding, Conn.; San Francisco and Sonoma, Calif.; and the campus of Elmira Collage in upstate New York. ⌂

LAURA INGALLS WILDER HISTORIC HOME
Where 'Little House' Books Were Penned

LOCATION Southwest Missouri in Mansfield, in the Ozark hills, 45 miles east of Springfield on US 60. In Mansfield, take US 60 to Highway 5/A south to Highway A east. The **Laura Ingalls Wilder/Rose Wilder Lane Historic Home and Museum** ($) is 1 mile east of Town Square.

The home and museum are open from March 1 through mid-November, Monday through Saturday, from 9 a.m. to 5 p.m., and on Sunday from 12:30 p.m. to 5:30 p.m. In June, July and August, the site closes at 5:30 p.m. Closed Easter. For more information, contact Laura Ingalls Wilder/Rose Wilder Lane Historic Home and Museum ($), 3068 Highway A, Mansfield, MO 65704. Tel. (417) 924-3626 or 1-877-924-7126. On the Net: www.lauraingallswilderhome.com.

FRAME OF REFERENCE Laura Ingalls "Bessie" Wilder and her husband, Almanzo, finished building their home on the Rocky Ridge Farm in 1913. Their daughter Rose gave the stone cottage, called The Rock House, to them in 1928 as a retirement home. The Wilders lived in the large house, built on the edge of the farm, until 1936. The couple then moved back into their original house and spent their remaining years there. Wilder died in 1957 and the historic site opened to the public that same year.

SIGNIFICANCE Wilder begin writing her *Little House* series of autobiographical books in her sixties while living at Rocky Ridge Farm. Her nine books about growing up on the American frontier had become classics of children's literature by the mid-1950s. Their publication made the Wilders well-known international literary characters.

Wilder's popularity culminated in the television series, *Little House on the Prairie,* which ran on NBC from 1974 through 1984. The late actor Michael Landon produced, starred in and sometimes directed the show and the *Little House* TV movie that preceded it. Two made-for-television movies also were made in the mid-1980s. A Broadway musical, *Prairie,* ran in 1982. The *Little House* set for the TV series burned to the ground during the California wildfires of 2003.

Although her books have been criticized as patriarchal, materialistic and racist, Wilder said that she wrote her stories to provide history lessons for new generations of children who no longer could experience the character-building prairie frontier. She wanted them to learn the values of home, love and personal courage from her stories. Wilder's books, which have never been out of print, have been published in 40 languages.

ABOUT THE SITE On the 163-acre Rocky Ridge Farm, you'll find Wilder's nine-room farmhouse; the English Tudor-style stone house given to her by Rose; and the museum, which is located next to the farmhouse. The two-story, white clapboard farmhouse began as a windowless, one-room log cabin the Wilders built with materials from the farm. The Wilders expanded the house through the years to eight rooms. The simple house, the same inside and outside just as Wilder left it, has a back porch and two large front windows flanking the front door.

Inside the farmhouse, you'll find the Wilders' 1920s furniture and belongings throughout the house. Of special note are Wilder's small, fold-down desk with letters and notepad as she left them; her sewing machine in the museum; the Adirondack chairs and the cypress stump table Almanzo made for the house's sunniest corner; the lap desk Almanzo made for Wilder and the clock he gave to his family at Christmas 1886. Wilder describes the lap desk in her book, *On The Way Home*, a diary of her trip from South Dakota to Mansfield. She said that $100 hidden in the desk served as down payment for their Mansfield farm, along with a bank loan.

Wilder told about the clock in *The First Four Years*. She said the clock traveled with them to Mansfield, and Almanzo wound it nightly before going to bed. Caretakers still wind the clock daily and it works "perfectly."

The farmhouse, completed in 1913, features open-beam ceilings, wood paneling throughout and picture windows (shades now protect the furnishings from sunlight) Wilder designed her house so that she could bring the outside in and see her outside surroundings, an idea that was unusual for that era in the Ozarks. At Wilder's insistence, a main fireplace in the front parlor was built of three massive fieldstones found on the farm, and her cozy yellow kitchen featured appliances and cabinets built to accommodate her diminutive height, 4 feet 10 or 11 inches.

She arranged the nearly all-white upstairs bedroom at Rocky Ridge Farm for company. Author Helen Boylston, who wrote the *Sue Barton* career nurse books, used the room from 1928-1931. The museum contains Wilder-related artifacts, family photographs, some of Wilder's hand-written manuscripts, and Pa's fiddle.

HOT TIPS In Mansfield you'll also find the Wilder Public Library, a bronze bust of Wilder in Mansfield Square, and the Wilder graves in Mansfield Cemetery at the end of Lincoln Street off Highway A. The gravesite is in the cemetery's center section. The Wilder farm hosts the annual Rocky Ridge Day on the Saturday closest to Oct. 15. For more on Wilder, look under South Dakota and Minnesota in this book.

THE BEST STUFF The museum at Rocky Ridge Farm displays Pa's fiddle, looking much as Charles Ingalls would have left it after playing a tune for his family. Pa Ingalls was the family dreamer, while Ma Caroline was the civilizer and stabilizer. When Pa sang, young Laura and her three sisters were transported to sweet places beyond the hardships of their pioneer life.

THE WRITER AND HER WORK

BORN: Feb. 7, 1867, in Pepin Wis.

DIED: Feb. 10, 1957, in Mansfield; buried Mansfield Cemetery

MARRIED: Almanzo James Wilder, 1885; one daughter, one son who died in infancy

IMPORTANT WORKS: *Little House in the Big Woods* (1932, about first years in Pepin, Wis.); *Farmer Boy* (1933, about Almanzo's childhood in Malone, NY); *Little House on the Prairie* (1935, Independence, Kan.); *On the Banks of Plum Creek* (1937, Walnut Grove, Minn.); *By the Shores of Silver Lake* (1939); *The Long Winter* (1940); *Little Town on the Prairie* (1941); *These Happy Golden Years* (1943). Wilder's manuscript of *The First Four Years* was published posthumously in 1971. The book tells about the early years of her marriage.

ACCOLADES: The American Library Association initiated the Laura Ingalls Wilder Medal for children's literature in 1954.

INTERESTING BIO FACT: Known as Bessie to her family, the ambitious, intelligent and individualistic farm girl became author Laura Ingalls Wilder late in life. Wilder's daughter, Rose, an accomplished writer, encouraged her to write about her family's adventures on the frontier. No publisher was interested in Wilder's first attempt at a book, *Pioneer Girl*, in 1930. But with Rose's help, Wilder rewrote her manuscript. It was published as *Little House in the Big Woods*, and Wilder's writing career took off. Bessie Wilder, however, continued to run her farm, read her Bible and participate in the rural way of life she loved.

FURTHER READING *The Little House Guidebook* By William Anderson (2002); *Becoming Laura Ingalls Wilder: The Woman Behind the Legend* by John E. Miller (1998); *The Little House Cookbook* by Barbara M. Walker (1995)

ELSEWHERE IN THE AREA Mark Twain National Forest is southeast of Mansfield ◢

'THE ELMS': BESS STREETER ALDRICH HOUSE

Home of Best-Selling Midwestern Writer

LOCATION Southeastern Nebraska, in Elmwood, along Highway 1, at 204 East F St.

From Lincoln, take US 34 16 miles to Highway 1 north 2 miles to F Street. The **Bess Streeter Aldrich House and Museum** is open May through October, on Wednesday, Thursday, Saturday and Sunday, from 2 p.m. to 5 p.m., and from November through April on Saturday only. Visitors also can take a self-guided **Walking Tour of Aldrich Homes** and Aldrich-related sites in tiny Elmwood.

For more information, contact the Bess Streeter Aldrich House, P.O Box. 167, Elmwood, NE 68349. Tel: (402) 994-3855. On the Net: www .lincolnne.com/nonprofit/bsaf.

FRAME OF REFERENCE Bess Geneva Streeter Aldrich lived in her prairie mansion, The Elms, which she and husband, Charles, built in 1922, until 1946, when she moved to Lincoln to live with her grown daughter. Aldrich lived in several homes in Elmwood prior to The Elms. Young Aldrich moved with her family to Elmwood in 1909.

SIGNIFICANCE During her 40-year career, Aldrich was among the best-selling and highest-paid writers of her time. Her success came largely from stories published such national magazines as The American, Saturday Evening Post, Ladies Home Journal, Collier's, Cosmopolitan and McCall's.

In addition to her 13 novels, Aldrich wrote 160 short stories and articles. Her works, several of which were made into movies, emphasized family values and told of Midwest pioneering. She is best known for her novel *A Lantern in Her Hand* (1928).

Other popular works include *Miss Bishop* (1933), *Song of Years* (1939) and *The Lieutenant's Lady* (1942). Aldrich's short story, *Why I Live in a Small Town*, printed in the Ladies Home Journal in 1933, remains particularly popular in Nebraska. Aldrich produced most of her work in Elmwood, which served as the setting for many of her stories and novels.

ABOUT THE SITE The Elms is a stately two-story, 10-room frame dwelling with white stucco upper level and brick lower level. Towering elms Aldrich herself planted once surrounded the house, but died years ago of disease. The house has a brick center chimney and low brick fence. Most of the home's furnishings belonged to Aldrich, but some symbolize Aldrich's life in Elmwood. The house displays an ice cream table from the former Greene's Drug Store that Aldrich often frequented. A legal bookcase came from the old Elmwood post office.

The four upstairs bedrooms are named for Aldrich's novels and are thematically decorated with a few pieces out of the story. The bedroom called *Lantern In Her Hand* features a Christmas tree next to a pump organ and rocking horse like those Aldrich described. In the master *Mother Mason* bedroom, articles on the dresser and the sewing machine are items Aldrich wrote about. You'll also find Aldrich's three-piece luggage set with brass initials.

The shrubbery and flowers around The Elms are labeled with the name of the book in which Aldrich mentioned them. Aldrich enjoyed tending her yard. When she moved to the house, she even planted 20 additional elms, now dead of Dutch-elm disease. The house also has a small gift shop.

The Elmwood walking tour encompasses five Aldrich houses, including The Elms, as well as The Elmwood Bank, at 102 S. Fourth, co-owned by Charles Aldrich. You also can visit the Aldrich family gravesite in Elmwood Cemetery along Highway 1, the Aldrich park next to the site, and the Aldrich Museum and Library downtown.

HOT TIPS Tours of The Elms are guided tours. The site hosts many special events, including an Aldrich Birthday Celebration in February, a Christmas holiday open house, and lawn concerts.

The site of the house where Streeter was born in **Cedar Falls, Iowa**, is located at 809 Franklin St. Bess and Charles also were married in the house. That structure has been demolished and the house that now occupies the site is a private residence and not open to the public. A house in Lincoln where Aldrich lived with her daughter is located on what is now Aldrich Drive.

THE BEST STUFF The study where Aldrich penned most of her writing on tablets contains her original writing desk, which opens to reveal a typewriter. Aldrich didn't type, but hired a local high school girl to type for her. On the desk, you'll see an article from a 1942 World Herald issue that shows Aldrich working in the room. An east-facing window above Aldrich's desk allowed her a view of "the rim of the prairie" as she wrote. Charles had coined the phrase, and Aldrich dedicated her second book,

The Rim of the Prairie, to her husband. He died just before its publication in 1925.

THE WRITER AND HER WORK

BORN: Feb. 17, 1881, in Cedar Falls, Iowa

DIED: 1954, in Lincoln, Neb.; buried Elmwood Cemetery

EDUCATED: Iowa State Normal School, 1901

MARRIED: Charles Aldrich, a captain in the Spanish-American War, 1907; four children

IMPORTANT WORKS: *Mother Mason* (1924); *The Rim of the Prairie* (1925); *The Cutters* (1926); *A Lantern in Her Hand* (1928); *A White Bird Flying* (1931); *Miss Bishop* !933); *Spring Came on Forever* (1935); *The Man Who Caught the Weather and Other Stories* (1936); *Song of Years* (1939); *The Drum Goes Dead* (1941); *The Lieutenant's Lady* (1942); *Journey Into Christmas* (1949)

ACCOLADES: Honorary degree, University of Nebraska, 1934; Iowa Authors Outstanding Contributions to Literature Award, 1949; Nebraska Hall of Fame, 1973

INTERESTING BIO FACT: Aldrich begin writing stories as a child and won prizes for her stories as a teenager. Her busy life as a wife and mother caused her to stop writing until she saw an announcement for a fiction contest in Ladies Home Journal in 1911.

While her baby napped in the afternoons, Aldrich penned a story that was one of six selected from 2,000 entries. Her first book of short stores followed in 1924.

When Charles Aldrich died of a cerebral hemorrhage, Bess had to support her family. Her writing not only enabled her to do so, but eventually paid for college educations for all four of her children.

FURTHER READING *Bess Streeter Aldrich: The Dreams Are Real* by Carol M. Peterson (1996); *Fulfilled Visions: The Life and Work of Bess Streeter Aldrich* by Patrick Keating (1990)

ELSEWHERE IN THE AREA Arbor Lodge State Historical Park southeast of Elmwood; The 25-mile MoPac East Recreational Trail traverses some of southeast Nebraska's finest wildlife habitat and Elmwood. ◪

'CATHERLAND'

Red Cloud Area Remembers Willa Cather

LOCATION The town of Red Cloud is located in south central Nebraska 6 miles north of the Kansas state line and 50 miles south of Grand Island, Neb. The town, in western Webster County, is located at the junction of US 281 and US 136 in the Republican Valley. The Nebraska State Legislature officially proclaimed the area "**Catherland**" in 1965 and erected a state historical marker as testimony 14 miles north of Red Cloud.

The **Willa Cather State Historic Site** and childhood home is located at 3rd and Cedar Streets in Red Cloud. The home is accessible as part of the guided **Willa Cather Walking Tour** ($) in Red Cloud. A self-guided, 1-mile version of the tour includes additional Cather-related sites. The guided Cather tours are available year-round, Monday through Saturday from 8 a.m. to 5 p.m., and on Sunday from 1 p.m. to 5 p.m. Last tour at 3 p.m. Closed Jan. 1, Easter, Thanksgiving, Dec. 25.

For more information, contact Willa Cather Pioneer Memorial and Educational Foundation, 326 N Webster, Red Cloud, NE 68970-2550. Tel. (402) 746-2653. On the Net: www.willacather.org. Or contact the Nebraska State Historical Society, P.O. Box 82554, Lincoln, NE 68501. E-mail: wcpm@gpcom.net.

FRAME OF REFERENCE Willa Siebert Cather lived in this home in Red Cloud from 1884 to 1890, when she left for college. The house was built circa 1876. Cather moved at age 9 from Virginia with her family to a farm in Webster County for 2 years before moving to nearby Red Cloud.

SIGNIFICANCE Cather — author, journalist, editor, short-story writer, poet, teacher, critic — is best known for her novels, *O Pioneers!* (1913), *My Antonia* (1918) and *Death Comes for the Archbishop* (1927). She wrote 12 novels, several made into popular movies, and excelled in her portrayals of human relationships and immigrant and pioneer life on the frontier West. Six of her books are set in Red Cloud, a Great Plains town of about 1,000 people, including *One of Ours* (1922), a scathing look at the world, which won the Pulitzer Prize. Cather, a proponent of Naturalism, drew on her childhood in the farming community for both plot and scenery.

Sinclair Lewis, on being awarded the Nobel Prize for Literature in 1930, declared Cather should have won it.

ABOUT THE SITE A tour of Webster County can take you to more than 190 Cather-related sites, making Catherland possibly the largest historic district dedicated to an author in the United States. Here are facts about the tours of Red Cloud:

WILLA CATHER WALKING TOURS You can choose between two guided tours of Cather-related sites: a three-building tour or a seven-building tour. Tours begin at the Willa Cather Pioneer Memorial bookstore in the renovated Red Cloud Opera House, built 1885, at 326 N Webster St. in Red Cloud. The three-building tour includes the Cather childhood home, the Opera House and the Garber Bank Building, which Cather wrote about in *Lost Lady*. Additional sites on the seven-building tour include the 1883 Miner Brothers' General Store, described in *Two Friends*; The Harling Home in *My Ántonia* (real home of the J. L. Miner family); The Rosen House of *Old Mrs. Harris*; the Cather family church. Other sites are also within walking distance.

You can also visit the **Willa Cather Memorial Prairie** 5 1/2 miles south of Red Cloud along Highway 281. The park offers hiking and riding trails through 610 acres of native grasslands. You also can walk the chalk cliffs of the Republican River, as well as the Pavelka farmstead and crossroads grave site, both described in *My Antonia.*

WILLA CATHER CHILDHOOD HOME The modest, 1 1/2-story light brown wood house has a full front porch and is surrounded by a white picket fence. The interior has been restored to its 1870s appearance with many rooms exactly as Cather described them. The house has some Cather family artifacts, including the family Bible, furniture, dishes and decorations.

Cather wrote of her childhood home in *Old Mrs. Harris* and *The Best Years*. In *Song of the Lark* she wrote of the house: "They turned into another street and saw before them lighted windows; a low story-and-a-half house, with a wing built on at the right and a kitchen addition at the back, everything a little on the slant — roofs, windows, and doors."

HOT TIPS Write for *A Walking Tour* map or pick it up at the Opera House, where you'll find a Cather art gallery and bookstore. The gallery displays paintings by John Blake Bergers illustrating scenes from Cather's writings. The Cather Archives at the site contain letters, photographs, early manuscripts and other historical items related to the Cather family and the real people behind the characters in Cather's writing. Researchers can visit the archives by appointment.

The foundation hosts special events year-round, including the annual Willa Cather Spring Festival in May, now in its 48th year, and a celebration of Cather's birthday the first weekend in December.

THE BEST STUFF The young Cather's attic bedroom where she wrote still features the wallpaper Cather hung long ago. In *Song of the Lark*, Cather described the wallpaper as having red and brown roses on a yellow background. The Cather children called this room "The Rose Bower."

THE WRITER AND HER WORK

BORN: Dec. 7, 1873, in Back Creek Valley, Va.

DIED: April 24, 1947, in New York City; buried in New Hampshire

EDUCATED: Lincoln State/University of Nebraska, 1895

IMPORTANT WORKS: *Alexander's Bridge* (1912); *O Pioneers!* (1913); *My Antonia* (1918); *Lost Lady* (1923); *Song of the Lark* (1915); *One of Ours* (1922); *The Professor's House* (1925); *My Mortal Enemy* (1926); *Death Comes for the Archbishop* (1927); *Shadows on the Rock* (1931); *Obscure Destinies* (1932, short stories); *Lucy Gayheart* (1935); *Sapphira and the Slave Girl* (1940)

ACCOLADES: Pulitzer Prize, 1923, for *One of Ours*; American Academy medal for *Death Comes for the Archbishop*; gold medal from the National Institute of Arts and Letters; numerous honorary degrees

INTERESTING BIO FACT: An accomplished journalist, Cather worked as an editor, then managing editor of McClure's magazine. While on an assignment for McClure's, Cather met author **Sarah Orne Jewett** (see Maine in the New England section of this book), who encouraged her to quit journalism and write books. Cather dedicated *O Pioneers!* to Jewett's memory.

FURTHER READING *Willa Cather and the Politics of Criticism* by Joan R. Acocella (2002); *Willa Cather and the American Southwest* edited by John N. Swift (2002); *Willa Cather: A Literary Life* by James Woodress (1989)

ELSEWHERE IN THE AREA Historic Round Barn, on US 136, 4 miles east of Red Cloud; 1914 Webster County Courthouse; Webster County Historical Museum, US 136

WEST NORTH CENTRAL *Nebraska*

• CATHER IN VIRGINIA •

Cather's childhood home near the town where she was born, **Gore, Va.**, (then called Back Creek Valley), stands along US 50 in northern Virginia near the West Virginia border. A commemorative plaque stands in front of the house, Willow Shade, built in 1858. Cather lived in the farmhouse from 1874 to 1883, when her immigrant parents moved to Nebraska. The house was the setting for the last chapters of Cather's novel *Sapphira and the Slave Girl*. The large house, which served as a Civil War field hospital, is privately owned and not open to the public.

On the Net: http://www.womenwriters.net/domesticgoddess/ catherhome.html. ◬

JOHN NEIHARDT CENTER

Honoring Poet Laureate Who Wrote 'Black Elk Speaks'

LOCATION Northeastern Nebraska, in Bancroft, about 30 miles southwest of Sioux City and west of US 77 at the intersection of Highways 51 and 16. The John Neihardt Center is located at 306 W. Elm. St., at Washington Street.

The center is open Monday through Saturday, from 8 a.m. to noon and 1 p.m. to 5 p.m., and on Sunday from 1:30 p.m. to 5 p.m. For more information, contact the John G. Neihardt Center, P.O. Box 344, Bancroft, NE 68004. Tel. (402) 648-3388 or 1-888-777-4667. E-mail: neihardt@gpcom.net. On the Net: www.ci.bancroft.ne.us/tourism.htm.

FRAME OF REFERENCE John Gneisenau Neihardt came to Wayne, Neb., in 1891 with his mother and sisters. The family moved to Bancroft in 1900 and Neihardt lived in the town for 20 years. He returned to Nebraska at age 88 and remained in the state until his death. The Neihardt Center, a branch museum of the Nebraska State Historical Society, was opened in 1976.

SIGNIFICANCE Neihardt was Nebraska's Poet Laureate for 52 years, but the writer, educator and philosopher is best known for his famous book, *Black Elk Speaks* (1932). The book, which recorded the life of the legendary Oglala Lakota (Sioux) Holy Man in his own words, is considered the most influential book ever written on American Indian culture and religion.

Neihardt interviewed Black Elk as a historical source for an epic poem he was writing on Wounded Knee. The two became friends, and Neihardt wrote fully of the respected tribal elder and spiritual leader in his book. Neihardt's other books include: *The Sacred Pipe: Black Elk's Account of the Seven Rites of the Oglala Sioux*; (1953) *The Sixth Grandfather: Black Elk's Teachings Given to John G. Neihardt* (1984).

In Bancroft, a town of 500 people, Neihardt began his epic poem, *The Cycle of the West*, in 1912. He completed the work in 1941. The epic poem comprises four parts: *The Song of Hugh Glass* (1915); *The Song of Three Friends* (1919); *The Song of the Indian Wars* (1925); and *The Song of the Messiah* (1941). These poems, published in 1949, earned Neihardt national attention. Neihardt wrote at least 13 of his major works in Bancroft.

ABOUT THE SITE The John Neihardt Center features exhibits that chronicle Neihardt's life, works and the times in which he lived. You'll find Neihardt's one-room, 8-foot by 10-foot study at the exact location as when he rented it in the late 1890s. The cabin was built circa 1880, possibly as a honeymoon cabin. You'll also see The Sacred Hoop Garden, a Sioux prayer garden that Neihardt designed. The garden contains symbolism from the vision of Black Elk and represents Neihardt's interest in American Indian customs and traditions.

Neihardt's study, inside a little, white wood cottage with front porch, stands near the garden, shaded by a towering tree. Inside, you'll find Neihardt's writing table, rocking chair and a pot-bellied stove. In the center, visitors can view videotapes of Neihardt reading his poetry, portraits of the author, and family sculptures by his wife, Mona, who studied under Auguste Rodin in Paris. Especially interesting are the sacred personal items that Black Elk gave Neihardt in 1931. These include his sacred pipe, drum, and coup stick.

HOT TIPS The center hosts the annual John G. Neihardt Spring Conference the last Saturday in April, and an outdoor festival, Neihardt Day, the first Sunday in August. The Sunday Afternoon at the Museum (SAM) offers special programs. For more on Black Elk, see Montana in the Mountain section of this book.

THE BEST STUFF The circular Sacred Hoop Garden comes from a vision of Black Elk and is a living symbol of the vastness of the universe. Neihardt wrote of the garden symbolism in *Black Elk Speaks*. The Oglala Lakota Holy Man said the Hoop of the World is "so big it has everything in it."

Visitors can stroll the garden's two intersecting "roads", one a hard black road beginning in the east and going west, and the other a red road that lies north and south.

The black road is the road of world difficulty. The red road, which makes the black road bearable, is one of spiritual understanding.

The intersecting paths divide the Hoop into four quarters: north, south, east west, each with individual meaning. The West, symbolized by the color blue or black, has the power of life and destruction. The North is white, symbolizing cleansing and healing. The quarter of the East is red, with the power of enlightenment; the South is yellow to symbolize the power to grow. Where the garden paths intersect, a crabapple tree of life — filled with leaves, blossoms and singing birds — protects man. In Black Elk's vision, the tree was a cottonwood.

THE WRITER AND HIS WORK

BORN: Jan. 8, 1881, near Sharpsburg, Ill.

DIED: Nov. 3, 1973 in Columbia, Mo.; ashes mingled with wife's and scattered from an airplane into Missouri River

EDUCATED: Nebraska Normal College (now Wayne State)

MARRIED: Mona Martinsen, 1908; four children

IMPORTANT WORKS: *The Devine Enchantment*, 1900; *A Bundle of Myrrh*, 1907; *The Lonesome Trail*, 1907; *Man Song*, 1909; *The River and I*, 1910; *The Stranger at the Gate*, 1912; *Two Mothers*, 1921; *Indian Tales and Other*, 1926; *The Song of the Messiah*, 1935; *The Song of Jed Smith*, 1941; *When the Tree Flowered*, 1951; *Patterns & Coincidences*, 1978

ACCOLADES: National Institute of Arts and Letters; Poetry Society of America national prize, 1919; gold medal from Poetry Center, 1936; Nebraska Poet Laureate, 1921; first civilian member Order of Indian Wars, 1925; Prairie Poet Laureate of America, 1968; Nebraska Poet Laureate in Perpetuity, 1982; and numerous honorary degrees

INTERESTING BIO FACT: The Illinois native's life-long interest in American Indians began when he moved to Bancroft in 1901. He was an assistant in a trader's office and worked closely with area tribes. He spent many hours in Indian camps learning their history, traditions and customs. Between 1944 and 1948, Neihardt worked in U.S. Bureau of Indian Affairs and also was co-owner and editor of a small weekly newspaper in Bancroft.

FURTHER READING *Interpreting the Legacy: John Neihardt and Black Elk Speaks* by Brian Holloway (2003); *The Black Elk Reader* edited by Clyde Holler (2000); *Black Elk and Flaming Rainbow* by Hilda Neihardt (1999)

ELSEWHERE IN THE AREA The Susan LaFlesche Picotte Center in Walthill, Neb. ◭

He is a word sender. This world is like a garden and over it go his words like rain, and where they go they leave everything greener. After his words have passed, the memory of them shall stand long in the West like a flaming rainbow.

— BLACK ELK on Neihardt

HAMLIN GARLAND MEMORIAL
Site of Writer's Farm Homestead

Hamlin Garland, the poet known for his *Middle Border* books, lived briefly on a homestead he claimed in 1881 near **Aberdeen, S.D.**, in northeastern South Dakota at US 12 and US 281. Garland's homestead was 5 miles west of his father, Richard's, homesteading farm near Ordway. The small wooden house that Garland built burned down in the early 1900s, but the site is now marked by a plaque on a 15-ton boulder. The plaque at the site of the **Hamlin Garland Homestead** was dedicated in 1936. Garland — novelist, short-story writer, biographer, poet, and essayist — authored 52 books and about 500 pieces for periodicals. The frontier author began his best-known work, *Main-Travelled Roads* (1891), an innovative collection of short stories, at his homestead near Aberdeen. Garland was awarded the Pulitzer Prize for best biography in 1921 for *Daughter of the Middle Border*, part of his *Middle Border* series that includes his memoir *A Son of the Middle Border* (1917). Garland's works, often autobiographical, tell of the hardships of pioneer life and the colorful social practices of the Midwest.

Main-Travelled Roads offered a harsh view of farming. Garland dedicated his widely acclaimed book to his parents "whose half-century pilgrimage on the main roads of life has brought them only toil and deprivation."

In June 1936, the Brown County Commissioners named a section of Brown County Highway 11 the Hamlin Garland Memorial Highway. The 10-mile section wends past the homestead of Richard Garland. The Garland Township near Ordway also was named in the poet's honor.

Garland (1860-1940), a Wisconsin native, also lived in Iowa, Boston, Chicago, the Hudson Valley and Los Angeles, Calif. For details on Garland, see Wisconsin in the East North Central section of this book. For more information on the Hamlin Garland Homestead, contact Aberdeen/Brown County Landmarks Commission, 123 S. Lincoln St., Aberdeen, SD 57401 or the Hamlin Garland Society, P. O. Box 405, Aberdeen SD 57401-0405. ◬

LAURA INGALLS WILDER'S DE SMET

Tour Tells of 'Little Town on the Prairie'

Fans of Laura Ingalls Wilder, who wrote the popular autobiographical series of *Little House* books, should put the town of De Smet, S.D. on their literary maps.

Wilder wrote of her life in De Smet in two of her books, *By the Shores of Silver Lake* (1939) and *The Long Winter* (1940). In De Smet, "The Little Town on the Prairie," the **Laura Ingalls Wilder Memorial Society Tour** ($) takes visitors to several Wilder-related sites. De Smet is located in east central South Dakota along US 14 between Huron and Brookings.

Guided tours include visits to **The Surveyors' House**, Laura's prairie home in Dakota Territory for one winter; a replica of the **Brewster School**, where Laura taught; **The Ingalls House,** called "The House That Pa Built" six blocks away; and the nearby **Ingalls Memorial,** which features an Ingalls Monument and five cottonwood trees planted more than 100 years ago by Pa Ingalls. Pa planted a tree on his homesteading property for each of "his girls."

In summer months, you also can attend the **Wilder Pageant**, an outdoor drama about Wilder's De Smet years. Wilder's parents and many of the people mentioned in her books are buried in the **De Smet Cemetery**. You'll also find many of the De Smet landmarks Wilder wrote about in her books.

Wilder (1867-1957) penned six of her nine *Little House* books about life in De Smet, where she moved with her family when she was 12 years old. The town of about 1,200 people retains Loftis Store on Main Street, where Laura and sister Carrie bought suspenders for Pa at Christmas; and you can visit the Big Slough and the site of Silver Lake, now drained. The home of Banker Ruth in De Smet still stands. It has been converted to a bed and breakfast.

The Surveyors' House is the oldest building in De Smet, a town that began as a community of railroad workers. The town, settled in 1880 near Silver Lake, was named for Father Pierre Jean De Smet, a Belgian Jesuit Priest known as "The Apostle of the Indians." The railroad surveyors, hired to work for the Chicago Northwestern (now the Chicago and Northwestern) Railroad, stayed in the four-room residence during the warm months. When they returned East for the winter of 1879, they asked Pa Ingalls and his family to live in the house to guard their tools.

Pa worked as storekeeper and timekeeper for the men working on the railroad grade.

When the surveyors returned in the spring of 1880, the Ingalls family moved to a shanty on their nearby, 160-acre homesteading claim. That shanty disappeared long ago but the story lives on in *The Long Winter*. Wilder's book tells of the harsh winter of 1880-1881, when trains were stopped for months and the town nearly starved to death.

In 1887, the Ingalls moved into a new house that Pa had built in De Smet. That two-story wood house at 210 3rd St. SW is called The Ingalls House. The house displays many artifacts and personal items of the Ingalls and Wilder families. Ma and Pa Ingalls lived in the house until their deaths.

Today, the Surveyors' House, originally built of board-and-batten, has been restored to resemble its appearance of the late 1800s. In 1940, a private owner covered the exterior with white siding and this remains. The three downstairs rooms, plus huge pantry and large upstairs room, now look much as they did when the Ingalls lived there. In the house, you'll see the original organ from the First Congregational church that Pa Ingalls helped establish, a family dresser and a special mantel clock. The clock belonged to David Gilbert, the man who delivered mail to the isolated Ingalls home during the harsh winter.

A Wilder gift shop is located in a restored old home next to the Surveyors' House, which the Wilder Memorial Society opened to the public in 1967.

The Ingalls Memorial is located 1 mile southeast of De Smet off US 14. The 1.12-acre, fenced-in site, which has never been plowed, features the five cottonwood trees and the Ingalls Memorial. The stone Ingalls monument stands at the possible site of the family's shanty. The monument features facts about the Ingalls' stay in De Smet. After her marriage, Wilder and her husband, Charles, lived in another homestead in De Smet until 1894, when they moved to Missouri.

Surveyors' House tours are offered daily in June, July and August from 9 a.m. to 5:30 p.m.; and Monday through Saturday in September, October, April and May, from 9 a.m. to 3:30 p.m. From November through March, tours are offered Monday through Friday from 9 a.m. to 3:30 p.m. There is no admission to the Ingalls Memorial.

For more tour information, contact the Laura Ingalls Memorial Society, Inc., P.O. Box 426 De Smet, SD 57231. Tel. 1-800-880-3383 Ext. 2. E-mail: laura@liwms.com. On the Net: www.liwms.com. For details about the Wilder Pageant, contact the Wilder Pageant Society, Box 154, De Smet, SD 57231. Tel. (605) 692-2108. On the Net: www.desmetpageant.org ◮

Robert Penn Warren House

FITZGERALD MUSEUM
F. Scott and Zelda's Alabama Home

LOCATION In the Alabama capital, Montgomery, at 919 Felder Ave. in the historic Cloverdale neighborhood just south of the downtown area. From I-85,take Exit 1 onto Decatur Street, left on Carter Hill Road at Alabama State University Acadome onto Dunbar Street, then left on Felder.

The F. Scott and Zelda Fitzgerald Museum (donation) is open Wednesday through Friday from 10 a.m. to 2 p.m. and Saturday and Sunday from 1 p.m. to 5 p.m. For more information, contact F. Scott and Zelda Fitzgerald Museum Association, P.O. Box 64, Montgomery, AL 36101. On the Net: www.fitzgerald-museum.org.

FRAME OF REFERENCE Francis Scott Key Fitzgerald and his wife, Zelda, a Montgomery native, lived in this leased house from Oct. 1931 to April 1932. Scott spent some of this period in Hollywood as a screenwriter, leaving Zelda and their daughter, Scottie, behind. When Zelda suffered another mental breakdown in February and was hospitalized in Baltimore, Fitzgerald returned and lived here with Scottie until April. Zelda's breakdowns and hospitalizations continued until her death in 1948. The 1901 house was privately owned until 1986. The museum opened in 1988.

SIGNIFICANCE Fitzgerald, novelist, short-story writer and Hollywood screenwriter, is recognized as one of the greatest talents of the generation of writers that brought American literature to world prominence. His writings recorded — and helped create — the flamboyant Golden Age of Jazz.

Fitzgerald's well-crafted novels tell of the social manners of a fading American aristocracy. *The Great Gatsby,* considered his masterpiece, was turned into a successful Broadway play, as well as three films in 1926, 1949 and 1974. America remembers Fitzgerald as much for his high living, tumultuous love for the emotionally unstable Zelda, and madcap antics as for his enduring literary contributions.

ABOUT THE SITE The Fitzgeralds, who met while Scott was stationed as an Army lieutenant in Montgomery, leased this two-story, brick and shingle Tudor with plans to settle down after living in Europe. They lived in the house only briefly. While here, Fitzgerald worked on his novel *Tender*

Is The Night and several short stories, often typing on the back patio. Zelda worked on her novel *Save Me The Waltz*.

Although Fitzgerald's residences are documented in several places in the United States, this house apparently is the only official Fitzgerald site open to the public. The museum memorializes Scott and Zelda's life and honors Fitzgerald's famous works.

Today the house comprises four apartments. The first-floor unit on the right houses the museum. The cream-colored rooms, with high ceilings and heavy dark wood moldings, are furnished with period furniture. Visitors can view Fitzgerald artifacts, photographs, two marble-topped tables from Zelda's childhood home, Zelda's original paintings (she was an accomplished writer, painter and dancer), newspaper articles, magazines, and letters the celebrity couple exchanged during courtship and marriage.

HOT TIPS Call ahead to confirm limited museum hours. On-street parking; handicapped accessible. You can find a sizable collection of papers of F. Scott and Zelda at Princeton University. For details, go to http://libweb.princeton .edu. The University of South Carolina also has a Fitzgerald collection. On the Net: http://www.sc.edu/fitzgerald/collection.

THE WRITER AND HIS WORK

BORN: Sept. 24, 1896, in St. Paul, Minn.

DIED: Dec. 21, 1940, in Hollywood, Calif.; buried in Rockland Union Cemetery in Rockland, Md. In 1975, Scott and Zelda's graves and marker were moved to Saint Mary's church cemetery in Rockland. The gravestone features the last sentence from *Gatsby*: "So we beat on, boats against the current, borne back ceaselessly into the past."

EDUCATED: St. Paul Academy; N.J. prep school; Princeton, class of 1917

MARRIED: Zelda Sayre, 1920; one child

IMPORTANT WORKS: *This Side of Paradise* (1920); *Flappers and Philosophers* (1921); *The Beautiful and the Damned* (1922); *Tales of the Jazz Age* (1922); *The Vegetable, Or from the Postman to President* (satirical play) (1923); *The Great Gatsby* (1925); *All the Sad Young Men* (1926); *Tender is the Night* (1934); *Taps At Reveille* (1935); *The Last Tycoon* (unfinished) edited by Edmund Wilson (1941); *The Crack-Up* edited by Edmund Wilson (1945). Short stories include: *The Jelly-Bean; Bernice Bobs Her Hair; The Camel's Back; Head and Shoulders; The Ice Palace; May Day; Myra Meets His Family; The Offshore Pirate.*

INTERESTING BIO FACT: Fitzgerald's first professional story sale was *Babes* *in the Woods,* published in the September 1919 issue of The Smart Set, co-edited by **H.L. Mencken.** (See Maryland in South Atlantic section of this book.) Fitzgerald wrote dozens of short stories for leading magazines of the period. Fitzgerald called Mencken "my current idol" in a letter to his aunt and uncle in 1920. Mencken, a proponent of realism and naturalism, encouraged Fitzgerald to write in this vein, which Fitzgerald did in such stories as *May Day* and in the novel *The Beautiful and Damned.* Fitzgerald's namesake and distant relative is **Francis Scott Key**, who penned what became America's National Anthem. (See Maryland.)

FURTHER READING *The Cambridge Companion to F. Scott Fitzgerald* by Ruth Prigozy (2002); *Some Sort of Epic Grandeur: The Life of F. Scott Fitzgerald* by Matthew J. Bruccoli (2002); *Sometimes Madness Is Wisdom: Zelda and Scott Fitzgerald: A Marriage* by Kendall Taylor (2001)

ELSEWHERE IN THE AREA Civil Rights Memorial, Washington and Hull streets downtown; historic Alabama State Capitol

• FINDING FITZGERALD •

You can see where Fitzgerald was born in St. Paul, Minn., at 481 Laurel Ave., as part of a walking tour of the city. In Great Neck, Long Island, N.Y., you can view the house where Scott and Zelda lived at 5 Gateway Drive, as well as the apartment house where they lived briefly in Buffalo, N.Y. The sites are not open to the public.

• WHAT IS 'THE JAZZ AGE'? •

The heady decade of 1920 through 1930 introduced post-World War I America to a bold new sound called jazz, prohibition and gangland crime, and a short-haired, short-skirted, wildly dancing libertine known as a "flapper" girl. It was the "roaring twenties," a time of new sophistication, fashion and mores for rebellious youth.

Young, smart and flamboyant, F. Scott Fitzgerald endures as the writer most identified with the Jazz Age. Others include Elinor Glyn (*It*) and Percy Marks (*The Plastic Age*). Fitzgerald also is identified with The Lost Generation of writers, epitomized by **Ernest Hemingway.** (See Florida in South Atlantic section of this book.) ◢

IVY GREEN

Birthplace of Helen Keller

LOCATION Northwest Alabama, 20 miles from the Tennessee border in Tuscumbia, at 300 W. North Commons near the downtown business area. Tuscumbia can be reached via US 72. Ivy Green is 2 miles north of US 72 and 2 miles west of US 43.

Ivy Green ($) is open Monday through Saturday 8 a.m. to 4 p.m., except for major holidays. Group reservations requested. For more information, contact Ivy Green, 300 W. North Commons, Tuscumbia, AL 35674. Tel. (256) 383-4066 or toll free at 1-800-329-2124. On the Net: www.helenkellerbirth place.org.

For information about the annual summer production of the play *The Miracle Worker*($) on the Ivy Green grounds or the weeklong Helen Keller Festival, contact the site. On the Net: www.helenkellerfestival.com.

FRAME OF REFERENCE Helen Adams Keller was born in this house in June 1880 and lived here until age 16, when she left to attend prep school. The house was built in 1820 by Keller's grandparents. Ivy Green was made a shrine and placed on the National Register of Historic Places in 1954, the last year Keller visited.

SIGNIFICANCE Keller, author, lecturer and humanitarian, is known worldwide as "America's First Lady of Courage" because she overcame extreme obstacles to become the first blind and deaf person to communicate effectively. This was largely due to her extraordinary teacher Anne Sullivan. Sullivan, a partially blind orphan, came to Tuscumbia when she was 21 to teach the spoiled, mute, 7 year-old Helen, who communicated largely through wild laughter or violent tantrums. Sullivan taught Helen to read and write in Braille and to "talk" with her hands. **Mark Twain** called Sullivan "the miracle worker."

Under Sullivan's tutelage, Keller learned to use a typewriter, speak and "hear" by placing her fingers on a speaker's lips or throat. Keller, who lost her sight and hearing at 19 months while suffering a febrile illness, became America's first blind and deaf person to complete college, graduating cum laude from Radcliffe.

The adult Keller traveled to 25 countries on five continents, dedicating herself not only to the sightless and the afflicted, but to humanity. During

387

World War II, she made countless trips to comfort those in military hospitals, calling this period "the crowning experience in my life." Her books tell of her courage and indomitable spirit. They continue to inspire millions around the globe.

ABOUT THE SITE Ivy Green, named for the abundant English Ivy that grew on the cotton plantation, was originally 640 acres. Today, the site's 10 acres brim with lush shrubs, colorful flowerbeds and formal gardens blooming throughout manicured grounds. Ivy Green survived untouched through the ravages of the Civil War and is maintained to the smallest detail in its original state.

Built in 1820, the green-shuttered main house is a simple, two-story white clapboard structure designed in typical Southern architecture. Towering English boxwoods more that 150 years old shade the estate, as well as magnolias and mimosa. Roses, honeysuckle and tulips bloom around the grounds. Outbuildings open for tour include the carriage house, where you'll she the original Keller buggy; a free-standing kitchen, filled with original equipment; and the famous well, where Sullivan spelled out "water" in Helen's hand and the child experienced her communication breakthrough. Visitors can peer through the doors and bay window of the two-room annex east of the main house where Keller and Sullivan lived. The annex was originally the plantation office and later a bridal suite.

Original Keller family furnishings, photographs and Helen's memorabilia fill four large rooms of the first floor, each opening to the wide main hall bisecting the house. Visitors will find the Kellers' burgundy velvet Victorian sofa, imported carpets, 200-year-old silver set and the few remaining square china plates that survived young Helen's dining room tantrums.

A back room, once a bedroom for Keller's aunt, functions as a fascinating museum. Here you'll see Helen's Braille books, Braille typewriter from the Perkins School for the Blind in Massachusetts, some of Helen's childhood clothing, and a note young Helen hand-wrote to her friends inviting them to a party. A small gift shop is tucked in a back room. The amphitheater where *The Miracle Worker* draws thousands each summer stands behind the carriage house.

HOT TIPS Watching (or re-watching) the 1962 film version of *The Miracle Worker* with Patty Duke as Keller and Anne Bancroft as Sullivan makes a visit to Ivy Green more meaningful. The movie was remade in 1979 staring an adult Duke as Sullivan. In 1959, *Worker* became a Broadway play, opening to rave reviews. It became a smash hit and ran for two years. In 1962, it was made into a film, and the actresses playing Anne and Helen both received Oscars for their performances.

If you go to the summer two-hour performance of William Gibson's Pulitzer-Prize winning play (1960) on the Ivy Green Grounds, be sure to take seat cushions to soften the wood bleachers or metal chairs. Park in front of the house. Keep off grass. Snacks are available in season.

THE BEST STUFF Of course it's the simple black well pump in the back yard where Helen's spirit was freed that attracts the most interest. Until that moment at the well with Sullivan, angry Helen had not yet fully understood the meaning of words. That all changed on April 5, 1887, at this very spot. As Anne frantically pumped the water over Helen's hand, she spelled out w-a-t-e-r in Helen's palm. Helen got it.

Everything had a name! A wooden shelter protects the black iron pump and a historic marker tells the story.

THE WRITER AND HER WORK

BORN: June 27, 1880, at Ivy Green

DIED: June 1, 1968, while napping in her home, Arcan Ridge, in Westport, Conn.

Her funeral service was held at the National Cathedral in Washington, D.C., where her ashes were buried next to those of Anne Sullivan and Polly Thomson. Thomson became Helen's teacher after Sullivan's death in 1936.

EDUCATED: Radcliffe College, 1904

ACCOLADES: Presidential Medal of Freedom, the nation's highest civilian award, 1964; Women's Hall of Fame 1965; Alabama Communication Hall of Fame. Keller's life was the subject of a Hollywood film, *Deliverance* in 1919, and a 1953 documentary, *The Unconquered*, which won an Oscar for best feature-length documentary. First woman to receive an honorary degree from Harvard

IMPORTANT WORKS: Books include *The Story of My Life* (1903); *Optimism* (1903); *The World I Live In* (1908); *Out of the Dark* (1913); *Midstream: My Later Life* (1929); *Journal* (1938); *Let Us Have Faith* (1940); *Teacher* (1955)

INTERESTING BIO FACT: When tested as a youth, Keller's IQ reportedly measured 160. The average IQ is 100. Helen might have been extremely intelligent, but her desperate family was having no luck educating and civilizing her until, with help from Alexander Graham Bell, inventor of the telephone, they found Anne Sullivan.

FURTHER READING *Helen Keller and the Big Storm* by Pat Lakin, et. al. (2002); *Helen Keller: A Life* by Dorothy Herrmann (1999); *Helen Keller: Courage In The Dark* by Johanna Hurwitz (1997); *Helen and Teacher* by Joseph P. Lash (1981)

ELSEWHERE IN THE AREA Alabama Music Hall of Fame, US 72; U.S. Space & Rocket Center and Alabama Constitution Village, both in Huntsville 60 miles east; restored log cabin birthplace of W.C. Handy, "Father of the Blues," the Coon Dog Cemetery, and Pettus Museum, all in nearby Florence. ◭

> *Literature is my utopia. Here I am not disenfranchised.*
>
> — HELEN KELLER

EAST SOUTH CENTRAL *Alabama*

MONROEVILLE COURTHOUSE
Preserving 'To Kill A Mockingbird' Scene

The courtroom that served as the model for the dramatic trial scene in Harper Lee's masterpiece, *To Kill A Mockingbird* (1960), welcomes visitors in **Monroeville, Ala.**. The courthouse is authentically restored at the **Old Courthouse Museum,** home to the Monroe County Heritage Museums in the historic town square. Rooms in the museum are dedicated to Lee and her childhood friend, writer Truman Capote, both Monroeville natives. Monroe ville is located in southern Alabama, 100 miles southwest of Montgomery.

Capote is famous for his best-selling books *Breakfast At Tiffany's* (1958) and *In Cold Blood* (1966). The sensational *In Cold Blood* was based on a six-year study of the murders of a rural Kansas family by two young drifters. Both books were made into popular movies. Lee's unforgettable *Mockingbird* became an instant best seller upon publication, with more than 13 million copies printed in 10 languages worldwide.

In 1997, the Alabama legislature designated Monroeville, population 7,000, and Monroe County as the Literary Capital of Alabama. The Alabama Bar Association placed a plaque in front of the courthouse commemorating Lee's heroic lawyer in *Mockingbird*, Atticus Finch. Finch, played in the 1962 movie by actor Gregory Peck, who won an Oscar for his role, defended a black man accused of rape. The museum opened to the public in 1991.

The museum includes rooms that serve as tributes to the two authors, featuring first-edition books, articles and movie posters. In the stark, two-story courtroom, with a pot-bellied stove, visitors can climb the stairs to the balcony. That's where Lee's characters Scout, Jem and Dill watched the trial of Tom Robinson. You can also take a Monroeville walking tour to 33 points of interest related to the authors, including the elementary school Lee and Capote attended.

The Heritage Museums consist of six locations, including The Old Monroe County Courthouse, Rikard's Mill Historical Park, Bethany Baptist Church, and the River Heritage Museum. A museum gift shop in the courthouse offers an array of unique *Mockingbird* items.

When movie rights were acquired in the sixties, the director, film crew and Peck came to Monroeville hoping to film there. Monroeville, however, had changed from the 1930s, the period of Lee's only novel. The courthouse was still in use for everyday legal proceedings. So the crew photographed and shot footage of the courthouse and the town, then recreated the setting in a Hollywood studio. The Montgomery Advertiser reported on Jan. 4, 1962, that Peck said, "I feel at home here. My hometown is very much like Monroeville."

After its California premier, *Mockingbird* opened at the Monroe Theatre for a one-week run on March 28, 1963. The theater advertised that it would pay $10 each to the first five customers bringing in a live mockingbird on Saturday, March 23. The film was held over two days due to popular demand.

Truman Garcia Capote (1924 -1984) wrote of his Monroe County experiences in such works as *Other Voices, Other Rooms* (1948) and *The Grass Harp* (1951) and *A Christmas Memory* (1949).

Nelle Harper Lee was born in Monroeville on April 28, 1926. She's still known around her hometown as Nelle but has lived in New York for much of her life. The reclusive Lee avoids publicity, although in 2002 at age 76, she made a rare public appearance in Birmingham, Ala., to accept the Alabama Humanities Award. On the site of Lee's former home in Monroeville there's now an ice cream stand.

The courthouse museum is open Monday through Friday from 8 a.m. to noon and from 1 p.m. to 4 p.m., and on Saturday from 10 a.m. to 2 p.m. For more information, contact Monroe County Heritage Museums, P.O. Box 1637, Monroeville, Alabama 36461. Tel.: (251) 575-7433. E-mail: mchm@frontiernet.net. On the Net: www.tokillamockingbird. com or www.frontiernet.net/~mchm/page2.html. **Hot Tip** Every May, the museum organization stages the play *To Kill a Mockingbird* with an all-local cast at the Old Courthouse. The play consistently sells out, but one night's production is set aside for those attending the **Alabama Writers Symposium** at Alabama Southern Community College in Monroeville. For more information, contact the college at Alabama Writers Symposium, Alabama Southern Community College, P.O. Box 2000, Monroeville, AL 36461. Tel.: (251) 575-3156, ext. 223. E-mail: dreed@ascc .edu. On the Net: www.ascc.edu/WritersSymposium/symp1.htm ♤

TUSKEGEE INSTITUTE

Booker T. Washington's Dream Realized

LOCATION Central Alabama in the town of Tuskegee. From I-85, take AL 81 south to Old Montgomery Road west. Go to second stoplight, turn right and follow signs.

Tuskegee Institute National Historic Site is open daily. Self-guided walking and driving tours of the Tuskegee Institute are allowed during daylight hours. Guided tours of **The Oaks**, Washington's home, are available daily. Times are posted at the National Park Service's headquarters at the corner of Old Montgomery and Franklin Roads at 1212 Montgomery Road. The George Washington Carver Museum on campus is open daily from 9 a.m. to 4 p.m.

For more information, contact Superintendent, Tuskegee Institute National Historic Site, P.O. Drawer 10, Tuskegee Institute, AL 36087. Tel. (334) 727-3200 or (334) 727-6390. E-mail: tuin_administration@nps.gov. On the Net: www.nps.gov/tuin.

FRAME OF REFERENCE Tuskegee Normal School for Colored Teachers was founded in the post-Reconstruction (1865-1877) era of growing segregation and disenfranchisement of African-Americans. Soon after the election of 1880, a former slave and successful tradesman, Lewis Adams, made a deal to deliver African-American voters. In return, the Alabama legislature passed a bill establishing the school. In 1881 at age 26, Booker Taliaferro Washington, also a former slave dedicated to education, established the school, becoming its first principal, visionary and fund-raiser. When the school opened, its enrollment was 30 students.

Washington wrote that he was able to spend only six months of each year at The Oaks, built by Tuskegee students in 1899, because of his extensive travels.

In 1965, Tuskegee Institute was designated a National Historic Landmark and in 1974 became a part of the National Park System. The private school received university status in 1985, and today Tuskegee University flourishes with about 3,000 students and a broad curriculum.

SIGNIFICANCE Washington, 19th-century author, statesman and leading educator of African-Americans, is known for his autobiography, *Up From Slavery* (1901), as well as for his many speeches and other writings. Washington wrote in *Up From Slavery* that he founded Tuskegee Institute in the "Black Belt of The South" as "a civilizing agent" to help the African-American by making "his skill, intelligence, and character of such undeniable value to the community in which he lived that the community could not dispense with his presence."

Tuskegee focused on preparing students of all ages for jobs in agriculture and other vocations, with emphasis on cleanliness, manners and pride. As Washington earned widespread support in both the North and South through tireless travel, speeches and personal appeals, Tuskegee prospered and grew.

Washington later became an important but controversial leader of his race at a time when increasing racism forced African-Americans to face a new era of legalized oppression. Washington saw education as the true emancipator. From 1895 to 1915, he was the most powerful and influential African-American in America. In his time he was maligned by black intellectuals for accommodating whites. Today he's regarded as a major leader in the civil rights struggle.

ABOUT THE SITE Two buildings are open for public tours: The Oaks and The George Washington Carver Museum across the street. The famous scientist Carver worked and taught at Tuskegee for 47 years after accepting Washington's invitation to head the new Department of Agriculture there. The school honored Carver with the museum in 1938.

Visitors can walk the historic part of the 58-acre Historic Campus District and see dozens of buildings built by students with the red bricks they also made. Architect R.R. Taylor, the first black graduate of MIT and a Tuskegee faculty member, designed most of the old buildings, as well as The Oaks, and supervised their construction.

Just west of the former Girl's Industrial Building stands The Booker T. Washington Monument, the campus centerpiece, by artist Charles Keck. The bronze statue depicts Washington pulling the veil of ignorance and superstition away from a crouching, half-concealed former slave . The ex-slave sits on an anvil and next to a plow, which represent the value Washington placed on manual labor. Washington's towering figure represents his dreams. A book represents the strength of mind.

An inscription on the monument base reads: "He lifted the veil of ignorance from his people and pointed the way to progress through education and industry." Washington's burial site is near the monument.

HOT TIPS Visitors should park behind The Oaks but spaces are limited, as is on-street parking. The best place to park is in the parking garage behind the convention center adjacent to the museum. Do not interfere with student activities while on a self-guided tour. Wear comfortable shoes and dress for the weather. Some walkways and steps are old and steep. Pedestrians have right-of-way on all campus roads.

Begin your tour at the orientation center in the Carver Museum, where you'll find audio-visual programs and park brochures. Call ahead to be sure that all park sites will be open when you visit. Accommodations available along I-85; food in adjacent town of Tuskegee. The campus bookstore sells Tuskegee shirts.

For Tuskegee's 25th anniversary in 1906, poet **Paul Laurence Dunbar** (look under Ohio in the East North Central section of this book) wrote a poem, at Washington's request, capturing the Tuskegee spirit. For details on Washington, look under Virginia in the South Atlantic section of this book.

THE BEST STUFF The restored interior of The Oaks lets visitors see the personal side of Washington. The three-story house has double front doors, a broad front verandah and four chimneys. The five downstairs rooms include the parlor, where table games and a stereopticon attest to the family's leisure activities. Above the gilded molding of the formal rooms are frieze murals, painted in 1908 by European artist E.W. Borman.

On the second floor, the bedrooms are filled with functional furniture, built by Institute students. Elegant, hand-carved furniture from the Orient decorates other rooms. In Washington's cream-colored study, you'll find his ornate Oriental desk (a gift), beloved library, his certificate from Hampton Institute and photographs of famous friends. All furnishings in the house belonged to the Washington family and the house looks much as it did when they lived there.

THE WRITER AND HIS TIMES

BORN: April 5, 1856, to a young slave mother called Jane, on a Hardy, Va., plantation

DIED: Nov. 14, 1915, in The Oaks; buried at Tuskegee

MARRIED: Fannie N. Smith, 1882, died 1884; Olivia Davidson, 1885, died 1889; Margaret James Murray, 1893; daughter and two sons

EDUCATION: Hampton Institute in Hampton, Va.

ACCOLADES: First African-American awarded honorary degree from Harvard

INTERESTING BIO FACT: Washington saw education as the way to lift himself and African-Americans up from the invisible chains that remained after slavery had been abolished. He believed that when African-Americans proved themselves economically, civil rights for blacks would follow.

FURTHER READING *The Art of the Possible: Booker T. Washington and Black Leadership in the United States 1881-1925* by Kevern Verney (2001); *Unshakable Faith: Booker T. Washington & George Washington Carver* by John Perry (1999); *Black-Belt Diamonds: Gems from the Speeches, Addresses and Talks to Students by Booker T. Washington* (1977)

ELSEWHERE IN THE AREA Tuskegee Airmen National Historic Site at Moton Field, training base for the first African-American aviators in World War II. The site, just outside Tuskegee on US 81 at Gen. Chappie James Avenue, includes a visitor center with museum, original red brick hangar and control tower. The famous airmen studied at Tuskegee Institute. ⌂

WEEDEN HOUSE MUSEUM
Celebrating Artist-Poet Maria Howard Weeden

It's worth a visit to the Weeden House Museum in **Huntsville, Ala.,** to see the illustrations and oils of 19th-century poet-artist Maria Howard Weeden. The two-story, six-room house of Federal design, is located at 300 Gates St. "Howard" Weeden turned to writing and painting to boost her income after the Civil War had left her family impoverished. Weeden wrote four volumes of poetry, *Shadows on the Wall, Songs of the South, Old Voices & Bandanna Ballads* and her most famous book, *Shadows on the Wall* (1898). (**Joel Chandler Harris** wrote the introduction to *Bandanna Ballads*.) Her verse, written in dialect, reflects the African-American philosophy of life and sense of humor. She illustrated the poetry herself and achieved world notice for her work. Many admirers thought she was a black man because she went by her middle name, Howard, and showed such sensitivity to African-Americans.

The Weeden House Museum ($) displays a comprehensive collection of Weeden's art, ranging from early illustrations to oil paintings in her mature years. Most noteworthy are her finely detailed watercolor portraits of African-American servants of her neighbors, as well as pictures of wild-flowers, painted in their natural settings. Weeden drew much inspiration for her paintings from her mother's flower garden that flourished on the east lawn of the house. In her *Book of Roses*, Weeden illustrated the many varieties in her mother's garden. Today, the Burritt Museum in Huntsville houses a large collection of Weeden's works.

Weeden was born in 1846 in this painted brick house with spiral stair-way, elaborately hand-carved woodwork and mantels, and a marvelous fan-shaped, leaded-glass window above the front door. The five-bay, white house with gabled roof, window blinds and a carved, leaf-patterned frieze, looks much as it did when built in 1819. It features elaborate interior woodwork, period furnishings and many Weeden pieces. Weeden's lifelong home/museum is located in Huntsville's historic Twickenham District, one of the South's largest neighborhoods of antebellum structures with more than 65 buildings.

A frail woman all her life, Weeden died on April 12, 1905. She is buried in Maple Hill Cemetery in Huntsville.

The Weeden House is open Monday through Friday 11 a.m. to 4 p.m. and Saturday by appointment. The site is available for weddings and parties.

For more information, contact The Weeden House Museum, P.O. Box 2239, Huntsville, AL 35801. Tel. (256) 536-7718. E-mail: weedendir @aol.com. On the Net: http://huntsville.about.com/cs/attractions/a/walkingtour_2.htm.

FURTHER READING *Maria Howard Weeden: the Gentle Artist of Huntsville* by Pamela C. Patrick (1989); *Shadows on the Wall: The Life and Works of Howard Weeden* by Francis C. Roberts and Sarah H. Fisk, 1962 ⌂

EAST SOUTH CENTRAL *Alabama*

HEMINGWAY'S HIDEAWAY
Family Home of Wife Pauline Pfeiffer

The barn studio where Ernest Hemingway wrote *A Farewell to Arms* and several short stories is preserved in **Piggott, Ark.**, at 1021 W. Cherry St. The **Hemingway-Pfeiffer Museum** and Educational Center in Piggott, a small town in northeast Arkansas, was the home of Hemingway's second wife, Pauline Pfeiffer, a journalist. Hemingway spent much time in Piggott between 1927 and 1939, the year he and Pauline divorced. Pauline's parents, Paul and Mary Pfeiffer, were prominent citizens who owned more that 60,000 acres of land and financially supported Hemingway's travel and writing.

Ernest and Pauline were married 13 years. During that time, they had two sons and Hemingway's career soared, due somewhat to the Pfeiffer family's support. The movie version of Hemingway's novel *A Farewell to Arms* had its world premiere at the Franklin Theater in Piggott in Dec. 1932.

The museum belongs to Arkansas State University, 60 miles south in Jonesboro, and functions as an off-campus program center. The rambling, white wood home and barn studio have been renovated in keeping with the 1930s era and most of the furniture is original. Visitors can view seven rooms on the first floor and five upstairs bedrooms, including Pauline's pink bedroom, where she and Hemingway slept on visits. The red barn studio still has the same poker table used by the writer and his pals, as well as his Welsh dresser and chairs. Hemingway mementos and pictures are scattered throughout the house. The site was placed on the National Register of Historic Places in 1982 and opened the public in 1992.

The Hemingway-Pfeiffer Museum and Educational Center also houses literature of the 1930s. It offers exhibits on world events of that era, as well as agricultural and social and economic developments of northeast Arkansas during the Depression and New Deal eras.

The museum is open to the public Monday through Friday 9 a.m. to 3 p.m. and on Saturday from noon to 3 p.m. For more information, contact the Hemingway-Pfeiffer Museum, 1021 W. Cherry St., Piggott, AK 72454. Tel.: (870) 598-3487. E-mail: dwebster@piggott. On the Net: http://hemingway.astate.edu. For details on Hemingway, see Florida and Illinois in this book. ◪

ROBERT PENN WARREN HOUSE

Birthplace of America's First Poet Laureate

LOCATION Southwest Kentucky, just north of the Tennessee state line in Guthrie. The small town is reachable from north and south via US 41 and north and south via US 79. The birthplace, at the corner of Third and Cherry streets, stands one block south of US 41, which becomes Park Avenue in Guthrie.

The Robert Penn Warren Birthplace House is open Tuesday through Saturday, 11:30 a.m. to 3:30 p.m., and on Sunday from 2 p.m. to 4 p.m. For more information contact Robert Penn Warren Birthplace House, P.O. Box 296, Guthrie, KY 42234. Tel. (270) 483-2683 or (270) 483-2986. On the Net: www.robertpennwarren.com/birthpla.htm.

FRAME OF REFERENCE Robert Penn Warren was born in this turn-of-the-century brick house in 1905 and lived here until age 5. Warren left Guthrie at age 16 to attend Vanderbilt University in 1921. The house opened to the public in 1989.

SIGNIFICANCE Warren — poet, novelist, literary critic, essayist, short-story writer, co-editor of numerous textbooks on literary criticism, and a founding editor of The Southern Review — won the Nobel Prize for literature and three Pulitzer Prizes. He was appointed America's first Poet Laureate in 1986. He taught at several universities, notably Louisiana State and Yale.

Warren's 60 years of writing include 10 novels (two made into movies), 16 volumes of poetry, short stories and a play. Though he lived many places and much of his later work was done in a converted barn in Connecticut, Warren never left his Kentucky roots behind. Much of his writing has a Southern bent and a sensitivity to small-town life.

ABOUT THE SITE The restored one-story, red brick house trimmed in white has a pitched roof, front bay and L-shaped porch and is of the "railroad bungalow" design. Inside, period antiques furnish the simple and sturdy house with original fireplaces and hardwood floors. Furnishings include his mother's secretary, a pair of wooden candlesticks Warren made as boy, family photographs and Warren's childhood books. A display case protects 35 foreign-language editions of Warren's books and the site's piéce de résistance: a complete set of Warren's works, all signed by the author.

You'll also find Warren's collection of newspaper clippings about his childhood chum Kent Greenfield, a pro baseball player with the Giants and Braves. Warren wrote a poem on Greenfield titled *American Portrait: Old Style*. The house has a small gift shop.

HOT TIPS Park on-street. The house is handicapped accessible. The house's library has a complete collection of Warren's works for on-site reading and study.

The **Robert Penn Warren Library** at Western Kentucky University in Bowling Green, 50 miles northeast of Guthrie, houses 2,700 volumes of papers from Warren's personal collection. The Warren family gave the collection to the school after the poet's death.

The library, on the second floor of the Kentucky building, features Warren's recreated study. The study includes his wooden desk, personal reference library — some with Warren's marginal notations — personal papers, about 300 photographs, and his bookcases filled with first editions and foreign-language editions of Warren's books. Memorabilia include the laurel wreath for his Poet Laureateship, ribbons, plaques and medals. On the Net: www.wku.edu/Library/dlsc/rpwlib.htm.

THE BEST STUFF In the house in Guthrie, you'll find a poster-sized enlargement of a Life magazine color photo of Warren taken after he had been named U.S. poet laureate. The photo shows Warren holding an American Beauty rose in the same year the rose was made the national flower. The house also displays original movie posters from *All The King's Men* and *Band of Angels*. A signed Annie Leibovitz photograph from Life magazine shows Warren with his shirt off.

THE WRITER AND HIS WORK

BORN: April 24, 1905, in Guthrie

DIED: Sept. 15, 1989; buried at Stratton, Vt. At Warren's request, a memorial stone stands in the Warren family gravesite in Guthrie.

EDUCATED: Vanderbilt University, magna cum laude, 1925; master's at Berkeley, 1927; graduate studies at Yale, 1927-28; Oxford as Rhodes Scholar, 1930

MARRIED: Emma Brescia, 1929, divorced 1951; Eleanor Clark, 1952; two children

IMPORTANT WORKS: Prose — *Night Rider* (1938); *At Heaven's Gate* (1943); *All the King's Men* (1946); *Blackberry Winter* (1946); *The Circus in the Attic, and Other Stories* (1948); *World Enough and Time* (1950); *Band of Angels* (1955); *The Cave* (1959); *Wilderness* (1960); *Flood* (1964); *Meet Me in the Green Glen* (1971); *A Place to Come To* (1977); *John Brown: The Making of a Martyr* (1929); *Who Speaks for the Negro?* (1965); *Homage to Theodore Dreiser* (1971); Poetry — *XXXVI Poems* (1935); *Eleven Poems on the Same Theme* (1942); *Brother to Dragons* (1953); *Promises: Poems, 1954-1956* (1957); *Incarnations* (1968); *Audubon: A Vision* (1969); *New and Selected Poems 1923-1985* (1985). Text books — *Understanding Poetry* (1938) and *Understanding Fiction* (1943), two influential examples of New Criticism.

ACCOLADES: Three Pulitzer prizes, one for fiction (*All the King's Men*) and two for poetry (*Promises*, 1957, and *Now and Then*, 1978), the only person to win in both categories; Bolingen Prize for Poetry, National Medal for Literature, Presidential Medal of Freedom; Sidney Hillman Award, the Edna St. Vincent Millay Memorial Award, the National Book Award; and a MacArthur Foundation "genius" grant.

Warren served as a Chancellor of The Academy of American Poets from 1972 until 1988 and was named America's first Poet Laureate in 1986. He received nine honorary degrees from American universities.

INTERESTING BIO FACT: In 1921, young Warren suffered an injury to his left eye when his younger brother threw a rock at him. The injury eventually led to removal of the eye. During the summer of 1921, Warren spent six weeks in Citizens Military Training Corp, Fort Knox, Ky., where he published his first poem, *Prophecy*, in The Messkit. He earlier had obtained an appointment to the U.S. Naval Academy but because of the blind eye the appointment was canceled. In the fall of 1921 at age 16, he entered Vanderbilt University. While there, he got involved in the Fugitives, a famous group of poets.

FURTHER READING *Racial Politics and Robert Penn Warren's Poetry* by Anthony Szczesiul (2002); *Robert Penn Warren, A Biography* by Joseph Blotner (1997)

ELSEWHERE IN THE AREA Jefferson Davis Monument; Guthrie Railroad Museum in nearby Fairview ◢

ROWAN OAK

Home of William Faulkner

LOCATION North central Mississippi in Oxford, 2 miles from the University of Mississippi campus. From Oxford Square, take South Lamar Street south to Old Taylor Road to the site on right. From MS 6, take Taylor Road north and right/east on Old Taylor Road to site on left.

Rowan Oak is open Tuesday through Friday, from 10 a.m. to noon and 2 p.m. to 4 p.m.; on Saturday 10 a.m. to 4 p.m.. and on Sunday noon to 4 p.m. Closed major holidays. Groups and special needs individuals should make advance reservations. Groups limited to 50.

For more information, contact the University of Mississippi, University, MS 38677. Tel: (662) 234-3284 or University Museums at (662) 915-7073. On the Net: www.rowanoak.net or www.mcsr.olemiss.edu/%7Eegjbp/faulkner/rowanoak.

FRAME OF REFERENCE William Cuthbert Faulkner (Faulkner restored the "u" that had been removed from the ancestral name) bought the mansion he later named Rowan Oak in 1930. He lived and wrote here until his death in 1962. Rowan Oak was built in 1840 by a pioneer settler. Ole Miss purchased the house in 1972 from Faulkner's daughter and later opened it to the public. After renovations, the house was to be reopened in late 2003.

SIGNIFICANCE Faulkner lived and worked at Rowan Oak for more than 30 years. Considered by many the greatest American writer of all time, few doubt that he belongs in the worldwide pantheon of major modern literary figures. The Nobel Prize and Pulitzer Prize-winning novelist, short-story writer, poet, essayist and Hollywood screenwriter published 19 novels, more than 80 short stories, two books of poetry and numerous essays.

Faulkner's landmark work experiments with narrative structure, often building on a complex, stream of consciousness narrative. He depicts the details of traditional society as large-scale human dramas, suggesting ties between the past and present and showing the conflict between the old and the new South. His principal setting is the fictional Yoknapatawpha County, his "little postage-stamp of native soil," actually Lafayette County in central Mississippi. Faulkner's decision to set his fiction in his native region profoundly affected his literary production and literature itself. Highway signs approaching Oxford proudly read "Yoknapatawpha County."

Faulkner, with novels in 13 languages, might be the most-studied author in the world, with more books, articles and papers written about his work than any other writer besides William Shakespeare.

ABOUT THE SITE Faulkner began renovations on the primitive Greek Revival-style house and 4 acres of oak and cedars when he bought the house in 1930. He also purchased options on the surrounding acreage, called Bailey's Woods, where he had played as a youth. Faulkner named his estate Rowan Oak after the Scottish legend of the Rowan tree, thought to bring good luck and peace, and the many oaks growing on the property.

Five buildings stand on the 32-acre grounds, four original and dating to the early 1840s. In addition to the white clapboard main house with green shutters, you'll find the stable that Faulkner, a horse lover, designed and built; a tenant house with kitchen that Faulkner used as a smokehouse; a barn; and a square-hewn log stable original to the property. Faulkner designed the formal gardens on the east side.

Faulkner items fill the fairly plain, functional house. He built the pine shelves in the first-floor library. Wife Estelle's Chickering piano dominates the parlor. In Faulkner's upstairs bedroom, you'll see his books, cameras, riding and field boots and his shoeshine kit. The number emblazoned on the mantle is the "64" Faulkner wore at a Virginia horse show.

HOT TIPS No smoking in the house or Bailey's Woods. Parking at the site is limited. Allow at least an hour for the tour. Try one of the quaint restaurants at Oxford Square for lunch.

Don't miss the **Faulkner Room** at University of Mississippi library, where you'll find Faulkner-related treasures, as well as letters and papers of other famous Southern writers. Ole Miss also hosts an annual Faulkner and Yoknapatawpha Conference: on the Net at www.ics.olemiss.edu/events/faulkner_yoknapatawpha .

At the University of Virginia Library in Charlottesville, you can find the **William Faulkner Collection** of manuscripts, letters and other papers. On the Net: www.lib.virginia.edu/speccol/collections/faulkner.

THE BEST STUFF In 1950, Faulkner added a small office to Rowan Oak that became his sanctuary. In the office, he prepared the outline for the novel *A Fable* and inscribed it on the white wall in his close, vertical handwriting. Today, you can view this carefully preserved outline above his cot. The office remains as it was at the time of the author's death. Faulkner's

Underwood portable typewriter sits near the window on a small table given to him by his mother. A fold-top desk that he made is in the corner with a bottle of horse liniment, a carpenter's pencil and a bottle of ink.

THE WRITER AND HIS WORK

BORN: Sept. 25, 1897, in New Albany, Miss.

DIED: July 6, 1962, in Oxford; buried in St. Peter's Cemetery in Oxford

EDUCATED: Dropped out of University of Mississippi to pursue writing career

MARRIED: Estelle Oldham, 1929; two stepchildren, one daughter

IMPORTANT WORKS: *Soldiers' Pay* (1926); *Father Abraham* (1926); *Mosquitoes* (1927); *Sartoris* (1929); *The Sound and the Fury* (1929); *As I Lay Dying* (1930); *Sanctuary* (1931); *Light in August* (1932); *Absalom, Absalom!* (1936); *The Unvanquished* (1938); *The Wild Palms* (1939); *The Hamlet* (1940, the first novel in a trilogy about the rise of the Snopes family); *Go Down Moses* (1942, a collection of Yoknapatawpha County stories of which the novella *The Bear* is the best known); *Intruder in the Dust* (1948); *Requiem for a Nun* (1951); *A Fable* (1954); *The Town* (1957); *The Mansion* (1959, which completed the Snopes trilogy); *The Reivers* (1962). Short Works: *These Thirteen* (1931); *Idyll in the Desert* (1931); *Knight's Gambit* (1949); *Collected Stories* (1950); *Notes on a Horsethief* (1950); *New Orleans Sketches* (1958); *The Wishing Tree* (1964). Poetry - *This Earth, a Poem* (1932); *A Green Bough* (1933). Screenplay for *To Have and Have Not* (1945) by **Ernest Hemingway** (See Florida in the Southeast section of this book).

ACCOLADES: Nobel Prize for literature, 1949; Pulitzer Prize, 1954 for *A Fable* and 1956 for *The Reivers*; Howells Medal, 1950

INTERESTING BIO FACT: In 1925, Faulkner moved to New Orleans, where he worked as a journalist, and met the American writer **Sherwood Anderson** (see Ohio in the East North Central section of this book). Anderson helped Faulkner find a publisher for his first novel, *Soldier's Pay,* and convinced him to write about the people and places he knew best. Faulkner recounted this in his essay *A Note on Sherwood Anderson.*

FURTHER READING *William Faulkner: His Life and Work* by David L. Minter (1997); *Reading Faulkner* by Stephen M. Ross (1996); *The Cambridge Companion To William Faulkner* by Phillip M. Weinstein, editor (1995); *Faulkner's Rowan Oak* by Dan Hise, photos by John Lawrence

(1993). Faulkner's Nobel Prize acceptance speech is available in print and on audiocassette.

ELSEWHERE IN THE AREA Cedar Oaks mansion, 601 Murray Drive; Square Books (late 1860s; Faulkner section), 160 Courthouse Square; J.E. Neilson Co., reportedly oldest continually operating department store in South, 119 Courthouse Square

• LONGSTREET GRAVE •

The 19th-century humorist **Augustus Baldwin Longstreet** is also buried St. Peter's Episcopal Cemetery. Longstreet is best known for his rowdy book *Georgia Scenes, Characters, Incidents, Etc. in the First Half Century of the Republic* (1835), a groundbreaking work praised by Edgar Allan Poe. The circuit-riding lawyer's *Georgia Scenes* included rich characters who spoke in dialect and told of rural Southern manners and moral conflicts. The book's 19 tales were immensely popular and had 11 editions between 1835 and 1897.

Longstreet's obelisk tombstone reads: "Born the day the sun went cross the line."

• FAULKNER TREASURES •

The William Faulkner Room in the main library on the **Ole Miss** campus in Oxford displays Faulkner's gold Nobel Prize medal, movie posters, a 1897 birth announcement for the author, and Faulkner first editions and letters. The library, in Room 318A, also houses the **Rowan Oak Papers**. This collection includes 1,800 pages of Faulkner manuscripts, newspaper clips, photographs and memorabilia. For details, go to www.olemiss.edu/depts/general_library .

A glass case in the Faulkner Room protects one especially interesting item: a yellowed letter the author typed in Oxford in Sept. 1935. Faulkner wrote a detailed letter to an aspiring writer, one of many admirers who sent him original manuscripts to critique. Faulkner's letter to "Mr. Dean," whose work obviously impressed him, explains why he thought publishers had rejected the story, titled *Black Orchid*.

"It is too long. It is too episodic. . . It is just a strung-out short story, all of which might have been told in a court room.," Faulkner wrote.

Faulkner tempered his harsh criticism by writing "This may offend you. If it does, you have no business trying to write at all. If it does not, and you follow this advice, you may get somewhere someday. . . If you don't want to write it, how about giving it to me?" ◿

WILLIAM JOHNSON HOUSE

Home of Antebellum African-American Diarist

A house in a National Park in **Natchez, Miss.**, tells the story of William T. Johnson, a freed slave turned well-to-do barber in pre-Civil War Natchez. Johnson, born circa 1809, earned his place in American literature and history by keeping a 2,000-page diary that includes some of his sketches. Johnson's writings give the most complete account of the life of a free African-American in the antebellum South. Johnson, who owned slaves himself, kept the diary from 1835 up to his death in 1851. The diary gives colorful details of contemporary life in Natchez.

Johnson's three-story house is part of the 80-acre Natchez National Historical Park at 212 State St. in downtown Natchez. The park features three units: Fort Rosalie, site of an 18th-century fortification built by the French and later occupied by the British, Spanish and Americans; Melrose, estate of wealthy Northerner John T. McMurran; and the William Johnson House.

After 13 years of study, restoration of the Johnson House complex was completed in fall 2005 and opened to the public. The 1841 Greek Revival-style, brick townhouse features exhibits on the first floor, where Johnson conducted business, and a bookstore. The second floor, occupied by the Johnson family, is furnished to the period when Johnson lived there, from 1841 to 1851. Johnson died in 1851 in an ambush resulting from a heated dispute over property lines. Johnson's personal furnishings also are displayed in the house.

The McCallum House, which shares a common wall with the Johnson House, will become a visitor center with restrooms and elevator to the second floor. Fort Rosalie is located several blocks from the Johnson House.

Johnson's edited diary was published in 1951 as *William Johnson's Natchez: The Antebellum Diary of a Free Negro*. Johnson's diary entries describe local theatrical performances, political campaigns, horse races, steamboat explosions, yellow fever epidemics and the Panic of 1837. Johnson was a trusted confidant to many prominent Natchez customers at his barber shop.

Although diarist Johnson was a member of the African-American aristocracy who owned property, businesses and slaves, his status as a free man was tenuous. He could not vote, sit on a jury or testify against whites. After his death, a white man involved in the boundary dispute concerning

Johnson's 2,000-acre plantation was charged with his murder. Despite public outrage at the crime, which necessitated a change of venue for the trial, the ambusher was acquitted. The only witnesses to the crime were black. They weren't allowed to testify.

The Natchez park is open Monday through Saturday, 8 a.m. to 5 p.m., and on Sunday from 9 a.m. to 4 p.m. Hours are extended in summer. The Johnson House is open from 9 a.m. to 4:40 p.m., Thursday through Sunday. Melrose mansion ($) is open daily, 8:30 a.m. to 5 p.m., with tours on the hour from 9 a.m. to 4 p.m.

For more information about the Johnson House, contact Natchez National Historical Park, 640 S. Canal Street, Box E, Natchez, MS 39120. Call the William Johnson House at 601-445-5345. E-mail: www.nps.gov/natc/pphtml/contact.html. On the Net: www.nps.gov/natc.

HOT TIP Johnson's correspondence, legal and financial documents, diaries, daybooks and other manuscripts are collected in 54 volumes at Louisiana State University in Baton Rouge. The **William T. Johnson Family Papers** are part of the school's Louisiana and Lower Mississippi Valley Collection. The collection also includes sheet music from 1839 to 1909 that belonged to the family. On the Net: www.lib.lsu.edu. Search for William T. Johnson Family Papers.

FURTHER READING *Chained to the Rock of Adversity* by Virginia M. Gould, editor (writings of Johnson women, 1998); *The Black Experience in Natchez* by Ronald L. F. Davis (1994); *The Barber of Natchez* by Edwin Adams et al (1973) ⏹

TENNESSEE WILLIAMS BIRTHPLACE

First Home of Famous Playwright

LOCATION Eastern Mississippi near the Alabama border in downtown Columbus, at 300 Main St. at College Street. The house serves as offices for the Mississippi Welcome Center for Columbus and Lowndes County. Reach Columbus via US 82 or US 45 to Main Street/Old Highway 82 exit. Follow signs.

The Tennessee Williams Home and the Tennessee Williams Room are open weekdays from 8:30 a.m. to 4:30 p.m., and on Sunday noon to 4:30 p.m. For more information contact the Mississippi Welcome Center, 300 Main St., Columbus, MS 39703. Tel. (662) 328-0222 or 1-800-327-2786. On the Net: www.columbus-ms.org.

FRAME OF REFERENCE Thomas Lanier Williams was born in 1911 in this Victorian house (circa 1876), then the rectory for St. Paul's Episcopal Church where his grandfather was minister. "Tom" lived here until age 3 with his mother and sister Rose until they moved to Nashville in 1914. The house was moved to its current site in 1995, renovated and opened to the public.

SIGNIFICANCE Williams fans can look at the privately owned Key West, Fla., cottage where Williams lived and wrote, or gawk at his New Orleans and Big Apple haunts, but this house in the playwright's hometown offers a unique, hands-on connection to the famous writer of stage and film. The house represents an era in Mississippi and the South, primary sources of inspiration for Williams' work, and glimpses the tension-filled Williams family that lived here. Williams brought to his audiences a slice of his own chaotic life and an unblinking look at southern culture.

Williams, two-time Pulitzer Prize winner, wrote plays, film scripts, short stories, novels and verse. He won numerous awards and global recognition as one of the greatest American playwrights of the 20th century. Best-known among his 25 plays are *The Glass Managerie* (1945), his first financial success, as well as *A Streetcar Named Desire* (1947) and *Cat On A Hot Tin Roof* (1954), for which he won Pulitzer Prizes. These and many other plays were popularized on stage and screen.

In addition to his 25 full-length plays, Williams wrote dozens of short plays and screenplays, two novels, a novella, 60 short stories, more than

100 poems and an autobiography. Williams' works are universal, vividly portraying the sexual tensions and suppressed violence of his tormented characters.

ABOUT THE SITE The two-story, seven-room, yellow and gray house has been restored to original appearance. The downstairs rooms, with 12-foot-high ceilings, iron fireplaces, cream-colored walls and pine floors, are furnished with period furniture, much of it from the old rectory. Local citizens, with help from various groups, moved the Victorian home from its original site next to St. Paul's Episcopal Church to its present location a block away. Only the first floor is open to the public. The two former upstairs bedrooms function as offices.

The Tennessee Williams Room, in what was the home's dining room, displays Williams-related photographs, playbills, books and souvenirs.

HOT TIPS Park behind the house. Restrooms are on site; handicapped accessible. The town of Clarksdale, Miss., where the playwright attended kindergarten (Williams moved 16 times in 15 years due to his father's notorious drinking), hosts the Mississippi Delta **Tennessee Williams Festival** every fall. The festival features performances of Williams' dramas, a literary conference, blues and gourmet food. For information on events and the drama competition, contact Tennessee Williams Festival, P.O. Box 1565, Clarksdale, MS 38614-1565; Tel. (662) 627-7337.

The five-day **Tennessee Williams/New Orleans Literary Festival** every spring also honors the playwright, who considered New Orleans his "spiritual home." For more information, call (504) 581-1144. On the Net: www.tennesseewilliams.net.

THE WRITER AND HIS WORK
BORN: March 26, 1911, in Columbus
DIED: Feb. 24, 1983, at the Hotel Elysee in New York City; buried in St. Louis
EDUCATED: University of Missouri; Washington University; University of Iowa, where he graduated in 1938
IMPORTANT WORKS: *The Vengeance of Nitrocis* (1928 short story); *American Blues* (1939); *The Glass Menagerie* (1945); *A Streetcar Named Desire* (1947); *One Arm and Other Stories* (1948); *Summer and Smoke* (1948); *The Roman Spring of Mrs. Stone* (1950); *The Rose Tattoo* (1951); *Camino Real* (1953); *Hard Candy, A Book of Stories* (1954); *The Cat On A Hot Tin*

Roof (1955); *In The Winter of Cities* (1956); *Baby Doll* (1956); *Orpheus Descending* (1957); *Suddenly Last Summer* (1958); *Sweet Bird of Youth* (1959); *A Period of Adjustment* (1960); *The Night of Iguana* (1962); *The Milk Train Does Not Stop Here Anymore* (1962); *Small Craft Warnings* (1973); *Where I Live: Selected Essays* (1978); *A House Not Meant To Stand* (1982); *Five O'Clock Angel* (1990)

ACCOLADES: Group Theater Award, 1939; Donaldson Award, New York Drama Critics Award and Pulitzer Prize, 1948, for *A Streetcar Named Desire*; Pulitzer Prize, 1955, for *Cat On A Hot Tin Roof*

INTERESTING BIO FACT: Williams was called Tom most of his life. He began calling himself Tennessee when he began his writing career in New Orleans. College acquaintances had jokingly used the name, referring to Williams' heritage as a Tennessee pioneer, his poverty and his deep Southern accent. While living in New Orleans, Williams fell in love with a man named Frank Merlo. Merlo, a World War II Navy veteran, was a calming influence in Williams' chaotic life. When Merlo died in 1961, Williams, who had long struggled with alcohol and drugs, went into a deep depression that lasted for a decade. He feared he would go insane, as did sister Rose.

FURTHER READING *Tennessee Williams* by Philip C. Kolin (1998); *The Kindness of Strangers: The Life of Tennessee Williams* by Donald Spoto (1997); *Tom: The Unknown Tennessee Williams* by Lyle Leverich (1995); *Tennessee Williams* edited by H. Bloom (1987); *Conversations with Tennessee Williams* edited by A.J. Devlin (1986)

ELSEWHERE IN THE AREA Temple Heights plantation townhouse and Gardens, 515 Ninth St. North; Waverley Plantation Mansion, off MS 50 between Columbus and West Point; Columbus Lock and Dam on the Tennessee-Tombigbee Waterway; Tombigbee Dundee Riverboat Tours, 1096 Island Rd. △

EUDORA WELTY'S JACKSON

Birthplace, Home Tell One Writer's Story

LOCATION Central Mississippi in the state capital, Jackson. The Welty birthplace and childhood home is located at 741 N. Congress St., a few blocks from the capitol. The house serves as headquarters for the Mississippi Writers Association and will function as a literary learning complex, the **Eudora Welty Writers Center.**

A second Welty house, where the writer lived 76 years and wrote most of her fiction, stands at 1119 Pinehurst St. The **Eudora Welty House** is undergoing renovation with completion expected by 2005. Days and hours of operation are not yet decided. For more information, contact Eudora Welty House, Museum Division, MDAH, 1119 Pinehurst St., Jackson. MS 39202-1812. Tel. (601) 353-7762. E-mail: mawhite@mdah.state.ms.us. Virtual tours are planned for the Net: www.eudorawelty.org and/or www.mdah.state.ms.us.

For information on the Eudora Welty Writers Center, contact Eudora Welty Writers-MS Chapter, P.O. Box 16483, Jackson, MS 39236. On the Net: ftp.ggi-project.org/wpercy/welty.center.html.

FRAME OF REFERENCE Eudora Welty was born in 1908 in the Congress Street house, where she spent her childhood. Her parents built the house in 1908. The dedication of the Eudora Welty Writers Center site was held May 1, 1996.

As an adult, Welty lived in the Pinehurst Street house, built in 1925, until her death in 2001.

SIGNIFICANCE Welty — novelist, short-story writer, essayist, poet and accomplished photographer — lived all her life in Jackson. She recalled many events that occurred in her Mississippi childhood home in her book, *One Writer's Beginnings* (1984).

Welty, regarded as one of America's finest storytellers, won a Pulitzer Prize, as well as six O. Henry awards. She also was awarded a host of other honors worldwide for her work. Her novels and stories have been translated into every major European language, as well as a half dozen others. Welty conferences are held in several countries.

Welty, who described her Southern childhood as "sheltered," said that her subject was human relationships. Her ability to capture the nuances of Mississippi life earned her global recognition and popularity.

ABOUT THE SITES Welty's Pinehurst Street home, a Tudor-style, two-story house amid towering trees, is undergoing renovation. Welty gave the rambling, high-ceilinged house, as well as her personal papers and manuscripts, to the Mississippi Department of Archives and History before her death. The department's museum division hopes the house will be the "most complete" literary site in America when fully restored. The home remains the same as when Welty lived there and is complete with her books and furnishings. The Welty garden also will be open for tours. Welty enjoyed gardening and alluded in her works to more than 150 plants, many of which are still in the garden.

The Welty birthplace and childhood home was privately purchased in 1979 and used as business offices. The rambling, beige wood, two-story house with front porch has a plaque to commemorate the site as Welty's birthplace. The restoration of Welty's birthplace and construction of the Writers Center will be funded by proceeds from the annual Eudora Welty Film and Fiction Festival and private donations.

HOT TIPS The Mississippi Department of Archives and History in Jackson at 100 S. State St. houses a **Welty Collection** of photographs, printed works and correspondence. Welty gave the collection to the agency before her death. The library is open weekdays, except for major holidays, 8 a.m. to 5 p.m. and on Saturday from 8 a.m. to 1 p.m.

THE WRITER AND HER WORK
BORN: April 13, 1908, in Jackson
DIED: July 23, 2001, in Jackson
EDUCATED: Mississippi State College for Women, 1927; University of Wisconsin, Madison, 1929; Columbia University School of Business, 1 year
IMPORTANT WORKS: *A Curtain of Green* (short stories, 1941); *The Robber Bridegroom* (1942); *The Wide Net and Other Stories* (1943); *Delta Wedding* (1946); *Music from Spain* (separately published short story, 1948); *The Golden Apples* (1949); *Selected Stories of Eudora Welty* (1954); *The Bride of the Innisfallen and Other Stories* (1955); *The Ponder Heart* (1954); *Place in Fiction* (essay, 1957); *The Shoe Bird* (children's story, 1964); *Thirteen Stories* (1965); *Losing Battles* (1970); *One Time, One Place: Mississippi in the Depression, A Snapshot Album*; *The Optimist's Daughter* (1972); *The*

Eye of the Story (essays, 1978); *One Writer's Beginnings* (1984); *Photographs* (1989)

ACCOLADES: Pulitzer Prize, 1973 for her novel *The Optimist's Daughter*; six O. Henry awards; French Legion of Honor medal; National Medal of Arts; Presidential Freedom Medal of Honor and the Presidential Medal of Arts; Library of America series; National Institute of Arts and Letters; Fellowship of Southern Writers; French Legion d'Honneur; many honorary degrees

INTERESTING BIO FACT: Welty's primary medium was language, but her talents also blossomed as a photographer. She began taking artistic photographs in the 1930s, when she worked as a junior publicity agent for the Works Progress Administration. She continued to use a camera until 1950, when she left her Rolleiflex on a bench in the Paris Metro. Angry at her carelessness, she did not replace it.

FURTHER READING *Welty: Collected Novels* (1999); *Welty: Collected Essays and Memoirs* (1999); *A Writer's Eye: Collected Book Reviews*, edited by Pearl Amelia McHaney (1994); *Eudora Welty* by Ruth Vande Kieft (1987); *Conversations with Eudora Welty*, edited by Peggy Prenshaw (1984); *Eudora Welty's Chronicle: A Story of Mississippi Life* by Albert Devlin (1983)

ELSEWHERE IN THE AREA Mississippi Agriculture and Forestry Museum, 1150 Lakeland Dr.; The Oaks, 823 N. Jefferson St.; Manship House Museum, site of surrender to Sherman, 420 E. Fortification St.; Smith Robertson Museum, Jackson's first African-American school; Old Capitol Museum, 100 S. State St. ◭

NATCHEZ AND ITS NATIVE SON

Richard Wright Remembered

Natchez has recognized its native son, novelist and poet Richard Wright with historic markers at the Wilson House, where young Wright lived with his grandparents, at 20 Woodlawn Ave., and with a memorial in **Natchez Bluff Park** along the Mississippi River at the edge of the city. The private home on Woodlawn Avenue, north of the downtown area, is not open to the public.

Wright, one of America's foremost black writers of the 20th century and the first widely read African-American man, also was among the first African-American writers to achieve literary fame and fortune — and the bestseller list. He was born Sept. 4, 1908, to a sharecropper father and schoolteacher mother on the Rucker family plantation, 20 miles east of Natchez. He died in Paris, France, in 1960.

Wright's novels *Native Son* (1940), *Black Boy* (1945) and *White Man, Listen!* (1957) shocked the literary world with stories of the black experience in America. *Native Son* has been adapted to stage and screen. PBS made *Black Boy*, his autobiography, into a documentary in 1995.

Wright's writing career began as a boy when a black newspaper in Jackson, Miss, where he lived, printed his first story *The Voodoo of Hell's Half Acre* in 1924.

Other works include: *Bright and Morning Star* (story, 1938); *The Outsider* (1953); *Savage Holiday* (1954); *The Long Dream* (1958); *Eight Men* (stories, 1961); *Lawd Today* (1963) and *American Hunger* (1977). Wright also authored about 4,000 haikus, edited and published posthumously in 1998 as *Haiku: This Other World*.

In April 1931, while living in Chicago, Wright published his first major story, *Superstition*, in Abbot's Monthly. The ties he forged in Chicago to the Communist Party continued after moving to New York in 1937. He became the Harlem editor of the party's newspaper Daily Worker and helped edit a short-lived literary magazine, New Challenge. In 1938 four of his stories were collected as *Uncle Tom's Children* (1938). He was twice married and had two children.

FURTHER READING *The Unfinished Quest of Richard Wright* by Michel Fabre (1973); *The Most Native of Sons* by John A. Williams and Dorothy Sterling (1970). You can find Wright papers and manuscripts at the Beinecke Rare Book and Manuscript Library at Yale University, and at the Northwestern and Kent State University libraries. For more on Wright, look under Tennessee in this book. ◢

ALEX HALEY HOUSE MUSEUM

Documenting Writer's 'Roots'

LOCATION Western Tennessee in Henning, 50 miles north of Memphis, at 200 S. Church St. From north and south, take US 51. From west take I-40 to U.S. 51 north. From east take I-40 to TN 19 north to the town.

The **Alex Haley State Historic Site and Museum** ($) is open Tuesday through Saturday, from 10 a.m. to 5 p.m., and on Sunday from 1 p.m. to 5 p.m. For more information contact Alex Haley House Museum, 200 S. Church St., Henning, TN 38041; Tel. (731) 738-2240. On the Net: www .suite101.com/article.cfm/literary_tour/26207. For information about the nearby **African Roots Museum**, contact African Roots Museum in Haywood County, TN 38041. Tel. (731) 772-6902.

FRAME OF REFERENCE Alexander Murphy Palmer Haley came with his parents as a 6-week-old infant to this house in 1921 and lived here as a child with his grandparents until 1929. Haley's grandfather, Will E. Palmer, built the house from 1918 to 1921.

SIGNIFICANCE Haley — biographer, scriptwriter and author — wrote the famous, Pulitzer Prize-winning *Roots* (1976), the culmination of 12 years of research. The book, now published in 37 languages, was adapted to a TV series that attracted a record-setting 130 million viewers. The series ignited an interest in genealogy, particularly among African-Americans. The master storyteller is also known for his book, *The Autobiography of Malcolm X* (1965). The story, told in Malcolm X's own words, sold more than six million copies worldwide by 1977.

At this modest house in Henning, young Alex often sat and listened attentively as relatives told stories about his ancestors. It was on the front porch here that Haley heard about Kunta Kinte and Queenie. "The front porch of this home is, in fact, the birthplace of Roots," Haley once said. Haley's childhood home was the first state-owned historic site devoted to African-Americans in Tennessee.

ABOUT THE SITE Visitors can tour the first floor of the restored two-story, 10-room bungalow, of gray wood on brick foundation. The house has been restored to reflect the home as it was when Haley was born. The upstairs is used as office space. The house has a mix of period furniture and some of the

1919 furniture that belonged to the Haley family, including Mother Haley's upright piano. The house displays the writer's childhood memorabilia, rare family books, photographs, audio tapes, Haley's eyeglasses, information about the people who inspired the characters in *Roots*, and a gift shop. Haley is buried in the front yard of the house.

HOT TIPS Park in a lot at the rear of the house. The site hosts story-telling sessions for children during the summer. Also, in **Annapolis, Md.**, you'll find the Kunta Kinte-Alex Haley Memorial at the foot of the city harbor. It is located directly across the street from the Market House, and within two blocks of both Maryland's State House and the U.S. Naval Academy. According to family history, Kunta Kinte landed with other Gambian Africans in "Napolis" (Annapolis), where he was sold into slavery. On the Net: www.kintehaley.org or info@kintehaley.org.

THE BEST STUFF Haley's final resting place on the front lawn features a black marble base topped by a flat granite slab. Etched in marble beneath Haley's name is a list of his books. In the house, you'll find a testament to Haley's roots: an original photograph of "Chicken" George Haley, the writer's great, great grandfather, taken in the late 1800s.

THE WRITER AND HIS WORK
BORN: Aug. 11, 1921, in Ithaca, N.Y.
DIED: Feb. 10, 1992, in Seattle, Wash.; buried in Henning
MARRIED: Nannie Branch, 1941; Juliette Collins, 1964; Myra Lewis 1972; three children
EDUCATED: Elizabeth City (N.C.) Teachers College; 20 years in U.S. Coast Guard
IMPORTANT WORKS: *The Autobiography of Malcolm X* (1965, film 1992); *Roots* (1976, TV films 1977, 1979); *Palmerstown, USA* (1980 TV collaboration with producer Norman Lear); *A Different Kind of Christmas* (1988); *Queen* (1993 with David Stevens); *Mama Flora's Family* (1998, with David Stevens); anthology of Haley's Playboy interviews 1962-1992
ACCOLADES: National Book Award and a special Pulitzer Prize for *Roots*, 1977
INTERESTING BIO FACT: While in the Coast Guard, Haley sent his stories to magazines for eight years, receiving countless rejection slips before being published. He learned the basics of his craft during this time. After 20 years of service, Haley left the Coast Guard in 1959 to become

a full-time writer. Success came as a staff writer for Playboy magazine, when he interviewed Malcolm X and other famous people.

FURTHER READING *Great African Americans in Literature* by Pat Rediger, et al. (1999); *Alex Haley & Malcolm X's the Autobiography of Malcolm X*, edited by Harold Bloom (1996); *Alex Haley*, edited by Nathan I. Huggins (1993)

ELSEWHERE IN THE AREA Fort Pillow State Historic Park, a Civil War museum, 3122 Park Road; Anderson-Tully Wildlife Management Area bordering park on the north ◮

KINGSTONE LISLE

Thomas Hughes' Tennessee Utopia

LOCATION Eastern Tennessee in Rugby, on the Cumberland Plateau along the Clear Fork River, 70 miles northwest of Knoxville, on Scenic Road 52. From I-75 north and south, take TN 63 to 52 west to the site. From east and west, take I-40 to TN 127 or TN 27 north to 52.

Kingstone Lisle ($) is open daily for walking tours. Times of guided tours, special events and workshops vary. Open in January by appointment only. For more information, contact Kingstone Lisle, P.O. Box 8, Rugby, TN 37733. Tel. (423) 028-2441. On the Net: www.historicrugby .org. or RugbyTn@Highland.net.

FRAME OF REFERENCE Thomas Hughes founded and dedicated Rugby colony, his agrarian Utopia for young British men in America, amid great fanfare on Oct. 5, 1880. The colony, based on the principles of Christian Socialism, survived only a decade. Hughes completed his cottage home, Kingstone Lisle, in 1885. He did not live in the house, but stayed there during annual visits to the colony. His last visit was in 1887.

By 1900, most original settlers, 500 at one point, had left the village. By the 1920s, about 100 remained. Most of the 70 buildings, including the magnificent, three-story Tabard Inn, were destroyed by fire or decay. The library and school were used locally through the 1950s, thanks to volunteer efforts. In the '60s and '70s historic restoration took place, and the site was placed in the National Register of Historic Places in 1972. Today, much of the historic village looks as it did more than 120 years ago.

SIGNIFICANCE Hughes — British author, statesman and social reformer — wrote *Tom Brown's School Days* (1857), one of the earliest books written specifically for boys and a classic of English literature. The book's success ensured the financial stability of London's Macmillan and Co. publishers, which later expanded to America. It also made Hughes very rich and famous.

Hughes invested much of the fortune he made on *School Days* in the Rugby colony, his "New Jerusalem." Hughes envisioned Rugby as a place where second sons of England's gentry — well-bred but without the inheritances of first-born sons — could flourish in a highly structured environment in the American wilderness.

Although the colony was zealously launched, most inhabitants proved more interested in recreation, swell luncheons, and afternoon teas than in Hughes' ideals and opportunity in a new world. Fights over land titles, harsh winters, a typhoid epidemic and drought proved final blows. The colony in the Land of Opportunity failed. Hughes' works and ideals persist at the site and in his work. At his desk in Kingston Lisle, Hughes might have written parts of his biographies of David Livingstone and James Fraser, the Bishop of Manchester. Today, his Victorian village of high-minded ideals stands as one of the most authentically preserved historic sites in America.

ABOUT THE SITE More than 20 of the original, decorative Victorian buildings survive at Rugby and the would-be Utopia remains relatively untouched by modern times. Visitors can join a guided interpretive tour of Christ Church, Kingstone Lisle and the 1882 Thomas Hughes Free Public Library. Admission includes daily guided walking tours to the library, the 1884 Kingstone Lisle and the 1887 Christ Church Episcopal. The restored schoolhouse functions as a visitor center.

Hughes' 1,200-square foot house, painted in its original colors of tan, brown and maroon, is based on an English Rural Style cottage drawn by the famous American landscape and architectural designer Andrew Jackson Downing. Like all Rugby's early buildings, it is built of the virgin pine, walnut and poplar that covered the Tennessee Plateau in the 1880s. A reproduction of the original picket fence surrounds the grounds, which brim with shrubs and flowers. The cottage's scalloped dormer gables, gabled bargeboards and battens trimmed with beaded edges are typical of other Rugby homesteads. The houses reflect Hughes' belief that buildings and natural surroundings should harmonize.

Kingston Lisle is furnished with a few of Hughes' belongings, including his mother's walnut sideboard in the dining room. Other original pieces came from surrounding Rugby homesteads. Visitors will see a carved, German chess set and Victorian-era kitchen utensils and cookstove.

Though Rugby declined, it was never deserted. About 85 residents live in Rugby today and help care for the site. Owners have restored private homes; other structures await restoration.

HOT TIPS To begin your visit, go to the Schoolhouse Visitor Centre. There you can view a 12-minute orientation video, interpretive exhibits, artifacts, dozens of historic photographs of early Rugby and a village map. Wear comfortable shoes for the walking tour. Historic Rugby hosts workshops and special events, which include a Spring Music and Crafts

Festival, Pilgrimage of Homes, Halloween Ghostly Gathering and Christmas at Rugby.

Check out lodging at the Newbury House B&B, a boarding house operating during the Rugby years. The house, which was in use by 1880, has been restored and reopened for guests in 1985. Other Victorian cottages are also open for overnight stays and meetings. Contact the site for details.

THE BEST STUFF The Hughes Free Public Library, which opened in Rugby in 1882, houses about 7,000 volumes of Victorian literature, one of the most complete collections in America today. The books were donated primarily by American publishers to honor Hughes. The small wooden structure remains virtually unchanged, painted its original gray and red colors.

Walk inside the swinging, green-baize-covered front doors with gilt lettering and you'll find rare Victorian travel books still tagged with the original spine labels and catalog slips intact on the floor-to-ceiling shelves.

THE WRITER AND HIS WORK

BORN: Oct. 22, 1822, in Uffington, Berkshire

DIED: 1896 in Brighton, England; buried there

EDUCATED: Rugby School; Oriel College, Oxford, 1845; later studied law

MARRIED: Francis (Fanny) Ford, 1847

IMPORTANT WORKS: *Tom Brown's School Days* (1857); *Tom Brown at Oxford*; *A Layman's Faith*; *The Scouring of the White Horse*; *Rugby, Tennessee-1778-1789* (1881); and several biographies of famous Victorian-era men.

INTERESTING BIO FACT: A proponent of Christian Socialism, Hughes co-founded the London Working Men's College, where he was principal and a boxing instructor from 1872 to 1883. He also helped start England's first trade unions.

FURTHER READING *Thomas Hughes* by George John Worth (1984); *Thomas Hughes, 1822-1896* by John Egram Little

ELSEWHERE IN THE AREA Highland Manor Winery, Pickett State Park, Historic Stearns and the Big South Fork Scenic Railway, Blue Heron Historical Museum, Muddy Pond Mennonite Community ⚑

COSSITT BRANCH LIBRARY
Recognizing Richard Wright

A library in downtown **Memphis, Tenn**., earned the title of Tennessee's first literary landmark in 1998 when it was recognized for the role it played in the life of American short-story writer, poet and novelist Richard Nathaniel Wright. Wright, as a poor youth in Memphis, secretly borrowed books from the whites-only library to continue his self-education, 1925 through 1927. Wright is best known for his milestone novel, *Native Son* (1940).

The Cossitt Branch Library, located at 33 South Front St., now displays a plaque recognizing its role in Wright's literary career. The plaque reads: *In the 1920s Richard Wright (1908-1960) was denied access to the library because of race. A sympathetic white man helped Wright use the library, thus nourishing his dream of becoming a writer. This story is told in Wright's famous autobiography, Black Boy.*

The library, on a bluff overlooking the Mississippi River, began in 1888 as the Cossitt-Goodwyn Institute. It was the first public library in the fledgling city of Memphis and now serves the city's inner-city population. The original, red sandstone Romanesque-style structure was built in 1893 and featured rounded wings, towering turrets and gables. The current building was built in 1959. The Library functions as home for the Memphis and Shelby County Archives and the Cossitt Art Gallery.

The Tennessee Library Association bestowed its first Literary Landmark status to the branch in 1998 and arranged for the plaque.

With the publication of *Native Son*, Wright became an important spokesman on conditions facing African-Americans. The controversial novel sold 215,000 copies in the first three weeks, making it an instant best seller. In 1950 it was made into a so-so movie with Wright in the lead role of the character Bigger Thomas. A 1986 remake with a star-studded cast including Oprah Winfrey drew better reviews.

In 1938, Wright's story *Fire and Cloud* won the O. Henry Memorial Award and his book, *Uncle Tom's Children*, helped Wright win a Guggenheim Fellowship, which enabled him to devote his full time to writing. In 1937, he moved to New York City to become editor of the Daily Worker. In 1949, Wright joined George Plimpton and others in founding the Paris Review. In 1959, he began composing haiku, producing almost 4,000 of the verses.

Wright was born in 1908 on a Natchez, Miss., plantation, the grandson of slaves. He drew on the poverty and segregation of his childhood in the South and early adulthood in Chicago for his writing. He died nearly penniless in Paris, France, on Nov. 28, 1960.

Wright's works include *Uncle Tom's Children* (1938); *Native Son* (1940; plays 1941, 51, and with playwright Paul Green 1980); *How Bigger Was Born* (1940); *Twelve Million Black Voices* (1941); *The Negro and Parkway Community House* (1941); *The Man Who Lived Underground* (1942-44); *Black Boy* (1945); *The God That Failed* (1950); *The Outsider* (1953); *Savage Holiday* (1954); *Black Power* (1954); *The Color Curtain* (1956); *Pagan Spain* (1957); *White Man, Listen!* (1957); *The Long Dream* (1958); *Eight Men* (1961); *Lawd Today* (1961); *Letters To Joe C. Brown* (1968); *What The Negro Wants* (1972); *Farthing Fortunes* (1976) and *American Hunger* (1977).

The Cossitt Branch Library is open Monday through Friday from 10 a.m. to 5 p.m. For more information, call the library at (901) 526-1712. On the Net: www.memphislibrary.lib.tn.us/about/libraries/cossitt.

FURTHER READING *Richard Wright: The Life and Times* by Hazel Rowley (2001); *Richard Wright and Racial Discourse* by Yashinobu Hakutani (1996); *Voice of a Native Son* by E. Miller (1990); *Notes of a Native Son* by James Baldwin (1955) ◭

O'Henry Home

KATE CHOPIN HOUSE
Home of Controversial Creole Novelist

LOCATION Northwestern Louisiana, in the village of Cloutierville, 20 miles south of Natchitoches, La., along Highway 1 near the Cane River. From I-49, take exit 119 for 2 miles northeast to Cloutierville (pronounced Cloochyville). The village is situated in Natchitoches Parish (Nak' uh tush) at the southern tip of Cane River Lake.

The **Bayou Folk Museum/Kate Chopin House** ($) is open Monday through Saturday, from 10 a.m. to 5 p.m., and on Sunday from 1 p.m. to 5 p.m. Closed Jan. 1, Thanksgiving, Easter, and Dec. 25. For more information, contact Kate Chopin House/Bayou Folk Museum, Cloutierville, LA 71416. Tel. (318) 379-2233. On the Net: www.natchitoches.net/melrose/chopin.htm.

The house is part of the Cane River Creole National Historical Park and National Heritage Area. The park includes landscapes, sites and structures associated with the development of Creole culture. For more information, contact Cane River Creole NHP, 400 Rapides Drive, Natchitoches, LA 71458. Tel. (318) 356-8441.

FRAME OF REFERENCE Catherine (Kate) O'Flaherty Chopin and her husband, Oscar, reared their children in this house for four years, beginning in 1879. After Oscar's death in 1882, Chopin briefly managed his plantation and nearby general store. In 1884, she returned to St. Louis with her six children and sold the Cloutierville property five years later. Slaves built the house between 1805 and 1809 for Alexis Cloutier, the town's French founder. The museum opened to the public in 1965.

SIGNIFICANCE Chopin did not begin to write until after her husband's death. Her first published poetry in 1899 was soon followed by her controversial masterpiece, *The Awakening* (1899). The novel tells the story of a wife and mother who must balance her ignited sexual passions with traditional duties to society and family. Novelist **Willa Cather** praised the book as "A Creole Bovary is this little novel of Miss Chopin's . . . Hers is a genuine literary style..." A "Creole" is a descendant of the original French settlers in Louisiana. The word also refers to the dialect and culture of these people.

Chopin's too-hot-to-handle novel was 75 years ahead of Victorian America's literary tastes, and the heat it engendered eventually suffocated

Chopin's promising career. Since the 1960s, *The Awakening* has been regarded as a benchmark for the transition of American women writers from the themes of romance and contented domesticity to the exploration of their emotional and sexual needs.

A master storyteller, many of Chopin's first works appeared in such periodicals as Vogue, Atlantic Monthly and Harper's Young People. These stories later were published as collections. Chopin's stories and poems reflected the open, independent nature of a writer who smoked, dressed smartly and flirted with married men, habits that raised eyebrows in Cloutierville despite Chopin's popularity. In her work, Chopin drew on memories of better times in New Orleans and the recollections of the bayou folks of Natchitoches Parish.

ABOUT THE SITE The restored white, two-story house is built of handmade brick, heart cypress and heart pine with square wood pegs and bousillage, a mixture of mud, Spanish moss and animal hair. The typical Creole-style "raised" house has green trim, a screen porch at the rear, and four fireplaces that share a single chimney. Original, double French doors open to the front balcony of the second floor, where the family lived. A wrought iron and brick fence surrounds the grounds decorated with stately magnolias.

The floors and walls of the house remain as when Chopin lived there, but furnishings today are period Cane River pieces. Only a dresser of the writer's is original. The Chopins' quarters were on the second floor, which was accessed from a front, side stairway to the balcony. Visitors today still gain access to the former living room, family bedroom and two smaller bedrooms this way. The ground level had a dirt floor and was used for storage. An inner staircase leads to the attic.

The original kitchen, stables, barn and cook's cabin are gone, but an old doctor's office was moved to the grounds in 1938 and restored with items that belonged to Cane River plantation doctors. A restored blacksmith shop from the 1800s displays farm tools and equipment.

HOT TIPS Park on the shoulder of the road near the site in front of the house. The second story is not handicapped accessible. **Grand Isle**, the get-away island off the Gulf coast of Louisiana where Chopin set much of *The Awakening*, attracts thousands of vacationers yearly. Located at the southern tip of Highway 1, the island bills itself as "The Sportsman's Paradise." For details, go to www.grand-isle.com

The Kate Chopin House at 4132 McPherson Ave., in **St. Louis,** Mo., is listed on the National Register of Historic Places. The house is privately owned and not open to the public.

THE BEST STUFF Like many old Bayou houses, the Chopin House harbors its ghost. Legend has it that the spirit of Alexis Cloutier searches for his tombstone at twilight. Visitors can sometimes join the site's "ghost watch" for Cloutier's restless specter.

THE WRITER AND HER WORK

BORN: Feb. 8, 1850, in St. Louis, Mo.

DIED: Aug. 22, 1904, in St. Louis

EDUCATED: St. Louis Academy of the Sacred Heart

MARRIED: Oscar Chopin, 1870; six children

IMPORTANT WORKS: *Bayou Folk* (1894); *A Night In Acadie* (1897); *The Awakening* (1899); *At Fault* (1890). Stories include: *Love on the Bon-Dieu*; *Beyond the Bayou*; *A Visit to Avoyelles*; *La Belle Zoraide*; *In Sabine*; *Ozeme's Holiday*; *A Matter of Prejudice*; *At Cheniere Caminada*; *A Respectable Woman*; *Regret*; *Athénaise*; *A Little Free Mulatto*; *Alone*; *An Embarrassing Position* (play); *The Night Came Slowly*; *The Going a...of Liza...*; *The Dream of an Hour*; *Emancipation, A Life Fable*; *The Maid of Saint Phillippe*; *The Storm: A Sequel to the 'Cadian Ball'*; *Two Portraits*

INTERESTING BIO FACT: When she wrote *The Awakening*, Chopin was an assertive, individualistic 48-year-old widow who had survived her husband's unexpected death from Swamp Fever, her beloved mother's death, financial hardship, and plenty of harsh gossip centering on her alleged affair with a local man. But the former debutante was hardly prepared for the controversy and censure her novel caused in Victorian America. Libraries banned her books. Her friends shunned her. Her publisher rejected her third collection of short stories. Rattled and disillusioned, Chopin abandoned her budding literary career.

FURTHER READING *Kate Chopin: A Literary Life* by Nancy A. Walker (2001); *Unveiling Kate Chopin* by Emily Toth (1999); *New Essays on The Awakening* by Windy Martin (1988)

ELSEWHERE IN THE AREA Visitation to Cane River Creole National Historical Park is by guided tour with reservation. The site includes 42 acres of Oakland Plantation and 18 acres of Magnolia Plantation outbuildings. Other Cane River plantations include Melrose and Little Eva Plantation, once owned by man who might have been the model for slave owner Simon Legree in **Harriet Beecher Stowe**'s *Uncle Tom's Cabin.* ◿

> *This little French village…was simply two long rows of very old frame houses, facing each other closely across a dusty roadway.*
>
> — CHOPIN'S description of Cloutierville

BEAUREGARD-KEYES HOUSE

Home of Best-Selling Writer of 1940s and 50s

The house where the queen of the New Orleans literary scene during the 1940s and 50s, **Frances Parkinson Keyes** (rhymes with skies), wintered for 25 years is open for guided tours. The Beauregard-Keyes House ($), at 113 Chartres St. in New Orleans, is open Monday through Saturday, except for major holidays, from 10 a.m. to 3 p.m. Guided tours on the hour. Keyes (1885-1970) is best known for her novels reflecting Louisiana life, including *Crescent City Carnival* (1942), *The River Road* (1945), *Dinner at Antoine's* (1948), *The Chess Players* (1960) and *Madame Castel's Lodger* (1962).

Keyes, a Virginia native, wrote 51 books in her lifetime, 29 of them in this historic cottage. In 1944, she rented the cottage in New Orleans' famed French Quarter where Confederate Gen. Pierre G. T. Beauregard had lived after the Civil War, from 1865-66. Keyes lived in the 1826 cottage, which a New Orleans group had preserved in honor of native hero Beauregard, during winters for the rest of her life.

Keyes furnished the cottage with several original Beauregard pieces and memorabilia, including his bedroom set, portraits, and trunk, as well as her own collections of hand fans, 200 dolls from around the world, and "veilleuses" (beverage warmers), all on display. The yellow house was built in the Palladian and Louisiana raised-cottage style, with living quarters on the second floor and an above-ground basement that was used for storage and as a wine cellar.

The house facade is of brick overlaid with stucco and features large windows with green shutters and a typical front porch with white columns. Inside, wide floor planks are of yellow pine. Ornate carved cypress woodwork around sliding doors and ceilings feature intricate medallions. The estate includes the original slave quarters and a carriage house, which Keyes converted into her study. The study remains as Keys left it, with her desk, thousands of books and original, handwritten manuscripts in school tables. Two joined buildings that served as her bedroom and library also are open to the public. Visitors now find a gift shop in the carriage house.

In 1948, the novelist hired the distinguished architectural firm of Koch and Wilson to restore the Beauregard house. Keyes wrote her book *Madame Castel's Lodger* about Gen. Beauregard. *The Chess Players* tells of world chess champion Paul Morphy, whose grandfather once owned her

New Orleans house. Local legend says the restless spirits of Gen. Beauregard and Keyes' cocker spaniel, Lucky, roam the house today.

For more information, contact the Beauregard-Keyes House, 1113 Chartres St., New Orleans, LA 70016. Tel. (504) 523-7257.

On the Net: www.123neworleans.com/beauregard-keyes-house.htm ◢

NEW ORLEANS, BY THE BOOK

A heady atmosphere fueled by Cajun food, flowing bourbon, hot jazz and a wild Mardi Gras has lured many famous writers to New Orleans. Mark Twain, Kate Chopin, Sherwood Anderson, William S. Burroughs, F. Scott Fitzgerald, Walker Percy and Truman Capote were among those who sought stimulation and inspiration in the Crescent City. William Faulkner and Tennessee Williams bought houses in the city's French Quarter. Lillian Hellman, John Kennedy Toole and Anne Rice were born in "N'awlins." And myriad modern writers, including John Grisham, Robert Olen Butler and Richard Ford have set their works in the sizzling city with a reputation as The Big Easy.

Book lovers who visit New Orleans might want to check out these literary sites:

FAULKNER BOOK HOUSE, 624 Pirates Alley, was once home to William Faulkner. The charming bookstore features a large collection of rare Faulkner books and first-edition classics. The Mississippi novelist wrote his first novel, *Soldier's Pay* in the house in 1925. The store serves as a focal point for the Pirate's Alley Faulkner Society. Its owners organized the city's first Faulkner Festival, now the annual Words and Music Festival. Tel. (504)-524-2940. E-mail: Faulkhouse@aol.com. On the Net: www.wordsandmusic.org.

THE LILLIAN HELLMAN HOUSE, not open to the public, is located in the Lower Garden District at 1712 Prytania St. The playwright and memoirist was born in 1905 in this white Victorian boarding house run by her aunts and lived there until she was 5 years old. In childhood, Hellman spent half of every year in New York City and the other half in Louisiana.

Although Hellman wrote only 12 plays, she is considered a leading voice in American theater. Her best-known works include *The Little Foxes* (1939), *The Children's Hour* (1934) and *Toys In The Attic* (1960). Her first memoir, *An Unfinished Woman*, was published in 1969. Hellman, who died in 1984, is also remembered for her lifelong relationship with the mystery writer **Dashiell Hammett**.

THE HOTEL MONTELEONE, 214 Rue Royale, in the French Quarter, was a hangout for Truman Capote, Eudora Welty, Faulkner and Williams. Tel. (504) 523-3341 or E-mail: reservations@hotelmonteleone.

THE NATIONAL D-DAY MUSEUM, 945 Magazine St., was founded by writer/historian Stephen Ambrose. The museum depicts the stories he tells in *D-Day, June 6, 1944* (1994) and *Band of Brothers* (1993). Before his

death in 2002, Ambrose authored more than 20 biographies and historical books. Ambrose is perhaps best known for his bestseller *Undaunted Courage* (1996) about the expedition of **Lewis and Clark**.
On the Net: www.ddaymuseum.org. (800) 535-9595.

TENNESSEE WILLIAMS HAUNTS. The playwright from Mississippi lived at several addresses in the French Quarter: 722 Toulouse, now a part of the Historic New Orleans Collection; 710 Orleans, where he wrote *Ten Blocks on the Camino Real* while gazing upon St. Anthony's Garden; 632 St. Peter, where he wrote *A Streetcar Named Desire*; and 1014 Dumaine. Among Williams' favorite haunts was Galatoire's Restaurant, 209 Bourbon St. Every year, New Orleans hosts the popular Tennessee Williams Festival. For details, go to: www.tennesseewilliams.net/adjunctevents .html.

GARDEN DISTRICT BOOK SHOP, 2727 Prytania St., uptown, features autographed books by New Orleans authors. Tel. (504) 895-2266.

SHERWOOD ANDERSON'S SALON at the Pontalba apartments, 540-B St. Peter St.

You can stroll by for a glimpse of this literary landmark where Katherine Anne Porter also rented a residence.

HOT TIP For information about tours of New Orleans literary sites, go to www.neworleansonline.com/tours-attractions/tours.

FURTHER READING *The Booklover's Guide to New Orleans* by Susan Larson et. al. (1999) ◮

RALPH ELLISON'S HOMETOWN

Oklahoma City Keeps Novelist Visible

LOCATION Central Oklahoma in the capital, Oklahoma City, at 2000 N.E. 23rd St. at M.L. King Boulevard in the northeast neighborhood of Ellison's youth known as Deep Deuce. Reach downtown Oklahoma City via I-44, I-40 or I-35.

The **Ralph Ellison Library** is open Monday through Thursday from 9 a.m. to 8 p.m., on Friday from 9 a.m. to 6 p.m., and on Saturday from 9 a.m. to 5 p.m. For more information, contact the Ralph Ellison Library, 2000 N.E. 23rd St., Oklahoma City, OK 73111. Tel. (405) 424-1437. On the Net: www.metrolibrary.org. Other Ellison-related sites can be viewed on self-guided tours.

FRAME OF REFERENCE Ralph Waldo Ellison was born in Oklahoma City in 1914 and graduated from the city's Douglass High School in 1931. He left his hometown in 1933 to study music at Tuskegee Institute in Alabama. Oklahoma City named its branch library in Ellison's old neighborhood after the novelist in 1975. The library became an Oklahoma Literary Landmark in 2002, which was officially The Year of Ralph Ellison in Oklahoma City.

SIGNIFICANCE Ellison — novelist, essayist, short-story writer, poet, literary critic, sculptor, journalist, teacher, photographer, and accomplished jazz musician — wrote the seminal novel, *Invisible Man* (1952). The book is considered one of the most important literary works of the 20th century. Ellison developed the notion of "social invisibility," a condition in which an individual is judged on the basis of superficial characteristics assigned by white men and not intrinsic values. His work influenced many notable American authors, including Joseph Heller, John Irving, Kurt Vonnegut and Saul Bellow. Ellison worked seven years to write *Invisible Man*, his first novel. The book, which brought him international acclaim, traces a black man's search for identity, what Ellison called the essential American theme.

Ellison, trained as a jazz musician, wrote in a richly symbolic and metaphorical language heavily influenced by frontier traditions and the tight-knit black community where he grew up in Oklahoma City. At the urging of novelist **Richard Wright**, who was introduced to him by Langston Hughes in New York in 1936, Ellison turned from music and sculpture to writing. In 1938, the Federal Writers' Project in New York City hired Ellison. With the publication of *Invisible Man*, he was hailed as a major voice for African-Americans, a writer who redefined black literature in America.

ABOUT THE SITE Eight Ellison-related sites are preserved in Oklahoma City, including the Ellison library and the site of the house where he was born, at 407 N.E. 1st St. Two of Ellison's later homes on N. Stiles Street are not open to the public. At 429 N.E. 1st, you'll find Avery Chapel, where the Ellison family lived in the parsonage after the death of Ralph's father. Ellison's mother was the housekeeper.

Other Ellison-related sites are the Douglass High School (named for **Frederick Douglass**), 200 E. California, where the future writer graduated in 1931; the site of the Dunbar Library (named for poet **Paul Lawrence Dunbar**), 609 N.E. 4th St.; and the Aldridge Theater, 305 E. 2nd St. The Aldridge, now closed, was the first movie theater built for African-Americans and was a locus for the city's jazz scene. Ellison played his trumpet here. The Dunbar library no longer stands.

The Ellison library features an exhibit on Ellison's life and work and displays several photographs, including an enlarged photograph of Ellison as a baby. The centerpiece is a contemporary stainless steel and bronze sculpture by New York sculptor Ed Wilson. The three-piece work dominates the library foyer above display cases of his books. It includes a relief sculpture of Ellison's face.

HOT TIPS To find Ellison-related sites, pick up the flier *Ralph W. Ellison in Oklahoma City* at the Ellison Library. The library has a small refreshment center in the foyer.

The Library of Congress in Washington, D.C. houses the Ralph Ellison Collection. The collection includes Ellison's manuscripts, drafts and notes, speeches, notebooks, lectures, subject files, photographs and recordings, as well as his personal working library acquired from his widow, Fanny. The Ellison papers also include correspondence from writers Saul Bellow, Kenneth Burke, John Cheever, James T. Farrell, Martin Luther King Jr., Archibald MacLeish, Budd Schulberg, Robert Penn Warren, Bernard Malamud and Richard Wright.

THE BEST STUFF Ellison's boyhood neighborhood, Deep Deuce, refers to Oklahoma City's Second Street, a one-time black commercial district known for innovative schools, churches, theaters and its prominent jazz and blues clubs. The city's rich jazz heritage was born in Deep Deuce, a product of Jim Crow laws and now an historic district. The legendary Oklahoma City Blue Devils (Count Basie's orchestra), Jimmy Rushing and guitarist Charlie Christian are part of the city's jazz heritage, which imbued Ellison's life. Two or three jazz festivals are held in the neighborhood each year, culminating in the Deep Deuce Jazz Festival on Second Street.

THE WRITER AND HIS WORK

BORN: March 1, 1914, in Oklahoma City

DIED: April 16, 1994, in Harlem, N.Y.

EDUCATED: Tuskegee Institute, 1936; studied music on scholarship

MARRIED: Fanny McConnell, 1946, second wife

IMPORTANT WORKS: *Invisible Man* (1952); *Shadow And Act* (1964); *Going To The Territory* (1985); *Collected Essays of Ralph Ellison* edited by John Calahan (1995). Ellison's novel *Juneteenth*, which he was researching when he died in 1994, was finished and edited posthumously by Ellison's friend and literary executor, John Callahan. It was published in 2000.

ACCOLADES: National Book Award; National Newspaper Publisher's Russwurm Award; Chicago Defender's Award, all 1953; fellow of the American Academy of Arts and Letters; Medal of Freedom, 1969; Chevalier de l'Ordre des Artes et Lettres, 1970; National Medal of Arts, 1985; Oklahoman of the Century award, 2000

INTERESTING BIO FACT: Ellison's father, Lewis, wanted his eldest son to be a poet and named him after Ralph Waldo Emerson. Ellison reportedly was embarrassed by his middle name and avoided using it all his life. As a youth Ellison mowed the lawn of conductor Ludwig Hebstreit in exchange for trumpet lessons and training in orchestration.

FURTHER READING *Ralph Ellison: Emergence of Genius* by Lawrence Jackson (2002); *Jazz Country: Ralph Ellison in America* by Horace A. Porter (2001)

ELSEWHERE IN THE AREA Oklahoma City National Memorial; National Cowboy and Western Heritage Museum ◮

The library is the university; it's the grade school of the novelist.

— RALPH ELLISON

WOODY GUTHRIE'S OKEMAH

Birthplace of Poet, Songwriter

Woodrow Wilson (Woody) Guthrie, the poet/pioneer folk singer/writer who brought us the ever-popular *This Land is Your Land*, was born in the oil boomtown of **Okemah, Okla**., on July 14, 1912, the year his namesake was elected U.S. president. In 2001, the Oklahoma Friends of Libraries designated Guthrie's hometown as a literary landmark, the first in Oklahoma. The organization placed a plaque honoring Guthrie at the historic Crystal Theater, where Guthrie performed as a teenager. The theater, built in 1921, is still in operation. Guthrie left Okemah for Texas when the oil boom went bust in 1931.

Okemah, in east central Oklahoma just north of I-40, also hosts the annual Woody Guthrie Folk Festival that coincides with the singer's birth date. The free music festival includes performances by well-known folk singers at the Crystal Theater ($). For more information, contact Woody Guthrie Coalition, P.O. Box 661, Okemah, OK 74859. Tel. (918) 623-2440. On the Net: www.woodyguthrie.com.

You can find photographs of the Guthrie family amid displays about area settlers and American Indians at the **Okfuskee County Historical Museum**, 407 W. Broadway, in Okemah. For more information, contact the museum at P.O. Box 409, Okemah OK 74859.

In addition to his more than 1,000 songs, Guthrie wrote poems, newspaper and magazine articles, and six books including his autobiography, *Bound for Glory* (1943). He traveled America during the 1930s and '40s performing his music, often hopping freight trains or hitchhiking. His protest songs drew attention to social injustice and became a rallying cry for action. In the 1930s, he recorded *Dust Bowl Ballads*, 12 records for the Library of Congress Folk Song Archive. In 2000, he was awarded the Lifetime Achievement Award at the 2000 Grammy Awards. Guthrie's song, *The Oklahoma Hills*, is Oklahoma's official state folk song.

Guthrie wrote *This Land Is Your Land* in response to Irving Berlin's beloved *God Bless America*. Guthrie's song has become one of the most frequently performed patriotic songs, its protest element forgotten. Guthrie died on Oct. 3, 1967, in a Queens, N.Y. hospital. His son is the composer and singer Arlo Guthrie.

FURTHER READING *Woody Guthrie: A Life* by Joe Kline (1999) ◬

WILL ROGERS BIRTHPLACE AND MEMORIAL

Hands-On Look at Famous Humorist's Life

LOCATIONS Northeast Oklahoma, in the towns of **Claremore** and nearby **Oologah**, 20 miles northeast of Tulsa. The **Will Rogers Dog Iron Ranch and Birthplace Home** is located on Lake Oologah, 2 miles east of Oologah, on US 169, 12 miles northwest of Claremore. The **Will Rogers Memorial Museum**, framing the Rogers tomb, is located in Claremore. Follow signs. To reach Claremore, take I-44 (Will Rogers Turnpike) or SH 66 to Route 88 north to the site.

Both the ranch and museum are open daily year-round. The museum is open from 8 a.m. to 5 p.m., and the ranch from dawn to dusk. For more information, contact the Will Rogers Memorial and Birthplace, P.O. Box 157, Claremore, OK 74018-0157. Tel: (918) 341-0719 or toll free at 1-800-828-9643.

FRAME OF REFERENCE William Penn Adair Rogers was born in a frontier log cabin in Oolagah, Indian Territory, on Nov. 4, 1879. Rogers' father, Clem, built the large "White House on the Verdigris" River one room at a time from a log core, completing it in 1875. Young Will spent his first 10 years on his family's ranch and lived there later between stints at boarding school. When Rogers' mother, Mary, died in 1890, Clem Rogers moved to Claremore.

After Rogers' death on Aug. 15, 1935, in a plane crash in Alaska, he was buried in Los Angeles. In 1944, his remains were moved to the family tomb in Claremore. The memorial museum opened in 1938. Ten years after Rogers' death, his family donated the ranch and house to the state of Oklahoma.

SIGNIFICANCE Rogers — professional rodeo performer, cowboy, trick roper, vaudeville comedian, actor, radio personality, newspaper columnist, author, humorist and aviator — loved to write. He wrote prolifically throughout his colorful career and excelled as a syndicated newspaper columnist. At his peak, he wrote for 350 daily and 200 Sunday newspapers across America, reaching 40 million readers. His writings filled 21 volumes, and he also authored six books.

Famous for his wit and expressions ("I never met a man I didn't like"), Rogers was celebrated for his horse and rope tricks. His career in vaudeville took him to Broadway and the Ziegfeld Follies. He then went to Hollywood to star in 71 movies (21 with sound), write his own newspaper column, and host his own radio show. He left behind about 2 million published words and still reigns as one of the most quoted writers in America.

ABOUT THE SITES

WILL ROGERS DOG IRON RANCH AND BIRTHPLACE HOME On this ranch, young Will learned to ride a horse, rope a calf and see first-hand the political and cultural life of the Oklahoma frontier. Today the working ranch of 400 acres tells visitors about Rogers' life on the ranch and offers a look at what cowboy and ranch life was in the 1870s. Authentically dressed ranch hands work 50 head of Texas Longhorns, and you can stroll to your heart's content among farm animals. Clem Rogers owned 60,000 acres at one point in the 1880s and up to 10,000 head of cattle roamed his range. The site's barn mirrors the 1879 barn that a wildfire destroyed. Amish farmer-carpenters rebuilt the barn in 1993 using rough-sawed oak with the notch-and-peg methods of the 19th century.

The original abode where the tight-knit Rogers family lived was built with 10-inch logs hand-hewed from indigenous oak, hickory and walnut trees. The house was typical of the Indian frontier territory. It had two main 16- by 16-foot front rooms connected by a "dog trot" that eventually became an enclosed foyer. The east front room doubled as the parlor, where Clem Rogers had his business desk and record books, and the master bedroom. Will was born in this log-walled room. Clem added a kitchen, dining room and spare bedroom.

Clem Rogers later added a second floor with two bedrooms and white clapboard siding to the growing abode, transforming it into a 2,200 square-foot Greek Revival-style house. He dubbed it "The White House on the Verdigris." Four open fireplaces stem from the house's two original stone chimneys. The Army Corps of Engineers moved the house from its original site near Lake Oologah to the current location in 1961.

Original family furnishings were lost in a fire in the 1890s, but the house now displays pieces the Rogers sisters bought years later for the house. A hall tree with mirror, however, did belong to the family. In young Will's day, the parlor also had a piano used for family and community celebrations as well as funerals. A piano typical of the era sits there now. Family photographs fill the log walls.

WILL ROGERS MEMORIAL MUSEUM The 16,652 square-foot museum in Claremore is built of fossilized limestone quarried locally. The museum comprises nine galleries filled with exhibits about the family and Will's life, including his saddle collection. Two theaters show the star's movies and a documentary on Rogers. A children's museum features interactive computer exhibits to learn about "Ambassador Will" and scenes from Rogers' movies. The museum houses a research library and an archive with 15,000 photographs, thousands of Rogers' original manuscripts, private letters, contracts and personal papers.

Rogers bought the 20-acre site on a green slope in 1911 as a place to build a retirement home. The grounds and sunken garden surround his tomb, where his wife, Betty, and his children are also buried. You also will find a larger-than-life size bronze of Will *Riding Into the Sunset* on his favorite horse, Soapsuds, by Electra Wagner.

A Rogers likeness stands in Statuary Hall in the U.S. Capitol in Washington, D.C.

HOT TIPS The Rogers ranch offers paved parking, picnic areas, a grass airstrip and RV hook-ups. Camping is available at Oologah Lake.

THE BEST STUFF A visit to the ranch and memorial shows the grounded, loving and vital roots of the boy who grew up to become America's most beloved humorist, social and political commentator and entertainer of his era. A rare photograph in the ranch house helps visitors understand the political, cultural and family background that helped mold the young, aimless cowboy into a world-famous journalist. The photograph shows Clem Rogers, a Cherokee senator and judge who helped write the Oklahoma Constitution, with members of the Cherokee Senate. For 15 years, the Rogers "White House" was a seat of power and community gathering place.

THE WRITER AND HIS WORK For details about Rogers, see California in the Pacific section of this book.

FURTHER READING *Will Rogers: A Biography* by Ben Yagoda (2003); *Will Rogers' World: America's Foremost Political Humorist Comments on the Twenties and Thirties—And Eighties and Nineties* by Bryan B. Sterling, et al (1993)

442　**ELSEWHERE IN THE AREA** JM Davis Arms and Historical Museum, 333 Lynn Riggs Blvd.; Totem Pole Park △

SEQUOYAH'S CABIN

Honoring Warrior Who Created Cherokee 'Alphabet'

The Cherokee warrior and silversmith who created an 86-character "alphabet" for his people worked in a one-room log cabin he built in 1829 in eastern Oklahoma. Today you can visit the cabin where he worked on the system of symbols that paved the way to American Indian literacy at **Sequoyah's Home Site** in Sequoyah County, named in the warrior's honor. The cabin, protected by a stone cover-structure, is located 10 miles north of **Sallisaw, Okla.**, along OK 101 just north of I-40 near the Arkansas border. From US 59, go east on OK 101 for 7 miles. The shrine is open Tuesday through Friday, except state holidays, from 9 a.m. to 5 p.m., and on Saturday and Sunday from 2 p.m. to 5 p.m.

Sequoyah (1776-1843) spent 12 years developing his system of symbols based on his realization that the Cherokee language is based on a specific number of recurring sounds. He then created a symbol for each sound, thus producing a "syllabary" rather than a traditional alphabet. He completed his syllabary in 1821, after enduring years of isolation and ridicule from his family and tribe.

Sequoyah, crippled son of a Cherokee mother and a white father, had the English name of George Gist. As a child, Sequoyah had observed white settlers reading from books, what he called "talking leaves." In his cabin, Sequoyah wrote with charcoal on "manuscripts" of bark. After he completed his invention, Sequoyah established a school in his log home. Within a year, every Cherokee who could speak the Cherokee language could read it. His achievement allowed American Indians a way to read and write, and paved the way for the founding of the Cherokee Constitution and the Cherokee Advocate newspaper. Sequoyah became an admired and respected leader, receiving many honors from both the Cherokee Nation and the white man.

In 1824 the Cherokee National Council at New Echota, Ga., honored him with a silver medal, which he proudly wore for the rest of his life, and later with an annuity of $300, which his widow continued to receive after his death. Sequoyah's statue stands in the U.S. Capitol's Statuary Hall in Washington, D.C. Georgia's state capitol also displays a statue of him. Two species of giant redwood trees and Sequoia National Park in California were named after him.

Sequoyah died in 1843 while searching for a band of Cherokees in

Mexico. The location of his grave is unknown. Today, a stone building protects his one-room log cabin, considered a shrine. Period furnishings include Sequoyah's own spinning wheel. The Works Progress Administration (WPA) built the cover structure in 1936. Workers also removed an addition to the cabin, built by later owners from logs Sequoyah cut, which now functions as the visitor center. Historians at the visitor center tell of the history of the Cherokees from 1600 to 1907 and the story of Sequoyah's alphabet. Visitors can get a computer printout of their names and common greetings in Cherokee.

For more information, contact Sequoyah's Home Site, Route 1, Box 141, Sallisaw, OK 74955-9735. Tel. (918) 775-2413. On the Net: www .ok-history.mus.ok.us/mus-sites/masnum26.htm.

HOT TIP For more on Sequoyah, visit the Sequoyah Birthplace Museum ($) in Vonore, Tenn., at 576 Highway 360 in the Great Smoky Mountains. For more information, contact the museum, P.O. Box 69, Vonore, TN 37885. Tel. (423) 884-6246.

ELSEWHERE IN THE AREA The nearby Sequoyah National Wildlife Refuge is winter home to nearly 1 million waterfowl. ⌂

ARMSTRONG BROWNING LIBRARY

English Poets Immortalized in U.S.A.

If you're interested in the Victorian poets Robert and Elizabeth Barrett Browning, you don't have to travel to England to find a treasure-trove of Browningiana. Look no further than **Baylor University** in **Waco, Texas**. The central Texas university has amassed the world's largest collection of manuscripts, books, letters (about 2,000) and artifacts relating to the famous English couple in the Armstrong Browning Library. The striking building occupies a block on the Baylor campus, at 9th Street and Speight Avenue, in Waco, 90 miles south of Dallas.

The Brownings are remembered not only for their outstanding verse, but for their legendary Victorian romance. Elizabeth is best known for her 44 *Sonnets from the Portuguese.* Her husband, Robert, is considered one of the greatest Victorian poets. *Sonnets from the Portuguese* is a collection of love poems the invalid Elizabeth wrote to Robert, whom she married in 1846 at age 40. Robert affectionately called Elizabeth "my little Portuguese" because of her dark complexion. Elizabeth Browning was England's most respected and successful woman poet of the Victorian period.

The collection began decades ago in one room of Baylor's library when the chairman of Baylor's English Department, Andrew J. Armstrong, donated his personal Browning collection to the school. The school opened the new library to house the growing collection in 1951. The elegant, Italian Renaissance-style, granite-and- limestone library features 56 stunning stained-glass windows designed to illustrate poems and themes from Robert or Elizabeth's works. The collection is believed to be the largest collection of secular stained glass in the world.

The bronze-paneled front doors depict 10 themes from Elizabeth's poems, including five from the *Sonnets.* The library's interior features walnut paneling, marble, hand-painted ceilings, parquet floors and a foyer with a brass-inlaid terrazzo floor. The Browning Corridor exhibits 26 portraits and busts of Robert, and the McLean Foyer of Meditation displays Harriet Hosmer's cast of the clasped hands of the two poets.

In the Elizabeth Barrett Browning salon, you'll find Elizabeth's writing desk and chairs, her fan, mementos, and shelves filled with first editions of her works and later publications. Two large, mahogany cabinets flanking an ornate mirror provide filing space for music composed to accompany the Brownings' poems. Above the cabinets, you'll see pastel likenesses of

Robert and Elizabeth, drawn by Lowes Dickinson, and on the walls, portraits of Elizabeth by Sir William Charles Ross, Fox-Briell, Edmund Havell, and Valentine Prinsep.

Elizabeth's chairs feature needlepoint with a *Bells and Pomegranates* design. Her afghan pattern is used in the large afghan on the divan and in the miniature afghan in the reproduction of the scene from *The Barretts of Wimpole Street*. The play (and several movies) immortalized Elizabeth and Robert's romance. You'll also find a portrait of actress Katherine Cornell, who played the part of Elizabeth in the play. Gallery paintings are related to Robert Browning's poems, and much of the displayed furniture in the center is associated with him or the Browning family.

Other noted works by Elizabeth Barrett Browning (1806-1861) include: *The Battle of Marathon* (1820); *Poems* (1844); *A Drama of Exile* (1845); *Casa Guidi Windows* (1851); *Aurora Leigh* (1857); *Napoleon III in Italy* (1860) and the anthology, *Prometheus Bound* (1833), translated from the Greek of Aeschylus.

Works by Robert Browning (1812-1889), who ranks with Tennyson as one of the foremost Victorian poets, include: *Pauline* (1833); *Bells and Pomegranates* (1841-46); *Dramatic Romances and Lyrics* (1845); *Men and Women* (1855); and *Aristophanes' Apology* (1875).

For more information, contact the Armstrong Browning Library, Baylor University, P.O. Box 97152, Waco, TX 76798-7152. Tel. (254) 710-3566. On the Net: www.browninglibrary.org. ◣

O. HENRY'S HOME IN AUSTIN

Museum Recounts Life of Master of Short Story

LOCATION Downtown Austin, Texas, at 409 E. 5th St. at Trinity Street. From I-38, go west on 6th Street to Trinity and turn left to the site. The museum is located a few blocks south of the state capitol.

The **O. Henry Home and Museum** is open Wednesday through Sunday, from noon to 5 p.m. For more information, contact the Friends of the O. Henry Museum, 409 E. Fifth St., Austin, TX 78701. Tel. (512) 472-1903. On the Net: www.ohenryfriends.com.

FRAME OF REFERENCE William Sidney Porter, pen name O. Henry, came to Austin in 1884. He lived in this 1886 house with his wife and daughter from 1893 to 1895. During this time, Porter worked at the First National Bank of Austin after working for a while at the General Land Office. After he lost his bank job under a cloud of embezzlement charges, he left Austin for Houston, then fled to New Orleans and then Honduras. He briefly returned to Austin in 1897 to care for his dying wife in her parents' house. Porter first came to Texas in 1882 at age 20 from North Carolina, settling in San Antonio. He spent a total of 16 years in the Lone Star State — 13 in Austin — before last leaving in 1898. The house became a National Literary Landmark in 1999.

When Porter lived in the cottage, it was located a few blocks away on 4th Street. Until 1930, it was a rental property and slated for demolition. A community group moved it to its present site and after restoration, the house opened to the public in 1934.

SIGNIFICANCE Porter, a newspaperman who began his short-story career in an Ohio federal prison while serving five years for embezzling from an Austin bank, reigns as one of America's favorite storytellers. His tale, *Gift of the Magi*, especially enjoys widespread popularity. O'Henry's first collection of short stories was *Cabbages and Kings* (1904) followed by a second collection, *The Four Million* (1906). The master storyteller then produced eight more collections between 1907 and 1910. Three additional collections were published posthumously and several stories have been made into Hollywood movies.

In the last eight years of his life, Porter published 381 short stories for The New York World Sunday Magazine. His skillful wit, keen characterizations and surprising plot twists earned him his enduring popularity. In

1918, The Society of Arts and Sciences established the O. Henry Award to honor Porter's considerable contribution to American literature. The award is given out annually to authors of the best stories printed in magazines.

While in Austin, Porter published the Rolling Stone newspaper and went to San Antonio on weekends to expand readership. He also worked briefly for newspapers in Houston and New Orleans.

ABOUT THE SITE The one-story, five-room Queen Anne-style Victorian cottage is built of wood, now painted tan with brown, the colors when O. Henry lived there. The front porch has gingerbread detailing and a white screen door and leaded glass inner door. Four original brick chimneys were rebuilt, a back bedroom added in 1900 and electrical wiring put in in 1934. The cottage is furnished with Victorian pieces, many belonging to O. Henry or his family. You'll find O. Henry's desk, felt fedora, ink wells, and porcelain shaving mug and brush, as well as daughter Margaret's doll furniture.

Porter was clearly moved by the power of the Texas landscape. He set several of his best stories in Texas, including *The Afternoon Miracle*. He wrote vivid and specific descriptions the Lone Star State's vegetation and animals.

HOT TIPS Visitors are asked to wear flat, soft-soled shoes in the house to prevent damage to the original longleaf yellow pine floors. Call ahead for special assistance. Reservations for 10 or more are requested. Parking is on-street only.

Be sure to pick up the brochure, *Will Porter In Austin,* at the museum. The brochure gives details on four other O. Henry sites open to the public in the capital city. The sites are: Old General Land Office building where Porter worked; the Lundberg Bakery, which he frequented; the Austin History Center, which features O. Henry first editions and memorabilia; and Scholz Garten, where Porter often relaxed.

The museum offers several special events, including a celebration of O. Henry's birthday every September. Call for specific date. For more on O. Henry, see North Carolina in the South Atlantic section of this book.

THE BEST STUFF Porter took the pen name O. Henry while serving time for embezzlement in an Ohio prison, using his literary moniker on the 12 stories he wrote behind bars. The pseudonym is said to have come from his frequent calling of the family cat, Henry, with the phrase "Oh, Henry!." Before leaving Texas in 1897, Porter's first nationally published short story, *The Miracle at Lava Canyon*, appeared under his new pen name.

THE WRITER AND HIS WORK
BORN: Sept. 11, 1862, Greensboro, N.C.; buried Riverside Cemetery, Asheville, N.C.

DIED: June 5, 1910, in New York City at age 47

EDUCATED: Trained as a pharmacist

MARRIED: Athol Estes, 1887; one daughter

IMPORTANT WORKS: Novels - *The Gift of the Magi* (1906); *Heart of the West* (2000). Collections - *Cabbages and Kings* (1904); *The Four Million* (1906); *The Voice of the City* (1908); *Options* (1909); *The Best Short Stories of O. Henry* (1952); *Complete Works Of O. Henry* (1953); *Stories by O. Henry* (1978); *41 Stories* (1984); *100 Selected Stories* (1993); *Tales of O. Henry* (1996)

INTERESTING BIO FACT: Porter never seemed to have a way with money. His mishandling of funds at the Austin bank might have been no more than usual carelessness. Despite his considerable success at writing, the former cowhand, bank teller, editor and convict-turned-writer died almost penniless.

FURTHER READING *O. Henry* by Eugene Current-Garcia (1993); *Cheap Rooms and Restless Hearts: A Study of Formula in the Urban Tales of William Sydney Porter* by Karen C. Blansfield (1988)

ELSEWHERE IN THE AREA Elizabeth Ney Museum, 304 E. 44th St.; George Washington Carver Museum, 1165 E. Angelina St.; 1856 Governor's Mansion; Jourdan-Bachman Pioneer Farm, 11478 Sprinkle Cut-off Road; LBJ Library and Museum, 2313 Red River St., all in Austin

• O. HENRY HOUSE IN SAN ANTONIO •

You'll find the house where William Sydney Porter lived briefly in San Antonio, Texas, at 601 Dolorosa St. at Laredo Street downtown. O. Henry spent weekends in the two-room, caliche block house with Spanish-tile roof while he tried to expand sales of his newspaper, The Rolling Stone, which he published in Austin. The house displays an original copy of the humor-filled weekly. A four-minute recording tells visitors about the house. Victorian-era pieces owned by O. Henry furnish the tiny abode and newspaper accounts of O. Henry hang on the walls.

The house was moved to its current site in the Military Historic District from the grounds of the Lone Star Brewing Co., which had bought the house in 1960.

The brewery purchased the house from the Conservation Society, which had saved it in 1959. The brewery moved the house from its original location at 904 S. Presa St. In 1998, a the house was privately purchased and moved to the historic district. The restored house opened to the public in May 1999.

While a number of O. Henry stories and sketches feature San Antonio, two specifically refer to San Antonio: *A Fog in Santone* and *The Enchanted Kiss*.

The O. Henry House is open Monday through Friday from 9 a.m. to 4 p.m. Docents are on hand to show visitors around.

HOT TIP The historic Menger Hotel, 204 Alamo Plaza in downtown San Antonio, boasts its association with O. Henry, Oscar Wilde and Theodore Roosevelt. ◮

KATHERINE ANNE PORTER HOUSE
Childhood Home of 'Ship of Fools' Author

LOCATION South central Texas, about 50 miles northeast of San Antonio in Kyle, at 508 W. Center St. From I-35, take Kyle exit 213. Go to the stop sign on the feeder road and take a right onto Center Street through downtown to site. The house is leased by Texas State University-San Marcos, which will use the house for a writer-in-residence program and literary events.

The **Katherine Anne Porter** Literary Center **Museum** is open by appointment only. For more information, contact the Katherine Anne Porter Museum, 508 W. Center St., Kyle, TX 78640. Tel. (512) 268-6637. E-mail: porterhouse@swt.edu. On the Net: www.swt.edu. Search for Porter.

FRAME OF REFERENCE When Callie Russell Porter's mother died in 1892, she and her siblings moved with their father, Harrison, to this house to live with her paternal grandmother. Porter lived in this house, built in 1880, until 1902. The renovated center opened to the public 2000.

SIGNIFICANCE The short-story writer, journalist and novelist who wrote under the pen name, Katherine Anne Porter, is best remembered for her short fiction collections, especially *Flowering Judas* (1930); *Pale Horse, Pale Rider* (1939), which included the short work, *Noon Wine*, as well as *The Leaning Tower* (1944). These works embodied Porter's recurring theme of human failure and the resulting evil. They established her as one of the most accomplished stylists of her time.

Porter's only novel, *Ship of Fools* (1962), was an allegory alluding to the 15th-century satire of the same title by Sebastian Brant. The best seller became a major motion picture in 1965, starring Vivian Leigh and Lee Marvin.

From 1919 to 1930 Porter wrote poetry, short stories and book reviews while making regular visits to Mexico. Although Porter lived in many places in the United States, as well as in Europe, some of her best works, including *Noon Wine,* are set in Central Texas and reflect her strong Texas roots. Porter won the Pulitzer Prize for fiction in 1966 for *The Selected Short Stories of Katherine Ann Porter*. Porter is considered Texas' first professional writer.

ABOUT THE SITE The white wood, one-story house with long, narrow front porch and large windows has been restored to its turn-of-the-century look. Restoration of the six-room house added such modern conveniences as indoor plumbing, electricity and air-conditioning for in-residence writers. The house retains original house walls, floors and windows. You can see the hole in the ceiling that vented the wood stove that kept the poor Porter family warm.

Period pieces and collections of works by Southwest writers, artists and poets fill the modest house. The center also features a collection of Porter photographs, recordings, videos, letters and manuscripts. Visitors can view the ottoman-size, granite "upping block" used by Porter's grandmother to mount and dismount horses in the yard, site of young Porter impromptu plays. A fig tree Porter wrote about still stands in the back yard.

HOT TIP Parking is available at Kyle Elementary School off Gross Street and at the Kyle Public Library across the street from the school. The museum is available for public meetings, classes and weddings with reservations. The Albert B. Alkek Library at Texas State University-San Marcos houses the **Paul Porter/Katherine Anne Porter Papers**. The collection includes letters, recipes, photographs and other published materials related to Porter from 1940 to 1998. For details, contact Archivist, Albert B. Alkek Library, 601 University Drive, San Marcos, TX 78666-4604. Tel. (512) 245-2313.

The University of Maryland's Katherine Anne Porter Library contains the writer's personal collection of nearly 4,000 titles. It includes copies of first editions of all her works and foreign language editions. Porter herself donated most of the collection, along with some of her personal papers and items of memorabilia.

THE BEST STUFF First Lady Laura Bush spoke at the dedication of the renovated Porter House as a Texas Literary Landmark in 2000. In her remarks, given on the front porch, Mrs. Bush noted Porter called the porch her "gallery. . .a wonderful venue for repose and conversation and iced tea and tall frosted beakers of mint julep, for the men, of course."

THE WRITER AND HER WORK
BORN: March 15, 1890, in Indian Creek, Texas
DIED: Sept. 18, 1980, in a Silver Springs, Md., nursing home; buried in Indian Creek Cemetery, Indian Creek, Texas.
EDUCATED: Thomas School in San Antonio
MARRIED: Four times; no children
IMPORTANT WORKS: *Flowering Judas* (1930); *Hacienda* (1934); *Flowering*

Judas and Other Stories (1935); *Pale Horse, Pale Rider* (1939, includes three short novels: *Old Mortality, Noon Wine,* and title work); *The Leaning Tower* (1944); *The Days Before* (1952); *Ship of Fools* (1962); *The Collected Stories of Katherine Anne Porter* (1965); *A Christmas Story* (1967); *The Collected Essays of Katherine Anne Porter* (1970); *The Never-Ending Wrong* (1977)

ACCOLADES: Pulitzer Prize and National Book Award, 1966; Guggenheim Fellowship; O. Henry Memorial Award; Gold Medal for Fiction from National Institute of Arts and Letters; appointment to American Academy of Arts and Letters, 1966; Emerson-Thoreau Gold Medal for Fiction

INTERESTING BIO FACT: In 1931, Porter received a fellowship to work in Germany. She began a 27-day voyage to Germany from Mexico that became the basis for her best-selling *Ship of Fools*. In the novel, a group of Germans return home by ship from Mexico as the Nazis are rising to power.

FURTHER READING *Katherine Anne Porter* by Harold Bloom (2000); *The Texas Legacy of Katherine Anne Porter* by James. T. F. Tanner (1991); *Katherine Anne Porter and Texas* by Clinton MacHann (1990) ◭

THE RANSOM CENTER

A Literary and Cultural Treasure Chest

Book-loving sleuths out to find the goods on literary America should map their way to the campus of the **University of Texas at Austin** and discover the tantalizing treasures of the **Harry Ransom Humanities Research Center.** The galleries, special exhibits and stacks at the center house 30 million literary manuscripts and 1 million rare books, along with 5 million photographs (including the world's first photograph), film, and more than 100,000 works of art.

The Center, located at 21st and Guadalupe streets in the capital city, is dedicated to scholarly research on primary materials and preserving rare and unique cultural acquisitions. The center offers special exhibitions, lectures, and performances. Its huge collection of literary and photographic artifacts rivals those of the Library of Congress and the New York Public Library.

At the Ransom Center, you'll find a replica of the California study where mystery writer Erle Stanley Gardner wrote his *Perry Mason* books; poet Anne Sexton's typewriter and fan mail; and Nobel Prize-winning author Isaac Bashevis Singer's Yiddish typewriter and manuscripts. The center also owns major manuscript collections of James Joyce, Ernest Hemingway, T.S. Eliot, D.H. Lawrence, Tennessee Williams, Robert Lowell, Graham Greene, Arthur Miller, Samuel Beckett, André Malraux, Ezra Pound and Pulitzer Prize-winning poets James Tate and Karl Shapiro. The center puts special emphasis on collecting works of major Jewish writers. In ddition to Singer's works, collections include manuscripts of Bernard Malamud, Leon Uris, Benjamin Appel and Jay Neugeboren.

The center's British theater collections include archives from playwrights Tom Stoppard, David Hare, Arnold Wesker and John Osborne.

Visitors also can see a real Gutenburg Bible (c 1450). The Gutenberg Bible, the first surviving book printed from movable type on a printing press, was printed in Johann Gutenberg's shop in Mainz, Germany. The center holds one of five complete copies extant in America.

The university began amassing its awesome collection in 1958 when Harry Ransom was chancellor of the school. With royalties from university-owned oil fields, the center bought every rare-book collection and author archive it could find. Today, the university houses its treasures in a 40,000 square foot building with galleries, reading rooms and a theater.

For more information, contact Harry Ransom Humanities Research

Center, The University of Texas at Austin, P.O. Drawer 7219, Austin, TX 78713-7219. Tel. (512) 471-9119. On the Net: www.hrc.utexas.edu/collections ◮

D. H. Lawrence Shrine

ZANE GREY CABIN

Museum Recalls Western Novelist

The cabin that belonged to western novelist Zane Grey is being recreated near **Payson, Ariz.** The cabin, which was situated under the Mogollon Rim, burned down in 1990. The Rim Country Museum has undertaken the project and fundraising continues. The museum's mission is to discover and preserve the natural and cultural history of the greater Payson area, known as the "Rim Country." Grey wrote many of his 89 books in his cabin amid the rugged beauty of the Mogollon Rim.

The Rim Country Museum ($) features a Zane Grey exhibit, which includes personal items such as chaps, saddle, guns, as well as books and posters.

The museum is located in Payson at 700 Green Valley Parkway. For more information, contact the museum at P.O. Box 2532, Payson, AZ 85541. Tel. (520) 474-3483. E-mail: rimmuseum@cybertrails.com.

For more about Grey, look under Ohio and Pennsylvania in this book. ⌂

SHARLOT HALL MUSEUM
Sharing the Feminist Poet's Interest in Nature

Frontier historian and poet Sharlot Mabridth Hall transformed her interest in mountain history and nature into a living monument by founding a museum in downtown **Prescott, Ariz.,** in 1928. The museum at 415 W. Gurley St. explores the diversity of regional heritage through festivals, living history events, outdoor theater performances, exhibits, publications and research services. The museum also houses a museum store, archives and library.

Hall, born Oct. 12, 1870, to a frontier family, expressed her fascination with Arizona frontier life through prose and poetry. Although self-educated, she wrote 10 books, more than 500 articles, short stories (she sold her first, *The Genesis of the Earth and Moon*, a Moqui folk tale, in 1891 for $4) and poems, including *Cactus and Pine* (1910) and *Poems of a Ranch Woman*. Both poems were published after her death on April 9, 1943. Her diary, *A Diary of A Journey Through Northern Arizona in 1911*, was republished in 1997.

In 1909, Hall was appointed territorial historian, becoming the first woman to hold territorial office. She was active in the national political arena, first as a lobbyist then as a presidential elector. In 1927, Sharlot moved her extensive collection of artifacts and documents into the Old Governor's Mansion and opened a museum. Her life-long work inspired others to preserve local history. After her death, a local istorical society continued her efforts to build the Prescott complex that bears her name.

The 3-acre museum complex comprises eight restored historic structures spanning the years from the founding of Prescott in 1864 to the present. The museum buildings, artifacts (including Hall's desk), photographs and documents tell the stories of those who settled Arizona and the West and of the area's rich natural environment. Public programs include four annual festivals, historical re-enactments in an outdoor amphitheater, heritage gardens, and education outreach opportunities.

The Sharlot Hall Museum is open in summer, Monday through Saturday, from 10 a.m. to 5 p.m., and on Sunday from 1 p.m. to 5 p.m. From November through March, hours are Monday through Saturday, 10 a.m. to 4 p.m., and on Sunday from 1 p.m. to 5 p.m. The archives and library are open Tuesday through Friday, noon to 4 p.m. and on Saturday from 10 a.m. to 2 p.m.

For more information, contact the Sharlot Hall Museum, 415 W. Gurley

St., Prescott AZ 86301. Tel: (928) 445-3122. On the Net: www.sharlot.org/
archives

FURTHER READING *A Passion for Freedom: The Life of Sharlot Hall* by
Margaret Maxwell (1995); *Sharlot Herself* by Nancy Wright (1992) ◮

COLORADO SPRINGS PIONEER MUSEUM

Remembering Helen Hunt Jackson

The novelist, poet, children's story writer and activist Helen Hunt Jackson, whose writings historians say called national attention to the plight of American Indians in the West, is remembered in **Colorado Springs, Colo.**, at the Colorado Springs Pioneer Museum ($). The museum is located in the former El Paso County Courthouse (1903) downtown, just east of I-25 in the central Colorado city.

In 1881 and 1882, Helen Hunt Jackson wrote *A Century of Dishonor*, a controversial book documenting mistreatment of American Indians in the old Spanish missions of Colorado. Jackson (1831-1885), a Massachusetts native whose personal life had been punctuated by the deaths of her children and husband, also penned the novel *Ramona* (1884). The book tells the poignant love story of two mission Indians. *Ramona* has enjoyed more than 300 printings in many different languages. Other Jackson works include: *Saxe Helm's Stories*; *The Rainbow*; *Nelly's Silver Mine*; *Sonnets and Lyrics*; *Glimpses of Three Coasts*; *Bits of Travel*; *The Indian Reform Letters of Helen Hunt Jackson*, 1879-1885 (edited by V. M. Mathes, 1998). Jackson's detailed and loving descriptions of the landscape, sky, and flowers of the mountainous country still inspire readers.

The pioneer museum features a reconstructed portion of Jackson's home, furnished with hundreds of her original possessions, rare dolls based on *Ramona* characters, and an oil portrait of Jackson. The museum also tells the history and culture of the Pikes Peak Region with more than 40,000 objects. The American Indian collection includes hundreds of items representative of the Ute, Cheyenne, and Arapaho cultures. The museum is open Tuesday through Saturday, 10 a.m. to 5 p.m., and on Sunday from 1 p.m. to 5 p.m., May through October.

For more information, contact Colorado Springs Pioneers Museum, 215 S. Tejon St., Colorado Springs, CO 80903. Tel: (719) 385-5990. Email: COSMuseum@ci.colospgs.co.us. On the Net: www.cspm.org.

FURTHER READING *Helen Hunt Jackson: A Literary Life* by Kate Phillips (2003); *Helen Hunt Jackson* by Evelyn E. Benning (1973) ◭

THOMAS HORNSBY FERRIL HOUSE

Home of 'Poet of the Rockies'

Thomas Hornsby Ferril quietly spent 42 years at the Great Western Sugar Company in **Denver, Colo.**, as publicity director and advertising manager. But in his off hours, he wrote a newspaper column, plays and poetry. In 1979, the multi-award-winning, 5th-generation Westerner was named Colorado's poet laureate. He loved Colorado and celebrated it in his poetry. Ferril's works include *Westering, I Hate Thursday* and *High Passage*. You can find his poetry in *New and Selected Poems* (1982).

Today Denver honors its hometown regular guy by preserving his Victorian house at 2123 Downing St. as the **Colorado Center for the Book**. Ferril's words also are inscribed in the rotunda of the State Capitol Building, and a bronze marker carries his words in a park at the confluence of the Platte River and Cherry Creek. Lake Ferril, named after the poet, dominates City Park.

Carl Sandburg (see North Carolina in South Atlantic section of this book) once called Ferril "the Poet of the Rockies," and "one of the great poets of America." **Robert Frost** (see New Hampshire under New England) immortalized Ferril, the "Denverite," in a poem.

For more information, contact the Colorado Center for The Book, 2123 Downing St., Denver, CO 80205. Tel.: (303) 839-8320. On the Net: www.coloradobook.org.

FURTHER READING *Thomas Hornsby Ferril and the American West* edited by Robert C. Baron, Stephen J. Leonard, and Thomas J. Noel; *The Great Poem of the Earth: A Study of Thomas Hornsby Ferril* by Andrew Elkins (1997) ◢

HEMINGWAY'S KETCHUM

Final Home, Memorial to Novelist

Ernest Hemingway came to Sun Valley in 1939 to work on his novel, *For Whom The Bell Tolls*, and lived his final years in a house in **Ketchum, Idaho.** He committed suicide in the resort town in 1961. Although the airy, concrete house where he lived is privately owned and not open to the public, Ketchum honored the famous and influential 20th-century novelist in 1966 with the Ernest Hemingway Memorial. A bronze bust of the writer stands amid a grove of aspen and willow trees overlooking Trail Creek.

You will find an exhibit on Hemingway at the Ketchum-Sun Valley Historical Society/**Ski and Heritage Museum**, 180 1st Street East in Ketchum. For more information contact the museum at Box 2746, Ketchum, ID 83340. Tel: (208) 726-8118. The small exhibit includes Hemingway's portable Royal typewriter and case, decorated with travel stickers; and the story of the writer's life in Ketchum. Some photos show Hemingway with his pal, actor Gary Cooper, who often visited in Sun Valley. Others show the Hemingway house interior as his widow Mary left it.

Hemingway is buried at the **Ketchum Cemetery** just north of Ketchum. His flat grave is centrally located in the cemetery, beneath two big trees. His wife, Mary, is buried nearby.

For more information about the Hemingway house, contact The Nature Conservancy of Idaho at (208) 788-8988. For information about the memorial, call (208) 726-3423. For an unofficial virtual tour of the Hemingway gravesite and memorial and an unofficial virtual tour of the Hemingway house, go to: www.usplanb.com/hemingway.cfm. For details about Ernest Hemingway, look under Florida and Illinois this book. ⌂

MOUNTAIN *Idaho*

EZRA POUND BIRTHPLACE

Avant-garde Poet's First Home

LOCATION South central Idaho, in Hailey, 10 miles south of Ketchum, at 2nd Avenue and Pine Street.

The Ezra Pound birthplace home, now known as **The Hailey Cultural Center**, is open only for public events by reservation. Plans to open the Pound house to the public during regular hours are on the horizon. You can arrange a private tour of the house by contacting the Ezra Pound Association, P.O. Box 1482, Hailey, ID 83333-1482. Tel.: (208) 578-1660. E-mail: jenwilson8@aol.com. On the Net: www.isu.edu/pound.

FRAME OF REFERENCE Ezra Loomis Pound was born in 1885 in this house, built in 1883. His family left rough-and-rowdy Hailey 15 months later, when Pound was an infant. The Ezra Pound Association acquired the house in 1998 and opened it to visitors on a limited basis in 2003.

SIGNIFICANCE Pound — poet, critic and editorialist — was an immensely influential 20th-century writer. He redefined poetry in the modernist movement through his terse and evocative style of rhythm and cadence. During decades in self-exile, he emerged as a central figure in the European literary avant-garde, testing the limits of poetry and helping renew English poetry in the 1910s. Pound began publishing verse in 1908. His first literary fame came with *Ripostes* in 1912.

Pound's most significant contribution to poetry begin with Imagism, a movement that derived its technique from classical Chinese and Japanese poetry. The form stressed clarity, precision, and economy of language. This type of poetry shunned traditional rhyme and meter to achieve what Pound called "the sequence of the musical phrase, not in the sequence of the metronome." Pound's work had a profound impact on poets T.S. Eliot and William Butler Yeats. Pound's later writing, refined over 50 years, focused on the expansive epic poem, *The Cantos*. Pound called *The Cantos* "a poem including history."

ABOUT THE SITE When the Pounds lived in the late-Victorian house, it had four rooms, two on the first floor and two on the second. Later, a south wing of the same vintage was built with four rooms on the first floor. A kitchen was added in the mid-20th century. The simple wood house on rock foundation is made of lath and plaster, painted white with dark gray trim. The house, now with eight rooms and two baths, has a front bay window and porch, as well as a back porch. A metal roof covers the original cedar shingles. A vintage shed stands behind the house.

The first floor has 10-foot high ceilings with vintage Victorian reproduction wallpaper, most of William Morris design. Vintage light fixtures decorate the whole home. The upstairs is used as an artists' residence.

The house exhibits several Pound-related items, including a life mask of Pound, scholarly books, a centennial plaque, and a bust provided by Pound's daughter. When wallpaper was removed from a bedroom ceiling during renovation, workers found newspapers that bore Homer Pound's signature. The father of the famous poet had signed his name near an article referring to his membership on the Fireworks Committee, circa 1886.

In 1993, poet Allen Ginsberg visited the decaying house and expressed the need to preserve the site a reminder of Pound's creative legacy. Two years later, the Ezra Pound Association formed to meet this goal. The Pound association has transformed the birthplace into a center for creativity cultural study, sponsoring poetry readings, lectures, concerts, dance performances, art exhibitions and a literary magazine.

HOT TIPS You can visit the Emmanuel Episcopal Church (1885) at 2nd Avenue and Bullion Street, Hailey's oldest church. Pound was possibly the first child ever christened there. At the Blaine County Museum, corner of Main and Galena streets, an exhibit documents Pound's life and work. Both sites are within walking distance of the Pound house. For information about the annual International Ezra Pound Conference, contact the site.

THE BEST STUFF The garden and lawn around the house are large and outstanding. Enormous evergreens shelter the property. The Idaho Centennial tree, an apple tree, dominates the front lawn amid flower gardens. An old iron fence, about 4 feet high and possibly original, surrounds the property on two sides. The original Pound home sat on six city lots, two of which were sold around 1950.

THE WRITER AND HIS WORK

BORN: Oct. 30, 1885, in Hailey
DIED: Nov. 1, 1972, in Venice, Italy
EDUCATED: University of Pennsylvania, M.S., 1906; Ph. D., Hamilton College, 1905

MARRIED: Dorothy Shakespear, 1914

IMPORTANT WORKS: Poetry — *A Lume Spento* (1908); *Personae* (1909); *Exultations* (1909); *Provenca* (1910); *Canzoni* (1911); *Ripostes* (1912); *In a Station at the Metro* (1916); *Lustra and Other Poems* (1917); *Quia Pauper Amavi* (1919); *Hugh Selwyn Mauberley* (famous sequence poem, 1920); *Umbra: Collected Poems* (1920); *The Cantos* (1925-1940); *Homage to Sextus Propertius* (1934); *The Pisan Cantos* (1948); *Patria Mia* (1950); Prose — *How To Read* (1931); *The ABC of Economics* (1933); *Social Credit and Impact* (1935); *What is Money For?* (1939); *The Spirit of Romance* (1953); Anthology — *Cathay* (1915); *The Classic Anthology Defined by Confucius* (1954)

ACCOLADES: Bollingen-Library of Congress Award, 1949, for *The Pisian Cantos*

INTERESTING BIO FACT: In 1924, Pound self-exiled to Italy and became involved in Fascist politics. He returned to America in 1946, after being indicted for treason for broadcasting Fascist propaganda by radio to the United States during World War II. He was acquitted, but declared mentally ill and committed to St. Elizabeth's Hospital in Washington, D.C. Released in 1958 as "incurable," he returned to Italy. Although Pound's contributions to poetry are undeniable, his personal legacy remains controversial. Some say his harsh politics damaged his high-minded view of art and civilization.

FURTHER READING *The Roots of Treason: Ezra Pound and the Secret of St. Elizabeth's* by E. Fuller Torrey, M.D. (1999); *A Companion to the Cantos of Ezra Pound* by Carroll F. Terrell (1993); *Ezra Pound: The Cantos* by George Kearns (1990)

ELSEWHERE IN THE AREA Ketchum Ski and Heritage Museum (Hemingway Exhibit), 180 1st Street East, Ketchum ◮

LITTLE BIGHORN BATTLEFIELD

Recalling Words of Black Elk

Black Elk was 13 years old when he fought Lt. Col. George Armstrong Custer and the U.S. 7th Cavalry at the battle of Little Bighorn in 1876. The legendary Oglala Sioux warrior also witnessed the massacre of the Sioux at Wounded Knee in 1890. American poet **John Gneisenau Neihardt** recorded Black Elk's life in his landmark 1931 book, *Black Elk Speaks.*

Neihardt interviewed Black Elk as a historical source for an epic poem he was writing on Wounded Knee. The two became friends, and Neihardt wrote fully of the respected tribal elder and spiritual leader in his book. Other books include: *The Sacred Pipe: Black Elk's Account of the Seven Rites of the Oglala Sioux*; (1953) *The Sixth Grandfather: Black Elk's Teachings Given to John G. Neihardt* (1984).

Black Elk's words now grace the side of the visitor center in Little Bighorn Battlefield National Monument in south central Montana. His famous sentiment, written in large, wooden letters painted black, read: *Know The Power That Is Peace.*

The Little Bighorn Battlefield National Monument ($) is located on the Crow Indian Reservation. Take I-90 (US 87/212) to exit 510. Watch for signs. Take US 212 one mile east to entrance. The monument is open daily, except Thanksgiving, Dec. 25 and Jan. 1, from 8 a.m. to 9 p.m., Memorial Day through Labor Day; in winter months, from 8 a.m. to 4:30 p.m.; and in fall and spring months, from 8 a.m. to 6 p.m. Self-guided tours and interpretative programs are available.

For more information, contact Little Bighorn Battlefield National Monument, P.O. Box 39, Crow Agency, MT 59022. Tel. (406) 638-3224. On the Net: www.nps.gov/libi. For more on Neihardt, see Nebraska in the West North Central section of this book. ◢

MOUNTAIN Montana

D. H. LAWRENCE RANCH AND SHRINE

English Writer's Home In America

English writer David Herbert Lawrence, author of the literary classics *Sons and Lovers* (1913), *Women in Love* (1920), and *Lady Chatterley's Lover* (1928), first came to New Mexico for a visit in Sept. 1922. He ended up living in the southwestern state briefly, on Kiowa Ranch near **Taos, N.M.**, where he was buried in 1934. The site is known today as the D.H. Lawrence Ranch and Shrine.

Lawrence's American sojourn began when an admiring New York socialite and friend, who had a home in Taos, invited him and his wife, Frieda, to visit her. Lawrence spent only 11 months altogether in New Mexico during three trips to the state, but on his second visit in 1924, he and Frieda lived for five months at Kiowa Ranch. The ranch, named for the Kiowa Indians and nestled in the Sangre de Christo Mountains, was a gift to Frieda from the friend. (Lawrence would not accept such an extravagant gift.)

Today the University of New Mexico owns the D. H. Lawrence Ranch and Shrine. The school uses the ranch, established in the 1880s by a homesteader, as an education and conference center. Only Lawrence's burial site and memorial chapel on the ranch are open to the public. The shrine is located along NM 522 between Santa Fe to the south and the Colorado state line.

While at the ranch, Lawrence and Frieda lived in the three-room, adobe Homesteader's Cabin on the 160-acre ranch, 20 miles northwest of Taos on Lobo Mountain. Lawrence came to New Mexico hoping to create a utopian society called Rananim, but the colony never took off. The simple cabin is built of Ponderosa pine and adobe plaster and has a tin roof. Lawrence and Frieda repaired the cabin and other buildings on the ranch.

In the cabin, Lawrence, born in 1885 in England, completed his short novel *St. Mawr*. The book celebrates the special quality and landscape of the Kiowa Ranch. Lawrence loved to write in the morning at a small table under a towering pine in front of the abode. The pine is now called The Lawrence Tree.

During his last visit to the ranch in 1925, Lawrence wrote the biblical drama, *David* and part of *The Plumed Serpent*. New Mexico figures prominently in other Lawrence essays and stories, including *The Woman Who Rode Away*, *The Plumed Serpent* and *Mornings in Mexico*.

In his two decades of writing, Lawrence wrote more than 40 volumes of narrative fiction, poetry, travel writing and social commentary. His work largely reflected his view that sexual relations were the decisive element in human behavior.

After Lawrence died near Vence, France, in 1930, Frieda returned to New Mexico and lived in the state with her new husband for the rest of her life. In 1934, she had Lawrence's body exhumed from his Vence grave and cremated. His ashes were brought to the ranch and enshrined in a small memorial chapel at the end of a rocky trail. At the top of the silver-painted, concrete altar embossed with leaves and flowers sits a statue of Lawrence's personal symbol, the phoenix. Frieda's grave is to the left of the memorial.

In 1955, not long before her death, Frieda gave the ranch to the University of New Mexico. For more information about the site, contact Public Affairs Department, Hodgin Hall, 2nd Floor, University of New Mexico, Albuquerque, NM 87131-0001. Tel. (505) 277-5813. E-mail: paaffair@unm.edu. On the Net: www.unm.edu/~taoconf/ranch.

HOT TIP Playwright **Tennessee Williams** (see Mississippi in East South Central section of this book) wrote the play *I Rise in Flame, Cried the Phoenix* as a tribute to Lawrence, dramatizing the events surrounding Lawrence's death. ◮

> *The big pine tree in front of the house, standing still and unconcerned and alive...the overshadowing tree whose green top one never looks at...One goes out of the door and the tree-trunk is there, like a guardian angel. The tree-trunk, the long work table and the fence!*
>
> — D. H. Lawrence

ERNIE PYLE HOUSE

Journalist's Home Preserved As Library

Famous WWII correspondent Ernie Pyle and his wife, Jerry, built the only house they ever owned in 1940, in **Albuquerque, N. M.,** at 900 Girard S.E. The six-room, wood-frame house today functions as the **Ernie Pyle Memorial Library**, as it has since 1947, when the city opened it as the first branch of its public library system. Librarians accommodate visitors with informal tours.

Though adobes dominate the quiet residential neighborhood, Pyle built his dwelling of wood to remind him of his childhood home in Indiana. Pyle had hoped to live in the house permanently, but he stayed there only briefly while on vacation from the war. He left it for the last time in Jan. 1945. In April that year, he was cut down by a Japanese sniper in Ie Shima, near Okinawa, while covering a battle. He was 44. Jerry, who suffered depression and had tried to kill herself twice in the Albuquerque house, died seven months later.

Today's branch library is crammed with books on floor-to-ceiling shelves. In a display case you'll find several items that belonged to Pyle. These include a typewriter; war correspondent patches; a 10-gallon hat, pewter mug and goggles he used in Africa; and his ring. You'll also find photographs, manuscripts, copies of Pyle's books, and the 1945 Albuquerque newspaper with headlines announcing Pyle's death. Pyle's former bedroom functions as the nonfiction room. The bathroom houses the periodical reading room. Parking is on-street.

The Ernie Pyle Memorial Library is open Tuesday through Saturday, from 10 a.m. to 6 p.m. For more information, contact the library at 900 Girard, S.E., Albuquerque, NM 87106. Tel. (505) 256-2065. For details on Pyle, look under Indiana in the East North Central region of this book. ◮

> *I have no home. My home is where my extra luggage is, and where the care is stored, and where I happen to be getting mail at the time. My home is America.*
>
> — ERNIE PYLE

Tor House

FORT CLATSOP

Where Lewis and Clark Edited Their Journals

LOCATION Coastal Oregon, on the banks of a Columbia River tributary, 6 miles southwest of Astoria and 91 miles northwest of Portland. From north and south, take US 101/26 to Business 101 at Astoria. Follow signs 3 miles to the park entrance. From east, take US 30, the Lewis and Clark auto tour route, to US 101 to Business 101 south. Follow signs to park entrance.

The Salt Works unit of the park is located in the resort town of Seaside, 15 miles southwest of Fort Clatsop. From US 101 take Avenue G toward the beach. Turn left on S. Beach Drive and go 5 blocks. Turn right on Lewis and Clark Way, a dead end. Park on-street. The Salt Works is on the left inside an iron fence.

Fort Clatsop National Memorial ($) is open daily except Dec. 25, from 8 a.m. to 6 p.m. in summer, and 8 a.m. to 5 p.m. the rest of the year. For information, contact Fort Clatsop National Memorial, Rt. 3, Box 604-FC, Astoria, OR 97103. Tel. (503) 861-2471. On the Net: www.life back.com/kidscafe/lewisclark.html. For the *Journals*, go to http://xroads .virginia.edu/~HYPER/JOURNALS/journals.html.

FRAME OF REFERENCE Lewis and Clark's Voyage of Discovery began in 1804 and ended in 1806. During the 2-year voyage, the co-commanders kept meticulous journals. The Expedition encamped at Fort Clatsop for 3 months in the winter of 1805-06. The men began building the fort on Dec. 8, 1805, and had shelter by Christmas Eve. The Expedition left the fort on March 23, 1806, to return to St. Louis.

SIGNIFICANCE The most valuable product of the Voyage of Discovery was Lewis and Clark's 1 million-word journals, recording "America's greatest epic." The voyage's co-commanders both regularly wrote detailed but fragmented and unpolished entries in an elk skin-bound field book and red morocco-covered journals. Lewis did most of the editing.

The voyage commanders, exceptional frontiersmen and writers, included elaborate descriptions of people, wildlife, plants and terrain, as well as weather, astronomical observations, tabulations of longitude and latitude, and maps. Their daily logs told the story of the struggles the group faced while traveling west and returning home. The voyagers, mostly military men, endured swift rivers, hot deserts, harsh storms, attacking animals, bitter mountain snow, lack of food, and once, hostile Indians. The captains also wrote of such housekeeping chores as hunting for food, extracting rotten teeth, and administering whippings for neglect of duty.

The famous journals, complete with misspellings, added 1,000 new words to the American vocabulary while expanding knowledge of the unknown West. President Thomas Jefferson, who commissioned the voyage, had just pulled off the Louisiana Purchase from France, and he wanted to know about the vast land his country had bought. He chose Meriwether Lewis to lead the exploratory expedition into the unknown wilderness. Lewis in turn selected his admired friend, William Clark, as co-commander. Both were native Virginians, as was Jefferson.

The voyagers built Fort Clatsop, named for the local Clat Sop Indians, on a site where the Columbia, the "Big River of the West," empties into the Pacific. The Expedition had completed half of its 28-month, 8,000-mile round trip to the west coast, mostly by water. The weary, 33-person Lewis and Clark party spent a soggy but important winter in their hand-hewn garrison.

The Voyage of Discovery team built Fort Clatsop on the Netul River, a Columbia tributary, near present-day Astoria. (The river's name is now Lewis and Clark River.) Astoria is named for John Jacob Astor, the New York financier who built a fur-trading fort, Fort Astoria, on the Columbia in 1811. Astoria was America's first permanent settlement west of the Rocky Mountains and its citizens helped pave the way for emigrants. {**Washington Irving** wrote about Astor's ill-fated commercial enterprise in the Pacific Northwest in his book, *Astoria* (1836)}.

During the weary winter at Fort Clatsop, Lewis and Clark reworked their journals. The captains reflected on their experiences and revised their return route. Their unique journals are sometimes called "our national poem." Their seven published volumes of journals and volume of maps are an American treasure.

ABOUT THE SITE Fort Clatsop today is an exact replica of the 50-foot square, log stockade with slanted roof that the Expedition built. It stands amid a forest of towering Sitka Spruce and Douglas Fir. The Astoria community, following Clark's sketches, reconstructed the fort in 1955. Two rows of seven connected rooms, each with central fireplace, line a 20 by 48-foot parade ground. An historically accurate American flag flies atop a log pole.

Mud and moss fill the spaces between the logs, just as in 1805. A thick mat of moss grows on the fort roof, a result of near-constant rainfall, which Lewis and Clark complained about in their journals. "We are all wet and disagreeable," Clark wrote. Of the 106 days the Corps spent at Fort Clatsop, only 12 were without rain.

One mile of wood-chip trails takes hikers from the visitor center to the fort, through a forest of moss-covered, colossal conifers, to a canoe launch, and then back through the 125-acre park. The canoe launch marks the place where the Lewis and Clark Expedition probably landed. Markers by the trail point out native trees and plants first identified in the captains' journals.

The spacious visitor center houses a museum, bookstore and large theater. Among museum artifacts are a knife and file believed to have belonged to John Shields, a private in the Expedition party. The theater offers a 17-minute orientation slide show and an excellent 32-minute film, *We Proceeded On: The Expedition of Lewis and Clark, 1804-1806*. The center's lobby has a video viewing area offering a selection of four videos about life at Fort Clatsop. There's also a guide to park fauna.

THE SALT WORKS The Salt Works in Seaside sits at the place where five men from Fort Clatsop boiled seawater to produce salt. The monument is a reconstruction of the rock oven with five brass kettles of saltwater on top and a marker. In December 1805, the men boiled 1,400 gallons of seawater over two months, producing 3 1/2 bushels of salt to season food, to trade and to take on their return trip. They built the salt camp where the sea had a high salt content, and wood and game were plentiful. Because there are few parking spaces near the Salt Works, it's wise to park in downtown Seaside and walk to the site.

HOT TIPS *The Journals of Lewis and Clark* is the best introduction to Fort Clatsop. It's especially interesting to read of the now-extinct Killamuck, Chinnook and Clatsop Indians. The journals also tell of the party's diet: wappato roots, spoiled elk meat, fish, and Clark's favorite, dog meat. "I think it an agreeable food and would prefer it vastly to lean Vinison or Elk," he wrote.

Allow two hours to visit the fort and 20 minutes to visit the Salt Works. Dress for wet weather and wear sturdy shoes. Use caution at the canoe launch site, which is slippery. Wood chips on the trail can be slick. The site has no beverages or snacks, but picnic tables are available. The site offers special events, seasonal programs and a Junior Explorer Program for kids. Ask for a brochure for the Columbia Estuary Driving Tour.

Camp River Dubois/Lewis and Clark State Historic Site, with a hands-on museum, is located at Rt. 3 at Poag Rd. Hartford, Ill. 62048, (618) 251-5811.

THE BEST STUFF For history buffs who've traveled the Lewis and Clark Trail, whether by car or literature-fed imagination, this rustic fort in the enchanted forest cements the journey, just as it did for the Corps of Discovery. Running your eyes over the hand-hewn cots, tables, chairs, and especially the writing desk in Lewis and Clark's personal quarters, you feel you've dropped in on America's greatest epic *in progress.*

Lewis and Clark's living quarters are on the right, next to the corner room of guide/interpreter Toussaint Charbonneau, his Shoshone wife, Sakakawea (Sacagawea) and their infant son Jean-Baptiste. Check out the Enlisted Men's Quarters left of the wooden gate. The soldiers spent a lot of time in their flea-riddled bunks, sick with colds and stomach pains. A big tree stump serves as a table. When the Expedition party arrived in 1805, they had trouble finding a clearing in the thick forest. To build Fort Clatsop, they felled several towering trees. Rather than removing the giant stumps, they simply designed the fort to accommodate the stumps as furniture.

Lewis and Clark saw trees over 300 feet tall with 40 foot circumferences at the base. Now after years of logging, later growths reach only 100 feet. The magnificent forests remain Oregon's economic lifeblood. Park rangers say some of the giant Sitka Spruce in the park are true survivors; they might have witnessed Fort Clatsop's original construction as saplings.

Northwest Oregon's coastal weather remains as it was when the Expedition visited: rain, rain and more rain. A coat of lush, green moss eerily engulfs nearly everything in sight, including trees, rocks, even mailbox posts. Rainfall averages nearly 63 inches annually. Temperatures are mild year-round.

Just right of the canoe landing site, neat rows of pilings stand watch in the river. The pilings are part of an active logging operation. Trucks drop newly cut logs into the river and they collect against the pilings. Boats then harvest them. Other estuary pilings are remains of 39 turn-of-the-century salmon canneries or boat facilities.

FURTHER READING *Lewis and Clark on the Trail of Discovery* by Rod Gragg (2003); *National Geographic Guide to the Lewis and Clark Trail* by Thomas Schmidt (2002); *Undaunted Courage* by Stephen Ambrose (1996)

ELSEWHERE IN THE AREA Ecola State Park west of Fort Clatsop (features the 7.5-mile Tillamook Trail, which traces the route Clark took over

"Clark's Mountain" to see a beached whale); 1896 Battery Russell; I-25 Monument, site of a Japanese submarine attack, all near Fort Clatsop; Fort Canby State Park north in Washington state (where the Expedition first camped before moving to the Fort Clatsop site, with museum dedicated to Lewis and Clark); Fort Columbia museum; Astoria Column on Coxcomb Hill in Astoria; America's tallest fir alongside US 26. ◬

BANCROFT RANCH HOUSE

Adobe Home of 'Historian of the West'

The adobe house once owned by Hubert Howe Bancroft, known as the "Historian of the West," now functions as a regional museum in **Spring Valley, Calif.** In the 1800s, Bancroft voluminously documented the history of the American West, an endeavor that earned him a national reputation. He intermittently lived in the adobe from 1885 until his death in 1918. Today, the Bancroft Ranch House museum occupies the house, built of sun-dried clay, at 9056 Memory Lane.

The museum, which opened to the public in 1963, displays Spring Valley artifacts, 1880s furniture and some Bancroft items. The Spring Valley Historical Society was founded to preserve a portion of Bancroft's farm after his death in 1918. In 1967, the society bought the adobe, now a California state landmark.

Bancroft, born in Ohio in 1832, began collecting Californiana in 1859. His interests quickly expanded to include all the Pacific states, the area from Alaska to Panama and states eastward to Texas. Eventually, he amassed 60,000 volumes of books, pamphlets, newspapers and manuscripts about the West. From 1874 to 1890, he published 39 massive volumes detailing the region's vast history, still considered the greatest collection of its kind. Bancroft, severely criticized for not crediting his assistants for their work, sold his histories by subscription, eventually grossing more than $1 million. He followed this project with eight volumes of subsidized biographies, volumes of essays and a book, *The Chronicles of the Builders* (1891).

Bancroft bought the adobe, built in 1863 as a two-room home, and 500 surrounding acres in 1885. He called his property Helix Farms, after a snail found nearby. Bancroft developed the ranch, planting orchards and building farm outhouses, including a stone structure now called Rock House. The structure is undergoing renovation. Bancroft might have spent time writing in Rock House, although it could have been used as a school for his children. Bancroft also built a family residence he called Cactus Cottage on a nearby hill in 1889. That house is now a private residence and not open to the public.

By the early 1900s, Helix Farms, managed by Bancroft's son, had become one of the largest olive ranches in southern California. Many of the farm's original olive trees still grow in the area. After Bancroft's death, his heirs sold the farm. Much of it was subdivided into La Mesa Country Estates.

For more information, contact the Bancroft Ranch House, 9056 Memory Lane, Spring Valley, CA 91977. Tel.: (619) 469-1480. E-mail: 4jrv@nethere.com.

FURTHER READING *Hubert Howe Bancroft: Historian of the West* by John Walton Caughey (1946, 1970) ◮

PACIFIC *California*

ZANE GREY PUEBLO

Hotel Was Once Western Novelist's Home

A hotel in **Avalon, Calif.**, on Catalina Island, has been fashioned from the former seaside vacation home of popular Western novelist Pearl Zane Grey (1872-1939). Grey authored 89 books, including more than 50 novels, most of them tales of adventure on the plains of the Old West. More than 13 million copies of his books were sold during his lifetime.

Grey was best known for his novel, *Riders of the Purple Sage* (1912). His other works include *The Last of the Plainsmen* (1908), *The Thundering Herd* (1925), *Code of the West* (1934), and *West of the Pecos* (1937). Nonfiction works include *Tales of Fishing* (1925) and *Tales of Swordfish and Tuna*, the latter written at his Avalon pueblo. Several of Grey's novels were turned into popular movies, and millions enjoyed his stories on the television series, Zane Grey Theater, which ran from 1956 to 1961.

Grey, a dentist-turned-novelist and big game sports fisherman, built the large sun-dried clay house, inspired by Hopi Indian pueblo architecture, on a cactus-covered hill in 1926. He used the adobe on the island south of Los Angeles as a vacation home. His primary home was located in Altadena, Calif., northeast of Los Angeles, where he moved to work closely with the developing motion picture industry. Many of his novels were being made into films. Grey spent much of his later life in Avalon writing and fishing until his death at age 67.

A long hall bisects the house, with some bedrooms overlooking the ocean and the others facing the rolling hills. When Grey vacationed in the house, a fireplace with log mantel dominated the living and dining room, which had open beam ceilings, a hewn plank door and oak dining table with heavy benches and a custom-made piano. Today, a pool occupies the dirt patio that separated the Grey home from that of the writer's brother, Romer.

In *What the Open Means to Me*, Grey described his getaway house as "a place for rest, dream, peace, sleep. I could write here and be at peace..."

For hotel information, contact the Zane Grey Hotel, P.O. Box 216, Avalon, CA 90704. Tel.: (310) 510-0966 of 1-800-3-PUEBLO. For details about Zane Grey, see Pennsylvania in the Middle Atlantic section of this book. Other Grey sites are under Ohio and Arizona. ◬

TOR HOUSE

Poet Robinson Jeffers' Home by the Sea

LOCATION On Carmel Point over Carmel Bay, along the Carmel-Big Sur Coast, in Carmel, Calif., at 26304 Ocean View Ave. Take CA 1 to Rio Road north past Carmel Mission Basilica to Santa Lucia Ave on left to Ocean View Avenue. The house, just south of Carmel Village, faces Scenic Road and is bounded by Stewart Way and Ocean View Avenue.

Tor House and Hawk Tower ($) is open for tours year-round on Friday and Saturday, from 10 a.m. to 3 p.m. Groups limited to six people; no visitors under age 12 for safety reasons. Reservations strongly recommended.

For more information contact Robinson Jeffers Tor House Foundation, P.O. Box 2713, Carmel, CA 93921. Tel.: (831) 624-1813 or (831) 624-1840. E-mail: thf@torhouse.org. On the Net: www.torhouse.org.

FRAME OF REFERENCE John Robinson Jeffers began building the cottage in 1918 and worked on it for 10 years. He moved in with his family in 1919. The writer died in Tor House in 1962. The Robinson Jeffers Tor House Foundation acquired the house in 1978.

SIGNIFICANCE Jeffers, poet and playwright, wrote his major poetical works at his desk in the attic of Tor House, named for the treeless, windswept, craggy knoll or "tor" on which it was built. These influential works included long narratives of "this coast crying out for tragedy," and his shorter meditative lyrics and dramas on classical themes. Jeffers' Naturalistic poetry praises "the beauty of things" in this scenic coastal setting and emphasizes his belief that such splendor demands tragedy.

Influenced by modern psychology, Jeffers combined old stories and modern themes. He based *The Tower Beyond Tragedy* (1924) on *Orestreia*, and *Solstice* (1935) and *Medea* (1946) on the ancient story of Medea. *Tamar* (1924) and *Dear Judas* (1929) were based on biblical stories. Jeffers called for a poetry of "dangerous images" which would "reclaim substance and sense, and psychological reality."

Jeffers' *Tamar and Other Poems* (1924) established his national reputation. The high point of his career came in 1947, when *Medea* became a successful Broadway play starring Dame Judith Anderson in the title role.

At Tor House, Jeffers continued his study of the classics and meditated on man's place in the universe. His unique home welcomed famous celebrities, artists and intellectuals of the day with glasses of Una Jeffers' Celtic wine. These included **Edgar Lee Masters**, **Sinclair Lewis** and **T .S. Eliot**.

ABOUT THE SITE Visitors can tour the original west wing of the granite house, small and close to the ground to withstand winter storms; the 40-foot Hawk Tower; and Una's restored English country garden. Jeffers built the house, modeled after a Tudor barn in England, with his own hands under the guidance of a building contractor and stonemason. The granite stones were drawn by horse from the little cove below the house. Oil lamps and candles lit the rooms until the Jeffers installed electricity in 1949.

The original wing contained two attic bedrooms, a main floor guest room, the living room, a tiny kitchen and a bathroom. Jeffers later added a sunken dining room from 1926 to 1930 and an east wing. His son, Donnan, finished the east wing after Jeffers' death. Today, the Jeffers foundation occupies the house's east wing.

Jeffers began Hawk Tower in 1920 as a retreat for Una and as a magical place for his sons to play. Working alone, he used wooden planks and a block-and-tackle system to move the stones and to set them in place. Some parts of the wall are nearly 3 feet thick. He completed Hawk Tower in 1924.

Tor House's furnishings, a mix of antiques and family pieces, are all original to the family. These include the family book collection, a Steinway piano, Una Jeffers' collections of Jugtown pottery, crystal balls, Mayan masks and unicorns, as well as Una's grandmother's early 19th-century spinning wheel from Ireland.

HOT TIPS Special events at the Tor House include a Fall Festival, poetry readings and an annual Tor House Prize for Poetry as a living memorial to Jeffers. For more information, contact the Tor House Foundation.

Jeffers' alma mater, Occidental College in Los Angeles, houses a 150-volume collection of his works plus letters, journals, photographs, manuscripts and galley proofs. Go to the College Library's Special Collections page on the Net: http://departments.oxy.edu/library/speccoll.

THE BEST STUFF If you look closely at the thick walls of Tor House, you'll detect embedded fossils, mineral specimens and even the head of a Cambodian figurine. Jeffers incorporated stones given to him by friends, including lava from Hawaii and marble from Greece. A rock at the very top of Hawk Tower came all the way from the Great Wall of China.

THE WRITER AND HIS WORK

BORN: Jan. 10, 1887 in Pittsburgh, Pa.

DIED: Jan. 20, 1962, in Carmel

EDUCATED: Occidental College; traveled throughout Europe; graduate student of literature at the University of Southern California; attended medical school at USC; studied forestry at University of Washington

MARRIED: Una Call Kuster, 1913 ; twin sons

IMPORTANT WORKS: *Flagons and Apples* (1912); *Californians* (1916); *Tamar and Other Poems* (1924); *Roan Stallion* (1925); *The Women at Point Sur* (1927); *Cawdo* (1928); *Poems* (1928); *Dear Judas* (1929); *Stars* (1930); *Descent To The Dead* (1931); *Thurso's Landing* (1932); *Give Your Heart to the Hawks* (1933); *Solstice* (1935); *The Beaks of Eagles* (1936); *Such Counsels You Gave Me* (1937); *Selected Poetry* (1938); *Two Consolations* (1940); *Be Angry at the Sun* (1941); *Medea* (1946); *The Double Axe* (1948); *Poetry, Gongorism and a Thousand Years* (1949); *The Tower Beyond Tragedy* (1950); *The Cretan Woman* (1951); *Hungerfield* (1954); *The Loving Shepherdess* (1956); *Themes in My Poems* (1956); *The Beginning and The End* (1963); *Not Man Apart* (1965); *The Alpine Christ and Other Poems* (1973); *Tragedy Has Obligations* (1973); *Brides of the South Wind* (1974); *In This Wild Water* (1976); *What Odd Experiments* (1981); *Songs and Heroes* (1988)

INTERESTING BIO FACT: During the late 1930s and 1940s, some said Jeffers' genius had faded. His references to World War II events and figures (Pearl Harbor, Hitler and Roosevelt) raised questions about his patriotism. *The Double Ax*, published in 1948, carried a disclaimer from the publisher.

FURTHER READING *Robinson Jeffers* by J. Karman (1995); *Robinson Jeffers: The Dimensions of a Poet* edited by R. Brophy (1995); *Critical Essays on Robinson Jeffers* edited by J. Karman (1990); *Robinson Jeffers and the Critics* by Jeanetta Boswell (1986); *Robinson Jeffers: Poet of Inhumanism* by A.B. Ciffin (1971)

ELSEWHERE IN THE AREA Monterey State Historic Park in nearby Monterey at Fisherman's Wharf includes the Robert Louis Stevenson House. ⚑

JACK LONDON RANCH
Home of Popular Adventure Novelist

LOCATION In northern California's Valley of the Moon, 60 miles northeast of San Francisco, in Glen Ellen, 12 miles east of Santa Rosa and 20 miles north of Sonoma, at 400 London Ranch Road. From Santa Rosa, take CA 12 to Glen Ellen, then take Jack London Ranch Road to the park. From Sonoma, turn left on Madrone Road, right on Arnold drive, left on London Ranch Road.

The **Jack London State Historic Park** ($), part of London's former 1,500-acre Beauty Ranch, is open daily from 9:30 a.m. to 5 p.m. standard time, and 9:30 a.m. to 7 p.m. daylight savings time. The House of Happy Walls is open from 10 a.m. to 5 p.m. daily, except Thanksgiving, Dec. 25, and Jan. 1. The London cottage is open to the public on Saturday and Sunday from noon to 4 p.m..

For more information, contact the Jack London State Historic Park, 2400 London Ranch Rd., Glen Ellen, CA 95442. Tel. (707) 938-5216 or 938-4827. E-mail: Jacklondonshp@aol.com. On the Net: www.parks.sonoma.net/JLPark.html.

FRAME OF REFERENCE John Griffith (Jack) London bought Beauty Ranch in 1905 and made his home here until his death in 1916 at age 40. He and wife, Charmian, lived in a cottage at the ranch while building their dream home on the property, Wolf House, which burned down in 1913. After Jack's death, Charmian built a second house, House of Happy Walls in 1919-26. She died in 1955. The park was created in 1959 on 40 acres of the original ranch and has expanded through the years to 1,400 acres.

SIGNIFICANCE London — a passionate and prolific novelist, short-story writer, lecturer, adventurer and rancher — was easily the most popular and highest paid American writer during the first decade of the 20th century. In the west-wing study of his Beauty Ranch cottage, he wrote some of his 50-plus books, as well as hundreds of short stories, articles and letters. Some of his books became popular motion pictures. At the ranch, London supervised his crops and animals, explored on horseback every canyon and vale of his vast land, and planned Wolf House. He also found time to write here, giving "two hours a day to writing and ten to farming."

The ruggedly handsome London's naturalistic works are considered

483

classics of their kind. They represent the archetypal struggle between the savage heart and civilization. London, whom some call "an early Hemingway," was a member of San Francisco's Bohemian Club, along with Joaquin Miller and Frank Norris.

Countless editions of London's writings remain in print and some have been translated into at least 70 languages. His best-known works are moving stories of conflict and adventure and include the short novels *The Call of the Wild* (1903) and *White Fang* (1906). He first achieved international fame for *Call* and *The Sea Wolf* (1904) at age 29.

ABOUT THE SITE The wooded park includes the London cottage; the charred ruins of Wolf House, London's grand stone and log dream house that burned down only days before the move-in date; the London gravesite; and the House of Happy Walls, which Charmian built in a redwood grove after Jack's death. Charmian's house is similar to what Wolf House was before its fiery end, with Spanish-style roof tiles and fieldstone walls. It is, however, smaller and more formal. The magnificent Wolf House, built for $80,000, a huge sum at the time, had a big-game room, library, outdoor pool to be stocked with mountain bass, a dining room that would have seated 50 guests, and an alcove for Charmian's grand piano and custom-built furniture. In The House of Happy Walls, you'll find some of that furniture, plus exhibits about London's life and works, early manuscripts, and artifacts from London's travels.

The park encompasses various ranch buildings, including the Sherry Barn, built by Chinese laborers in 1884 and used as a stable for London's English shire horses; the Stallion Barn; concrete silos; the ruins of a former winery; and the "Pig Palace," which London designed for his animals. Many of the buildings are in disrepair.

A trail to these sites also takes visitors to the white, wood cottage with green trim where London wrote much of his later work. The Londons expanded the cottage to about 3,000 square feet after they bought it. After Wolf House burned down, they added a wing to the cottage as a study for Jack, who had become very depressed over the loss. In the study, London wrote 1,500 words each morning. Charmian edited and typed her husband's writing the next day. The cottage features photo panels and a video describing London's life and adventures.

Visitors also can take a 3/4-mile trail to a dam and the 5-acre lake London created, as well as a bathhouse. Other trails traverse fir and oak woodlands to views of the Valley of the Moon. One leads to the place where Jack's ashes are buried under a mossy boulder of red lava near the Wolf House ruins.

HOT TIPS Allow three hours for your visit. Restoration projects may change tour times, so check ahead. The park's upper parking lot provides access to a picnic area, London's cottage, stables, stone barns, silos and pig palace. Bicycling and horseback riding are permitted on some trails. A summer horseback riding concession provided.

Camping available at nearby Sugarloaf Ridge State Park. Stay on trails and watch for rattlesnakes and poison oak. Weather is changeable so wear layered clothing. Special hikes, tours and events offered. A visitor center sells books by and about London.

In **San Francisco,** a plaque marks the site of London's birthplace at 615 Third St. A fire destroyed the house in 1906.

THE BEST STUFF The London's custom-built furniture, some of which they designed for Wolf House, now has a home in the House of Happy Walls museum. These include two rocking chairs made from spiral-grained koa wood Jack found on one of his voyages. In the library, you'll find the roll-top desk and Dictaphone from Jack's study.

THE WRITER AND HIS WORK
BORN: Jan. 12, 1876 in San Francisco
DIED: Nov. 22, 1916 in Glen Ellen
EDUCATED: High school degree and self-taught writing skills; one semester University of California
MARRIED: Bessie Maddern, 1900, divorced 1904, two daughters; Charmian Kittredge, 1905
IMPORTANT WORKS: *The Son of the Wolf* (1900); *The God of His Fathers* (1901); *Children of the Frost* (1902); *The Cruise of the Dazzler* (1902); *A Daughter of the Snows* (1902); *The Kempton-Wace Letters* (1903); *The Call of the Wild* (1903); *The People of the Abyss* (1903); *The Faith of Men* (1904); *The Sea Wolf* (1904); *War of the Classes* (1905); *The Game* (1905); *Tales of the Fish Patrol* (1905); *Moon-Face and Other Stories* (1906); *White Fang* (1906); *Before Adam* (1907); *Love of Life and Other Stories* (1907); *The Iron Heel* (1908); *Martin Eden* (1909, autobiographical); *Lost Face* (1910); *Revolution and Other Essays* (1910); *Burning Daylight* (1910); *When God Laughs and Other Stories* (1911); *South Sea Tales* (1911); *The House of Pride and Other Stories* (1912); *A Son of the Sun* (1912);

Smoke Bellew (1912); *The Night-Born* (1913); *The Abysmal Brute* (1913); *John Barleycorn* (1913); *The Valley of the Moon* (1913); *The Strength of the Strong* (1914); *The Mutiny of the Elsinore* (1914); *The Scarlet Plague* (1915); *The Star Rover* (1915); *The Little Lady of the Big House* (1916); *The Turtles of Tasman* (1916); *The Human Drift* (1917); *Jerry of the Islands* (1917); *Michael Brother of Jerry* (1917); *The Red One* (1918); *On the Makaloa Mat* (1919); *Hearts of Three* (1920); *Dutch Courage and Other Stories* (1922)

INTERESTING BIO FACT: An illegitimate only child who grew up in poverty, London gained celebrity as much for his colorful personality and personal exploits as for his writing. As a teen gang leader at the Oakland, Calif., docks, he chronicled his experiences in boys adventure stories, such as *Tales of the Fish Patrol* (1905). He then went on to write adventure stories based on time spent on a sailing ship. He later sought gold during the Klondike Gold Rush in Alaska, the basis of many of his best short stories, including *The Son of the Wolf.*

FURTHER READING *Jack London: A Biography* by Daniel Dyer (2002); *Jack London, Star Warrior* by David Bischoff (2002); *A Pictorial Biography of Jack London* by Russ Kingman (1992)

ELSEWHERE IN THE AREA Sugarloaf Ridge State Park, Adobe Canyon Road ⚲

JOHN MUIR HOUSE AND RANCH
Home of Naturalist Writer

LOCATION Northern California, in Martinez, 25 miles northeast of San Francisco, at 4202 Alhambra Ave. From I-680 or I-80, take CA 4 (John Muir Parkway) to Alhambra Avenue exit toward Martinez. Site is at foot of ramp. For detailed directions and maps, go to www.nps.gov./jomu/directions.htm.

The **John Muir National Historic Site** ($) is open Wednesday through Sunday, from 10 a.m. to 5 p.m., for self-guided tours of grounds. Guided tours and group tours of the Muir House are offered daily at 2 p.m., and weekends at 1, 2 and 3 p.m. Groups of 10 or more must make reservations. Closed Thanksgiving, Dec. 25 and Jan. 1. Mount Wanda natural area is open daily from sunrise to sunset.

For more information, contact John Muir National Historic Site, 4202 Alhambra Ave., Martinez, CA 94553. Tel.: (925) 228-8860. E-mail: JOMU_Interpretation@nps.gov. On the Net: www.nps.gov/jomu/muirhouse.htm.

FRAME OF REFERENCE John Muir lived in this mansion, built by his father-in-law in 1882, from 1890 to his death 1914 at age 76. Muir operated the citrus ranch from 1880 to 1890, making a fortune. The house and grounds became a National Historic Site in 1964.

SIGNIFICANCE Probably America's most famous conservationist and naturalist, Muir wrote his most influential works in this intriguing house on the picturesque fruit ranch where he worked, frequently entertained, and enjoyed nature walks. After many passionate and public battles on behalf of the environment, he retired here with his wife and children to devote the majority of his time to his journals.

Known as the father of the national park system for his campaign to preserve forests and animal refuge areas, Muir wrote more than 300 magazine articles and 10 major books in his lifetime. His writings moved presidents, congressmen and everyday Americans to action. They also popularized a radically new concept in American land use — to conserve and enjoy the natural world — when the prevailing climate was to slash and burn for expansion.

Muir was personally involved in creating seven national parks, including Grand Canyon, Sequoia, Kings Canyon, and Mt. Rainier National Parks.

This was due largely to his influence with three U.S. presidents, especially outdoorsman Teddy Roosevelt. Muir also helped preserve Yosemite.

The writer, lecturer, geologist, botanist, glacier expert, explorer, school teacher, Sunday School teacher, efficiency expert and inventor founded the Sierra Club in 1892 and was its president until his death in 1914.

ABOUT THE SITE The 9-acre park includes Muir's two-story, 17-room Italianate Victorian house; the historic 1849 Martinez Adobe; surrounding lands with various grapevines, fruit and nut trees; the 325-acre Mount Wanda area with its oak forest and stunning views of the Carquinez straits; and a visitor center and bookstore at the Mount Wanda area.

The 10,010-square-foot, wood-frame mansion (including porches, attic and basement) has been restored to what it might have looked like when Muir lived there. The house displays some Muir family objects, as well as Victorian-era furnishings. Furnishings in Muir's second-floor office, what he called his "scribble den," include only a few of Muir's belongings, including his wooden desk, Alaskan Indian fish spear and throwing stick, and honorary degrees from Yale, Harvard, and Universities of California Berkeley and Wisconsin. His suitcase is displayed in his bedroom. Wall coverings in the rooms, all with 12-foot ceilings, reflect the period. The floors are Douglas fir painted to look like golden oak, a technique of wood feathering popular in the 1800s. The banister railing, fashioned from black walnut, goes all the way to the third floor attic.

The house originally featured seven coal-burning fireplaces, indoor plumbing, gas lighting, a telephone as early as 1884, and an electrical system installed just before Muir's death. Three of the imported Italian marble fireplaces remain. A three-story addition in back supports a large, steel water tank to run Muir's innovative plumbing. The original 5,000-gallon attic tank was made of redwood and collected rainwater from the roof and from three wells. Today's tank is steel.

The first floor has a dark-paneled library (which Muir said was too dark and small for writing about nature) that served as his father in law's office; two parlors, entrance hall, dining room with conservatory, and a kitchen. Six bedrooms take up the second floor, along with a bathroom and water closet. On the roof, a large, square cupola with arched windows houses a bell that marked the fruit farm's workday. The Muirs used the attic to store farm tools and furniture. A pair of palm trees guard the grand, double burgundy front door and a three-sided front porch.

John Muir's burial site is in a quiet, tree-shaded spot near the banks of Alhambra Creek next to his wife. Their headstones are made of Black Academy Granite with Raymond Granite bases. Both display an ornate floral design, possibly of thistle, the national emblem of Muir's Scottish homeland. The gravesite is not open to the public.

The site's Martinez Adobe, built by Don Vincente Martinez, son of the commandant of the Presidio of San Francisco, has a foundation of rough stone. The walls are sun-dried adobe brick ranging in thickness from 24 to 30 inches. The roof was covered with shingles of either cedar or redwood. Muir's father-in-law bought the adobe in 1874 and made it a residence for ranch employees. In 1906, Muir's daughter, Wanda, and her husband made it their home. The first floor is open to visitors and tells of early California history.

The entrance gate for the Mt. Wanda area and Muir Nature Trail is located by the "Park and Ride" lot on Franklin Canyon Road and Alhambra Avenue. The two highest points in the park are the 660-foot Mount Wanda and the 640-foot Mount Helen, named for Muir's daughters. Muir often took them on outings to this part of the ranch to study the wildflower varieties that still cover the park.

HOT TIPS Begin your visit at the visitor center with the 28-minute orientation video, *John Muir: Earth, Planet, Universe*. Picnic tables are in the park. Food and lodging is within walking distance. The mansion's first floor is wheelchair accessible. Take water and snack for Mt. Wanda 1-mile loop trail, which is steep. Wear sturdy shoes and layered clothing. No toilets on trail. No pets are allowed in buildings and must be on leash in park. The site's bookstore sells a self-guiding tour booklet for $1 and Muir books. All fire roads in the Mount Wanda area dead-end at private property. There is currently one way in and one way out. Do not climb fences.

Special events include John Muir's Birthday Celebration each May, full-moon walks on Mt. Wanda in summer, bird and flower walks in spring, Junior Ranger Program for ages 8 to 12, Victorian piano programs and special holiday events.

THE BEST STUFF You'll find Muir's original, flat-top desk amid bookcases in his "scribble den." Muir spent long hours writing at his cluttered desk, placed in front of the room's tall, north windows that commanded a splendid view of the Alhambra Valley. Muir, easily distracted, found writing tedious. He sometimes rented a room in a San Francisco hotel to concentrate on his work.

489

THE WRITER AND HIS WORK

BORN: April 21, 1838, in Dunbar, Scotland

DIED: Dec. 25, 1914, in Los Angeles; funeral in the Muir House; buried 1 mile south of mansion

EDUCATED: Self-educated; briefly attended University of Wisconsin

MARRIED: Louie Strentzel, 1880; two daughters

IMPORTANT WORKS: *Picturesque California and the Region West of the Rocky Mountains, from Alaska to Mexico (1888-1890)*. (Muir edited this complete text of his writings.) *The Mountains of California* (1894); *Our National Parks* (1901); *Stickeen: The Story of a Dog* (1909); *My First Summer in the Sierra* (1911); *Edward Henry Harriman* (1911); *The Yosemite* (1912); *The Story of My Boyhood and Youth* (1913); *Letters to a Friend* (1915); *Travels in Alaska* (1915); *A Thousand-Mile Walk to the Gulf* (1916); *The Cruise of the Corwin* (1917); *Steep Trails* (1919); *John of the Mountains* (1938); *Studies in the Sierra* (1950 reprint of 1874 serial)

INTERESTING BIO FACT: President **Theodore Roosevelt**, himself a conservationist and author (see New York in this book), established the Muir Woods National Monument in Marin County, Calif., to honor Muir's achievements.

FURTHER READING *John Muir: Nature's Visionary* by Gretel Ehrlich (2000); *Guide to the John Muir Trail* by Thomas Winnett and Kathy Morey (1998)

ELSEWHERE IN THE AREA Mt. Diablo State Park; Nancy Boyd park off Pleasant Hill Road ⌂

FRANK NORRIS GRAVE

Author of 'McTeague,' 'The Octopus'

You can find the grave of Benjamin Franklin Norris, a noted pioneer of literary Naturalism and social realism, in **Mountain View Cemetery** in **Oakland, Calif.** The cemetery was designed by Frederick Law Olmsted, the landscape architect who designed the grounds of the U.S. Capitol in Washington, D.C., Central Park in New York City, and parks in Boston. (Olmsted also wrote *The Cotton Kingdom* in 1861, a result of his travels in the American South.)

Novels by Norris, born in 1870 in Chicago, include *Blix* (1899), *The Pit* (1903), *The Octopus* (1901), and his masterpiece, *McTeague* (1899). *McTeague*, the story of a San Francisco dentist and his money-hungry wife, was made into a motion picture, *Greed*, in 1925. The writer/journalist was a member of San Francisco's Bohemian Club, along with Joaquin Miller and **Jack London**. Norris died in 1902, at age 32. At the time, he was writing a trilogy of San Francisco, which included *McTeague*, *Blix* and *Vandover the Brute*. *Brute* was published posthumously in 1914. Norris might have chosen San Francisco for the stories of moral ruin because of the city's violent and depraved reputation after the Gold Rush of the 1800s.

An 8-foot tablet in the Arts and Crafts style marks Norris' grave, shaded by four Irish yews. The writer's fraternity brothers at the University of California placed the monument in the Norris family plot. The tablet bears the name "Frank" and three blades of wheat, in tribute to his epic novel, *The Octopus*, about the struggle of the San Joaquin Valley wheat farmers against the Southern Pacific monopoly. His burial place is located at the foot of Piedmont Avenue at Site 11 on the cemetery's map of "Graves of Noted Persons."

FURTHER READING *Harbingers of a Century: The Novels of Frank Norris* by Lawrence E. Hussman (1998); *Frank Norris Revisited* by Joseph R. McElrath (1992) ◮

TAO HOUSE

Eugene O'Neill's 'Final Harbor'

LOCATION California, in the San Ramon Valley 26 miles east of San Francisco, in Danville, at 1000 Kuss Road. From San Francisco, take I-80 (Bay Bridge) to I-680 south to Danville. From San Jose take I-680 north to Danville. From Sacramento take I-80 west to Fairfield, then I-680 south to Danville.

The **Eugene O'Neill National Historic Site** is open Wednesday through Sunday for tours beginning at 10 a.m. and 12:30 p.m., by reservation only. Call at least two weeks in advance. Closed Thanksgiving, Dec. 25 and Jan. 1. The National Park Service provides a free shuttle van to the site from a pickup point in Danville. No private vehicles are allowed access. Tour specifics given when you call for a reservation.

For more information, contact Eugene O'Neill National Historic Site, P.O. Box 280, Danville, CA 94526. Tel. (925) 838-0249 for tour reservations. E-mail: EUON_Administration@nps.gov. On the Net: www.eugeneoneill.org or www.nps.gov/euon/ or www.eoneill.com/eof/index.htm.

FRAME OF REFERENCE Eugene Gladston O'Neill and wife, Carlotta, purchased 158 acres in the San Ramon Valley in 1937 and moved into their new house in December of that year. O'Neill lived in Tao House for 7 years, until ill health forced him to sell the home in 1944. O'Neill's sojourn at the house was the longest the restless playwright had ever lived in one place. The Eugene O'Neill Foundation bought and renovated the site in the early 1970s, opening it to the public in 1984 in cooperation with the National Park Service.

SIGNIFICANCE O'Neill, considered America's pre-eminent playwright, led the country's fledgling, early 20th-century theater into the mainstream of world drama. The Nobel Prize winner wrote 40 plays, including *Anna Cristie* (1922), *Desire Under the Elms* (1924), *Mourning Becomes Electra* (1931), *Long Day's Journey Into Night* (1956) and *The Iceman Cometh* (1946). Ten plays became successful motion pictures.

At Tao House, O'Neill wrote five of his greatest plays, including the autobiographical *Long Day's Journey*, which was awarded a Pulitzer Prize posthumously in 1957. Although plagued with health problems, O'Neill worked furiously in long stretches, often for weeks. He considered Tao House his "final harbor."

In addition to three more Pulitzer Prizes, O'Neill, a bold experimenter, also won the Nobel Prize for literature in 1936, the only American playwright ever to do so. His plays hold up a mirror to society and range from satire to tragedy. His characters often depict people with no hope of controlling their destinies.

Many scholars of the theater rank O'Neill alongside Shakespeare and Shaw as the three greatest playwrights in the English-speaking world.

ABOUT THE SITE The restored, 7,000-square-foot Tao House and courtyard is the 13.19-acre park's centerpiece. The park also has a barn, shed and chicken coop. The O'Neills built their new home with Eugene's Nobel Prize money. The house is built of specially made concrete blocks, the size of adobe brick, that Carlotta purchased from Portland Cement Co. She wanted to use these blocks inside and outside the house.

Tao House was built in the California Monterey style with primitive Spanish as well as Chinese touches that incorporated Eastern philosophy. The O'Neills had visited China in 1928, and they named their new home after the Chinese spiritual term for "The Way." The Way refers to the primal reality that gives birth to the visible world. O'Neill felt an affinity with the Taoist idea of nature influencing humans, and his home — and many of his plays — reflect his view that man must be in harmony with nature.

Tao House is located at the end of a long, private road. You enter the home's courtyard through a heavy, black gate adorned with Chinese lettering, which translates to Tao House. The house's exterior strikingly combines Carlotta's baselite blocks, a black-tile roof, and earthy red doors and shutters. Rolling hills protect the house, which fits snugly into the landscape of a plateau affording spectacular views. The jasmine-scented courtyard with winding brick walkway mirrors the Taoist gardens the O'Neills toured in China. The garden has indirect paths, "guardian rocks," and hidden entryways.

The house's shadowy interior also reflects Eastern philosophy. You will find deep blue ceilings, dark-tiled or black-stained floors, red doors, colored mirrors and glass, and period pieces throughout. One of the few remaining original pieces in the partially furnished house is the playwright's rosewood bed (actually an antique Chinese opium couch), an Italian bird bath on the patio, carved wood dog posts, and O'Neill's writing desk. Possibly in keeping with feng shui practices, no stairways face exterior doors.

O'Neill's isolated, fully furnished study has a bare-beamed ceiling, thick walls and three doors through private rooms leading to it. Here, you'll see

O'Neill's writing desk and chair. The O'Neills rarely spent a night away from their home, preferring to quietly garden, swim in the pool, and play with their beloved Dalmatian, Blemie.

HOT TIPS Allow three hours for a guided tour of the house and courtyard and a self-guided tour of the grounds, barns, shed, pool and Blemie's grave, marked by an inscribed, granite headstone. The site's visitor center houses a small bookstore and exhibits. The first floor of the house and the visitor center are wheelchair-accessible. O'Neill's study on the second floor is reached only by a stairway. Lodging is available in the valley communities of Danville, Livermore and Walnut Creek. Camping available at nearby Mount Diablo State Park.

The foundation offers many educational programs and plays, as well as a reading room. Contact the site for details. For a list of O'Neill collections, including the vast repository at Yale's Beinecke Rare Book and Manuscript Library, go to the Electronic Eugene O'Neill Archive at www.eoneill.com/index. For another O'Neill site, see Connecticut in the New England section of this book.

THE BEST STUFF O'Neill built a special room on the main floor for his player piano, which he named Rosie. The original Rosie was green with pink painted flowers and reputedly came from a New Orleans bordello. The piano you'll see today in what O'Neill called "Rosie's Room" is a period piece. The sunny room is informally furnished to evoke a tavern atmosphere and includes a tavern-style overhead light original to the house.

THE WRITER AND HIS WORK

BORN: Oct. 16, 1888, in New York City, in a Broadway hotel

DIED: Nov. 27, 1953, in a Boston hotel

EDUCATED: Princeton; suspended for a prank

MARRIED: Kathleen Jenkins, 1909, 1 son, divorced; Agnes Boulton, 1918, son and a daughter, Oona, who married actor Charlie Chaplin, divorced; Carlotta Monterey, 1929

IMPORTANT WORKS: *Bread and Butter* (1914); *Children Of The Sea* (1914); *Bound East for Cardiff* (1916); *The Long Voyage Home* (1917, film 1940); *In The Zone* (1919); *Where the Cross Is Made* (1919); *The Rope* (1919); *Moon of the Caribees* (1919); *Gold* (1920); *The Dreamy Kid* (1920); *Emperor Jones* (1920); *Beyond The Horizon* (1920); *The Straw* (1921); *Hairy Ape* (1922, film 1944); *Anna Christie* (1922, film 1931); *Welded* (1924);

All God's Chillun Got Wings (1924); *The Fountain* (1925); *Desire Under the Elms* (1925, film 1958); *The Great God Brown* (1926); *Strange Interlude* (1928); *Lazarus Laughed* (1928); *Marco Millions* (1928); *Dynamo* (1929); *Mourning Becomes Electra* (1931, film 1948); *Nine Plays* (1932); *Ah! Wilderness* (1933, film 1935); *Days Without End* (1933); *The Iceman Cometh* (1946, film 1973); *Lost Plays* 1913-15 (1950); *Long Day's Journey Into Night* (1956, film 1966); *A Moon for the Misbegotten* (1957); *A Touch of the Poet* (1958); *Hughie* (1958); *Inscriptions* (1960); *Ten Lost Plays* (1964); *More Stately Mansions* (produced 1967); *Poems 1912-1944* (1979); *A Tale of Possessors Dispossessed* (1982, unfinished)

ACCOLADES: Nobel Prize for literature, 1936; Pulitzer Prizes for *Beyond the Horizon* in 1920, for *Anna Christie* in 1922, for *Strange Interlude* in 1928, and posthumously for *Long Day's Journey Into Night* in 1957.

INTERESTING BIO FACTS: O'Neill spent his early years in hotel rooms and theaters. He was the son of an actor father, known for his role as the Count of Monte Cristo, and a mother addicted for 25 years to morphine that a quack doctor had prescribed for her after Eugene's birth. The writer's youth was marked by a strict Catholic upbringing and family upheaval; young O'Neill ran away from his family for travels and adventure. After landing with tuberculosis in a sanitarium at age 24, he began writing plays. Health problems plagued him throughout life, and a hand tremor forced him to give up writing in 1943.

FURTHER READING *Eugene O'Neill and His Eleven-Play Cycle* by Donald Clifford Gallup (1998); *Eugene O'Neill's Creative Struggle* by Doris Alexander (1992); *Staging O'Neill* by Ronald Harold Wainscott (1988); *Conversations with Eugene O'Neill*, edited by Mark W. Estrin (1990); *Down the Nights and Down the Days* by Edward Lawrence (1996)

ELSEWHERE IN THE AREA Los Trampas Park and Mount Diablo State Park ◭

WILL ROGERS RANCH

Home of Columnist, Hollywood Superstar

LOCATION In the central Santa Monica mountains in Pacific Palisades, Calif., just before Sunset Boulevard meets the ocean, at 1500 Will Rogers State Park Rd.

The **Will Rogers State Historic Park** grounds are open daily from 7 a.m. until sunset for access to the stable and corral areas, riding ring, roping arena, polo field and riding and hiking trails. Guided tours of the main ranch house are expected to resume in late 2006 upon completion of a major renovation project.

For more information, contact Will Rogers State Historic Park, 1501 Will Rogers State Park Rd., Pacific Palisades, CA 90272. Tel. (310) 454-8212. On the Net: http://parks.ca.gov or www.willrogers.org.

FRAME OF REFERENCE William Penn Adair Rogers bought this California property in 1924. His family moved permanently to the ranch from Beverly Hills in 1928, when he was the nation's top male movie star. The site became a California state park in 1944, after wife Betty Rogers' death.

SIGNIFICANCE Rogers — professional rodeo performer, cowboy, trick roper, vaudeville comedian, actor, radio personality, newspaper columnist, author, humorist and aviator — loved to write. He wrote prolifically throughout his colorful career and excelled as a syndicated newspaper columnist. At his peak, he wrote for 350 daily and 200 Sunday newspapers across America, reaching 40 million readers. His writings filled 21 volumes, and he also authored six books.

Famous for his wit and expressions ("I never met a man I didn't like"), Rogers was also celebrated for his horse and rope tricks. His career in vaudeville took him to Broadway and the Ziegfeld Follies and then on to Hollywood to star in 71 movies (21 with sound), write his own newspaper column, and host his own radio show. He left behind about 2 million published words and remains one of the most quoted writers in America.

ABOUT THE SITE The 186-acre park includes Rogers' two-story, 31-room ranch house, renovated stables, corrals, riding ring, roping arena, and remains of the family four-hole golf course. Rogers' polo field might be the only remaining outdoor polo field in Los Angeles county and is a popular movie location. Riding and hiking trails afford spectacular views of the ranch, Pacific Ocean, mountains and Los Angeles from Inspiration Point. The ranch is the southern terminus of the Santa Monica Mountains' Backbone Trail.

The visitor center, being fashioned from the ranch's garage, will feature a film on Rogers' life, as well as newsreels, exhibits and an audio tour of the site. The ranch buildings and grassy grounds are maintained as they were when the Rogers family lived there.

The white wooden main house, an early example of the California ranchhouse-style architecture, has 11 bathrooms and seven fireplaces. The spacious living room of the main ranch house features Will's collection of Indian rugs and baskets, his extensive collection of Western art, and the humorist's unmistakable personal touches. In the center of the living room, you'll find the porch swing from Rogers' Beverly Hills house. The swing was Will's favorite seat, so it came with him when he moved here. You'll also see a mounted calf on casters, humorously given to Rogers to encourage him to use the calf for roping practice instead of his friends necks. Rogers practiced in the living room for hours, ensnaring the calf's head so often that it eventually lost its ears.

The house's north wing contains the family bedrooms, Will's study with private staircase and view of the golf course, and the sunroom, Betty's favorite room. The Rogers used their large patio with outside fireplace for dining and entertaining.

HOT TIPS Picnic areas in the park. A fee is charged for the parking lot, which is next to the polo field. Dress for hot to mild weather and bring water when hiking. No smoking. Dogs must be on leash and only on trails.

The Will Rogers Birthplace and Rogers Memorial, where the humorist was born, lived the first 10 years of his life, and is buried are located in **Oologah and Claremore, Okla**. See Oklahoma in the West South Central section in this book.

THE BEST STUFF Will and Betty Rogers often would retreat to their private quarters on the second floor, where a rustic room served as his study, the famous "Will Rogers Den." The room, adorned with photographs of favorite friends, features Rogers' desk, his globe with his pencil markings, maps mounted over his desk, and his portable typewriter on which he pecked out his columns. Rogers was known to never be early and never to be late meeting deadlines. Betty spent long hours in the adjacent sunroom. Here, she managed family business affairs, read or sewed while Will worked.

THE WRITER AND HIS WORK

BORN: Nov. 4, 1879, in Oologah, Indian Territory, Okla.

DIED: Aug. 15, 1935, in a plane crash in Alaska; first buried in Los Angeles; remains moved to Claremore in 1944

EDUCATED: Self-educated; dropped out of school after grade 10

MARRIED: Betty Blake; three children

IMPORTANT WORKS: *Rogerisms: The Cowboy Philosopher on The peace Conference* (1919); *Rogerisms: The Cowboy Philosopher on Prohibition* (1919); *Ether and Me; Illiterate Digest* (1924); *Letters of a Self-Made Diplomat; There's Not A Bathing Suit in Russia* (1927); *Will Rogers' Political Follies* (1929); plus 4,000 newspaper columns

ACCOLADES: Top Male Movie Star (1933,34,35 - Motion Picture Herald); Aviation Hall of Fame

INTERESTING BIO FACT: Rogers was famous for his simple and pithy ad-libs, which he liberally sprinkled into his radio commentaries, as well as his writings and his 10-year vaudeville stint with the Ziegfeld Follies. He especially loved to ad-lib in his movies. His rope tricks, documented in several books, earned him a spot in the Guinness Book of Records and his self-proclaimed title of "Poet Lariat."

FURTHER READING *Will Rogers: An American Legend* by Frank Keating (2002); *Cookin' With Will Rogers* by Sharon McFall, et. al. (2000); *Will Rogers* by Betty Rogers (reprint 2000)

ELSEWHERE IN THE AREA Santa Monica Heritage Museum, 2612 Main St., Santa Monica; El Pueblo de Los Angeles Historic Monument and a host of museums and attractions in Los Angeles; Hollywood Boulevard's Walk of Fame; J. Paul Getty Museum in Malibu ⬧

> *When I first started out to write and misspelled a few words, people said I was just plain ignerant. But when I got all the words wrong, they declared I was a humorist, and said I was quaint.*
>
> — ROGERS' description of his writing career

UPTON SINCLAIR HOUSE
Muckraking Journalist's Former Home

The house where famous muckraking journalist and social critic Upton Beall Sinclair lived is located 15 miles northeast of Los Angeles in **Monrovia, Calif.**, at 464 N. Myrtle Ave. The private residence, listed on the National Register of Historic Places, is not open to the public. Sinclair (1878-1968) lived in the 1923 Spanish Colonial Revival house for 24 years and finished his Pulitzer Prize-winning novel, *Dragon's Teeth* (1943), there. Architect Frederick H. Wallis designed the two-story, seven-room, 2,380-square-foot house for hotel magnate Louis B. Vollmer and his wife.

Sinclair, best known for his novel *The Jungle* (1906), an exposé of the appalling conditions of the Chicago stockyards, bought the two-story, seven-room house in 1942. By then Sinclair was already famous and wealthy. He was nationally known as a novelist, essayist, playwright, short-story writer, children's book writer, failed candidate for governor of California (1934) and leader of the crusading, 20th-century journalists known as the muckrakers. *The Jungle* led to the implementation of the Pure Food and Drug Act in 1906, and might have had the deepest social impact in America since **Harriet Beecher Stowe**'s *Uncle Tom's Cabin*. (See Connecticut in the New England section of this book.)

Sinclair's more than 100 published books also criticized mining monopolies, American journalism and education, prohibition, the film industry, the justice system, and corruption in Washington. He also wrote about venereal disease in his novel *Damaged Goods* (1913). Many of Sinclair's books became movies, including *Dragon's Teeth* and his *Lanny Budd* series.

Other important works include: *Prince Hagen* (1903); *Manassas* (1904); *A Captain of Industry* (1906); *The Money Changers* (1908); *King Coal* (1917); *Damaged Goods* (1913); Sylvia (1913); *They Call Me Carpenter* (1922); *The Brass Check* (1919); *The Goose-Step* (1923); *The Goslings* (1924); *The Millennium* (1924); *Oil!* (1927); *Money Writes* (1927); *Boston* (1928); *Mental Radio* (1930); *The Wet Parade* (1931); *Upton Sinclair Presents William Fox* (1933); *I, Candidate For Governor, And How I got Licked* (1935); *Little Steel* (1938); *Dragon Harvest* (1945); *Another Pamela* (1950); *My Lifetime in Letters* (1960); *Affectionately Eve* (1961); *The Autobiography of Upton Sinclair* (1962); *World's End* (1940). *End* was the first of 11 novels about fictional Lanny Budd, a confidant of international leaders in World War I and II.

The Sinclair House features an ornate arched and bracketed doorway, flanked by two high-arched windows. The concrete-block facade is topped by a Mission Revival parapet. The front door is covered with ornate bronze grillwork depicting the initial "V" for Vollmer. Pocket doors, a stone fireplace and Batchelder tile decorate the interior of the house, which has a basement.

A fireproof storage building, which long housed Sinclair's collection of nearly half a million letters and manuscripts, and the original garage, now a guest house, still stand on the property, along with the detached two-car garage Sinclair built. Sinclair used the garage as his writing studio.

For more information, go to www.goss.com/mohpg/98sincla.htm.

FURTHER READING *Upton Sinclair* by James Diedrick (1998); *The Campaign of the Century: Upton Sinclair's Race for Governor of California and the Birth of Media Politics* by Greg Mitchell (1992); *Upton Sinclair: Literature and Social Reform* by Dieter Herms (1990)

HOT TIP Occidential College in Los Angeles houses a 1,000-volume **Upton Sinclair collection**. The College Library's Special Collections page is on the Net at http://departments.oxy.edu/library/speccoll. ◮

STEINBECK'S SALINAS

Birthplace, Museum Tell of Nobel Winner

LOCATION Oldtown Salinas, Calif., 50 miles south of San Jose and 17 miles east of Monterey. **The Steinbeck House,** which operates as a nonprofit, gourmet luncheon restaurant, is located at 132 Central Ave., at Stone Street. **The National Steinbeck Center**, featuring interactive Steinbeck exhibits and programs, is located at One Main Street and Central Avenue. Both are just south of CA 183/Market Street. The Steinbeck House serves lunch Monday through Saturday, from 11:30 a.m. to 2 p.m., and on Sunday, from 1 p.m. to 3 p.m., through Labor Day. Tours are offered in the summer. For more information, contact the Valley Guild, 132 Central Ave., Salinas, CA 93901. Tel. (831) 424-2735.

The National Steinbeck Center ($) is open daily, except Jan. 1, Easter, Thanksgiving and Dec. 25, from 10 a.m. to 5 p.m. For more information, contact The Steinbeck Center, One Main St., Salinas, CA 93901. Tel.: (831) 796-3833. Information line: (931) 775-4720. On the Net: www.steinbeck .org.

FRAME OF REFERENCE John Ernst Steinbeck was born in the house on Central Avenue in 1902 and he lived there until he left for Stanford University in 1919. Steinbeck's father bought the house, built in 1897, in 1900. After Steinbeck's parents' death, the house changed hands several times before opening to the public in 1974. The Steinbeck Center opened in 1998.

SIGNIFICANCE Among the greatest American writers of the 20th century, Steinbeck was awarded the Nobel Prize for Literature in 1962. In 1940, he won the Pulitzer Prize for his masterpiece, *The Grapes of Wrath*, a 20th-century classic. The impact of the book, a bitter story of Oklahoma tenant farmers who become fruit pickers in California during the Depression, has been compared to the storm caused by **Harriet Beecher Stowe**'s *Uncle Tom's Cabin* in the 1800s. (See Connecticut in the New England section of this book.) Salinas turned its back on Steinbeck, more or less driving him out of town, but *Grapes* inspired federal legislation to protect migrant workers. Steinbeck's books have been translated into 30 languages.

The Modernist writer used his profound concern for the poor, eccentric and social outcasts to write allegories about the human condition. Many of

Steinbeck's novels have been made into successful Hollywood and made-for-TV movies, including his first success, *Tortilla Flat*. *Of Mice and Men* was both, as well as a Broadway play.

Steinbeck returned to his Salinas house for a few months in the 1930s to care for his ill mother. During that time he worked on his first successful novel, *Tortilla Flat,* and *The Red Pony*. In these books, Steinbeck turned to the Salinas Valley and the Monterey Bay waterfront for his settings and characters, as he would do over and over again. In his book *East of Eden*, he wrote of his family and described his childhood home.

In the Old Salinas house, Steinbeck's mother, Olive, a schoolteacher, taught her son to love literature. She read to baby John and arranged family evenings to read in the living room, the only heated room in the house until 1912. Olive introduced her only son to Sir Thomas Malory's *Morte d'Arthur*, which Steinbeck said ignited an appreciation of language and influenced his writing style. Steinbeck spent much of his last years writing a modern version of *Morte d'Arthur*. Although incomplete when he died, it was published posthumously as *The Acts of King Arthur and His Noble Knights*.

ABOUT THE SITES

THE STEINBECK HOUSE The two-story 15-room, Victorian house of Queen Anne style is irregularly shaped and features a steeply pitched roof with gables, turret, and intricate spindlework. A delicate, white fence surrounds the small lawn. Only the first floor is open to the public. Dining tables fill all rooms of the house, except the restaurant's reception room and service area. A nonprofit, volunteer organization, The Valley Guild, has operated the Steinbeck House restaurant since 1974. All profits from home tours and the restaurant, featuring seasonal, Salinas Valley produce, go to charities in the Salinas Valley and to birthplace maintenance.

The restaurant's reception room, which features a Steinbeck display, is located in what once was the parents' bedroom, where the writer was born. In *East of Eden*, Steinbeck described the pleasant bedroom of his grandmother as "crowded with photographs, bottles of toilet water, lace pincushions, brushes and combs, and the china and silver bureau-knacks of many birthdays and Christmases." The restaurant's service area is located in the Steinbecks' former dining room, where the family gathered at a large, round table for meals.

In the reception area, you'll find several items that once belonged to the Steinbecks when they lived in the house: a marble-top chest and a marble-top dresser; family photographs; and the deed of sale for the house dated 1900. A curio cabinet protects the family's teapot and china dishes, as well as young Steinbeck's glasses, harmonica and silver baby cup. You'll also find a marble sink that father Steinbeck installed for use by his daughters.

Other rooms now used for public dining include the parlor, a formal room with piano used only for special occasions (John was baptized here); a guest room; and the cozy living room which the Steinbecks used as a family room. The fireplace in the living room provided the only heat in the house until 1912.

After his sisters left for college, young John moved in 1906 from his parents' blue, front bedroom to a bedroom upstairs. When the Steinbecks bought the house, the second floor was unfinished. John, his sisters and frequent playmates would roller skate across its hardwood floors before it was remodeled as bedrooms.

THE NATIONAL STEINBECK CENTER Interactive, multi-sensory exhibits at the 37,000-square-foot Steinbeck Center bring Steinbeck's novels to life in seven themed galleries. You can walk into the lettuce boxcar of *East of Eden*, smell the sardines at Monterey's *Cannery Row,* trace the journey to the *Sea of Cortez*, and stroll the Mexican Plaza from *The Pearl.* The gallery, titled *Growing Up East of Eden*, features a replica of Steinbeck's bedroom with books he owned and original letters.

Sights and sounds at the museum include a likeness of Steinbeck's writing studio from his Long Island, N.Y., home and a recording of the author's Nobel Prize acceptance speech. Visitors hear the speech through a speaker next to a giant photo of Steinbeck receiving the prize, along with recorded anecdotes from his wife, Elaine.

Large-screen theaters show clips from films of Steinbeck's works. The center also has permanent exhibits, a wing for special programs, a museum store and a research room. The center's archive contains more than 40,000 Steinbeck first editions, posters, photographs, manuscripts, historical documents and films.

HOT TIPS An appointment is needed to visit the archives at The Steinbeck Center. Park across the street or in nearby parking lots. One Main Street Café at the center is open daily for lunch from 11 a.m. to 3 p.m. The site hosts many programs and events, including the annual Steinbeck Festival, Day of the Dead celebration, and writing competitions. Luncheon reservations are recommended for The Steinbeck House. The house is open for private functions.

To find the homes and haunts of Steinbeck in **Pacific Grove, Calif.,** the seaside town where he lived and drew inspiration for many of his most famous works, go on the Net to www.93950.com/steinbeck. As a child, Steinbeck vacationed at his family's cottage on 11th Street in Pacific Grove. He moved back to the cottage in 1930 with his bride, Carol, and wrote several famous works there. The cottage, built by Steinbeck's father, is privately owned and not open to public tours.

THE BEST STUFF The bed in which Steinbeck was born is now displayed in the Best Cellar Gift Shop downstairs at the Steinbeck House restaurant. Here, you often can find first-edition Steinbeck books for sale.

Want to get your kids interested in Steinbeck? Let them mount The Red Pony (not a real horse, of course) or brush his mane in an authentic barn recreated in the exhibit titled *An Livin Off the Fat of the Lan* at the Steinbeck Center. And everyone should enjoy peering inside Rocinante, the actual camper that Steinbeck wrote about in *Travels with Charley.* Steinbeck named the camper after his horse.

THE WRITER AND HIS WORK

BORN: Feb. 27, 1902, in Salinas

DIED: Dec. 20, 1968, in Sag Harbor, N.Y.; buried in the Garden of Memories Memorial Park, Salinas

EDUCATED: Stanford, 1920 and 1926; no degree

MARRIED: Carol Henning, 1930, divorced 1942; Gwyndolyn Conger; two sons, divorced 1949; Elaine Scot, 1950

IMPORTANT WORKS: *Cup of Gold* (1929); *The Pastures of Heaven* (1932); *To A God Unknown* (1933); *Tortilla Flat* (1935, film 1942); *In Dubious Battle* (1936); *Saint Katy The Virgin* (1936); *Nothing So Monstrous* (1936); *Of Mice and Men* (1937); *The Red Pony* (1937); *Their Blood Is Strong* (1938); *The Long Valley* (1938); *The Grapes of Wrath* (1939); *A Letter to the Friends of Democracy* (1940); *The Sea of Cortez* (1941); *The Forgotten Village* (1941); *Bombs Away!* (1942); *The Moon Is Down* (1942, film 1943); *How Edith McGillicuddy Met R.L.S.* (1943); *Cannery Row* (1945, film 1982); *The Wayward Bus* (1947, film 1957); *The Pearl* (1947, film 1946); *A Russian Journal* (1948) *Burning Bright* (1950); *East of Eden* (1952, film 1954); *Sweet Thursday* (1954, musical); *The Short Reign of Pippin IV* (1957); *The Crapshooter* (1957); *Once There Was A War* (1958); *The*

Winter of Our Discontent (1961); *Travels With Charley* (1962, TV movie 1968); *Letters To Alicia* (1965); *America and Americans* (1966, TV movie 1967); *Journal of a Novel* (1969); *The Acts of King Arthur and His Noble Knights* (1976); *Amnesia Glasscock* (1976); *Letters to Elizabeth* (1978); *The Harvest Gypsies* (1988); *Working Days* (1989)

ACCOLADES: Nobel Prize for literature, 1962; Pulitzer Prize, National Book Award for *Grapes of Wrath*, 1940

INTERESTING BIO FACT: While writing, Steinbeck worked as a manual laborer to support himself. He also worked as an apprentice hood-carrier, apprentice painter, estate caretaker, surveyor and fruit-picker. While on a job as a house watchman in the High Sierra, he wrote his first book, *Cup of Gold* (1929). Steinbeck later traveled around California migrant camps in 1936 to research *Grapes of Wrath*. When published, a congressman attacked the book, calling it "a lie, a black, infernal creation of a twisted, distorted mind." The Swedish Academy, in awarding the Nobel, termed it "an epic chronicle."

In later years Steinbeck did much special reporting abroad and reported from Vietnam on the war. He also did much of his writing in New York City while hobnobbing with the social elite.

FURTHER READING *John Steinbeck* by Ellyn Sanna, et. al. (2003); *John Steinbeck and Edward F. Ricketts: The Shaping of A Novelist* by Richard Astro (2002); *John Steinbeck, Writer* by Jackson Benson (1990)

ELSEWHERE IN THE AREA The Monterey Bay Aquarium, Maritime Museum, the Custom House, Fisherman's Wharf, and the shops, galleries and restaurants in old cannery building of Steinbeck's Cannery Row. All are in Monterey. ◭

STEVENSON IN CALIFORNIA

Sites Recall Scottish Writer's U.S. Sojourn

The Scot who brought us the adventure novels *Treasure Island* (1883), *Kidnapped* (1886) and the horror story, *The Strange Case of Dr. Jekyll and Mr. Hyde* (1886), spent a couple of months in the western United States in the late 1800s. Several sites in California now commemorate the famous author, including an adobe where Robert Louis Balfour Stevenson (1850-1894) rented an upstairs room in **Monterey**, and a museum in **St. Helena**, near where he spent his honeymoon. Both are open to the public.

THE STEVENSON HOUSE The 1830 **Stevenson House** ($) in Monterey, at 530 Houston St., sheltered the love-smitten Stevenson from September to December 1879. Stevenson came to America to await the divorce of Fanny Van de Grift Osbourne, whom he had met in an artist colony in France. He eventually married her, and the couple returned to Scotland. While in the sleepy old town, Stevenson wrote *The Old Capitol* and worked on *The Amateur Emigrant*, the story *Pavilion on the Links*, and an essay on Thoreau. He also worked for a local newspaper, The Californian. The beautiful Monterey coastline where Stevenson often strolled might have inspired his *Treasure Island* scenery.

The grand adobe was built as a private home, but through the years various businesses have occupied the site. For a time it was known as The French Hotel. In 1937, private citizens bought the house and gave it to California in 1941 as a memorial. Today the house/museum and flower garden surrounded by an adobe wall are part of **Monterey State Historic Park** ($) on the Monterey Peninsula, 300 miles north of Los Angeles. The park features many historic buildings, including the old Monterey Custom House.

Manuela Giradin, the owner of the large rooming house when Stevenson was there, renamed her house to capitalize on its famous boarder. The mud-brick house with green trim now displays Stevenson memorabilia, including furniture, first-edition books, manuscripts, Stevenson's mother's scrapbooks and his baby blanket. The house, with a sola (parlor) and seven bedrooms, also displays Stevenson's cigarette case and Samoan Tapas from his stay in the South Pacific, where he died in 1894. You'll find Fanny's painting of the bridge at Grez, portraits of Stevenson (by Fanny, Joe Strong and A.J. Daplyn), Fanny's Samoa diary, four of Stevenson's mother's scrapbooks of reviews, photographs, family silverware, and memorabilia given by members of his family.

The house is open daily, except Wednesdays, from 10 a.m. to 11 a.m. and from 1 p.m. to 4 p.m. Reservations required. For more information, contact Monterey State Historic Park, Stevenson House, P.O. Box 2562, Monterey, CA 93942. Tel. (831) 649-7172. On the Net: http://users.dedot .com/mchs/stevensonhouse.html. Renovation is ongoing and might mean tour cancellations.

THE SILVERADO MUSEUM at 1490 Library Lane in **St. Helena, Calif.**, occupies a wing of the St. Helena Public Library Center, 65 miles north of San Francisco. The museum, which opened at this site amid vineyards in 1979, displays more than 8,000 items relating to Stevenson. This internationally distinguished collection includes his wedding ring, his large desk from his last home in Samoa, his lead soldiers, a box he made as a boy, and rare letters and manuscripts. The site is especially proud to display Stevenson's manuscript of *Dr. Jekyll and Mr. Hyde* in his own handwriting.

The museum also features paintings and sculptures of the author, and an exhibit on the Stevenson works that have been made into movies. The exhibit includes illustrations, movie stills, photographs, playbills, and theater programs. The Silverado Museum is open Tuesday through Sunday, except major holidays, from noon to 4 p.m. For more information, contact The Silverado Museum, P.O. Box 409, St. Helena, CA 94574-0409. Tel.: (707) 963-3757. On the Net: www.silverado museum.org.

STEVENSON STATE PARK A marker on the slopes of 4,343-foot Mount St. Helena pinpoints the site where Stevenson and Fanny honeymooned in a bunkhouse at the old Silverado Mine in 1880. Stevenson recalled their stay on Mount St. Helena in *The Silverado Squatters*. Hikers today at **Robert Louis Stevenson State Park**, 18 miles northwest of St. Helena, can take the 5-mile trail to the mountain's summit for spectacular views of the Napa Valley. Take CA 29 to the entrance 8 miles north of Calistoga, Calif.

Stevenson also stayed briefly in a cottage **Saranac, N.Y.**, now called the Robert Louis Stevenson Cottage. See the Middle Atlantic section of this book for details.

HOT TIP In addition to extensive library collections in the United Kingdom, several American universities house Stevenson collections. They include the Yale, Princeton, Harvard, Columbia and the University of South Carolina. Many collections are online. ⌂

MARK TWAIN CABIN

Where Writer Stayed During Gold Rush

Mark Twain (Samuel Langhorne Clemens) briefly stayed in a log cabin in **Tuolumne County, Calif**., in the Central Sierra during the last gasp of the Great Gold Rush in the mid-1800s. The cabin site is located in a remote area southeast of Sonora along The Mother Lode. Here, Twain finished his story, *The Celebrated Jumping Frog of Calaveras County*. The tale brought him his first national recognition and put the California site on the literary map.

The weathered cabin, rebuilt in 1922, today barely survives atop Jackass Hill, within the boundaries of the New Melones Reservoir Project Area, just south of Calaveras County. (This also is the setting of many of writer Bret Harte's Gold Rush stories, including *Roaring Camp*.) Long after Twain left, a fire destroyed the original cabin. It was reconstructed on its original foundation.

Twain arrived on Jackass Hill in Dec. 1864 and left in late Feb. 1865, returning to San Francisco. The cabin was owned by acquaintances of Twain's, the Gillis brothers — James, Stephen and William. Twain had worked with Stephen Gillis on newspapers in Nevada and San Francisco. The writer lived with the Gillis brothers in their cabin during his three months on Jackass Hill. Now the second, simple cabin, with front door flanked by two windows, has a sunken roof, crumbling walls and leans to the left. A cyclone fence surrounds the site.

For more information about the Mark Twain Cabin, contact the Tuolumne County Historical Society, 158 W. Bradford Ave., Sonora, CA 95370. Tel. (209)-532-1317. For more about Twain, look under Missouri, Connecticut and New York in this book. ◭

SAN FRANCISCO, BY THE BOOK

Mark Twain, Bret Harte, Robert Louis Stevenson, Dashiell Hammett, Allen Ginsberg and Jack London are among the literary luminaries who once wandered the hilly streets of San Francisco. Today, with a little effort, you can find places associated with these and other writers. Plaques mark some spots. Other literary settings are private, while some operate as businesses and welcome the public.

Here are some of these San Francisco literary sites:

STEVENSON'S BOARDING HOUSE: A plaque on a narrow, three-story wooden building at 608 Bush St., where Robert Louis Stevenson rented a room in August 1879, commemorates the Scot's stay in San Francisco. While in the boarding house, Stevenson wrote essays on Benjamin Franklin and William Penn, as well as a dime novel he later discarded. A memorial at Portsmouth Square also remembers the man who wrote *A Child's Garden of Verses.*

JACK LONDON BIRTHPLACE: A plaque mounted on a rock marks the birthplace of novelist Jack London at 615 Third St. near Brannan. Fire following the earthquake of 1906 destroyed the house. A small street near South Park is also named for the most popular and well-paid American writer of the early 20th century. London's home in nearby Oakland is a private residence and local landmark.

DASHIELL HAMMETT'S APARTMENT: The influential noir detective writer who brought us *The Maltese Falcon* (1930) and *The Adventures of Sam Spade* (1945), lived in the Tenderloin district apartment building located at 891 Post St. Hammett worked as a private eye for the Pinkerton National Detective Agency in the Flood Building o Market Street. You'll find the 1908 John's Grill, a *Maltese Falcon* setting, at 63 Ellis St.

SITE OF NEWSPAPER WHERE TWAIN, BRET HARTE WORKED: The offices of the Golden Era newspaper, where Mark Twain and Bret Harte (*Luck of the Roaring Camp*) worked in the 1860s, stood at 732 Montgomery St., now in the Jackson Square Historical District. Twain lived at the Occidental Hotel at Montgomery and Sutter streets in the present-day Financial District.

GINSBERG READING SITE: In Oct. 1955, Beat poet Allen Ginsberg gave the first public reading of his controversial poem *Howl* at the Six Gallery, 3119 Fillmore St. The reading officially kicked off the "Beat movement." A business now occupies the building.

THE MONTGOMERY BLOCK: Where the towering Transamerica Pyramid now stands, a four-story building once stood. That building, built in 1853 for offices in what was known as the Montgomery Block or "Monkey Block," later became studios for thousands of bohemian artists and writers in the late 19th and early 20th centuries. These included Ambrose Bierce, Kathleen Norris, Joaquin Miller, Gelett Burgess, W.C. Morrow, George Sterling and James Hopper.

CITY LIGHTS BOOKS: The bookstore, at 261 Columbus Ave., was founded in 1955 by Lawrence Ferlinghetti, San Francisco's first Poet Laureate. The landmark boasts many literary firsts and hosts numerous events. ◿

BIBLIOGRAPHY

Albert, Janice. "Frank Norris." Online 19 Nov. 2003. Available http://www
.cateweb.org/CA_Authors/Norris.html.

Allaback, Steven. "Henry Wadsworth Longfellow," Dictionary of Literary
Biography: The American Renaissance in New England. edited by Joel
Myerson. vol. 1 Detroit: Gale Research Company, 1978. 117-124.

Allen, Anne Wallace. "Rudyard Kipling's Sojourn in Vermont." Chatam
News (Chatam, NY) Online. 31 Dec. 1997. Available http://www
.s-t.com/daily/12-97/12-28-97/e04li201.htm.

American Heritage Guide: Historic Houses of America,. New York: American Heritage Publishing Co., Inc., 1971.

"America's Historic Places." Readers Digest. Pleasantville, NY: St. Remy
Press, 1995.

"Annals of San Francisco, The: Chapter VIII." Online. 16 Nov. 2003. Available http://www.zpub.com/sf50/sf/hbannidx.htm.

"Armstrong Browning Library at Baylor University." Handbook of Texas
Online. 4 Dec. 2002. Available http://www.tsha.utexas.edu/hand
book/online.

Bartin, Nina, et al. Norton Anthology of American Literature. New York:
W.W. Norton and Co., 1989.

Bengtsson, Gunnar. "Vachel Lindsay." American Poems Home - Poets. Online. 2003. Available http://www.americanpoems.com.

Blair, Walter and Hornberger, Randall, Theodore and Stewart. The Literature of the United States. Chicago: Scott, Foresman and Co., 1953.

Brosi, George. "A John Fox, Jr. Bibliography." Online. 30 September 1997.
Available at http://www.english.eku.edu/services/kylit/fox.htm.

Brown, Katherine Tandy. "A Place to Go To: Visit the birthplace of the nation's first poet laureate." The Lane Report, Kentucky Business Online.
June 2001. Available http://www.kybiz.com/lanereport/departments
/tourism/exploring_ky601.html.

Brown, Lawrence. "Homage to the DH Lawrence Ranch in Taos, New
Mexico." Online. 1997. Available http://web.ukonline.co.uk/rananim
/lawrence/brown1.html.

Burghardt, Renie. "Hemingway And Piggott Arkansas." The Nomad Group
Online. 2003. Available http://www.literarytraveler.com/hemingway
/piggott.htm.

Burke, Michelle Prater, Ideals Guide to Literary Places in the U.S. Nashville, TN: Ideals Publications Inc., 1998.

Butler, Joseph T. "Washington Irving: Squire of Sunnyside." Historic Hudson Valley Online. 15 Nov. 2003. Available http://www.hudsonvalley.org/web/sunn-wash.html.

Caldwell, Erskine, Tobacco Road. Athens, Ga.: University of Georgia Press. 1995.

Caudle, Bill. "The Fitzgerald Walking Tour." Online. July 1998. Updated Jan. 2003. Available http://home.att.net/~caudle/fscotwlk.htm.

Caviness, Rochelle. "Helen Keller - A Role Model for the World." Online 29 July 2002. Available http://www.largeprintreviews.com/kellerhome.html.

"Chesnut, Mary Boykin Miller." Online 07. Nov. 2000. Available http://docsouth.unc.edu/chesnut/about.html.

Chopin Kate, The Awakening and Other Stories, New York: The Modern Library. 2000.

Claffey, Charles E. "Sinclair Lewis, USA: Dropping by Main Street 60 Years Later." Boston Globe Online 11 Oct. 1980. Available http://www.boston.com/globe/search/stories/nobel/1980/1980p.html.

Columbia Encyclopedia, Sixth Edition, 2003.

"Crane, (Harold) Hart," Microsoft Encarta Online Encyclopedia 2003 http://encarta.msn.com.

Cunningham, Noble E., Jr. "Thomas Jefferson." World Book Online. 22 Feb. 2000. Available http://www.worldbookonline.com/ar?/na/ar/co/ar286800.htm.

DeCredico, Mary A. Mary Boykin Chesnut: A Confederate Woman's Life. Madison, Wis.: Madison House Publishers, Inc., 1996.

Depp, Michael. "Off To See The Wizard." American Profile Online. 05 May 2003. Available http://www.americanprofile.com/issues/20030525/20030525_3063.

Donat, Hank. "Literary San Francisco." Online 2001. Available http://www.mistersf.com/literary/litmain.htm.

"Dorothy Parker's New York." Online. 12 Oct. 2003. Available http://www.dorothyparkernyc.com.

"Dreadful Murder in Natchez." The Concordian Intelligencier (Natchez, Miss.) Online. 21 June 1851. Available http://mshistory.k12.ms.us/features/feature4/johnsonobit.htm.

Duyckinck, Evert A. "William Gilmore Simms." NA. Cyclopaedia of American Literature, 1856.

"Edgar Allen Poe National Historic Site." Online. 8 July 2003. Available www.ushistory.org/tour/tour_poe.htm.

Bibliography

"Edgar Lee Masters (1868-1950)." The Columbia Encyclopedia, Sixth Edition. 2001.

"Edith Wharton's World." Smithsonian Institution Online. 2000. Available http://www.npg.si.edu/exh/wharton/whar3.htm.

Edwards, Rebecca. "William Allen White." Online. 2000. Available http://www.http://iberia.vassar.edu/1896/white.html.

"Edwin Arlington Robinson." Gardiner Public Library Online. 2000. Available http://www.gpl.lib.me.us.

"E. E. Cummings." Online. 2 Nov. 2003. Available http://www.empirezine.com/spotlight/cummings/cummings.htm.

Eldred, Eric. "The Old Manse." Online 21 Sept. 1999. Available http://eldred.ne.mediaone.net/nh/hawthorne.html.

"Ernest Taylor Pyle: August 3, 1900 – April 18, 1945." Online. 2 July 2003. Available http://www.scripps.com/foundation/programs/pyle/pyle.htm.

"Ernie Pyle in England, 1944." National Archives, Washington, D.C., 1999. Online. Available http://normandy.eb.com/normandy/articles/Pyle_Ernie.htm.

"Eugene O'Neill." Encyclopædia Britannica Online. 2000. Available http://search.britannica.com/search?query=Eugene+O'Neill.

"Faulkner, William," Microsoft Encarta Encyclopedia. Online. 2003. Available http://encarta.msn.com.

"Frank Norris." Cambridge: Bentley Publishers. Online 2003. Available http://www.bentlypublishers.com/author.htm?who=Frank_Norris.

"Frederick Douglass National Historic Site." America's National Parks. Washington, D.C.: National Park Foundation, 2003, 130.

Fredrix, Emily. "William Allen White house to be renovated, reopened." Associated Press Online. 05 July 2003.

Gehman, Mary and Ries, Nancy. "Women and New Orleans: A History." Online 1996. Available http://margaretmedia.com/women_and_new_orleans/contents.htm.

Giddens, Tharon A. "Local road remains testiment to hard times." The Augusta Chronical (Augusta, Ga.). Online. Available http://augustachronicle.com/stories/040897/fea_tobaccoroad.html.

Givner, Joan. "Katherine Ann Porter." Handbook of Texas Online. 16 Oct. 2003. Available http://www.tsha.utexas.edu/handbook/online/articles/view.

"Greenfield Village", The Columbia Electronic Encyclopedia. Online. 2001. Available http://www.aol.bartleby.com/65/gr/GreenfieV.html.

Grolier Encyclopedia of Knowledge, Danbury, Conn.: Grolier Inc., 1991.

Hanna, John. "Editor's house has future in tourism." The Topeka Capital-Journal Online. 21, May 2001. Available http://cjonline.com/stories/052001/kan_whitehome.shtml.

"Harper Lee accepts award with few words," The State (Columbia, S.C.) May 2003: 2.

"Harriet Beecher Stowe House: A Bed and Breakfast." Online 11 Sept. 2003. Available http://TheInnkeeper.com!

"Hawthorne in Salem." Online. 9 Nov. 2003. Available http://www.hawthorneinsalem.org/page/11425.

"Henry Wadsworth Longfellow." The Columbia Encyclopedia. 1995.

"History of Dr. Seuss 1904 -1991." Online. 2000. Available http://store.yahoo.com/ftcollect/noname9.html.

Hovde, Karen. "Gene Stratton-Porter." St. James Encyclopedia of Popular Culture. 2002. Online. Available http://www.findarticles.com/g1epc/bio/2419201172/p1/article.jhtml.

Hurwitz, Howard L. An Encyclopedic Dictionary of American History. New York: Washington Square Press, 1970.

"James Thurber," St. James Encyclopedia of Popular Culture. Gale Group. Feb. 2000.

"John R. Dos Passos." Online. 1994. Available http://:www.english114.com/eds/edseli/text/text/DosPassos.htm.

"John Steinbeck (1902-1968)." Online. 2000. Available http://todayin literature.com/biography/john.steinbeck.asp.

Keating, Francis A. Will Rogers: An American Legend. New York: Silver Whistle, 2002.

Kecuyer, Kate. "Vermont history revealed at Rokeby Museum." Online. 12 Nov. 02. Available http://journalism.smcvt.edu/echo/12.11.02/Rokeby.htm.

Kelso, Dorothy Honiss. "William Bradford." Online. 18 Sept. 2000. Available http://www.pilgrimhall.org.

Larson, Susan. The Booklover's Guide to New Orleans. Baton Rouge: LSU Press, 1999.

"Lincoln Home National Historic Site." America's National Parks. Washington, D.C.: National Park Foundation, 2003, 183.

Liukkonen, Petri. "Robinson Jeffers." Author's Calendar Online. 2003. Available http://www.biblion.com/litweb/biogs/jeffers_robinson.html.

Long, Thomas L. "Life of William Byrd II." Online, October 1998. Available http://www.tncc.vccs.edu/faculty/longt/byrd.

Maltin, Leonard, editor. Leonard Maltin's Movie and Video Guide. New York: Signet. 2000.

"Mark Twain At Rest; Buried Beside Wife." The New York Times. April 25, 1910: 1.

Marley, Donna. "Eugene Field." Online June 2003. Available http://www.empirezine.com/spotlight/field/field1.htm.

Martich, Michale and Dorothy. "Sojourner Truth." A BiographySite. Online. 1996. Reprinted courtesy of the Battle Creek Historical Society. Available http://www.geocities.com/Athens/Oracle/9840/index.html.

"Martin Luther King, Jr. National Historic Site." America's National Parks. Washington, D.C.: National Park Foundation, 2003, 165.

Mattson, Arthur S. "Whittaker Chambers' Home in Lynbrook." Online. Nov. 2001.

Available http://members.aol.com/lynhistory/lhps/chambers.htm.

McBryde, John. "Alabama's Literacy Capital (Monroeville)." American Profile Online. 12 Dec. 2001. Available http://www.americanprofile.com/issues/20011125/20011125se_15.

McGovern, Linda. "Footprints in Cloutierville: The Chopin Home and Bayou Folk Museum. Online 9 July 2003. Available http://www.literarytraveler.com/summer/south/clout.htm.

McNutt, Randy. "Miami professor helped shape American education." The Cincinnati Enquirer. Online. 31 March 1999. Available http://www.enquirer.com/editions/1999/03/31/loc_mcguffey_deserves.html.

Miller, Joel. "Unitarians, Universalists, Communities and Communes: A Sermon." Online 2001. Available http://www.revjm.com/communes.htm.

"Monkingbird, the Film." To Kill a Mockingbird Online. 7 Nov. 2001. Available Jane Kansas + kansas@chebucto.ca.

"Monte Cristo Cottage in New London, Connecticut." The New London Gazette (New London, CT) 24 Oct. 2003. Available http://www.newlondongazette.com/monte.html.

Morris, Anne. "$600,000 donated to center for writers." Austin American-Statesman, Sept. 1, 1999: B1, B5.

Norris, Walter Biscoe, Jr., Westmoreland County Virginia 1653-1983. Montross, Virginia: Westmoreland County Board of Supervisors, 1983.

Page, David and Koblas, Jack. "F Scott Fitzgerald in Minnesota: toward the summit."

North Star Press of St. Cloud Online. 1966. Available http://www.north starpress.com/fscottfitzgerald.htm.

Paschke, Jean. "Sauk Centre, Minnesota." by Jean Paschke. Historic Traveler (March 1998); 18-20; 86-88.

Peschel, Bill. Edwin Arlington Robinson's Life and Career. New York: Oxford University Press, 1999.

Petersen, Carol Miles. "Bess Streeter Aldrich (1881-1954) Elmwood." Online. 21 Sept. 2003. Available http:// www.lincolnne.com/nonprofit/bs.

"Portsmouth's Bad Boy." SeacoastNH Online. 10 Oct. 2003. Available http://www.seacoastnh.com/aldrich/index.html.

Potter, Michelle. "Zora Neale Hurston: A Literary Life." The Nomad Group Literary Traveler. Online 2003. Available http://www.literarytraveler .com/hurston/hurston.htm.

"Rawlings, Marjorie Kinnan," Microsoft Encarta Encyclopedia. Online. 2003.

Reuben, Paul P. "Joel Chandler Harris." Perspectives in American Literature. Online. 03 Sept. 2003. Available http://www.csustan.edu/english /reuben/pal/chap5/harris.html.

Reuben, Paul. P. "Vachel Lindsay (1879-1931)." Perspectives in American Literature. Online. 23 October 2003. Available http://www.csustan .edu/english/reuben/pal/chap7/lindsay.html.

"Riley, James Whitcomb." Encarta Online Encyclopedia. Online. 2003. Available http://encarta.msn.com.

"Robert Frost Trail." Online Sept. 2003. Available http://www.amherst common.com/recreation/rftrail.html.

Robinson, Ella. "Alex Haley State House Museum." Online 12 Oct. 1999. Available http://www.suite101.com/print_article.cfm/4054/26207.

Robinson, Ella. "Katherine Anne Porter Museum." Online. 30 Nov. 1999. Available http://www.suite101.com/article.cfm/literary_tour/29373.

"Robinson Jeffers." The Academy of American Poets. Online. 2003. Available http://www.poets.org/poets/poets.cfm?prmID=203.

Robinson, Ray. American Original: A Life of Will Rogers. Oxford University Press, 1996.

Ross, Don. "UNC Now Home to Charles Kuralt's Office." WTVD-TV Inc. Online. 04 July 2001. Available http://abclocal.go.com/wtvd/features /070401_DR_kuraltoffice.

"Sagamore Hill National Historic Site." America's National Parks. Washington, D.C.: National Park Foundation, 2003, 311.

"Sarah Orne Jewett." Columbia Encyclopedia. Online. 2002. Available http://www.bartleby.com/65/je/Jewett-S.html.

Schafer, Elizabeth D. "Laura Ingalls Wilder." St. James Encyclopedia of Popular Culture Online. 19 Jan. 2002. Available http://www.find articles.com/cf_0/g1epc/bio/2419201304/p1/article.jhtml.

Schur, Joan Brodsky. "New York: A Magnet for Wordsmiths." Online. June 2003. Available http://www.ncteamericancollection.org/litmap/new _york.htm.

Scotchie, Joe. "Christopher Morley Fest in Roslyn." The Roslyn News (Roslyn, NY) Aug. 31, 2001.

Seidlitz, Anne. "Ralph Ellison." American Masters series (PBS) Online. August 2003. Available http://www.pbs.org/wnet/americanmasters /database/ellison_r.h.

"Sinclair Lewis' Boyhood Home Tells A Story." Sauk Centre Herald Online. 16 July 1996. Available http://www.saukherald.com/lewis/home.

Singhania, Lisa. "Sojourner Truth sculpture dedicated in Battle Creek." The Detroit Free Press. Online. 26 September 1999. Available http://www .freep.com.

Skinner, Winston. "The Erskine Caldwell Birthplace and Museum." Online. 23 Nov. 2003. Available http://www.newnan.com/ec.

Slappey, DeDe. "History of the Mary Gay House Restoration Project." 1982.

Steichin, Paula. My Connemara. Washington, D.C.: Eastern National, 1989.

Stoddard, R.H. et. al. Poets' Homes. Chicago: The Interstate Publishing Co., 1877.

Stokes, Allen. "Library Acquires Williams-Chesnut-Manning Papers." Online 1999. Available http://www.sc.edu/library/socar/uscs/99spr /manning.html.

Straw, Deborah. "Rokeby and The Robinson Family." Online. 2003. Available http://www.literarytraveler.com/special/rokeby.htm.

"The Magnificent Mr. Morley: With Christopher Morley in Roslyn Harbor."

Poetry Bay Online Magazine. Summer 2002. Available http://www.poetry bay.com/summer2002/morley.htm.

"Thurber, James Grover," Microsoft Encarta Encyclopedia. Online. 2003. Available http://encarta.msn.com.

Trent, William P. William Gilmore Simms. New York : Haskell House Publishers, 1968.

Tubergen, Jan. " 'L' is For Lloyd." Online. 2003. Available. /www.winnetka history.org/Gazette/Winnetka%20From%20A%2.

Washington, Booker T., Up From Slavery. New York: Dover Publishing Co., 1995.

"W.E.B. Du Bois River Garden." Online 2002. Available http://www.gbriver walk.org/riverwkDuBoisGarden.html.

"What is the Lost Generation?" PageWise, Inc. 2002. Online. Available http://ok.essortment.com/whatlostgenera_nkj.htm.

Wiencek, Henry. "The Road to Modern Atlanta", American Heritage (April 1996): 82–92.

"Willa Cather (1873–1947) Red Cloud, Nebraska." Nebraska Department of Travel and Tourism Online. Sept. 2003. Available http://info.neded .org/stathand/parttwo/cather.htm.

"William Gilmore Simms." Academic Affairs Library. Chapel Hill: The University of North Carolina, 1998. Available http://docsouth.unc .edu/simms/about.html.

"William Gilmore Simms Society." Online 08 August 2000. Available http://www.westga.edu/~simms.

Williams, Thomas E. Q. "A Short Biography of America's Children's Poet." Greenfield, Ind.: Old Home Society, 1913.

Wilson, Charles Reagan and Ferris, William, editors. Encyclopedia of Southern Culture. Chapel Hill: University of North Carolina Press (1989).

Woodbury, Chuck. "It Wasn't a Happy Time" Out West Newspaper Online. 2002. Available http://www.outwestnewspaper.com/erniepyle.html.

Woodward, C. Van and Muhlenfeld, Elisabeth. The Private Mary Chesnut: The Unpublished Civil War Diaries. New York: Oxford University Press, 1984.

"Zora Neale Hurston." St. James Encyclopedia of Pop Culture. Online. 2002 Available http://www.findarticles.com/g1epc/bio/2419200577 /p1/article.jhtml.